The New Relationship between the United Kingdom and the European Union

Emmanuel Guinchard • Carlo Panara
Editors

The New Relationship between the United Kingdom and the European Union

Springer

Editors
Emmanuel Guinchard
Liverpool John Moores University
Liverpool, UK

Carlo Panara
University of Leicester
Leicester, UK

ISBN 978-3-031-70651-6 ISBN 978-3-031-70652-3 (eBook)
https://doi.org/10.1007/978-3-031-70652-3

This Springer imprint is published by the registered company Springer Nature Switzerland AG
The registered company address is: Gewerbestrasse 11, 6330 Cham, Switzerland

Acknowledgements

The editors would like to thank wholeheartedly the publisher for supporting this project and the authors of the individual chapters for their contribution.

The editors are also grateful to Liverpool John Moores University, and particularly to Professor Timothy Nichol Pro Vice Chancellor of the Faculty of Business and Law, for their support through the duration of this project.

The editors would like to thank Dr Majida Ismael and Dr George William Lamb for their wonderful research assistance and, in the case of George, also for an outstanding and thought-provoking chapter.

Carlo Panara would like to dedicate this book to Rachel, Niamh and Alessandra.

Emmanuel Guinchard would like to dedicate this book to his family.

Contents

About the Editors

Emmanuel Guinchard is Principal Lecturer at Liverpool John Moores University, where he leads the Academic LLMs and PhD programmes. His teaching and research focus on Private International Law, European Union law, World Trade Organization law and Competition Law. He has published widely in the field of European Civil Justice. His publications include the edited books "Le nouveau règlement Bruxelles I bis" (Bruylant, 2014) and "Rome I and Rome II in practice" (Intersentia, 2020).

Carlo Panara is Chair & Head of the Law School at Leicester University. He is widely published in the fields of European and Comparative Law. His publications include the monograph "The Sub-national Dimension of the EU: A Legal Study of Multilevel Governance" (Springer, 2015) and the edited books "The Role of the Regions in EU Governance" (Springer, 2011, with Alexander De Becker) and "Local Government in Europe" (Routledge, 2013, with Michael Varney). He is the Co-Editor-in-Chief of the European Public Law Review (Kluwer).

Introduction

Carlo Panara and Emmanuel Guinchard

The referendum of 23 June 2016, that triggered the departure of the United Kingdom from the European Union after over 40 years of membership ('Brexit'), will no doubt remain one of the landmark dates in British and European history. The exit of the UK from the EU had a huge impact on life in the UK and the EU, both in the private sphere (e.g. on workplace and job market dynamics) and in the public sphere (e.g. as citizens). All dimensions were impacted: political, economic, financial, psychological, cultural, and of course legal. Law, as a sociological phenomenon that permeates and largely regulates our collective life and endeavours has been hugely affected by the UK's decision to leave the EU. A study that focuses on the impact of Brexit on key aspects of the law in the UK and the EU is therefore an important contribution to the understanding of this absolutely crucial period in European history.

The UK's departure from the EU is the first, and to date only, case of member state leaving the EU after joining.[1] The UK was and still is the second economy by GDP in Europe after Germany, back in 2016 c.45% of its export went to the EU and over 60% of its import came from the EU, not to mention the key role played by the UK since the 1970s in shaping important aspects of the EU including the development of the law and particularly the case law of the Court of Justice of the EU. The

[1] Greenland's departure from the European Economic Community (EEC) in 1985 is not comparable to the later departure of the UK from the EU. Greenland is part of the Kingdom of Denmark, and as a result joined the EEC alongside Denmark in 1973. After becoming an autonomous territory following the introduction of the home rule in 1979, Greenland decided to leave the EEC and left in 1985. However, the UK remains the first and to date only sovereign state to have left the EU.

C. Panara (✉)
University of Leicester, Leicester, UK
e-mail: cp481@leicester.ac.uk

E. Guinchard
Liverpool John Moores University, Liverpool, UK
e-mail: E.R.Guinchard@ljmu.ac.uk

E. Guinchard, C. Panara (eds.), *The New Relationship between the United Kingdom and the European Union*, https://doi.org/10.1007/978-3-031-70652-3_1

UK was the second country by population in the EU at the time of leaving and, alongside France, was the only nuclear power and permanent member of the UN Security Council among the member states of the EU. At the time of the referendum there were around 3.5 million EU citizens who resided in the UK and 1.2 million UK citizens who resided in the EU. All of this illustrates very clearly why Brexit was nothing less than an earthquake both in the UK and the EU.

Eight years after the referendum an analysis can be conducted taking stock of what has happened until now, both in relation to the implementation of the measures triggered by Brexit and regarding its impact on economy, society, politics, and obviously law in the UK and the EU. Additionally, after 8 years it is finally possible to analyse Brexit as a historical and sociological phenomenon with more rationality, the appropriate distance, and without the acute albeit legitimate emotions that accompanied in particular the aftermath of the 2016 referendum. Since 2016 two new UK Parliaments have been elected, in 2017 and 2019, and five British Premierships have taken place. All were significantly impacted on by the political upheaval originating from the referendum and by the need to establish a renewed cooperation between the UK and the EU.[2] Eight years after the referendum, the time seems also ripe to reflect on a new relationship between the UK and the EU at the dawn of a likely new political era, ushered by a new EU Parliament and EU Commission following the June 2024 elections and a new UK Parliament and Prime Minister following the July 2024 elections, and in the light of the forthcoming review of the Trade and Cooperation Agreement in early 2026.[3]

The book has been conceived as a research handbook that covers the most important areas of the new relationship between the UK and the EU. The authors are all specialists in their respective fields and we are pleased that alongside internationally known and established academics, we were able to involve in this project some exceptionally bright mid- and early career scholars from the UK and overseas. We are particularly pleased that some high-profile public servants were able to contribute to this book either as authors or as participants in the research. We deeply thank all of them for their valued contributions.

Due to its research handbook nature and scope, the book covers a wide range of topics under three major headings. The first concerns 'The Background to the New Relationship between the UK and the EU' (Part I of the book). The chapters under this heading critically explore the history of the UK membership in the EEC and EU and the historical facts that led to the present position (Birkinshaw), as well as key aspects of the impact of Brexit on UK constitutional law and politics (Stanford), on human and fundamental rights (Varney). In relation to human rights, it is important to note that these are the subject of a heated debate in light of the criticism in particular from Tory party circles of the rights originating from the European

[2] These are the premierships of David Cameron (2010–2016) who supported the continuing membership of the EU and who resigned after the referendum, Theresa May (2016–2019), Boris Johnson (2019–2022), Liz Truss (2022) and Rishi Sunak (2022-present).

[3] Trade and Cooperation Agreement, Article 776: "The Parties shall jointly review the implementation of this Agreement and supplementing agreements and any matters related thereto five years after the entry into force of this Agreement and every five years thereafter".

Convention on Human Rights, and of the proposal in June 2022 to replace the Human Rights Act 1998 with a UK bill of rights.[4]

The second part of the book covers the most important aspects of 'The New Relationship as Shaped by the 2019 and 2020 Agreements' and features eight chapters on the rights of EU citizens in the UK and of UK citizens in the EU (Bradshaw), trade in goods between the UK and the bloc (Repyeuski), commercial transactions (Renaudin), the absolutely important areas of police and counterterrorism cooperation (Lowe), public procurement (Bovis), the Northern Ireland Protocol (McMahon), the status of UK Overseas Territories (Bell & Waddington) and the procedures in place for dispute settlement (Tasnim Ahmed).

The third part of the book looks at aspects that are not covered by the 2019 and 2020 Agreements and where, therefore, there is 'A New Relationship to Forge'. This part comprises seven chapters on security and defence cooperation (Lamb), the post-Brexit international trade agreement of the UK (Collins), the cooperation in the field of environmental protection and climate change (Olmos Giupponi), the cooperation in the field of civil justice (Mukarrum Ahmed), the area of critical importance to the UK economy of financial services (McCarthy), the cooperation in the field of research (Kortese & Garben) that received a boost in 2023 after the agreement that enabled the UK to join Horizon Europe as an associate member, and finally the activities of the European offices of UK local authorities and devolved administrations in Brussels after Brexit (Panara).

Each chapter has a triadic structure. The first part considers the regime prior to Brexit; the second analyses the current regime; and the third discusses ongoing and predictable trends. These makes all the chapters broadly comparable in terms of structure and type of content. We have, however, where appropriate, allowed for flexibility, because academic freedom and research do not always and necessarily lend themselves to rigid structures.

The authors are all legal scholars, accordingly the methodology used in the various chapters is mostly doctrinal. Some chapters rely on the direct experience of public officials and one chapter (18) engaged in qualitative research typical of socio-legal studies. The employed research methods reflect the broad spectrum of topics this book covers, with some chapters at the intersection in particular between Law and Politics (Stanford, Panara), Law and History (Birkinshaw, Lamb), and Law and Economics (Repyeuski, Collins).

The concluding chapter by Guinchard attempts to identify some themes likely to impact on the forthcoming preparation of the 2026 review.

---

[4] Bill of Rights Bill introduced by the Ministry of Justice on 22 June 2022. The bill has been withdrawn on 27 June 2023 due to the growing opposition to the bill not only in parliament but in the wider British society.

Part I
The Background to the New Relationship Between the UK and the EU

An Historical Perspective of the UK in the EU

Patrick Birkinshaw

1 The UK Entry into a European Community

What we now term the European Union (EU) was forged in the ashes of the second world war in Europe. A motivating factor was to interlink the economies of the members so closely that war between members would become in Robert Schuman's words 'not only unthinkable but materially impossible'. France, West Germany, Italy and the three Benelux countries (Belgium, the Netherlands and Luxembourg) signed the Treaty on Coal and Steel creating a common market, common objectives and institutions in 1951–1952, linking and regulating the market in power and steel, the tools of war. The Treaty of Rome was signed by the same parties in March 1957, establishing the European Economic Community along with a parallel treaty, the Atomic Energy Community (Euratom). The EEC was inaugurated in 1958 and is today the EU. The UK signed the European Free Trade Association treaty in 1959 and joined the Organisation for European Economic Cooperation in 1961 working towards reduction of trade restrictions between the member states. These developments did not make up for non-membership of the EEC and the UK's efforts to join the EEC were twice frustrated by French President de Gaulle in 1963 and 1967 who feared the input of US influence through UK membership.

Whether Prime Minister Macmillan's aim in joining the EEC was to act as a counter to the emerging Franco-German alliance and to preserve the UK's ascendancy in Europe, now that the 'wind of change' was blowing through former British colonies, the rapid economic advances made by France and Germany incentivized his desire to join the EEC. McMillan claimed that membership involved merely minor commercial negotiations and the Lord Chancellor in 1967 declared that EEC

P. Birkinshaw (✉)
Hull University, Kingston upon Hull, UK
e-mail: P.Birkinshaw@emeritus.hull.ac.uk

E. Guinchard, C. Panara (eds.), *The New Relationship between the United Kingdom and the European Union*, https://doi.org/10.1007/978-3-031-70652-3_2

law had 'little direct effect on the life of ordinary citizens'.[1] By 1971, the government asserted 'there is no question of any erosion of essential national sovereignty' (UK government 1971). It was left to Edward Heath to oversee UK admission to the EEC in 1973 after the death of de Gaulle. There was no national referendum before membership. That was to wait until the 1975 UK referendum. The 1974 Wilson government was unhappy with the terms of EEC membership. A substantial UK majority voted in favour of continued membership.

Parliament, as a representative chamber, was legally in control of accession through the European Communities Act 1972 (ECA). Under this legislation Parliament clearly bound itself voluntarily to the jurisprudence of the ECJ (ss 2(1) and (4)), which for a decade had promoted both legal sovereignty of EEC law over national law, in limited but ever-growing areas of competence, and the twin doctrine of direct effect of EEC law.[2] Under the latter directly enforceable rights of Community law under the treaties, regulations and directives could be encashed in domestic courts by individuals. All UK legislation was to be read as being bound by the terms of relevant EEC law. This was all there in the ECA which Parliament had agreed but it was to await almost 20 years for the full impact to be seen. When it was made explicit in *Factortame No 2*,[3] Euroscepticism grew from a whimsical obsession of oddballs and eccentrics to a major force in British politics.

2 A Movement from a Community to a Union

The first major revision of the Treaty of Rome came with the Single European Act (1986) signed by the now 12 members. This was a significant revision which brought an extension of qualified majority voting (QMV), which meant a state may have its opposition to new laws overridden by a qualified majority in the subject areas covered, a cooperation agreement for the European Parliament and Council and legislation enhancing that Parliament's locus in law-making, and a commitment to European Union and monetary union. A single market was being superseded by a 'federal Europe' opponents claimed. Mrs. Thatcher nonetheless signed the treaty.

In 1988, Mrs. Thatcher made her famous Bruges speech.[4] Over the centuries, she exclaimed, the UK has fought to prevent Europe from falling under the dominance of a single power, which she now saw the EEC becoming. Our destiny is in Europe, as part of the Community. A willing and active cooperation between independent sovereign states is the best way to build a successful European Community, she continued. We have not successfully rolled back the frontiers of the state in Britain through privatisation, only to see them re-imposed at a European level with a

[1] HL Debs col. 1197 at col 1203 8/05/67. For an alternative view see Sked (2015), founder of UKIP.

[2] Case 26/62 *Van Gend en Loos* [1963] ECR 1 and Case 6/64 *Costa v. ENEL* [1964] ECR 545.

[3] *Factortame No 2* [1991] 1 All ER 70 (HL and ECJ).

[4] Thatcher (1988).

'European super-state' exercising a new dominance from Brussels (Young 1999). This became the rallying cry for anti-communitarians.

For the euro-sceptics the context was only to deteriorate dramatically. The Treaty on European Union signed at Maastricht (1992–1993) by the 12 members marked a 'new stage in the process of European Integration'. The treaty also ushered in the age of rejection of EU treaties by national plebiscites. It envisioned a shared European citizenship, eventual introduction of a shared European currency, the UK had left the exchange rate mechanism in 1992, and a European Central Bank and a European Union involving the EC, a Common Foreign & Security Policy (CFSP) and Cooperation in Justice & Home Affairs (JHA), presaged an increasingly globalized world and how the Community was to react to that on one hand, as well as posing a serious threat to national sovereignty on the other. Both the CFSP and JHA emerged from earlier initiatives and were intergovernmental and required unanimity in voting. This was a complex three-pillar structure only the EEC component of which was legally binding in national law. The treaty emerged after the dissolution of the Soviet Union and the unification of Germany. The UK opted out of social policy, the Schengen immigration system and the third stage of monetary union—a single currency.

Maastricht gave a clear indication of the problems that lay ahead for Conservative governments in securing Parliamentary approval of EU treaties. The fact that Parliament had to approve treaties increasing the power of the European Parliament (s 6, European Assembly Elections Act 1978) meant that where domestic courts were inclined to give a generous ruling on locus standi, questions could be raised in the courts about the legality of the treaties signed by the government where Parliamentary approval had not allegedly been obtained in proper form.[5] These matters would previously have been confined to an unreviewable prerogative power. The legal challenge, brought by the then editor of the *Times*, was unsuccessful. John Major had threatened to ratify the social policy provisions of Maastricht by prerogative but then linked it to a vote of confidence precipitating a general election if Conservatives voted against it. He won the vote and Maastricht was ratified with Parliamentary approval.

After incremental changes at Amsterdam (1997) and Nice (2001), the next significant step in integration proved a step too far. A Treaty establishing a Constitution for Europe was a single consolidated text embracing a written constitution replacing the existing EU treaties and containing a legally binding part (Charter of Fundamental Rights (CFR)) dedicated to fundamental human rights for the EU. It followed a European Convention and Intergovernmental conference. The text was agreed by (now) all 25 member states but before ratification could be completed it was rejected by French and Dutch voters in referenda in 2005. Prime minister Blair had undertaken to allow a UK referendum on the treaty but when it was rejected by the French and Dutch, he took this as a signal to abandon the Constitution.

Lisbon 2007, comprising the TEU and TFEU, followed a 'period of reflection' after the abandonment of the Constitution. Basically, Lisbon achieved a significant number of the proposals in the Constitution although some provisions fell by the

[5] *Rees-Mogg* [1994] 1 All ER 457.

wayside. Prominent developments included the further extension of qualified majority voting in at least 45 policy areas in the Council of Ministers, a change in calculating such a majority to a new double majority, a more powerful European Parliament forming a bicameral legislature alongside the Council of Ministers under the ordinary legislative procedure, a consolidated legal personality for the EU and the creation of a long-term President of the European Council and a High Representative of the Union for Foreign Affairs and Security Policy.

The Treaty also made the Union's bill of rights, the CFR, legally binding. The UK and Poland added a national qualification to the CFR which was essentially meaningless. For the first time, the treaty gave member states the explicit legal right to leave the EU, and established a procedure by which to do so through Art 50 TEU. A TEU component set out the constitutional basics of the EU, the CFSP and the JHA. These three now became an integrated part of the EU although the CFSP still maintains significant intergovernmental components. The three-pillar structure is gone and the EU as a legal entity covers all three areas. The EU can sign documents in its own name and becomes in its own right a member of the WTO. There is an enhanced role for national parliaments in advance scrutiny of EU legislation. Exclusive, shared and supporting competences of the EU were spelt out, Member states retain competences not conferred upon the Union: TEU Art. 4. The UK opted out of JHA with opt back in provision. Lisbon foresees possibility of future defence cooperation.

Lisbon is still the governing treaty although simplified procedures introduced in Lisbon allow for specified revisions. Emergency monetary measures in the wake of the financial crisis have been taken within the treaties and via new non EU based financial instruments, such as the European Stability Mechanism which the ECJ interpreted with a relaxed approach,[6] an approach that was not initially accepted by the Bundesverfassungsgericht in other EU financial policies (OMT case law).[7] Refugee immigration policy has been directed by Germany and other national political leaders in discussion with third country states. Opposition to war in Ukraine and Russia's invasion has been directed by the Commission and has shown a united front despite the serious consequences of loss of Russian energy resources for some states including Germany and differences on placing restrictions on Russian travellers to the EU. The Council adopted a fifth package of sanctions against Russia on April 8 2022 following reports of atrocities committed by Russian invading troops in Ukraine and a sixth package proposed a total ban by member states on Russian oil imports. By February 2024, there were thirteen packages. In relation to Brexit, the EU has shown unity in its future relationship with the UK set out in the Written Agreement (WA) and Trade and Cooperation Agreement (TCA) despite UK efforts to negotiate terms with individual members.

---

[6] *Pringle* EU:C:2012:756.

[7] BVerfG, Judgment of the second Senate of 05 May 2020–2 BvR 859/15 bond purchasing by the ECB.

3 The UK's Road to Exit

By 2009, the UK's semi-detached status within the EU had long been apparent. The old Labour dislike of a commercial union that it believed anti-worker had given way to a more positive acceptance by Labour of a union that was increasingly dedicated to protecting social rights, equality and human rights. Blair opted into the social policy provisions of Maastricht on coming to office. Corbyn still displayed an obvious ambivalence towards Europe in the Brexit referendum. But on the Tory side the divisions were becoming ever more rancorous and took on increasing significance in David Cameron's premiership.

The sceptics' efforts were focused on symbolic 'victories' such as Parliamentary sovereignty with no efforts to unpack what sovereignty meant. The UK's 2011 European Union Act states that any directly applicable or effective EU law was effected via an act of Parliament (section 18). What Parliament gives Parliament may take back. The 2011 Act, it has been argued, itself establishes a new form of self-embracing sovereignty in so far as Parliament had bound its future action on many Union initiatives to a popular referendum. Bogdanor (2012) has argued that the people are now a constituent part of Parliament. Taking treaty changes, for instance, section 2(1) provides that a treaty amending or replacing the TEU or TFEU is not to be ratified until a statement has been laid before Parliament in accordance with section 5, Parliament has approved the treaty and the referendum or exemption condition is satisfied. All significant treaty reforms and EU developments were to be subject to a popular referendum. The mood in the country was becoming increasingly anti-European and this would act as a real bar to UK ratification of treaty reforms. Brexit made the act redundant.

While our relationship with the Union has often been a strained one, several factors combined to curdle domestic perspectives on the UK's relationship with Europe. Sovereignty, or rather loss of sovereignty, as we have seen, had been a persistent complaint.

Loss of power, over-regulation and bureaucratic expansionism have been other long-standing gripes. Being different, never really trusting European initiatives or initiatives in Europe and harping back to halcyon days of a self-sufficient Commonwealth were often repeated. Complaints grew of loss of commercial freedom and enterprise, loss of autonomy in international trade negotiations and loss of resources such as fisheries. The UK opted out of Union policies, in particular those of monetary union and the Schengen Agreement on abolition of internal border controls, and the non-Union financial stability measures although it was not alone in these opt outs. The pre-Lisbon Justice and Home Affairs provisions on criminal law and justice were opted out off only for the more important measures to be opted back into.

To these were added complaints of a Union that somehow transmuted from an economic association and a common market to a fully-fledged political union claiming not just political sovereignty but also legal sovereignty including sovereignty over national constitutions. These latter themes began to unravel in the top courts of Member States. There is no doubt, however, that the Union absorbed more and more characteristics of a multi-nation state so that federalism was often used to describe the relationship between the members and the union. These developments were accompanied by what some saw as increasingly interventionist social and employment policies including Union citizenship and human rights protection as well as a Union criminal law to protect an area of freedom, security and justice. While some saw these as the necessary corollaries of societies working more closely together and consequential residence rights based on free movement, others deeply resented what they chose to view as globalised alienation.

As so often in the UK's past, immigration came to be seen as a cause of deep felt discontent and a subject on which it is easy to foment nationalist and racist fears. Now the threat was not from the new Commonwealth but from the new members of the EU, especially Eastern Europe. These fears were fanned by political parties. Both Labour and Conservative supporters had significant anti-EU elements but the emergence of a populist and anti-immigration party UKIP (United Kingdom Independence Party) initially appeared to eat into the Conservative vote. It subsequently became a threat to Labour.

There is no need to recount the well-known UKIP onslaught on Europe. UKIP spoke on behalf of the frustrations of swathes of English voters who felt threatened by globalization and accompanying immigration with effects on employment, wage restraint, public services and housing. Some of its message was simply racist. The loss of 'control' and the feeling of being left behind and not being listened to in the wake of a global bandwagon alienated many who were not racist but who blamed the EU for their woes. The ideological anxieties of UKIP were echoed by Conservative party politicians who were fearful of self-preservation through UKIP inroads into Conservative constituencies. They had just cause to be worried but from 2019 the populism unleashed by UKIP and its successor, the Brexit Party, became an even greater problem for Labour in its traditional heartlands.

In January 2013, David Cameron outlined his ideas for EU treaty reform which he then hoped to negotiate successfully with EU partners before putting the results to an in/out referendum vote for the British people.[8] A referendum became a manifesto pledge. In his speech, Cameron opined 'I have no illusions of the scale of the task ahead.'

Despite his reasoned package of reforms which included a UK opt-out from 'ever closer union' and a red card block on EU legislation by national parliaments, the most publicised development in Tory policy was in freedom of movement of EU workers and a desire to 'reclaim our borders'. By 2015, the Conservative Party manifesto for the general election contained proposals for restrictions on EU freedom of movement involving benefits, job-seeking support, social housing, restrictions on unemployment benefit, child benefit return by EU workers after 6 months if unemployed, restrictions on child benefit and child tax credits, stronger powers of deportation and restrictions on non-EU spouses. Restrictions covered free movement

[8] https://www.gov.uk/government/speeches/eu-speech-at-bloomberg.

rights for new Member States. This was just as Europe faced the refugee crisis of 2015 which UKIP used to fan the flames of xenophobia.

In October 2015, the EU state leaders requested that Cameron's reforms be put in writing. Cameron's letter to the President of the EU Council in November 2015 seemed modest. It met with a hostile reaction from members of his own party.

The May 2015 general election led to a Conservative majority of 12 in the House of Commons. In the event, only one UKIP MP was elected to Parliament despite gaining 3,881,099 (12.6 pc of the total) UK votes. The election result meant that a referendum on membership of the European Union would take place by 2017—pressure immediately grew for such a referendum to take place within 2016, which was the case. The European Union Referendum Bill was introduced in the House of Commons on 9 June 2015. The question initially proposed to be put to those entitled to vote in the referendum was modified (the electorate was that of a UK Parliamentary general election with modifications allowing peers to vote as well as Commonwealth and Irish Republic citizens in Gibraltar). Following a recommendation from the statutory Electoral Commission it was agreed to change the wording to one which did not, the Commission believed, favour a vote in favour of the status quo. The Commission recommendation was: 'Should the United Kingdom remain a member of the European Union or leave the European Union?' David Cameron allowed a ministerial free vote on in or out of the EU despite the government policy of negotiating terms supporting an in vote. The freedom to campaign against collective government policy arose after the terms of renegotiation were agreed. Boris Johnson became the most prominent Brexit campaigner.

By 2016, the pro-European initiative had been waning throughout the Union. The level of opt-outs by member states from Union policies and the multi-layered nature of the EU enterprise even post Lisbon made it an opaque edifice. The efforts and vision required to bring Europe back from catastrophe post-1945 seemed consigned to history. So too were the memories of more recent European dictatorships and not too distant Soviet hegemony in newer Member States. Events in the Ukraine since 2014 and the invasion of 2022 have reforged memories of the latter. The EEC and its successors have produced peace in western Europe for over 70 years and assisted in the transformation of 13 former dictatorships to EU members since 1980. A war in Europe between nations seemed unthinkable. But the craving for European peace and security that impelled economic integration almost 70 years ago seemed no longer there in 2016.

The Eurozone financial crisis brought austerity measures that were accused of bringing the European ideal to its knees and overriding national democratic will. Where lies the balance between supranationalism and national democratic will? The refugee crisis stretched solidarity to breaking point. In most cases the benefits of union were not weighed by those who were to vote in favour of Brexit. It may be the benefits would count for little in their calculations in any event. Regaining sovereignty and control of 'our borders' were seen as ends worth justifying in the face of economic restrictions that come with 'freedom'.

4 The People Vote

David Cameron was not alone in suggesting that a referendum on European membership would be necessary. The then Labour leader Ed Miliband qualified his assurance on a referendum stating this would occur if there were a further transfer of powers to the Union. The Liberal Democrats came to support a Union referendum despite their avowed support for the European Union. Above all the rhetoric there was a sense that the argument had to be addressed that the people of the United Kingdom had not agreed in the 1975 EEC referendum, or subsequently, to the European Union of 2015 and that the narrative was no longer the same. The changes required approval by plebiscite.

Professor Biondi and I wrote that now that a referendum was to take place, the people should vote on full, impartial and undistorted information on the pros and cons of continuing membership.[9] The debate was supposed to be informed by the coalition government's balance of competencies' review between the EU and Member States. This was hailed by the government as the most extensive analysis ever undertaken of the UK's relationship with the EU. The House of Lords Select Committee on the EU (2014–2015, paras 25–28) described the 32 reports as 'ambitious' and 'unprecedented' and 'for the most part' 'fair and neutral assessments'. But the reports had not been well publicised and contained, the committee reported, omissions and displayed over-emphasis of the government position.

Under the Referendum Act 2015 s 6, the government had to publish a statement setting out what has been agreed by member states following negotiations relating to the United Kingdom's request for reforms to address concerns over its membership of the European Union, and the opinion of the government of the United Kingdom on what has been agreed. This was published in February 2016 (UK government 2016). The European Council published its agreed terms if the UK expressed a desire to remain in the EU.[10] Under s 7, the secretary of state had to publish a report which included information about rights and obligations that arise under European Union law as a result of the UK's membership of the European Union.

The referendum outcome of 23 June 2016 decided by 51.9pc to 48.1pc for the UK to leave the European Union. This was from a 77.2 pc turn-out of eligible voters. There was no specification about the manner or terms of departure. Bitter and acrimonious controversy arose concerning the gross misrepresentation of the leave campaign and a completely inept performance by the government to advance the case for remain. Subsequently, evidence emerged of foreign (Russian) interference with the referendum through social media a House of Commons select committee claimed (DCMS Committee 2017–2019, ch 5). The Brexit vote divided the country in a manner not seen since the English civil war of the 1640s. The UK and its political institutions seemed gripped by paralysis incapable of determining which way to proceed.

---

[9] Birkinshaw and Biondi (2016).

[10] European Council Brussels, 19 February 2016 EUCO 1/16: CO EUR 1 CONCL. 1.

The immediate consequence was the resignation of David Cameron. He was facing forces within his own party and the country at large that were irresistible. The Remain campaign he led was beneath inept and faced a Leave campaign orchestrated by lies and malign efficiency (Shipman 2016). Mrs. May became leader of the Conservative Party and Prime Minister. In 2017, she called a general election hoping to build on Cameron's tiny majority. She emerged with the loss of an overall majority in the Commons and was forced to rely upon a 'confidence and supply' agreement to govern with the Northern Ireland Democratic Unionist Party who immediately played their small hand for all it was worth. On this basis, she faced a Commons that was split down the middle in terms of in or out.

Her position was pitiful. She miscalculated on every turn, starting with the notification to the European Council under Article 50 TEU of the UK's intention to leave the EU. There was no plan in place for such a world-changing decision. In the 2019 European Parliament elections the Brexit Party under the charismatic demagogue Nigel Farage (Crick 2022) was the clear winner in the UK's European elections, while the pro-EU Lib Dems came second. The Conservatives and Labour suffered heavy losses, with the former getting less than 10% of the vote. Nigel Farage said he was ready to 'take on' the main parties in a general election.

5 Withdrawal

Under TEU Article 50, a member state that has decided to withdraw from the Union 'in accordance with its own constitutional requirements' may notify the European Council of its intention. The Supreme Court famously concluded that this requirement necessitated an authorization through legislation and that acting under the prerogative was not sufficient (*Miller No 1* below). The EU and the withdrawing state shall conclude an agreement setting out the arrangements of its withdrawal taking account of the framework for its future relationship with the Union. That agreement and statement were agreed between the UK government and EU in November 2019 and included a transition period (TP) under which EU law would operate within the UK. Under the European Union Withdrawal Act 2018 (EUWA) section 13, the agreement and statement have to be agreed by the House of Commons. If agreed by the Commons, the agreement will then have to be concluded by the Council acting by a qualified majority after obtaining the approval of the European Parliament. If agreed, a trade agreement between the UK and EU will then be negotiated under different procedures.

Under Article 50, where an agreement does not materialize, then the UK leaves the EU 2 years after first giving notice. This would have originally have been 29 March 2019, but that date was extended by agreement of all member states until, 31 January 2020. If the UK left on a no-deal, there is no TP. If no new trade agreement is concluded before 31 December 2020, the UK will leave the Union without a trade deal, unless the TP is once again extended by agreement. If a no-deal departure, this would clearly sour relations between the UK and EU and would place in doubt the good-will, and time, necessary for a post Brexit trade deal.

The House of Commons rejected May's negotiated withdrawal agreement on three occasions inflicting the greatest ever Commons defeat on a government. After her third defeat, Mrs. May announced her resignation leading to the election of Boris Johnson as party leader by Conservative party members and prime minister. Faced with the divided House of Commons, which increasingly began acting more like an executive than a legislature, he sought to dissolve Parliament. But he was straightjacketed by Cameron's Fixed Term Parliaments Act and he failed to get Corbyn's consent to override that legislation. The Commons, assisted by the Speaker, asserted its mastery over BJ's government and behaved as the governor controlling the Commons Order paper and determining the PMs actions even in the terms of correspondence with the EU President seeking an extension of the TP. It sought to avoid a no-deal exit at all costs. When BJ was frustrated by the Commons, he sought to prorogue Parliament a move which the Supreme Court unanimously ruled unlawful and a judgment which Johnson labelled as 'wrong'. BJ negotiated a new agreement with the EU which the Commons approved but he wished for an accelerated procedure for the necessary bill through the Commons and on failing to achieve this Jeremy Corbyn finally agreed to a bill to seek the Queen's consent to dissolve Parliament and call a general election.

6 WA and TCA

With an election secured BJ achieved a commanding Commons majority of 80. Farage had declared that the Brexit Party would not contest seats held by Tories. BJ's will was Parliamentary law and his mandate and mantra were to get Brexit done. In most respects the WA negotiated by Johnson was the same as that negotiated by Mrs. May and rejected by Parliament although Johnson, together with several prominent Eurosceptics, did vote for the May agreement on her third attempt.

There were two crucial differences in Johnson's WA which he described as 'the greatest single restoration of national sovereignty in parliamentary history' (19/11/19). Firstly, the 'political statement on future relationships was far more qualified from the UK perspective. The UK had watered down its future commitments.

The other change was the replacement of the protocol containing what became known as the 'backstop' by the Northern Ireland Protocol (NIP). BJ described the NIP as the best possible solution' to the Irish question; a 'good solution'. The NIP leaves NI in a single market and a de facto customs union with the EU in order to avoid a border between NI and the Republic on the mainland of Ireland. This is to maintain one of the outcomes of the Good Friday peace agreement in Ireland in 1998. Under the backstop, GB and NI (UK) would have been left under EU law to avoid an Irish border. The backstop may never have materialized if a WA were agreed that avoided this necessity—ie a 'soft Brexit'. The Parliamentary convolutions before the 2019 election were aimed at preventing a no deal Brexit and all its consequences. The NIP is there as a reality in Johnson's agreement and necessitated a border in the Irish sea (ports of entry) for goods, food products and livestock coming from GB to NI. The NIP also means that NI (but not GB) is under EU law for whole swathes of subject areas, EU law is sovereign and of direct effect and courts may make references to the ECJ on matters covered by the NIP. But NI has no say in EU laws, no EU judges and no EU officials.

In 2018, Theresa May as PM told the House of Commons that 'no UK Prime Minister could ever agree' to a customs and regulatory border down the Irish Sea.' Johnson made a similar pledge while his majority depended upon the DUP for parliamentary support. When that ceased to be the case the DUP were sold down the river and had no veto over the NIP. The DUP had been robust supporters of Brexit. With the NIP, BJ agreed because he was no longer beholden to the DUP. The DUP had voted against the WA and also voted against the TCA. The party had moved from power broker to political failure and saw its prime objective of undivided union with the rest of the UK betrayed and the prospect of a united Ireland enhanced, a prospect reinforced by Sinn Fein's electoral success in 2022.

The NIP has been a running sore for BJ. Either he didn't understand what he signed up to and praised, he did not listen to advice on its content, or as Ian Paisley Jr. has disclosed, he said he intended to tear it up even though Parliament had voted in favour of it and a general election majority had supported it. The latter might be consistent with his threats on numerous occasions to take unilateral action against the NIP if the Union will not renegotiate its terms. The latter's stance is understandably *pacta sunt servanda*. The attorney general and foreign secretary had agreed that this involves no breach of international law because Johnson will be invoking Parliamentary sovereignty in new legislation. The usual presumption is that Parliament acts in support of international law not in defiance of it! Bluff was a Johnson ploy.

Untrammelled by his pre-election position of weakness, BJ was able to renegotiate the WA which the Commission said was 'unopenable'—and conclude the TCA at breakneck speed and have them approved by Parliament in legislation paving the way for signature. With the reduction of opposition MPs in 2019, Parliament's position was demoted after the 2019 election so that its statutory oversight of negotiations on the future relationship as under the EU(WA) Bill was removed. Parliament had to approve the WA in law. Scotland, Wales and Northern Ireland refused to give consent motions to the WA bill. This did not prevent the bill becoming law.

The TCA—a 'tariff and quota free' trade deal—removes EU law and influence from the UK's future trade, commercial, environmental and FSJ activities though the actual parameters of Global Britain's freedoms are set out below. The TCA contains numerous level playing-field provisions covering competition, state aids, data protection, environmental protection, employment rights and human rights.

7 UK Courts and Europe

The advent of EC law was described by Lord Denning as an 'incoming tide'[11]; in fact it was to become more like a tsunami. By Act of Parliament, Union law has become a part of 'our law' said Lord Denning and although not 'supplanting English law' (sic) it 'overrides any part that is inconsistent with It'.[12]

The sourness of the political relations, which was coloured by nationalistic sensitivities, has to be contrasted with the legal relationship between the EU and UK courts and how our courts adapted to a new legal regime which promoted concepts of EC legal sovereignty and direct effect, doctrines crafted by the ECJ, so that fundamentals of the unwritten UK constitution were called into question including the non-application by the courts of an act of Parliament itself,[13] injunctions to prevent EU law being overridden by ministers of the Crown in subjects covered by Crown immunity [ditto] and use of treaties by UK and EU individuals (non-state actors) in UK courts.[14]

From the earliest years of the UK membership the courts had embraced the new system of law and new methods on interpretation constructively and had generally, if not universally, followed the lead given by the ECJ in the interpretation of treaty provisions and directives. *Von Colson* and *Marleasing*[15] duties of consistent construction of domestic measures with EU provisions, especially where the national laws pre-dated the EU measures, caused problems as they did for all national courts but the courts stuck to their task of interpreting domestic measures in the light of EU law (occasionally baulking at what we might term political correctness—rights of pregnant women in employment,[16] or placing limits on consistent construction with non-binding TEU Title Three measures).[17] But in legal cases of significant complexity brought about by effluxion of time, complex and shifting statistical evidence and its impact on discrimination the courts sought to uphold the dictates of s2(1) and (4) ECA and uphold EU law's sovereignty.[18]

Judicial review in UK domestic laws became highly influenced by principles developed in EU law, invariably by way of national laws (Birkinshaw 2020). Strains in the ECJ methods of construction given in a single judgment and the generalised and compromised nature of EU legislation compared with the more specific terms of

---

[11] (*Bulmer v Bollinger* [1974] EWCA Civ 14).

[12] *Macarthys v. Smith* [1981] 1 All ER 111 at 120.

[13] Lord Bridge *Factortame* [1990] UKHL 7.

[14] *McCarthys v Smith* above; *Garland v British Engineering* [1983] 2 All ER 751 (HL); *EOC v SoS Employment* [1994] 1 All ER 910 (HL); *Rees-Mogg* above note 5.

[15] *Von Colson* Case 14/83; *Marleasing* Case C 106/89.

[16] *Webb v EMO* [1995] 4 All ER 577 (HL).

[17] *Assange v Swedish Prosecution Authority* [2012] UKSC 22 the majority did not apply such limitations; the minority Lord Mance and Lady Hale did.

[18] An exception was *R v SoS Employment ex p Seymour-Smith* [1997] 2 All ER 273 (HL) and in the court of appeal [1996] All ER (EC) 1.

Parliamentary legislation were apparent.[19] But the sovereignty of EU law in its areas of competence was not doubted as it had been by the Conseil d'Etat in France[20] and more recently by the German Bundesverfassungsgericht where the ECJ has been criticised for acting in an ultra vires manner, and in Poland.[21] What was called into question were the claims of overriding sovereignty of EU law over national constitutional fundamentals. In its sphere of competence, UK courts steadfastly accepted that EU norms enjoyed supremacy over domestic law.[22]

Questions were asked on whether there were boundaries to the ECJ defining its own limits and jurisdiction, including its power to overrule national constitutional fundamentals[23] or for the domestic courts to allow EU law to do something that not even Parliament could do—entrench itself.[24] The legacy of this legal appraisal forged a new outlook among UK judges so that the courts became exponents on the constitution and case law became enriched by analysis of issues that had hitherto been the preserve of political institutions in the UK. Courts started to grapple with questions of sovereignty and what it means not only in relation to the EU[25] but also in relation to the relationship between the executive and prerogative and legislature as witnessed by the famous Gina Miller litigation on the limits of the prerogative[26]—cases on leaving the Union and prorogation of Parliament. The Crown, the supreme court ruled, could not simply assert a prerogative power to leave the EU or to prorogue Parliament. These assertions had to be legally reasoned to justification. The assertions of government were found to be legally wanting.

The ancient political constitution was becoming judicialised and legalised, a factor bitterly resented by Boris Johnson who after 2019 set in motion a review of judicial review and human rights legislation with the aim of curbing the reach of the courts, both in judicial review and in human rights. The reforms in judicial review are actually quite minor, though not unimportant, although press reports emerged of further reforms, and in human rights reforms are geared more to reducing the influence of the CHR and confining its impact and in making procedures more prolonged in domestic courts than in removing substantive rights of the ECHR. Described as 'politically unworkable' the bill reforming human rights was immediately dropped by the incoming PM Truss. No other PM has undermined the conventions of the UK constitution as had Johnson and exposed the delicate basis on which our constitutional fundamentals rest when a headstrong PM is determined to have his way. How much of his influence will survive his resignation remains to

[19] HS2 [2014] UKSC 3 per Lord Reed.

[20] The position until changed by *Nicolo* CE 20 October 1989.

[21] Decision of 7 October 2021 Polish Constitutional Tribunal Case K/321: TEU breaches the Polish constitution.

[22] *Miller No 1* [2017] UKSC 5.

[23] *Pham* [2015] UKSC 19 Lord Mance.

[24] *Thoburn* [2002] 4 All 156.

[25] *Thoburn; HS2*; *Pham* above.

[26] *Miller No 1* above and *No 2* [2019] UKSC 41.

be seen. The short chaotic premiership of Truss led to her resignation and the appointment of Rishi Sunak as prime minister. His appointment of Dominic Raab as justice secretary led to the possibility of revival of the controversial Bill of Rights bill to repeal the Human Rights Act. Raab's resignation in disgrace led to the cessation of the bill.

8 Retaining and Removing EU Law[27]

Meanwhile, there is the vast legacy of EU law in UK law. The government has set about reviewing this corpus of law to adjust its content to the needs of global Britain and to re-mould the domestic regulatory relationship which was governed by EU law. It is a task of enormous complexity.

The EU (Withdrawal) Act 2018 (EUWA) (and now see 2020 EUWA Act) was passed to ensure a smooth transition for the UK's legal system after Brexit. This meant that all EU law (except the Charter of Fundamental Rights), together with pre-Brexit general principles of EU law and the pre-Brexit case law of the ECJ, was converted into UK law on 31 December 2020 as 'retained EU Law' (REUL). The general principles may be used in a 'purposive way' by UK courts but not to disapply UK laws post Brexit or to 'create rights of action'. While the CFR is not maintained by deliberate choice this does not remove any underlying fundamental rights or principles which exist, and EU law which is retained will continue to be interpreted in light of those underlying rights and principles. The rule in *Francovich* on liability for breaches of EU law does not apply after 31 December 2020.

Under EUWA, REUL takes precedence over conflicting provisions of pre-Brexit UK law. After Brexit, Parliament can pass laws to repeal or modify any REUL it no longer wishes to be bound by. Parliament can pass a law to reverse any judicial decisions giving primacy to EU law. The Supreme Court and Court of Appeal and Scottish equivalents may also diverge from erstwhile EU binding judgments.[28] It was recommended that this power should be widely extended to lower courts and this was avidly advocated by Lord Frost. The outcome found its way in complex provisions in the Retained EU etc Law Act 2023. In short since 31 December 2020, the UK is no longer bound by past EU law if it chooses not to be and is not bound by future EU law. Northern Ireland differs.

The Trade and Cooperation Agreement (TCA) stipulates that each side sets its own policies in areas such as social, commercial, environmental matters and criminal justice. However, the safety net for the parties, referred to as level playing field provisions, means that if this creates a material impact on trade or investment, the EU (or UK) may take retaliatory action. The TCA is replete with dispute mechanisms

---

[27] For a short introduction see Barnard (2022).

[28] SI 2020 No 1525 EUWA etc. Regs. for the courts included.

involving consultation, negotiation, and arbitration as well as 'rebalancing' measures (Birkinshaw 2021).

The ECJ retains an important role under the WA: under the provisions on citizens' rights UK courts may make a preliminary reference to the ECJ about the interpretation of the WA until 2028. The general dispute resolution mechanism (DRM) provides for political consultation and then arbitration; however, if a point of EU law is at issue, a reference must be made to the ECJ. Provision is made for litigation commenced before 31 December 2020. Under the NIP, the ECJ continues to have the same role as it did before Brexit in matters covered by the protocol. So, for example, the Commission can bring enforcement proceedings against the UK (Article 258 TFEU below) and national courts can make references to the ECJ (Article 267 TFEU) on points covered by the NIP. The EU law that applies under the WA on citizens' rights and the NIP is pre-31 December 2020 law, so it includes the Charter of Fundamental Rights, the general principles and EU methods of interpretation including EU sovereignty.[29]

The Commission commenced proceedings under the NIP before the ECJ when the UK unilaterally extended 'smoothing provisions' for the protocol's introduction. On 29 January 2021, the European Commission caused surprise by announcing plans to invoke Article 16 NIP 'in order to avert serious societal difficulties due to a lack of supply threatening to disturb the orderly implementation of the covid vaccination campaigns in the member states.' The move, according to Pow, 'achieved the relatively rare feat of uniting all of Northern Ireland's main five parties – unionist, nationalist and other – along with the British and Irish Governments' in opposition to the Commission's intemperate action (Pow 2021).

The UK government complained in its White Paper in July 2021 (UK government 2021a) that the ECJ should have no role under the NIP—the same protocol the terms of which the UK government had agreed to. The UK wants the DRM that applies under the TCA to apply to the NIP. Yet because the TCA contains no elements, with minor exceptions, of EU law, the TCA's DRM could be based on the model found in more standard trade agreements (political consultation and then arbitration, with no role for the ECJ). One possible compromise might be that the Withdrawal Agreement's general DRM be applied to the NIP as well suggests Barnard (2022). The 2021 paper mooted the possibility of invoking Article 16 of the NIP to exert leverage although the Article was not intended to allow either party to suspend provisions of the protocol permanently or in their entirety and is subject to review by the Joint Committee.

The NIP, agreed by Johnson and forced on the DUP, had been an albatross dangling around Johnson's neck. He was prepared to legislate for change unilaterally. This has been threatened previously and had the attorney general's support that such action would not breach international law because of parliamentary sovereignty. This is a crude misunderstanding of international and domestic law. The US

[29] *SSWP v AT* [2023] EWCA Civ 1307 and *NIHRC, Re Application for Judicial Review* [2024] NIKB 35; WA Arts 2a and 4; EU (WA) 2020 and Retained EU Law etc Act 2023 ss 9, 11, 12 & 13.

urged the UK to reach a compromised settlement. Both the EU Commission and Labour opposition said that such unilateral action would breach international law. The Commission emphasised that the NIP created bi-lateral legal obligations. Such breaches would reverberate badly at a time when Russia was acting in defiance of international law. Sinn Fein supported the NIP and its observance; the DUP wanted resolution of the protocol's 'problems' before power sharing could recommence in NI. The UK stand on the NIP did not prevent the UK initiating legal proceedings against the EU for alleged breaches of the TCA in relation to access to EU research and scientific programmes involving £100 billion funding.

In February 2023, Sunak agreed the Windsor Framework with the EU Commission President in an effort to resolve the disputes left by the NIP. The UK bill which had threatened unilaterally to breach the NIP was halted in the House of Lords, although Sunak adverted to the fact that future contingencies might cause its revival.[30] In respect of post-Brexit ECJ cases, we have seen UK courts and tribunals are not bound by them, and preliminary references to the ECJ are no longer permissible absent NIP. But a UK court or tribunal may have regard to anything done on or after the end of the transition period (31/12/2020) by the ECJ 'so far as it is relevant to any matter before the court or tribunal'. In other words, UK courts can take post-Brexit ECJ case law into account when interpreting REUL. This provision will be watched with keen interest.

9 Further Action on REUL

The UK government prioritised UK regulatory autonomy in the TCA. Lord Frost as Brexit minister thought the presence on the UK statute book of volumes of REUL was unacceptable. In his final resignation speech to Parliament in December 2021, he said he wanted to give REUL a 'more appropriate status within the UK legal system for the purposes of amendment and repeal'. This prompted concerns that if this resulted in downgrading all REUL to secondary legislation (some of it is currently considered primary legislation), thus making it much easier to repeal, Parliamentary scrutiny would be inadequate, especially if, as proposed, an 'accelerated process' for change is involved. In *its Benefits of Brexit* policy paper (UK government 2021b), the government reiterated Lord Frost's ambition to allow 'changes to be made to retained EU law more easily'. 'Our intention is to ensure that this foreign-derived body of law has the appropriate status given that we are no longer a member of the EU'. A 'targeted power' would provide a mechanism to allow REUL to be amended in a 'more sustainable way to deliver the UK's regulatory, economic and environmental priorities' (p. 34). The government also

[30] HMG *Legal Position: Windsor Framework* p. 2 https://assets.publishing.service.gov.uk/government/uploads/system/uploads/attachment_data/file/1139419/HMG_Legal_Position_The_Windsor_Framework.pdf.

wanted to give Parliament the power to define in a more precise way the relationship between retained EU law and UK law. This involved removing the supremacy of pre-Brexit EU and EU derived law over pre-Brexit UK law (covering 2376 UK acts p. 34). This will raise complex issues of legitimate expectation and entitlement.

A Brexit Freedoms Bill was announced in the Queen's Speech in May 2022 to further these aims along with reforms in data protection, financial regulation, public procurement covering £300 billion pa and live exportation of animals. Space for reform will be limited by the level playing field provisions of the TCA and the realities of economic co-existence under the TCA. In addition, there are concerns about regulatory divergence within the UK, particularly given the inhibitions imposed by the NIP; and manufacturers, financiers, professionals, entertainers, scientists and so on who in many cases are fretful of divergence and who do not see benefits in divorce from Europe from their business, occupational or research point of view. In his budget address to the Commons in September 2022, the new chancellor spoke of an automatic 'sunset' of 'EU regulations' by December 2023 to restore the primacy of UK legislation in his boost for economic growth. The Retained EU Law etc. Bill of September 2022 makes provision for far-reaching and precipitate changes to the duration and status of EU law in a manner that is bound to cause confusion and uncertainty. One major concession by the government meant that instead of the repeal of all but exempted REUL measures by the end of 2023, the cull was limited to those measures set out in schedule 1 to the bill – about 600 items. Domestic courts are also given wide powers to depart from pre Brexit EU case law and EU derived domestic case law. After 2023, REUL is to become 'assimilated law'. The Labour government introduced a Product Regulation and Metrology Bill which could involve wide compliance with EU measures.

The die is cast. The UK is out. With an eye on lost Labour voters, Keir Starmer has stated that the task is now to make Brexit a success and not to hark back to EU membership, free movement of persons, the single market or a customs union. The UK is on its own and it is unclear what the future holds for the UK or what countries will comprise the UK in the longer term. As in the 1950s and 1960s, the UK is looking for its place in the world.

References

Barnard C (2022) UKCE Constitution and Governance in the UK. https://ukandeu.ac.uk/wp-content/uploads/2022/03/UKIN-Constitution-Governance-Report_FINAL-PROOF.pdf. p. 72

Birkinshaw P (2020) European public law: the achievement and the Brexit challenge. Wolters Kluwer, Alphen aan den Rijn

Birkinshaw P (2021) Brexit and the trade and cooperation agreement: endgame or prolegomenon. Eur Public Law 27(2):229

Birkinshaw P, Biondi A (2016) Introduction. In: Birkinshaw P, Biondi A (eds) Britain alone! The implications and consequences of United Kingdom exit from the RU. Wolters Kluwer, Alphen aan den Rijn

Bogdanor V (2012) Imprisoned by a doctrine: the modern Defence of parliamentary sovereignty. Oxford J Legal Stud 32:179

Crick M (2022) One party after another: the disruptive life of Nigel Farage. Simon & Schuster, New York

Digital, Culture, Media & Sport Committee (2017–2019) Disinformation and 'fake news': Interim Report, Commons DCMS Committee, Fifth Report of Session 2017–19, HC 363, 2018, Chapter 5

House of Lords Select Committee on the EU (2014–2015) Twelfth Report HL 140 (2014–15)

Pow J (2021). https://ukandeu.ac.uk/the-dup-and-the-protocol/

Shipman T (2016) All out war. William Collins, Glasgow

Sked A (2015). https://ukandeu.ac.uk/how-a-secretive-elite-created-the-eu-to-build-a-world-government/

Thatcher M (1988). https://www.margaretthatcher.org/document/107332

UK government (1971) The UK and European Communities Cmnd 4715 (1971)

UK government (2016) The Best of Both Worlds: the United Kingdom's special status in a reformed European Union, HMG, 2016

UK government (2021a). https://assets.publishing.service.gov.uk/government/uploads/system/uploads/attachment_data/file/1008451/CCS207_CCS0721914902-005_Northern_Ireland_Protocol_Web_Accessible__1_.pdf

UK government (2021b). https://assets.publishing.service.gov.uk/government/uploads/system/uploads/attachment_data/file/1054643/benefits-of-brexit.pdf

Young H (1999) This blessed plot; Britain and Europe from Churchill to Blair 1999 revision. Macmillan, London

The Restraint, Reassertion and Realities of Parliamentary Sovereignty: Reassessing the United Kingdom's Post-Brexit Constitutional Identity

Ben Stanford

1 Introduction

Normative values and principles play an essential role in shaping and influencing constitutions. In one respect, some have even suggested that the very purpose of a constitution is to 'articulate and preserve a society's fundamental moral principles'.[1] This may be more obviously apparent in democratic states that allow broad societal political participation in the form of elections and free speech, but values and principles still help to determine the constitutional identity of all states regardless of any particular form of government or the involvement of society.

Whilst some fundamental values underpin the constitutions of all liberal democracies to some extent, for example a basic conception of the rule of law,[2] each state's constitutional identity is unique and differs from the next. For Gary Jacobsohn, a constitutional identity is really a reflection of both continuity and societal aspirations.[3] By this he meant that a 'constitution acquires an identity through experience...[and thus] emerges dialogically and represents a mix of political aspirations and commitments that are expressive of a nation's past, as well as the determination of those within the society who seek in some way to transcend that past'.[4]

Identifying the constitutional identity of states and organisations is, on the face of it, an easier task when that entity has a codified constitution or, particularly in the

[1] Loveland (2021), p. 4.

[2] See eg. Arajärvi (2021), pp. 173–175; Etherton (2018); Chesterman (2008), pp. 331–342.

[3] Jacobsohn (2010), p. 7.

[4] Ibid.

B. Stanford (✉)
Liverpool John Moores University, Liverpool, UK
e-mail: b.j.stanford@ljmu.ac.uk

E. Guinchard, C. Panara (eds.), *The New Relationship between the United Kingdom and the European Union*, https://doi.org/10.1007/978-3-031-70652-3_3

case of an international organisation, documents in the form of founding treaties. For example, Article 2 of the Treaty on the European Union (TEU) provides that the EU is founded on:

> the values of respect for human dignity, freedom, democracy, equality, the rule of law and respect for human rights, including the rights of persons belonging to minorities. These values are common to the Member States in a society in which pluralism, non-discrimination, tolerance, justice, solidarity and equality between women and men prevail.[5]

These values are, to some extent, further reflected in the Copenhagen criteria, which candidate accession countries must demonstrate when seeking to join the EU. These include *inter alia* the need for 'stable institutions guaranteeing democracy, the rule of law, human rights and respect for and protection of minorities', 'a functioning market economy' and 'the ability to take on and implement effectively the obligations of membership, including adherence to the aims of political, economic and monetary union'.[6] In recent years the Court of Justice of the EU (CJEU) has grappled with the concept of constitutional identity amidst clashes between EU law and the national identities of member states,[7] which the EU has the obligation to respect owing to the so-called 'national identity clause' in Article 4(2) of the TEU.[8] The declining rule of law standards in member states such as Hungary and Poland has attracted particular attention recently,[9] but a landmark CJEU judgment in 2018 confirmed that member states must guarantee and respect the independence of their national courts and tribunals.[10]

Owing in part to the absence of a codified constitution or foundational document, the United Kingdom has a particularly unique and opaque constitutional identity which is more difficult to identify. Recognising the importance and role of history in the UK's constitutional development, Edmund Burke famously spoke of the continuity of the UK Constitution 'made by the peculiar circumstances, occasions, tempers, dispositions, and moral, civil, and social habitudes of the people'.[11] A good starting point when attempting to identify the UK's constitutional identity is to consider the various sources of the UK's Constitution, not least of all statutes, common law, the royal prerogative and constitutional conventions, but also the informal yet vitally important normative principles underpinning it. Amongst these are the rule of law, accountable government, human rights and democracy, but

[5]Consolidated Version of the Treaty on European Union [2008] OJ C115/13, Art. 2. See also the Charter of Fundamental Rights of the European Union [2000] OJ C364/1, Preamble para. 2.

[6]European Commission, Conditions for Membership https://ec.europa.eu/neighbourhood-enlargement/enlargement-policy/conditions-membership_en accessed 1 November 2023.

[7]See e.g. de Witte (2021), Schnettger (2019) and Schill and von Bogdandy (2011).

[8]Consolidated Version of the Treaty on European Union [2008] OJ C115/13, Art. 4(2).

[9]See e.g. Pech (2022), Ovádek (2022) and Bonelli and Claes (2018).

[10]C-64/16 *Associação Sindical dos Juízes Portugueses* [2018] ECR I-117.

[11]Burke (1782).

perhaps the most important and unique of all is parliamentary sovereignty which establishes the supremacy of Parliament in the UK's constitutional system.

In that respect, the UK's 47-year membership and subsequent departure from the EU in January 2020 was undoubtedly one of the most important and historic episodes for its legal and political system, impacting the UK's constitutional framework and overall constitutional identity in significant ways.[12] Often described as a constitutional 'shock',[13] Brexit has triggered or played a role in the resignation of two Prime Ministers, provoked major disagreements between political parties, as well as between national and devolved governments, and even within successive governments, over the future of the UK-EU relationship. It has also exposed the fragile nature of the UK's Constitution and broader constitutional identity. Insofar as the principle of parliamentary sovereignty is concerned, few issues have attracted as much attention and debate as the impact of EU membership and the supremacy of EU law,[14] the 2016 Referendum vote to leave and subsequent process of withdrawal,[15] and, since then, broader questions about the nature of referendums, different notions of sovereignty and the role of the principle within the UK Constitution.[16] That said, whilst the notion of parliamentary sovereignty undoubtedly played a role in discussions leading up to and following the 2016 Referendum, the debate has been heavily obfuscated by misleading or over-simplified political rhetoric and commentary, seen most obviously with the official Leave Campaign's slogan 'take back control'.[17]

Following this introduction, the second section outlines the principle of parliamentary sovereignty and how it was effectively 'restrained' during the UK's membership of the EU, whilst also providing a brief overview of the background to Brexit. The third section considers how, despite the blurring of the notions of sovereignty in the Referendum debate, parliamentary sovereignty was ultimately 'reasserted' with Brexit. The fourth section then considers the 'realities' of current trends and likely future developments impacting parliamentary sovereignty and other constitutional values underpinning the UK Constitution. Ultimately this chapter argues that whilst the UK's constitutional identity has generally been stable, notwithstanding its vulnerabilities, membership of the EU provided some stability and predictability which has now been removed. Owing to the reality of this governance vacuum and the approach of successive UK Governments which has expanded executive sovereignty, the UK's constitutional identity is now experiencing a period of upheaval, challenging its long held constitutional values in a direct, and in some ways, alarming manner.

---

[12] See e.g. Birkinshaw (2020).

[13] Blick (2019).

[14] See e.g. Barber (2011), Allan (1997), Wade (1996), Laws (1995) and Craig (1991).

[15] See e.g. Ewing (2017), Young (2017), Craig (2016) and Douglas-Scott (2016a). See also Public Law Brexit Special Extra Issue 2017.

[16] See e.g. Barnard (2022), Gordon (2020), Bickerton (2019) and Bogdanor (2019).

[17] See e.g. Douglas-Scott (2016b).

2 Parliamentary Sovereignty Restrained (1973–2020)

2.1 The UK Constitution and EU Membership

As is well-known, the Constitution of the United Kingdom is a patchwork of both legal and non-legal sources supplemented by an array of normative constitutional principles. Foremost amongst these legal sources are what Lord Justice Laws famously termed 'constitutional statutes',[18] such as Magna Carta 1215, the Bill of Rights 1689, the Human Rights Act (HRA) 1998 and the various 1990s devolution Acts. Another crucial legal source is the common law and principles that derive from landmark judicial decisions, with cases such as *Attorney-General v De Keyser's Royal Hotel Limited* and *Pickin v British Railways Board* confirming the supremacy of Parliament,[19] though obiter comments in *R (Jackson) v Attorney General* suggested that there may be some limitations,[20] which this chapter will address later. Whilst undoubtedly more restrained in the present day, the royal prerogative also demonstrates the power held by the UK executive to carry out many important and symbolic tasks.

Constitutional conventions and official documents such as the Ministerial Code also play a pivotal role as non-legal sources,[21] though their relevance today can certainly be questioned in light of inconsistent political enforcement and accusations of democratic backsliding. Nonetheless, these formal sources of the UK Constitution are all subject to the constraints of normative constitutional principles, chief amongst them parliamentary sovereignty.

The essence and traditional conception of parliamentary sovereignty was most famously captured by A.V. Dicey writing in the late nineteenth century:

> The principle of Parliamentary sovereignty means neither more nor less than this, namely, that Parliament...has, under the English constitution, the right to make or unmake any law whatever; and, further, that no person or body is recognised by the law of England as having a right to override or set aside the legislation of Parliament.[22]

In other words, Parliament is legally unrestrained and the dominant law-making institution in the UK constitutional system, able to enact law on any subject matter which cannot be challenged. Put most directly by Vernon Bogdanor, this traditional view of parliamentary sovereignty meant that the UK Constitution could be summed up in eight words—'what the Queen in Parliament enacts is law'.[23] Such a literal and absolute position would, however, both simplify and complicate the UK's

---

[18] *Thoburn v Sunderland City Council* [2002] EWHC 195 (Admin), paras. 60–62.

[19] *Attorney-General v De Keyser's Royal Hotel Limited* [1920] UKHL 1; [1920] AC 508; *Pickin v British Railways Board* [1974] UKHL 1; [1974] AC 765.

[20] *R (Jackson) v Attorney General* [2005] UKHL 56; [2006] 1 AC 262.

[21] HM Government, Ministerial Code. https://www.gov.uk/government/publications/ministerial-code accessed 1 November 2023.

[22] Dicey (1885/1985), p. 40.

[23] Bogdanor (2009), p. 13.

constitutional identity, as Paul Craig reflected when concluding that this would mean the rejection of any other facets of constitutional identity in the UK.[24]

Nevertheless, as constitutional lawyers have discussed in much depth, our understanding of parliamentary sovereignty changed drastically in 1973 when the UK joined the (then) European Community. As a dualist state, an Act of Parliament was needed for European law to have binding effect in UK domestic law. Sections 2 and 3(1) of the European Communities Act (ECA) 1972 were unquestionably the most significant and controversial provisions in that respect. First, these established that European law which was directly applicable, or had direct effect, would be automatically incorporated and binding in UK domestic law,[25] and second, that Government Ministers could enact secondary legislation to give effect to European law which lacked direct applicability or direct effect.[26] Third, on the specific impact of European law on UK domestic law, and therefore the status of parliamentary sovereignty itself, the Act made it clear that all statutes passed before and since the Act would have to be construed and applied subject to the requirements of European law.[27] Fourth, the ECA 1972 also established that in legal proceedings, any question over the meaning or effect of European law had to be referred to the CJEU.[28]

Whilst a number of cases to reach the CJEU before the UK joined had already confirmed the supremacy of European law over domestic law,[29] the case most often discussed in the context of the UK Constitution and parliamentary sovereignty is the *Factortame* litigation which began in 1989. In this case, following a reference for a preliminary ruling to the Court of Justice,[30] the House of Lords held that the Merchant Shipping Act 1988 had to be disapplied in favour of European Community law, as the former was discriminatory and breached (then) Article 52 of the EEC Treaty. Lord Bridge delivered perhaps the most well-known passage of the judgment, saying that 'whatever limitation of its sovereignty Parliament accepted when it enacted the European Communities Act 1972 was entirely voluntary'.[31] For Lord Bridge, membership of the European Community (and later Union) thus represented a voluntary restraint on parliamentary sovereignty.

The implications for parliamentary sovereignty were profound, with subsequent debate generally focusing on whether this amounted to constitutional revolution or

---

[24] Craig (2019), p. 288.

[25] ECA 1972, s. 2(1).

[26] ECA 1972, s. 2(2).

[27] ECA 1972, s. 2(4).

[28] ECA 1972, s. 3(1).

[29] See in particular, C-26/62 *NV Algemene Transport—en Expeditie Onderneming van Gend en Loos v Nederlandse Administratie der Belastingen* [1963] ECR 1; C-6/64 *Flaminio Costa v ENEL* [1964] ECR 585; C-11/70 *Internationale Handelsgesellschaft mbH v Einfuhr- und Vorratsstelle fur Getreide und Futtermittel* [1970] ECR 1125.

[30] C-213/89 *R v Secretary of State for Transport ex parte Factortame Ltd* Case [1990] ECR I-2433.

[31] *R (Factortame Ltd) v Secretary of State for Transport (No 2)* [1990] UKHL 13; [1991] 1 AC 603, para. 659.

evolution. Arguing the former more drastic result, Sir William Wade suggested that '[w]hile Britain remains in the Community we are in a regime in which Parliament has bound its successors successfully, and which is nothing if not revolutionary'.[32] For Nicholas Barber, in light of the pre-1991 traditional interpretation of parliamentary sovereignty, it was 'clear that the rule ceased to be a feature of the British constitution after *Factortame*'.[33] Other arguments were not so bold and instead suggested constitutional evolution, for example Sir John Laws suggested that the ECA 1972 provided a new rule of construction whereby subsequent UK legislation would have to be interpreted as 'compatible with rights accorded by European law'.[34] Trevor Allan took a different stance, accepting that parliament's sovereignty had been curtailed during EU membership, but this was an example of evolution as British courts would take a purposive approach when interpreting legislation to 'avoid a result thought unacceptable on general constitutional grounds'.[35]

Whilst the UK's membership of the EU was undoubtedly the principal challenge to the traditional conception of parliamentary sovereignty, as a voluntary (and temporary) restraint, other issues which raise questions about the limits of sovereignty have persisted and outlived Brexit. Recognising this to some extent, Lord Hope delivered one of the most famous obiter comments in recent times in *R (Jackson) v Attorney General*, saying that whilst the UK constitution is dominated by the sovereignty of Parliament, it is 'no longer, if it ever was, absolute'.[36] In the same case, Lord Steyn suggested that the Scotland Act 1998 'points to a divided sovereignty' and that the HRA 1998 incorporating the ECHR has 'created a new legal order', ultimately suggesting that 'the classic account given by Dicey of the doctrine of the supremacy of Parliament, pure and absolute as it was, can now be seen to be out of place in the modern United Kingdom'.[37] The traditional and orthodox view of parliamentary sovereignty is, therefore, not easy to reconcile with the legal and political realities of the twenty-first century.

2.2 The Road to Brexit

Rather than being confined exclusively to the past decade, considerable opposition to the UK's membership of the European Union actually existed throughout its 47-year history and was particularly strong at certain moments.[38] Prior to the decisive 2016 EU Referendum itself, the UK's commitment to membership was

---

[32] Wade (1996), p. 571.

[33] Barber (2011), p. 152.

[34] Laws (1995), p. 89.

[35] Allan (1997), p. 447.

[36] *R (Jackson) v Attorney General* [2005] UKHL 56; [2006] 1 AC 262, para. 104.

[37] *R (Jackson) v Attorney General* [2005] UKHL 56; [2006] 1 AC 262, para. 102.

[38] Usherwood (2002).

tested just 3 years after the UK joined, in 1975, with the first nationwide referendum on the UK's membership of the then European Communities which resulted in a decisive two-third majority decision to remain.[39]

Other key moments which challenged the UK's level of support include the negotiation of several treaty changes, most significantly the Treaty of Maastricht in 1992 which established the European Union and signified the growth of its status as a 'political union'. To facilitate this an amendment to the ECA 1972 was necessary, prompting the introduction of the European Communities (Amendment) Bill in 1992. The Government encountered significant disruption as the so-called Conservative Party 'Maastricht Rebels' voted against the Bill during its passage, before its eventual enactment in 1993.[40] A legal challenge even followed, arguing that the Government could not legally ratify the Maastricht Treaty as it would transfer prerogative powers to Government and that the Treaty would increase the powers of the European Parliament without UK Parliament approval, but the judicial review was unsuccessful.[41] The Treaty of Lisbon in 2007, which implemented several democratising reforms and established the EU's full legal personality, also provoked considerable controversy in light of political pledges and debate to hold a referendum on UK constitutional change and even EU membership itself.[42] Despite the Treaty embodying only minor changes from the originally proposed Constitutional Treaty, the Labour Government proceeded without holding a referendum.

The immediate origins of Brexit, however, began in 2015 when the Conservative Party pledged in their General Election Manifesto to give the public 'a say over whether we should stay in or leave the EU, with an in-out referendum by the end of 2017'.[43] Following their election victory and formation of a majority Government, the European Union Referendum Act 2015 was passed, pledging to hold the referendum no later than 31 December 2017.[44]

Consequently, the 2016 EU Referendum, held on 23 June 2016, resulted in a narrow victory for the leave campaign with just under 52% of the vote.[45] The Prime Minister, David Cameron, announced his resignation the next day as the result became clear, succeeded by Theresa May in July 2016. Several months of uncertainty followed before Theresa May indicated in October 2016 that the Government would trigger Article 50 of the TEU in early 2017, and thus begin the formal process of leaving the EU. However, in one of the most constitutionally significant cases in

[39]The result was approximately 67.2% in favour of remaining in the European Community to 32.8% against. See Walsh (2016).

[40]Bowcott (2018).

[41]*R v Secretary of State for Foreign and Commonwealth Affairs, ex p Rees-Mogg* [1994] QB 552.

[42]See Miller (2009).

[43]The Conservative Party Manifesto (2015), p. 72.

[44]European Union Referendum Act 2015, s. 1.

[45]BBC News (2016).

recent times, first the High Court in November 2016,[46] and then the Supreme Court in January 2017,[47] both confirmed that an Act of Parliament would be needed for the Government to have the legal authority to trigger Article 50 of the TEU, placing parliamentary sovereignty at the heart of the judgment. The European Union (Notification of Withdrawal) Act 2017 soon followed in March 2017, beginning the formal process of withdrawal. Thus, despite its restraint during EU membership, parliamentary sovereignty as a fundamental principle of the UK Constitution played a significant role from the very conception of Brexit, and this fact did not change during the withdrawal process and aftermath.

3 Parliamentary Sovereignty Reasserted (2020-)

3.1 The Blurred Notion(s) of Sovereignty

At this point it is important to consider the very meaning of sovereignty as a 'multidimensional, elastic concept',[48] given that three different conceptions—national, popular and parliamentary—all played an important role during the various stages of Brexit. As Neill Nugent recognised long before Brexit was set in motion, 'sovereignty' is an emotive word associated with 'notions of power, authority, independence, and the exercise of will', giving rise to several different meanings.[49] Moreover, as complex notions in their own right, each conception of sovereignty has generated tensions between fundamental constitutional principles of the UK Constitution which the process of Brexit has further exposed.[50]

First, with respect to *popular* sovereignty, in its most basic sense meaning the power of the people to rule, the prime focus here is on the status of the 2016 EU Referendum itself. Despite repeated assertions from some politicians that the Referendum represented the biggest democratic vote and mandate in the history of the UK,[51] and a small minority claiming that it had binding status,[52] the commonly accepted position from a *legal* perspective was that it was an advisory mechanism with no legally binding force. The European Union Referendum Act 2015 made no reference to the status of the Referendum, which the High Court confirmed in *Miller*

[46] *R (Miller) v Secretary of State for Exiting the European Union* [2016] EWHC 2768 (Admin) (hereafter '*Miller I*').

[47] *R (Miller) v Secretary of State for Exiting the European Union* [2017] UKSC 5 (hereafter '*Miller I*').

[48] Barnard (2022), p. 13.

[49] Nugent (1996), p. 3.

[50] Bickerton (2019).

[51] See e.g. 27 June 2016 vol. 612, col. 22 per David Cameron; 5 September 2016 vol. 614, cols. 38 and 44; 10 October 2016 vol. 615, cols. 50 and 54; 7 November 2016 vol. 616, cols. 1259 and 1265 per David Davis; 7 December 2016 vol. 618, col. 321 per Kwasi Kwarteng.

[52] See e.g. Lee (2017).

1, finding that 'a referendum on any topic can only be advisory for the lawmakers in Parliament unless very clear language to the contrary is used in the referendum legislation in question'.[53] The situation was of course very different from a *political* perspective, which the UK Supreme Court acknowledged in *Miller 2*, finding that:

> Technically, the result was not legally binding. But the Government had pledged to honour the result and it has since been treated as politically and democratically binding. Successive Governments and Parliament have acted on that basis.[54]

Second, with respect to *parliamentary* sovereignty, which according to the traditional Diceyan understanding reflects the supreme law-making power of Parliament as already discussed, we can look to the judgments of the High Court and Supreme Court in *Miller 1*,[55] and subsequent legislation as key constitutional moments whereby parliament's supremacy was asserted during the process of withdrawal. However, during the various stages of the withdrawal process, considerable difficulties arose about the scope and purpose of parliamentary sovereignty.

For some, there was a perception that Parliament was obstructing Brexit, or in other words, there was a clash between the demands of popular sovereignty and the strength of parliamentary sovereignty within the UK Constitution. Controversy in this area dogged Brexit throughout the withdrawal process, particularly between 2017 and 2019 with accusations that the situation amounted to a clash between the people and parliament, with some Government Ministers repeatedly suggesting that Parliament was frustrating the 'will of the people'.[56] Geoffrey Cox, the then Attorney General, reflected the Government's clear frustration with Parliament at the time, saying 'Twice they have been asked to let the electorate decide whether they should continue to sit in their seats, while they block 17.4 million people's votes. This Parliament is a disgrace'.[57] However, as will be discussed further below, it has been questioned whether parliamentary sovereignty has truly been reasserted following the final departure of the UK, or whether a form of *executive* sovereignty is now superseding it, particularly given the sudden gaps in the UK legal system previously occupied by EU law.

---

[53] *Miller 1* [2016] EWHC 2768 (Admin), para. 106. The ability (or inability) of parliament to bind itself to the result of a referendum is beyond the scope of this chapter and much has been written about this already. See eg. Gordon (2020).

[54] *R (Miller) v The Prime Minister; Cherry and others v Advocate General for Scotland* [2019] UKSC 41 (hereafter '*Miller 2*'), para. 7 per Lady Hale and Lord Reed.

[55] See notes 46–47 above.

[56] See e.g. 13 July 2017 vol. 627, col. 432; 8 April 2019 vol. 658, col. 83; 11 April 2019 vol. 658, col. 476; 25 April 2019 vol. 658, col. 914 per Andrea Leadsom; 7 February 2017 vol. 621 Committee; 6 July 2021 vol. 698, cols. 788–789 per Michael Gove; 25 July 2019 vol. 663, col. 1480; 3 September 2019 vol. 664, col. 40 per Boris Johnson.

[57] 25 September 2019 vol. 664, col. 660 per Geoffrey Cox.

3.2 National Sovereignty and 'Freedom Day'

The third notion of sovereignty, *national* sovereignty, understood by Damian Chalmers as the sole power to rule, to subjugate, and to represent and protect the national political community,[58] was undoubtedly a massive factor driving the referendum campaign. Several studies have found that sovereignty in this sense, especially in the context of a state's ability to impose immigration controls, was one of the most decisive factors influencing leave voters.[59] During the referendum campaign, the issue of sovereignty took centre-stage in the official Leave Campaign, albeit in a politicised and simplified form as the Group's slogan 'take back control'.[60] Whilst the word 'control' seemingly engaged the notion of sovereignty, the key word 'back' was emotionally provocative as it signified the loss of something once owned or, as the Vote Leave campaign director Dominic Cummings put it, the term played into a 'strong evolved instinct – we hate losing things, especially control'.[61] The phrase featured in parliamentary discourse too, both in the build up to and the aftermath of the Referendum. Despite its pivotal role in the referendum debate and leave campaign, however, the vast majority of mentions of 'take back control' in Parliament have actually occurred in the years following the Referendum, peaking in 2018 with more than 275 mentions compared to just 83 mentions in 2016, the year of the Referendum, according to Hansard.[62] This may simply reflect grievances at the various stages of political impasse during the withdrawal period and negotiations between the UK and the EU, but also perhaps frustration at the approach taken by successive UK governments in delivering Brexit.

To facilitate the departure and mitigate the vacuum that would be caused by the undoing of over 40 years of European legislation, the European Union (Withdrawal) Act 2018 was passed in June 2018. Dubbed the 'Great Repeal Act', this provided that the European Communities Act 1972 would be repealed on exit day,[63] but also, crucially, that all existing European law would be preserved in domestic law.[64] The Act also addressed parliamentary sovereignty more directly in several ways, providing that the House of Commons would have to approve the negotiated withdrawal agreement,[65] that the principle of the supremacy of EU law would not apply to laws

[58] Chalmers (2021), p. 286.

[59] See e.g. Lord Ashcroft (2019).

[60] Craig (2016), p. 447.

[61] Cummings (2017).

[62] A simple text search of 'take back control' via Hansard reveals the following: 83 mentions in 2016; 189 mentions in 2017; 276 mentions in 2018; 216 mentions in 2019; 240 mentions in 2020; 103 mentions in 2021; 80 mentions in 2022, and 83 mentions in 2023 as of 1 November 2023.

[63] European Union (Withdrawal) Act 2018, s. 1.

[64] European Union (Withdrawal) Act 2018, ss. 2–4.

[65] European Union (Withdrawal) Act 2018, s. 13(1).

passed on or after exit day,[66] but it would still apply if relevant for UK laws passed before exit day.[67]

Thus, with national sovereignty in mind, after several years of negotiations and three extensions to the withdrawal period, the UK formally left the EU at 11 pm GMT (12 am CET) on 31 January 2020 and entered into an 11-month transition period, during which the UK remained in the single market and customs union. The date 31 January 2020 was dubbed 'Freedom Day' by some, with prior parliamentary debates even taking place to celebrate the UK's departure,[68] and an attempted early day motion to ensure that Big Ben chimed at the exact moment of departure.[69] Whilst the engagement and relevance of the notion of *national* sovereignty would then appear to have concluded following the UK's final withdrawal and expiration of the transition period on 31 December 2020, issues still remain over the implementation of the Withdrawal Agreement, particularly with respect to the Northern Ireland Protocol and the prospect of legal action against the UK for breaching its requirements.[70]

4 The UK's Post-Brexit Constitutional Identity

4.1 A Power Vacuum

Turning to the status of parliamentary sovereignty and the United Kingdom's post-Brexit constitutional identity, it is arguable that significant change is now underway and that a shift of values may be occurring. First, as previously discussed, the UK's membership of the EU undoubtedly acted as a restraint upon parliamentary sovereignty, as much of the UK's legal system was determined or at least influenced by EU law. The UK's departure, therefore, immediately and directly impacted the position of parliamentary sovereignty within the UK Constitution and led to its reassertion as the dominant normative principle in the UK constitutional system. Second, Brexit has opened and exposed a governance vacuum which had previously been occupied by EU law. During the Referendum debate, concerns over a potential 'governance gap' arose particularly in the context of certain sectors such as environmental protection and employment rights,[71] and later at the prospect of the UK's departure without a formal withdrawal agreement, i.e. a no-deal Brexit.[72]

[66] European Union (Withdrawal) Act 2018, s. 5(1).

[67] European Union (Withdrawal) Act 2018, s. 5(2).

[68] 9 January 2020, 'Marking Exit Day', vol. 669, cols. 585–588.

[69] Big Ben Chiming on Day of Brexit, EDM 2 tabled on 19 December 2019.

[70] European Commission (2022).

[71] See eg. House of Lords European Union Committee (2017) and Trades Union Congress (2016).

[72] See e.g. Fella (2019) and Jozepa et al. (2019).

In that respect, as already discussed, the European Union (Withdrawal) Act 2018 was passed to facilitate the UK's departure and allow for EU law to be incorporated into domestic law for possible replacement or eventual repeal. During its passage however, the Bill generated considerable controversy for the sweeping 'Henry VIII' powers—legislative clauses that 'enable ministers to amend or repeal provisions in an Act of Parliament using secondary legislation, which is subject to varying degrees of parliamentary scrutiny'[73]—that would be conferred upon Government Ministers. This was perceived by many as a weakening of parliamentary sovereignty, somewhat undermining and muddying the Leave campaign's pledge to 'take back control'. During the legislative process, Stephen Kinnock, a Labour MP, remarked:

> Brexit was supposed to be about Britain and her sovereign Parliament taking back control. Whatever a vote for Brexit meant, it was surely not a vote for the degradation of our fundamental constitutional values. The first principle of our constitution is parliamentary sovereignty under a constitutional monarch. That means that it is Parliament, not the Executive, that determines the rules and laws that govern this country. The Bill seeks to turn that fundamental principle on its head. Without substantial amendment, this Bill will usurp the sovereign power of this House, giving Ministers the absolute powers of feudal lords, and the Prime Minister the power of a 16th century monarch. It would emasculate this House, giving the Government, who were denied a majority in this House at the ballot box just three months ago, unaccountable power.[74]

Similar concerns arose as the transition phase of Brexit drew to a conclusion, with suggestions that the UK Government may conduct a 'power grab' to the detriment of Parliament and the devolved administrations as powers previously exercised by the EU were returned to the UK.[75] Thus, despite a central tenet of the Leave campaign focusing on the issue of sovereignty, the delivery of Brexit itself has provoked criticisms that successive UK Governments have accumulated further powers and expanded executive sovereignty to the detriment of Parliament and its ability to properly exercise scrutiny.

The pivotal European Union (Withdrawal) Act 2018 is perhaps the most obvious statute which conferred considerable powers upon Government Ministers to be able to amend primary legislation, but it is certainly not the only example. The European Union (Withdrawal Agreement) Act 2020 and United Kingdom Internal Market Act 2020 are further examples of legislation directly linked to the withdrawal process conferring greater executive power. During the Brexit withdrawal process, other examples included the Data Protection Act 2018 which implemented the EU's General Data Protection Regulation, and the Sanctions, Anti-Money Laundering Act 2018 enacted to enable the continuation of various sanctions regimes previously established and directed by the EU.[76] More recently, in response to the COVID-19 global pandemic, the Coronavirus Act 2020 received criticism for conferring

---

[73] UK Parliament, Henry VIII Clauses https://www.parliament.uk/site-information/glossary/henry-viii-clauses/ accessed 1 November 2023.

[74] 11 September 2017 vol. 628, col. 546.

[75] Torrance (2020).

[76] Pasculli and Stanford (2023).

immense power upon Government Ministers to issue delegated legislation. In that respect, the growth of delegated legislation generally since Brexit has attracted critique from the Hansard Society,[77] the House of Lords Select Committee on the Constitution,[78] and academics.[79]

Some, however, have viewed the post-Brexit power vacuum favourably as an opportunity for the UK to assert its sovereignty once more in several major areas previously influenced or determined by EU law, all of which featured in the Referendum debate to some extent. First, given its prominent position in the debate preceding Brexit, the UK's decision to end free movement (and leave both the single market and customs union)[80] with the restored ability to fully manage and limit immigration from EU member states is perhaps the most obvious example.[81] That said, the UK has recently recorded record high net migration in 2022, with the UK's population jumping by over 600,000 in 1 year, predominantly due to rising non-EU migration.[82] Second, more specifically, the UK chose to leave the EU's Common Agricultural Policy and Common Fisheries Policy,[83] thus leading to greater control over UK agricultural and fishing policies. Parliament has been involved in these pivotal decisions to some extent, primarily by consenting to the European Union (Withdrawal Agreement) Act 2020 which ratified the UK-EU Withdrawal Agreement. Third, the ability to negotiate trade agreements with non-EU states is another significant example, with entirely new agreements since Brexit having been negotiated with Australia and New Zealand,[84] with some pre-existing EU arrangements being rolled over, for example with Japan, Singapore, Mexico and Canada,[85] and further negotiations ongoing with several other states. Parliament's involvement here has been limited to providing scrutiny, rather than any binding authority, given the generally accepted position that the negotiation and ratification of treaties remains within the royal prerogative. In that respect, the UK-Australia Free Trade Agreement and the new UK-Singapore Digital Agreement have both been laid before Parliament pursuant to the Constitutional Reform and Governance Act 2010, and various parliamentary committees have robustly engaged in providing scrutiny during the negotiation process for these agreements.[86]

---

[77] The Hansard Society (2021).

[78] See e.g. House of Lords Select Committee on the Constitution (2017).

[79] Barnard (2022).

[80] HM Government (2018), p. 1.

[81] Immigration and Social Security Co-Ordination (EU Withdrawal) Act 2020.

[82] BBC News (2023).

[83] HM Government (2018), p. 1.

[84] Webb (2022).

[85] UK-Japan Comprehensive Economic Partnership Agreement; UK-Singapore Trade Agreement; UK-Mexico Trade Continuity Agreement; UK-Canada Trade Continuity Agreement.

[86] Webb (2022).

4.2 Constitutional Identity Cast Adrift

Brexit undoubtedly symbolised a watershed moment for the United Kingdom's constitutional system and has provided an opportunity for significant reform in ways that would impact its constitutional identity. As Eleni Frantziou recently argued, the UK's decision to leave the EU 'carried precisely the narratives about self-determination that lie at the heart of secessionist movements'.[87] It is exactly moments of this kind in a state's history which allow for a reconsideration of its values and principles, perhaps even with a new or revised codified constitution. Whilst this may be unlikely in the UK, or that the UK would drastically diverge from constitutional values shared by the EU and its member states, it is at least arguable that some significant changes and reforms are now occurring.

In that respect, recent legislative reforms and developments in the UK have engaged matters concerning the rule of law, accountability, democracy and human rights, all of which have increased the power of the executive or otherwise limited measures of scrutiny. For example, the Overseas Operations (Service Personnel and Veterans) Act 2021 has imposed a statutory presumption against the prosecution of soldiers for alleged offences committed in the course of duty which occurred more than 5 years prior,[88] as well as introducing additional hurdles and time limits for bringing a criminal or civil case.[89] The Covert Human Intelligence Sources (Criminal Conduct) Act 2021 allows for a 'Criminal Conduct Authorisation',[90] essentially authorising conduct which would amount to a crime and thus guaranteeing immunity for undercover agents who break the law in the conduct of their role.

In April 2022, a package of constitutionally significant Bills received Royal Assent on the same day as the 2020–22 parliamentary session ended. This included the Elections Act 2022 which has reduced the independence of the Electoral Commission and introduced voter identification requirements for polling station voting[91]; the Judicial Review and Courts Act 2022 which has reformed the scope of judicial review and availability of remedies[92]; the Nationality and Borders Act 2022 which has reformed resettlement routes, as well as introducing offshore refugee processing facilities and the possibility to revoke citizenship without notice[93]; and the Police, Crime, Sentencing and Courts Act 2022 which allows the police to impose significant restrictions upon static protests, for example with start and finish times as well as maximum noise limits.[94] More recently, the Public Order Act 2023,

[87] Frantziou (2022), p. 69.

[88] Overseas Operations (Service Personnel and Veterans) Act 2021, s. 2. This presumption does not, however, apply to genocide, crimes against humanity, and war crimes (Schedule 1 to the Act).

[89] Ibid. Parts 1 and 2.

[90] Covert Human Intelligence Sources (Criminal Conduct) Act 2021, s. 1.

[91] Elections Act 2022, Part 3 and Schedule 1 respectively. See also Stanford (2021).

[92] Judicial Review and Courts Act 2022, ss. 1–2 respectively.

[93] Nationality and Borders Act 2022, Part 2; Schedule 4; and s. 10 and Schedule 2 respectively.

[94] Police, Crime, Sentencing and Courts Act 2022, Part 3.

passed in May 2023, has introduced new criminal offences concerning protest such as 'locking on' and obstructing major transport works, as well as expanding police stop and search powers and the ability to ban people from participating in protests.[95]

The previous UK Government led by the Conservative Party, defeated in the July 2024 General Election, had also been edging closer towards a conflict with the European Court of Human Rights with respect to the deportation of illegal migrants and failed asylum seekers in particular. The Illegal Migration Act 2023, passed in July 2023, goes even further than the Nationality and Borders Act 2022 and, if its main provisions enter into force, effectively removes the right to access refugee protection in the UK for people who enter the UK illegally or via a 'safe country' as their claims are deemed inadmissible,[96] whilst an obligation has also been placed on the Home Secretary to deport people in this position to their country of origin or a safe country such as Rwanda,[97] which can only be challenged in limited circumstances.[98]

More specifically with UK-EU relations in mind, the Retained EU Law (Revocation and Reform) Act was passed in June 2023 to enable the UK to easily amend law inherited from the EU, with enormous power being given to Government Ministers to this end.[99] Amongst other reforms, the Act has revoked nearly 600 legislative instruments of EU origin,[100] revoked all retained directly effective EU law such as rights and obligations formerly conferred directly under EU treaties or directives,[101] and revoked the principle of supremacy of EU law in the UK legal system,[102] with all remaining retained EU law to be called 'assimilated law'.[103] The Act also makes it easier for the UK courts to depart from legacy caselaw of the Court of Justice of the EU,[104] and for the Government to amend or revoke retained EU law by using delegated powers with less parliamentary scrutiny.[105] Lastly, UK Government ministers and devolved authorities will be given wide discretion on key decisions about the substance and future of retained EU law, namely, to restate, reproduce, revoke or replace certain aspects of it.[106]

These reforms are arguably the most significant from the perspective of constitutional identity, but each Act has reformed many other areas of law necessitating specific and much deeper analysis in the future. Further controversial reforms

---

[95] Public Order Act 2023, s. 1; s. 6; ss. 10–11; and Part 2 respectively.

[96] Illegal Migration Act 2023, s. 5.

[97] Ibid. s. 2.

[98] Ibid. s. 42.

[99] Cowie (2023).

[100] Retained EU Law (Revocation and Reform) Act 2023, s. 1 and Schedule 1.

[101] Ibid. s. 2.

[102] Ibid. s. 3.

[103] Ibid. s. 5.

[104] Ibid. s. 6.

[105] Ibid. s. 9.

[106] Ibid. ss. 11–16.

impacting law-making, democracy and accountability have been considered or are currently on the horizon. For example, the now-dropped Northern Ireland Protocol Bill was introduced in June 2022 and proved highly contentious amidst concerns that the UK would seek to unilaterally amend the formal UK-EU agreement, thus violating international law in the process.[107]

The future of the HRA 1998 has also been subject to fierce debate for at least 15 years with successive Governments threatening its reform or replacement with a so-called British Bill of Rights. In June 2022, the Bill of Rights Bill was introduced with the purpose of repealing and replacing the HRA 1998,[108] drawing much criticism for the likely reduction of effective human rights protection. According to the then Government, 'mission creep has resulted in human rights law being used for more and more purposes, with elastic interpretations that go way beyond anything that the architects of the [European] Convention had in mind', whilst the new Bill will 'reinforce our tradition of liberty whilst curtailing the abuses of human rights, restoring some common sense to our justice system, and ensuring that our human rights framework meets the needs of the society it serves'.[109] However, with Cabinet reshuffles as well as political and economic crises in the UK and beyond dominating the agenda and either resetting Government priorities or stalling progress, plans to progress the Bill were formally dropped in June 2023.[110]

Taking a step back for a moment, these reforms can also be framed within the context of a developing 'culture war' in the UK and other liberal democracies, that is—a clash between values and beliefs which impact various contentious issues. Whilst the issue to attract the most media attention in this context was Brexit and the EU between 1997–2020,[111] which to some extent has now reached a conclusion, other issues are now provoking debate about values and identity. Examples include the mandated wearing of face masks during the COVID-19 pandemic, Black Lives Matter and Extinction Rebellion protests, trans rights, and the legacies of empire and slavery.[112] Whilst each concerns a distinct issue, they all engage constitutional values not least of all the rule of law, human rights, and democracy.

Given that Brexit has signified a constitutional watershed moment, with choices to be made about the future direction of the UK's legal and constitutional system, an alternative future might be possible. In 2015, the UK's Political and Constitutional Reform Committee reviewed the UK's constitutional framework to consider potential reforms and further stimulate debate.[113] Whilst this was, of course, pre-Brexit

---

[107] UK Parliament, Northern Ireland Protocol Bill at https://bills.parliament.uk/bills/3182 accessed 1 November 2023.

[108] UK Parliament, Bill of Rights Bill at https://bills.parliament.uk/bills/3227 accessed 1 November 2023.

[109] Ministry of Justice (2022).

[110] Hyde (2023).

[111] Duffy et al. (2021).

[112] Ibid. p. 17.

[113] House of Commons Political and Constitutional Reform Committee (2015).

and the EU Referendum, it nevertheless provided some useful food for thought on the issue of constitutional identity. Following wide public consultation, a progressive suggestion for a Preamble to a potential codified constitution was put forward. This incorporated many values and principled objectives, including the recognition of every citizen as an equal partner in government; fair and equitable treatment under the law; equality of opportunity for all citizens; to eradicate poverty; to protect and cultivate community identities within the UK's four nations; to preserve the environment for future generations; to safeguard freedom of thought, conscience, and assembly; and to protect fundamental rights against the encroachment of tyranny and the abdication of reason.[114] Assuming that it would have a superior status to ordinary law, the introduction of a codified constitution would obviously prompt a momentous change in the UK's constitutional framework and the status of parliamentary sovereignty, challenging its core tenets and even the supremacy of Parliament. Notwithstanding the unlikelihood of a codified constitution in the immediate future, the realisation and deliverance of these ambitious values and principles in the UK's post-Brexit constitutional identity appears anything but certain amidst growing concerns of culture wars and democratic backsliding.

5 Conclusion

Brexit was undoubtedly a constitutional shock and watershed moment for the United Kingdom's legal and political systems, only complicated by the patchwork nature of the UK's Constitution and broader constitutional identity which lacks legal certainty and predictability despite its relatively stable historic nature. Insofar as parliamentary sovereignty is concerned, the single biggest restraint upon this principle—the UK's membership of the EU—has now been removed. In the short term this has led to the apparent reassertion of parliamentary sovereignty in its traditional, orthodox sense and confirmation of the superiority of Parliament as the UK's dominant law-making institution. However, the withdrawal process following the 2016 Referendum was dogged with problems, primarily with clashes between Parliament and Government, but also between devolved administrations and the UK Government, and even within the UK Government itself.

The notion of sovereignty played a critical yet confused role throughout this process. Moreover, claims of Brexit 'being done' only paint part of the picture, with questions remaining over the future of retained or 'assimilated' EU law and, most significantly, whether the UK will seek to override the Northern Ireland Protocol or amend the withdrawal agreements. Turning to events since Brexit, it is arguable that the UK's constitutional identity has been significantly impacted and that the reassertion of parliamentary sovereignty has actually led to a growth of executive power and sovereignty. Other reforms, proposals and recent developments have

---

114 Ibid. p. 3.

placed normative values and principles under further pressure. The future of the UK's constitutional identity is anything but certain.

References

Allan TRS (1997) Parliamentary sovereignty: law, politics, and revolution. Law Q Rev 113(3): 443–452
Arajärvi N (2021) The Core requirements of the international rule of law in the practice of states. Hague J Rule Law 13(1):173–193
Barber NW (2011) The afterlife of parliamentary sovereignty. Int J Const Law 9(1):144–154
Barnard C (2022) Taking Back control? Rule by law(s) and the executive in the post-Brexit world. Oxf Rev Econ Policy 38(1):11–26
BBC News (2016) EU Referendum Results. https://www.bbc.co.uk/news/politics/eu_referendum/results. Accessed 1 Nov 2023
BBC News (2023) Migration too High Says Sunak, as total hits record level. https://www.bbc.co.uk/news/live/uk-65669832. Accessed 1 Nov 2023
Bickerton C (2019) "Parliamentary", "popular" and "pooled": conflicts of sovereignty in the United Kingdom's exit from the European Union. J Eur Integr 41(7):887–902
Birkinshaw P (2020) European public law: the achievement and the Brexit challenge, 3rd edn. Kluwer Law International, Alphen aan den Rijn
Blick A (2019) Stretching the constitution: the Brexit shock in historic perspective. Bloomsbury, London
Bogdanor V (2009) The new British constitution. Hart, Oxford
Bogdanor V (2019) Beyond Brexit: towards a British constitution. Bloomsbury, London
Bonelli M, Claes M (2018) Judicial serendipity: how Portuguese judges came to the Rescue of the Polish Judiciary. Eur Const Law Rev 14(3):622–643
Bowcott O (2018) John Major had a "Full Gloat" after defeating rebels on Maastricht. The Guardian. https://www.theguardian.com/politics/2018/jul/24/john-major-full-gloat-defeating-rebels-maastricht-european-union. Accessed 1 Nov 2023
Burke E (1782) Speech on Reform of Representation of the Commons in Parliament
Chalmers D (2021) National Sovereignty and European Union law. Eur Law Rev 46(3):285–305
Chesterman S (2008) An international rule of law? Am J Comp Law 56(2):331–361
Cowie G (2023) Retained EU Law (Revocation and Reform) Act 2023. House of Commons Library Briefing Paper 09841
Craig P (1991) Sovereignty of the United Kingdom parliament after Factortame. Yearb Eur Law 11(1):221–255
Craig P (2016) Brexit: a Drama in six acts. Eur Law Rev 41(4):447–468
Craig P (2019) Constitutional identity in the United Kingdom. In: Calliess C, van der Schyff G (eds) Constitutional identity in a Europe of multilevel constitutionalism. Cambridge University Press, Cambridge
Cummings D (2017) On the referendum #21: branching histories of the 2016 referendum and the "Frogs before the Storm". https://dominiccummings.com/2017/01/09/on-the-referendum-21-branching-histories-of-the-2016-referendum-and-the-frogs-before-the-storm-2/. Accessed 1 Nov 2023
de Witte B (2021) Article 4(2) TEU as a protection of the institutional diversity of the member states. Eur Public Law 27(3):559–570
Dicey AV (1885/1985) Introduction to the study of the law of the constitution, 10th edn. Macmillan, London
Douglas-Scott S (2016a) Brexit, article 50 and the contested British constitution. Mod Law Rev 79(6):1019–1040

Douglas-Scott S (2016b) Brexit, the Referendum and the UK Parliament: Some Questions about Sovereignty. The Constitution Unit. https://constitution-unit.com/2016/06/29/brexit-the-referendum-and-the-uk-parliament-some-questions-about-sovereignty/. Accessed 1 Nov 2023
Duffy B et al (2021) "Culture Wars" in the UK. The Policy Institute, King's College London. https://www.kcl.ac.uk/policy-institute/assets/culture-wars-in-the-uk.pdf. Accessed 1 Nov 2023
Etherton T (2018) The universality of the rule of law as an international standard. Israel Law Rev 51(3):469–483
European Commission (2022) Protocol on Ireland/Northern Ireland: commission launches four new infringement procedures against the UK. https://ec.europa.eu/commission/presscorner/detail/en/IP_22_4663. Accessed 1 Nov 2023
European Commission, Conditions for Membership. https://ec.europa.eu/neighbourhood-enlargement/enlargement-policy/conditions-membership_en. Accessed 1 Nov 2023
Ewing E (2017) Brexit and parliamentary sovereignty. Mod Law Rev 80(4):711–726
Fella S (2019) Planning for a no-deal brexit. House of Commons Library Briefing Paper 8733
Frantziou E (2022) Was Brexit a form of secession? Global Pol 13(Suppl. 2):69–78
Gordon M (2020) Referendums in the UK constitution: authority, sovereignty and democracy after Brexit. Eur Const Law Rev 16(2):213–248
HM Government (2018) The future relationship between the United Kingdom and the European Union. Cm 9593
HM Government, Ministerial Code. https://www.gov.uk/government/publications/ministerial-code. Accessed 1 Nov 2023
House of Commons Political and Constitutional Reform Committee (2015) The UK Constitution: a summary, with options for reform
House of Lords European Union Committee (2017) Brexit: Environment and Climate Change (Session 2016–17, HL Paper 109)
House of Lords Select Committee on the Constitution (2017) The "Great Repeal Bill" and delegated powers (Session 2016–17, HL Paper 123)
Hyde J (2023) Raab's bill of rights officially killed off. Law Society Gazette. https://www.lawgazette.co.uk/news/raabs-bill-of-rights-officially-killed-off/5116465.article. Accessed 1 Nov 2023
Jacobsohn GJ (2010) Constitutional identity. Harvard University Press, Cambridge
Jozepa I et al (2019) No deal Brexit: trade. House of Commons Library Briefing Paper 8636
Laws J (1995) Law and democracy. Public Law Spring: 72–93
Lee G (2017) The culture secretary said the EU referendum was binding—It wasn't. Channel 4 FactCheck. https://www.channel4.com/news/factcheck/the-culture-secretary-said-the-eu-referendum-was-binding-it-wasnt. Accessed 1 Nov 2023
Lord Ashcroft (2019) How the UK voted on Brexit, and why—a refresher. https://lordashcroftpolls.com/2019/02/how-the-uk-voted-on-brexit-and-why-a-refresher/. Accessed 1 Nov 2023
Loveland I (2021) Constitutional law, administrative law, and human rights: a critical introduction, 9th edn. Oxford University Press, Oxford
Miller V (2009) The Treaty of Lisbon: Government and Parliamentary views on a Referendum. SN/IA/5071. https://researchbriefings.files.parliament.uk/documents/SN05071/SN05071.pdf. Accessed 1 Nov 2023
Ministry of Justice (2022) Bill of rights: bill documents, Policy Paper. https://www.gov.uk/government/publications/bill-of-rights-bill-documents. Accessed 1 Nov 2023
Nugent N (1996) Sovereignty and Britain's membership of the European Union. Public Policy Admin 11(2):3–18
Ovádek M (2022) The making of landmark rulings in the European Union: the case of National Judicial Independence. J Eur Publ Policy. https://doi.org/10.1080/13501763.2022.2066156
Pasculli L, Stanford B (2023) Form and flexibility: the normalisation of 'Magnitsky sanctions' in the face of the rule of law. Hague J Rule Law 15(1):109–142
Pech L (2022) The rule of law as a well-established and well-defined principle of EU law. Hague J Rule Law 14(2–3):107–138

Schill SW, von Bogdandy A (2011) Overcoming absolute primacy: respect for National Identity under the Lisbon treaty. Common Market Law Rev 48(5):1417–1453

Schnettger A (2019) Article 4(2) TEU as a vehicle for National Constitutional Identity in the shared European legal system. In: Calliess C, van der Schyff G (eds) Constitutional identity in a Europe of multilevel constitutionalism. Cambridge University Press, Cambridge

Stanford B (2021) The elections bill: the arrival of voter ID (and a whole lot more). Coventry Law J 26(2):46–54

The Conservative Party Manifesto (2015) Strong leadership, a clear economic plan, a brighter, more secure future

The Hansard Society (2021) Delegated legislation: the problems with the process. London

Torrance D (2020) EU powers after Brexit: 'Power Grab' or 'Power Surge'? House of Commons Library Insight. https://commonslibrary.parliament.uk/eu-powers-after-brexit-power-grab-or-power-surge/. Accessed 1 Nov 2023

Trades Union Congress (2016) UK employment rights and the EU. https://www.tuc.org.uk/research-analysis/reports/uk-employment-rights-and-eu. Accessed 1 Nov 2023

Usherwood S (2002) Opposition to the European Union in the UK: the dilemma of public opinion and party management. Gov Oppos 37(2):211–230

Wade HWR (1996) Sovereignty: revolution or evolution? Law Q Rev 112:568–575

Walsh J (2016) Britain's 1975 Europe Referendum: What was it like last time? The Guardian. https://www.theguardian.com/politics/2016/feb/25/britains-1975-europe-referendum-what-was-it-like-last-time. Accessed 1 Nov 2023

Webb D (2022) Progress on UK Free Trade Agreement Negotiations. House of Commons Library Briefing Paper 9314

Young A (2017) The constitutional implications of Brexit. Eur Public Law 23(4):757–786

The Impact of Brexit on the Protection of Human Rights and Fundamental Rights (Including General Principles of Law)

Mike Varney

1 Introduction

The impact of the United Kingdom's exit from the European Union on the protection of human rights and fundamental rights is perhaps less obvious than its impact on other areas of law. At first blush, the major protections for human and fundamental rights in the UK come from the Human Rights Act 1998, which incorporates certain of the provisions from the European Convention on Human Rights and Fundamental Freedoms 1950 into UK law and from the common law.[1] Although proposals have been put forward to repeal the Human Rights Act 1998 and replace the Act with a British alternative,[2] these are not a direct consequence of Brexit, though some will no doubt have been fired or inspired by a degree of anti-European sentiment, reflected in the Brexit process. Ultimately, these proposals were abandoned by government and at present, it appears that the Human Rights Act 1998 will remain as the primary mechanism of human rights protection in UK law.

It is important, however, to note that on a broader view of human and fundamental rights than the (primarily) political and civil rights protected by the Human Rights Act 1998 and the nascent development of common law fundamental rights, the impact of European Union law on the protection of individual rights is more significant. Equality law, social rights in respect of employment, rights of data

[1] See *e.g. R (UNISON) v. Lord Chancellor* [2017] UKSC 51; [2017] 3 WLR 409, where the Supreme Court decided that the employment tribunal fees that were required to be paid before an individual could bring a claim before the Employment Tribunal was an infringement of the fundamental right of access to justice, recognised by the common law. See also Lienen (2018).

[2] See *e.g.* the Bill of Rights Bill 2022-2023, available at https://publications.parliament.uk/pa/bills/cbill/58-03/0117/220117.pdf (accessed 25th May 2024).

M. Varney (✉)
Lincoln Law School, The University of Lincoln, Lincoln, UK
e-mail: MVarney@lincoln.ac.uk

E. Guinchard, C. Panara (eds.), *The New Relationship between the United Kingdom and the European Union*, https://doi.org/10.1007/978-3-031-70652-3_4

protection and protections for migrants have all been heavily influenced by developments in European Union Law. Furthermore, there is little doubt that membership of the European Union and the corresponding opportunities to engage with the jurisprudence of Member State courts in the European Union has had a significant impact on the development of the principles of judicial review in the United Kingdom, which is an important mechanism for the vindication of such rights.[3] It remains to be seen whether the UK's withdrawal from the European Union will lead to a reduction in the future influence of European legal systems on the development of the principles of judicial review, though it is unlikely that there will be a judicial retreat from the developments that have been influenced by European systems in the past. As Birkinshaw argues, European influence is "...too deep rooted to be extirpated either by Brexit or departure of the UK from European Union or Council of Europe."[4]

This chapter will proceed in three parts. It will first examine the impact of the UK's membership of the European Union on the protection of human and fundamental rights prior to Brexit. It will then move on and consider the impact of the Brexit process on the protection of human and fundamental rights and the final section will look at the prospects for the law in the future.

2 The Impact of EU Membership on the Protection of Human Rights and Fundamental Rights

As noted earlier, prima facie, EU membership has not had an extensive a role in the protection of human and fundamental rights in the United Kingdom as membership of the Council of Europe. The Human Rights Act 1998 implements rights from the European Convention on Human Rights and Fundamental Freedoms[5] and the Human Rights Act 1998 is the primary mechanism of human rights protection in the United Kingdom. In addition to the rights protected under the Human Rights Act 1998, we can also identify rights protected by common law, including the decision of the Supreme Court in *UNISON*.[6] None of these protections are directly impacted by Brexit, although the public sentiment that led to the referendum vote to withdraw from the European Union has served to embolden those who wish to promote a withdrawal from European and international organisations and a more insular, domestically focused, approach to human rights protection, which, in the case of the Bill of Rights Bill 2022–2023, delivered what many argued to be a diminished level of protection.[7]

[3] Birkinshaw (2020), p. 783.

[4] Ibid.

[5] See the Human Rights Act 1998, section 1 and schedule 1.

[6] See above, note 1.

[7] Amos (2024).

Membership of the European Union facilitated some important developments in the protection of human rights. The coming into force of the Charter of Fundamental Rights of the European Union (CFR)[8] in 2009 as part of the Treaty of Lisbon offered an additional avenue for the protection of human rights, though it is important to note that according to Art. 51 of the Charter of Fundamental Rights, these extend "to the Member States only when they are implementing Union law." The contours of this limitation have been explored by the courts where individuals have sought the protection of the Charter of Fundamental Rights in domestic legal proceedings, with claimants often seeking to rely on the Charter and its more expansive approach to the definition of fundamental rights. In *Sandiford*,[9] the Court of Appeal held that the claimant could not rely on the Charter of Fundamental Rights to support her claim that the UK government should fund the provision of legal representation in a case where she was detained in Indonesia on charges of narcotics trafficking because, although her counsel argued that her position had a connection to EU law through Council Framework Decision 2004/757/JHA, it was held that the Framework Decision and thus the requirements of the CFR could not extend to offences committed outside of the European Union. Similarly, in *Jagoo*,[10] the Court of Appeal declined to consider a challenge to the rules on local taxation levied by a local authority due to its lack of connection with EU law.

The need to demonstrate a connection with the implementation of EU law imposed some limitation on the impact of the CFR in UK law, but we can observe that it still had an important impact on cases brought in a range of areas, including immigration, asylum and the treatment of third country nationals,[11] state immunity in the context of employment disputes,[12] effective remedies where there was a breach of a right granted by EU law[13] and a number of cases drawing on the provisions of the CFR to claim data protection and data privacy rights.[14]

In each of these areas, it is possible to argue that the claimants may have been able to derive the same or similar protections from the ECHR, but the CFR has significance because it contains a wider range of rights and protections than might be found in the ECHR and, furthermore, it may sometimes be the case that the protection offered by the CFR is more comprehensive.[15] It is important not to

---

[8] Charter of Fundamental Rights of the European Union [2012] OJ C 326/02.

[9] *R (Sandiford) v. Secretary of State for Foreign and Commonwealth Affairs* [2013] EWCA Civ 581; [2013] 1 WLR 2938.

[10] *Jagoo v. Bristol City Council* [2019] EWCA Civ 19; [2019] PTSR 555.

[11] See *e.g. ZZ v. Secretary of State for the Home Department* [2014] EWCA Civ 7; [2014] QB 820.

[12] *Benkharbouche v Embassy of the Republic of Sudan* [2015] EWCA Civ 33; [2016] QB 347.

[13] *R (Evans) v. Attorney General* [2014] EWCA Civ 254; [2014] 2 WLR 1334.

[14] See *e.g. Vidal-Hall v. Google Inc.* [2015] EWCA Civ 311; [2015] 3 WLR 409; *R (National Council for Civil Liberties) v Secretary of State for the Home Department and others (National Union of Journalists intervening)* [2023] EWCA Civ 926; *R (Open Rights Group and another) v Secretary of State for the Home Department and another (Liberty and another intervening)* [2021] EWCA Civ 800; [2021] 1 WLR 3611.

[15] See *e.g.* Douglas Scott (2011), pp. 655—658; Birkinshaw (2020), pp. 793—794.

overstate this point, as in the vast majority of cases, the UK courts have found that where the provisions of the CFR broadly mirror the requirements of the ECHR, the protections offered by the two instruments are in alignment, as envisaged by Art. 52(3) of the CFR.

In *ZZ*,[16] a case concerning a challenge to a decision of the Secretary of State to prevent the re-entry of a French national who had previously been lawfully resident in the UK on public security grounds, ZZ's counsel sought to argue that the protection offered by Article 47 of the CFR, when considered alongside provisions of Directive 2004/38/EC[17] imposed stronger requirements on the Secretary of State to disclose the information on which the refusal to grant re-entry was based than Art. 6 ECHR. ZZ had been refused details of the reasons for refusal on public security grounds, and the appeal that he brought against the refusal were heard primarily under the 'closed material' procedure, where the evidence against the claimant is not disclosed in open court. The Court of Appeal found that ZZ was entitled to receive details of the reasons for refusal, subject to appropriate restrictions to protect national security. In considering whether the CFR offered greater protection than the ECHR in this respect, the Court of Appeal noted that the approaches are in alignment.[18] In the case of *Tariq*, Lord Mance JSC observed that "A national court, faced with an issue of effective legal protection or, putting the same point in different terms, access to effective procedural justice, can be confident that both European courts, Luxembourg and Strasbourg, will have the same values and will expect and accept similar procedures."[19]

Despite the similarities in protection offered by the ECHR and the CFR, it might be argued that the CFR has sometimes emboldened the UK courts to protect individual rights. In the UNISON case, the Supreme Court considered the importance of the principle of effectiveness and effective judicial protection in the context of the general principles of law and the CFR.[20] These principles offered important support to the ultimate conclusion that the fees applicable to claims before the Employment Tribunal were a disproportionate barrier to access to justice.

From the above, it is plain that the CFR had considerable impact on UK law. Much like other aspects of EU law, it is also possible to argue that as the CFR becomes embedded into EU law and is considered more frequently in UK case law, the 'overspill' of principles into domestic law cases, not concerning EU law or rights conferred by EU law is likely.

In addition to the Charter of Fundamental Rights, membership of the European Union also injected the general principles of law into the UK's legal system. As these

---

[16] *ZZ*, above, note 11.

[17] Directive 2004/38/EC of the European Parliament and of the Council of 29 April 2004 on the right of citizens of the Union and their family members to move and reside freely within the territory of the Member States [2004] OJ L 158/77.

[18] *ZZ*, above, note 11 at [30].

[19] *Tariq v Home Office* [2011] UKSC 35; [2012] 1 AC 452 at [23].

[20] *UNISON*, above, note 1, [105]—[117].

are primarily drawn from the constitutional traditions of the Member States, we might also observe that the UK has made a contribution to the development of these principles, particularly in the context of the rights of defence. In seeking to define the general principles, we can find consensus amongst authors that the general principles of law include the supremacy of EU law and direct effect, protection of human rights, proportionality, adherence to the rule of law and principles of good administration, legal certainty, equality and non-discrimination, openness and transparency, state liability and the giving of reasons.[21]

There is ample evidence of the impact of the general principles of law on the UK legal system. The UK adhered to the principle of the supremacy of EU law, adopting both the duty of consistent interpretation[22] and, where necessary, disapplying provisions of primary legislation.[23] Human rights protection in the UK has been primarily drawn from the ECHR under the Human Rights Act 1998, although the discussion above illustrates that human rights protection under EU law has also had an impact in the UK legal system.

We can also see how the principle of legality in domestic law cases has been significant impacted by the general principles of law. Proportionality as a concept has found its way into English law through the interpretation of Convention rights[24] and also through its application in cases where the proportionality of interference with rights derived from EU law was required.[25] These decisions have delivered domestic impact and has expanded the potential for more intensive scrutiny of administrative action than that envisaged by the test originally conceived of in *Wednesbury*.[26] Over time, the proportionality principle has informed a notable change in approach to the review of the rationality of administrative decisions, with the intensity of review depending on the case at hand, and some of the tools and techniques deployed in the proportionality test informing the approach of the courts.[27]

---

[21] See *e.g.* Birkinshaw (2020), p. 157; Tridimas (2007).

[22] See, for example, *Garland v British Rail Engineering Ltd* [1982] 2 AC 75, *McCarthy's v Smith* [1981] 1 All ER 111 and *Litster v Forth Dry Dock* [1989] 1 All ER 113.

[23] *Factortame Ltd. v. Secretary of State for Transport (No. 2)* [1991] 1 A.C. 603.

[24] *A and Others* v. *Secretary of State for the Home Department* [2005] 2 AC 68, *Bank Mellat* v. *HM Treasury* [2013] UKSC 39; [2014] A.C. 700.

[25] *R.* v *Secretary of State for Health Ex p. Eastside Cheese Co* [1999] 3 C.M.L.R. 123, *R (Mabanaft Ltd.)* v. *Secretary of State for Energy and Climate Change* [2009] EWCA Civ 224; [2009] Eu. L.R. 799 and, more recently, the examination of the application of the proportionality principle in respect of rights derived from EU law in *Lumsdon* v. *Legal Services Board* [2015] UKSC 41; [2016] A.C. 697.

[26] *Associated Provincial Picture Houses* v. *Wednesbury Corporation* [1948] 1 KB 223.

[27] See e.g. *R (Mahmood)* v. *Home Secretary* [2001] 1 WLR 840, *R* v. *Secretary of State for the Home Department, ex parte Simms* [2000] 2 AC 115 and *R* v. *Secretary of State for the Home Department, ex parte Daly* [2001] UKHL 26, [2001] 2 AC 532. The current approach is perhaps best exemplified by *Kennedy* v. *Information Commissioner* [2014] UKSC 20; [2015] A.C. 455. See also Craig (2013).

Similarly, one might identify several other developments in the principles of judicial review, brought about through the interface with EU law. The development of the principle of legitimate expectation (both procedural and substantive), owes at least some of its existence from the inspiration of EU law.[28] The legitimate expectation principle has supported the development of openness and transparency in its procedural form,[29] and has supported the principle of legal certainty in its substantive form.[30] Similarly, reason-giving has become increasingly important in English law, driven in part by the requirements of EU law.[31] Transparency has also been aided by the requirements of EU law in different areas of decision-making, with the Environmental Information Regulations in the UK,[32] implementing the Directive on access to environmental information being a prime example of an area where transparency has been supported by European legislation.[33]

European Union law on equality and non-discrimination, both in terms of legislation and the jurisprudence of the EU courts, has proven to be an important source of inspiration for the development of the law in the UK. From the time of joining the EEC, when the Equal Pay Act 1970 was passed to pave the way to EU membership, to the time of Brexit, the UK courts had been willing to ensure compliance with the requirements of EU law,[34] The Equality Act 2010 is a significant piece of legislation in the UK, with important constitutional impacts. It brings together equality and non-discrimination law into a single piece of legislation, pulling together all of the forms of prohibited conduct and protected characteristics and prohibiting discrimination in employment, in the provision of services and also bringing in a public sector equality duty.[35]

We can also identify EU law as an important source of rights in relation to data protection and data privacy. The General Data Protection Regulation and its precursor Directives offered the basis for data protection law in the UK, with the enactment of the Data Protection Act 1998 and subsequently the Data Protection Act 2018 as

---

[28] See e.g. *R* v. *Ministry of Agriculture, Fisheries and Food, ex parte Hamble* [1995] 1 C.M.L.R. 533, *R* v. *North and East Devon Health Authority, ex parte Coughlan* [2000] 3 All ER 850 and *In the matter of an application by Geraldine Finucane for Judicial Review (Northern Ireland)* [2019] UKSC 7.

[29] See *R (Moseley)* v. *Haringey LBC* [2014] UKSC 56; [2014] 1 W.L.R. 3947.

[30] *R (on the Application of Niazi) v Secretary of State for the Home Department* [2008] EWCA Civ 755 and *Hamble*, above note 28.

[31] See e.g. *R (on the application of Hoverspeed Ltd)* v *Customs and Excise Commissioners* [2002] EWCA Civ 1804. *R (on the application of Manchester Airports Holdings Ltd)* v *Secretary of State for Transport* [2021] EWHC 2031 (Admin) and *Dover DC* v *Campaign to Protect Rural England (Kent)* [2017] UKSC 79, per. Lord Carnwath at [54]-[55].

[32] SI 2004/3391 The Environmental Information Regulations 2004.

[33] Council Directive 2003/4/EC on public access to environmental information [2003] OJ L 41/26.

[34] See the cases cited above at note 22 and the case of *Webb v EMO Air Cargo Ltd* [1995] 4 All ER 577 as examples.

[35] For a valuable account of the development of the Equality Act 2010 and the importance of EU law to the development, see Hepple (2011), chapter 1.

domestic legislation to deal with data protection issues. The UK courts have taken a number of important decisions, driven by data protection law, enhancing the rights available to individuals in the context of data protection and privacy. These include the decision in *Vidal-Hall,*[36] extending the tort of misuse of private information for data protection breaches and *Bridges*, finding that the introduction of facial recognition technology by a police force was not compatible with Art. 8 ECHR, but also raised issues of legality when EU law and the public sector equality duty in the Equality Act 2010 were considered.[37]

The above discussion has sought to demonstrate that the UK's membership of the EU delivered many developments that enhanced the protection of fundamental rights in the United Kingdom. The CFR was impactful in several areas, particularly in its requirement of an effective remedy and in its protection of data protection rights and its elaboration of protections which sometimes go beyond those offered in the ECHR. The general principles of law have assisted the development of domestic judicial review and have supported the development of principles of good administration that have supported effective judicial protection for individuals and we can also see a significant impact on the prohibition of discrimination and the development of equality and in the field of data protection. The next section of this chapter will aim to consider how Brexit has impacted these areas.

3 The Impact of Brexit on Protection of Human Rights and Fundamental Rights Influenced by EU Law in the UK

The impact of withdrawal from the EU and the Brexit process on the protection of fundamental rights depends somewhat on the source of the protection. Where the rights were derived from legislation, in the initial legislative scheme governing departure from the EU under the European Union Withdrawal Act 2018 (EUWA), Regulations and EU tertiary legislation became part of UK law under ss. 2 and 3 of the Act and the associated provisions in Schedule 1 of the Act. Such law was known as 'retained' EU law. This has subsequently been revisited by the Retained EU Law (Revocation and Reform) Act 2023, which made a number of important amendments to the EUWA and, in particular for the purposes of this discussion, renamed 'retained' EU law and now defines it as 'assimilated law'. The CFR was not to be treated as retained EU law according to the provisions of the EUWA, so its

[36]See above, note 14. N.B. the decision in *Google LLC* v. *Lloyd* [2021] UKSC 50; [2022] A.C. 1217, clarifying that damages can be claimed only when a contravention of any of the requirements of the Act by a data controller can be shown to have caused material damage or distress.

[37]*R (Bridges)* v. *Chief Constable of South Wales Police* [2020] EWCA Civ 1058; [2020] 1 W.L.R. 5037. See [62]—[65] for the EU law dimension.

immediate legal effects in the UK legal system were negated by Brexit.[38] In s. 5 (4) EUWA, the Act sought to retain the effects of any "any fundamental rights or principles which exist irrespective of the Charter".

Schedule 1 of the EUWA provides for the retention of the general principles of law as they existed at the end of the implementation period for Brexit,[39] so any general principles determined by the EU courts after IP completion day could not form a part of UK law. In reality, the significance of this restriction is very limited, because Paragraph 3 of Schedule 1 of the EUWA was as follows:

(1) There is no right of action in domestic law on or after IP completion day based on a failure to comply with any of the general principles of EU law.
(2) No court or tribunal or other public authority may, on or after IP completion day

    (a) disapply or quash any enactment or other rule of law, or
    (b) quash any conduct or otherwise decide that it is unlawful, because it is incompatible with any of the general principles of EU law.

As such, the ability to bring proceedings based on a failure to comply with the general principles of law was effectively removed by the EUWA after IP completion day. The Act retained a limited saving, contained in Paragraph 39 of Schedule 8 of the Act, permitting legal proceedings to be brought for up to 2 years after IP completion day, but only where the act or decision complained of occurred before IP completion day. This period has now expired, so the ability to bring litigation in respects of infringements of the general principles of EU law is removed and has since been repealed by the Retained EU Law (Revocation and Reform) Act 2023. However, as noted above, many of these principles have influenced or have been absorbed into common law, so although the direct right to bring a claim in respect of a breach of the general principles of EU law is removed, where judicial review of administrative action is available, many of the principles might still be relied upon to the extent that they are reflected in UK domestic law.

The EUWA retains another route through which the general principles of law and, perhaps, the CFR, could still retain some influence in UK law. Section 6 EUWA sets out the powers available to the court in the interpretation of retained EU legislation, with s. 6(1) making it clear that courts or tribunals in the UK are not bound by any decision of the EU courts made after IP completion day and also that after that date, no matter can be referred to the EU courts. However, s. 6(2) provides that "...a court or tribunal may have regard to anything done on or after IP completion day by the European Court, another EU entity or the EU so far as it is relevant to any matter before the court or tribunal." This provision offered an avenue for the UK courts to consider decisions of the EU courts decided after Brexit, though only in the interpretation of what was known under the EUWA as 'retained' legislation and is

---

[38] See section 5(4) EUWA.

[39] This was known as 'IP completion day'—11 pm on 30 December 2020. See the European Union (Withdrawal Agreement) Act 2020, s. 39(1).

known now, following the Retained EU Law (Revocation and Reform) Act 2023 as 'assimilated' legislation.

Section 6(3) of the EUWA provides that any question as to the "validity, meaning or effect" of assimilated (previously retained EU law) should be determined, provided that the assimilated law has not been modified before or after IP completion day, in accordance with the assimilated (previously retained) case law of the EU courts (i.e. that decided prior to IP completion day). Section 6(4) of the EUWA excepts the Supreme Court from this requirement, stating that the Supreme Court is not bound by assimilated EU case law, though if the Supreme Court wishes to depart from assimilated case law,[40] it must apply the same test as it would apply to depart from its own case law. Section 6(5) EUWA gives the executive the power, through delegated legislation, to extend the power to depart from assimilated case law to other courts. This opportunity has been taken and the power has been extended to a number of other courts, most notably the Court of Appeal.[41]

It is important to note one change that has been brought about by the Retained EU Law (Revocation and Reform) Act 2023. In section 6(3) of the EUWA as it was originally enacted, the courts were given the power to interpret assimilated EU legislation in light of the retained general principles of law (i.e. those in place prior to IP completion day). This power is removed by s. 4(3)(a) of the Retained EU Law (Revocation and Reform) Act 2023 as of January 1 2024. The precise impact of this change is difficult to determine, given that the general principles of law will inform the case law that is to be applied in s. 6(3) and also that s. 6(2) offers a broad potential for courts to consider decisions of the EU courts made after IP completion day.

The Retained EU Law (Revocation and Reform) Act 2023 makes some changes to the EUWA in order to try and reduce the impact of the general principles of EU law. These amendments took effect on 1 January 2024. The first notable amendment is in s. 4(2)(a) of the 2023 Act, which adds a new s. 5(A4) of the EUWA, which provides "No general principle of EU law is part of domestic law after the end of 2023." Section 5(4) of the EUWA as enacted, which provided that fundamental rights or principles which existed irrespective of the CFR were retained in UK law is also repealed by s. 4(2)(b) of the 2023 Act. Given that many of these principles have now become a part of the common law, it is not evident that these changes will bring significant practical changes to the approach of the courts, not least because they only become relevant when assimilated law is under consideration.

[40] The definition of 'assimilated' (previously known as 'retained EU case law', is to be found in s. 6 (7) EUWA.

[41] See SI 2020/1525 The European Union (Withdrawal) Act 2018 (Relevant Court) (Retained EU Case Law) Regulations 2020, Reg. 3. The Court of Appeal has used its power to depart from retained case law in *Industrial Cleaning Equipment (Southampton) Ltd v Intelligent Cleaning Equipment Holdings Co Ltd* [2023] EWCA Civ 1451; [2024] Bus. L.R. 103, concerning the enforcement of Trade Marks.

An examination of the decision in *Harris*[42] suggests how the repeal of reference to the general principles in s. 5(4) may make a difference in the future. In this case, the claimant sought a remedy against the Environment Agency for its failure to comply with the Habitats Directive,[43] as implemented in UK law by Regulations.[44] Johnson J. said "Here, the claimants have not just a presumptive common law right to a remedy, but also a statutory right. . . The effect of regulation 9(3) of the Habitats Regulations and article 6(2) of the Habitats Directive must be determined in accordance with retained general principles of EU law: section 6(3)(a) of the 2018 Act."[45] The removal of the reference to the general principles of EU law may remove the putative 'statutory' right to remedy, though as Johnson J. observed in the case, in a judicial review case where unlawful action has been found, the claimant will be presumed to have a common law remedy in any case, so the practical impact of s. 4 (3)(a) of the Retained EU Law (Revocation and Reform) Act 2023 is likely to be limited.

Of the other rights discussed above, the impact of Brexit on the Equality Act 2010, or the UK courts' ability to consider the jurisprudence of the EU courts in their decisions is small. Although the courts are not obliged to follow decisions of the EU courts given that the supremacy of EU law is abolished by s. 3 of the Retained EU Law (Revocation and Reform) Act 2023, they may choose to consider cases before the EU courts and be guided by them should they see fit. One potential future problem is that the UK will no longer be bound to implement any revisions to EU non-discrimination and equality law, so the Equality Act 2010 will remain representative of EU law as it was at the time of Brexit unless the UK Parliament decides to amend to 2010 Act. This may mean that the UK falls behind the state of the art in protections from discrimination at the EU level.

In data protection law, upon exit from the EU, the GDPR was retained in domestic law, subject to minor amendments, reflecting the UK's departure from the EU. The legislation is known as the 'UK GDPR' and, much like the point made in respect of the Equality Act 2010, should be considered to be a 'snapshot' of the GDPR at the time of Brexit. It will not be amended in line with changes at the EU level unless the UK Parliament chooses to make amendments to reflect changes at the EU level, so the UK may fall behind the state of the art at the EU level on data protection. However, there may be some incentive for the UK to align its data protection law with that of the EU because it will wish to maintain the adequacy decision for international data flows pursuant to Article 45 GDPR in the future.[46]

---

[42] *Harris v Environment Agency* [2022] EWHC 2606 (Admin); [2023] 2 C.M.L.R. 8.

[43] Council Directive 92/43/EEC of 21 May 1992 on the conservation of natural habitats and of wild fauna and flora [1992] OJ L 206/7.

[44] SI 2017/1012 The Conservation of Habitats and Species Regulations 2017.

[45] *Harris*, above, note 42, [7].

[46] Commission Implementing Decision (EU) 2021/1772 of 28 June 2021 pursuant to Regulation (EU) 2016/679 of the European Parliament and of the Council on the adequate protection of personal data by the United Kingdom [2021] OJ L 360/1.

However, decisions of the Court of Appeal already illustrate some of the challenges that have been brought about by Brexit in relation to the GDPR. *Open Rights Group*[47] concerned an exception (hereafter the 'immigration exception'), contained in Schedule 2 Part 1 paragraph 4 of the UK Data Protection Act 2018, which allowed data controllers to depart from the data protection principles in some situations where such departure was for the purpose of the maintenance of immigration controls, or the investigation of activities that would undermine effective immigration controls. The Court of Appeal held that this exception was unlawful as it was incompatible with the requirements of Article 23 of the UK GDPR, which provides a framework through which restrictions on the data protection principles can be imposed and, in particular, allows restrictions only when "...when such a restriction respects the essence of the fundamental rights and freedoms and is a necessary and proportionate measure in a democratic society."

The Court of Appeal found that the immigration exception was unlawful because it failed to comply with the requirements of Art. 23(2) of the UK GDPR, which laid down specific requirements that should be fulfilled and issues that should be addressed by any legislation seeking to create an exception to the data protection principles, at the Data Protection Act 2018 failed to do this. Furthermore, the Court held that the broad exception did not meet with the requirements of proportionality and necessity when the case law of the EU courts was considered.[48] Erdos notes that this case illustrates some substantial concerns about the power of the executive to modify assimilated legislation through delegated legislation under s. 8 of the EUWA, as the subsequent efforts to modify the UK GDPR in order to allow the exceptions to stand give the executive substantial power to reduce the protections available under the UK GDPR with limited Parliamentary scrutiny.[49]

4 Conclusions: What Might the Future Bring?

This paper has illustrated the contribution of EU Law to the protection of human and fundamental rights in the UK, including a consideration of the impacts of the general principles of law. It has sought to illustrate that the CFR, the jurisprudence of the EU courts that has developed the general principles of law and action in specific areas, such as non-discrimination and equality law and data protection law have all had a significant impact on the protection of individual rights in the UK. One might argue that some of these effects might be considered to be indirect, in the sense that the

[47] *Open Rights Group* v *Secretary of State for the Home Department* [2021] EWCA Civ 800 and, in respect of the remedies *Open Rights Group v Secretary of State for the Home Department* [2021] EWCA Civ 1573.

[48] *Open Rights Group* v *Secretary of State for the Home Department* [2021] EWCA Civ 800, [31]-[33] and [36]-[47].

[49] Erdos (2023), p. 799 et seq.

influence of EU law has altered the approach of the common law, so that some of the general principles of EU law are now embedded in the jurisprudence of the UK courts.

The Brexit process has led to some important diminutions in the protection previously available The CFR was removed from UK law on IP completion day, although it may be that it can still be called upon in appropriate cases due to the relatively broad scope of s. 6(2) EUWA. It is also the case that many of the provisions of the CFR are protected elsewhere in UK legislation, whether through the Human Rights Act 1998 and the alignment of the CFR and ECHR on many issues, through the Equality Act 2010. The common law will also give effect to some of the rights in the CFR, such as the right to an effective remedy, as illustrated by the *UNISON*[50] case.

In other areas, it is so far difficult to determine the precise impact of Brexit, as although the impact of the general principles of law has been abolished by the Retained EU Law (Revocation and Reform) Act 2023 and there are other limits on the judicial reference to EU law and an expanded potential for courts other than the Supreme Court to depart from EU law where they deem it appropriate to do so, the impact of this has so far been small. It remains to be seen whether the courts take a more expansive approach to these powers in the future.

A particular concern moving forward may be the dilution of rights granted by EU law through the extensive powers to modify legislation via delegated legislation contained in s. 8 EUWA. It may be that this, rather than the judicial freedom to depart from EU law, is the more pressing challenge.

References

Amos M (2024) Democratic state, autocratic method: the reform of human rights law in the United Kingdom. Int Comp Law Q 73:1–27. https://doi.org/10.1017/S0020589323000441

Birkinshaw PJ (2020) European public law: the achievement and the Brexit challenge, 3rd edn. Wolters Kluwer, Alphen aan den Rijn

Craig PP (2013) The nature of reasonableness. Current Legal Problems 66:131–167. https://doi.org/10.1093/clp/cut010

Douglas-Scott S (2011) The European Union and human rights after the treaty of Lisbon. Human Rights Law Rev 11:645–682. https://doi.org/10.1093/hrlr/ngr038

Erdos D (2023) The UK GDPR, the immigration exception and Brexit: interrogating open rights group v secretary of state for the home department and its aftermath. Modern Law Rev 86:785–800. https://doi.org/10.1111/1468-2230.12784

Hepple B (2011) Equality: the new legal framework. Hart Publishing, Oxford

Lienen C (2018) Common law constitutional rights: public law at a crossroads? Public Law:649

Tridimas T (2007) The general principles of EU law, 2nd edn. Oxford University Press, Oxford

[50] UNISON, above, note 1.

Part II
The New Relationship as Shaped by the 2019 and 2020 Agreements

When Citizens Become Foreigners: The Changing Fortunes of Citizens in the Post-Brexit Environment

Jules Bradshaw

> Two roads diverged in a yellow wood,
> And sorry I could not take them both
> And be one traveller, long I stood
> And looked down one as far as I could,
> To where it bent in the undergrowth;
> ROBERT FROST[1]

Citizenship's story is ancient, perceived as a gradually developing entity, expanding or contracting as needed, to encompass those defined as members of a polity. It is seldom thought of as subject to radical or sudden alteration and yet twentieth century Europe is littered with such occurrences: redrawn borders; a wall rising and falling; new organisations with new political ramifications emerging.[2] Overnight, after more than 30 years of a quasi-status developing through Court of Justice (ECJ, later CJEU) jurisprudence, the European Union (EU) birthed something novel: a supra-national manifestation that emphasised ties beyond the national arena that can and do bind peoples together.[3] Thus it disproved Aron's assertion that "there are no such animals as European Citizens... only French, German, or Italian"[4] ones.

It was expected that this novel, overarching status would apply to all who possessed it forever. Brexit, or Member State (MS) withdrawal, was not seriously contemplated: while Greenland departed the European Community (EC) in 1985, it remained an overseas country and territory and its citizens maintained a relationship

[1] Frost (1915), available at https://hdl.handle.net/2027/chi.19147394?urlappend=%3Bseq=235%3Bownerid=13510798902328987-245 last accessed 25/10/2023.

[2] See generally Richards and Waibel (2014).

[3] Article 3 TEU (ex.Article 2).

[4] Aron (1974), p. 653.

J. Bradshaw (✉)
LJMU, Liverpool, UK
e-mail: J.E.Bradshaw@ljmu.ac.uk

E. Guinchard, C. Panara (eds.), *The New Relationship between the United Kingdom and the European Union*, https://doi.org/10.1007/978-3-031-70652-3_5

with the organisation, even holding EU Citizenship (UC). It had acceded to the EU alongside Denmark, because it was part of the Kingdom of Denmark and its status altered because its relationship with Denmark changed. Denmark was, and remains, the MS. A MS leaving, having voluntarily joined the Union, was not seriously envisaged. Yet in 2016, while riding what might be termed the "nationalist wind of doctrine",[5] the UK made such a decision (albeit one that various of its constituent parts rejected) and its withdrawal was finalised in January 2020. Again overnight, UC was subject to a radical change, although the precise extent and nature of that change would be negotiated over a period of years.

Citizenship's elasticity, demonstrated by centuries of ebb and flow, proved capable of withstanding such alteration. However, the citizens themselves have had to prove as adaptable in navigating the changes of circumstance that have since befallen them, as well as trying to anticipate those which may follow. This chapter will outline the position EU Citizens (EUCs) enjoyed before Brexit, the nature of the changes enforced by Brexit on EUCs resident in the UK and EU-based UK nationals (UKCs), and will do so by highlighting key themes relating to the enjoyment of citizenship rights: given the vast field in question, the chapter serves to provide the reader a general overview.[6] It will close with an assessment of possible future developments for citizens in the coming years.

The rights and wrongs of Brexit aside, it provided an unexpected and unusual opportunity for both parties to reflect on and reconsider their relations with external parties, their values and the place of the individual in their societies. The avenues they therefore chose to pursue are instructive.

1 A 'European' Citizenship

"Union citizenship is destined to be the fundamental status of nationals of the Member States",[7] proclaimed the ECJ in 2001. This is a bold claim to make for a status that is not generated directly by the EU. Member States are UC's gatekeepers, as it is a derivative of MS nationality, a province over which the same ECJ has repeatedly held the MS have sole dominion.[8] Nonetheless, once the litmus test of

[5] Kostakopoulou (2020), p. 8.

[6] Northern Ireland and the Common Travel Area between Ireland and the UK will not be considered as part of this chapter. Likewise, the many facets of citizenship, such as access to social advantages, non-discrimination in broad equality terms, students' rights, the linkage between citizenship and worker rights and more must be considered in the broadest of terms (if at all) owing to limitations of space.

[7] C-184/99 *Grzelczyk v. Centre public d'aide sociale d'Ottignies-Louvain-la-Neuve* [2001], at para. 31.

[8] See *inter alia* C-369/90 *Micheletti and others v/ Delegación del Gobierno en Cantabria* [1992], C-135/08 *Rottman v. Friestaat Bayern* [2010], C-200/02 *Zhu & Chen v. Secretary of State for the Home Department* [2004] etc.

relevant nationality is met, UC deviates from standard international law conceptions of citizenship, i.e., the "genuine connection" test outlined in *Nottebohm*[9] and the "close connection"[10] of the Hague Convention, by creating a new concept of "Community rights".[11] Although emerging from an underlying nationality, UC further departs from standard international law in two ways: first it forbids discrimination amongst MS citizens based on nationality,[12] flying in the face of centuries of relationship-building between states and their nationals and the 'othering' of non-nationals; and second, it created an international status directly enforceable by its subjects before the courts (national and institutional), reiterating the EU's intention to create directly enforceable rights destined to become part of people's "legal heritage".[13]

UC was, therefore, an unprecedented addition to the international arena, creating parity amongst disparate peoples from which emerged a 'people', albeit that the new entity was subject to criticism both for its timidity and over-reach.[14] The Commission emphasised that UC is a "source of legitimation of the process of integration, by reinforcing the participation of citizens, and a fundamental factor in the creation among citizens of a sense of belonging",[15] building on Advocate General Jacobs' vision of a realm where individuals could invoke the phrase '*civis europeus sum*' as protection against fundamental rights violations.[16] It established a system of enforceable rights that built upon the pre-existing framework supporting workers' rights and so-called special rights,[17] and which developed significantly until the eve of Brexit. The evolving wording of the Treaties during this period deserves consideration: the 'citizenship article'[18] subtly changed after its first iteration. In 1992 the citizenship article defined UC in terms of its derivative nature but, following the Treaty of Amsterdam it became "complementary" and, after Lisbon, it is described as an

[9] CIG *Nottebohm* (April 6, 1955), full text available at https://www.icj-cij.org/sites/default/files/case-related/18/018-19550406-JUD-01-00-EN.pdf last accessed 25/10/2023.

[10] Article 5, The Hague Convention on Certain Questions Relating to the Conflict of Nationality Laws 1930.

[11] *Micheletti.*

[12] Art.18 TFEU.

[13] C-26/62 *Van Gend en Loos v. Nederlandse Administratie der Belastingen* [1963] at para.4.

[14] See *inter alia* Kostakopoulou (1998), pp. 639–656.

[15] European Commission "Third Report on Citizenship of the Union" 2001, in Magnette (2007), p. 669.

[16] C-168/91 *Konstantinidis v. Stadt Altensteig - Standesamt and Landratsamt Calw* [1992] - AG Opinion, at para.46: "In my opinion, a Community national who goes to another Member State as a worker or self-employed person . . . is entitled not just to pursue his trade or profession and to enjoy the same living and working conditions as nationals of the host state; he is in addition entitled to assume that, wherever he goes to earn his living in the European Community, he will be treated in accordance with a common code of fundamental values, in particular those laid down in the European Convention on Human Rights. In other words, he is entitled to say 'civis europeus sum' and invoke that status in order to oppose any violation of his fundamental rights".

[17] See Wiener (1998).

[18] Article 17 ECT, later Art. 20 TFEU.

"additional" status. The changing descriptions may seem inconsequential but reflect the developing judgments of the ECJ, responding to MS' actions and reflecting their role as UC gatekeepers. Whilst the issue of acquisition remains largely uncontested, in that MS retain an unfettered right to determine who attains nationality – and other MS are bound to respect that determination – the issue of citizenship loss is more nuanced and must be considered later in this chapter.

In terms of acquisition, it is not wholly correct to assert that nationality and citizenship are interchangeable terms, or that a citizen is, necessarily, a 'full citizen' so that all MS citizens are, therefore, EUCs. Some states, particularly those with colonial pasts like the UK, have rules delineating full membership and 'other' nationals. Thus Denmark recognises Faro Islanders as Danes, but not as "nationals for the purposes of Community law".[19] Similarly, long before Brexit emerged as a threat, the UK revisited the nature and classification of its citizenship under the *British Nationality Act* 1981. The changes began in the 1960s (pre-EU membership), with the *Commonwealth Immigration Acts*[20] and were crystallised with the *Kaur*[21] case. Here the UK effectively stratified its citizenship rendering Kaur unable to enforce UC rights (despite holding British nationality and residing in British territory), a move the ECJ respected and upheld.

Notably Arendt warned that possibly "humanity will conclude quite democratically – namely by majority decision – that for humanity as a whole it would be better to liquidate certain parts thereof"[22] and it has been argued that this citizenship restructuring is not liquidation but, rather, dilution of the "citizen pool".[23] Similarly, MS can delineate the potential scope of UC. However, a question arises regarding whether, instead of limiting the field, they might choose to expand the 'pool' massively, extending MS citizenship to a class, or classes, of people who would otherwise not qualify,[24] or limit it yet further, as a matter of "national discretion".[25]

The substance of UC, as opposed to its method of conferral, also requires consideration. UC contains both 'personal' and 'institutional' rights – institutional rights being those afforded to all, regardless of the degree of engagement with the EU or locus of residence, and the personal being those triggered, to a lesser or greater degree, by a EUC's actions.[26] Thus, institutional rights include: consular protection abroad by any MS in the absence of diplomatic or consular presence of the

---

[19]Protocol n.2 to the Act of Accession, relating to the Faro Islands, art.4, 1972 (OJ L 73163).

[20]For a discussion, see, Bradshaw (2016), p. 277.

[21]C-192/99 *R. v. Secretary of State for the Home Department ex. parte Manjit Kaur* [2001].

[22]Arendt (1951), p. 40.

[23]Bradshaw (2016), p. 278.

[24]Hughes (2020), https://www.ft.com/content/0cf70de8-fd10-4a5c-8303-fbd2b0b3811e. Last accessed 25/10/23.

[25]Kostakopoulou (2018), p. 861.

[26]These institutional rights are argued by some to be the sole truly 'supranational' elements of UC: see Mindus (2017).

originating state[27]; petitioning the European Parliament[28] (EP) or the Ombudsman[29]; addressing the EU in any official language and receiving a response in the same[30] – a right that will be unaffected by Brexit given that English will remain an official language. More tangible rights bestowed this way include political rights: the right to vote in EP elections in any MS and the right to vote in municipal elections in the host state,[31] the latter being a significant illustration of UC's inclusive nature – local elections generally being beyond the reach of resident non-nationals. Furthermore, a right founded upon the very cross-border nature of the EU, the citizens' initiative,[32] afforded EUCs a form of direct participation, contingent on support from a million fellow citizens based across seven states, to seek to direct EU policy and indicate popular support for specific new legislation, albeit that the institution was not bound to pursue a successful proposal.

The rights above can be enjoyed by any EUC. The enjoyment of a right of movement – and then residence – is a significant personal right that EUCs may choose to avail themselves of and which will form the basis of much of the post-Brexit considerations later in this chapter. Movement rights are not uncontested, despite their inclusion in Treaties[33] and within the citizenship article itself.[34] Their application has led to the CJEU being called "Janus-faced",[35] extending rights in some cases, restricting them in others. The TFEU specifies that restrictions may apply: the CJEU has confirmed it. Early examples of this *volte-face* can be found in decisions like *Grzelczyk,*[36] *Baumbast,*[37] *Collins*[38] and *Bidar,*[39] where the CJEU promulgated a rights-based approach to social assistance, or financial support, on the basis of 'genuine links' to the state, where individuals could demonstrate a degree of societal integration, only for it to be undone with *Förster*'s[40] insistence on sufficient residency before accessing assistance, which initially appeared to be an awkward exception[41] to the previous line of cases, but has become the norm.

---

[27] Art. 20(2)(c) TFEU.

[28] Art. 227 TFEU.

[29] Art. 228 TFEU.

[30] Art. 20(2)(d) TFEU.

[31] Art. 20(2)(b) TFEU.

[32] Art. 11 TEU.

[33] Art. 21 TFEU, Art.3 TEU.

[34] Art. 20(2)(a) TFEU.

[35] Carter and Jesse (2018), p. 1202.

[36] C-184/99 *Grzelczyk v. Centre Public d'aide Sociale d'Ottignies-Louvain-la-Neuve* [2001].

[37] C-413/99 *Baumbast and R v. Secretary of State for the Home Department* [2002].

[38] C-138/02 *Collins v. Secretary of State for Work and Pensions* [2004].

[39] C-209/03 *The Queen (on the application of Danny Bidar) v. London Borough of Ealing, Secretary of State for Education and Skills* [2005].

[40] C-158/07 *Jacqueline Förster v. Hoofddirectie van de Informatie Beheer Groep* [2008].

[41] Nic Shuibhne (2017), p. 162.

Subsequently, having previously indicated that the "genuine enjoyment" of UC should not be limited in *Zambrano,*[42] the later *Dano,*[43] *Alimanovic*[44] and *Garcia-Nieto*[45] decisions specified that MS could not be prevented from restricting access to certain benefits for non-nationals. Commentary following *Commission v UK*[46] leads to the troubling notion that MS may indirectly discriminate against resident non-nationals by reassessing legality of residence in cases where non-discretionary social assistance has been sought,[47] and instigate expulsion proceedings as a result.[48] These cases effectively curtailed so-called 'benefit tourism', by underlining the requirements in Directive 2004/38 (the 'Citizenship Directive') that citizens should not become an unreasonable burden on the host state.[49]

The issue of 'burden' is important, affecting residence, education and family reunification. The *prima facie* prohibition on nationality-based discrimination is illusory, unexpectedly complex. There are desirable migrants and undesirable ones. While all EUCs may cross borders for up to three months,[50] longer stays demand sufficient economic activity or means,[51] albeit that unexpected unemployment or illness may warrant an extension of legal residence for six months or more.[52] Thus, while the Citizenship Directive proclaims the desirability of fostering integration[53] and the CJEU has held that obstacles to the exercise of the right to residence for EUCs and their family members must be abolished,[54] the barrier of the 'economic capacity' requirement hinders residence beyond three months and arguably leads to strata of citizenship, as the Court has moved to safeguard MS from the possibilities that citizenship had to offer citizens.[55]

This stratification is emphasised following the *Dano* case line as host states may interpret 'reasonableness' of the possible burden imposed very differently: *Alimanovic* shows that a MS can base decisions not on a single assistance application, but on the *potential* 'cumulative effect' of such applications.[56] The Court has

[42] C-34/09 *Geraldo Ruiz Zambrano v. Office National de l'emploi* [2011] at paras. 40 and 42.

[43] C-333/12 *Elisabeta Dano, Florin Dano v. Jobcenter Leipzig* [2014].

[44] C-67/14 *Jobcenter Berlin Neukölin v. Nazifa Alimanovic and Others* [2015].

[45] C-299/14 *Vestische Arbeit Jobcenter Kreis Recklinghausen v. Johanna García-Nieto and Others* [2016].

[46] C-308/14 *Commission v. United Kingdom* [2016].

[47] In this case a child benefit available upon satisfaction of objective criteria and not subject to discretionary oversight.

[48] See *inter alia* Carter and Jesse (2018), pp. 1179–1208; Nic Shuibhne (2016), pp. 908–936.

[49] Art 7(1)(b) Directive 2004/38.

[50] Art. 6(1) Directive 2004/38.

[51] Art. 7(a) and (b) Dir. 2004/38.

[52] Art. 7(3) Dir. 2004/38.

[53] The preliminary paragraphs discuss this notion directly.

[54] C-424/98 *Commission v. Italian Republic* [2000] at para.35.

[55] Nic Shuibhne (2017), p. 168.

[56] *Alimanovic* at para.62.

hereby seemingly abandoned a core EU principle: there is no application of proportionality[57] in relation to UC rights, leading Kochenov to conclude that UC "virtually never protects the weak and needy"[58] instead projecting the "dogmatic ideal of a 'good market citizen'".[59] The fragility of UC is thus exposed: it can withstand external shock (Brexit), but not internal trials when movement is attempted by all, regardless of 'personal circumstance', shifting its focus from generating a formal status of equality to one of "social affiliation".[60] Consequently, all EUCs are equal, but some are more equal than others,[61] or, as Verschueren asserts more bluntly, "EU citizenship is not for the poor".[62] Therefore, the EU has latterly created internal 'othering', undermining (or "thinning"[63]) the post-*Grzelczyk* 'fundamental' legal status the CJEU had earlier striven to fortify.[64]

For those who can overcome the 'burden' issue both the Citizenship Directive and the CJEU indicate that longer residence can confer significant advantages, both to individual citizens and their extended family. The Directive defines 'family' members[65] and provides that relationships not expressly covered therein should be examined by the proposed host state, effecting the broadest impact possible to the free movement right. UC allows both EUC and third-country-national (TCN) spouses to join citizens exercising lawful residence in host states, limiting MS' capacity to restrict that right to reunification,[66] including when TCNs join EUC spouses returning 'home'.[67] Moreover, UC can extend rights absent in the state of origin, as seen in *Coman,*[68] where a mobile EUC met and married a TCN same-sex partner. Their union was recognised in the host state, but not the originating state: the CJEU ruled that the free movement right precludes originating state authorities from

---

[57] O'Brien (2017), p. 49; Hooton (2021), p. 160.

[58] Kochenov (2020), p. 51.

[59] ibid., at p. 52.

[60] Kostakopoulou and Thym (2020), p. 319.

[61] Paraphrasing Orwell (1945), p. 97 (electronic version).

[62] Verschueren (2014).

[63] Kochenov (2020), p. 41.

[64] For further discussion see Reynolds (2020), pp. 80–81; Minterhoud and Mantu (2020), pp. 191–207.

[65] Art. 2 Dir. 2004/38.

[66] See: C-459/99 *Movement Contre le Racisme. L'antisémitisme et la xénophobie ASBL (MRAX) v. État Belge* [2002], C-127/08 *Blaise Bahenten Metock v. Minister for Justice, Equality and Law Reform* [2008], C-109/01 *Secretary of State for the Home Department v. Akrich* [2003], etc., for the rights of third country national spouses to reside in a host state.

[67] C-456/12 *O v. Minister voor Immigratie, Integratie en Asiel and Minister voor Immigratie, Integratie en Asiel* [2014].

[68] C-673/16 *Coman and Others v. Inspectoratul General pentru Imigrari* [2018]: the judgement has not been implemented, thus the extension of rights is theoretical rather than implemented, but as a principle it is significant. This reflects the situation with the earlier C-148/02 *Garcia Avello v. État Belge* [2003] where Belgian authorities delayed giving effect to the CJEU's rulings in law for some years.

refusing residency to TCNs "on the ground that the law of that Member State does not recognise marriage between persons of the same sex".[69]

Extension of rights flows, controversially, both horizontally from spouse to spouse *and* vertically, from minor child to parent, with so-called "anchor babies".[70] *Baumbast and R*[71] affected EUCs and TCNs alike: in both cases residence rights extended to an adult based on the child's acquired rights. When *Chen*[72] allowed a TCN parent to remain with an infant child – particularly as the birthplace was specifically chosen to activate citizenship rights[73] – it led to national rules being redrawn, fearing that the decision could 'open a floodgate'. By generating the "genuine enjoyment" test in *Zambrano*[74] the CJEU appeared to be formulating a rights-based approach to citizenship, promoting family unity and advocating for an active role for minors.[75] The curtailment of the 'genuine enjoyment' focus in later cases[76] does not remove the *capacity* for minors to extend rights, not for dependants but those they depend on, but rather forces preliminary consideration of the existence of that dependency before the rights are extended[77] and, latterly, an assessment as to

[69] ibid., at para. 51.

[70] King (2019), p. 357. See further discussion in Guild (2016), pp. 231–249.

[71] C-413/99 *Baumbast and R v. Secretary of State for the Home Department* [2002].

[72] C-200/02 *Zhu & Chen v. Secretary of State for the Home Department* [2004].

[73] ibid., at para.11.

[74] C-34/09 *Geraldo Ruiz Zambrano v. Office National de l'emploi* [2011] at paras.42 and 44.

[75] See C-480/08 *Maria Teixeira v. Lambeth LBC* [2010] and C-310/08 *Harrow LBC v. Nicole Hassan Ibrahim, Secretary of State for the Home Department* [2010]. See also: C-451/19 and C-532/19 *Subdelegación del Gobierno en Toledo v. Xu (C-451/19) and QP (C-532/19)* [2022] where complex family units, similar but not the same as that in *Zambrano* came under review and extended rights horizontally and vertically. The Court held: "Article 20 TFEU must be interpreted as meaning that a relationship of dependency capable of justifying the grant of a derived right of residence under that article to a minor child, who is a third-country national, of the spouse, who himself or herself is a third-country national, of a Union citizen who has never exercised his or her right of freedoms of movement exists where the marriage between that Union citizen and his or her spouse produces a child who is a Union citizen who has never exercised his or her right of freedom of movement, and where that child would be forced to leave the territory of the European Union as a whole if the minor child who is a third-country national were forced to leave the territory of the Member State concerned".

[76] For examples specifically relating to parental residency, see C-40/11 *Iida v Stadt Ulm* [2012], where the Court did not extend a residence right to the TCN parent resident in Germany, of a child resident with her mother in Austria and; C-256/11 *Dereci v. Bundesministerium für Inneres* [2011], wherein the ECJ effectively ruled that States' refusals to allow children to live with their TCN fathers—in their originating states, having not practiced free movement—was not an infringement of the "genuine enjoyment of the substance of the rights" conferred by virtue of their status as EUCs and that it would only become so if the children had to leave Union territory completely in order to achieve reunification; and, C-87-12 *Ymeraga and Others* [2013]. 'Curtailment' more generally refers to the tests applied in the *Dano* line onwards.

[77] Nic Shuibhne (2020), p. 229.

whether the adult has sufficient resources to satisfy the Citizenship Directive's conditions.[78]

On the eve of Brexit, then, UC provided powerful benefits to those who exercised their rights, politically, socially and economically, more so to those who had secured permanent residence in a host state. Brexit looked to rupture that state of affairs, threatening to remove a sense of safety from those who expected it and leaving in limbo those who had yet to accrue sufficient residence to qualify for permanent status. As a status it enabled political and economic engagement in host societies, protected those whose sexual relationships might have been threatened had they not moved, and extended rights from individuals to their family members. The extent to which those protections were to be – or will be – damaged, or lost altogether, forms the basis of the subsequent discussion.

2 After Brexit: Re-defining Relations

"Brexit means Brexit"[79]: therefore, the two principal questions arising the morning after the referendum were 'what will Brexit be?', and 'when will Brexit be?'. For EUCs[80] these questions were critical. They had to be made aware of potential timeframes in which they must make decisions affecting the rest of their lives and personal and employment relationships: they needed information upon which to base those decisions. Moreover, if UC was both 'fundamental' and 'additional' might it be possible for UKCs who so desired to maintain UC in the wake of Brexit? Furthermore, while the EU already had a framework covering relationships of TCNs[81] with the Union, was it right to 'demote' those who previously enjoyed legitimate equal status as EUCs? If not, was there some special intermediate, or associate, status that could be developed and implemented,[82] especially where there

[78] See C-86/12 *Adzo Domenyo Alokpa and Others v. Minister du Travail, de l'Emploi et de l'Immigration* [2013], wherein the ECJ confirmed that its ruling in *Chen* remained good law, but that it was not unreasonable for a host state (Luxembourg) to remove Ms. Alopka to another state (France, where her two minor children had nationality) which would be obliged to provide work and residence permits to her, otherwise her children would be forced to quit Union territory completely, thereby losing the "genuine enjoyment of the substance of their rights" as outlined in *Zambrano*.

[79] Theresa May pushes for citizenship guarantees in early Brexit talks (2016), https://www.independent.co.uk/news/uk/politics/theresa-may-brexit-means-brexit-conservative-leadership-no-attempt-remain-inside-eu-leave-europe-second-referendum-a7130596.html. Last accessed 25/10/2023.

[80] And recall that UK citizens retained EU citizenship in the meantime.

[81] Thus the main focus of this section will lie on the new arrangements emerging in the UK, as UKCs' status changed, but to one that had developed over several decades, rather than one requiring much novel consideration.

[82] For such discussions see, *inter alia*, Coutts (2018), pp. 231–247; Kostakopoulou (2018), pp. 854–869; Cambien (2018), pp. 1344–1346; Shaw (2016), p. 1–4, c.f., Kochenov and van den Brink (2019), pp. 1366–1382.

had been no act of wrongdoing, or where personal desire to retain the threatened status was expressed[83]?

Citizenship loss now requires consideration: *Kaur* definitively demonstrates that MS can exclude citizens from the supranational arena, but *Rottmann*[84] illustrates that this power is not to be exercised indiscriminately. Once EUCs have become accustomed to the rights flowing from UC, should MS be able to withdraw the status at whim? Or, in the case of state withdrawal, should a political decision have such extreme consequences in what Kelsen termed the "personal sphere of validity",[85] whereby millions lose their 'fundamental' status, without recourse[86]? The CJEU argued against such a simplistic formulation: in *Rottmann* the Court highlighted that it was imperative EU principles (e.g., proportionality) were considered in decision-making[87] relating to citizenship loss, later reaffirmed in *JY*.[88] Acquisition is an unfettered right at MS discretion: removal is, to a degree, circumscribed. Regardless, UC, a *sui generis* EU creation is not in the gift of the institution itself, such that the impact of voluntary withdrawal by a MS cannot be countermanded – for those wishing to retain status – automatically. Following many arguments from UKCs remaining in the EU seeking to retain their EUC status,[89] in *Préfet du Gers* the CJEU crushingly reaffirmed its lack of capacity to assert UC's existence—or its concomitant rights – independently,[90] affirming the *Rottmann* position.

Hence, while legally nothing changed immediately following the referendum, EUCs in the UK and UKCs in mainland MS faced uncertainty.[91] Having exercised

---

[83] Given the close nature of the referendum result, at least 48% of the UK population who voted did not vote to lose citizenship and UK citizens resident in the EU for longer than 15 years (who presumably would not have chosen to lose a status according them parity in their chosen place of residence) were not permitted to vote. Minors—those most affected by the decision in the long-term—were also excluded. Interestingly, a proponent of the Leave vote, Steve Baker MP has recently conceded that a vote of such significance should have been subject to a supermajority, at which point the Uk would not have met a threshold sufficient to trigger Article 50 Forrest (2023), https://www.independent.co.uk/news/uk/politics/brexit-referendum-supermajority-vote-tory-baker-b2434582.html. Last accessed 25/10/2023.

[84] C-135/08 *Janko Rottmann v Freistaat Bayern [*2010] at para.55.

[85] Kelsen (1945).

[86] Such occurrences have confronted the EU before: when Russian-speaking citizens became non-citizens in Estonia and Latvia in 2004, and subsequently when the *izbrani* were created in Slovenia (a group who failed to apply for Slovenian citizenship in the appropriate timeframe following the break-up of Yugoslavia, and who subsequently were erased from the register of permanent residents), EU citizenship law was not capable of providing solutions. For further discussion see *inter alia*: Vetik (2011); Bradshaw (2013), pp. 195–215; Bradshaw (2016), pp. 290–317; Mindus (2017), pp. 68–70; Kostakopoulou (2020), pp. 61–66.

[87] *Rottmann*, at para.55. Ultimately, the ECJ demonstrated that it could not prevent the withdrawal of nationality by the MS and subsequent UC loss.

[88] C-118/20 *JY v. Wiener Landesregierung* [2022].

[89] Ferbrache (2019), pp. 81–88.

[90] C-673/20 *EP v Préfet du Gers & INSEE* [2022].

[91] For qualitative accounts of their feelings about the uncertainty following the vote see, Remigi and Martin (2020) and Remigi (2020).

legal rights and made personal and professional decisions based upon them, they now seemed destined to be removed, presumably without their consent and contrary to the legitimate expectations held upon their exercise. For that reason, once withdrawal negotiations were required, Theresa May[92] wanted citizens' rights to form an early part of the 'divorce' discussions[93] and EU negotiator Michel Barnier was issued instructions to seek lifetime protection of rights for EUCs resident in the UK at that time.[94] Barnier later stated, "[w]hen the moment arrives for the separation that the British have chosen, we must guarantee the rights of European Citizens in the UK and British citizens in the EU",[95] presenting the desired outcome as one of balance. If pre-Brexit status and recognition were to form part of those guaranteed rights, the EU wanted *status quo* for those who had moved already.

Negotiations began in 2017, concluding in October 2019, with a preliminary Joint Text of Agreement published in March 2018. Withdrawal Agreement (WA) negotiations played a critical role in determining the scope of, and rights attaching to, the 'new reality' to emerge on January 31st, 2020. "Citizens' Rights" form Part Two of the final WA underscoring their significance in the discussions and future relationship. The WA contained an effective 'sunset clause', however, with a 'transition period' beginning on the UK's exit on 31st January, 2020 and terminating on December 31st, 2020: the intervening period allowed EUCs and UKCs to manoeuvre and position themselves to be covered by the terms agreed in the WA. The WA affords "life-long"[96] protection to those covered under its citizens' rights provisions and is intended to be subject to direct effect,[97] extending Union law as part of the "legal heritage"[98] of all those caught by its provisions. It covered EUCs resident in the UK and UKCs in the EU[99] – provided they remained in the same state—as well as making reference to their family members[100] in terms reflecting definitions previously outlined in the Citizenship Directive. It included rights relating to family reunification,[101] a restatement of non-discrimination on nationality grounds[102] and protection for those who had already attained a right of permanent residence as defined under the Citizenship Directive.[103]

[92] British Prime Minister 13th July, 2016 to 24th July, 2019.

[93] Theresa May pushes for citizenship guarantees in early Brexit talks (2016).

[94] Michel Barnier rebuffs Theresa May on Brexit talks (2017).

[95] "Paradoxically, Brexit Has Also United Europe", Michel Barnier, Speech delivered at the "Obbligati a crescere-l'Europa dopo Brexit" conference, Rome, November 9th, 2017.

[96] Article 39 Withdrawal Agreement.

[97] Article 4 Withdrawal Agreement.

[98] Peers (2020), pp. 131–132.

[99] Article 10 Withdrawal Agreement.

[100] Article 9 Withdrawal Agreement.

[101] Article 10 Withdrawal Agreement.

[102] Article 12 Withdrawal Agreement.

[103] Article 11 Withdrawal Agreement.

The WA also preserved rights of entry and exit in terms comparable to ongoing Union membership[104] for at least five years following the end of the transition period and sought to preserve a route to securing permanent residence along the same lines outlined in the Citizenship Directive,[105] whilst protecting individuals from possible punitive action in the event of personal status changes, such as becoming a student, having been a worker, or entering into self-employment, or ceasing work entirely.[106] Interestingly, the WA also protects dependants of EUCs and UKCs even once they are no longer dependants.[107] In the event of inappropriate behaviour by an individual protected by the WA, expulsion is framed in the pre-existing terms of the Citizenship Directive,[108] whilst rights relating to social benefits,[109] worker rights,[110] self-employed status[111] and mutual recognition of qualifications[112] all reflect pre-Brexit norms.

The WA seems to have achieved *status quo* for those enjoying 'acquired rights', both personally and for associated family members for life i.e., EU law and rights will continue to apply to them[113] just as Barnier was instructed to achieve and in spite of the UK's initially more restrictive desires.[114] It was a tool to secure legal certainty, thus permanent residence in the EU was guaranteed for those UKCs who had accrued five years' residence – and would be accorded to those who achieved that milestone in the coming years.[115] In the UK, reality has not reflected that intent, principally with problems arising under the EU Settlement Scheme (EUSS).

The EUSS is a government vehicle, compulsory for EUCs[116] resident in the UK before January 1st, 2021 seeking to secure their right to remain in the UK. Successful applicants received either 'settled' status (i.e., indicating a permanent right to remain[117]) or the more complex 'pre-settled' status. The EUSS was criticised for

---

[104] Article 14 Withdrawal Agreement.

[105] Articles 13, 15 and 16 Withdrawal Agreement.

[106] Article 17 Withdrawal Agreement.

[107] ibid.

[108] Article 20 Withdrawal Agreement.

[109] Article 24 Withdrawal Agreement.

[110] ibid.

[111] Article 25 Withdrawal Agreement.

[112] Article 27 Withdrawal Agreement.

[113] Peers (2020), pp. 154–166.

[114] Polak (2021), pp. 991–992.

[115] Not all Member States would require UK nationals to make an application to remain: those that would require an application would assist applicants with their applications in accordance with the Withdrawal Agreement and issue biometric residence cards upon completion of the process. The EU provided guidance online for UK nationals at https://europa.eu/youreurope/citizens/residence/brexit-residence-rights/uk-nationals-living-in-eu/index_en.htm. Last accessed 25/10/2023.

[116] Also for EEA nationals (Iceland, Liechtenstein and Norway) as well as Swiss nationals in the UK, but excluding Irish nationals.

[117] Having satisfied the requirement of 5 years' residence, in line with provisions under Directive 2004/38.

closing in June 2021,[118] not least owing to difficulties with timely processing of applications and the volume of those who remained 'pre-settled' at the expiration of the application window.[119] 'Pre-settled' status lacks security and certainty: it is valid only for five years, meaning applicants must reapply – successfully – for settled status before this period expires; it can be nullified by periods of absence[120]; it precludes contemporaneous applications for British citizenship; it did not amount to a 'right to reside' as required to access UK welfare benefits.[121] This issue was particularly relevant for economically inactive EUCs, who might have been denied access to the NHS on the grounds they lacked 'comprehensive sickness insurance'[122] despite otherwise being eligible for it. In a significant but awkwardly timed decision, the ECJ ruled that "once a Union citizen is affiliated to... a public sickness insurance system in the host Member State, he or she has comprehensive sickness insurance".[123] As the UK had not, to that point, implemented legislation requiring EU migrants to possess 'private' medical insurance, the decision protects 'pre-settled' citizens in this regard: it potentially exposes the UK to cases from thousands who unnecessarily purchased private insurance.

The vulnerability to deportation of those with pre-settled status in the event of failure to reapply for settled status was controversial and affected some 2.2 million individuals.[124] The vulnerability stemmed from the government's assertion that failure to reapply for a permanent right to remain once five years' residence accrued would lead to the individual "overstaying",[125] i.e., being present illegally.[126] The High Court held that there was "no basis"[127] in the WA to require individuals to make multiple applications to remain and, ultimately, the EUSS breached citizens' rights. The Government later declared it did not intend to appeal.[128]

Those exercising rights to move prior to the transition period ending have been provided for, those migrating thereafter face new arrangements. As *Préfet du Gers*

[118] Fernández-Reino and Sumption (2022), https://migrationobservatory.ox.ac.uk/resources/reports/how-secure-is-pre-settled-status-for-eu-citizens-after-brexit/. Last accessed 25/10/2023.

[119] Criticism is relevant owing to the vulnerability of the 'pre-settled' to deportation.

[120] Covid-19 emerged during this time and is viewed as a legitimate reason for absence from the country for a prolonged period, as is compulsory military service, amongst other exceptions.

[121] Fernández-Reino and Sumption (2022), https://migrationobservatory.ox.ac.uk/resources/reports/how-secure-is-pre-settled-status-for-eu-citizens-after-brexit/. Last accessed 25/10/2023.

[122] The UK interpreted 'Comprehensive sickness insurance' routinely as meaning the possession of private medical insurance - this was arguably a discriminatory interpretation, given that many insurers will not cover all conditions, with a disproportionate impact on the disabled.

[123] C-247/20 *VI v Commissioner's for Her Majesty's Revenue & Customs* [2022].

[124] *Independent Monitoring Authority v. Secretary of State for the Home Department* [2022] EWHC 3274 (Admin) at para.76.

[125] ibid., at para.140.

[126] In contravention of s.24 Immigration Act 1971.

[127] *Supra.* N.124 at para.179.

[128] Fox (2023), https://www.independent.co.uk/news/uk/high-court-government-European-commission-Robert-jenrick-secretary-of-state-b2283505.html. Last accessed 25/10/2023.

stated, UKCs became TCNs immediately upon the UK's withdrawal.[129] The European Council suggests that 34 million EU inhabitants were born outside EU territory – some 8% of the total population.[130] The EU has encountered TCNs for longer than it has acknowledged UC and has been long criticised for not extending membership to them[131]: the presence of outsiders brought with it the challenge of diversity and the EU had to formulate a regulatory framework in response to "demands for respect for 'unassimilated otherness'",[132] albeit one that is criticised for being "fragmented"[133]: UKCs now fall under it.

For basic travel needs of 90 days or fewer in a 180-day period, UKCs will not require a visa to enter EU territory,[134] although passport checks at borders have become mandatory, travellers must possess sickness insurance, and passports must have adequate time remaining on them *after* the date of return to gain entry.[135] This adds expense, delay and inconvenience to what had been a fairly simple border-crossing experience.[136] Furthermore, from 2025, the EU intends to implement new biometric documentation (ETIAS[137]) for visa-exempt TCN travellers: it incurs a (small) fee, will be linked to travel documentation (e.g., passports) and will be required before booking entry to EU territory, although border checks at points of

---

[129] *Préfet du Gers* at para.56.

[130] European Council, "Integration of third-country nationals", updated 10/12/22 https://www.consilium.europa.eu/en/policies/eu-migration-policy/integration-policy/.These numbers have risen: by 2008, there were more than 19 million TCNs in the EU—5.3% of the total population. (Maas 2008, p. 583) and 23.7 m by 2021 (5.3% of the total population. "Communication from the Commission to the European Parliament, the Council, the European Economic and Social Committee and the Committee of the Regions: Attracting Skills and Talent to the EU", 27.4.22, https://eur-lex.europa.eu/legal-content/EN/TXT/PDF/?uri=COM:2022:657:FIN) all last accessed 25/10/2023.

[131] Kostakopoulou (1998), p. 640.

[132] ibid., at p. 641.

[133] Guild (2020), p. 361.

[134] https://www.gov.uk/travel-to-eu-schengen-area#:~:text=You%20do%20not%20need%20a,or%20for%20certain%20other%20reasons. Last accessed 25/10/2023.

[135] Schengenvisa Info "UK Citizens Travelling to the EU, Switzerland, Norway, Iceland or Liechtenstein", https://www.schengenvisainfo.com/uk-citizens-travelling-to-the-eu-switzerland-norway-iceland-or-liechtenstein/#:~:text=known%20as%20ETIAS.-,Requirements%20for%20British%20Citizens%20Travelling%20to%20the%20EU,your%20stay%20in%20the%20EU. Last accessed 25/10/2023. Note that adequate remaining time on a passport can vary depending on the state of travel.

[136] The Guardian, 'I was in tears': Briton with valid passport barred from flight over Brexit rules (2023), https://www.theguardian.com/money/2023/apr/29/briton-valid-passport-barred-from-flight-brexit-rules-eu. Last accessed 25/10/23; Euronews.travel, "UK passport holders urgently wanted to check expiry date before summer flights (2023), https://www.euronews.com/travel/2023/02/20/post-brexit-travel-uk-passport-holders-warned-to-urgently-check-expiry-date-after-rule-cha last accessed, 25/10/23; Politico, Brexit wrecked Britain's school holiday trips abroad (2023), https://www.politico.eu/article/brexit-britain-school-holiday-europe-travel-dover-port-checks/. Last accessed 25/10/2023.

[137] European Travel and Authorisation System.

entry will still be the final determinant of a right to enter.[138] Residency for longer than 90 days will be subject to the entry requirements[139] of the intended host state (which in the case of work permit applications can be costly[140]) and there is no initial guarantee of intra-EU mobility.

Once such residency is obtained, the EU framework[141] has developed to include limited mobility rights,[142] non-discrimination provisions[143] and extended family rights,[144] as well as rules regarding and rights attached to acquiring long-term resident status[145] that to a considerable degree mirror those contained in the Citizenship Directive. Moreover, TCNs can apply to the Ombudsman[146] and European Parliament[147] (as well as deriving rights from EUC family members, as explored above). Added to this, the underlying Union commitment to equal treatment[148] and rights protections (whether through the Charter of Fundamental Rights (CFR) or obligations attaching to the ECHR) have steadily enhanced the position of TCNs in, or entering, Union territory, such that it has become easier for TCNs to move within EU territory and to enjoy family rights.[149] Thus the EU has not replicated citizenship for TCNs, but has generated a system of parallel *denizenship*: regardless of desires to be included,[150] TCNs face political exclusion, partial social and civil inclusion and therefore partial 'othering', what Thym calls a 'cosmopolitan' outlook on non-nationals, consistent with human rights considerations based on the assumption

---

138 "New Requirements to Travel to Europe" https://travel-europe.europa.eu/etias/what-etias_en. Last accessed 28/05/2023.

139 A general presumption being that the individual is moving for employment purposes, or that they have sufficient means to be independent: the idea of burden on the host state is, again, a significant consideration.

140 Mussche and Lens (2019), p. 1257.

141 As with citizenship law and, it is a framework constructed on legislative and jurisprudential bases.

142 For instance, enhancing rights and removing restrictions for TCN workers posted from one state to another, see: C-445/03 *Commission v. Luxembourg, posted workers* [2004]; C-244/04 *Commission v. Germany* [2006]; C-168/04 *Commisison v. Austria, posted workers* [2006]; C-319/06 *Commission v. Luxembourg, posted workers II* [2008]: however, there is no equivalent free movement right akin to Art.21.

143 Directive 2004/43 Implementing the Principle of Equal Treatment between persons irrespective of racial or ethnic origin, subject to limitations of Article 3(2), and Directive 2000/78 establishing a general framework fir equal treatment in employment and occupation, subject to the limitations of Article 3(2).

144 Directive 2003/86 on the Right to Family Reunification.

145 Directive 2003/109 Third-country nationals who are long-term residents (available after 5 years' legal residence, Art.4(1) and acquired following lodging an application for the status (Art.7)).

146 Art.228 TFEU.

147 Art.227 TFEU.

148 See Weiler (1992), pp. 65–81.

149 Fernandez (2012), p. 155.

150 Sime and Behrens (2022), p. 5.

that all humans share "equal moral worth".[151] The same approach was advocated for in the UK's approach to EUC integration post-Brexit, by Ashcroft and Bevir,[152] as they highlighted the importance of pluralism to prevent Britain "sliding into inward-looking and exclusionary forms of populism", and the dangers of the "racism and xenophobia that has been released – and in the minds of many, legitimised – by Brexit".[153]

In the event, post-WA EU migrants to the UK also face changes, and less favourable conditions.[154] Short term visits (stays of less than six months for family visits, job interviews, tourism and suchlike) remain possible without application for a visa, albeit subject to criminality checks – an additional hurdle that may not have been proportionate under EU movement rules. For longer periods of residence, the UK has instituted a points-based immigration programme (PBS), applicable to all seeking to live, study, or work in the UK[155] and it is a system in flux. It is founded on the economic desirability of the proposed immigrant, reflected in the salary threshold imposed to classify as a 'skilled worker' and has received negative commentary for its limited scope for family unity.[156]

Economic desirability is further underscored by the nature of the application process: through an online application, the government expressly informs potential applicants that they will need to use a phone – for which we can read 'smartphone' – to complete identification verification.[157] Whilst unusual, not all individuals have access to such technology. Furthermore, applications — which are not guaranteed to be successful – have considerable upfront costs attached.[158] It is also a system with a high administrative burden: applicants must provide prospective employers with a code to check their immigration status: the code is valid for short

[151] Thym (2016), pp. 296–316.

[152] Ashcroft and Bevir (2016), p. 358.

[153] ibid., at p. 356 and p. 358 respectively.

[154] Note, Irish citizens are not affected by these changes, as they maintain the rights they enjoyed before Brexit as part of the Common Travel Area: this reciprocal arrangement also applies to UK nationals moving to reside in Ireland - onward movement from Ireland into EU territory will trigger third-county national rules.

[155] H.M. Government 2021, https://assets.publishing.service.gov.uk/government/uploads/system/uploads/attachment_data/file/971253/6.7209_HO_Right_to_Work_leaflet__PBS__V14.pdf. Last accessed 25/10/2023.

[156] Meyer and Bridgen (2022).

[157] UK Government, "The UK's Points-Based Immigration Process: Application Guidance", https://assets.publishing.service.gov.uk/government/uploads/system/uploads/attachment_data/file/1015798/The_UK_s_points-based_immigration_system_-_Application_guidance.pdf. Last accessed 25/10/2023.

[158] Visa applications range from a a starting price of £100 (£247 for a work visa), up to £3250, depending on the type of visa sought, with possible additional administration costs attached. Source: "Home Office Immigration and Nationality fees: 6 April 2022", updated 15 September 2023, https://www.gov.uk/government/publications/visa-regulations-revised-table/home-office-immigration-and-nationality-fees-6-april-2022. Last accessed 25/10/2023.

periods and must be renewed frequently and conveyed to possible employers (and potentially landlords) prior to entering the country.

The PBS fundamentally changes the position for job-seekers from the pre-Brexit position: whereas EUCs could move between states for up to six months in search of employment, one must now be in possession of a valid employment offer, departing from EU standards. Students also face some upheaval: in addition to new visa requirements, the Government has announced its intention to prevent overseas students bringing family with them.[159] In addition, access to social advantages that would previously have been available to EUCs may no longer be,[160] further underscoring the emphasis placed under the UK regime on the economic capacity of 'good' migrants.

For all, access to healthcare has become a further financial consideration, with the government asserting that "you might need"[161] to pay a healthcare surcharge (the immigration health surcharge) at the same time as making an application. Cumulatively, the costs incurred – and limitations on enjoyment of private and family life – in the application process recalls Kochenov's earlier critique of the state of UC,[162] except that emphasis on possession of arbitrarily determined adequate means is a deliberate deterrent for those deemed 'undesirable' in broader immigration policy.

Of course, Brexit has ramifications beyond movement and residence, as outlined in the first part of this chapter. The political and social ramifications are also keenly felt, regardless of the WA. Municipal voting rights will disappear[163]: for some individuals this may mean complete disenfranchisement[164] and, stemming from that political disconnection to the community, a weakening of a sense of belonging in that community, or the reinforcement of 'othering'. Whether as a result of status changes or not, EUCs appear to be disinclined to remain: at a time when net

---

[159] Except those undertaking post-graduate courses designated as research programmes: Rogers (2023), https://news.sky.com/story/home-office-to-stop-students-from-brining-family-to-uk-in-bid-to-curb-migration-12887545. Last accessed 25/10/2023.

[160] H.M. Government (2018b), https://assets.publishing.service.gov.uk/government/uploads/system/uploads/attachment_data/file/766672/The-UKs-future-skills-based-immigration-system-accessible-version.pdf. Last accessed 25/10/23 and Meyer and Bridgen (2022).

[161] Gov.uk, "Pay for UK healthcare as part of your immigration application", https://www.gov.uk/healthcare-immigration-application last accessed 28/05/2023.

[162] Supra, n.58 Kochenov (2020), p. 51.

[163] Except where reciprocal municipal voting arrangements have been agreed: currently, that means Spain, Portugal, Luxembourg and Poland. Pickard (2023), https://www.ft.com/content/d18fff3f-d396-43c1-bffa-43aee03a6477. Last accessed 25/10/2023.

[164] For instance, British nationals resident outside the UK for 15 years or more.

migration overall to the UK is rising – and when jobs traditionally undertaken by EU migrants are being left undone[165] – net migration from the EU stands at minus 51,000 for the year 2021–2022.[166]

3 Assessing the Future

For Leave campaigners, Brexit meant "taking back control" – an ambiguous phrase commonly perceived as targeting immigration control[167] that found its way into later government policy.[168] For the EU it highlighted the need to renew focus on unity[169] and citizenship, leading to policy initiatives from the Committee of the Regions[170] and to some EU leaders reflecting that it "symbolises the crisis of Europe",[171] calling for broader reconceptualisation of the Union itself.[172] Academics have reignited the debate about the possibilities UC has to offer.[173] The remainder of this chapter will focus on potential outcomes for citizens and citizenship in the post-Brexit era: like

---

[165] Chorley and Desave (2022), https://www.thetimes.co.uk/article/fruit-and-vegetables-rot-in-farmers-fields-despite-rising-food-bills-x2k73vv3f; Butler (2022), https://www.theguardian.com/environment/2022/aug/15/pounds-60m-in-uk-crops-left-to-rot-lack-of-workers-nfu-farming; Age (2020), https://www.ageuk.org.uk/our-impact/campaigning/care-in-crisis/brexit/. All last accessed 28/05/2023.

[166] ONS (2023), https://www.ons.gov.uk/peoplepopulationandcommunity/populationandmigration/internationalmigration/bulletins/longterminternationalmigrationprovisional/yearendingdecember2022. Last accessed 25/10/2023.

[167] Gietel-Basten (2016), p. 673.

[168] H.M. Government (2018a). https://assets.publishing.service.gov.uk/government/uploads/system/uploads/attachment_data/file/759792/28_November_EU_Exit_-_Taking_back_control_of_our_borders__money_and_laws_while_protecting_our_economy__security_and_Union__1_.pdf. Last access 25/10/23.

[169] "Paradoxically, Brexit Has Also United Europe", Michel Barnier, Speech delivered at the "Obbligati a crescere-l'Europa dopo Brexit" conference, Rome, November 9th, 2017.

[170] European Committee of the Regions (2019). It includes calls to follow three key principles to bring the EU closer to the citizens: the principle of "active subsidiarity" (at p. 9), "multi-level governance" (at p. 10), to enhance feelings of trust on the part of the citizenry and ensure active participation and enhance social and economic progress; and, "permanent dialogue" (at p. 11) to reduce accusations of a democratic deficit by enhancing opportunities for dialogue between citizens and EU institutions to feed citizen consultation directly into policy-making.

[171] Macron (2019), https://www.elysee.fr/en/emmanuel-macron/2019/03/04/for-european-renewal. Last accessed 25/10/2023.

[172] Mallet and Fleming (2019), https://www.ft.com/content/44075d7c-888d-47c3-837e-862195906a1a. Last accessed 25/10/2023.

[173] See *inter alia:* Kostakopoulou (1998), pp. 639–656; Bradshaw (2013), pp. 195–215; Acosta Arcarazo (2015), pp. 200–219; Strumia (2016), pp. 417–447; Kostakopoulou (2020); Weingerl and Tratnik (2022), pp. 13–38, c.f. Kochenov and van den Brink (2019), pp. 1366–1382.

all fortune-telling it comes with a warning that what is foretold may not come to pass and is by nature hypothetical and theoretical.[174] *Caveat emptor*!

For the EU, Brexit has become a footnote to its daily operation. Whilst the operation of the WA has faced challenges, particularly publicly in Sweden where the absence of a valid passport seemed likely to lead a British grandmother with Alzheimer's to be deported,[175] attention has turned to the future. Brexit was a cause of contraction but may herald the next great round of enlargement and with it a considerable population – citizen – influx. 2022 saw upheaval for Europeans *en masse* with war erupting following Russia's invasion of Ukraine following the disruption caused already by a global pandemic. The EU's reaction could have been one of introversion, or more generous open-handed dealing: it chose the latter and EUCs responded positively.[176] Subsequently, Ukraine, Moldova and Bosnia-Herzegovina enjoy candidate status, whilst negotiations have opened with North Macedonia and Albania. EU membership, and with it EUC, are desirable statuses.

The Ukrainian war suggests how a more expansive (non-nationality) approach to citizenship and its associated rights may be enacted. By activating the Temporary Protection Directive,[177] attempting to prevent MS asylum procedures becoming swamped and TCNs in desperate need of rapid protection facing danger, the EU demonstrated an uncommon degree of fleetness of foot. The extension of a *quasi*-citizenship status that followed the Directive's activation – and popular support for the EU's action – demonstrate that, handled correctly, immigration and integration on a broader basis than that currently in operation is achievable. Ukrainians moving into Europe enjoy rights such as residence, access to education and employment, banking facilities, family reunification, access to medical attention and suitable housing – as well as rights to intra-EU movement. They are being given the opportunity to put down roots and to integrate in their communities, as well as having their human rights acknowledged and protected.

Part of the wider discussion, before the Ukrainian war, surrounding citizenship's development and evolution, centred on notions pertaining to TCNs and recognition of their fundamental rights, their social engagement and integration, and included consideration of developing political rights.[178] The UN Human Rights Committee accepts that individuals may develop strong "personal and emotional" links to

[174] Furthermore, owing to space constraints, it is a limited discussion of potential developments: there is, inevitably, more to be said on the topic.

[175] Rhodes-Paul (2023), https://www.bbc.co.uk/news/uk-65180538. Last accessed 25/10/2023: this situation has now been rectified satisfactorily.

[176] Euro barometer polls show 74% of EUCs support the EU's response to Ukraine and 72% of citizens believe their country has benefitted from EU membership: https://webgate.ec.europa.eu/ebsm/api/public/deliverable/download?doc=true&deliverableId=84907. Last accessed 25/10/2023.

[177] European Commission: https://home-affairs.ec.europa.eu/policies/migration-and-asylum/common-european-asylum-system/temporary-protection_en. Last accessed 25/10/2023.

[178] Iglesias Sánchez (2020).

countries other than their own, that may be stronger than the bonds of nationality[179] and this can equally apply in the EU realm to resident TCNs. In the presence of the Long-Term Residence Directive, and viewing UC through the lens of transnational status operable in a supranational sphere, rather than a purely supranational status, it is possible to construct a fresh citizenship paradigm that eschews the nationality requirement and which can evolve as a process of integration, or rootedness, on the part of the emerging citizen. Such a reconceptualisation would reflect UC's cosmopolitanism,[180] but would also build on the traditional Marshallian notion of the social rights of citizenship benefitting society as a whole,[181] allowing the notion of solidarity in Union life to form the basis of future UC and what it can offer – and what, other than solidarity and humaneness, was the purpose of welcoming Ukrainians to the EU?

Earlier parts of this chapter might suggest that such reformulation is unlikely: the thrust of CJEU jurisprudence in relation to EUCs lacking sufficient means indicates a more restrictive interpretation of UC than that now suggested. Likewise, the glacial response to the refugee crisis at an institutional level is not promising. Nonetheless, long-term resident TCNs can show a degree of integration and (usually) contribution through taxation that would warrant access to some benefits on terms equal to MS nationals, in spite of hostility to such access at national level.[182] Likewise, it could be argued that those TCNs establishing families in Union territory, learning its languages and engaging in "citizenship activism"[183] exemplify the very pluralistic values that underpin the Union's *raison d'etre*[184] and in so doing actively have been pushing the bounds of what citizenship means anyway, acting as stakeholders[185] in society. The CJEU's restriction of UC rights on the one hand could yet be counterbalanced by more inclusive expansion institutionally, what Kostakopoulou and Thym term the "non-simultaneous evolution"[186] of citizenship. The EU's commitment to human rights, both through the ECHR and its own CFR surely mean that revisiting the citizenship issue, and a de-coupling from the nationality requirement, are warranted: in light of the Union's perennial desire to prevent discrimination and promote respect for equality, it is wise to recall Arendt's assertion that equality stems from group membership[187] and that if the "right to have rights"[188] is predicated on citizenship then the EU could enhance its own legitimacy

[179] Human Rights Committee, Views of 1 November, 1996, communication no.538/1993 *Charles E. Stewart v. Canada* in Strumia (2018), p. 753.

[180] Coutts (2018), p. 236.

[181] Marshall (1992).

[182] de Vries (2020).

[183] MacClancy (2019), pp. 368–389.

[184] Article 2 TEU.

[185] Baubock (2005), p. 686.

[186] Kostakopoulou and Thym (2020), p. 319.

[187] Arendt (1951), pp. 42–43.

[188] ibid., at p. 37.

and emerge as a greater power on the world stage with such a bold reimagining of its 'fundamental' status.

Turning now to the UK, for 'Remainers' there is a sense of *schadenfreude* about Nigel Farage's pronouncement that "Brexit has failed",[189] a sense of victory albeit a pyrrhic one. For, while Brexit was heralded by some as precipitating a new era of 'Global Britain',[190] it has proven costly in citizenship terms and is likely to wield further damage without a radical change of political direction. In addition to narrowing the scope of citizenship rights, benefits and opportunities of the British people, it also radically reduced the value of British citizenship internationally, causing "a loss of 30% of UK nationality's value".[191] Nonetheless, the British former Tory government asserted that Brexit is an opportunity to "[plant] the British flag on the world stage"[192] and reassert the 'historic' British values of freedom and democracy.[193]

In light of those values, it may seem strange that a key policy emerging in the wake of 'taking back control' has been tougher rules on immigration. Earlier, this chapter highlighted the PBS introduced in the UK and its focus on migrants' economic desirability: spousal visas to join UK spouses in the UK require the UK spouse to have significant income (which increases if there are children from the relationship) and documentation that – for non-national spouses based outside the UK at the time of applying – may be impossible to provide.[194]

Post-Brexit flagship legislation relating to immigration and border control, including the *Nationality and Borders Act* (NBA) and the *Illegal Migration Bill* (IMB), alongside the new PBS and the removal of protections for "*Zambrano*-carers",[195] has cumulatively caused concern about diminishing standards for UK nationals and foreign alike and aroused criticism about human rights protections,

---

[189] Parker and Foster (2023), https://www.ft.com/content/e6682422-67cb-47a8-a7d0-fb47f09d4301. Last accessed, 25/10/2023.

[190] D. Raab, "Foreign Secretary's introduction to the Queen's Speech debate", 13 January, 2020 https://www.gov.uk/government/speeches/foreign-secretary-introduction-to-queens-speech-debate last accessed 25/10/2023.

[191] Kochenov (2017), https://verfassungsblog.de/brexit-and-the-argentinisation-of-british-citizenship-taking-care-not-to-overstay-your-90-days-in-rome-amsterdam-or-paris/; see also Kuper (2020), https://www.ft.com/content/5529fbc0-3cb0-11ea-b232-000f4477fbca. Last accessed 25/10/2023.

[192] *Per* Boris Johnson in H.M. Government, "The Benefits of Brexit. How the UK is taking advantage of leaving the EU", January 2022 at p. 6 https://assets.publishing.service.gov.uk/government/uploads/system/uploads/attachment_data/file/1054643/benefits-of-brexit.pdf. Last accessed 25/10/2023.

[193] ibid., at p. 105.

[194] Such as evidence of shared utility bills, joint savings, tenancy agreements: https://www.gov.uk/uk-family-visa/partner-spouse. Last accessed 25/10/2023.

[195] I.e., parents caring for British citizenship children who are not British nationals themselves. Solanke (2020), p. 148.

particularly on human dignity and family life grounds.[196] These developments follow the 'hostile environment' developed in 2010 and the NBA was passed with the then-Home Secretary citing Brexit as underpinning its migration restrictions.[197]

However, the NBA also contains provisions relating not just to extending citizenship, but stripping it from UKCs. Chillingly, the new provisions permit the Home Secretary[198] to remove citizenship from a British national[199] without notification, removing opportunities to appeal the decision. Meanwhile, the IMB has drawn considerable condemnation for weakening the UK's commitment to human rights standards, provoking the Joint Committee on Human Rights to launch an inquiry into its terms[200] (and the negative response to government policy did not get better following a speech by the Home Secretary Suella Braverman, questioning international human rights norms[201]). When proposed to Parliament, the Home Secretary could not confirm the IMB was *Human Rights Act* compliant[202] and, while under debate in the House of Lords, the then-Archbishop of Canterbury called it "morally unacceptable".[203] For *Zambrano*-carers, the perception is of reduced citizenship status for UKCs on largely racial lines. The families involved fell beyond the

[196] For consideration of human dignity and migration more generally see Brownsword (2021), pp. 6–28.

[197] "The British people have repeatedly voted to take back control of our borders. They finally have a government that is listening to them". P. Patel, "Home Secretary Opening Speech for Nationality and Borders Bill", 19 July 2021, https://www.gov.uk/government/speeches/home-secretary-opening-speech-for-nationality-borders-bill last accessed 25/10/2023.

[198] Under the newly revised s.40(5A)(b) *British Nationality Act* 1981.

[199] For further discussion of UK citizenship-stripping, see Bradshaw (2016).

[200] "Inquiry into Illegal Migration Bill launched—Home Secretary asked to appear before Committee", 16 March 2023, https://committees.parliament.uk/committee/93/human-rights-joint-committee/news/194241/inquiry-into-illegal-migration-bill-launched-home-secretary-asked-to-appear-before-committee/. Last accessed 25/10/2023.

[201] Braverman attacked the UN 1951 Refugee Convention in a speech at the American Enterprise Institute in Washington DC on September 26, 2023 (reanscript available: https://www.aei.org/wp-content/uploads/2023/09/230926-Keynote-Address-by-UK-Home-Secretary-Suella-Braverman-Transcript.final_-1.pdf?x91208. Last accessed 25/10/23). The UNHCR took the unusual step of issuing a press release that expressly rebuked her comments ("UNHCR News Comment on the Importance of the International Refugee Convention", 26 September, 2023, https://www.unhcr.org/uk/news/press-releases/unhcr-news-comment-importance-international-refugee-convention. Last accessed 25/10/2023.

[202] *Illegal Migration Bill*at p. 1 https://bills.parliament.uk/publications/50885/documents/3348. Last accessed 28/05/2023.

[203] HL Deb, 10 May 2023, Vol. 829 Col.1787 the Archbishop of Canterbury's coming in response to the so-called 'Rwanda plan', to deport 'illegal' migrants to Rwanda to await processing, which the Equality and Human Rights Commission warned "risks breaching" UK obligations under international law and "undermining ... the universality of human rights" (Equality and Human Rights Commission "Statement following the announcement of the Illegal Migration Bill", 7 March, 2023 https://www.equalityhumanrights.com/en/our-work/news/statement-following-announcement-illegal-migration-bill. Last accessed 25/10/2023).

consideration of WA negotiations, are largely black[204] and poor, and their access to a range of benefits has been restricted creating, for the affected children, "a second class citizenship demarcated by race".[205] When challenged on the UK's post-Brexit declining commitment to the ECHR and the European Court of Human Rights' rulings, Rishi Sunak failed to commit to upholding ECHR standards, instead acceding to his party's calls to ignore legal decisions,[206] which received little sympathy internationally.[207]

Brexiteers promised a 'bonfire of the laws', culminating in the *Retained EU Law (Revocation and Reform) Bill 2022* on the basis that "[t]here is no place for EU law concepts in our statute book".[208] EU laws were to be effectively subject to a sunset clause—the end of 2023—and while the scope of this mass repeal has been scaled back,[209] the ultimate impact of the great repeal is uncertain, potentially impacting a huge range of laws affecting employment and social rights, particularly in equalities/discrimination fields. This uncertainty is unhelpful, but the impact of repealing such legislation could impact both UKCs and EUCs: without the constraining hand of EU oversight, the *potential* for social stratification and discriminatory practice resulting from removal of EU law is huge, even if it will eventually be unrealised.

Of prime concern to resident EUCs, in light of failures to process applications under the EUSS correctly[210] and previous examples of incorrect determinations about reasons for entry and subsequent detention,[211] is that the IMB again criminalises those considered to be illegally resident and repeats calls for deportation. As processing the EUSS has a chequered past and continues to provide uncertainty for the 'pre-settled' – potentially exposing them to calls to repay welfare benefits, with resultant poverty implications[212] – relations with Brussels in the post-Brexit era have soured. In light of the *Windrush* scandal (caused in no small part by Home Office destruction of physical documents[213]) and with the absence of certainty

[204] Solanke (2020), p. 148.

[205] ibid., at p. 151.

[206] Gallardo and Bloom (2023), https://www.politico.eu/article/eu-rishi-sunak-against-push-bypass-echr-human-rights-english-channel-migration-bill/. Last accessed 25/10/2023.

[207] Quinn (2023), https://www.theguardian.com/law/2023/may/16/cool-response-in-iceland-as-rishi-sunak-urges-europes-leaders-to-back-rwanda-plan. Last accessed 25/10/2023.

[208] Gov.uk "The Retained EU Law (Revocation and Reform) Bill 2022, 22 September 2022 https://www.gov.uk/government/news/the-retained-eu-law-revocation-and-reform-bill-2022. Last accessed 25/10/2023.

[209] HC Deb, 11 May 2023, Vol.732, Cols.437-451.

[210] Bounds et al. (2023), https://www.ft.com/content/13026db9-1251-41f2-beea-de8f6c08a44f, Last accessed 25/10/2023.

[211] Wright (2021), https://www.ft.com/content/04ba2bbd-c430-4f59-9ce2-2506a3f6256c. Last accessed 25/10/2023.

[212] Bounds et al. (2023), https://www.ft.com/content/13026db9-1251-41f2-beea-de8f6c08a44f, Last accessed 25/10/2023.

[213] "Windrush Scandal Explained", Joint Council for the Welfare of Immigrants, https://www.jcwi.org.uk/windrush-scandal-explained. Last accessed 25/10/2023.

for UK-based EUCs and perceived hostility to all outsiders generated by post-Brexit migration-related legislative trends, the UK's desirability as a locus of EUC residence has undoubtedly reduced, a position that looks unlikely to alter without considerable political ideological change.

4 Conclusion

Brexit was a watershed moment. Fifty years of integration and overarching policy alignment was abruptly terminated. The WA secured a legacy of the rights previously enjoyed for a small proportion of those actually affected by the 'divorce' and those rights will naturally peter out over time. For the EU, it has meant a period of contemplation, followed by largely liberal responses[214] to emerging crises and renewed engagement with the idea of what citizenship does, and can, mean. In the UK, Brexit was heralded as an era of freedom, opportunity and emerging as a global force. Unfortunately for individuals it has generated uncertainty, restrictions and a reduction in global significance.

Ultimately, when addressing questions concerning future status for UKCs migrating to the EU and EUCs migrating to the UK, there are stark conclusions to be drawn. In the former case, the EU has generated numerous protections and inclusion mechanisms for TCNs: you will be respected and can expect fair dealing, but the surest route to securing your rights is to find and marry an EU citizen. For EUCs, the message is less positive: your fortunes are likely to change with political winds, but the hostile environment created under previous Tory governments and propensity to breach international law demonstrated by more recent administrations indicate that the best advice you can be offered, in order to protect your rights and enjoy legal certainty, is to stay safely in the loving arms of the EU.

References

Journals/Books

Acosta Arcarazo D (2015) Civic citizenship reintroduced? The long-term residence directive as a post-National Form of membership. Eur Law J 21(2):200–219

Arendt H (1951) The perplexities of the rights of man. In: The portable Hannah Arendt. Penguin Classics, London, p 2003

Aron R (1974) Is multinational citizenship possible. Soc Res 14(4):638–656

Ashcroft R, Bevir M (2016) Pluralism, National Identity and citizenship: Britain after Brexit. Polit Q 87(3):355–359

[214] The global pandemic caused world-wide restrictions on free movement: it was (hopefully) a once-in-a-lifetime occurrence and the EU's response was in line with global responses.

Baubock R (2005) Expansive citizenship: voting beyond territory and membership. Polit Sci Politics 38(4):683–687
Bradshaw J (2013) Emerging from the Chrysalis: union citizenship must escape its nationality-based shortcomings. Liverpool Law Rev 34:195–215
Bradshaw J (2016) Stateless in Europe: the unbearable lightness of being an Unperson in the EU. In: Ferreira N, Kostakopoulou D (eds) The human face of the European Union: are EU law and policy humane enough? Cambridge, Cambridge University Press
Brownsword R (2021) Migrants, state responsibilities, and human dignity. Ratio Juris 34(1):6–28
Cambien N (2018) Residence rights for EU citizens and their family members: navigating the new Normal. Eur Papers 3(3):1133–1352
Carter D, Jesse M (2018) "The '*Dano* evolution'":assessing legal integration and access to social benefits for EU citizens. Eur Papers 3(3):1179–1208
Coutts S (2018) Citizens of elsewhere, everywhere and... nowhere? Rethinking union citizenship in light of Brexit. Northern Ireland Legal Q 69(3):231–247
de Vries KM (2020) The integration exception: a new limit to social rights to third-country nationals in European Union law. In: Thym D (ed) Questioning EU citizenship: judges and the limits of free movement and solidarity in the EU. Hart, Oxford
European Committee of the Regions (June 2019) Working together to bring the EU closer to its citizens: EU cities and regions
Ferbrache F (2019) Acts of European citizenship: how Britons resident in France have been negotiating post-Brexit futures. Geography 104(Part 2 Summer):81–88
Fernandez C (2012) Patriots in the making? Migrants, citizens, and demos building in the European Union. Int Migration Integr 13:147–163
Fernández-Reino M, Sumption M (29 March 2022) How Secure is Pre-Settled Status for EU Citizens After Brexit?, The Migration Observatory, https://migrationobservatory.ox.ac.uk/resources/reports/how-secure-is-pre-settled-status-for-eu-citizens-after-brexit/
Frost R (August 1915) The Road Not Taken, The Atlantic Monthly, https://hdl.handle.net/2027/chi.19147394?urlappend=%3Bseq=235%3Bownerid=13510798902328987-245
Gietel-Basten S (2016) Why Brexit? A toxic mix of immigration and austerity. Population Dev Rev 42(4):673–680
Guild E (2016) Free movement of EU citizens and their family members. New J Eur Criminal Law 7(2):231–249
Guild E (2020) Promoting the European way of life: migration and asylum in the EU. Eur Law J 26(5–6):355–370
H.M. Government (November 2018a) EU exit: taking back control of our borders, money, and laws while protecting our economy, security and Union
H.M. Government (December 2018b) The UK's future skills-based immigration System
H.M. Government (2021) Understanding your right to work in the UK, EU, EEA and Swiss Citizens
H.M. Government. The UK's Points-Based Immigration Process: Application Guidance
Hooton V (2021) A tale of two citizens: the *Brey-Dano* proportionality gap in UK courts and tribunals. Eur J Soc Secur 23(2):144–171
Iglesias Sánchez S (2020) The constitutional status of foreigners and European Union citizens: loopholes and interactions in the scope of application of fundamental rights. In: Thym D (ed) Questioning EU citizenship: judges and the limits of free movement and solidarity in the EU. Hart, Oxford
Kelsen H (1945) General theory of law and state. Harvard University Press, Cambridge. (Electronic version)
King DH (2019) *Zhu and Chen* revisited: and update on the ECJ's jurisprudence on the derivative rights of third-party nationals. Loyola Los Angeles Int Comp Law Rev 43(3):357–569
Kochenov D (24 June 2017) Brexit and the Argentinianisation of British Citizenship: Taking care not to overstay your 90 days in Rome, Amsterdam or Paris, https://verfassungsblog.de/

brexit-and-the-argentinisation-of-british-citizenship-taking-care-not-to-overstay-your-90-days-in-rome-amsterdam-or-paris/
Kochenov D (2020) The citizenship of personal circumstances in Europe. In: Thym D (ed) Questioning EU citizenship: judges and the limits of free movement and solidarity in the EU. Hart, Oxford
Kochenov D, van den Brink M (2019) Against associate EU citizenship. J Common Mark Stud 57(6):1366–1382
Kostakopoulou T (1998) European citizenship and immigration after Amsterdam: openings, silences, paradoxes. J Ethn Migr Stud 24(4):639–656
Kostakopoulou D (2018) *Scala Civium:* citizenship templates post-Brexit and the European Union's duty to protect EU citizens. J Common Mark Stud 56(4):854–869
Kostakopoulou D (2020) EU citizenship law and policy: beyond Brexit. Elgar European Law, Cheltenham
Kostakopoulou D, Thym D (2020) Conclusion: non-simultaneous evolution. In: Thym D (ed) Questioning EU citizenship: judges and the limits of free movement and solidarity in the EU. Hart, Oxford
Maas W (2008) Migrants, states and EU Citizenship's unfulfilled promise. Citizsh Stud 12(6):583–596
MacClancy J (2019) Before and beyond Brexit: political dimensions of UK lifestyle migration. J R Anthropol Inst 25:368–389
Macron E (4th March 2019) For European Renewal, Eylsée
Magnette P (2007) How can one be European? Reflections on the pillars of European civic identity. Eur Law J 13(5):664–679
Marshall TH (1992) Citizenship and social class, Pluto Classics
Meyer T, Bridgen P (2022) Open for the childless skilled only: the poverty risks of migrant workers under the UK points-based immigration system. J Poverty Soc Justice 30(1):9–36
Mindus P (2017) European citizenship after Brexit: freedom of movement and rights of residence. In: Palgrave studies in European Union politics. Palgrave Macmillan, London
Minterhoud P, Mantu S (2020) Back to the roots? No access to social assistance for union citizens who are economically inactive. In: Thym D (ed) Questioning EU citizenship: judges and the limits of free movement and solidarity in the EU. Hart, Oxford, pp 191–207
Mussche N, Lens D (2019) The ECJ's construction of an EU mobility regime—Judicialization and posting of third-country nationals. J Common Mark Stud 57(6):1247–1261
Nic Shuibhne N (2016) What I tell you three times is true: lawful residence and equal treatment after *Dano*. Maa J Eur Comp Law 23(6):908–936
Nic Shuibhne N (2017) Recasting EU citizenship as Federal Citizenship: what are the implications for the citizen when the polity bargain is privileged? In: Kochenov D (ed) EU citizenship and federalism: the role of rights. Cambridge University Press, Cambridge, pp 147–177
Nic Shuibhne N (2020) Integrating union citizenship and the charter of fundamental rights. In: Thym D (ed) Questioning EU citizenship: judges and the limits of free movement and solidarity in the EU. Hart, Oxford, pp 209–239
O'Brien C (2017) Unity in adversity: EU citizenship, social justice and the cautionary tale of the UK. Hart Publishing, Oxford
ONS (May 2023) Long-term international migration, provisional: year ending December 2022
Orwell G (1945) Animal farm: a fairy tale. Penguin Classics, London
Peers S (2020) The end—or a new beginning? The EU/UK withdrawal agreement. Yearb Eur Law 39(1)
Polak P (2021) Who had their cake and ate it? Lessons from the UK's withdrawal process and its impact on the post-Brexit trade talks. German Law J 22:983–998
Remigi E (2020) Limbo too: Brexit Testimonies from UK citizens in the EU. Spokesman Books, Nottingham
Remigi E, Martin V (eds) (2020) In limbo: Brexit Testimonies from EU citizens in the UK, 2nd edn. Spokesman Books, Nottingham

Reynolds S (2020) (De)constructing the road to Brexit: paving the way to further limitations on free movement and equal treatment? In: Thym D (ed) Questioning EU citizenship: judges and the limits of free movement and solidarity in the EU. Hart, Oxford, pp 57–87
Richards MD, Waibel PR (2014) Twentieth century Europe: a brief history, 3rd edn. Oxford, Wiley-Blackwell
Shaw J (2016) Citizenship, migration and free movement in Brexit Britain. German Law J 17(S1: Brexit Special Supplement):99–104
Sime D, Behrens S (2022) Marginalized (non)citizens: migrant youth political engagement, volunteering and Performative citizenship in the context of Brexit. Ethn Racial Stud:1–25
Solanke I (2020) The impact of Brexit on black women, children and citizenship. J Common Mark Stud 58:146–159
Strumia F (2016) European citizenship and EU immigration: a Demoi-critic bridge between the third country nationals' right to belong and the member states' power to exclude. Eur Law J 22(4):417–447
Strumia F (2018) From alternative triggers to shifting links: social integration and protection of supranational citizenship in the context of Brexit and beyond. Eur Papers 3(2):733–759
Thym D (2016) 'Citizens' and 'foreigners' in EU law. Migration law and its cosmopolitan outlook. Eur Law J 2(3):296–316
Verschueren H (14–16 March 2014) Free movement of EU citizens: also for the poor. In: 21st International Conference of Europeanists, Washington DC
Vetik R (2011) The statelessness issue in Estonia. In: Sawyer C, Blitz B (eds) Statelessness in the European Union: displaced, undocumented and unwanted. Cambridge University Press, Cambridge
Weiler J (1992) Thou shalt not oppress a stranger. Eur J Int Law:65–81
Weingerl P, Tratnik M (2022) Climbing the wall around EU citizenship: has the time come to align third-country nationals within intra-EU migrants? Eur J Int Law 33(1):13–38
Wiener A (1998) 'European' citizenship practice: building institutions of a non state. Westview Press, Boulder

Newspapers

'I was in tears': Briton with valid passport barred from flight over Brexit rules (29th April 2023) The Guardian
Age UK (4 November 2020) Brexit could worsen broken care system for older people
Bounds A, Fleming S, Foster P (7 February, 2023) Brussels demands answers after UK abruptly rejects residence for thousands of EU citizens, Financial Times
Brexit wrecked Britain's school holiday trips abroad (6 April 2023) It doesn't have to be this way, Politico
Butler S (15 August 2022) Up to £60m in UK crops left to rot owing to lack of workers, says NFU, The Guardian
Chorley M, Desave C (15 August 2022) Fruit and vegetables rot in farmer's fields despite rising food bills. The Times
Forrest A (23rd October 2023) Brexit Should Have Been Called Off Because Too Few Voted For It, Says Chief Tory Brexiteer, The Independent
Fox A (16 February 2023) Government not challenging judgement that rules on EU citizens in UK are not unlawful, The Independent
Gallardo C, Bloom D (26 April 2023) EU warns Rishi Sunak against plans to bypass human rights court, Politico
Hughes L (28 May 2020) UK opens door to citizenship for 300,000 HK residents. Financial Times

Kuper S (January 23 2020) Brexit, blue passports and the declining value of Britishness. Financial Times
Mallet V, Fleming S (9 May 2019) Macron calls for European 'community' including Ukraine, Financial Times
Michel Barnier rebuffs Theresa May on Brexit talks, Financial Times, May 3rd, 2017
Parker G, Foster P (12 May 2023) Rishi Sunak faces ire of Brexiters after ditching 'trivial' EU-era laws
Pickard J (14 May 2023), Keir Starmer scales back plan to extend voting rights to EU citizens, Financial Times
Quinn B (16 May 2023) Cool Response in Iceland as Rishi Sunak urges Europe's leaders to back Rwanda plan, The Guardian
Rhodes-Paul A (4 April 2023) Grandmother with Alzheimer's faces deportation from Sweden, BBC News
Rogers A (23rd May 2023) Home Office to stop overseas students bringing family to UK in bid to curb migration, Sky News
Theresa May pushes for citizenship guarantees in early Brexit talks, Financial Times, November 30th, 2016
Theresa May says 'Brexit means Brexit' and there will be no attempt to remain inside the EU, *The Independent*, June 11th, 2016
UK passport holders urgently wanted to check expiry date before summer flights (20th February 2023) Euronews.travel
Wright R (28 July 2021) UK immigration: Global Britain or the hostile environment?, Financial Times

Cases

C-109/01 Secretary of State for the Home Department v. Akrich [2003]
C-118/20 JY v. Wiener Landesregierung [2022]
C-127/08 Blaise Bahenten Metock v. Minister for Justice, Equality and Law Reform [2008]
C-135/08 Janko Rottmann v. Friestaat Bayern [2010]
C-138/02 Collins v. Secretary of State for Work and Pensions [2004]
C-148/02 Garcia Avello v. État Belge [2003]
C-158/07 Jacqueline Förster v. Hoofddirectie van de Informatie Beheer Groep [2008]
C-168/04 Commisison v. Austria, posted workers [2006]
C-168/91 Konstantinidis v. Stadt Altensteig - Standesamt and Landratsamt Calw [1992]
C-184/99 Grzelczyk v. Centre public d'aide sociale d'Ottignies-Louvain-la-Neuve [2001]
C-192/99 R. v. Secretary of State for the Home Department ex. parte Manjit Kaur [2001]
C-200/02 Zhu & Chen v. Secretary of State for the Home Department [2004]
C-209/03 The Queen (on the application of Danny Bidar) v. London Borough of Ealing, Secretary of State for Education and Skills [2005]
C-244/04 Commission v. Germany [2006]
C-247/20 VI v Commissioner's for Her Majesty's Revenue & Customs [2022]
C-256/11 Dereci v. Bundesministerium für Inneres [2011]
C-26/62 Van Gend en Loos v. Nederlandse Administratie der Belastingen [1963]
C-299/14 Vestische Arbeit Jobcenter Kreis Recklinghausen v. Johanna García-Nieto and Others [2016]
C-308/14 Commission v. United Kingdom [2016]
C-310/08 Harrow LBC v. Nicole Hassan Ibrahim, Secretary of State for the Home Department [2010]
C-319/06 Commission v. Luxembourg, posted workers II [2008]

C-333/12 Elisabeta Dano, Florin Dano v. Jobcenter Leipzig [2014]
C-34/09 Geraldo Ruiz Zambrano v. Office National de l'emploi [2011]
C-369/90 Micheletti and others v. Delegación del Gobierno en Cantabria [1992]
C-40/11 Iida v. Stadt Ulm [2012]
C-413/99 Baumbast and R v. Secretary of State for the Home Department [2002]
C-424/98 Commission v. Italian Republic [2000]
C-445/03 Commission v. Luxembourg, posted workers [2004]
C-451/19 and C-532/19 Subdelegación del Gobierno en Toledo v. Xu (C-451/19) and QP (C-532/19) [2022]
C-456/12 O v. Minister voor Immigratie, Integratie en Asiel and Minister voor Immigratie, Integratie en Asiel [2014]
C-459/99 Movement Contre le racisme. L'antisémitisme et la xénophobie ASBL (MRAX) v. État Belge [2002]
C-480/08 Maria Teixeira v. Lambeth LBC [2010]
C-67/14 Jobcenter Berlin Neukölin v. Nazifa Alimanovic and Others [2015]
C-673/16 Coman and Others v. Inspectoratul General pentru Imigrari [2018]
C-673/20 EP v Préfet du Gers & INSEE [2022]
C-86/12 Adzo Domenyo Alokpa and Others v. Minister du Travail, de l'Emploi et de l'Immigration [2013]
C-87-12 Ymeraga and Others [2013]
CIG Nottebohm (April 6, 1955)
Independent Monitoring Authority v. Secretary of State for the Home Department [2022] EWHC 3274

Trade in Goods Between the UK and the EU Post-Brexit

Pavel Repyeuski

1 Introduction

After 47 years of being part of the European common market, the United Kingdom has left the European Union on 31 January 2020.

When the UK first joined the European Communities in 1973, the soon-to-be European Union was still at a relatively early stage of European integration.[1] However, by the time of Brexit the EU has grown into a full scale political and economic union, comprising of the world's largest single (internal) market[2] guaranteeing free movement of goods, people, services, establishment, and capital between its Member States.[3] For trade in goods this means that goods can move freely inside the EU with no tariff or non-tariff barriers and with minimum (and mostly harmonised) regulatory requirements.[4]

Leaving the EU has brought the UK out of the EU's single market. Even though as of the national GDP, the UK's economy is heavily dominated by services,[5] for international trade, the value of goods and services annually exported from the

[1] See Pinder (1998).

[2] https://european-union.europa.eu/priorities-and-actions/actions-topic/trade_en#:~:text=The%20European%20Union%20is%20one,up%20world%20trade%20as%20well. Accessed 12 October 2023.

[3] Art 3 TFEU.

[4] For a detailed overview of the legal aspects of Free Movement of Goods and the workings of the Customs Union within the EU see Gormley (2009).

[5] Latest UK national accounts can be found in ONS., UK National Accounts: the Blue Book 2022 https://www.ons.gov.uk/economy/grossdomesticproductgdp/compendium/unitedkingdomnationalaccountsthebluebook/2022 Accessed 12 October 2023.

P. Repyeuski (✉)
Leeds Law School, Leeds Beckett University, Leeds, UK
e-mail: P.Repyeuski@leedsbeckett.ac.uk

E. Guinchard, C. Panara (eds.), *The New Relationship between the United Kingdom and the European Union*, https://doi.org/10.1007/978-3-031-70652-3_6

United Kingdom is nearly equal.[6] And with the EU being the UK's main trading partner,[7] to avoid the Brexit cliff edge,[8] as a 'no deal Brexit' was commonly referred to, it was important to agree on the post-Brexit trade regime between the two trading partners.

The Trade and Cooperation Agreement (TCA)[9] between the EU and UK, signed on 30 December 2020, has set out the terms of such a trade regime. Notwithstanding some transitional arrangements and temporary easements, the EU has introduced a full customs control with the UK from 1 January 2021. The UK Government, however, has been phasing out and putting off the full introduction of the control measures ever since, with the latest target date for the full-scale import control in the UK (at the time of this publication) have been moved to the end of 2024.[10]

This chapter focuses on the dynamics of the UK-EU relationship in trade in goods following the UK's departure from the European Union. We will start by briefly summarising the pre-Brexit rules on trade in goods, which were in operation whilst the UK was still part of the EU's common market. The chapter will then examine how the trade in goods regime has changed following the UK's departure from the EU by considering the new rules put in place by the UK-EU Trade and Cooperation Agreement (TCA)[11] and outlining existing issues and difficulties.

It is no surprise that the post-Brexit trade relationship between the UK and the EU remains challenging.[12] Brexit has caused a 'major shock to the UK-EU trade,'[13] as even though, thanks to the TCA, the trade in goods between the two parties, technically, remains tariff and quota free under the agreed 'zero-tariff, zero-quota' rules, the UK is no longer part of the European common market, which means more read tape, non-tariff barriers, customs controls and enhanced paperwork for the

[6] https://www.gov.uk/government/statistics/uk-trade-in-numbers/uk-trade-in-numbers-web-version#uk-trade-summary-statistics Accessed 12 October 2023.

[7] See Office for National Statistics Pink Book Data for 2017, where UK's trade with EU totalled more than non-EU https://www.ons.gov.uk/economy/nationalaccounts/balanceofpayments/datasets/9geographicalbreakdownofthecurrentaccountthepinkbook2016 Accessed 12 October 2023.

[8] Clement-Davies (2019), pp. 125–127.

[9] Trade and Cooperation Agreement between the European Union and the European Atomic Energy Community, of the one part, and the United Kingdom of Great Britain and Northern Ireland, of the other part *OJ L 149, 30.4.2021, p. 10–2539.*

[10] New Customs Rules for trade with the EU, UK House of Commons Library, 12.05.23 https://commonslibrary.parliament.uk/new-customs-rules-for-trade-with-the-eu/ Accessed 12 October 2023.

[11] Trade and Cooperation Agreement between the European Union and the European Atomic Energy Community, of the one part, and the United Kingdom of Great Britain and Northern Ireland, of the other part *OJ L 149, 30.4.2021, p. 10–2539.*

[12] Foster (2022).

[13] BBC, New Brexit Rules caused major shock to UK-EU Trade-report, https://www.bbc.co.uk/news/business-61237225 Accessed 12 October 2023.

traders. The Northern Ireland (NI) Protocol[14] (which was part of the UK Withdrawal Agreement[15]) aimed to facilitate for there being no hard border or checks on goods between the Northern Ireland and the Republic of Ireland, has further complicated the trade relationship. Whilst Northern Ireland, technically, remains outside the EU single market, the Protocol has created a *de facto* sea border between the NI and rest of the UK, which some feared may have become an irresolvable Brexit trilemma,[16] making it impossible for the UK to achieve its goal of leaving the EU single market and customs union, avoiding dividing the Island of Ireland with a hard border, and not having border checks between the NI and rest of the UK, thus maintaining UK's unity. This trilemma has now been addressed by the Windsor Framework,[17] which replaced the Protocol in February 2023 and opened opportunities for further negotiations in this area.

Whilst the *status quo* of the UK-EU post-Brexit trade relationship has been described by some as 'a gun on the table,'[18] this chapter concludes by analysing the ongoing trends and considering the possible developments and needs of further cooperation in the post-Brexit trade in goods between the UK and the EU.

2 Trade in Goods Between UK and EU Pre-Brexit

Notwithstanding of Brexit, the European Union has been and remains today the UK's biggest trade partner, accounting for approximately 50% of the UK's export of goods.[19] In fact, before the UK has left the EU, the Union was a net importer, having been supplying around £220 billion worth of goods annually to the UK, whilst the UK been exporting around £150 billion into the EU (the data here is from 2014, by means of an example).[20] Even though the actual degree of Brexit's impact on the UK's trade remains contested,[21] there is no doubt that leaving the EU has resulted in

---

[14] https://www.gov.uk/government/publications/the-northern-ireland-protocol Accessed 12 October 2023.

[15] Agreement on the withdrawal of the United Kingdom of Great Britain and Northern Ireland from the European Union and the European Atomic Energy Community, OJ C 384I, 12.11.2019, pp. 1–177.

[16] See Barnard and Leinarte (2021).

[17] Northern Ireland Protocol: The Windsor Framework, House of Commons Library, 23.03.2023 https://commonslibrary.parliament.uk/research-briefings/cbp-9736/ Accessed 12 October 2023.

[18] BBC, UK Brexit legislation is a gun on the table, says EU negotiator Maros Šefčovič, https://www.bbc.co.uk/news/uk-politics-61984708 Accessed 12 October 2023.

[19] https://policy.trade.ec.europa.eu/eu-trade-relationships-country-and-region/countries-and-regions/united-kingdom_en#:~:text=The%20EU%20is%20the%20UK's,the%20United%20States%20and%20China Accessed 12 October 2023.

[20] HM Revenue and Customs, UK Overseas Trade statistics with the EU January 2015, https://www.uktradeinfo.com/media/pwjloupi/release_ots_eu_jan15.pdf Accessed 12 October 2023.

[21] https://ukandeu.ac.uk/uk-trade-in-the-wake-of-brexit/ Accessed 12 October 2023.

a considerable disruption and decline of the UK-EU trade.[22] To evaluate the post-Brexit changes for the rules on trade in goods between the UK and the EU and the ongoing issues with trade, this section starts by first summarising the key EU rules, which the UK was subject to before leaving the European Union. These are the EU's mandatory trade rules, which the UK had to follow before Brexit.

The EU is based on the idea of a single (also, common or internal) market,[23] which is its principal economic rationale.[24] Established by article 3 of the Treaty on the European Union (TEU)[25] and defined in article 26 of the Treaty of the Functioning of the European Union (TFEU),[26] the internal market comprises '*an area without internal frontiers in which the free movement of goods, persons, services and capital is ensured.*'[27] For trade in goods between the EU Member States (including, previously, the UK) that, essentially, means removing physical, technical and fiscal barriers in trade between the Member States,[28] as well as facilitating varied harmonized measures enacted by the Union[29] aiming to smoothen the cross-border trade.

The core rules on the free movement of goods, established by the TFEU[30] and supplemented by various Court of Justice of the European Union (CJEU) cases,[31] cover duties and charges[32] (tariff barriers external to the Member States), discriminatory tax provisions[33] (internal tariff barriers), as well as quantitative restrictions and similar measures[34] (non-tariff barriers).

Customs union is the founding element of the EU and is essential for the proper functioning of the single market.[35] Provided for in Articles 28 and 30 TFEU, there is a *'prohibition between Member States of customs duties on imports and exports and of all charges having equivalent effect.'*'[36] Article 30 TFEU's prohibition is strict—any tax, duty or charge caught under the article is unlawful regardless of its

[22] Freeman (2022).

[23] For an overview of various stages of European economic integration see Swann (1992).

[24] For a good selection of publications on EU single market see Barnard and Scoot (2002).

[25] Art 3 TEU.

[26] Art 28 TFEU.

[27] Art 26 TFEU.

[28] On harmonization and removing barriers to trade see Egan (2001).

[29] As per art 114 TFEU.

[30] Treaty on the Functioning of the European Union [2012].

[31] Such as C-8/74 *Procureur du Roi v Dassonville* [1974] ECR837; C-120/78 *Rewe-Zentrale AG v Bundesmonopolverwaltung fur Branntwein* (Cassis de Dijon) [1979] ECR 649; C-267 & 268/91 *Keck and Mithouard* [1993] ECR I-6097.

[32] Articles 28-30 TFEU.

[33] Article 110 TFEU.

[34] Articles 34-36 TFEU.

[35] https://taxation-customs.ec.europa.eu/customs-4/eu-customs-union-facts-and-figures/eu-customs-union-unique-world_en Accessed 12 October 2023.

[36] Art 28 TFEU.

purpose.[37] However, even though it is not possible to justify custom duties or border taxes imposed between the Member States, the CJEU does permit imposition of limited charges for mandatory inspection fees or services offered to traders. This derogation is extremely strict—for the services, the charge in question should not exceed the cost of the provided service and the service should be of individual and tangible benefit to a trader.[38] And for an inspection fee, this should be mandated by the EU and should not exceed the cost of the inspection.[39] In addition to the limited capacity of the Member States to impose duties and charges when goods cross the internal frontiers, the customs union rules also oblige the EU Members to maintain a common customs tariff on goods imported from outside of the EU,[40] facilitated by the Union's Customs Code,[41] aiming to create a paperless and fully automated customs system.

Whilst articles 28–30 TFEU regulate external tariff barriers between the EU Member States, article 110 TFEU covers internal taxes. The restriction here is far less strict: only discriminatory (both, direct[42] and indirect[43] discrimination) internal tax on similar products is prohibited,[44] as well as taxes benefiting other goods.[45] Non-discriminatory internal taxation, varied taxation on non-similar products[46] or protective taxation justifiable by an imperative requirement in the public interest[47] are permitted.

It is worth noting that even though articles 28–30 and 110 TFEU rules appear to be mutually exclusive[48] (one catches external taxation when goods cross the border, the other internal fiscal policies), the CJEU has applied both sets of provisions systematically to ensure that there is no gap between them, as these rules are in

[37] See C-7/68 *Commission v Italy* [1968] ECR 423 in relation to tax on art items protecting artistic heritage.

[38] C-87/75 *Bresciani v Amministrazione Italiana delle Finanze* [1976] ECR 129.

[39] C-18/87 *Commission v Germany* [1988] ECR 5427—Germany was able to charge a veterinary inspection fee as prescribed by an EU Directive.

[40] Art 28 (2) TFEU.

[41] Regulation (EU) No 952/2013 of the European Parliament and of the Council of 9 October 2013 laying down the Union Customs Code (recast) (OJ L 269 10.10.2013, p. 1) http://data.europa.eu/eli/reg/2013/952/2020-01-01 Accessed 12 October 2023.

[42] In C-21/79 *Commission v Italy* [1980] ECR 1 Italy was unable to impose different tax on domestic and foreign regenerated oil.

[43] In C-112/84 *Humblot v Directeur des Services Fiscaux* [1985] ECR 1367 and C-433/85 *Feldain v Directeur des Services Fiscaux* [1987] ECR 3536 sharp increase of car tax rates by France was found indirectly benefiting French cars.

[44] Art 110(1) TFEU.

[45] Art 110(2) TFEU; in C-170-78 *Commission v United Kingdom* [1983] ECR 2265 the UK tried to tax wine 5 times more than beer, which was a violation.

[46] In C-243/84 *John Walker v Ministeriet for Skatter og Afgifter* [1986] ECR875 ECLI:EU:C:1986:100 whiskey was found not similar to liquor fruit wine, hence could be taxed differently.

[47] In C-196/85 *Commission v France* ECLI:EU:C:1987:182 France was allowed to tax natural sweet wines lower than liquor wines to encourage production on poor soils.

[48] Craig and De Burca (2020), p. 717.

place to prevent fiscal discrimination between goods when they enter and are sold in the Member States.

Articles 34-36 TFEU further cover non-tariff barriers in trading goods between the EU Member States. The rules prohibit quantitative restrictions (*'measures which amount to a total or partial restraint of…import, export or goods in transit'*)[49] on imports[50] and exports,[51] as well as measures having equivalent effect to quantitative restrictions (MEQRs). MEQRs are defined by the CJEU widely, to include *'all trading rules enacted by Member States which are capable of hindering, directly or indirectly, actually or potentially, intra-Community trade.'*[52] The Court did not stop there, having ruled that Article 34 TFEU's prohibition covers direct[53] and indirect[54] discrimination as well as non-discriminatory (indistinctly applicable)[55] restrictions.

Non-tariff barriers can be justified by article 36 TFEU's derogations,[56] which are interpreted and applied by the Court rather strictly.[57] The reason for the derogation must be warranted[58] and the restriction must be proportionate.[59] Additionally, non-discriminatory restrictions (i.e. indistinctly applicable rules) can be justified by the Member States using mandatory requirements,[60] an open-ended exception to the principle of mutual recognition,[61] which should be reasonable, objective and proportionate. And certain selling arrangements,[62] which apply indistinctly, do not hinder trade, impede market access, or impose an additional economic burden on

---

[49] As per C-2/73 *Geddo v Ente Nazionale Risi* [1973] ECR 865.

[50] Art 34 TFEU.

[51] Art 110(1) TFEU.

[52] C-8/74 *Procureur du Roi v Dassonville* [1974] ECR 837, para 5.

[53] In C-8/74 *Procureur du Roi v Dassonville* [1974] ECR 837 the requirement to provide certificate of origin applied only to non-Belgium products.

[54] In C-249/81 *Commission v Ireland* [1982] ECR 4005 the State sponsored 'Buy Irish' campaign indirectly benefited domestic products.

[55] C-120/78 *Rewe-Zentral AG v Bundesmonopolverwaltung für Branntwein* [1979] ECR 649 (Cassis de Dijon).

[56] Art 36 TFEU includes public morality, policy, security, protection of life and health, national treasures, etc.

[57] For the detailed overview of the application of article 36 TFEU restrictions see Barnard (2019) Chapter 5.

[58] In C-174/82 *Officier van Justitie v Sandoz BV* [1983] ECR 2445 muesli bars containing vitamins were not harmful for human consumption.

[59] In C-72/83 Campus Oil Ltd v Minister for Industry and Energy [1984] ECR 2727 the CJEU accepted the Irish law requiring importers to buy 35% of petrol from state-owned refineries as proportionate.

[60] As per C-120/78 *Rewe-Zentral AG v Bundesmonopolverwaltung für Branntwein* [1979] ECR 649 (Cassis de Dijon).

[61] for a good overview, see Pelkmans (2003).

[62] As per cases C-267 and 268/91 *Criminal Proceedings against Keck and Mithouard* [1993] ECR I-6097.

traders, do not require justification by the Member States and are mostly permitted.[63]

These core EU rules covering tariff and non-tariff barriers on movement of goods between the Member States play a key role in the realization of the single market. Despite some controversies[64] and its somewhat expanding nature,[65] the European single market is rightfully seen as one of the greatest EU's achievements, having fuelled economic growth and made the everyday life of European business and consumers easier.[66]

The *status quo* of the UK-EU trade relations was irrevocably changed by Brexit. 'Taking back control' of the UK's laws, borders, money, trade, and fisheries by leaving the EU single market has become one of the main Brexit's slogans. Yet, as the actual Brexit's date loomed, both parties became increasingly conscious of the potential consequences of the UK severing the ties with the European Union without having in place a trade deal. At the eleventh hour, after eight months of negotiations, the EU-UK Trade and Cooperation Agreement (TCA),[67] outlining the future trade relationship between the two parties, was finally signed. The following section considers the trade in goods rules between the UK and EU as provided for by the TCA, comparing these with the EU internal market rules.

3 Trade in Goods Between the UK and the EU Under the TCA

Having voted to leave the European Union in a referendum on 23 June 2016,[68] and following the Withdrawal Agreement having received the Royal Assent on 23 January 2020,[69] the UK has formally left the European Union on 31 January 2020.[70] To avoid a 'no-deal Brexit' (in which case all the EU law and existing EU-UK agreements would have ceased to apply) both sides were keen to reach an agreement to secure uninterrupted continuation of trade.[71] Finalised on Christmas Eve 2020, having entered into force after just one day of debate in the UK Parliament

[63] For some reflections on the Keck rule see Connor (2005).

[64] See Kingsont (2006–2007).

[65] Schutze (2017).

[66] https://single-market-economy.ec.europa.eu/single-market_en Accessed 12 October 2023.

[67] Trade and Cooperation Agreement between the European Union and the European Atomic Energy Community, of the one part, and the United Kingdom of Great Britain and Northern Ireland, of the other part *OJ L 149, 30.4.2021, p. 10–2539.*

[68] See the key Brexit dates here: https://commonslibrary.parliament.uk/research-briefings/cbp-7960/ Accessed 12 October 2023.

[69] Agreement on the withdrawal of the United Kingdom of Great Britain and Northern Ireland from the European Union and the European Atomic Energy Community OJ C 384I, 12.11.2019, pp. 1–177.

[70] For some detailed overview of the Brexit process see Craig (2020).

[71] Tauwhare (2017), pp. 89–96.

and 2 days before the end of the transition period provided for in the Withdrawal Agreement, the UK-EU Trade and Cooperation Agreement[72] have set hopes high for the future UK-EU trade relationship aiming to *'create a predictable commercial environment and prevent distortion of trade and unfair competitive advantages.'*[73]

Notably, whilst when it comes to international trade, having a regional free trade agreement is usually more economically beneficial to the trading parties than not,[74] as it was famously put by then the UK Prime Minister Theresa May, '*no deal is better than a bad deal*,'[75] thus the details and the effect of the of a trade agreement do matter. As of the TCA, however, there is a feeling amongst many that the Agreement may not be such a great deal: it appears to be much more about autonomy than economy, and the Agreement is seen as raising obstacles instead of enhancing co-operation.[76] It has been suggested that in the long run the TCA will significantly reduce the UK's trade.[77] This suggestion has, of course, some merit if comparing the post-Brexit trade rules with when the UK was part of the EU's common market. Fabrini et al,[78] for example, rightfully suggest that the mere reintroduction of customs formalities at the EU-UK borders following the Brexit alone may have caused an unprecedented fall in the UK exports to the EU (40.7%) and 28.8 fall in the UK imports from the EU in January 2021.[79] And the latest research highlights that at least 30% of the spiralling food price inflation which hit the UK post-Covid can actually be attributed to Brexit, whilst *'leaving the European Union has added an average of £210 to household food bills over the two years to the end of 2021, costing UK consumers a total of £5.8 billion.'*[80]

It is not, however, appropriate to expect the pre-Brexit *status quo* in trade between the UK and the EU to be maintained post-Brexit, as the TCA does not fully replicate the EU internal market rules. Acknowledging that the actual fall in trade between the UK and the EU after the UK has left the Union must have been caused by multiple reasons (including the COVID-19 pandemic), it is submitted that the most likely contributing factor here would be that the rules on the movement of goods under the

[72] Trade and Cooperation Agreement between the European Union and the European Atomic Energy Community, of the one part, and the United Kingdom of Great Britain and Northern Ireland, of the other part *OJ L 149, 30.4.2021, p. 10–2539.*

[73] Trade and Cooperation Agreement between the European Union and the European Atomic Energy Community, of the one part, and the United Kingdom of Great Britain and Northern Ireland, of the other part *OJ L 149, 30.4.2021, p. 10–2539.*

[74] Sager (1997), pp. 239–252.

[75] Brexit: 'No deal is better than a bad deal' says Theresa May, 21.09.2018 https://www.theguardian.com/politics/video/2018/sep/21/brexit-no-deal-is-better-than-a-bad-deal-says-theresa-may-video. Accessed 12 October 2023.

[76] Editorial (2021), pp. 1–2.

[77] Fussachia et al. (2022), pp. 27–49.

[78] Fabrini (2021), p. 22.

[79] See UK Office for National Statistics UK Trade: January 2021 https://www.ons.gov.uk/economy/nationalaccounts/balanceofpayments/bulletins/uktrade/january2021 Accessed 12 October 2023.

[80] Bakker et al. (2023).

Agreement do not come anywhere near the EU Single Market arrangements. In fact, many of the TCA provisions do not go far off the World Trade Organisation (WTO) Agreements (what would have been a 'no deal' scenario), which, as helpfully suggested by Barnard and Leinarte, represents a 'WTO plus' rather than 'free movement of goods minus' TCA approach.[81] So, the reduction of trade in goods between the parties, whilst not welcome, is to be expected. The big question is what can be done to minimize Brexit's negative effect on trade in goods between the UK and the EU and whether what has been achieved under the Trade and Cooperation Agreement thus far is enough.

This section briefly summarises the TCA rules on free movement of goods, comparing these with the EU Single Market and assessing some of the major drawbacks in the UK-EU trade in goods relationship post-Brexit.

Whilst the TCA is quite extensive in its scope and covers a wide range of issues (including institutional framework, services, capital, travel, fisheries, transport, law enforcement, cooperation in criminal matters, dispute settlement, etc), the rules on goods are located in Heading 1 titled 'Trade'—this contains 107 articles (out of the 783 articles of the main TCA body).

The TCA provisions on goods, aiming at liberalisation and facilitation of trade,[82] do cover most of the relevant trade policy issues, as one would expect of an international trade agreement, namely tariff reduction, elimination of quotas and other non-tariff barriers to trade (Technical Barriers to Trade (TBT) and Sanitary and Phytosanitary Measures (SPS)), as well as unfair subsidies and public procurement. There is some significant correlation with the EU rules here, as many key provisions of the EU's free movement of goods are retained by the TCA. However, overall the Agreement is very much modelled on the WTO framework, thus being quite distant from the EU law internal market regime.

In line with the EU Single Market, article 21 TCA prohibits custom duties on goods originating in the other Party (same as article 30 TFEU). Article 22 TCA outlaws other external and internal tariff barriers, including duties, taxes and charges in connection with export and internal taxes in excess of those imposed on like goods[83] (same as charges having equivalent effect (CEEs) under article 30 TFEU and internal taxes under article 110 TFEU). Article 23 TCA limits any fees and formalities in connection with import and export, which are to be approximate to the cost of the services rendered to the traders[84] (which is very much alike to the rules on the CEEs mandated by the CJEU case law). The "zero-tariff, zero-quotas' policy introduced by the TCA also extends to some non-tariff barriers, namely quotas on

---

[81] Barnard, Catherine and Leinarte, Emilija, Movement of Goods Under the TCA (November 1, 2021). University of Cambridge Faculty of Law Research Paper No. 31/2021, Due in 'Global Policy' eds. U. Staiger & R Schuetze (Forthcoming), Available at SRN: https://ssrn.com/abstract=3967061 Accessed 12 October 2023.

[82] Art 15 TCA.

[83] Art 22-23 TCA.

[84] Art 23 TCA.

import and export, which are prohibited by article 26 TCA (same to article 34 TFEU).

But this is where the similarity between the TCA and EU law ends. As even though article 19 TCA incorporates the national treatment principle in line with the WTO's Article III of GATT[85] (the UK and the EU should afford the same treatment to each other's domestically produced goods), the TCA does not prohibit regulatory restrictions and non-discriminatory measures (like measures having equivalent effect to quantitative restrictions (MEQRs) under article 34 TFEU), and there are no rules on mutual recognition or market access principle included into the Agreement.

When it comes to trade in goods, the rules on mutual recognition are an important part of the EU single market, as these guarantee market access to goods from all the Member States even in absence of the EU's harmonising measures. According to this principle, goods lawfully sold in one EU Member State could be lawfully sold in other Member States, subject to some limited, objective and reasonable exceptions.[86] Unfortunately, the UK and the EU were not able to agree on these, so no mutual recognition rules are included in the TCA. Instead, the WTO's Agreement on Technical Barriers to Trade (TBT) is directly incorporated into the TCA by article 90, meaning that the UK-EU trade in goods is subject to domestic product requirement of both Parties and that the UK traders must meet the regulatory requirements of all the 27 EU Member States (and same for the EU traders exporting to the UK).

Similar situation is with the Sanitary and Phytosanitary (SPS) measures: even though the WTO's SPS Agreement does allow the Member States to enter into bilateral agreements on recognition of the equivalence of specified SPS measures—in relation to the TCA this was rejected by the EU. This has put the burden on the UK agricultural exporters to meet all the EU's SPS import requirements (and *vice versa*), and the need for traders to obtain various documentation (such as Export Health Certificates), creating extensive border checks, customs formalities and further obstructing the trade. Even though the levels of the actual physical products border checks do vary (these range between 1% and 30% depending on a product),[87] and some low and medium risk products benefit from a simplified border and customs regime between the UK and the EU, the TCA rules on TBT and SPS represent a '*a far cry from enhanced mutual recognition,* '[88] as in this respect the TCA here offers little more than the WTO membership, i.e. 'a no deal' scenario.

---

[85] Article III GATT.

[86] C-120/78 *Rewe-Zentral AG v Bundesmonopolverwaltung für Branntwein* [1979] ECR 649 (Cassis de Dijon).

[87] See Press Release https://www.gov.uk/government/news/uk-secures-listed-status-to-protect-5-billion-animal-export-market#:~:text=The%20Department%20for%20Environment%2C%20Food,than%20%C2%A35%20billion%20a. Accessed 12 October 2023.

[88] Barnard, Catherine and Leinarte, Emilija, Movement of Goods Under the TCA (November 1, 2021). University of Cambridge Faculty of Law Research Paper No. 31/2021, Due in 'Global Policy' eds. U. Staiger & R Schuetze (Forthcoming), Available at SRN: https://ssrn.com/abstract=3967061 Accessed 12 October 2023.

Having to comply with the mutual safety standards of the EU and the UK is itself a barrier to trade. Many goods exported to the EU have to bear the CE (*Conformite Europeenne*) mark, certifying that the product is compliant with the EU safety standards for it to be sold in the European Single Market. And even though one would have hoped that after Brexit the divergence of safety standards between the UK and the EU would not suddenly spiral, there had been a change in the rules on product marking: from the 1st January 2021 for the products to be imported into the UK from the EU the CE marking should have started to be replaced with the UKCA (UK Conformity Assessed) marking to show compliance with the UK safety standards.[89] However, due to complexity and various technical issues, the compliance deadline for goods accessing the UK market has been moved by the UK government many times, with the latest extension up until 31 December 2024, four years from the originally set deadline. At the end of the day, to further ease the cross-border trade, the UK Government has now confirmed that they intend to introduce legislation to extend recognition of goods which meets the EU requirements, including CE marking, for many products indefinitely.[90]

Another area creating trade complications are the rules on origin of goods. These rules are covered in detail by Chapter 2 of the TCA. As the preferential trade regime under the Agreement only applies to goods originating in the UK and the EU, the need for traders to certify the goods' origin resulted in additional paperwork and border control measures. This had also significantly disrupted the existing supply and manufacturing chains, as during the EU membership many companies based in the UK operated as a supply hub, where goods (as intermediate products)[91] were entering from the third counties for further transformation in the UK to then be being sold in the European Single Market. Once the UK, having left the EU, had become a third country itself, for the goods to originate here (and thus benefit from the zero-tariff treatment when sold to the EU) the manufacturers now need to demonstrate a substantial degree of transformation.[92] This prompted changes in imports and re-organisation of supply chains,[93] where some third country manufacturers (in particular, consumer-goods-manufacturing, medical-technology, and pharmaceutical companies)[94] are choosing to sell directly to the EU, thus omitting the UK.

---

[89] See Newson, C., CE Marking vs UKCA Marking, https://www.makeuk.org/insights/blogs/ce-marking-vs-ukca-marking Accessed 12 October 2023.

[90] https://www.gov.uk/guidance/using-the-ukca-marking Accessed 12 October 2023.

[91] See Johnson and Noguera (2012), pp. 224–236.

[92] See article 40 TCA on Cumulation of origin rules.

[93] See part 2 of Bakker, J, et al, Post-Brexit imports, supply chains and the effect on consumer prices, UK in Changing Europe, 25 April 2022, https://ukandeu.ac.uk/wp-content/uploads/2022/04/UKICE-Supply-Chains-Report_Final.pdf Accessed 12 October 2023.

[94] McKinsey & Company interviewed executives at about 50 UK firms, see Gusegom, W., Brexit: The bigger picture—Rethinking supply chains in a time of uncertainty, https://www.mckinsey.com/featured-insights/europe/brexit-the-bigger-picture-rethinking-supply-chains-in-a-time-of-uncertainty Accessed 12 October 2023.

Adding to the onerous and time-consuming issues of the certificates of origin and the extra border controls is the disruption of the transportation logistics and the problems with the groupage of goods. Pre-Brexit logistics companies would consolidate multiple small loads of goods into a single lorry exporting to the EU—a service which was used by many small and medium-sized exporters, who would otherwise not be able to send their goods individually. Now, inadequate paperwork on one product in the consignment can end up delaying the entire lorry, so most transportation companies in the UK have halted this service.[95]

The above are just some of the main problematic areas of the UK-EU trade in goods. One of the key, and, probably, the most complicated issues which had been adversely affecting the post-Brexit trade relations is the Northern Ireland (NI) Protocol.[96] As the NI Protocol is discussed elsewhere in this book, there will be just a brief summary here.

Part of the UK Withdrawal Agreement,[97] the NI Protocol immediately proved to be contentious, as it threated the Belfast Agreement (also known as the Good Friday Agreement, a peace deal between the British and Irish Governments as well as Northern Ireland's political parties, securing the NI peace process). Many commentators feared that Brexit could affect many rights under the Belfast Agreement[98] and these fears prove to be true. Even though introducing border measures between Northern Ireland and Republic of Ireland is not directly prohibited by the Belfast Agreement, Brexit has ended the operation of the EU single market rules in the UK and re-introduced border control on the movement of goods between the UK and the EU, thus affecting the situation and position of Northern Ireland.[99] Due to the high sensitivity of the issue, both the UK and the EU committed to maintain the 'soft' border arrangement between Northern Ireland and the Republic of Ireland. To avoid the hard border, the NI Protocol has kept Northern Ireland in the EU's single market for goods, which resulted in border checks being performed on goods when they enter Northern Ireland from the UK, thus creating a *de facto* border in the Irish sea, which is seen by some as separating Northern Ireland from the UK. This had further complicated the trade in goods as the EU and the UK were having difficulties agreeing which goods crossing the border are at risk and should be subject to checks

---

[95] Holmes (2021).

[96] https://assets.publishing.service.gov.uk/government/uploads/system/uploads/attachment_data/file/840230/Revised_Protocol_to_the_Withdrawal_Agreement.pdf Accessed 12 October 2023.

[97] Agreement on the withdrawal of the United Kingdom of Great Britain and Northern Ireland from the European Union and the European Atomic Energy Community, OJ C 384I, 12.11.2019, p. 1–177.

[98] See Prof McCrudden, The Good Friday Agreement, Brexit and the Rights, A Royal Irish Academy-British Academy Brexit Policy Discussion Paper, 2017, https://www.thebritishacademy.ac.uk/publications/europe-good-friday-agreement-brexit-and-rights/ Accessed 12 October 2023.

[99] For comprehensive discussion of the issues see the study by Phinnemore and Hayward (2017).

and how the checks to be carried out, as well as the required infrastructure/institutions to be put in place for the 'invisible border.'[100]

The continuous negotiations by both Parties trying to resolve the issues had not been easy or straightforward. On 3 March 2021 the UK has decided to unilaterally suspend some checks on trade in goods from Great Britain to Northern Ireland—a move, which the EU Commission has called to be a violation of both, the Protocol and the Withdrawal Agreement. Compromising, the EU suggested the October 2021 package[101] offering some flexibility in terms of border checks and documentation for certain types of goods. This was not seen as a sufficient measure by the UK.[102] Further on, the UK Government has proposed a Northern Ireland Protocol Bill containing a provision suggesting that the UK should be able to unilaterally change the Trade and Cooperation agreement—this provision (albeit later having been dropped from the bill)[103] was, understandably, not received well by the EU.[104]

The above highlights the degree of complexity of the relationship and the need for further negotiation and agreement. There were some EU-UK 'technical level' talks over the NI protocol restarting in October 2022.[105]

A significant break-through in attempts to resolve the issues was made by the Parties having agreed the Windsor Framework[106] on 27 February 2023. The Framework created a new system of checks on goods moving from Great Britain to Northern Ireland where goods designed to stay in NI will go through a 'green' lane (thus having fewer checks and controls) and goods moving on to Ireland and/or the rest of the EU will go through a 'red' lane, being subject to full control and checks. This should significantly facilitate the trade in goods and address some of the 'Irish sea border' arguments. The green/red lane system became operational on 30th September 2023 and has been reported so far to be operating smoothly.[107]

The Windsor Framework, even though a significant achieving, had, however, stopped shy from allowing the NI to fully benefit from the same tax rules as elsewhere in the UK, as currently the NI businesses must follow the EU rules on

[100] See Gasiorek and Jerzewska (2020).

[101] See https://ec.europa.eu/info/strategy/relations-non-eu-countries/relations-united-kingdom/eu-uk-withdrawal-agreement/protocol-ireland-and-northern-ireland_en#october-2021-package Accessed 12 October 2023.

[102] Curtis, J., Northern Ireland Protocol: Implementation, grace periods and EU-UK discussions (2021-2022), House of Commons Library, number 9333, https://researchbriefings.files.parliament.uk/documents/CBP-9333/CBP-9333.pdf Accessed 12 October 2023.

[103] See https://www.bbc.co.uk/news/uk-politics-61790248 Accessed 12 October 2023.

[104] Questions and answers on the Commission's reaction to the United Kingdom's bill overriding core parts of the Protocol on Ireland/Northern Ireland, 15 June 2022, https://ec.europa.eu/commission/presscorner/detail/en/qanda_22_3679 Accessed 12 October 2023.

[105] See https://www.bbc.co.uk/news/uk-northern-ireland-63081585 Accessed 12 October 2023.

[106] Northern Ireland Protocol: The Windsor Framework, House of Commons Library, 23.03.2023 https://commonslibrary.parliament.uk/research-briefings/cbp-9736/ Accessed 12 October 2023.

[107] https://www.drapersonline.com/news/windsor-framework-so-far-so-good-for-northern-irish-indies Accessed 20 October 2023.

state aid and VAT, meaning that any UK government payments to help firms in the Northern Ireland and any tax breaks must be within the limits set by the EU). The Framework, notably, did provide for some zero VAT rates, mostly for energy-saving products, and tightened up the circumstances under which the EU can bring action against the UK for subsidies in NI under the EU's State aid rules.[108]

As the Northern Ireland situation remains important and ever fragile, many believe that the fate of the TCA may have became inevitably entangled with the challenges connected to the faithful implementation of the Withdrawal Agreement.[109]

Summarising, as the analysis here shows, by having eliminated tariffs and quotas on goods in the UK-EU trade, the TCA does reduce the uncertainty over the future trading relations following the UK's departure from the EU. However, not aligning non-tariff barriers and other measures equivalent to quantitative restrictions and the restrictive approach to the origin of goods means that there being *de facto* no free movement of goods between the UK and the EU, as most goods now need to go through the complex border and compliance checks.

Despite the drop in trade, fears of some that the new trade regime might significantly curtail the trade activities, as these may no longer be profitable in their current format,[110] did not materialise, even though it is hard to disagree with the view that, unfortunately, the TCA has created only a shallow trade relationship between the UK and the EU.[111] The need for further compromise is evident, but the problem is that many of the objectives of the UK and the EU are, seemingly, in conflict and there remains a significant amount of red tape for the both Parties.

The next, concluding section, will consider the future of the UK-EU trade in goods with the view of how this can be improved.

4 Post-Brexit Trade in Goods Between UK and EU: The Future

It has been submitted that so far Brexit has had a modest, yet considerable,[112] impact on trade between the UK and the EU, with the adaption process still ongoing on both sides of the Channel.[113] It remains, however, the point of acute debate whether the Trade and Cooperation Agreement is a good deal, at least for the United

[108] Northern Ireland Protocol: The Windsor Framework, House of Commons Library, 23.03.2023 https://commonslibrary.parliament.uk/research-briefings/cbp-9736/ Accessed 12 October 2023.

[109] Fabrini (2021), p. 21.

[110] Buesa et al. (2021).

[111] Fussachia et al. (2022), pp. 27–49.

[112] Fussachia et al. (2022), pp. 27–49.

[113] Minenna (2021).

Kingdom[114]—on one hand, it retained the core rules of the EU internal market (namely, the zero-tariff zero-quota provisions), on the other hand the traders now must undergo customs border checks and comply with the product-specific rules of origin, which is costly and onerous. One must agree with the view that the overall picture looks somewhat more favourable to the EU than the UK,[115] and the recent UK Parliament's report has concluded that '*while most trade is tariff-free, it is not simple.*'[116] It would, however, undermine the certainty of the Agreement if the TCA was viewed as a 'living' instrument, open to further re-negotiations and amendments. As the Agreement is, in essence, an international treaty, any modification would require good will and acceptance by both Parties.

Fairness is key in trade relations, as trading partners are to act in good faith and not to be seen taking unfair advantage of each other. It is, however, inevitable that governments provide support to many sectors of national economy. One of the key TCA provisions is the commitments to a Level Playing Field,[117] which are said to be the most extensive seen in any free trade agreement to date.[118] These cover areas like state aid, environmental law, labour rights, and are there to ensure that businesses located in one trading partner do not gain unfair competitive advantages and undercut rivals from another. The TCA requires both the UK and the EU to have an effective system of subsidy control, as the rebalancing mechanism under the Level Playing Field could allow either Parties to impose tariffs and other countervailing measures in cases where there is unfair competition.

The fact that the UK and the EU do not have to comply with each other's rules, just to follow the common 'broad principles,' can be viewed as a positive aspect of the Agreement, giving some reassurance to the Parties. To foster frictionless trade, the Parties should, however, try to avoid having to trigger the Level Playing Field mechanism unless absolutely necessary, as this can result in the imposition of further tariff and non-tariff barriers in trade in goods (subject to arbitration), as well as it is liable to dampen the spirit and good-will of the trading Parties. Thus, it is crucial to have a transparent subsidy control regime, as both Parties will be keen to support the domestic businesses in the early years of Brexit and beyond.[119] When it comes to the dispute settlement, the TCA has created a bespoke mechanism, involving consultations, recourse to an independent arbitration tribunal, and temporary cross-retaliation, with no CJEU involvement except the NI Protocol disputes.

---

[114] UK Parliament, Trade in goods significantly harder under Brexit deal, 25 March 2021 https://committees.parliament.uk/committee/445/eu-goods-subcommittee/news/153116/trade-in-goods-significantly-harder-under-brexit-deal/ Accessed 12 October 2023.

[115] Minenna (2021).

[116] House of Lords, Paper 249, Beyond Brexit: trade in goods, 25 March 2021 https://publications.parliament.uk/pa/ld5801/ldselect/ldeucom/249/249.pdf Accessed 12 October 2023.

[117] Title IX TCA.

[118] Ares et al. (2021).

[119] The UK, for example, in 2021 offered grants for small and medium size businesses new to import/export https://www.gov.uk/guidance/grants-to-help-small-and-medium-sized-businesses-new-to-importing-or-exporting Accessed 12 October 2023.

The rules of origin under the Agreement continue presenting a challenge for the free flow of goods, as only products originating or mostly originating in either the EU or the UK now qualify for the zero tariff. The rules of origin under the TCA provide for the 'bilateral cumulation' only, which means whilst one Party is allowed to use products originating in another Party without the final goods losing its originating status (i.e. goods manufactured/assembled in the UK using the EU components and materials will be treated as UK-made), the 'diagonal cumulation' is not allowed (i.e. goods manufactured/assembled in the UK using third country (non-EU) components and materials are not treated as UK-made, thus are not eligible for the zero tariff when being exported into the EU). To ease the trade, the TCA does allow self-certification of origin,[120] however there is a concern that in absence of the 'diagonal cumulation' some of the third country suppliers (which previously used the UK as an assembly hub) would now supply directly to the EU, thus cutting the UK out of the supply chains.

The reason for this restriction is clear: it prevents trade deflection, unfair competition, loss of customs revenues and stops one Party collecting duties on imported goods from a third country and then exporting the same goods duty free to the other Party.[121] Agreeing on the 'diagonal cumulation' or even 'full cumulation' (where the rules of origin would be satisfied when the goods are 'sufficiently processed' in either the UK or the EU), however, would have helped to further facilitate trade, yet the EU was not willing to go this far. On a fair point, some commentators point that the TCA does provide for much more favourable origin rules compared to the WTO (no-deal) agreements, and these rules are way ahead of the most other trade agreements the EU has made so far.[122] Yet, there are precedents when some 'diagonal' and/or 'full cumulation' rules of origin were agreed by the EU with a number of other trading partners, including EFTA, some Balkan and Mediterranean countries and Turkey–so, there is scope for further negotiation here.

It is also unfortunate that the Parties could not agree on the mutual recognition rules when it comes to technical barriers to trade, measures having equivalent effect to quantitative restrictions (including sanitary and phytosanitary measures) and other relevant standards. Multiple testing requirements, double certification, having to comply with the regulatory requirements of all the 27 EU Member States, as well as the UK, is placing a significant administrative and financial burden on the traders and in many cases (for example, trade in animal and plant products) risk becoming permanent barriers to trade.

Acknowledging that the full-scale re-negotiation of these provisions is highly unlikely, the Parties should at least try to refrain, where possible, from introducing significant regulatory divergence, so that the goods from the UK remain as conformant to the EU standards as possible, and *vice versa*. The regulatory divergence does not only create red tape, but it is harmful to the Level Playing Field and

[120] Art 18-19 TCA.

[121] Tauwhare (2017), pp. 89–96.

[122] Tauwhare (2017), p. 95.

competition. This suggestion may be easier to implement for the UK (if there is a good will and considering that the net balance of trade is in favour of the EU),[123] as it may be hard to expect every one of the 27 EU Member States to be particularly mindful of the UK's regulatory standards.

Divergence in standards between the Parties also carries another threat: in case of significant impact on trade, both Parties have the right to take countermeasures under the rebalancing mechanism for the Level Playing Field, which are subject to arbitration. That means that if one Party raises its standards and the other does not, the former can take reciprocal actions. These rebalancing measures could include temporary suspension of parts of the Agreement, imposition of tariffs or even the possibility of the entire trade part of the Agreement being suspended[124]—something both Parties should be keen to avoid.

Related to the lack mutual recognition, the UK government has pointed out[125] that overly complicated and varied VAT rules in different EU Member States have been, so far, amongst the most problematic non-tariff barriers to trade in goods between the UK and the EU, which has prompted the United Kingdom to unilaterally postpone the accounting scheme. This measure, which does help the VAT-registered traders (but the small-sized exporters may still be affected) is only temporary and, moving forward, it is pivotal to enhance the understanding of the VAT system for traders across both borders. Other measures (such as a trusted trader scheme, green/red corridors, UK's Authorised Economic Operator, Groupage Export Facilitation schemes) could further facilitate the cross-border trade.

Another key issue needing addressing is the UK-EU border infrastructure, which, despite there had now been over 7 years following the Brexit vote, remains underprepared and under-invested. Brexit-related UK border crossing issues have made many news headlines,[126] when lorries have had to wait days to cross the Channel, traders losing money and fresh foodstuff deteriorating.[127] Both sides acknowledge and try to tackle the issues, yet the progress on this is way too slow.

On one hand, the UK acknowledges that increased investment in the physical border infrastructures as well as the customs intermediary sector is needed, as the staff numbers dealing with the increased border checks are too low,[128] yet the government had previously opposed the Port of Dover inland border facility

[123] Minenna (2021), p. 3.

[124] Buesa et al. (2021).

[125] https://committees.parliament.uk/committee/445/eu-goods-subcommittee/news/153116/trade-in-goods-significantly-harder-under-brexit-deal/ Accessed 12 October 2023.

[126] See https://www.independent.co.uk/news/uk/politics/brexit-dover-lorry-drivers-queues-b2016650.html from 17.02.2022 Accessed 12 October 2023.

[127] See https://www.reuters.com/world/uk/britains-dover-delays-damaging-fresh-produce-exports-producers-warn-2022-04-11/ Accessed 12 October 2023.

[128] https://committees.parliament.uk/committee/445/eu-goods-subcommittee/news/153116/trade-in-goods-significantly-harder-under-brexit-deal/ Accessed 12 October 2023.

expansion having deemed it to be adequate.[129] The blame for the border delays is being passed on back and forth between the UK and the EU counterparts (France),[130] which is not helping with further cooperation.

Enhancing use of IT and innovative digital technologies may be the way forward here—there are some successful examples of the EU initiatives leaded by France, including the 'smart border' project (where the system anticipates the customs formalities before loading the means of transport and provides for the largely automated processes and checks), 'logistic envelop' (a tool, that groups multiple customs declarations under a single barcode) and 'zero kilometer customs' (a streamlined administrative procedure, that allows the exporter to obtain the authorization of approved places other than the customs areas at which to carry out the formalities relating to export).[131] Further harmonisation of the customs procedures and appropriate investments into physical and digital borders, as well as increasing awareness of traders, would have smoothened the trade in goods between the Partners.

As one can see, there are multifarious factors affecting and shaping up the future of the EU-UK relation in the trade of goods and to maintain the free flow of trade, a great degree of good will, cooperation and compromise is needed on both sides of the English Channel.

5 Conclusion

Brexit was, no doubt, a major shock to the UK-EU trade in goods and it had significantly disrupted the trade. Both Parties are still adapting to the new trade regime whilst achieving and maintaining frictionless in trade remains important.

At the eleventh hour to avoid 'the cliff edge' of the no-deal Brexit, the Parties have signed the Trade and Cooperation Agreement, providing for a transition from the UK being part of the EU's internal market onto the 'zero tariff-zero quota' post-Brexit trade arrangement. The TCA is quite an atypical trade agreement due to the dis-integration nature of Brexit and, comparing to the EU single market, the Agreement is seen as raising the trade barriers rather than removing them.[132] Yet, having to resort to the basic WTO rules would have hit the UK-EU trade in goods much harder, thus, even though the TCA may not be perfect, it is important.

One of the main TCA's achievements are the rules on tariff-free and quota-free trade in goods, as well as other agreed areas of trade cooperation between the Parties.

---

[129] See https://www.export.org.uk/news/608834/Proposed-Port-of-Dover-inland-border-facility-axed-by-HMRC-with-current-capacity-deemed-enough.htm Accessed 12 October 2023.

[130] https://www.theguardian.com/politics/2022/jul/23/dover-travel-delays-who-is-to-blame Accessed 12 October 2023.

[131] Minenna (2021), p. 22.

[132] See Fabrini (2021).

The Agreement, however, contains some major omissions, namely the lack of mutual recognition on technical and other standards, rather inflexible rules on origin of goods and various complexities surrounding the Northern Ireland Protocol and the Windsor Framework. All these create controls, certifications, red tape, paperwork, and related border issues. Having extensive regulatory obstacles to trade is, indeed, more harmful than just imposing customs duties,[133] and the success of the Agreement is measured by its ability to facilitate trade and avoid disruptions.

Commenting on the latest UK Government Report on Trade in Goods Beyond Brexit[134] Baroness Verma has admitted that the TCA has left a lot of unfinished business between the two Parties. She suggested that *"the [UK] Government must take an ambitious approach to trade ties with the EU...Ongoing dialogue will be crucial to achieving smoother trade. The TCA should be treated as the start, not the end of the UK's new relationship with the EU."*[135]

The Agreement is, indeed, a work in progress as it has left many details of the new EU-UK trade relationship to be further determined by the TCA institutions (the Partnership Council and various joint committees and working groups). And even though the UK Government had ruled out another trade deal with the EU which would rely on EU law alignment,[136] further converging of cross-border trade in goods between the EU and the UK is not merely desirable, but is inevitable. Thus, one would hope that the two trading Partners will continue smoothing things over and removing the existing barriers to trade.

References

Ares E et al (2021) The UK-EU Trade and Cooperation Agreement: Level Playing Field, Briefing Paper number 9190, 20 May 2021, https://researchbriefings.files.parliament.uk/documents/CBP-9190/CBP-9190.pdf. Accessed 12 Oct 2023

Bakker J et al (2023) Brexit and consumer food prices: 2023 update. Centre for Economic Performance, 24 May 2023. https://cep.lse.ac.uk/textonly/_new2014/news/releases/2023_05_25_i508.pdf. Accessed 12 Oct 2023

Barnard C (2019) The substantive law of the EU: the four freedoms, 6th edn. OUP, Oxford. Chapter 5

Barnard C, Leinarte E (2021) Movement of goods under the TCA (November 1, 2021). University of Cambridge, Faculty of Law Research Paper No. 31/2021, https://doi.org/10.2139/ssrn.3967061. Accessed 12 Oct 2023

Barnard C, Scoot J (2002) The law of the single European market: unpacking the premises. Hart

[133] Mariani and Secerdoti (2021), p. 27.

[134] UK Parliament, European Union Committee, *Beyond Brexit: Trade in Goods, HL Paper 249, 25 March 2021* https://publications.parliament.uk/pa/ld5801/ldselect/ldeucom/249/249.pdf Accessed 12 October 2023.

[135] UK Parliament, Trade in goods significantly harder under Brexit deal, 25 March 2021 https://committees.parliament.uk/committee/445/eu-goods-subcommittee/news/153116/trade-in-goods-significantly-harder-under-brexit-deal/ Accessed 12 October 2023.

[136] See https://www.bbc.co.uk/news/uk-politics-63700905 Accessed 12 October 2023.

Buesa A, Kataryniuk I, ĹHotellerie-Fallois P, Moreno S (2021) The EU-UK Trade and Cooperation Agreement (TCA) (March 22, 2021). Banco de Espana Article 08/21, Available at SSRN: https://ssrn.com/abstract=3821574. Accessed 12 Oct 2023

Clement-Davies C (2019) BREXIT—plunging over the cliff-edge. IELR 5:125–127

Connor T (2005) Accentuating the positive: the "selling arrangement," the first decade, and beyond. ICLQ 54:127

Craig P, De Burca G (2020) EU law: text, cases and materials, 7th edn. OUP, Oxford

Craig PP (2020) Brexit, A Drama: the Endgame -- Part I (February 20, 2020). European Law Review. Oxford Legal Studies Research Paper No. 10/2020, Available at SSRN: https://ssrn.com/abstract=3541896. Accessed 12 Oct 2023

Editorial (2021) The UK-EU trade and cooperation agreement: Brexit is done, long live Brexit! Eur Law Rev 46(1):1–2

Egan M (2001) Constructing a European market. OUP, Oxford

Fabrini F (2021) The law and politics of Brexit: volume III: the framework of the new EU-UK relations. OUP, Oxford

Foster P (2022) UK-EU trade relationships tumble after Brexit, Financial Times, 26 April https://www.ft.com/content/b0860ee6-e06e-4fc4-bd87-d56dcc7ee946 Accessed 12 Oct 2023

Freeman R et al (2022) Unravelling Deep Integration: UK Trade in the Wake of Brexit, UK in a Changing Europe. Working Paper 26 April 2022. https://ukandeu.ac.uk/wp-content/uploads/2022/04/FPMS_March_2022_Final.pdf. Accessed 12 Oct 2023

Fussachia I et al (2022) The consequences of the trade and cooperation agreement for the UK's international trade. Oxford Rev Econ Policy 38(1):27–49. https://doi.org/10.1093/oxrep/grab052

Gasiorek M, Jerzewska A (2020) The Unresolved difficulties of the Northern Ireland Protocol. UK Trade Policy Observatory, briefing paper 41, June 2020 https://blogs.sussex.ac.uk/uktpo/files/2020/06/BP-41-final.pdf. Accessed 12 Oct 2023

Gormley L (2009) EU law of free movement of goods and customs union. OUP, Oxford

Holmes H (2021) Logistics companies Halt EU exports due to post-Brexit red tape. The Grocer, 13 January 2021. https://www.thegrocer.co.uk/brexit/logistics-companies-halt-eu-exports-due-to-post-brexit-red-tape/652022.article. Accessed 12 Oct 2023

Johnson RC, Noguera G (2012) Accounting for intermediaries: production sharing and trade in value added. J Int Econ 86(2):224–236. https://doi.org/10.1016/j.jinteco.2011.10.003

Kingsont S (2006-7) The boundaries of sovereignty: the ECJ's controversial role applying internal market law to direct tax measures. CYELS 9:287

Mariani P, Secerdoti G (2021) Trade in goods and level playing field. In: Fabrini F (ed) The law and politics of Brexit: volume III: the framework of the new EU-UK relations. OUP, Oxford

Minenna M (2021) A Look at EU-UK Trade Relations in Light of Brexit, Pandemic and the Trade and Cooperation Agreement (April 9, 2021) at p 3. Available at SSRN: https://ssrn.com/abstract=3823333. Accessed 12 Oct 2023

Pelkmans J (2003) Mutual recognition in goods and services: an economic perspective. ENEPRI, Working Paper No16, March 2003. http://aei.pitt.edu/1852/1/ENEPRI_WP16.pdf. Accessed 12 Oct 2023

Phinnemore D, Hayward K (2017) UK Withdrawal ('Brexit') and the Good Friday Agreement, AFCO, European Parliament, November 2017, https://www.europarl.europa.eu/RegData/etudes/STUD/2017/596826/IPOL_STU(2017)596826_EN.pdf. Accessed 12 Oct 2023

Pinder J (1998) The building of the European Union, 3rd edn. OUP, Oxford

Sager M (1997) Regional trade agreements: their role and the economic impact on trade flows. World Econ 20(2):239–252. https://doi.org/10.1111/1467-9701.00068

Schutze R (2017) From international to federal market: the changing structure of European law. OUP, Oxford

Swann D (1992) The economics of the common market, 7th edn. Penguin

Tauwhare R (2017) Brexit: achieving near-frictionless trade. Int Trade Law Regul 23(3):89–96

Perspectives on the Regulatory Framework for Commercial Transactions in the UK and in the EU Pre and Post Brexit

Muriel Renaudin

1 Introduction

The United Kingdom (UK) left the European Union (EU) on 31st January 2020 (an event that has become known as Brexit) with a transition period which ended on 31st December 2020. The European Union (Withdrawal Agreement) Act 2020[1] effectively transferred existing EU law into domestic legislation. This body of laws took the name of retained EU law (REUL). In the international context, the Trade and Cooperation Agreement (TCA) now regulates cross-border trade relationships between the UK and the EU.[2] Brexit has noticeably generated, and continues to generate, significant impact on cross-border trade between the UK and the EU. The legal framework underpinning commercial transactions underwent systemic changes triggered by Brexit, in particular by the TCA. This chapter therefore proposes a discussion of the extent to which Brexit has impacted the law governing commercial transactions in the UK and the EU. It further proposes to discuss whether it might be possible to foresee a trend as to its future trajectory. From the outset, it is noticeable that the law governing commercial transactions is national in nature and remains largely unaffected by Brexit. This is because European harmonisation remains limited in this field. Much of the harmonisation occurred in specific areas such as consumer law, the fight against tax fraud, transparency of financial markets and the

[1] The European Union (Withdrawal Agreement) Act 2020. https://www.legislation.gov.uk/ukpga/2020/1/contents/enacted. Accessed 20 April 2023.

[2] The Trade and Cooperation Agreement was signed on 30 December 2020, provisionally applied as of 1 January 2021 and entered into force on 1 May 2021. https://commission.europa.eu/strategy-and-policy/relations-non-eu-countries/relations-united-kingdom/eu-uk-trade-and-cooperation-agreement_en. Accessed 20 April 2023.

M. Renaudin (✉)
School of Law and Politics, Cardiff University, Cardiff, UK
e-mail: RenaudinM1@cardiff.ac.uk

E. Guinchard, C. Panara (eds.), *The New Relationship between the United Kingdom and the European Union*, https://doi.org/10.1007/978-3-031-70652-3_7

supervision of credit institutions. As a result, Brexit did not have a significant impact on the regulatory framework for commercial contracts. However, Brexit ineluctably impacted the party's autonomy by triggering unforeseen negative economic externalities such as the imposition of new tariffs and additional formalities for cross-border traders. National commercial and contract laws had to be applied in the context of unforeseen economic changes such as financial costs and less profitable gains. Although, the strict approach to the doctrine of frustration did not envisage Brexit as a ground which would allow the parties to escape their contractual obligations, some judicial opinions and governmental recommendations seem to suggest the need for more lenience and flexibility within contractual performance in the UK. Such flexibility already existed in the contract law of most EU Member states pre Brexit, such as France for example.[3]

Although it is possible to recognise some changes that have already occurred within the national legal framework underpinning commercial transactions in both the UK and the EU, the exact shape of its future regulatory landscape is still unclear. Will the UK depart or continue to align to EU's standards? Will the EU's harmonisation endeavours be facilitated by Brexit? Clearly, Brexit created new regulatory opportunities for legislatures on both sides. The EU without the UK now sees an opportunity to pursue deeper economic integration, thanks to the proposal for a European Business Code. Such an endeavour, it is argued, would contribute to the achievement of the Single Market, increase the accessibility of EU commercial law rules and push further towards the symbolic goal of European integration. The UK outside the EU lost its access to the EU Single Market and Custom Union, but regained its freedom to regulate (national parliamentary sovereignty). As such, Brexit may create opportunities for the UK to rethink some of its commercial and contract law principles and to innovate in new legal areas such as digital finance. However, both the UK and the EU are also likely to face significant regulatory challenges in navigating the post Brexit era. The extent to which the UK will depart from EU's standards is still unclear, yet regulatory divergence was at the epicentre of the Brexit narrative.[4] As the UK and the EU will inevitably continue to trade with each other, divergent regulatory framework for commercial transactions may lead to barriers to trade, extra costs and legal uncertainty for businesses.

This chapter is organised in two parts. Part two discusses whether and to what extent Brexit has already changed aspects of the regulatory framework for commercial transactions in the UK and the EU. Whilst it is acknowledged that the law governing commercial contracts remains predominantly national in nature and unaffected by Brexit, supranational regulatory pressures such as those contained in the TCA have to a certain extent, impacted national laws and, in particular, the bargain struck by the parties. Part three discusses future regulatory opportunities and

---

[3]See the French theory of '*imprévision*' for example which found some application in the context of Brexit. On the operation of 'imprévision', see Pédamon (2017).

[4]See for example, Boris Johnson's speech on the EU referendum (2016). https://conservativehome.com/2016/05/09/boris-johnsons-speech-on-the-eu-referendum-full-text/. Accessed 20 April 2023.

challenges for both the UK and in the EU, in particular, the prospect of a new European Business Code and whether it might be possible to foresee a trend as to the future trajectory of commercial contract law in the UK and the EU.

2 General Overview of the Impact of Brexit on the Regulatory Framework for Commercial Transactions in the UK and the EU

2.1 National, European and Transnational Legal Frameworks for Commercial Contracts: The State of Play at Brexit

If the harmonisation of the law of all EU Member states remains the ultimate ambition of the European Union, particularly for the achievement of the Single Market, one cannot but notice that, at the point of Brexit, it remained far from complete. This was the conclusion of the *Association Henri Capitant Pour la Culture Juridique Française* (the *Association Capitant*), which published in 2016 an inventory of the *acquis communautaire* in twelve areas of commercial law (internal market law, e-commerce law, corporate law, secured transactions, enforcement procedures, insolvency law, banking law, insurance law, financial markets law, intellectual property law, labour law and tax law).[5] The inventory concludes that European commercial law suffers from a significant lack of accessibility and clarity which may prevent businesses from developing.[6] The EU regulatory approach in commercial law has focused on crucial issues such as the protection of consumers, the fight against tax fraud, transparency of financial markets, supervision of credit institutions,[7] but the *Association Capitant* concedes that it has not sufficiently addressed the everyday practices of European traders and entrepreneurs, and more generally of anyone who is involved in a commercial transaction.[8]

Insofar as attempts have been made to harmonise contract and commercial law within the EU, this has been pursued through the enactment of soft law instruments such as with the Common Frame of Reference (CFR)[9] which is based on the Principles of European Contract Law (PECL).[10] The PECL is a non-binding

[5] *Association Henri Capitant* (2016).

[6] Hence the pursuit of the proposal for a European Business Code.

[7] See the EU Consumer law Acquis which includes the Doorstep Selling Directive 85/577, the Package Travel Directive 90/314, the Unfair Contract Terms Directive 93/13, the Timeshare Directive, 2008/122/EC, the Distance Selling Directive 97/7, the Price Indication Directive 98/6, the Injunctions Directive 98/27 and the Consumer Sales Directive 99/44).

[8] Dupichot (2016).

[9] See Eidenmüller (2008).

[10] PECL is available at https://www.trans-lex.org/400200/_/pecl/. Accessed 20 April 2023.

instrument which predominantly aims to assist national legislators and judges to reform the law towards European standards.[11] Nevertheless, it is possible to identify several European Directives, which have been transposed into the national laws of the UK and of the EU Member States, and thus harmonised the law. Examples include the Consumer sales or the Unfair Terms and Unfair Commercial Practices Directives. These legal instruments remain in place (for now) regardless of Brexit through the REUL.[12] However, and given the perceived reluctance of English law makers to reform contract law along the lines of continental Civil law jurisdictions principles (such as those contained in the PECL), the UK may view Brexit as an opportunity to repeal and/or replace all or parts of these EU derived legislations. This reluctance stems from principles of security, certainty and needs of commerce which dominate English contract and commercial laws,[13] and which principles are often irreconcilable with the moralist and individual approaches adopted by most continental European contract laws.[14]

Despite the limited impact of European derived laws on English contract and commercial laws, it is to be acknowledged that some European continental law doctrines, such as the controversial good faith principle, have had a non-negligible influence (exacerbated by Brexit and the Covid-19 pandemic)[15] on English contract and commercial laws through judicial interpretation. Traditionally, Civil law jurisdictions recognise a duty to negotiate and perform commercial contracts in good faith,[16] but Common law jurisdictions such as England and Wales have always resisted the incorporation of such principle into the laws governing contracts.[17] The concept is generally said to be too abstract, too uncertain for contractual parties and too difficult to interpret and enforce in courts.[18] The good faith principle intruded

---

[11] On this point see Vogenauer and Weatherill (2006).

[12] The retained European Union Law (REUL) was created by the EU (Withdrawal) Act 2018 (EUWA) as amended by the EU (Withdrawal Agreement) Act 2020 (EUWAA) and came into existence at the end of the post-Brexit transition period (the end of 2020). The Consumer Act 2015, Parts 1 and 2 and the Consumer Protection from Unfair Trading Regulations 2008, Part 4 A are part of the retained EU law. There are also other EU derived law still in force in the UK such as the Commercial Agents (Council Directive) Regulations 1993 (SI 1993/3053).

[13] See for example see Irvine (2001).

[14] *Ibid.*

[15] See for example the UK Government 'Guidance on Responsible Contractual Behaviour In the Performance and Enforcement of Contracts Impacted by the Covid-19 Emergency'(2020). https://www.gov.uk/government/publications/guidance-on-responsible-contractual-behaviour-in-the-performance-and-enforcement-of-contracts-impacted-by-the-covid-19-emergency. Accessed 20 April 2023.

[16] See for example Article 1104 of the French Civil code which provides that: 'Contracts must be negotiated, formed and performed in good faith'.

[17] See for example comments of Bingham L.J. in *Interfoto Picture Library Ltd v Stiletto Visual Programmes Ltd* [1989] 1 Q.B. 433, para 439.

[18] Giliker (2022).

into English law mainly through European Directives in consumer contract law.[19] But the principle has arguably also found some application in the performance of commercial contracts where the courts have had to deal with the recognition of express and implied duties of good faith. English courts generally recognise, through a narrow construction, the validity of a term containing an express duty of good faith.[20] But, some attempts have also been made by courts to recognise an implied duty of good faith in contractual performance. Mr Justice Legatt in the famous decision *Yam Seng Pte Ltd v. International Trade Corporation Ltd.*[21] suggested the existence of an implied duty of good faith in a long-term distributorship contract, but he also conceded that parties could decide to exclude such duty by express or implicit term included in the contract.[22] In the case of *Sheikh Tahnoon v Kent*, Legatt went further to suggest that a duty of good faith could be implied in all relational contracts. While Legatt's comments were obiter, they opened up the debate as to the recognition of implied duties of good faith in commercial contracts[23] leading some academics to recognise that the good faith principle (contractual performance) may have found some application in English contract law under certain circumstances.[24] Conversely, other commentators have cautioned that this duty of good faith should not be generalised to all commercial contracts.[25]

2.2 Party Autonomy and Its Limits: The Impact of Brexit on the Bargain Struck by the Parties

The legal framework governing commercial contracts does not only derive from national sources such as legislation and case law, it also derives from international law instruments such as the United Nations Convention on Contracts for the International Sale of Goods (CISG), and from the party's agreement itself.[26] The implications of Brexit in respect of International treaties and Conventions are relevant to any discussion of the future EU-UK legal framework for commercial

---

[19] The Unfair Terms in Consumer Contract Directive (Council Directive 93/13/EEC of 5th April 1993) states that a term is deemed unfair if contrary to the requirement of good faith, it causes a significant imbalance in the parties' rights and obligations under the contract to the detriment of the consumer.

[20] Hoskins (2014), p. 159.

[21] *Yam Seng Pte Ltd v. International Trade Corporation Ltd* [2013] EWHC 111 (QB), [2013] 1 ALL ER (comm) 1321. See paras 119–154.

[22] *Ibid at* paras 149 and 150.

[23] See *Sheikh Tahnoon Bin Saeed Bin Shakhboot Al Nehayan v Kent* [2018] EWHC 333 (Comm) and *Essex CC v UBB Waste* [2020] EWHC 1581 (TCC).

[24] Giliker (2022), McKendrick (2015), pp. 196–209 and Saintier (2017).

[25] Whittaker (2013), p. 468 and Bell and McCunn (2021), p. 16.

[26] Smits (2021).

transactions[27] but, because of space constraints, the following discussion will focus on the implications of Brexit for the rights and obligations arising out of the contractual agreement, in other words the party's agreement.

In the context of cross-border commercial transactions, the principle of party autonomy which is recognised by most legal systems in Europe,[28] means that the parties can freely decide how to organise their legal relations according to their respective wills. In other words, they can freely choose the applicable law and jurisdiction.[29] However, the freedom of the will is not unlimited. Contractual parties are subject to limitations such as those contained in the *jus cogens* in the international context[30] and to mandatory rules dictated by the chosen supranational or chosen national contract law. Party autonomy is further limited by public economic regulations affecting the market (such as trade, competition, intellectual property and securities) or society (health, environmental and social protection) as well fundamental rights in fields of private law. Brexit has already affected some of these regulations (e.g. TCA) which triggered repercussions for the party's agreement, in particular, on the economic bargain struck by the parties. For example, before Brexit, businesses in the UK benefitted from a range of preferential market access opportunities under the terms of the Single Market and the EU Custom Union legal framework. The EU Customs Union is an agreement between countries which makes it easier for EU companies to trade, and which harmonises customs duties on goods coming from outside the EU. It means that once the goods are imported within the EU, there are no further custom duties, quotas or declarations as goods can move freely around Member States. The EU Customs Union is different from the Single Market, which is a broader agreement to accept free movement of goods,

[27] On this point, see Ramses (2018).

[28] On this point, see Ruhl (2007).

[29] Article 3 of the 1980 Convention on the Law Applicable to Contractual Obligations (Rome Convention) fully recognises this principle of party autonomy. Under Article 3 the parties are free to choose whichever law they deem appropriate to govern their contractual relationship. It is not even necessary for the transaction to display some connection with the chosen law. Before Brexit, the UK was bound by the rules for choice of law set out in the Rome I Regulation (593/2008) (with respect to contractual obligations) and in the Rome II Regulation (864/2007) (choice of law for non-contractual obligations). The Law Applicable to Contractual Obligations and Non-Contractual Obligations (Amendment etc.) (EU Exit) Regulations 2019 (the "Regulations") were approved by Parliament in February 2019. Under the Regulation, both Rome I and Rome II, the UK continues to apply the rules set out in Rome I and Rome II to determine the proper law of the contract and the law governing non-contractual obligations. The Regulations set out some minor exceptions arising from the different status of the UK following Brexit where they may apply differently to Rome I and Rome II, for instance in the case of non-derogable mandatory rules or certain insurance contracts. But, apart from these exceptions, the Regulations continue to apply the rules set out in Rome I and Rome II.

[30] The United Nations define *jus cogens* as follows: 'A peremptory norm of general international law (*jus cogens*) is a norm accepted and recognized by the international community of States as a whole as a norm from which no derogation is permitted and which can be modified only by a subsequent norm of general international law having the same character.' https://legal.un.org/ilc/reports/2019/english/chp5.pdf. Accessed 20 April 2023.

services and persons.[31] Article 26(2) TFEU provides that: 'The internal market shall comprise an area without internal frontiers in which the free movement of goods, persons, services and capital is ensured.'[32] These trade arrangements entitled pre-Brexit EU-UK contractual parties to preferential customs duties for goods and/or to a reduction in import tariff rates across a variety of goods and services. Since Brexit, the UK-EU TCA which is now in place since 1st January 2021, also guarantees zero tariffs and quotas on goods moving between the EU and UK but only if those goods meet the Rule of Origin (RoO).[33] These are goods which have been obtained and/or transformed in the EU or in the UK, or in both. However, if UK businesses re-export goods obtained from third countries, tariffs may become imposable. Research undertaken by the UK Trade Policy Observatory (UK TPO) demonstrates that the RoO can be onerous for traders. The UK TPO recognises that because the rules are so specific for particular products and because of the complexities and paperwork costs, some businesses prefer to pay the required tariff rather than to claim the zero tariff.[34] In addition to tariffs, the new UK-EU customs processes may add further costs on the parties.[35] The EU introduced full customs controls from 1st January 2021, whilst the UK introduced phased customs controls for goods imports from the EU.[36] The UK has now also implemented digital solutions and new technologies to reduce friction and costs for businesses and consumers.

[31] The European Commission defines the European Single Market as follows:

> The Single Market refers to the EU as one territory without any internal borders or other regulatory obstacles to the free movement of goods and services. A functioning Single Market stimulates competition and trade, improves efficiency, raises quality, and helps cut prices. The European Single Market is one of the EU's greatest achievements. It has fuelled economic growth and made the everyday life of European businesses and consumers easier.

[32] Article 26(2) Treaty on the Functionning of the European Union (TFEU). https://www.legislation.gov.uk/eut/teec/article/2a. Accessed 20 April 2023.

[33] The RoO determine the 'economic nationality' of goods based on where the products or materials (or inputs) used in their production come from. They prevent goods manufactured in third countries being routed through the UK (or the EU) to avoid paying third country tariffs.

[34] The UK TPO estimates that for the period January-July 2021, the TCA has reduced goods exports to the EU by 14% and by 24% for imports from the EU. The reduction in trade brought about an estimated combined hit to the UK economy of around £44 billion with £32.5 billion lost in potential imports to the UK and £11 billion in exports to the EU. For the first seven months of 2021, between 26–32% of UK exports to the EU that could have entered under a zero-tariff did not do so. Despite the zero-tariff, zero-quota trade agreement of the TCA, firms end up paying tariffs to avoid the bureaucratic costs of claiming zero tariff. The TCA has also had an adverse effect on services trade with the EU: we estimate a TCA effect on the exports and imports of services to the EU equal to −11.5% and −37% respectively, for the first half of 2021.

[35] Customs controls ensure duties are paid on goods moving across the border, and check compliance with safety, security, health and environmental requirements.

[36] For a comprehensive guide on the new customs controls between the UK and the EU, see the Border Operating Model published by the UK Government in https://www.gov.uk/government/publications/the-border-operating-model. Accessed 20 April 2023.

2.3 The Adverse Impact of Brexit on Contractual Economic Gains: Financial Difficulties and the Implications for the Legal Principles Governing Contractual Remedies

The imposition of extra formalities, extra costs and cross border trading tariffs applicable to commercial contracts trading goods between the EU and the UK may significantly affect the rights and duties arising from commercial agreements leading to potential financial and economic constraints on the parties.[37] As a result, the contractual economic gain which was generated and facilitated by existing EU legislations and trade agreements preceding Brexit, may lead to potential financial costs and loss of profitability on contracting parties. National laws have arguably had to deal with these unforeseen circumstances triggered by Brexit. It is therefore useful to question whether relevant national contractual law principles underpinning performance have changed, if at all, to accommodate financial difficulties caused by Brexit. Under English contract law, the debtor cannot in principle, be excused from performing his contractual obligations, no matter the reason. This is a strict liability.[38] Nevertheless, English contract law is prepared to recognise in certain situations that the debtor should be excused from performance where the contract has become impossible to perform 'because the circumstances in which performance is called for would render it a thing radically different from that which undertaken by the contract'.[39] The contract is said to have been frustrated because one essential element of the contract has been destroyed.[40] To provide relief from liability for non-performance of contractual obligations does to a certain extent undermine and contravene the principles of security and predictability of agreements and also places the risk of non-performance on the promisee. It is thus not surprising that English judges have been quite reluctant to use this doctrine to excuse non-performance.[41] Beale and Twigg-Flesner explain that:

> [T]he doctrine of frustration is quite narrow. It will not apply to many cases in which the impossibility is only temporary or partial; and it will not apply when the contract no longer serves one party's purpose, or has become very much more burdensome to perform. Lastly,

---

[37] On this point see European Commission (2018) 'Notice to stakeholders - withdrawal of the United Kingdom and EU rules in the field of import/export licences for certain goods'.

[38] See *Nicolene Ltd v Simmonds* [1952] 2 Lloyd's Rep. 419 at para 425 where Sellers J explained that:

> It does not matter whether the failure to fulfil the contract by the seller is because he is indifferent or wilfully negligent or just unfortunate. It does not matter what the reason is. What matters is the fact of performance. Has he performed or not?

[39] Lord Radcliffe in *Davis Contractors Ltd v Fareham Urban District Council* [1956] AC 696 at para 729. See also McKendrick (2013), Chapter 2.

[40] *Taylor V Caldwell* [1863] 3 B&S 826.

[41] See for e.g. *British Movietonenews Ltd v London and District Cinema* [1952] A.C. 166; *Tsakiroglou & Co. Ltd. V Noblee Thorl G.m.b.H.* [1962] A.C. 93; *The Nema* [1982] A.C. 724 and *J. Lauritzen A.S. v Wijsmuller B.V. (The Super Servant Two)* [1990] 1 Lloyd's Rep. 1.

> it is an "all-or-nothing" doctrine: if it applies, the parties are automatically discharged, but if it does not apply, a party who does not perform will be liable for breach of contract unless there is a force majeure or similar clause in the contract that covers the events that have taken place.[42]

As a result, a change in the economic bargain of the contract struck by the parties, such as those created by Brexit, is unlikely to excuse the debtor from performing the contract. Although, the contract may become more costly or more difficult to perform for the parties, the promisor will not be excused from performance simply because a contract has become more onerous to perform because of Brexit. Unless the promisor can demonstrate that performance of the contract has become impossible because one element of the contract has been destroyed, the promisor will not be able to escape liability for non-performance. An illustration of this narrow approach in the context of Brexit can be found in the case of *Canary Wharf (BP4) T1 Ltd v. European Medicines Agency*[43] where the European Medicine Agency argued that a 25-year lease of premises at Canary Wharf in London as their headquarters which begun in 2011 was frustrated by Brexit. In this case, the judge did not find that Brexit made the contract radically different from what was originally agreed. The doctrine of frustration did not apply as a result. A similar strict approach was adopted in the context of the Covid-19 pandemic.[44] Nonetheless, in the latter situation, it is worth noting that some incentives were placed on contractual parties to show more understanding regarding contractual performance affected by Covid-19.[45]

If frustration cannot help contracting parties, the allocation of risks could be expressly agreed by the parties thanks to a *force majeure* or Material Adverse Change clause (MAC) to cover unforeseen financial difficulties caused by Brexit. *Force majeure*, though an unfamiliar concept for the common law, is a well-established French law doctrine which excuses the promisor from performance

[42] Beale and Twigg-Flesner (2021), p. 471. See also Bridge (2021), p. 580.

[43] [2019] EWHC 335 (ch).

[44] See *Salam Air SAOC v. Latam Airlines Group SA* [2020] EWHC 2414 (comm) 6-year lease of three aircraft grounded as a result of pandemic legislation in Oman found to remain in full force and effect; referred to with approval in the non-covid frustration case of *Iris Helicopter Leasing Ltd v Elitaliana SRL, Point Holding SPA* [2021] EWHC 2459 (Comm), para. 26 (Jacob J.)); *Bank of New York Mellon (international) Ltd v Cine-UK Ltd* [2021] EWHC 1013 (QB) (landlord of leases of three commercial properties held entitled to full payment of overdue rent). On the application of frustration during the pandemic, Morgan (2021). See also *Commerz Real Investmentgesellschaft MBH v TFS Stores Ltd* [2021] EWHC.

[45] See for example, the UK Government's 'Guidance on Responsible Contractual Behaviour in the Performance and Enforcement of Contracts Impacted by the Covid -19 Emergency Pandemic Implications on contract' (2020) or the 'breathing space' concept which was referred to in the concept notes of the British Institute of International and Comparative Law (BIICL). BIICL highlighted the distinctive rules of continental European systems allowing courts to adapt contracts and noted that these could be more readily invoked in the Covid 19 context than the Common Law rules on frustration. https://www.biicl.org/projects/breathing-space-concept-notes-on-the-effect-of-the-pandemic-on-commercial-contracts. Accessed 20 April 2023.

under certain circumstances.[46] Article 1218 of the French Civil code defines *force majeure* as an irresistible and unforeseeable event. There is no definition *per se* of *force majeure* in English law but such clause will, in practice, often be agreed by the parties to escape liability for non-performance under certain circumstances.[47] McEndrick explains that:

> An event will be force majeure event if it constitutes a legal or physical restraint on the performance of the contract (whether or not occurring through human intervention, although it must not be caused by the act, negligence, omission or default of the contracting party) which is both unforeseen and irresistible.[48]

Relying on a *force majeure* clause in the event of Brexit to escape liability for non-performance is however uncertain. English Courts have generally held that changes in a party's economic circumstances will not qualify as *force majeure* events.[49] The fact that economic hardship will be suffered is not normally sufficient to claim relief from performance. The interpretation of the clause by English courts will depend on the exact wording of the applicable clause and it is possible that some types of clauses, for example, MAC clauses, could be wider than a standard *force majeure* clause and could potentially be triggered by financial hardship suffered as a result Brexit. MAC clauses enable the parties to renegotiate the terms of their contracts or to terminate the contractual agreement upon the occurrence of certain events. The changes in circumstances following the supervening event must be material, that is sufficiently substantial and significant to trigger a change in material circumstances. The question of whether the changes in circumstances caused by Brexit will be caught by a MAC clause will depend upon the drafting of the clause itself.

The application of these contract law principles in the context of Brexit demonstrates and supports the claim that the law of contract remains largely national in nature and remains unaffected by the departure of the UK from the EU. The same conclusion can be drawn in respect of the contract laws of European Member States where the application of contract law principles in the context of Brexit produced different outcomes, but remained largely unchanged. For example, French contract law seem to offer more flexibility to the contractual parties facing financial difficulties triggered by Brexit, through the doctrine of *imprévision*,[50] the good faith principle, *force majeure* clauses and the principle of *caducité*.[51] These contractual

---

[46] On this point see McKendrick (2013), Chapter 2.

[47] Donaldson explained in *Thomas Borthwick (Glasgow) Ltd. V Faure Fairclough Ltd.* ([1968] 1 Lloyd's Rep. 16, at p. 28.) that: "The precise meaning of the term, if it has one, has eluded lawyers for years."

[48] McKendrick (2013), p. 5.

[49] See *Tandrin Aviation Holdings Ltd v Aero Toy Store LLC and another* [2010] EWHC 40 (Comm).

[50] On the French theory of '*imprévision*' see Pédamon (2017).

[51] Article 1186 French Civil code provides that: 'A validly formed contract becomes null and void if one of its essential elements disappears.'

principles also demonstrates the more moralist approach to French contract law when compared with English contract law.[52]

3 Developing Projects for the Future Regulatory Framework for Commercial Transactions in the EU and UK Post-Brexit

3.1 The Harmonisation of Commercial Law in the EU: The Proposal for a European Business Code

3.1.1 The Context

Since Brexit, the European aspiration to harmonise the law seems to have regained some support from academics and European law makers.[53] The European Commission issued a White Paper in 2017 on the Future of Europe which proposed, *inter alia*, the codification of European business law. This idea of a European Business Code was politically endorsed in the context of the Franco-German bilateral relationship thanks to two key treaties, namely the Élysée Treaty[54] and the Aix-La-Chapelle Treaty.[55] The former formally recognises the willingness of the two countries to create a Franco-German economic area governed by harmonised rules, especially in areas of Company law, Tax law and Insolvency.[56] The Aix-La-Chapelle Treaty goes further and proposes the draft of a European Business Code to govern business transactions in the EU. A collective of European legal academics from the *Association Henri Capitant* network produced a first Draft European Business Code which was presented to the Italian Representation of the European Parliament in Rome on 29th September 2023, in the presence of a large number of lawyers, diplomats, members of parliament and eminent public figures from the Italian civil society.[57] The project's aims are clear; to achieve a deeper European integration, complete the Single Market, provide better accessibility for small and

[52] On a comparison between French and English contract laws in their respective approach to difficulties of contractual performance, see Pédamon (2021).

[53] On this point, see Dupichot (2016); Bélanger (2017) and Dupichot (2021).

[54] Élysée Treaty of 22nd January 2018 which establishes a closer cooperation between the French and German Parliaments (French *Assemblée Nationale* and German *Bundestag*) https://www.assemblee-nationale.fr/dyn/15/textes/l15t0072_texte-adopte-seance. Accessed 20 April 2023.

[55] Traité Franco-Allemand D'Aix-La-Chapelle adopted on 22nd January 2019. https://www.elysee.fr/emmanuel-macron/traite-franco-allemand-aix-la-chapelle. Accessed 20 April 2023.

[56] See fn 55.

[57] See the Draft European Business Code. https://www.henricapitant.org/actions/projet-de-code-europeen-des-affaires-2/ Accessed 20 October 2023.

medium enterprises (SMEs) and reinforce economic attractivity in Europe.[58] The next sections will critically discuss and evaluate these ambitions.

3.1.2 Deeper European Integration and the Achievement of the Single Market

The approximation of commercial law is instrumental to the success of market integration for economic organisations. Arguments in support of the approximation of law range from arguments based on a costs-benefit analysis (eg reduction of negative externalities such as transaction costs and judicial interface)[59] to arguments based on values linked to the principles of fairness and transparency within international transactions.[60] It is not the aim of the present chapter to revisit the case for the approximation of commercial laws,[61] but the following examples will support the claim that it can constitute an enabling factor to the success of market integration for economic organisations. The success of the American Uniform Commercial Code (UCC) is an interesting example of a common market which adopted a corresponding harmonised legislative approach to the regulation of businesses and commercial transactions.[62] The UCC was first published in 1952 and comprehensively unifies the laws governing all commercial transactions in the US. Although codification may be seen as an unusual legislative method for a Common law jurisdiction, it has proved very successful since all fifty states of America spontaneously adopted the UCC.[63] Other successful examples of common markets which have adopted uniform commercial rules include the Organisation for the Harmonisation of Business Law in Africa (OHADA) and the Common Market of the South (*Mercado Comùn Del Sur* or MERCOSUR). In the EU, numerous directives and regulations have successfully harmonised specific areas of commercial law such as consumer law and banking.[64] However key areas such as contract law, secured credit law[65] or sales law have not been harmonised. Yet, these areas truly are the backbone of commerce. One may therefore wonder why the European

---

[58] See www.codeeropeendesaffaires.eu. Accessed 20 April 2023.

[59] On this point see Schmitthoff (1968); Goode (1991); Fox (1991–1992); Leebron (1996); Kronke (2000); Goode (2001); Smits (2002); Kronke (2003) and Lando (2003).

[60] See Leebron (1996) and Renaudin (2018): pp. 223–250.

[61] For a detailed account of the literature on this point see references in fn 60.

[62] On this point, see for example Friel and Murphy (2017).

[63] Louisiana adopted the UCC in 1990 but not in its entirety. Louisiana didn't adopt Article 2 (Sale of goods).

[64] For an overview of the EU acquis in commercial law, see *Association Henri Capitant* (2016).

[65] The harmonisation of secured credit law in the EU is not totally absent but remains very limited to the definitions of financial instruments (Directive 2002/47/EC on financial collateral arrangements (Financial Collateral Arrangements Directive), as amended by Directive 2009/44/EC on settlement finality and financial collateral arrangements (Settlement Finality and Collateral Arrangements Directive) and Directive 2014/59/EU on Bank Recovery and Resolution (BRRD).

Single Market and its single currency is still operating under different commercial law rules. Many reasons can be brought forward such as the impossibility of reconciliating legal differences, legal culture, lack of political support, and national sovereignty.[66] As a result, there has been no comprehensive harmonisation of commercial law in the EU. So, to what extent does the project for the codification of business law in Europe differ from past endeavours? The *Association Henri Capitant* has emphasised it is not seeking to comprehensively unify the whole of commercial law as such, but to systemise and codify the *Acquis Communautaire*. It has also pointed out that it would attempt to harmonise selected areas of commercial law[67] only if it is desirable and feasible, for example with the proposal of a European form of company.

3.1.3 Political Aim of a European Business Code: Digitalisation and Sustainability

One of the central ideas underpinning the Draft European Business Code is to establish a harmonised legal framework for businesses (particularly SMEs) to operate within the EU Single Market. The focus on SMEs was justified by the fact that this type of company is the most predominant form in the EU.[68] To this end, the Draft European Commercial Code in Book 4, proposes a unique form of European company which would be fully operating online with a single legal regime; a type of 'transnational company' based on accessible and simple rules.[69] This proposal of a European standardised form of company would better support cross-border European businesses and would also support them becoming more sustainable. This political aim is in line with the current European Industrial Strategy (EIS) Package.[70] The EIS Package aims to make the EU globally competitive through the development of a climate-neutral digitalised economy and society. This ambition rests on two pillars: the green and digital ('twin') transitions which, according to the European Commission, require 'new products and services, markets and business models, which must be grounded in our European values and our social market economy.'[71] A European form of company operating online would contribute to

---

[66] On this point, see for example Boodman (1991).

[67] Thirteen working groups were created to work in selected areas of commercial law including insolvency, a model of European company, internal market and Banking law. See the Draft European Commercial Code. https://www.henricapitant.org/actions/projet-de-code-europeen-des-affaires-2/ Accessed 20 October 2023.

[68] In 2019, 98,9% of European businesses forming part of the non-financial business economy were micro or small enterprises employing less than 50 persons. https://ec.europa.eu/eurostat/web/products-eurostat-news/-/edn-20220627-1.

[69] See Book 4 of the Draft European Commercial Code. https://www.henricapitant.org/wp-content/uploads/2023/10/Livre-4-Droit-des-societes.pdf Accessed 20 October 2023.

[70] https://ec.europa.eu/commission/presscorner/detail/en/qanda_20_418. Accessed 20 April 2023.

[71] *Ibid.*

these ambitions. The European Commission further emphasised that the Covid-19 pandemic accelerated the digitalisation of the European economy including that of its companies. But, at the same time, it recognised that a proportion of SMEs have lagged behind.[72] The proposal for a European company fully operating online would thus fill this gap and enable SMEs to modernise.[73]

3.1.4 Challenges and Constraints

The project of a European Business Code is ambitious but may be limited. Putting aside the questions of compatibility with European principles such as rules on competences and the principle of subsidiarity,[74] the question of its feasibility raises further issues such as the substantial scope of the code, the approximation of law methods and the type of instrument to be adopted. The memory of the past failed harmonisation project for a Common European Sales Law (CESL)[75] may convince some commentators that the project of a European Business Code is also doomed to failure.[76] In terms of its substantial scope, some difficulties may arguably also arise from the absence of a clear definition of 'business law' or 'commercial law'. If business law can be broadly described as the rules and institutions governing the organisation of the entrepreneurial project and the development of this project towards third parties, then the scope of a European Business Code should arguably go beyond selected areas of commercial law.[77] A fragmentary approach aimed at the codification of specific areas of commercial law may undermine the harmonisation efforts and the need for more accessibility.[78] Furthermore, given that the nature of commerce is to provide for flexibility, security and greater predictability for businesses, the choice of a code as legal receptacle, may go against the spirit of these principles and against the freedom of the will.[79] The codification of European

[72] See The 2021/2022 Digitalisation in Europe Report (2022). https://www.eib.org/en/press/all/2022-214-the-2021-2022-digitalisation-in-europe-report-the-pandemic-has-made-the-digital-transformation-an-integral-part-of-european-society. Accessed 20 April 2023.

[73] The European Commission already introduced two legislative initiatives to upgrade rules governing digital services in the EU: the Digital Services Act (DSA) and the Digital Markets Act (DMA) in December 2020 and on 25 March 2022 respectively. The DMA entered into force on 1 November 2022, and the DSA entered into force on 16 November 2022. Together they form a single set of new rules that will be applicable across the whole EU to create a safer and more open digital space.

[74] Lehmann (2020). See also D'Avout (2019), p. 1004.

[75] https://www.europarl.europa.eu/legislative-train/theme-connected-digital-single-market/file-common-european-sales-law. Accessed 20 April 2023.

[76] See for example, D'Avout (2019).

[77] The *Association Henri Capitant* set up thirteen working groups in selected areas of commercial law including insolvency, the model for a European type of company and Banking law.

[78] Although, it has to be acknowledged that the American UCC is an example of successful harmonisation of selected areas of commercial law.?

[79] On the codification of commercial law, see Goode (1988).

Business law could also potentially lead to more regulatory interventions within the current commercial legal framework[80] which, some will argue, can lead to market and economic inefficiencies.[81] Finally, some may further question whether the European Court of Justice would be a suitable forum to deal with commercial litigation arising from the application of this European Business Code. Despite a marked enthusiasm from academics and from politicians and law makers, it is difficult to predict whether this project for a European Business Code will come to fruition.

3.1.5 Reinforcing Economic Attractivity in Europe: Legal Competitivity and Law as an Economic Tool

Mirabeau said: ‘law is the ruler of the world.’[82] In the current context of the internationalisation of commercial transactions, this postulate has never been so true. National entities have been compelled to become more legally and economically competitive so as to attract more entrepreneurial business ventures and more profit opportunities. Numerous financial literatures support the argument that the modernisation of national commercial laws would contribute to the promotion of market efficacy and the development of legal competitivity.[83] The postulate that national commercial law frameworks should become more legally and economically competitive also reinforces the idea that, from an economic perspective, law can be conceptualised as an economic competitive tool.[84] This idea is central to numerous international initiatives such as those undertaken by the World Bank *Doing Business reports* for example.[85] The US has also without a doubt engaged with initiatives to use law as a tool to develop its legal and economic competitivity. The US legal and economic hegemony has been growing out of its legal education system

---

[80] Particularly, if the project goes beyond the codification of the acquis Communautaire and introduces significant law reforms through the harmonisation of law.

[81] On this point, see in general the ‘Law and Finance literature’, in particular La Porta et al. (1997) and (1998) which have grounded the methodology used in the World Bank Reports. For example, the 2004 Doing Business Report provides at p 83 that: ‘Heavier regulation of business activities generally brings bad outcomes, while clearly defined and well-protected property rights enhance prosperity’. https://www.doingbusiness.org/content/dam/doingBusiness/media/Annual-Reports/English/DB04-FullReport.pdf. Accessed 20 April 2003.

[82] “Le droit est le souverain du monde.”

[83] On this point, see Wood (2008).

[84] On this point, see Renaudin (2013).

[85] The *Doing Business* program is an initiative run by the International Financial Corporation (IFC) which is an institution created by the World Bank. The *Doing Business* Reports have ranked the quality of national legislation for doing business yearly since 2004. These reports are available at <http://www.doingbusiness.org/. However, in September 2021, the decision was made to discontinue the publication of the Doing Business Reports initiative.

(e.g. Academies),[86] legal transplants[87] and foreign policies aimed at providing legal training and legal assistance programmes overseas.[88] These initiatives demonstrate that American law has truly become a global legal engine for trade. It is possible that European business law could develop in a similar fashion and also develop a legal influence globally, hereby attracting more business ventures. At a very minimum, Brexit offers this opportunity to revisit commercial law from a more continental perspective.

3.2 The Future for the Law Governing Commercial Transactions in the UK Post Brexit

3.2.1 Example of New Opportunities for Legal Innovations in Commercial Law: Fintech and Digital Finance

The UK has also signalled an eagerness to explore new legal opportunities in areas of commercial law since Brexit. For example, the UK Government and financial regulatory authorities have been keen to continue developing the governing legal framework for fintech and digital finance (eg cryptoassets).[89] The joint HM Treasury-Financial Conduct Authority (FCA)-Bank of England Cryptoassets Taskforce published a Report in 2018 which sets out the UK's approach to crypto assets and distributed ledger technology (DLT) in financial services.[90] The FCA's published a Final Guidance in 2019, which established that Cryptoasset firms aiming to do business in the UK would require authorisation according to the specific design of a given token.[91] In the EU, similar initiatives can be identified including the proposed Regulation on Markets in Crypto-Assets (MiCA).[92] MiCA is part of a broader EU digital finance package, which, *inter alia*, also includes the Digital

---

[86] Moliterno (2008).

[87] Mertus and Breier-Sharlow (2003).

[88] On this point, see for example Wiegang (1996); Mattei and Monti (2001) and Mattei (2003).

[89] HM Treasury, 'Government Sets out Plan to Make UK a Global Cryptoasset Technology Hub' (2022) https://www.gov.uk/government/news/government-sets-out-plan-to-make-uk-a-global-cryptoasset-technology-hub, accessed. Accessed 20 April 2023. The Law Commission also published its Final Report on 'Digital Assets' which was published on 28th June 2023. https://lawcom.gov.uk/project/digital-assets/ Accessed 30 October 2023.

[90] https://www.gov.uk/government/publications/cryptoassets-taskforce. Accessed 20 April 2023.

[91] https://www.fca.org.uk/publication/policy/ps19-22.pdf. Accessed 20 April 2023.

[92] https://www.europarl.europa.eu/thinktank/en/document/EPRS_BRI(2022)739221. Accessed 20 April 2023.

Operational Resilience Act (DORA)[93] and the DLT Pilot Regime Regulation.[94] Given that digital finance and crypto are relatively new legal areas and have not been regulated within the EU pre Brexit (except in areas of payment services and electronic money), retained EU legislation is non-existent in these areas. As a result, from the UK's viewpoint, it might be easier to introduce legal reforms from a 'blank canvass' than to detangle existing EU retained legislations to accommodate new reform proposals. As a result, it may be the case that UK and EU laws in these areas will diverge over the coming years. In particular, the UK has indicated a willingness to capitalise on the potential benefits offered by crypto and to take the opportunity to strengthen their position as a world-leader in fintech, generate economic growth and boost innovation.[95] The UK Government also believes that crypto technologies can have a profound impact across financial services. In view of this, it is certainly an area where legal divergence will need to be carefully watched.[96]

3.2.2 Limitations to Regulatory Changes

The Retained EU law (Revocation and Reform) Act 2023[97] will automatically revoke most EU retained law by the end of 2023, but that any law that is still applied after the end of 2023 would be renamed as assimilated law. It is still unclear which laws will be affected by the legislation and how far the UK will depart from EU law as a result of it. The future regulatory landscape for commercial transaction in the UK is thus unclear. Nevertheless, the proposed legislation supports the clear and unambiguous signal that the UK is prepared to engage in meaningful legal reforms which could indicate future divergences with EU's standards. The proposed legislation also reinforces the UK Government's Brexit narrative of its regained regulatory sovereignty. The UK Government has framed the Brexit political debate as an opportunity to depart from EU standards. But how far the UK will be able to innovate and depart from EU's standards is uncertain. From a theoretical point of view, the return to the idea of the Nation State operating in accordance with models of nineteenth Century self-regulation seems quite illusory in our modern liberal economic models. Even if Brexit reinstated domestic sovereignty (supremacy of

---

[93] *Regulation (EU) 2022/2554 of the European Parliament and of the Council of 14 December 2022 on digital operational resilience for the financial sector available at* https://eur-lex.europa.eu/legal-content/EN/TXT/?uri=CELEX%3A52020PC0595. Accessed 20 April 2023.

[94] Regulation (EU) 2022/858 Of The European Parliament And Of The Council of 30 May 2022 on a pilot regime for market infrastructures based on distributed ledger technology, and amending Regulations (EU) No 600/2014 and (EU) No 909/2014 and Directive 2014/65/EU available at https://eur-lex.europa.eu/legal-content/EN/TXT/PDF/?uri=CELEX:32022R0858. Accessed 20 April 2023.

[95] The UK Government issued a Consultation and Call for Evidence on 'Future Financial Services Regulatory Regimes for Crypto Assets' in February 2023.

[96] It may create risks linked to unlevel playing fields and regulatory arbitration.

[97] https://www.legislation.gov.uk/ukpga/2023/28/enacted. Accessed 30 October 2023.

parliamentary sovereignty) and the ability for the UK to enter into trade agreements with other states on their own terms, there are external economic, geographical, political and legal pressures on sovereignty which cannot be avoided. The TCA may create regulatory limitations to future commercial law innovations and reforms in the UK. For example, the TCA requires that parties remain on an 'equal regulatory footing with a view to preventing unfair competition for foreign investment and trade while acknowledging that the purpose of the agreement is not to harmonize the standards of the parties'.[98] To this end, the TCA provides for level playing field (LPF) obligations in specific areas such as competition policy, subsidy control, and environmental protection. These obligations ensure an open and fair competition among businesses. The LPF obligations were fundamental during the TCA negotiations to avoid the feared 'race to the bottom' in standards post Brexit. In particular, there was a fear that the UK would become a less regulated economy which could have undermined EU's efforts in regards to the environment, employment law and other matters.[99] The LPF obligations do not in principle mean that legal innovations and reforms in the UK cannot diverge from EU standards.[100] But, the regulatory implications of the LPF obligations effectively mean that any future divergence with EU standards will have to safeguard fair and open competition in these areas. The extent to which LPF obligations may limit regulatory innovations in the UK will depend upon their operation and interpretation. For example, among the LPF commitments are 'non-regression' undertakings in relation to employment and environmental law.[101] If either the UK or the EU 'weakens or reduces' the level of protection in these areas,[102] with the effect of distorting UK-EU trade or investment by significantly reducing the cost to businesses, this could trigger mechanisms enabling "rebalancing measures" under the LPF. Such weakening or reduction in standards could occur because of regulatory divergence or a failure to regulate. The specialised 'rebalancing' measures contained in Article 411.2 TCA provide for remedies in case of a 'significant divergences' and in case of a 'material impact on trade and investments'. What will amount to 'significant divergences' or 'material

---

[98] Collins (2021), p. 618.

[99] On this point see for example, Freedman and Loutzenhiser (2022), pp. 188–204.

[100] See Article 355.4 of the TCA which provides that: "The parties affirm their common understanding that their economic relationship can only deliver benefits in a mutually satisfactory way if the commitment relating to a level playing field for open and fair competition stand the test of time, by preventing distortions of trade or investment, and by contributing to sustainable development. However, the parties recognise that the purpose of this Title is not to harmonise the standards of the Parties. The Parties are determined to maintain and improve their respective high standards in the areas covered by the Title."

[101] Regression measures can be found in the TCA at Article 387-2 for labour law and Article 391-2 for Environmental law.

[102] *Ibid.*

impact' is still unclear,[103] but some commentators argue that the 'rebalancing measures' triggers are quite narrow, and may only have limited implications on the regulatory agenda of the UK.[104] Bronckers and Gruni explained that:

> [...] having to prove that a lowering of labour or environmental protection actually has trade or investment effects may appear so formidable a condition as to render the disciplines of the non-regression and non-enforcement clauses illusory.[105]

If the regulatory framework (eg TCA) can affect trade (with free tariffs for example), trade can also affect the regulatory framework. As such if the interests of businesses are to continue frictionless trade within the EU, departing from EU standards may create difficulties within EU-UK trading relationships (eg through rebalancing measures and increased tariffs). Trade disruptions within the UK internal market and within the EU-UK markets are already substantial.[106] The benefits of legal innovations and reforms which diverge significantly from EU standards will therefore have to be carefully weighed against the economic costs for businesses and the economy at large.

4 Conclusion

This chapter claims that the current legal framework underpinning commercial transactions in the UK and in the EU remains predominantly national in nature and is unaffected by Brexit. However, Brexit ineluctably impacted the party's autonomy and the bargain struck by the parties by triggering unforeseen negative economic externalities such as the imposition of new tariffs and additional formalities for cross-border traders. One may thus conclude that Brexit has merely brought added costs (e.g. tariffs and extra formalities) to a pre-existing framework of largely national rules nevertheless shaped to some extent by transnational influences within Europe and beyond. However, this chapter also acknowledges that both EU and the UK have broad aspirations for regulatory change that is seen by some as having the potential to transform economic and legal competitiveness on each side. If these projects are pursued vigorously, they are likely to lead to greater regulatory divergence. But there are good reasons for each side to hesitate in wholeheartedly

---

[103] Vienna Convention on the Law of Treaties, Art 60(3)b (23 May 1969) provides that a 'material breach' is one which violates 'a provision essential to the accomplishment of the object or purpose of the treaty.'

[104] On this point, see for example, Bronckers and Gruni (2021). See also Mitchell and Munro (2019), p. 630.

[105] *Ibid.*

[106] See for example, The Office for National Statistics report 'impacts of EU exit and the coronavirus on UK trade in goods' (2021) https://www.ons.gov.uk/businessindustryandtrade/internationaltrade/articles/theimpactsofeuexitandthecoronavirusonuktradeingoods/2021-05-25. Accessed 20 April 2023.

pursuing such a course. For the UK, the consequences may be greater trade friction with its biggest trading partner if they violate the LPF obligations. For the EU, the gamble would be to put its faith in a commercial law more rooted in continental Civil law traditions as an alternative to the historic dominance of Common law principles in international commercial trade. But creating greater divergence between established Common law commercial practices and those in the EU might also have its costs.

References

Association Henri Capitant (2016) La construction européenne en droit des affaires: acquis et perspectives (Lextenso)
Beale H, Twigg-Flesner C (2021) COVID-19 and English contract law. In: Hondius E et al (eds) Coronavirus and the law in Europe. Intersentia, Cambridge. ISBN 9781839700828
Bélanger L (2017) Un code européen des affaires, le droit au Coeur de la consolidation de l'Europe. JCP 16(17):790–795
Bell AJ, McCunn J (2021) Professional negligence in 2020: the year in review. J Prof Neglig 37:5–20
Boodman M (1991) The myths of harmonization of law. Am J Comp Law 39(4):699–724
Bridge MG (2021) Frustration and excused non performance. LQR 137:580–603
Bronckers M, Gruni G (2021) Retooling the sustainability standards in EU Free Trade Agreements. J Int Econ Law 24(1):1–27
Collins D (2021) Standing the test of time: the level playing field and rebalancing mechanism in the UK-EU trade and cooperation agreement (TCA). J Int Disp Settlement 12:617–636
D'Avout L (2019) L'étonnante initiative en faveur d'un Code Européen des Affaires. La Semaine Juridique ed. Générale 21(22):1002–1005
Dupichot P (2016) Du Brexit au Code Européen des Affaires Droit et Patrimoine 262: https://www.codeeuropeendesaffaires.eu/2022/01/03/dessiner-un-droit-des-affaires-commun/. Accessed 20 Apr 2023.
Dupichot P (2021) Designing a common European business law. Revue Européenne du Droit 3(2): 108–113
Eidenmüller H et al (2008) The common frame of reference for European private law – policy choices and codification problems. Oxford J Leg Stud 28:659–708
Fox EM (1991-1992) Harmonization of law and procedures in a globalized world: why, what, and how? Antitrust Law J 60:593-600
Freedman J, Loutzenhiser G (2022) Tax policy in the UK post-Brexit. Oxford Rev Econ Policy 38(1):188–204. https://doi.org/10.1093/oxrep/grab050
Friel RJ, Murphy WJ (2017-2018) Article 9 of the uniform commercial code: an export success story, a model for change, and challenge ahead. Uniform Commer Code Law J 47: 461-492
Giliker L (2022) Contract negotiations and the common law: a move to good faith in commercial contracting? Liverpool Law Rev 43(2):175–202
Goode RM (1988) The codification of commercial law. Monash Univ Law Rev 14(3):135–157
Goode RM (1991) Reflections on the harmonisation of commercial law. Unif Law Rev 1:54–75
Goode RM (2001) Insularity or leadership? The role of the United Kingdom in the harmonisation of commercial law. Int Law Comp Law Q 50:751–766
Hoskins H (2014) Contractual obligations to negotiate in good faith: faithfulness to the agreed common purpose. Law Quart Rev 130:131–159
Irvine L (2001) The law: an engine for trade. Mod Law Rev 64(3):333–349

Kronke H (2000) International uniform commercial law conventions: advantages, disadvantages, criteria for choice. Unif Law Rev 5:13–21
Kronke H (2003) Congrès du 75ème Anniversaire d'UNIDROIT – Harmonisation Mondiale du Droit Privé et Intégration Economique Régionale: Hypothèses, Certitudes et Questions Pendantes. Unif Law Rev 8:11–27
La Porta R, Lopez-de-Silanes F, Shleifer A, Vishny RW (1997) Legal determinants of external finance. J Financ 52:1131–1150
La Porta R, Lopez-de-Silanes F, Shleifer A, Vishny RW (1998) Law and finance. J Polit Econ 106: 1113–1155
Lando O (2003) Principles of European contract law and UNIDROIT principles: moving from harmonisation to unification? Unif Law Rev 8:123–113
Leebron DW (1996) Claims for harmonization: a theoretical framework. Can Bus Law J 27:63–107
Lehmann M (2020) EU law making 2.0: the prospect of a European business code. Eur Rev Priv Law 28(1):73–106
Mattei U (2003) A theory of imperial law: a study on US hegemony and the Latin resistance. Indiana J Legal Stud 10(1):383–448
Mattei U, Monti A (2001) Comparative law and economics: borrowing and resistance. Glob Just Front 1(2):11–25
McKendrick E (2013) Force majeure and frustration of contract. Informa Law From Routledge, Chapter 2
McKendrick E (2015) Good faith in the performance of a contract in English law. In: Di Matteo L, Hogg M (eds) Comparative contract law: British and American perspectives. Oxford University Press, Oxford, pp 196–209
Mertus J, Breier-Sharlow E (2003) Power, legal transplants and harmonization. Univ Detroit Mercy Law Rev 81:477–489
Mitchell A, Munro J (2019) No retreat: an emerging principle of non-regression from environmental protections in international investment law. Georgetown J Int Law 50:625–708
Moliterno JE (2008) Exporting American legal education. J Legal Educ 58(2):274–289
Morgan J (2021) Frustration and the pandemic. LQR 137:563–568
Pédamon C (2017) The paradoxes of the theory of imprevision in the New French law of contract: a judicial deterrent? Amicus Curiae 112:10–17
Pédamon C (2021) Contractual performance in covid-19 times: does Anglo-French legal history repeat itself? Eur Rev Priv Law 29(1):3–37
Ramses AW (2018) Consequences of Brexit for international agreements concluded by the EU and its Member States. Common Mark Law Rev 55(2):101–131
Renaudin M (2013) The modernisation of French secured credit law: law as a competitive tool in global markets. Int Company Commer Law Rev 24(11):385–392
Renaudin M (2018) Approximation of secured credit laws in global economies: methodological challenges. In: Lee J, Heidemann M (eds) The future of the commercial contract in scholarship and law reform: European and comparative perspectives. Springer, pp 223–250
Ruhl G (2007) Party autonomy in the private international law of contracts: transatlantic convergence and economic efficiency. CLPE Research Paper No. 4/2007. In: Gottschalk E et al (eds) Conflict of laws in a globalized world. Cambridge University Press
Saintier S (2017) The elusive notion of good faith in the performance of a contract, why still a bête noire for the civil and the common law? J Bus Law:441–460
Schmitthoff CM (1968) The unification or harmonisation of law by means of standards and general conditions. Int Comp Law Q 17(3):551–570
Smits JM (2002) The harmonisation of private law in Europe: some insights from evolutionary theory. Ga J Int Comp Law 31(1):79–100
Smits JM (2021) Contract law: a comparative introduction, 3rd edn. Edward Elgar
Vogenauer S, Weatherill S (2006) The European Community's competence to pursue the harmonisation of contract law—an empirical contribution to the debate. In: Vogenauer S, Weatherill S (eds) The harmonisation of European contract law. Hart

Whittaker S (2013) Good faith, implied terms and commercial contracts. Law Quart Rev 129:463–469
Wiegang W (1996) Americanization of law: reception or convergence. In: Friedman LM (ed) Legal culture and legal profession, ch.6. Routledge
Wood PR (2008) Maps of financial law, 6th edn. Sweet & Maxwell

'Legal Issues Related to UK Policing Agencies Working with Europol Post-Brexit'

David Lowe

1 Introduction

A perception several European Union (EU) politicians like Guy Verhofstadt claim is that Brexit means the UK has left Europe.[1] This is not the case, the EU is not Europe, and the UK is still part of the continent of Europe that consists of 45 countries. Brexit resulted in the UK leaving the EU consisting of 27 Member States that in relation to the EU has made the UK a third country. As such, post-Brexit the UK's co-operation and working alongside the EU's Member States policing agencies has changed dramatically. Prior to leaving the EU in January 2020, as a Member State the UK was very active Member State in engaging with the EU's policing agency Europol and UK citizen, Sir Rob Wainwright, was Europol's director from 2009 to 2018. Since leaving the EU the UK no longer has access to the European Arrest Warrant, Europol's intelligence system, the Schengen Information System, or Europol's European Counter Terrorism Centre. With political wrangling still ongoing between the UK and the EU, especially on border issues between Northern Ireland and the Irish Republic (commonly referred to as the Northern Ireland protocol), it is important to note criminals and terrorists are no respecters of geographical boundaries and political agreements (or in the case of Brexit, many disagreements). This point is of paramount importance as they will continue to carry out their criminality between the UK, EU Member States and the rest of Europe.

Examining the impact of this criminality and terrorist activity, the chapter commences by looking at the creation and development of the EU's policing agency, Europol, covering its key roles and how post the 2009 Lisbon Treaty Europol

[1]Katie Harris (2022), retrieved from https://www.express.co.uk/news/politics/1710253/brexit-news-guy-verhofstadt-uk-rejoin-eu [accessed 1 March 2023].

D. Lowe (✉)
Leeds Law School, Leeds Beckett University, Leeds, UK
e-mail: D.Lowe@leedsbeckett.ac.uk

E. Guinchard, C. Panara (eds.), *The New Relationship between the United Kingdom and the European Union*, https://doi.org/10.1007/978-3-031-70652-3_8

became an official EU body. This leads to an examination of the UK's relationship with the EU in dealing with serious organised crime and terrorism with the access to the Schengen Information System, analysing Europol's role in intelligence exchange between EU Members States and third countries. One important and growing function in counter-terrorism and serious organised crime investigations is the surveillance of electronic communications. The chapter examines EU law surrounding data protection and privacy, analysing the compatibility of UK legislation, (mainly the Investigatory Powers Act 2016) with EU law as this is important regarding intelligence exchange. As such, the chapter assesses if the Court of Justice of the European Union (CJEU) will still impact on UK police investigations that involves intelligence gathering on suspects that cross the UK and EU borders. Examining how intransigent politicking between UK and EU politicians can inadvertently lead to an increase in terrorist and criminal activity, the chapter examines how negotiations over the Northern Ireland/Irish border that resulted in the Northern Ireland Protocol regarding the movement of goods and customs tariffs resulting in EU law still being applicable in the country has led to the threat of a return to terrorist activity by Northern Irish loyalist groups as they see this leading to an erosion of their national sovereignty..

2 The Creation of Europol

During the UK's membership of the EU, its policing agencies worked closely with the EU's policing agency Europol on both major counter-terrorism investigations and investigations into serious organised crime such as drug trafficking and people trafficking. Europol plays an important role in combating terrorism and organised crime with both Member States and Third countries' policing agencies. Europol's existence can be traced to article K.1(9) TEU which covered the topic of police co-operation. Article K.1(9) states that the EU established the principle that a European police office was needed to meet the challenge of transnational organised crime with police co-operation being required:

> ...for the purposes of preventing and combating terrorism, unlawful drug trafficking and other serious forms of international crime, including if necessary certain aspects of customs cooperation in connection of a union-wide system for exchanging information within a European Police Office.[2]

Although Europol's remit has expanded considerably since its first operational years, Europol remains primarily an intelligence agency based in The Hague supported by liaison officers.[3]

Since its inception Europol has developed at quite a pace. This is demonstrated in Europol's 2003 Annual Report which states that there was a significant increase in

---

[2]Elvins (2003), p. 31.

[3]Bigo (2000), pp. 77–79.

operational activities for the agency, as 2002 saw a 40% increase in the information exchange between Europol and the Member States.[4] Examples of how Europol's role is expanding can be seen in the reports they produce regarding their current remit. Concerning the trafficking in human beings, it states that its mandate is to support the work of the Member States, adding that while Europol's activity in connection with combating trafficking in human beings is in relation to sexual exploitation, Europol also recognises that people trafficking in relation to labour exploitation is just as important for Member States.[5] Regarding illegal immigration into the EU, Europol offers assistance to law enforcement activities in Member States on an operational footing by producing assessments of the threat from organised immigration as well as initiating and/or supporting cross-border investigations with analytical and operational expertise and detecting criminal activity within the EU.[6] Since the 1999 Tampere Agreement and the introduction of the Hague Programme, the direct role of Europol in investigating crime and facilitating co-operation between the policing agencies has increased considerably from the role which was originally perceived it would be carrying out. In addition to its workload increasing, the introduction of the Treaty of Lisbon 2009 also increased Europol's authority and role. Regarding its workload, Europol is required to publish two annual reports instead of the one it was originally obliged to publish. These reports cover two areas, terrorism, in its Terrorism Situation and Threat Assessment report (TE-SAT), and organised crime, in its Organised Crime Threat Assessment report (OCTA). In order to monitor terrorist activity Europol created the European Counter-Terrorism Centre (ECTC) in January 2016. Consisting of 38 staff and five national experts, the ECTC focuses on:

1. Tracking foreign fighters;
2. Sharing intelligence and expertise on terrorism financing;
3. Monitoring online terrorist propaganda and extremism;
4. Illegal arms trafficking;
5. International co-operation among counter-terrorism authorities.[7]

The formation of the ECTC followed on from another unit created at Europol 6 months earlier in July 2015, the Internet Referral Unit. The Unit was introduced to combat terrorist propaganda and related violent extremist activities on the internet where, in essence, it identifies and refers relevant online content towards concerned Internet Service Providers and supports Member States with operational and

[4]Europol (2004) 'Europol Annual Report 2003', retrieved from www.europol.eu.int [accessed 1 February 2023], p. 3.

[5]Europol (2005) 'Trafficking in human beings for sexual exploitation in the EU: a Europol perspective', retrieved from www.europol.eu.int [accessed 1 February 2023], p. 1.

[6]Europol (2005) 'Organised illegal immigration into the European Union', retrieved from www.europol.eu.int [accessed 1 February 2023], p. 4.

[7]Europol (2004) 'European Counter terrorism Centre', retrieved from https://www.europol.europa.eu/about-europol/european-counter-terrorism-centre-ectc [accessed 2 February 2023].

strategic analysis.[8] In its relatively short existence, the role and influence of Europol has expanded beyond its original remit as a drugs intelligence unit to one moving closer to the original idea of Europol becoming a federal policing agency, but without the operational powers.

3 Legislative Changes Making Europol an EU Body

One issue that could cause a blockage to these agreements is the current position of Europol in relation to working with Member States' intelligence services. Two important documents have raised the importance of the role Europol plays in assisting in counter-terrorism and crime investigations: the EU Council Decision of 6 April 2009 establishing Europol[9] and articles 87 and 88 of the Lisbon Treaty. The 2009 Council Decision in effect transformed Europol into a European agency, as evidenced by its funding by the EU budget, the formalising of Europol's staffing structure and changes regarding Europol's co-operation with third countries and organisations.[10] The 2009 Council Decision also gives Europol a legal personality[11] where it states that Europol's objective is to support and strengthen action by the competent authorities of the Member States and their mutual co-operation in combating terrorism (and organised crime and other forms of serious crime).[12] Even with these developments, there are two problems that continue to exist in relation to Member States' attitudes towards sharing intelligence with Europol. They are the ability for Member States to negotiate their own bilateral or multilateral agreements and the fact that it appears there is no obligation on Member States' national intelligence services to co-operate with Europol.

---

[8] Europol (2015) 'Europol's Internet Referral Unit to combat terrorist and violent extremist propaganda', 1 July, retrieved from https://www.europol.europa.eu/newsroom/news/europol%E2%80%99s-internet-referral-unit-to-combat-terrorist-and-violent-extremist-propaganda [accessed 2 February 2023].

[9] Council Decision 6 April 2009 establishing the European Police Office (Europol) (2009/371/JHA).

[10] Kaunert and Leonard (2011), p. 294.

[11] Council Decision 2009 establishing the European Police Office (Europol) (2009/371/JHA), retrieved from https://www.europol.europa.eu/publications-documents/council-decision-of-6-april-2009-establishing-european-police-office-europol [accessed 2 February 2023] article 2(1).

[12] *Ibid*, article 3.

4 UK-EU Relationship in Dealing with Crime and Terrorism Pre-Brexit

Although the UK was never part of the Schengen Agreement as it wanted to maintain control of its borders, following the Treaty of Amsterdam 1997, the UK did sign up to the Schengen *acquis*. The Schengen *acquis* was an important development as it took a previous inter-state agreement that was outside the control of the EU within the EU's remit, thereby allowing police co-operation to be carried out on a formal EU and legal footing. Peers noted that Protocol 2 of the Convention was aimed at allocating the entire Schengen *acquis* to either the EC or the EU Treaty.[13] The impact of the potential benefits the *acquis* in enhancing crime and security investigations can be seen in March 1999 where the two Member States who refused to sign up to the 1990 Convention, the UK and Ireland, asked to take part in some aspects of Schengen. As it has been throughout its membership of the EU, the UK was reluctant to adopt the border control and immigration issues contained within the *acquis* but did want to participate in the police and legal co-operation and the fight against drugs. In May 2000 the Council agreed to the UK and Ireland's request. For Ireland, the request to take part in the implementation and operation of the EU's intelligence system, Schengen Information System (SIS), was granted in 2002. While the UK had a degree of reluctance to incorporate the Schengen Treaty in full on matters of border control, asylum and immigration, the Irish government has no problem with the Treaty *per se*, but as its rationale for opting out of the Treaty is due to the fact that 75% of travel to and from its borders are with the UK, it was deemed necessary to keep in line with the UK's intention to opt out in order to maximise the freedom of movement into and out of Ireland. The Irish government has declared that it will implement all measures of Schengen that are compatible with the Common Travel Area between itself and the UK.[14]

In addition to the EU Member States, Iceland and Norway also signed up to the Schengen *acquis*. While these two states are not members of the EU, they are members of the Nordic Passport Union and in 1999 the Justice and Home Affairs Council concluded an agreement with Norway and Iceland setting out the procedures for their association with the Schengen *acquis* and the measures building upon it being implemented.[15] As a result, in 2001 the Council decided the Schengen *aquis* would apply to the countries of the Nordic Passport Union.[16] The ten Member States that joined the EU in May 2004 had to sign up to the Schengen *acquis* as a condition of joining.[17] Since the UK left the EU in January 2020, the 27 remaining

---

[13] Peers (2000), p. 57.

[14] European Movement: Ireland (2000) 'The fight against crime and drugs in the EU', retrieved from www.europamovement.ie/am [accessed 1 February 2023].

[15] Peers (2000), p. 57.

[16] Europa – Justice and Home Affairs Department (2003) 'EU level cooperation crucial for national forces', retrieved from www.europa.eu.int [accessed 1 February 2023].

[17] Rawlinson (2003), p. 132.

Member States along with Iceland and Norway are active in the Schengen *acquis* and all the relevant policing agencies within these states are permitted to have access to information on the Schengen Information System (SIS). One of the main benefits of access to SIS is in giving those states' policing agencies to ability liaise a lot closer thereby enhancing policing co-operation. With terrorists and criminals involved in organised crime operating the continent of Europe they are no respecters of geographical boundaries, and it matters not to them if a state is a member of the EU. Under the provision of Protocol 2 of the Treaty of Amsterdam it ensured that police co-operation operated within an EU legal framework. However, a potential deficit in transparency and accountability of police co-operation was weakened as any form of redress or accountability was limited to the Justice and Home Affairs Council who made all the decisions. This had issues around transparency and accountability because, consisting of relevant ministers of state among the EU Member States, the Council is not a truly democratic body of the EU and, as it came under the former Third Pillar,[18] it evaded scrutiny by the CJEU and the EU's Parliament. This position changed following the Treaty of Lisbon, which is covered below in the examination of Europol.

5 The EU's Intelligence System: The SIS

The original SIS was a computer network system containing information on wanted persons, stolen objects and vehicles. The system contained six main categories of information:

1. Persons wanted for arrest and extradition (since 1 January 2004 the SIS has included those wanted for transfer under the European Arrest Warrant);
2. Third-country nationals to be refused entry into the Schengen area;
3. Missing persons (both minors and adults) to locate their whereabouts;
4. Witnesses and persons required to appear before the judicial authorities to locate their whereabouts;
5. Persons or vehicles to be put under surveillance for specific checks;
6. Certain categories of objects (e.g. identity documents, vehicles, firearms, bank notes), stolen, misappropriated or lost.[19]

The SIS can be consulted by police, border police, customs officers and partially by authorities responsible for delivering visas and residence permits.[20] The SIS is a compensatory measure that has generally been considered to be the most significant

[18] Following the Treaty of Lisbon 2009 the three Pillars of Union were dispensed with.

[19] Peers (2000), pp. 212–213.

[20] Europa – Justice and Home Affairs Department (2005) 'Free movement of people calls for increased cross-border police co-operation', retrieved from www.europa.eu.int/comm.justice [accessed 2 February 2023].

innovation of the EU's Justice and Home Affairs Commission as it is designed to facilitate quick information exchange between the countries concerned. There were technical difficulties in its initial stages, but these have been overcome, and the SIS now allows national policing agencies access to the most up-to-date information.[21] Member States supply the network with information through national networks (N-SIS) that are connected to a central system (C-SIS) based in Strasbourg.

Following the expansion of the Member States to 27, an updated version of SIS, SIS II, was installed and became operational by the end of 2006.[22] The aim of SIS II is to make the system as flexible a tool as possible by being a hit/no hit system allowing for information exchange with a view to policing the free movement of persons as well as maintaining public security, in particular to assist national authorities in the fight against transnational crime.[23] Only allowing national intelligence agencies to input information on SIS II helps to ensure consistency of information and policy procedures, thereby reducing inconsistencies that arise due to cultural traditions both at national and international level.[24]

The existence and running of SIS II raise some interesting issues, most of which can be covered under one topic for examination consisting of two key themes. First, establishing what information is stored on the system. Although the six categories above have been expanded in SIS II, the question goes deeper than that; it centres upon the quality and accuracy of the information that is stored on the SIS database. Second, establishing the criteria for access to that information. The database is accessed not solely by policing agencies, but also on a freedom of information request by citizens in the EU to check that information stored on them is accurate.[25] On this second point, Gill highlights the lack of transparency and accountability of the information stored on the SIS database, which represents a part of the democratic deficit in the EU.[26] In 2002, ten million people were listed on the SIS database and the majority of those entries were related to forged or stolen passports or identity cards. In addition to this, 1.3 million convicted and suspected criminals were flagged on the SIS alert system.[27] The reason there was so much information related to passports stored on the SIS database is that the system's roots were in immigration and border control as opposed to actual criminal activity. As a result, the original focus of the SIS was on assisting border control agencies in dealing with refugees

[21] Genson (1998), p. 137.

[22] Europa – Justice and Home Affairs Department (2003) 'The Schengen *acquis* and its integration into the Union', retrieved from www.europa.eu.int/comm.justice [accessed 2 February 2023].

[23] Justice and Home Affairs Bulletin, JHA 9845/03.

[24] Sheptycki (2004), p. 325.

[25] Home Office (UK) (2015) 'Second generation Schengen Information System (SIS II): general information', 13 April, retrieved from https://www.gov.uk/government/uploads/system/uploads/attachment_data/file/421540/SISII_General_Information_document.pdf [accessed 2 February 2023].

[26] Gill (2000), p. 53.

[27] Lewis (2005), p. 106.

and asylum seekers.[28] It was only following the Tampere Conference in 1999 on Justice and Home Affairs matters that it was realised the SIS could also be used to assist policing agencies in investigating criminal matters. SIS II has remedied some of these issues. Not all of the EU's Member States were connected to SIS II in 2006. For example, when it was an EU Member State, it was only in April 2015 that the UK connected to the system, and as the UK maintained control of its borders outside the Schengen Treaty, it only connected to the SIS in relation to law enforcement aspects.[29] What SIS II can do is enable EU Member States to share and receive law enforcement alerts in real time for:

1. Persons wanted for arrest for extradition purposes, for which a warrant has been issued;
2. Missing persons who need to be placed under police protection or in a place of safety, including minors and adults not at risk;
3. Witnesses, absconders or subjects of criminal judgments to appear before the judicial authorities;
4. People or vehicles requiring specific checks or discreet surveillance;
5. Objects that are misappropriated, lost or stolen and which may be sought for the purposes of seizure or for use as evidence (e.g. firearms, passports, etc.).[30]

SIS II is not a system that grants access to read or input information to all law enforcement officers in the EU and its Member States; it only allows access to identified staff. Currently the UK and the EU have stated their commitment to a security partnership comprising of law enforcement and judicial co-operation as a 'second tier membership' to Europol, similar to the relationship with the US and Denmark, which is observer status on Europol's management board and have indirect access to databases on a case-by-case basis.[31] In comparison to the access the UK had to databases like SIS II this system is fettering the UK policing agencies to police terrorist activity and organised crime effectively. This point was not lost on the British media who reported that Brexit resulted in the UK losing access to SISII resulting in the UK losing access to approximately 40,000 alerts regarding investigations in other European countries.[32] Pearson raised a valid point regarding the UK's lack of access to SISII. He points out that with the UK no longer having access it has also adversely lessened the capability fo EU Member States' policing agencies to effectively police terorist and organised crime groups and appreciate the wider

[28] Lodge (2002), p. 111.

[29] Home Office (UK) (2015) 'Second generation Schengen Information System (SIS II): general information', 13 April, retrieved from https://www.gov.uk/government/uploads/system/uploads/attachment_data/file/421540/SISII_General_Information_document.pdf [accessed 2 February 2023], paragraph 1.

[30] *Ibid*, paragraph 2.

[31] Hoxhaj (2020), retrieved from https://www.globalpolicyjournal.com/blog/02/07/2020/uks-policy-response-serious-and-organised-crime-after-brexit [accessed 6 July 2022].

[32] BBC (2021), retrieved from https://www.bbc.com/news/uk-politics-56529359 [accessed 20 September 2023].

European criminal risk.[33] Prior to Brexit the UK was one of the biggest contributors to SISII and other EU criminal justice cooperation mechanisms and EU security cooperation, which, no denied to the UK the result is the 27 EU Member State policing agencies and Europol are missing vital intelligence.[34] Pearson rightly stresses the safety and security of *all* European citizens is an issue of greater importance than political dogma adding that:

> ...police officers in both the UK and the EU should be allowed to do what they do best – work collaboratively to keep people safe from those that would cause them harm.[35]

6 Intelligence Exchange Between the EU AND Third Countries: The Role of Europol

Due to the international terrorist threat and organised crime, it is important that states' intelligence and policing agencies work in co-operation to counter the threat. One way this is achieved is in international terrorism intelligence exchange between the respective states' agencies. Since the Al Qaeda attack on the US (9/11), the international sharing of intelligence between counter-terrorism policing and states' intelligence agencies at international level has increased. As regards intelligence sharing between policing agencies, third countries this has invariably been carried out through Europol. Post-Brexit, now being a third country, the UK will have to negotiate separate agreements with EU Member States and this should include Europol with a mandate to collect, store, process, analyse and exchange intelligence.[36] Any arrangement with the UK should come under the 2009 Treaty of Lisbon (ToL) which states that Europol's mission:

> is to support and strengthen action by Member States police authorities and other law enforcement agencies through mutual co-operation in preventing serious crime affecting two or more Member States, *terrorism* and forms of crime which affect interest by EU Policy.[37] (my emphasis)

Following 9/11 the EU prioritised the fight against terrorism and within 10 days of the attack the EU's Justice and Home Affairs Commission adopted an action plan in the fight against terrorism resulting in acceleration in the development and implementation of measures to counter the threat posed by international terrorism.[38] The agreement between Europol and the US signed in 2001 is the most advanced of its

[33] Pearson (2021), retrieved from https://ukandeu.ac.uk/policing-capabilities-lessened-after-brexit/ [accessed 20 September 2023].

[34] Mitsilegas and Guild (2023), p. 2528.

[35] Pearson (2021), retrieved from https://ukandeu.ac.uk/policing-capabilities-lessened-after-brexit/ [accessed 20 September 2023].

[36] Berenskoetter (2012), p. 41.

[37] Treaty of Lisbon Article 88.

[38] Joffe (2008), p. 158; Kaunert (2010), p. 653.

kind as it authorises both parties to sign international agreements. Intelligence is shared between the EU's Member States' policing agencies and specified US agencies,[39] including the FBI, the US Secret Service, the Drug Enforcement Administration and the US Postal Inspection.[40] Part 3 of the Trade and Cooperation Agreement signed between the UK and the EU in 2020 does enable UK liaison officers to be present in Europol's headquarters to facilitate cross-border cooperation.[41] Due to the close geographical proximity and the fact that criminals involved in serious organised crime and terrorism between the two, it is imperative that a similar agreement is made between the UK and the EU thereby enabling Europol to share intelligence with specified UK agencies such as the National Crime Agency regarding organised crime and the UK's Counter-Terrorism Units. This will enhance the safety of citizens and the security of the UK and EU Member States.

7 Bilateral Agreements Undermining Europol

Coolsaet observes that the involvement of more actors in the counter-terrorism endeavour at Europol has 'reignited the traditional reluctance of Member States to transfer confidential information to the organisation'.[42] Added to this, what is hindering Europol's effective functioning as Europe's primary law enforcement agency is Member States' national preference for bilateral relationships and the parallel participation in informal, practitioner-led networks.[43] The effect of this is to limit the capability of Europol's co-operation, and that is not just between EU Member States but also in Europol's co-operation agreements with third countries. As Kaunert and Leonard point out, while Europol has described its co-operation with the US counter-terrorism agencies as excellent, '[Europol] has acknowledged that its cooperation with the FBI has been more limited so far, because the FBI has been encouraged to prioritise its bilateral liaison network of legal attachés in the embassies of EU Member States'.[44]

The establishment of bilateral agreements and the lack of full co-operation between EU Member States and Europol can be traced over the last decade, even up to the present day. Examples of these close international relations on terrorism-related issues include the UK with Pakistan and France with Algeria as well as Germany allowing US prosecutors and FBI agents to carry out investigations with a

---

[39] Kaunert (2010), p. 664.

[40] Den Boar et al. (2008), p. 10.

[41] UK Parliament (2022) 'Beyond Brexit: policing, law enforcement and security', House of Lords Library, 7 February, retrieved from https://lordslibrary.parliament.uk/beyond-brexit-policing-law-enforcement-and-security/ [accessed 20 October 2023].

[42] Coolsaet (2010), p. 864.

[43] *Ibid*, p. 864.

[44] Bassong (2014), p. 71.

German federal prosecutor.[45] Perhaps the prime example of how until 2010 EU Member States undermined Europol is through the signing of multilateral agreements outside the EU. The best two examples are seen with the 2003 G6 Agreement and the 2005 Prum Treaty. The G6 was established in May 2003 and consists of the six largest EU Member States (UK, France, Germany, Italy, Spain and Poland, who joined in 2006) who out of frustration with the EU's bureaucratic Justice and Home Affairs structures set up the G6 group to discuss issues of internal security, including terrorism.[46] The G6 was not simply a talking shop. In 2005 it agreed to create a common database of individuals suspected of connections to terrorist organisations, and in March 2006 it agreed to create multilateral police support teams in cases of serious terrorist attacks, as well as joint investigation teams to investigate terrorism and organised crime.[47] In May 2005 seven EU Member States, the Netherlands, Belgium, Luxembourg, Austria, France, Germany and Spain, signed the Prum Treaty to step up cross-border co-operation, particularly in combating terrorism, and the Treaty includes an exchange system of DNA profiles, fingerprints, vehicle registration data and data on aircraft security.[48] As a result, Europol's work has been seen as merely complementing a Member State's intelligence services' own analysis and the multilateral co-operation established with other services.[49]

However, there have been positives in Europol developing agreements with third countries in the European Neighbourhood Policy (ENP), as seen in the Middle East and the Maghreb, resulting in agreements between Europol and Morocco, Jordan, Algeria[50] and Israel that have built up strong co-operation in the area of counter-terrorism.[51] Even with these Southern Mediterranean ENPs, there are obstacles to developing co-operation on terrorism issues. There are two key reasons for this. One reason Western states' involvement in conflicts in the Middle East and North Africa which included EU Member States, such as the invasion of Iraq in 2003 by the US and the UK military. Second, many of the Southern Mediterranean ENP states are not democratically elected governments and those with authoritarian tendencies are more likely to try to enhance their popularity by not complying with Western requests for co-operation.[52] In relation to international terrorism, while the EU has some responsibilities for strategic decision-making, it does not play a significant operational or practical role in the fight against terrorism.[53] This could help to explain why there is a reluctance to share fully terrorism-related intelligence both amongst EU Member States and between the EU and third countries.

---

[45] Keohane (2008), pp. 128–129.

[46] Bures (2008), p. 506; Argomaniz (2012), pp. 51–52.

[47] Den Boar et al. (2008), p. 117.

[48] Bures (2008), pp. 506–507; Argomaniz (2012), p. 52.

[49] Muller-Wille (2008), p. 58.

[50] Joffe (2008), p. 164; Kaunert (2010), p. 660.

[51] Kaunert (2010), p. 661.

[52] Den Boar et al. (2008), p. 104.

[53] Muller-Wille (2008), p. 69.

8 Accountability of Europol and the Rule of Law

Emanating from the changes to the legal instruments governing Europol, there is a reason to be optimistic about future developments in the role of Europol and terrorism-related intelligence exchange. These changes regarding Europol's role are important for two reasons that centre on accountability. First, through the hierarchy of agencies associated with the EU's Justice and Home Affairs Commission, Europol has a vertical legal legitimacy that is identifiable when compared with the horizontal role of agencies made under the multilateral agreements.[54] This is important regarding accountability as the Treaty of Lisbon provisions brings Europol under the jurisdiction and scrutiny of the CJEU. The second reason why this development is important concerns the actions of Europol within the legal principle of the rule of law. As Murphy states, it is important that Europol's actions are scrutinised under the rule of law: 'The constitutive role of the rule of law relates to the means by which the community is governed: through law. The law regulates social relationships and therefore effective enforcement of the law is constitutive for the rule of law.'[55] This form of accountability would satisfy the requirement that intelligence gathering and exchange is operating within a legal framework balanced by the law governing rights to privacy and data protection.

In its desire to ensure that it can be an effective international actor, the EU's counter-terrorism measures in particular have led to an increased divergence of Member States' law, which can be achieved by replacing the Framework Decisions with Regulations and Directives that are more effective.[56] Supporting this and the Treaty of Lisbon, the Stockholm Programme[57] mapped out the 2010–2014 plan to provide an open and secure Europe, serving and protecting citizens.[58] This programme stressed that during this period EU criminal law and counter-terrorism measures would be pursued on the basis of the constitutional arrangements brought into place by the Treaty of Lisbon. This included co-operation in the collection, storage, processing, analysis and exchange of relevant information between EU Member State competent authorities.[59] The rationale for this, as Murphy's study recognised, was that as the volume of EU criminal law and counter-terrorism measures would increase rapidly during this period, stricter adherence to mutual co-operation between the Members States and Europol would be required, as well as enhancing the reputation and reliability of Europol's role as an international actor

[54] Murphy (2012), p. 106.

[55] *Ibid*, p. 35.

[56] *Ibid*, p. 255.

[57] 2010/C 115/01.

[58] The UK's House of Lords is already calling for input to the JHA's next five year agenda that is likely to be the 'Rome Plan', retrieved from http://www.parliament.uk/business/committees/committees-a-z/lords-select/eu-home-affairs-sub-committee-f-/news/rome-cfe [accessed 3 September 2022].

[59] Treaty of Lisbon, article 87.2(a).

with Member States and third countries.[60] The situation has not changed since the end of the Stockholm period, especially in relation to counter-terrorism. A number of EU Member States have suffered terrorist attacks where the period between 2015–2017 saw intensive Islamist inspired attacks that included the Paris marauding firearms attack in November 2015 where 130 people were killed,[61] Nice lorry attack killing 86 people,[62] to the attacks in Westminster, UK, in March 2017,[63] Manchester Arena bombing May 2017,[64] London Bridge/Borough Market attack in June 2017 (where 36 people were killed in total) and Stockholm, Sweden, in April 2017, where four people were killed.[65] The attacks carried out in this period resulted in Member State governments and the EU to review their counter-terrorism measures. This led to the Justice and Home Affairs Commission in 2017, findings that the increase in counter-terrorism measures are more rapid than ever.[66] It was realised that the way forward to deal with an international terrorist threat One way forward would be for the police community to move from the traditional position of regarding intelligence exchange on the 'need to know' paradigm to a 'need to share' paradigm.[67] As Occhipinti points out, the advantage of moving to a sharing culture regarding terrorism intelligence is that intelligence data is unlocked from a fragmented technology infrastructure allowing it to be accessed by multiple intelligence agencies. This makes intelligence readily discoverable and accessible from the earliest point at which an analyst can add value.[68] With the main aim of any counter-terrorism activity being to prevent acts of terrorism occurring, thereby protecting the right to life of citizens, and with the threat of international terrorism increasing, this is the most logical way forward to counter terrorism. We have seen a development in international terrorist activity from the Islamist groups like Al Qaeda and Islamic State inspiring many attacks in Europe and they are not the only ones. Since 2016

---

[60] Murphy (2012), p. 241.

[61] BBC News (2015) 'Paris attacks: What happened on the night', BBC News Website 9 December 2015, retrieved from https://www.bbc.co.uk/news/world-europe-34818994 [accessed 27 February 2023].

[62] BBC News (2016) 'Nice attack: What we know about the Bastille Day killings', BBC News Website, 19 August 2016, retrieved from https://www.bbc.co.uk/news/world-europe-36801671 [accessed 27 February 2023].

[63] Dodd and Ross (2017), retrieved from https://www.theguardian.com/uk-news/2017/mar/24/nine-custody-westminster-terrorist-attack-police-arrests [accessed 28 November 2022].

[64] BBC News (2018) 'Manchester Arena attack: Bomb injured more than 800', BBC News Website, 16 May 2018, retrieved from https://www.bbc.co.uk/news/uk-england-manchester-44129386 [accessed 27 February 2023].

[65] BBC News (2017) 'Stockholm attack: arrested man was lorry driver, police say', BBC News Website 8 April 2017, retrieved from http://www.bbc.co.uk/news/world-europe-39536174 [accessed 9th April 2017].

[66] Council of the European Union (2017) 'Outcome of the Council Meeting Justice and Home Affairs: 3258th Meeting' 7688/17 retrieved from www.consilium.europa.eu/en/meetings/jha/2017/03/st07688_en17_pdf [accessed 8 January 2023].

[67] Bures (2013), p. 70.

[68] Occhipinti (2013), p. 152.

there has been a steady increase in the internationalisation of extreme far-right groups (neo-Nazis). An example of this is the US extreme far-right group, Atomwaffen has encouraged an internationalisation of neo-Nazis with encouragement in the formation of the group Sonnenkreig Division in the UK and Feurekreig Division in continental Europe. This led to Sonnenkreig Division being proscribed in the UK as a terorist organisation in 2020[69] and Atomwaffen proscribed in April 2021.[70] This internalisation of the extreme far-right has inspired several attacks in Europe that includes the assassination of politicians as seen in the murder of UK MP, Jo Cox in June 2016[71] in Germany with the murder of leading German politician Walter Lubcke in June 2019 by male connected to the group Combat 18 Deutschland.[72] Another concern of policing cooperation post-Brexit is between Northern Ireland and the Republic of Ireland where the Police Service of Northern Ireland and An Garda Siochana have cooperated for many years dealing with both terrorist groups (mainly dissident republican groups like the New IRA and the INLA) and organised crime groups on the island of Ireland. The concern of the Northern Ireland Affairs Committee in the House of Commons is there now exists a cumbersome extradition processes and possible intelligence blind spots for criminals and terrorists to exploit.[73]

As stressed in this chapter, terrorists do not recognise geographical or political borders, all European states are vulnerable to terrorist attacks. This is equally applied to criminals involved in serious organised crime, in particular the trafficking offences. While Brexit has implications in relation to trade and freedom of movement of goods and services, when it comes to terrorism and serious organised crime, it should never have become a bargaining chip during Brexit negotiations. The UK should be treated as partners with the EU in preventing international inspired terrorist attacks and serious organised crime like the non-EU members of the Nordic Passport Scheme such as Norway and Iceland, and Switzerland as terrorism and organised crime is not about finance and tariffs, it is about the safety of *all* European citizens, not just EU member States' citizens. In doing so, as terrorism and serious organised crime investigations heavily involve the surveillance of electronic

[69] 'Neo-Nazi Group Sonnenkreig Division Proscribed', Counter-Terrorism Unit website, 28 February 2020 https://www.counterterrorism.police.uk/neo-nazi-group-sonnenkrieg-division-proscribed-counter-terrorism-police/ (accessed 21 February 2023).

[70] 'White supremacist group, Atomwaffen Division, banned in the UK', Home Office website, 23 April 2021, retrieved from https://www.gov.uk/government/news/white-supremacist-group-atomwaffen-division-banned-in-the-uk [accessed 21 February 2023].

[71] BBC News (2016) 'Jo Cox: Man jailed for 'terrorist' murder of MP', BBC News Website, 23 November 2016, retrieved from https://www.bbc.co.uk/news/uk-38079594 [accessed 27 February 2023].

[72] Deutsche Welle (2020), retrieved from https://www.dw.com/en/raids-in-6-states-as-germany-bans-combat-18-neo-nazi-group/a-52116504 [accessed 21 May 2020].

[73] House of Commons Northern Ireland Affairs Committee (2021) 'Cross-border co-operation on policing, security and criminal justice after Brexit', HC 766, 28 April 2021, retrieved from https://committees.parliament.uk/publications/5650/documents/55754/default/ [accessed 20 September 2023].

communications, it is important to assess if the UK can meet EU law on data protection and the right to privacy.

9 EU Data Protection and Right to Privacy Laws

Many states have some form of legislative protection of citizens' personal data and rights to privacy. However, there is a wide variation in the stringency they apply to protecting those rights and prohibiting state agencies from interfering with them. As covered later in this chapter, the US has little legislative protection of those rights, with the EU having the most stringent. As EU law must be followed by its current 27 Member States, one could argue that globally its legislation provides strong protection and strictly controls the circumstances in which state agencies can legally interfere with those rights. This section will provide an overview of the EU's legislation which is followed by two recent important cases from the CJEU where its decisions had far-reaching consequences in regard to international relations with third countries.

In relation to data protection, article 16 of the Treaty on the Functioning of the EU (TFEU) states that everyone has the right to the protection of personal data concerning them. Under article 16 TFEU, the European Parliament and the Council must act in accordance with ordinary legislative procedure, laying down rules protecting the processing of personal data by Union institutions, bodies, offices and agencies when carrying out activities that fall within the scope of EU law. This legal obligation is also present in article 39 in the Treaty of Union. Underpinning these articles' provisions is the EU's Charter of Fundamental Rights and Freedoms (CFRF). Since the Treaty of Lisbon 2009 came into force, the CFRF has become a legally binding document ensuring all EU institutions and Member States apply the Charter's principles when implementing EU law. Article 8 CFRF states that everyone has the right to the protection of personal data concerning them. When EU institutions or Member States access the data, it 'must be processed fairly for specified purposes on the basis of consent of the person concerned or some other legitimate basis laid down by law'.[74]This is in addition to the respect they must have for a person's right to their private and family life, home and communication.[75]

The 1995 Data Protection Directive[76] states that personal data can only be collected for specified, explicit and legitimate purposes and must not be processed in a way incompatible with these purposes.[77] Member States can only derogate from the 1995 Directive where it is necessary to safeguard national security, defence, public security and the prevention, investigation, detection or prosecution of

---

[74] Article 8(2) CFRF.

[75] Article 7 CFRF.

[76] European Parliament and Council Directive 95/46/EC.

[77] *Ibid*, article 6(1)(b).

criminal offences.[78] The Directive on the protection of personal data processed for the purposes of preventing, investigating, detecting or prosecuting criminal matters[79] came into force on 5 May 2016 for Member States to transpose into their national law by 6 May 2018.[80] In the preamble it is recognised that rapid technological developments and globalisation have brought new challenges for the protection of personal data where the scale of collecting and sharing this data has increased significantly and this directly applies to agencies involved in the prevention, investigation or detection of criminal offences.[81] The Directive states that in the processing of personal data these agencies can only collect it for specific, explicit and legitimate purposes,[82] and to be lawful the processing of personal data has to be necessary in the prevention, investigation or detection of criminal offences.[83] The Directive is also very clear that when processing personal data fundamental rights and freedoms must be protected, especially the right of the protection of personal data.[84] This requirement follows the CJEU decision in *Google Spain SL, Google Inc. v Agencia Espanola de Proteccion de Datos (APED)*,[85] which held that data retention without any link to risk or suspicion is not proportionate. Important in protecting personal data are the safeguards present in any legislative provision. In the 2016 Directive this includes:

1. Member States and the EU itself shall create a 'controller'[86] who have a number of obligations under the Directive to oversee the processing and exchange of personal data. This includes ensuring the requests by relevant agencies for personal data are proportionate to the purposes of processing the data,[87] and integrating the necessary safeguards in to the processing of the data[88];
2. Member States shall provide a data protection officer[89] whose roles include advising the controller and employees from agencies carrying out the processing of personal data and monitoring compliance with the Directive[90];

[78] *Ibid*, article 13(1).
[79] Directive 2016/680.
[80] European Commission (2016) 'Reform of EU data protection rules', retrieved from http://ec.europa.eu/justice/data-protection/reform/index_en.htm [accessed 19 January 2023].
[81] Directive 2016/680, paragraph 2.
[82] *Ibid*, paragraph 29.
[83] *Ibid*, paragraph 35.
[84] *Ibid*, article 1(2).
[85] (2014) Case C-131/12.
[86] Directive 2016/680, article 3(8).
[87] *Ibid*, article 19.
[88] *Ibid*, article 20.
[89] *Ibid*, article 32.
[90] *Ibid*, article 34.

3. Where the data subject conspires their personal protection rights have been infringed, Member States must ensure data subjects have the right to an effective judicial remedy (which in practice will be through a judicial review process).[91]

The transfer of personal data to a third country has to meet the requirements of being necessary and proportionate for the purposes of preventing, investigating or detecting criminal offences,[92] and it is therefore of paramount importance that the third country to whom the data is transferred has an adequate level of protection of personal data.[93] If there is an absence of adequate protection in a third country, transfer of personal data under the 2016 Directive can only occur where such conditions are implemented under a negotiated legally binding instrument.[94] With the 2016 Directive having to be introduced by EU Member States by May 2018, the UK has not introduced it into its domestic legislation. This is unfortunate, as by doing so it would help to guarantee that intelligence generated by UK agencies has sufficient safeguards in relation to personal data protection. This would ease intelligence exchange with EU Member States post-Brexit as the EU would be satisfied there was an adequate provision for data protection in the UK that would satisfy the statutory provisions contained within EU law.

10 Intelligence and Evidence Gathering Via Surveillance of Communications

In the UK intelligence and evidence gathering during police investigations is acquired through various methods ranging from the traditional static and mobile surveillance, which is governed as directed surveillance and intrusive surveillance under sections 27 and 32 of the Regulation of Investigatory Powers Act 2000 (RIPA) respectively. Another method is in the use of covert human intelligence sources, commonly referred to as informants, which is governed by section 29 RIPA. UK law in the use of informants is changed with the introduction of the Covert Human Intelligence Sources (Criminal Conduct) Act 2021. The Home Office stated that the Act would not be providing a new capability, rather it would provide a clear legal basis for a longstanding tactic that is vital for national security and the prevention and detection of crime.[95] The Home Office see the participation in criminal conduct by informants as essential by allowing them to work their way into the heart of

[91] *Ibid*, article 54.

[92] *Ibid*, article 35.

[93] *Ibid*, article 36(1).

[94] *Ibid*, article37.

[95] Home Office Factsheet (2020) Covert Human Intelligence Sources (criminal Conduct) Bill, retrieved from https://assets.publishing.service.gov.uk/government/uploads/system/uploads/attachment_data/file/920714/CHIS_Factsheet.pdf [accessed 6th July 2021].

groups that would cause harm to the public, especially informants involved in terrorist organisations.[96]

Introducing section 29B RIPA, it allows for the Secretary of State to authorise an informant to carry out criminal conduct. In most cases where informants are linked to terrorist activity handled by the police and the Security Service it will be the Home Secretary and if it is the Secret Intelligence Service (MI6), it will be the Foreign Secretary. The authorisation tasking the informant to carry out criminal conduct must be granted at the same time as an authorisation is granted to handle the informer under section 29 RIPA.[97] Compared to the grounds for authorising the handling of an informant under section 29, the grounds for an authority tasking an informant to carry out criminal conduct is limited and can only be authorised where it is necessary:

1. When it is in the interests of national security;
2. For preventing or detecting crime or of preventing disorder; or
3. When it is in the interests of the economic well-being of the UK.[98]

The conditions for this authority are that, what is sought to be achieved cannot be achieved by conduct that would not constitute a crime[99] and that the criminal conduct that will be carried out is necessary and proportionate to what is being sought to be achieved.[100] The authorised criminal conduct is conduct that is carried out in connection with the informant that is specified in the authorisation, that is carried out for the purpose of or in connection with the investigation or operation specified or described in the authorisation.[101] Among the agencies that can apply for a criminal conduct authorisation, includes:

1. Police;
2. National Crime Agency;
3. Serious Fraud Office;
4. Intelligence services;
5. Armed forces;
6. HM Revenue and Customs[102]

When reading the limitations when the authorisations are granted governing the use of these powers, one can see the influence of the European Convention on Human Rights (ECHR) as serious consideration is given to various human rights when granting authorities to the police.

---

[96] *Ibid.*

[97] Section 29B(3) RIPA.

[98] Section 29B(5) RIPA.

[99] Section 29B(6) RIPA.

[100] Section 29B(4) RIPA.

[101] Section29B(8) RIPA.

[102] Section 4, Covert Human Intelligence Sources (Criminal Conduct) Act 2021.

Similar consideration is seen in the UK's Investigatory Powers Act 2016 that grants the police and security services (and where applicable the military, Her Majesty's Revenue and Customs, and Border Agency) powers to obtain targeted interceptions warrants, warrants to obtain and retain communications data, bulk interception warrants and bulk interference warrants (lawful hacking of communications devices). Globally the use of electronic communications in society has grown exponentially, more so during the COVID-19 pandemic with the expansion in the use of online meetings facilities such as Zoom and Microsoft Teams, shopping and banking online. It is not just legitimate use of the various forms of communication that has expanded, both terrorists and organised crime gangs use and exploit electronic communications, especially in the use of deeply encrypted forms of communication. As such, powers granting policing agencies (including the security services) access to unlawful use of electronic communications is necessary, provided those powers are balanced with consideration of the protection of human rights such as rights to privacy and data protection. In the 2016 Act again we see the ECHR influence in the granting of these intrusive powers provided they are balanced with protecting relevant human rights. The authorities to interfere with these rights are only granted on the grounds of necessity, that is where it is under an act prescribed by law and necessary in a democratic society under certain grounds. These grounds include:

1. the interests of national security (this ground is certainly relevant to terrorism investigations);
2. the prevention of disorder or crime;
3. public safety; and
4. the protection of rights and freedom of others.

In relation to terrorist investigations the protection of the rights and freedom of others will include the right to life (article 2 ECHR), hence why intrusive investigative powers into the lives of citizens are necessary to prevent terorist attacks from taking place. It is not only ECHR provisions we see in relation to the protection of rights, but there is also consideration of the EU's CFRF and two important CJEU case decisions influenced the drafting of the statutes. The relevance of this is with the UK being a third country, its law must be adequate in relation to the protection of human rights, as legislation like the Investigatory Powers Act was introduced while an EU member state, this Act is most likely to meet that criterion. Whether this also applies to Covert Human Intelligence Sources (Criminal Conduct) Act 2021 consideration has to be given to the following CJEU cases.

11 *Digital Rights* and *Tele 2* Cases

Digital Rights: The 2006 Directive on Retention and Access to Communications Data and the Data Retention and Investigatory Powers Act 2015.

In *Digital Rights*[103] the CJEU examined the now repealed Directive 2006/24/EC that laid down an obligation on publicly available electronic communications services or public communications networks to retain certain data generated or processed by them. As the Directive allowed EU member states' intelligence and policing agencies to collect bulk data, the CJEU examined the acceptable limits of mass surveillance and the function of data protection in relation to compatibility with articles 7 (respect for private and family life) and 8 (protection of personal data) CFRF. The CJEU declared that the 2006 Directive was invalid on two important legal issues saying to ensure personal data is protected:

1. EU legislation must lay down *clear* and *precise* rules governing the scope and application of the measure in question;
2. Minimum safeguards are imposed to provide sufficient guarantees effectively protecting personal data against the risk of abuse and against unlawful access and use.

Under the 2006 Directive member states could retain bulk and personal data only when it was necessary and proportionate to do so. The CJEU held this phrase lacked the required specificity to allow lawful interference with that data and did not place a high enough level of protection of personal data, nor did it ensure there was an irreversible destruction of the data at the end of the data retention period. In *Digital Rights* the CJEU acknowledged data retention is an important strand in terrorism and serious crime investigations to ensure public safety and stated these specific grounds could be a justification. Article 52 allows for limitations in the exercise of CFRF rights where, subject to proportionality, limitations can only be made where they are necessary and genuinely meet the objectives of general interest recognised by the EU. The CJEU held the retention of telecommunications data to allow competent national authorities to have possible access must satisfy an objective of general interest under article 52 CFRF but added in doing so it is necessary to verify the proportionality of the interference found to exist.

It was the latter point on proportionality where the 2006 Directive failed as the CJEU found it was too broad as to the conditions and requirements as to why telecommunications data had to be retained and regarding access to it by competent authorities. As the retention included persons' personal data who had not nor were they suspected of being involved in any form of criminal or terrorist activity, the retention of the data was being carried out in an indiscriminate manner. The requirement under member state law that telecommunications data be retained by communications and internet service providers, it is essential the requirement to do so has to be for specific reasons, that includes defining what is meant by serious crime and disclosure/access to the data has to be necessary to assist in achieving the aim of an investigation and it must be proportionate. As a result of *Digital Rights* many member states repealed their domestic legislation governing the surveillance of electronic communications and retention of telecommunications data. This

[103] [2014] 3 WLR 1607.

included the UK. It repealed the provisions in RIPA and introduced the Data Retention and Investigatory Powers Act 2015 (DRIPA) that was drafted with consideration to the *Digital Rights* decision, but in *R (on the application of Davis and others) v Secretary of State for the Home Department and others*[104] the UK's High Court held that DRIPA did not comply with the decision in *Digital Rights*. The Court held that DRIPA did not lay down clear and precise rules regarding the access and use of communications data, and, on safeguards, the Court held that judicial approval was important to ensure surveillance authorities are not abused in order to protect citizens' rights.

12 *Tele2* and Directive on Privacy and Electronic Communication 2002/58/EC

In *Tele2 Sverige AB,* now referred to as *Tele2*[105] the CJEU were requested to provide a primary ruling on the interpretation of Article 15(1) Electronic Communications Directive 2002/58/EC concerning e-privacy and electronic communications and its compatibility with Member States' national law regarding the retention and access to telecommunications data. In the full title of the case, it included the *Davis* case heard at the High Court mentioned above that was referred to the CJEU. In *Tele 2* the CJEU examined citizens' rights under the CFRF, mainly articles 7, 8, and 52.

The aim of the 2002 e-Privacy Directive is to protect fundamental rights and freedom in relation to privacy when processing personal data in electronic communications, thereby ensuring the free movement of that data and electronic communications and services in the EU, especially in relation to the protection of subscribers to communications companies' services because in EU law subscribers are legal persons. The Directive is clear that its provisions shall not apply to activities concerning:

> ...public security, defence, State security (including the economic well-being of the State when the activities relate to State security matters) and the activities of the State in areas of criminal law.

Article 5 states that member states must ensure the confidentiality of communications, including related traffic data by means of a public communications network and publicly available electronic services through their national legislation. This includes the prohibition of listening, tapping, storage or other kinds of interception or surveillance of communications and related traffic data by persons other than the users without the consent of the users concerned. Article 5 contains an exception to this where such activity is legally authorised in accordance with article 15(1) of the

[104] [2015] EWHC 2092 (Admin).

[105] [2016] All ER (D) 107.

2002 Directive. Article 15(1) allows member states to legislate to restrict the privacy, rights and freedoms related to electronic communications when it is a:

> …necessary, appropriate and proportionate measure within a democratic society to safeguard national security (i.e. state security), defence, public security, and the prevention, investigation, detection and prosecution of criminal offences…

In *Tele2* the CJEU pointed out these restrictions laid down in member states' national legislation to privacy only apply only if the member states adopt and meet all the conditions laid down in the Directive. Although recognising that fighting serious crime, especially organised crime and terrorism, depends to a great extent on the use of modern investigation techniques where telecommunications data evidence can be effective, the CJEU added:

> …such an objective of general interest, however fundamental it may be, cannot in itself justify that national legislation providing for the general interest and indiscriminate retention of all traffic and location data should be considered to be necessary for the purposes of that fight.

While acknowledging the importance the role the retention of telecommunications data plays in the fight against serious crime, the CJEU's guidance in relation to this matter is it should be read in light of articles 7, 8, 11 and 52(1) CFRF by adopting legislation permitting as a preventative measure targeted retention of traffic and location data for the purpose of fighting crime. The important points in article 52(1) that must be considered are:

1. The limitation of the exercise of rights and freedoms must be provided for by law; and
2. The limitations must be subject to the principles of proportionality; and
3. The limitations must be necessary; and
4. The limitations must meet the general interest recognised by the EU.

The CJEU added the retention of the data must be limited to the categories for data to be retained, the means of communication affected, the persons concerned, and the retention period adopted, with all limitations being strictly necessary. Regarding UK legislation the Investigatory Powers Act 2016 is likely to be compatible with EU law. While founded on ECHR principles, applying these cases to the Covert Human Intelligence Sources (Criminal Conduct) Act 2021 it is likely the CJEU would like to see increased safeguards in place, although it should recognise the general interest under article 52(1) CFRF. However, while the UK is a party to the ECHR this should ensure there is a degree of cooperation between UK and the EU Member States policing agencies echoed by the CJEU that held the importance of the UK being party to the ECHR for post-Brexit cooperation.[106] The danger is should the UK withdraw from the ECHR, if not followed by a legislative substitute, be potentially considered as a deficiency big enough to trigger a suspension in cooperation.[107]

---

[106] *Minister for Justice and Equality v RO* (2018) Case C-327/18 PPU, ECLI:EU:C:2018:73.

[107] Mitsilegas and Guild (2023), p. 2533.

13 The Current Operational Situation Between the UK and the EU

While an EU member state, UK policing agencies had access to EU's policing agency Europol, including its European Counter Terrorism Centre (ECTC) that focuses on:

1. Providing operational support upon a request from an EU member state for investigations;
2. Tackling foreign fighters;
3. Sharing intelligence and expertise on terrorism financing;
4. Dealing with terrorist propaganda and extremism;
5. Dealing with illegal arms trafficking;
6. International co-operation among counter-terrorism authorities.

The UK's loss of direct access to the ECTC, while frustrating in having to have access as a third country, due to the UK's Joint Terrorism Analysis Centre (JTAC), this does not mean the UK suffered a major loss in its ability to investigate and counter terrorist activity. Established in 2003 and based at MI5's headquarters at Thames House (although not part of MI5), JTAC analyses and assess all intelligence relating to terrorist activity. It brings together counter-terrorism expertise from the police, the security services and governmental departments and agencies so information is analysed and processed in a shared basis to assess the nature and extent of the terrorist threat to the UK. Using this system, between 2017–2020 UK counter-terrorism agencies foiled 25 terrorism plots in the UK and this included passing on intelligence that foiled four terrorist plots in other EU member states in 2018. Although the UK would now come under working with the ECTC under international co-operation, this is not the same as being part of it, especially in relation to immediacy in intelligence sharing and support.

The UK's loss of access to the Schengen Information System II is frustrating as it allows Member States' policing agencies to:

1. Share biometric information such as DNA, facial images and fingerprints;
2. Share information on persons and objects involved in terrorism related activities;
3. Share information related to organised crime.

Perhaps one of the biggest losses of the UK becoming a 'third country' post-Brexit is losing access to the European Arrest Warrant. The EAW is a rapid form of extradition that takes on average between 14 to 17 days compared to the average of just over a year with traditional extradition treaties. The UK was a prolific user of EAW's and it was not just one-way usage. In relation to the EAW, the UK assisted many EU member states' investigations, a process that was beneficial to both UK and EU member states policing agencies. At the time of writing there is a degree of optimism that a separate agreement will be made producing a variant of the EAW for use between the UK and the EU. Now UK policing agencies will have to apply for extradition via the longer process of agreeing extradition treaties with respective EU

Member States. This equally frustrating as granting the UK access to EAW's would not only benefit the UK, but the 27 Member States as it is a two-way process. While Brexit has created new trade agreements and borders, Brexit means little to terrorists and criminals and the UK will still have to work with their EU Member State policing agencies, none more so than between the UK and the Republic of Ireland were An Garda Siochana constantly work closely with the Police Service of Northern Ireland, the UK's Counter-Terrorism Units and the National Crime Agency in relation to serious organised crime.[108] Co-operation and intelligence exchange is an important issue and cannot be stressed enough.

14 Post-Brexit the Northern Ireland Protocol Issue and the 2023 Windsor Framework Agreement: The Potential for a Return to Loyalist Terrorist Violence

An example of how Brexit negotiations caused an issue is in relation to the border with Ireland resulting in an important for politicians in Northern Ireland, the UK, Ireland and the EU. During the EU Referendum the Irish border issue was one that appeared to be overlooked by most in Britain, certainly among the electorate. It was only post the referendum result was it was an issue the EU negotiators raised, that suggests the EU were conveniently silent on during the respective campaigns leading up to the referendum. As a result, it has raised issues not just regarding the border between Northern Ireland and Ireland, but it is bringing into question the future of the UK as a united kingdom consisting of four countries as there is the potential that Northern Ireland, not just to depart, but it may trigger a referendum in all 32 Irish counties as to whether Northern Ireland become part of the Irish Republic.

Following the 1998 Good Friday Agreement (GFA) that saw a ceasefire from the Provisional IRA and a relative peace established in Northern Ireland, with both the UK and Ireland then being EU member states the freedom of people, goods and services applied allowing post the 1969–1998 Northern Irish Troubles an end to the hard border patrolled by the British Army and the police to allow a greater ease in crossing the border. However post-Brexit this has caused a problem as, along with the freedom of movement, EU customs law would only apply in Ireland and not in Northern Ireland. To ensure no hard border was formed, an agreement between the UK, Ireland and the EU was to place the border in the Irish Sea resulting in the anomaly that although part of the UK, Northern Ireland was still subject to EU customs law, freedom of movement of goods and the jurisdiction of the Court of

[108] House of Commons Northern Ireland Affairs Committee (2021) 'Cross-border co-operation on policing, security and criminal justice after Brexit', HC 766, 28 April 2021, retrieved from https://committees.parliament.uk/publications/5650/documents/55754/default/ [accessed 20 September 2023].

Justice of the European Union, with goods coming over to Northern Ireland from Britain being checked at the ports like Belfast and Larne before entering Northern Ireland. At the time of writing this position has not been resolved and has polarised positions among Northern Irish political parties and communities.

Brexit has caused an issue in relation to the border with Ireland resulting in a complex conundrum for politicians in Northern Ireland, the UK, Ireland, the EU and beyond. Following the GFA, with both the UK and Ireland, then both being EU member states, the freedom of people, goods and services applied allowing post the Troubles ease in crossing the border. However post-Brexit this has caused a major socio-political problem as, along with the freedom of movement, EU customs law would only apply in Ireland and not in Northern Ireland. To ensure no hard border was formed, an agreement between the UK, Ireland and the EU was to place the border in the Irish Sea resulting in the anomaly that although part of the UK, Northern Ireland was still subject to EU customs law, freedom of movement of goods and the jurisdiction of the CJEU, with goods coming over to Northern Ireland from Britain being checked at the ports like Belfast and Larne before entering Northern Ireland. At the time of writing this position, although under intense discussions and scrutiny, has yet to be resolved and has polarised positions among Northern Irish political parties and communities.

While the majority of Northern Ireland's electorate voted Remain in the 2016 Referendum, two thirds of the unionist/loyalist electorate voted Leave in the belief that leaving the EU would enable them to regain their sovereignty and oppose further integration between Ireland and Northern Ireland.[109] The fact the Protocol is still in place, for loyalists and most unionists, it is seen as an issue that not only erodes their sovereignty but is a step to ending the state of Northern Ireland with further integration with Ireland that will ultimately lead to unifying all 32 counties. Recent Northern Irish elections is beginning to show cracks in the unionist block as people in unionist communities are increasingly shunning unionist politicians, who they see as leading them into poverty and Protocol pessimism and are opting for either progressive political parties like the Alliance party or, of greater concern, into the arms of loyalist paramilitaries.[110] Regarding the latter, during the centenary year of the creation of the state of Northern Ireland under the Government of Ireland Act 1920, young males from loyalist communities carried out violent protests around the peace gate in Springfield Road and other parts of Belfast regarding their opposition to the Protocol as they felt unionist parties were not defending Norther Ireland's place in the UK, with working class loyalists feeling forgotten and marginalised.[111] This is building on the loyalists' narrative that the rot set in after the GFA where Sinn Fein and its allies used the agreement to chip away at Northern Ireland, removing royal symbols, remove the union flag from Belfast City Hall and erect Irish language

[109] Sean Brennon (2021), p. 758.

[110] Sean Brennon and Aaron Edwards (2022), p. 118.

[111] Roy Carroll (2021), retrieved from https://www.theguardian.com/uk-news/2021/apr/11/despair-fuels-the-flames-of-young-loyalist-anger-in-northern-ireland [accessed 6 November 2022].

signs.[112] As seen in the 2012 flag protests, once more loyalist groups recruited and used young people to carry out violent protests.

In March 2021 the Loyalist Community Council (LCC), a legal organisation that represents loyalist terrorist groups the Ulster Defence Association (UDA), Ulster Volunteer Force (UVF) and Red Hand Commando, wrote to the UK Prime Minister saying they were withdrawing its support for the GFA. Although the LCC's chairman, David Campbell, said the LCC was determined that loyalist opposition to the Protocol should be peaceful and democratic,[113] there is the underlying, veiled threat that loyalist opposition may not always be through peaceful protest, as seen in the April 2021 protests. At that time, Billy Hutchinson, the leader of the Progressive Unionist Party (the UVF's political wing) said that while loyalists were angry, the political process needs to take these fears away adding that in relation to the prospect of loyalist violence, '...it's not the time to rachet all this up'.[114] The impasse in forming an Executive in the Northern Ireland Assembly at Stormont following the May 2022 elections, where the DUP is currently refusing to form an Executive by submitting a Deputy First Minister to Sinn Fein's First Minister, which the DUP says in over the Protocol issue adding it needs to be resolved before they will form an Executive. This has led the Secretary of State for Northern Ireland, Chris Heaton-Harris having to make decisions to overcome the impasse. Consideration is being given to having another Assembly election in 2023. Another alternative is direct rule of Northern Ireland from Westminster, with one other consideration mooted being a joint rule between Westminster and the Irish Government in the Dail. The latter is a total anathema to loyalists and as a result, in November the LLC wrote to all the leaders of the unionist parties warning of 'dire consequences' should joint rule of UK and Irish governments be imposed on Northern Ireland. Loyalist blogger, Jamie Bryson sees the Northern Ireland Protocol as a powder-keg situation saying the Irish Sea border should not be tolerated as it results in an economically united Ireland causing further erosion of unionist/loyalist culture and sovereignty.[115]

The threat of a return to terrorist activity by loyalist groups emerged in March 2022 when two suspected UVF members hi-jacked a lorry at gunpoint and forced the driver to drive a device, he thought was a live IED, to Holy Cross church in north Belfast, close to where the Irish Foreign Minister, Simon Coveney was speaking at a peacebuilding event.[116] This forced Coveney to abandon his speech and leave the area immediately, although, it was later found to be a hoax device. On 20 November 2022 four East Belfast UVF members were arrested and charged with possession of a

---

[112] *Ibid.*

[113] 'Loyalist group withdraws support for Good Friday Agreement', BBC News website, 4 March 2021, retrieved from https://www.bbc.com/news/uk-northern-ireland-56276653 [accessed 6th November 2022].

[114] Sean Brennon (2021), pp. 760–761.

[115] Sean Brennon (2021), p. 761.

[116] Black and McCurry (2022), retrieved from https://www.irishnews.com/news/republicofirelandnews/2022/04/06/news/simon-coveney-looking-forward-to-returning-to-northern-ireland-soon-2636028/ [accessed 8 November 2022].

firearm with intent to endanger life[117] following a PSNI operation where they seized eight handguns and three pipe bombs.[118] While the Holy Cross incident can be perceived as making a sabre rattling statement of their intent, albeit a dangerous intent, the November 2022 arrest of UVF members reveals that loyalist groups do have the ability and the ambition to carry out terrorist acts. It is worth noting the PSNI did not charge the four UVF members with terrorist offences such as planning or preparing terrorist acts,[119] as this was part of an investigation into organised crime. It does reveal that loyalist groups have access to both firearms and IED's should they wish to carry out a terrorist attack. Following the bomb hoax in March 2022, terrorism is a move loyalist groups could take, especially when the Taoiseach, Leo Varadkar at Fine Gael's November 2022 Ard Fheis said the Irish government needs to engage more with all communities in Northern Ireland, adding the current stalemate at Stormont is 'not a realistic option'.[120] As seen with the Coveney incident, loyalist groups will see this as both as interference in Northern Ireland by the Irish government and further erosion of their sovereignty, potentially triggering loyalist groups to return to terrorist violence, as indicated in the LCC's letters to unionist party leaders.

At the time of writing, it remains to be seen if the Windsor Framework on the Protocol issue agreed between the UK and the EU in February 2023 will be accepted by all parties in Northern Ireland. The Windsor Framework is agreement between the UK and the EU made in February 2023.[121] In essence, the Windsor Framework Agreement has created a greater freedom of movement between goods entering Northern Ireland from Britain staying in Northern Ireland that are not subject to EU law and movement of goods that are transported from Britain to Ireland via Northern Ireland, that will be subject to EU law.[122] The main focus of the Windsor Framework is to safeguard Northern Ireland's place within the UK by changing and rewriting the core dynamic text as it stood in the old Protocol that entrenched democratic oversight and the prospect of damaging new goods rules being imposed on Northern Ireland.[123] A recent poll revealed that while 66% of Northern Irish people would back

[117] Section 16A Firearms Act 1968.

[118] 'East Belfast UVF: Four charged after gun and pipe bomb seizures', BBC News website, 20 November 2022, retrieved from https://www.bbc.co.uk/news/uk-northern-ireland-63693749 [accessed 20 November 2022].

[119] Section 5 Terrorism Act 2006.

[120] 'More engagement needed with NI communities – Varadkar', BBC News website, 19th November 2022, retrieved from https://www.bbc.co.uk/news/articles/cl5vnz7n24lo [accessed 20 November 2022].

[121] BBC News (2023) 'Brexit: What does Windsor Framework mean for business?', BBC News website 28 February 2023, retrieved from https://www.bbc.co.uk/news/uk-northern-ireland-64793597 [accessed 28 February 2023].

[122] *The Windsor Framework: a new way forward*, London: HMSO, retrieved from https://assets.publishing.service.gov.uk/government/uploads/system/uploads/attachment_data/file/1138989/The_Windsor_Framework_a_new_way_forward.pdf [accessed 29 February 2023], p.4.

[123] *Ibid*, p.5.

the deal, 75% DUP voters would not and this will have no doubt had some in influence the DUP's position to vote against the agreement,[124] along with a number of Eurosceptic Conservative MP's who view the Agreement as 'practically useless'.[125] In turn, this will also affect the loyalist groups' response too with an increased potential in them returning to political violence. If this occurs it will not only be demonstration of how irresponsible some politicians can be when it comes to issues surrounding the EU, it will have serious consequences for the hard fought for peace contained in the GFA, on the twenty-fifth anniversary of the Agreement being signed. While focusing on a country within the UK with a population of 1.8 million, that some may see as a minor backwater state when compared to other issues ongoing within wider Europe, the Protocol issue demonstrates the damage caused by irresponsible politicking. In relation to Brexit, it is the same on both sides, especially with the application of populist politics, especially during the premiership of Boris Johnson that has alienated EU politicians and with the EU who no doubt has shown disdain for the UK's EU referendum result and treat the UK punitively as an example to other Member States' governments that are considering also leaving the EU. I return to the point that terrorism and organised crime activity is the most serious issue that politicians deal with as this is not about finance, it concerns the safety of European citizens whether they reside in states regardless as to whether they are or not members of the EU.

15 Conclusion: Current Impact of CJEU Decisions and EU Law on the UK

In relation to the surveillance of electronic communications, the UK's Investigatory Powers Act 2016 took cognizance of the CJEU's decisions in both *Digital Rights* and *Tele2*, as well as the High Court decision in *R (on the application of Davis and others)*. Throughout the Act it consistently states the granting of authorities must be proportionate and necessary with the general interest being to allow relevant state agencies to interfere with those rights on the grounds:

1. of the interests of national security;
2. to prevent or detect serious crime; or,
3. in the interests of the economic well-being of the UK when those interests are relevant to the interests of national security.

[124] Suzanne Breen (2023), retrieved from https://www.belfasttelegraph.co.uk/news/politics/two-thirds-back-windsor-framework-but-73-of-dup-voters-say-no-to-deal/866342991.html [accessed 11 March 2023].

[125] BBC News (2023) 'Brexit-backing Tory MPs undecided on Rishi Sunak's Northern Ireland deal vote', BBC News website, 21 March 2023, retrieved from https://www.bbc.co.uk/news/uk-politics-65024165 [accessed 21 March 2023].

It is clear the general interest covered in the Act relates to serious criminal and terrorist activity. Being a third country, this is important as in *Maximillian Schrems v Data Protection Commissioner*[126] the CJEU held when dealing with third countries the EU must ensure there are adequate levels of data protection and privacy rights. The CJEU added this is an ongoing obligation to ensure there are no changes made by the third country and the EU Commission has a duty to regularly review a third country's level of protection. Unlike many other third countries the EU deal with, like the EU's member states, the UK is a signatory to the ECHR that is enshrined into UK law through the Human Rights Act 1998. Under this Act the UK public authorities must act in a way and its statutes are compatible with the ECHR, thereby ensuring another adequate level of protection of human rights.

In relation to intelligence and evidence gathering this is important as on matters of serious organised crime and terrorism, the UK will still have to work in co-operation with EU member states. While it is submitted that the UK's current legislation relating to investigations into these activities provide more than adequate levels of human rights protection, in fact they could be seen as comparable, it will be future legislation introduced by the UK Parliament that could be a cause for concern. This returns us to the question raised at the beginning of this article, would CJEU have jurisdiction on UK law? While the CJEU would not have jurisdiction, its decisions could have an impact on future UK/EU policing agencies co-operation as seen in the *Schrems* decision that brought an end to the EU-US Harbour Agreement (although following that decision a new agreement was quickly drafted and agreed on). Returning to the point that organised crime gangs and terrorists have no respect for borders, the UK is a major player in investigations into this activity and it is not one-way activity with the UK solely benefiting from the EU, the 27 EU member states also benefit from UK co-operation. There was hope after the signing of the Windsor Framework Agreement that there would be a thawing in the political relations between the UK and the EU, that would go wider than dealing solely with the protocol issue. At the time of writing there is a possibility that the Framework Agreement will not be accepted either at Westminster or at the Northern Ireland Assembly in Stormont. It is on this point there is optimism a future agreement will be made in relation policing co-operation and that on these matters the UK Parliament will ensure that any future legislation governing policing activity will provide adequate protection of rights acceptable to the EU. If this occurs, it will result in increased co-operation between the UK's policing agencies and Europol in dealing with terrorism and serious organised crime. Until an agreement on co-operation can be made between the UK and the EU in relation to terrorist and criminal activity like that between the EU and other European third countries like Norway or Iceland, the UK will have to rely on the likes of time-consuming extradition orders when dealing with EU Member States' policing agencies and vice versa, which is not an ideal situation when it comes to the safety of *all* European citizens.

[126] [2014] IEHC 310.

References

Argomaniz J (2012) The EU and counter-terrorism: politics. Polity and policies after 9/11. Routledge, London, pp 51–52

Bassong R (2014) EU cooperation on terrorism prevention and violent radicalisation: frustrated ambitions or new forms of EU security governance? Camb Rev Int Aff 27(1):66–82

BBC (2021) Brexit: UK lost 'significant' access to EU policing data under deal, report warns. BBC News Website, 26 March 2021

Berenskoetter F (2012) Mapping the field of UK_EU policing. J Common Mark Stud 50(1):37–53

Bigo D (2000) Liaison officers in Europe: new officers in the European security field. In: Sheptycki J (ed) Issues in transnational policing. Routledge, London, pp 77–79

Black R, McCurry C (2022) Simon Coveney 'looking forward' to returning to Northern Ireland soon. The Irish News website, 6 April 2022

Breen S (2023) Two-thirds back Windsor Framework, but 73% of DUP voters say 'No' to deal. The Belfast Telegraph website, 10 March 2023

Brennon S (2021) From warrior regimes to illicit sovereigns: Ulster loyalist paramilitaries and security implications for Brexit. Small Wars Insurgen 32(4–5):747–771

Brennon S, Edwards A (2022) Alleviating the courses of direct and structural violence in Northern Ireland peace process. J Soc Stud 34(1):111–119

Bures O (2008) Europol's fledgling counterterrorism role. Terror Polit Viol 20(4):498–517

Bures O (2013) Europol's counter-terrorism role: a chicken-egg dilemma. In: Kaunert C, Leonard S (eds) European security, terrorism and intelligence: tackling new security challenges in Europe. Palgrave, London, p 70

Carroll R (2021) Despair fuels the flames of young loyalist anger in Northern Ireland. The Guardian Website, 11 April 2021

Coolsaet R (2010) EU counterterrorism strategy: value added or chimera? Int Aff 86(4):857–873

Den Boar M, Hillebrand C, Nolke A (2008) Legitimacy under pressure: the European web of counter-terrorism networks. J Common Mark Stud 46(1):101–124

Dodd V, Ross A (2017) Westminster attack: police scramble to piece together past of London killer. The Guardian, 25 March 2017

Elvins T (2003) Europe's response to transnational organised crime. In: Edwards A, Gill P (eds) Trans-national organised crime: perspectives on global security. Routledge, London, p 31

Genson R (1998) The Schengen agreements—police cooperation and security aspects. In: Cullen PJ, Gilmore WC (eds) Crime sans frontieres: international and European legal approaches. Edinburgh University Press, Edinburgh, p 137

Gill P (2000) Rounding up the usual suspects: developments in contemporary law enforcement intelligence. Ashgate, Aldershot, p 53

Harris K (2022) 'Obsessed' Guy Verhofstadt insists UK will rejoin EU as he lashes out at Brexit travesty. The Daily Express Website

Hoxhaj A (2020) The UK's policy response to serious and organised crime after Brexit. Global Policy Website

Joffe G (2008) The European Union, democracy and counter-terrorism in the Maghreb. J Common Mark Stud 46(1):147–171

Kaunert C (2010) Europol and EU counterterrorism: international security actorness in the external dimension. Stud Conflict Terrorism 33(7):652–671

Kaunert C, Leonard S (2011) EU 'counterterrorism and the European neighbourhood policy: an appraisal of the southern dimension. Terror Polit Viol 23(2):286–309

Keohane D (2008) The absent friend: EU foreign policy and counter-terrorism. J Common Mark Stud 46(1):125–146

Lewis N (2005) Expanding surveillance: connecting biometric information systems to international police cooperation. In: Zureill E, Salter M (eds) Global surveillance and policing: Borders, security, identity. Willan Publishing, Cullompton, p 106

Lodge J (2002) Freedom, security and justice: pillar III and protecting the "internal *acquis*". In: Crawford A (ed) Crime and insecurity: the governance of safety in Europe. Willan Publishing, Cullompton, p 111

Mitsilegas V, Guild E (2023) Police and criminal justice cooperation after Brexit. J Eur Publ Policy 30(11):2519–2539

Muller-Wille B (2008) The effect of international terrorism on EU intelligence co-operation. J Common Mark Stud 46(1):49–73

Murphy CC (2012) EU counter-terrorism law: pre-emption and the rule of law. Hart Publishing, Oxford, p 106

Occhipinti J (2013) Availability by stealth? EU information-sharing in transatlantic perspective. In: Kaunert C, Leonard S (eds) European security, terrorism and intelligence: tackling new security challenges in Europe. Palgrave, London, pp 143–184

Pearson J (2021a) Policing capabilities lessened after Brexit. UK in a Changing Europe Website, 24 March 2021

Peers S (2000) EU justice and home affairs law. Pearson, Harlow, p 57

Rawlinson J (2003) Bad boys in the baltics. In: Edwards A, Gill P (eds) Transnational organised crime: perspectives on global security. Routledge, London, p 132

Sheptycki J (2004) Organisational pathologies in police intelligence systems: some contributions to the lexicon of intelligence-led poling. Eur J Criminol 1(3):319–338

Welle D (2020) Raids in 6 states as Germany bans "Combat 18". Deutsche Welle Website, 23 January 2020

Public Procurement Regulation in EU and UK

Christopher Bovis

1 Introduction

A liberalised and integrated public procurement is an essential component of the Single Market in the EU.[1] The origins of the regulation of public procurement in the European Union derive from soft law which identified purchasing practices of Member States as considerable non-tariff barriers and as hindering factors for the functioning of a genuinely < competitive market.[2] The need for competitiveness and transparency in public procurement markets has been also considered as a safeguard to fundamental Treaty principles,[3] such as the free movement of goods and services, the right of establishment and the prohibition of discrimination on grounds of nationality. Economic justifications for regulating public procurement have pointed towards introducing competitiveness into the relevant markets to increase cross-border trade of products and services destined for the public sector and to achieve price transparency and price convergence across the European Union, thus achieving

[1] Communication to the European Parliament, the Council, the Economic and Social Committee and the Committee of the Regions, *Towards a Single Market Act,* COM (2010) 608 final.

[2] *White Paper for the Completion of the Internal Market*, COM (85) 310 fin, 1985; also Green Paper on Public Procurement in the European Union: *Exploring the way forward*, European Commission 1996; also Commission, Communication on Public Procurement in the European Union, COM (98) 143.

[3] Cases C-223/99 *Agora Srl v Ente Autonomo Fiera Internazionale di Milano* and C-260/99 *Excelsior Snc di Pedrotti Runa & C v. Ente Autonomo Fiera Internazionale di Milano,* [2001] ECR 3605; C-360/96, *Gemeente Arnhem Gemeente Rheden v. BFI Holding BV*, [1998] ECR 6821; C-44/96, *Mannesmann Anlangenbau Austria AG et al. v. Strohal Rotationsdurck GesmbH,* [1998] ECR 73.

C. Bovis (✉)
Hull University, Hull, UK
e-mail: C.Bovis@hull.ac.uk

E. Guinchard, C. Panara (eds.), *The New Relationship between the United Kingdom and the European Union*, https://doi.org/10.1007/978-3-031-70652-3_9

significant savings.[4] The strategic importance of public procurement for the European integration process has been recognised by the 1986 Single European Act and the 2011 Single Market Act[5] which have prompted a series of reforms to the EU Public Procurement *acquis*.[6] These reforms have been cumulated by linking directly public procurement with the European 2020 Strategy on Growth and Competitiveness.

Following the exit of the UK from the EU, the UK government sought to transform public procurement adopting a deregulatory approach which is substantially relies on discretion and guidance through soft law. The UK public procurement framework consolidates all regulatory thematics derived from previous domestic statues implementing the EU public procurement acquis in the name of simplification yet inviting a de facto de-standardisation of administrative law by leaving substantial parts of regulation to government guidance and an unspecified margin of appreciation in priorities and even preferences of public sector and utilities procurement. The UK public procurement framework projects a legal system which reduces standardisation and consistency in administrative practice and embeds several key principles (non-discrimination and equal treatment) and objectives (value for money, maximising public benefit, transparency and integrity). De-regulation could provide an environment for growth and simplification resulting in efficiencies and cost savings but has the potential of generating an erosion of legal certainty. Procurement regulation in the UK is covered by and compliant with several international trade agreements including the WTO GPA with the possibility of future updating through targeted delegated powers. The Procurement Bill which was introduced in 2022, has been enacted becoming the Procurement Act 2023.

This chapter intends to offer an evolutional trajectory of the functional of public procurement regulation as applied to the UK prior its withdrawal from the EU in its first part. In its second part, the chapter will examine the procedural and substantive differentiation on public procurement regulation in the UK pending the introduction of the UK public procurement legal framework. In its final part, the chapter will focus on regulatory deficits by identifying shortcomings in both regimes. In the Conclusions the chapter will attempt a synthesis of future trends in both regimes, despite the infancy status of the UK public procurement framework.

---

[4]See Commission (1988). Also the Cechinni Report *1992 The European Challenge*, (Wildwood House, 1988).

[5]Communication: Europe 2020, A strategy for smart, sustainable and inclusive growth, COM (2010) 2020 final.

[6]Green Paper on the modernization of EU public procurement policy: Towards a more efficient European Procurement Market, COM (2011) 15/47.

2 Public Procurement Regulation in the UK Before Brexit

A different regulatory treatment to public sector procurement and utilities procurement has been justified on the dynamic nature of the utilities sector as well as the beneficial effects of the process of codification of administrative law. For the regulation of procurement of utilities, irrespective of their public or privatised ownership, a relaxed regime, has been justified and accepted because of the positive effects of liberalization of network industries which has stimulated sectoral competitiveness.[7] However, the public sector procurement received a codified set of rules, covering supplies, works and services procurement in a single legal instrument[8] which aimed at producing legal efficiency, simplification and compliance in order to achieve the opening up of the relatively closed and segmented public sector markets. Codification of administrative law served as a concentrated force to break uncompetitive and fragmented markets for the public sector, whereas a flexible and light application of the procurement acquis in the utilities showed the ultimate environment of EU Public Procurement regulation and its functioning conditions. The regulation for concessions procurement recognises their special nature and characteristics which are different than those of public contracts. Concessions are usually long term, complex arrangements, subject to avoidance of market foreclosure and restriction of competition, where the concessionaire assumes responsibilities and risks traditionally borne by the contracting authorities and normally falling within their remit. Concessions procurement regulation applies a light regulation which balances the freedom of Member States to organise delivery of their public services through exclusive rights granted to public undertakings with the imperative of the principle of transparency in the award of public contracts which ensures market access and competition in the delivery of public services. Concession contracts presuppose two features; first, consideration for the provision of services consists either solely in the right to exploit the service or in that right together with payment and secondly, the concessionaire assumes operational risk.[9] The essence of the definition of public service concessions under the public procurement Directives is that a service concession is a contract which meets the definition of a service contract except for the fact that the consideration for the provision of services consists either solely in the right to exploit the service or in that right together with payment. That corresponds to the Court's criterion of remuneration which comes not from the public authority concerned, but from sums paid by third parties. However, in addition, the Court has stressed that an essential feature of a public service concession is that the concession holder assumes the risk of operating the services in

[7] See Bovis (2006), pp. 461–495.

[8] See Directive 2004/18, *op.cit.*

[9] See Cases C-231/03, *Consorzio Aziende Metano (Coname). v. Comune di Cingia de' Botti* [2005] ECR I-7287; C-382/05 *Commission* v *Italy* [2007] ECR I-6657, paragraph 34; C-437/07 *Commission* v *Italy* [2008] ECR I-0000, paragraph 29; C-206/08 *WAZV Gotha v. Eurawasser Aufbereitungs* [2009] ECR I-8377.

question.[10] The Court has given further guidance on the type and degree of transfer of risk is required for a contract to be categorised as a service concession. In *Eurawasser*,[11] it ruled that in relation to a contract for the supply of services, the fact that the supplier does not receive consideration directly from the contracting authority, but is entitled to collect payment from third parties, is sufficient for that contract to be viewed as a service concession, where the service provider assumes all, or at least a significant share of the operating risk. The Court took the view that what matters is not that the operating risk should be significant in itself but that whatever risk is already assumed by the contracting authority should be transferred, either fully or to a significant extent, to the service provider.

The Defence and Security Procurement Directive[12] prompted by the European Court's case-law,[13] has homogenised the treatment of the procurement of military equipment with the principles of the public procurement *acquis*.

A decentralized enforcement of the public procurement rules has been introduced by the procurement Remedies Directives,[14] which suffered from serious deficiencies. These deficiencies were pointed at by the Court in numerous instances,[15] which resulted in the amending Remedies Directive[16] introducing a clear divide between pre-contractual and post-contractual stages, a balance between effective review of public contracts and need of efficient public procurement, a strict standstill requirement for contract conclusion, including direct awards by contracting authorities and extensive communication and monitoring requirements.

The reforms of public procurement have focused on standardisation of regulation for the award of public contracts and concessions. Regulatory standardisation faces a significant challenge. The desirability of regulating concessions and public contracts alike is counterbalanced with the difficulty of the regulation of concessions which emanates from the inability of such relations to fit into a procedural uniformity like that for the award of public contracts.

Public procurement regulation is a decision-making process which is based on objective, transparent and uniform procedures for selecting contractual partners to deliver public services. In concessions, the award process is heavily influenced by innovation, which as a concept emerges in risk-based contractual relations and it is not likely to appear in traditional public contracts. The concessions relations are

---

[10] See case C-382/05 *Commission* v *Italy* [2007] ECR I-6657, paragraph 34, and case C-437/07 *Commission* v *Italy* [2008] ECR I-0000, paragraph 29; see also Commission Interpretative Communication on Concessions under Community Law (OJ 2000 C 121, p. 2).

[11] See case C-206/08, *WAZV.Gotha* v. *Eurawasser Aufbereitungs*, [2009] ECR I-8377.

[12] See Directive 2009/81/EC, OJ L 2009, 216.

[13] See case *T-26/01 Fiocchi* Munizioni *v Commission* [2003] ECR II-3951 187; Case C-252/01, *Commission v. Belgium,* [2003] ECR I-11859; Case C-337/05, *Commission v. Italy*, (Agusta Helicopters,) [2008] ECR I-7313; Case C-284/05, *Commission v Finland,* [2009] ECR I-11705.

[14] See the Public Sector Remedies Directive 89/665 OJ 1989, L 395/33, and the Utilities Remedies Directive 92/13, OJ 1992, L 76/14.

[15] See Bovis (2012).

[16] See Directive 2007/66, O.J. 2007, L335/31.

conducive to development processes and systems which create new ground and advanced delivery and finance methods. Partner motivation in concessions creates an environment which is conducive for innovation. Environmental conduciveness in concessions and PPPs for innovation exhibits a balancing exercise of factors such as price, cost, risk, quality, performance, and continuous improvement which underpins the value for money (VFM) principle in public service delivery. The VFM is supported through incentivisation in concessions, by mechanisms which create profit or revenue driven notions such as gain and profit sharing and through value engineering, for the determination of specifications and standards and the development of solutions utilising R&D functions of the private partner.

The concept of concessions represents a genuine attempt to revolutionise the delivery of public services by introducing the private sector as strategic investor and financier of public services. First, the private sector assumes a direct responsibility in serving the public interest, as part of its contractual obligations *vis-à-vis* the public sector. The motive and the intention behind such approach focus on the benefits which would follow because of the private sector's involvement in the delivery of public services. Efficiency gains, qualitative improvement, innovation, value-for-money and flexibility appear as the most important ones, whereas an overall better allocation of public capital resources sums up the advantages of engaging with the private sector in delivery of public services. Concessions and public-private partnerships as a concept of public sector management have changed the methodology of assessing delivery of public services both in qualitative and quantitative terms.

2.1 Judicial Activism and Doctrinal Interpretation of Public Procurement Law

The Court's judicial activism has evidently influenced public procurement law-making.[17] It has also positioned public procurement as a regulatory instrument which creates compliance safeguards by authenticating established principles of European Union law[18] and which verifies compatibility links with European policies.[19] The Court's judicial activism in public procurement reveals an approach based on a doctrinal creation and a *rule of reason* which has defined essential public procure-

[17] See Bovis (2005a), pp. 607–630.

[18] See Craig (2010).

[19] See Bovis (2005b), pp. 79–109.

ment concepts such as public contracts,[20] contracting authorities,[21] the remit of selection and qualification criteria,[22] and the parameters for contracting authorities to use environmental and social considerations[23] as award criteria.

The doctrines of public procurement regulation which have been developed by the Court of Justice throughout the evolution of the public procurement acquis are pivotal to the interpretation of concepts in public procurement regulation and consecutively its applicability of the EU Public Procurement Directives. These doctrines have been utilised to construct the interpretation of concepts of the public procurement Directives include the doctrine of objectivity, the doctrine of effectiveness, the doctrine of flexibility, the doctrine of procedural autonomy and the doctrine of procedural equality.

---

[20] See cases C-399/98 *Ordine degli Architetti and Others* [2001] ECR I-5409; C-324/98 *Telaustria and Telefonadress,* [2000] ECR I-10745; C-59/00 *Vestergaard* [2001] ECR I-9505; C-26/03 *Stadt Halle and RPL Lochau* [2005] ECR I-1; C-264/03, *Commission v. France* [2005] E.C.R. I-8831; C-231/03, *Consorzio Aziende Metano (Coname). v. Comune di Cingia de' Botti* [2005] ECR I-7287; C-507/03, *Commission v Ireland,* (An Post) [2007] ECR I-9777; C-231/03 *Coname* [2005] ECR I-7287; C-458/03 *Parking Brixen* [2005] ECR I-8585; C-264/03 *Commission* v *France* [2005] ECR I-8831; C-412/04 *Commission* v *Italy* [2008] ECR I-0000; C-295/05, *Asociación Nacional de Empresas Forestales (Asemfo) v Transformación Agraria SA (Tragsa) and Administración del Estado,* [2007] ECR I-2999; C-220/05, *Jean Auroux and Others v Commune de Roanne,* [2007] ECR I-385; C-382/05 *Commission* v *Italy* [2007] ECR I-6657; C-6/05 *Medipac-Kazantzidis AE v Venizelio-Pananio (PE.S.Y. KRITIS),* [2007] ECR I-4557; C-480/06, *Commission v Germany,* [2009] ECR I-04747; C-148/06, *SECAP SpA* and *Santorso Soc. coop. arl* [2008] ECR I-3565; C-220/06, *Asociación Profesional de Empresas de Reparto y Manipulado de Correspondencia v Administración General del Estado,* [2007] ECR I-12175. C-324/07, *Coditel Brabant SA v Commune d'Uccle, Région de Bruxelles-Capitale,* [2009] 1 CMLR 29; C-437/07 *Commission* v *Italy* [2008] ECR I-0000; C-147/06 *Commission* v *Ireland* [2007] ECR I-0000; C-206/08 *WAZV Gotha v. Eurawasser Aufbereitungs* [2009] ECR I-8377.

[21] See cases C-31/87 *Beentjes* [1988] ECR 4635; C-343/95 *Diego Cali et Figli* [1997] ECR 1-1547; C-44/96 *Mannesmann Anlagenbau Austria,* [1998] ECR I-73; C-360/96 *BFI Holding* [1998] ECR I-6821; C-360/96, *Gemeente Arnhem Gemeente Rheden v. BFI Holding BV,* [1998] ECR 6821; C-380/98 *University of Cambridge* [2000] ECR I-8035; C-107/98 *Teckal* [1999] ECR I-8121; C-470/99 *Universale-Bau and Others* [2002] ECR I-11617; C-237/99 *Commission* v *France* (OPAC), [2001] ECR I-939; C-223/99, *Agora Srl v Ente Autonomo Fiera Internazionale di Milano,* and case C-260/99 *Excelsior Snc di Pedrotti runa & C v. Ente Autonomo Fiera Internazionale di Milano,* [2001] ECR 3605; C-373/00 *Adolf Truley* [2003] ECR-193; C-26/03, *Stadt Halle, RPL Recyclingpark Lochau GmbH v Arbeitsgemeinschaft Thermische Restabfall- und Energieverwertungsanlage TREA Leuna* [2005] ECR I-1; C-18/01 *Korhonen and Others* [2003] ECR I-5321.

[22] See cases C-176/98 *Holst Italia* [1999] ECR I-8607; C-324/98 *Telaustria and Telefonadress,* [2000] ECR I-10745; C-399/98 *Ordine degli Architetti and Others* [2001] ECR I-5409; C-285/99 and C-286/99 *Lombardini and Mantovani* [2001] ECR I-9233; C-315/01, *(GAT) and Österreichische Autobahnen und Schnellstraßen AG (ÖSAG),* ECR [2003] I-6351; C-314/01 *Siemens and ARGE Telekom & Partner* [2004] ECR I-2549; C-57/01 *Makedoniko Metro and Mikhaniki* [2003] ECR I-1091; C-126/03, *Commission v Germany,* [2004] ECR I-11197.

[23] See case C-31/87, *Gebroeders Beentjes B.V. v. State of Netherlands* [1988] ECR 4635; case C-225/98, *Commission v. French Republic (Nord-Pas-de-Calais),* [2000] ECR 7445; case C-513/99, *Concordia Bus Filandia Oy Ab v. Helsingin Kaupunki et HKL-Bussiliikenne,* [2002] ECR 7213; C-448/01, *EVN AG, Wienstrom GmbH and Republik Österreich,* [2003] ECR I-14527.

The concept of contracting authorities (contracting entities in utilities procurement) and the concept of public contracts are the two concepts which are fundamental to the application of public procurement Directives. The Court developed and utilised the doctrine of *effectiveness* and the doctrine of *flexibility* to interpret the above concepts and as a result, through reliance on the former doctrine, to ensure the applicability of public procurement Directives, whereas through recourse to the latter doctrine, to provide the parameters for the non-applicability of the Directives.

The doctrine of *objectivity* intends to provide a restrictive interpretation of rules governing selection procedures (quantitative and qualitative suitability criteria) and award procedures, in particular negotiated procedures as well as with the support of the test of *equivalence,* eliminate non-tariff barriers in the fields of technical standards, product specification and standardization.

The doctrine of *effectiveness* results in the applicability of public procurement Directives and is verified by the test of *functionality*, interpreting the term contracting authority in broad and functional terms[24] and encompassing as contracting authorities private law entities,[25] private entities for industrial and commercial development,[26] entities meeting needs of general interest retrospectively,[27] semi-public undertakings,[28] state commercial companies[29] and statutory sickness funds.[30] The doctrine of effectiveness is also verified by defining a body governed by public law as an effective concept of EU law which must receive an autonomous and uniform interpretation throughout the EU[31] based on the tests of *dualism*[32] and *commercialism.*[33] The test of dualism refers to the ability of

[24]Case C-44/96 *Mannesmann Anlagenbau Austria and Others*, [1998] ECR I-73, paragraphs 20 and 21; case C-470/99 *Universale-Bau and Others* [2002] ECR I-11617, paragraphs 51 to 53; case C-214/00 *Commission* v *Spain* [2003] ECR I-4667, paragraphs 52 and 53; and case C-283/00 *Commission* v *Spain* [2003] ECR I-11697, paragraph 69.

[25]Case C-214/00 *Commission* v *Spain* [2003] ECR I-4667, paragraphs 54, 55 and 60; and case C-283/00 *Commission* v *Spain* [2003] ECR I-11697, paragraph 75.

[26]Case C-18/01, *Arkkitehtuuritoimisto Riitta Korhonen Oy, Arkkitehtitoimisto Pentti Toivanen Oy, Rakennuttajatoimisto Vilho Tervomaa and Varkauden Taitotalo Oy,* , [2003] ECR I-5321 paragraphs 48 and 59; also case C-373/00, *Adolf Truly*, [2003] ECR-193, paragraph 66.

[27]Case C-470/99 *Universale-Bau and Others* [2002] ECR I-11617, paragraphs 51 to 53.

[28]Case C-26/03, *Stadt Halle, RPL Recyclingpark Lochau GmbH* v. *Arbeitsgemeinschaft Thermische Restabfall- und Energieverwertungsanlage TREA Leuna*, [2005] ECR I-1.

[29]Case *C-283/00, Commission v Spain*, [2003] ECR I-11697. Cases *Adolf Truley*, paragraph 42, and *Korhonen*, paragraphs 51 and 52, op.cit.

[30]Case C-300/07, *Hans & Christophorus Oymanns GbR, Orthopädie Schuhtechnik*, v. *AOK Rheinland/Hamburg,* [2009] ECR I-4779.

[31]Case C-44/96 *Mannesmann Anlagenbau Austria and Others*, [1998] ECR I-73, paragraphs 20 and 21; case C-470/99 *Universale-Bau and Others* [2002] ECR I-11617, paragraphs 51 to 53; case C-214/00 *Commission* v *Spain* [2003] ECR I-4667, paragraphs 52 and 53; and case C-283/00 *Commission* v *Spain* [2003] ECR I-11697, paragraph 69.

[32]Case C-44/96 *Mannesmann Anlagenbau Austria,* [1998] ECR I-73, paragraphs 17 to 35.

[33]Cases C-360/96, *Gemeente Arnhem Gemeente Rheden v. BFI Holding BV, op.cit*; C-44/96, *Mannesmann Anlangenbau Austria AG et al. v. Strohal Rotationsdurck GesmbH, op.cit.*

contracting authorities to pursue market-oriented activities without losing their classification as contracting authorities for the purposes of public procurement law. The test of commercialism indicates that profitability and commercially motivated decision-making on the part of an undertaking render the public procurement directives inapplicable. Contracting authorities are free to set up legally independent entities if they wish to offer services to third parties under normal market conditions. If such entities aim to make profit, bear the losses related to the exercise of their activities, and perform no public tasks, they are not to be classified as contracting authorities.[34] The doctrine of effectiveness applies also with a view to meeting the requirements of swift dispute resolution at national level and of enforceability of decisions of national courts or tribunals. The doctrine of effectiveness presumes that national remedies, which are left to the discretion of Member States, must be effective in adhering to and observing public procurement law and EU law by reference to enforcement mechanisms. Effectiveness is measured by the ability to enforce public procurement law.

The doctrine of *flexibility* which is defined through the tests of *dependency*[35] and *competitiveness*[36] provides the parameters for the inapplicability of the public procurement Directives. The test of dependency reveals two distinctive features: the similarity of control of an undertaking to that exercised by contracting authorities over their own departments and the operational connection of the undertaking's activities to the objectives of the contracting authority. The test of competitiveness indicates that any element of competition from private undertakings in the activities of an undertaking, dilutes the assumption that for that undertaking to be considered as a body governed by public law, it must be established for the specific purpose of meeting needs in the general public interest not having an industrial or commercial character. The doctrine of flexibility is also reflected in legislative provisions of both the public sector and utilities procurement Directives respectively. The flexibility doctrine is reflected on the award criteria of public contracts, through the test of *compatibility* of socio-economic and environmental policies with the economic approach to public procurement regulation.

The doctrine of *procedural autonomy*, depicted through the wide discretion afforded to Member States to create the appropriate *fora* to receive complaints against decisions of contracting authorities and utilities, as well as actions for damages.

The doctrine of *procedural equality,* expressed through the explicit obligation conferred to Member States to avoid introducing review procedures for public procurement disputes, as well as procedures for actions for damages which differ,

---

[34] Case C-18/01 *Korhonen and Others* [2003] ECR I-5321, paragraph 51.

[35] Case C-107/98, *Teckal Slr v Comune di Viano*, [1999] ECR I-8121; case C-237/99, Commission v. France, case C-380/98, *The Queen and H.M. Treasury, ex parte University of Cambridge*, [2000] ECR I-8035.

[36] Joined cases C-223/99 & C-260/99, *Agora Srl v. Ente Autonomo Fiera Internazionale di Milano and Excelsior Snc di Pedrotti Runa & C v. Ente Autonomo Fiera Internazionale di Milano*, [2001] ECR I-3605; also case C-18/01 *Korhonen and Others* [2003] ECR I-5321, paragraph 51.

in a discriminatory context, from other review procedures and procedures for actions for damages under national law. The doctrine of procedural equality is a boundary of Member States' discretion in their autonomy to establish remedies for enforcing public procurement rules. Procedural equality presumes that the procedural autonomy for public procurement remedies granted on Member States must not result in differentiated systems when compared with redress procedures for other disputes within their legal orders.

2.2 Discretion in the Application of Public Procurement Rules

Discretion has been inherent in public procurement *acquis*. Firstly, through harmonisation, discretion appears as the most influential factor in the evolution of public procurement regulation and its decentralised application. Directives have been entrusted to carry the principles and concepts of the regime. Secondly, discretion is evident in the procurement concepts, such as contracting authorities and public contracts and the process itself, such as the selection and qualification phase, the award procedures and the award criteria phases. Thirdly, discretion in the application of public procurement regulation is verified by CJEU's jurisprudence, where judicial doctrines attempt to align it with the underlying EU legal principles.

Discretion in public procurement surfaces through two judicially developed doctrines, the doctrine of flexibility in the application of substantive public procurement rules and the doctrine of procedural autonomy in the application of remedies in the award of public contracts. The doctrine of *flexibility* has been applied in order to determine the remit and thrust of public procurement rules, particularly in relation to the concept of contracting authorities and the ability to use socio-economic and environmental policies as award criteria. The doctrine of *procedural autonomy* is depicted through the wide discretion afforded to Member States to create the appropriate *fora* to receive complaints against decisions of contracting authorities and utilities, as well as actions for damages.

3 The UK Public Procurement Framework After Brexit

Following the exit of the UK from the European Union, the UK Government set to reform the United Kingdom's public procurement regime to create a simpler and more transparent system which is not based on transposed EU Directives. The United Kingdom joined the World Trade Organisation's Agreement on Government Procurement (GPA) on 1 January 2021. The UK public procurement legal framework will replace several existing statutory instruments, notably the Public Contracts Regulations 2015, Utilities Contracts Regulations 2016, Concession Contracts

Regulations 2016 and the Defence and Security Public Contracts Regulations 2011, which are largely drawn from EU Directives. The new regime envisaged streamlined new procedures and several sector-specific features, including tailored rules for defence and security procurement, and amending Part 2 of the Defence Reform Act 2014 which regulates single source contracts (contracts for goods, works or services for defence purposes awarded other than through competition).

The UK public procurement framework gives effect to the policies and principles that were set out in the Government's Green Paper 'Transforming Public Procurement' published in December 2020, namely value for money, public good, transparency, integrity, equal treatment and non-discrimination and the Government's response to the consultation published in December 2021. The Procurement Act 2023 comprises of the general principles of the envisaged legal system, a strategy for the simplification of the regulatory statutory design through the establishment of a consolidated and uniform framework, procedural reform, including a reduction in the number of available tender procedures and the introduction of a 'competitive flexible procedure' for contractor selection and to contract award, a set of new commercial options for contracting such as open framework agreements and dynamic purchasing systems; review of the available remedies, including limitation of damages awards; rules for contract management and modification; and the possibility of high-level Government policy directions that could have binding effect on contracting authorities (National Procurement Policy Statement); a new oversight unit entrusted with monitoring procurement.

3.1 Administrative Consolidation

The UK has a complex body of public procurement legislation, much of which was derived from EU law. The principal legislation on public procurement in England, Wales and Northern Ireland, the UK Public Procurement Act 2023, will repeal over 350 individual regulations derived from EU and create a single, uniform framework for public procurement in the UK. The Procurement Act 2023 does not cover procurements by the Security Service, the Secret Intelligence Service, the Government Communications Headquarters or the Advanced Research and Invention Agency

The Public Contracts Regulations 2015 will be repealed and new rules on procurement will be set out in the new regime. Most central government departments, their arms-length bodies and the wider public sector including local government, health authorities and schools will have to follow the procedures set out in the Procurement Act 2023 in awarding a contract with a value above set thresholds, to suppliers.

The Utilities Contracts Regulations 2016 will be repealed and new rules applicable to utilities procurement will be set out in the new regime. The single framework for procurement set out in the Procurement Act 2023 will generally apply to the award of utilities contracts, with some limited differences, for example, in relation to "utilities dynamic markets" and the duration of "closed frameworks". The Procurement Act 2023 applies to the award of contracts by utilities operating in the water, energy and transport sectors. Utilities can be: contracting authorities; public undertakings (bodies that operate commercially but are subject to public authority oversight); or private entities authorised to carry out the utility activity, due to being granted "special and exclusive rights" by a competent authority. The Government does not wish to regulate where utility activities are exposed to competition. The Procurement Act 2023 therefore includes a power, where it is satisfied that this is the case, for an appropriate authority to make regulations exempting a particular utility activity from regulation in the future. The Procurement Act 2023 also includes a power to further reduce the regulatory burden for private utilities wherever possible and consistent with the UK's international procurement obligations.

The Concession Contracts Regulations 2016 will be repealed and the single framework for procurement set out in the Procurement Act 2023 will generally apply to the award of concession contracts, with some limited differences. A concession contract is a contract for the supply, for pecuniary interest, of works or services to a contracting authority where at least part of the consideration is the right to exploit the works or services and under which the supplier is exposed to a real operating risk such as a car park or a hospital shop. There are specific provisions covering the definition of a concession contract, how a concession contract is to be valued, as well as some specific exemptions from the regime of certain types of concession contracts.

The Defence and Security Public Contracts Regulations 2011 ("DSPCR") will be repealed and rules on defence and security procurement will be set out in the new regime. The separation between defence and security and other procurements will largely disappear but the Procurement Act 2023 provides for particular derogations for defence to deal with the differences in the defence and security sector and to aid the delivery of the Defence and Security Industrial Strategy. These include the duration of "closed frameworks", greater flexibility to amend contracts to consider updates to technology as well as to ensure there are no gaps in the provision of goods, works or services which would have unacceptable operational impacts. There is greater flexibility to award contracts directly to specific suppliers to allow transportation of the armed forces where procurement timescales cannot be met and to deal with the interaction between the procurement rules on contract modifications and having the ability to enter into new contracts when needed under the Single Source Contract Regulations 2014. Direct award is also possible where necessary to enhance or maintain the operational capability, effectiveness and safety of the armed forces.

Single Source Contract Regulations, which are covered by Part 2 of the Defence Reform Act 2014 (DRA) are a framework for regulating defence contracts and sub-contracts which have not been the subject of a competition. Such contracts account for a substantial part of Defence procurement spend in the UK, which is equivalent to over £8 billion per year. The Single Source Contract Regulations 2014 (S.I. 2014/3337) (SSCRs), made under the DRA, are engaged when a defence contract is awarded with a value over £5 million without any competition, unless one or more of the specific exclusions set out in the SSCRs apply. These are known as qualifying defence contracts (QDCs) or qualifying sub-contracts (QSCs). There is a general power under section 14(7) of the DRA for the Secretary of State to direct that a particular contract which would otherwise meet the requirements should not be subject to the SSCRs. The DRA does not specify whether a contract should be competed. Where the DRA and SSCRs are engaged they make provision for the pricing of SSCs. They also make provision for transparency and record-keeping requirements, from the beginning of an SSC to its completion. The DRA also creates an arm's length body, the Single Source Contracts Office (the SSRO) which issues guidance on the application of the regime and adjudicates on disputes between the Secretary of State and contractors. The Government set out its broad policy objectives for reform of the regulatory regime in the DRA and SSCRs in a Command Paper published on 4 April 2022 (Defence and Security Industrial Strategy: Reform of the Single Source Contract Regulations). This set out changes centred around three main themes: providing greater choice and flexibility in procurement; speeding-up and simplifying the procurement process and promoting innovation. It also included several technical changes designed to address problems that have been identified.

3.2 Reform, De Regulation and Discretion

The Procurement Act 2023 embeds several key reforms which have been introduced to support small and medium-sized enterprises (SMEs), including a duty for contracting authorities to have regard to reducing and removing barriers to SME participation in procurement, and removing unnecessary obstacles relating to audited accounts and insurance in the conditions of participation.

The Procurement Act 2023 requires the evaluation of tenders to be based on award criteria that identify the 'Most Advantageous Tender' and will require contracting authorities to have regard to delivering value for money and maximising the public benefit from the contract. The Procurement Act 2023 sets out new procedures for awarding public contracts which allow for more negotiation with suppliers to deliver innovative solutions in partnership with the public sector.

Powers in the Procurement Act 2023 will allow Regulations to require all contracting authorities to use a single digital platform for supplier registration, ensuring businesses will only have to submit certain types of information to demonstrate their credentials once to be considered for a public sector procurement. There is a duty on a Minister of the Crown to establish and operate such an online system for this purpose and for the purpose of publishing notices, documents and other information.

To support prompt payment, 30 day payment terms will be passed down through public sector supply chains and private and public sector payment reporting will be aligned to allow comparison of how quickly different organisations pay their suppliers. The Procurement Act 2023 aims to make it easier for buyers to take account of previous poor performance by suppliers. There are clearer and broader grounds to allow for the exclusion of suppliers who pose unacceptable performance risks. The Procurement Act 2023 also includes provision for a centralised debarment list of suppliers which the Government considers must or may be excluded from procurements.

The Procurement Act 2023 introduces new arrangements for how procurement should be conducted in an emergency. There is a new power for Ministers to make provision in regulations allowing the direct award of contracts when necessary to protect life so that contracting authorities can procure at pace. The Procurement Act 2023 will ensure greater transparency of data to make it easier to scrutinise procurement decisions. Notices will need to be published at each stage of the commercial lifecycle in an open, accessible format. The Procurement Act 2023 integrates the existing "Light Touch Regime" for social, health, education and certain other services into the broader provisions but with a series of exceptions to recognise that "Light Touch Contracts" may require different treatment.

4 The Deficiencies of EU and UK Public Procurement Regulation

At first sight, a main deficiency of EU public procurement has been the discretion of member states and the *de lege ferenda* interpretation of public procurement Directives. There is no legal framework which could provide a platform upon which Member States can effectively implement uniformly the procurement *acquis* into domestic legal systems. Although the deficiencies and conceptual limitations of the public procurement Directives have been recognised, jurisprudence has pointed towards the strategic goal to arm the regime with direct effect, in order to enhance access to justice at national level, to improve compliance and to streamline public procurement regulation by introducing a minor element of uniformity in its application.

The most pronounced deficiency of the public procurement Directives is their porosity which is caused by non-exhaustive harmonisation. The porosity of the public procurement Directives undermines their effectiveness by preventing their applicability to certain contractual situations and as a result restricting a *de lege ferenda* extension of their provisions.

Non-exhaustive harmonisation excludes *de lege lata* from the scope of the public procurement Directives public contracts below certain thresholds and certain contractual relationships which reflect inter-administrative interfaces in the public sector or contractual relations based on dominant influence between utilities and affiliated undertakings and in particular public contracts based on exclusive rights, public contracts in pursuit of services of general economic interest and in-house contracts. Non-exhaustive harmonisation reflects the mutual exclusivity of the public sector Directive and the Utilities Directive as well as their non applicability in cases of public contracts awarded pursuant to international rules, or secret contracts and contracts requiring special security measures or contracts related with the protection of Member States' essential interests. In addition, the public sector Directive also does not cover public contracts of which their object is to provide or exploit public telecommunications networks; contracts for the acquisition or rental of land; contracts related to broadcasting services; contracts related with financial securities, capital raising activities and central bank services; employment contracts; and research and development contracts which do not benefit the relevant contacting authority. The Utilities Directive does not apply to contracts awarded in a third country; contracts awarded by contracting entities engaged in the provision or operation of fixed networks for the purchase of water and for the supply of energy or of fuels for the production of energy; contracts subject to special arrangements for the exploitation and exploration of oil, gas, coal or other solid fuels; contracts and framework agreements awarded by central purchasing bodies, contracts of which their object activity is directly exposed to competition on markets to which access is not restricted and contracts related to works and service concessions.

Non-exhaustive harmonisation in *lex specialis* legal instruments such as the public procurement Directives cannot impose limits on the application of primary EU law to supplement their legal thrust. The *lacuna* in the limited effectiveness of the procurement Directives and particularly in areas which cannot *de lege ferenda* be conducive to regulatory control and the need for conformity with EU law has been noted. Although the application of primary European law is not precluded in the presence of exhaustive provisions of secondary law,[37] it has been explicitly recognised that the *lex specialis* character of the procurement Directives aims at complementing fundamental freedoms of EU law. The treatment of the porosity of the procurement Directives is administered through the necessity to supplement their remit with *acquis* deriving from fundamental principles of EU law. Thus, the supplementary applicability of primary EU law intends to close the gap that exists in contracts falling outside the procurement Directives, such as sub-dimensional contracts[38] and in contracts which fall within the remit of the Directives but escape from the full thrust of the principles enshrined therein.[39] The need to increase

[37]Case C-37/92 *Vanacker and Lesage* [1993] ECR I-4947, paragraph 9; Case C-324/99 *DaimlerChrysler* [2001] ECR I-9897, paragraph 32; and case C-322/01 *Deutscher Apothekerverband* [2003] ECR I-14887, paragraph 64.

[38]Case C-231/03 *Coname* [2005] ECR I-7287, paragraph 16, and case C-264/03 *Commission* v *France* [2005] ECR I-8831, paragraph 32.

[39]See case 45/87 *Commission* v *Ireland* [1988] ECR I-4929, paragraph 27, where the Court held that the inclusion in the contract specification of a clause stipulating exclusively the use of national specifications infringe Article 30 EC; Case C-243/89 *Commission* v *Denmark (Storebælt)* [1993] ECR I-3353, where the Court found that contract clauses concerning preference to national specifications and nominated sub-contractors infringe Articles 30, 48 and 59 EC; Case C-158/03 *Commission* v *Spain*, and Case C-234/03 *Contse and Others* [2005] ECR I-9315, where the content of tendering specifications, and in particular sub-criteria for the award of contracts ran contrary to Article 49 EC; Case C-92/00 *HI* [2002] ECR I-5553, paragraph 42, where the Court ruled that contracting authorities' decisions are subject to fundamental rules of Community law, and in

compliance of contracting authorities by promoting the objectivity of the procurement Directives and enhancing their jusdiciability, whilst in parallel limiting their inherent flexibility has been manifested.

The porosity of the EU public procurement Directives has been treated further by relying on the principle of transparency for their interpretation and application. The principle of transparency is surrogate to the principle of equal treatment and both principles encapsulate the fundamental EU law principles which underpin public procurement, such as the free movement of goods, the right of establishment and the freedom to provide services, as well as the principle of non-discrimination. The conceptual link between transparency and the principle of equal treatment is evident from jurisprudential developments. Transparency intends to ensure the effectiveness of equal treatment in public procurement by guaranteeing the conditions for genuine competition. As the principle of equal treatment is a general principle of EU law, Member States are required to comply with the duty of transparency, which constitutes a concrete and specific expression of that principle. The duty of transparency represents a concrete and specific expression of the principle of equal treatment,[40] which assumes that similar situations should not be treated differently unless differentiation is objectively justified.[41]

Despite the rhetorical crescendo on the transformative nature of public procurement framework in the UK after its exit from the EU and the disapplication of the EU public procurement acquis, the imminent legal framework reveals its regulatory proximity with the principles, concepts and procedures applied by the previous regime. Deregulation of public procurement in the name of simplification could increase transactional costs in purchasing form the public and utilities sectors as a result of loss of legal certainty and legitimate expectation from the application of the rules. The flexibility and discretion which diachronically existed in the EU public procurement acquis in a balanced manner, could be jeopardised in the UK by a skeletal version of procurement regulation in statute which is relying on a disproportionate volume of soft law in the form of guidance.

A final point in deficiency between the two regimes relates to their administrative interoperability and the levels of divergence or convergence in their regulatory

---

particular to the principles on the right of establishment and the freedom to provide services; Case C-244/02 *Kauppatalo Hansel Oy* [2003] ECR I-12139, paragraphs 31 and 33, where the Court confirmed the principle under which primary law is to be taken into account in a supplemental capacity for evaluating the effectiveness of the public procurement Directives; Case C-57/01 *Makedoniko Metro and Mihaniki* [2003] ECR I-1091, paragraph 69, where the Court held that even if the Community directives on public procurement *do not contain specifically applicable provisions*, the general principles of Community law ... govern procedures for the award of public contracts; Case C-275/98 *Unitron Scandinavia* [1999] ECR I-8291, paragraph 30 et seq, where the Court held that Community law principles such as the principles of transparency and the prohibition of discrimination on grounds of nationality must embrace the remit of the public procurement Directives.

[40] Joined cases C-117/76 and C-16/77 *Ruckdeschel and Others* [1977] ECR 1753, paragraph 7.

[41] Joined cases 201/85 and 202/85 *Klensch and Others* [1986] ECR 3477, paragraph 9, and case C-442/00 *Rodríguez Caballero* [2002] ECR I-11915, paragraph 32.

outcomes. The EU public procurement acquis, which was the regime applicable prior to the UK's exit from the EU was fully compatible with ordo-liberal outcomes in pursuit of public policy such as socio-economic, innovative and environmental solution in delivering public services. The regulatory outcomes of the UK public procurement framework after Brexit are unknown due to the fact that the system has not been applied and domestic or international judicial precedent is not generated. Retained law on public procurement in the form of case law from the CJEU will act as a yardstick in formatting the applicability parameters of the new rules.

5 Conclusions

The challenge of the European public procurement system is twofold: first, to introduce innovation in traditional public contracts and mimic the collective motivation relations between public and private sectors which are found in concessions; secondly, to capture innovation during the procurement process and allow it to influence the selection process and be decisive factor in the award of public contracts. Public procurement regulation is channelled through three phases: selection, tendering and award. Innovation could possibly emerge in the award phase, as the selection phase is confined to objectively determined and standardised processes. Innovation could also emerge in the tendering phase when utilising negotiations between public and private sectors in competitive dialogue and innovation partnerships award procedures. The regulatory success of concessions rests on the relative efficiency and innovation capacity of the private sector. This efficiency must demonstrate itself in a dynamic mode, reflecting the need for competition in the provision of the relevant services. Innovation can provide for such efficiency. In traditional public contracts, the inherently oligopolistic yet contestable market is ripe for innovation as a feature which will facilitate new entries or offerings.

The UK public procurement framework presents a strong regulatory calibration to the EU acquis, despite the complete eradication of the statutory instruments which have been implemented the EU Directives in England, Wales and Northern Ireland. The regime has limited transformation aspirations, as most themes, concepts and procedures of procurement are similar with those of the EU acquis. The Procurement Act 2023 does not regulate issues such as the treatment of contracts subsidised by contracting authorities; use of electronic procurement tools such as electronic auctions and e-catalogues; detailed rules on the operation of centralised and collaborative purchasing, and an omission of the possibility to engage in cross-border collaboration beyond the UK; use of labels; rules on testing and third-party certification; rules on variants; rules on single procurement documents and cross-border recognition and other means of proof; use of quality assurance and environmental management standards; treatment of life-cycle costing; treatment of abnormally low tenders; rules on contract performance and post-contractual requirements.

References

Bovis C (2005a) The new public procurement regime of the European Union: a critical analysis of policy. law and jurisprudence. Eur Law Rev 30:607–630

Bovis C (2005b) Financing services of general interest, public procurement and state aids: the delineation between market forces and protection. Eur Law J 11(1):79–109

Bovis C (2006) Developing public procurement regulation: jurisprudence and its influence on law making. Common Mark Law Rev 43:461–495

Bovis C (2012) Redress of public contracts. In: Trybus M, Caranta R, Edelstam G (eds) EU law of public contracts. Bruylant

Commission (1988) The cost of Non-Europe, basic findings, Vol.5, Part. A; The Cost of Non-Europe in public sector procurement. Official Publications of the European Communities

Craig P (2010) Specific powers of public contractors. In: Noguellou R, Stelkens U (eds) Comparative law on public contracts. Bruylant

Brexit and NI: A Tale of Two Unions?

Joseph A. McMahon

1 Introduction

> It was the best of times, it was the worst of times, it was the age of wisdom, it was the age of foolishness, it was an epoch of belief, it was an epoch of incredulity, it was the season of Light, it was the season of Darkness, it was the spring of hope, it was the winter of despair, we had everything before us, we had nothing before us, we were all going direct to Heaven, we were all going direct the other way – in short, the period was so far like the present period, that some of its noisiest authorities insisted on its being received, for good or for evil, in the superlative degree of comparison only.

These introductory words to *A Tale of Two Cities* by Charles Dickens seem oddly appropriate to the problems arising from the arrangements made to facilitate the exit of the United Kingdom (UK) from the European Union (EU), especially as they apply to NI as a result of a special protocol to the withdrawal agreement.

In the wake of the June 2016 referendum result to leave the EU, the UK Prime Minister (Theresa May) visited NI the following month which in turn prompted the First Minister and Deputy First Minister to write to her in August 2016. The letter highlighted a number of issues of particular significance to NI which post-Brexit would be the only part of the UK with a land border with the EU.[1] It indicated that that border should "not create an incentive for those who wish to undermine the peace process and/or the political settlement." That settlement, enshrined in the Belfast/Good Friday Agreement, provided for the establishment of devolved Government in NI, alongside North-South and East-West cooperation. The letter acknowledged the importance of the agri-food sector; indeed, cooperation had created the island of Ireland as a single epidemiological unit for the purposes of

[1] Available at Letter to PM from FM & dFM - 10 August 2016 (executiveoffice-ni.gov.uk).

J. A. McMahon (✉)
UCD Sutherland School of Law, University College Dublin, Dublin, Ireland
e-mail: joseph.mcmahon@ucd.ie

E. Guinchard, C. Panara (eds.), *The New Relationship between the United Kingdom and the European Union*, https://doi.org/10.1007/978-3-031-70652-3_10

animal health and welfare. It also advocated that, as far as possible, "the ease with which currently trade with EU Member States" should be retained. The letter read as a plea that, as much as possible, the *status quo* should be maintained.

The trade statistics for 2016, according to the NI Statistics and Research Agency (NISRA) reveal the import statistics as £13.4 billion of purchases from Great Britain with total imports amounting to £6.8 billion of which £2.3 billion came from Ireland; as for sales and exports, Great Britain accounted for £14 billion of dales and of total exports of £10.1 billion some £3.4 billion were sent to Ireland.[2] Recently released trade statistics for 2021 from NISRA indicate that NI sales to Great Britain amounted to £12.8 billion, which was 2.5 times greater than exports to Ireland (£5.2 billion).[3] The import statistics reveal that Great Britain accounted for £14.4 billion of external purchases and imports which totalled £22.4 billion. Overall, it is clear from the statistics that Great Britain has remained the most important market for NI with Ireland remaining first in the list of external trading partners. So, economically it is very important to sustain the link with the rest of the UK whilst the link with Ireland, through the absence of a hard border on the island, is important politically. As a member of the EU, it was possible to balance these economic and political realities but this balance has been upset by Brexit. The Northern Ireland Protocol was the first attempt to maintain this balance with the Windsor Framework representing an attempt to finetune the balance between those two realities and between the two Unions that are at the heart of the balancing problem—the Acts of Union 1800 creating the United Kingdom of Great Britain and Ireland and the European Union.

This Chapter traces the development of the arrangements made for NI in the context of Brexit beginning with a discussion of the progress of the negotiations ahead of the final agreement reached for the withdrawal of the UK from the EU (Sect. 2). The terms of the NI protocol are then examined (Sect. 3) before discussion turns to the recently agreed Windsor Framework (Sect. 4) and some tentative conclusions on whether the correct balance has been struck (Sect. 5).

2 Before Brexit

Reflecting on the outcome of the referendum, the NI political parties expressed their views on Brexit with three of them making a case for Special Status (Sinn Fein, Social Democratic and Labour Party and the Alliance Party); neither of the two

---

[2] Import and Export Statistics are available at Sectoral Analysis (nisra.gov.uk) and Sectoral Analysis (nisra.gov.uk).

[3] Available at Overview of Northern Ireland Trade (nisra.gov.uk). Other studies paint a similar picture, see Gasiorek M and Tamberi N *The impact on NI arising from the UK's exit from the EU: Partial Equilibrium Modelling* available at The impact on NI arising from the UK's exit from the EU: Partial Equilibrium Modelling (economy-ni.gov.uk) and Duparc-Portier and Figus (2022), p. 1404.

largest Unionist parties argued for such status.[4] In her Lancaster House speech in January 2017 setting out the UK's Brexit negotiating priorities the Prime Minister, in relation to NI, stressed the need to maintain the Common Travel Area, which was established before either Ireland or the UK were members of the EU, and the need for a "new, comprehensive, bold and ambitious free trade agreement" with the EU.[5] An early position paper of the UK Government recognised the need to avoid a hard border so as to uphold the Good Friday Agreement.[6] As to how this was to be achieved, a later paper suggested a highly streamlined customs partnership between the UK and the EU.[7] So, whilst there would be customs formalities in UK-EU trade, specific measures would need to be taken to facilitate trade between NI and Ireland (e.g. a cross-border trade exemption) but it was also emphasised that avoiding a hard border between NI and Ireland should not lead to the imposition of a new customs border between NI and Great Britain.[8]

The first phase of the negotiations on the UK's departure from the EU would cover three topics, one of which was the "framework for addressing the unique circumstances in NI" and the Joint Report on those negotiations was issued in December 2017.[9] After affirming support for the Good Friday Agreement, the principle of consent in that Agreement and the operation of the institutions established under the Agreement, the Joint Report offered a commitment to avoiding a hard border. It continued:[10]

> The United Kingdom remains committed to protecting North-South cooperation and to its guarantee of avoiding a hard border. Any future arrangements must be compatible with these overarching requirements. The United Kingdom's intention is to achieve these objectives through the overall EU-UK relationship. Should this not be possible, the United Kingdom will propose specific solutions to address the unique circumstances of the island of Ireland. In the absence of agreed solutions, the United Kingdom will maintain full alignment with those rules of the Internal Market and the Customs Union which, now or in the future, support North-South cooperation, the all-island economy and the protection of the 1998 Agreement.

The following paragraph indicated that in the absence of agreed solutions the UK would ensure that no new regulatory barriers would develop between NI and Great

[4] For further discussion see McMahon (2018), pp. 2–4.

[5] Available at The government's negotiating objectives for exiting the EU: PM speech - GOV.UK (www.gov.uk). See also May 2017 policy Paper from the Department for existing the EU adding further details to these negotiating objectives, available at The United Kingdom's exit from, and new partnership with, the European Union - GOV.UK (www.gov.uk).

[6] Available at 6.3703_DEXEU_Northern_Ireland_and_Ireland_INTERACTIVE.pdf (publishing.service.gov.uk), para 2.

[7] Available at Future customs arrangements - a future partnership paper - GOV.UK (www.gov.uk), para 2.

[8] Above n 3, paras 45 and 52.

[9] Available at Joint_report_on_progress_during_phase_1_of_negotiations_under_Article_50_TEU_on_the_United_Kingdom_s_orderly_withdrawal_from_the_European_Union.pdf (publishing.service.gov.uk).

[10] Ibid, para 49.

Britain. The paragraph concludes by affirming NI's access on unfettered terms to the UK internal market and to complicate matters further, paragraph 51 of the Joint Report provides: "Both Parties will establish mechanisms to ensure the implementation and oversight of any specific arrangement to safeguard the integrity of the EU Internal Market and the Customs Union."

Although the Joint Report was sufficient to move the negotiations on the Withdrawal agreement to the next stage, there was very little detail on the nature of solution to the "unique circumstances in Northern Ireland." However, paragraph 46 of the Joint Report is worth noting, it provides:

> The commitments and principles outlined in this joint report will not pre-determine the outcome of wider discussions on the future relationship between the European Union and the United Kingdom and are, as necessary, specific to the unique circumstances on the island of Ireland. They are made and must be upheld in all circumstances, irrespective of the nature of any future agreement between the European Union and United Kingdom.

The second sentence stands in contrast with paragraph 5 of the Joint Report which offered the caveat that "nothing is agreed until everything is agreed" and is "without prejudice to discussion on the framework of the future relationship."[11] So, at the time of the Joint Report what was envisaged was a deep and comprehensive free trade agreement, or, if that could not be concluded, a solution proposed by the UK, or, if that was not acceptable, "full alignment" (it was not clear that there was any agreement on the meaning of this phrase). As for which of these outcomes was most likely, when the Joint Report was published the Prime Minister offered six commitments to NI including support to its status as an integral part of the UK so there would no borders between NI and Great Britain and, despite leaving the single market and customs unions there would be no hard border between NI and Ireland.[12]

As negotiations progressed, a contrast emerged with the EU arguing for a NI-specific solution whilst the UK Government argued for a solution applicable to all parts of the country. In July 2018, a Government White Paper proposed an economic partnership based on a free trade area for goods accompanied by a common rulebook with the EU for goods and the phased introduction of a Facilitated Customs Arrangement.[13] This proposal was enshrined in the Draft Withdrawal Agreement which in Articles 6 to 8 would have established a single UK-EU customs territory with regulatory alignment to ensure that there would be no hard border between NI and Ireland.[14] So, the EU's Customs Code would apply to goods from NI allowing them free circulation within the EU but at the same time such goods would also benefit from unfettered access to the rest of the UK. Checks on industrial goods would be undertaken by the relevant authorities, either on the marketer or at a

---

[11] Ibid, para 96

[12] Available at prime-ministers-commitments-to-northern-ireland.pdf (publishing.service.gov.uk).

[13] See Microsoft Word - Technical_Note_-_temporary_customs_arrangement_document_final_clean (11).docx (publishing.service.gov.uk).

[14] Available at Microsoft Word - 14 November Draft Agreement on the Withdrawal of the United Kingdom of Great Britain and NI from the European Union.docx (publishing.service.gov.uk).

traders' premises; as for agricultural goods, given Ireland's status as a single epidemiological area, existing checks would continue to protect animal and public health. This backstop solution was viewed as offering protection to both the UK's internal market and the EU single market thus avoiding a hard border between NI and Ireland.

Finding political agreement on the Draft Withdrawal Agreement was problematic; the House of Commons rejected the agreement before passing an amendment (the Brady amendment) that would replace the NI backstop with "alternative arrangements to avoid a hard border."[15] Attempts to renegotiate this part of the Protocol were to prove fruitless though they did yield a unilateral Declaration by the UK which suggested that the Protocol would cease to be temporary if it was not possible to conclude an agreement that superseded all or part of it. It also suggested that the UK could suspend its obligations under the Protocol subject to the proviso that it would uphold its obligation under the Good Friday Agreement and would avoid a hard border.[16] Attempts to get the Draft Withdrawal Agreement approved by the House of Commons were unsuccessful leading to the resignation of Theresa May as leader of the Conservative Party and the election of Boris Johnson as her successor and hence the new UK Prime Minister. It would fall to him to get Brexit done!

It was clear that the UK Parliament would not accept the NI backstop as part of the Withdrawal Agreement and with the deadline for Brexit (31 October 2019) fast approaching the UK Government finally made a proposal for a new Protocol.[17] Under the proposal there would be no regulatory checks on trade in goods between NI and Ireland as both would be part of an all-island regulatory zone. NI would remain part of the UK customs territory and all customs processes necessary to ensure compliance with UK and EU customs regimes would largely be undertaken electronically. Despite the initial rejection discussions continued leading to an eventual agreement.[18] On 23 January 2020, the European Union (Withdrawal Agreement) Act 2020 received Royal Assent with ratification of the Withdrawal Agreement by the Council of the EU taking place one week later.

---

[15] Available at European Union (Withdrawal) Act 2018 - Hansard - UK Parliament. The House of Commons also passed an amendment preventing a no-deal Brexit (the Spelman Amendment), available at European Union (Withdrawal) Act 2018 - Hansard - UK Parliament.

[16] See Microsoft Word - 2019-03-11 Unilateral Declaration.docx (publishing.service.gov.uk).

[17] Available at PM_letter_to_Juncker_WEB.pdf (publishing.service.gov.uk). See also Explanatory Note, available at Explanatory_Note_Accessible.pdf (publishing.service.gov.uk).

[18] See Brexit (europa.eu) for Michel Barnier's reaction to the proposal.

3 The Brexit Arrangements

The Protocol on Ireland/NI in the Withdrawal Agreement differs from the backstop solution proposed by Theresa May in a number of respects, but it also recognises that "the unique circumstances on the island of Ireland" require a unique solution which will protect the Good Friday Agreement by avoiding the creation of a hard border whilst ensuring that trade between NI and the rest of the UK remains unrestricted. The latter is confirmed in Article 4 which provides that "Northern Ireland is part of the customs territory of the United Kingdom" and so it can be included within the territorial scope of agreements concluded by the UK with third countries.

However, a different impression is created by Article 5 on the payment of customs duties, especially paragraphs 3 and 4. Article 5(4) references Annex 2 of the Protocol which lists a number of nearly 300 EU measures that will apply with respect to NI (e.g., the EU's Customs Code in Regulation 952/2013), thus making NI part of the EU customs territory.[19] Weatherill offers the following conclusion:[20]

> So although the Protocol says that NI is part of the customs territory of the UK, that is not what it does. The Protocol treats NI for most purposes as part of the EU's customs territory. Once it is appreciated that the Protocol contains misleading advertising, it is easier to understand.

Returning to the earlier provisions of Article 5, at first glance, a distinction is drawn between goods entering NI that are at risk of entering the single market and those that are not. EU customs duties will apply in the first instance with paragraph 2 indicating that goods will be assumed to be at risk of entering the single market if "(a) they are not subject to commercial processing in NI" and (b) they meet criteria established by the Joint Committee.[21]

If the impression created by Article 4 is inaccurate, is this also the case with respect to the provisions of Article 6 of the Protocol which is entitled "Protection of the UK internal market"? Article 6(1) provides;

---

[19] Ibid, Article 13(1) provides: "Notwithstanding any other provisions of this Protocol, any reference to the territory defined in Article 4 of Regulation (EU) No 952/2013 in the applicable provisions of the Withdrawal Agreement and of this Protocol, as well as in the provisions of Union law made applicable to and in the United Kingdom in respect of NI by this Protocol, shall be read as including the part of the territory of the United Kingdom to which Regulation (EU) No 952/2013 applies by virtue of Article 5(3) of this Protocol." Decision 3/2020 of the Joint Committee amended annex 2 [2020] OJ L 443/3 adding a number of measures.

[20] "Interpreting the Protocol" in McCrudden (2022), Chapter 6, p 73.

[21] The fourth sub-paragraph to Article 5(2) provides: "Before the end of the transition period, the Joint Committee shall by decision establish the criteria for considering that a good brought into NI from outside the Union is not at risk of subsequently being moved into the Union. The Joint Committee shall take into consideration, inter alia: (a) the final destination and use of the good; (b) the nature and value of the good; (c) the nature of the movement; and (d) the incentive for undeclared onward movement into the Union." See Decision 4/2020 of the Joint Committee on the determination of goods not at risk, [2020] OJ L 443/6.

> Nothing in this Protocol shall prevent the United Kingdom from ensuring unfettered market access for goods moving from NI to other parts of the United Kingdom's internal market. Provisions of Union law made applicable by this Protocol which prohibit or restrict the exportation of goods shall only be applied to trade between NI and other parts of the United Kingdom to the extent strictly required by any international obligations of the Union. The United Kingdom shall ensure full protection under international requirements and commitments that are relevant to the prohibitions and restrictions on the exportation of goods from the Union to third countries as set out in Union law.

What is different this time is that in the previous version, the customs arrangements applied to all parts of the UK. Article 6(2) indicates that this unfettered market access will take place "in accordance with applicable legislation and taking into account their respective regulatory regimes as well as the implementation thereof." The applicable legislation includes, by virtue of Article 5(3), that relating to the formalities of goods leaving the EU's customs territory, thus, a border is created between NI and the rest of the UK.

After the first meeting of the Joint Committee on March 30, the European Commission indicated that:[22]

> There is an urgent need to present a detailed timetable and proceed with the necessary measures, such as preparing for the introduction of customs procedures for goods entering NI from Great Britain, and ensuring that all necessary sanitary and phytosanitary controls as well as other regulatory checks can be carried out in respect of goods entering NI from outside the EU.

At the next Joint Committee meeting in June 2020, various specialised committees were established including a sub-committee on NI and doubts were expressed about the operational details in the UK Government's Command Paper on its approach to the Protocol.[23] That Paper set out a four-point plan to protect NI's place in the UK's customs territory.[24] First, there would be legislation to guarantee unfettered access for NI's goods to the UK internal market, so there would be, for example, no import customs declarations or safety and security declarations as goods enter the rest of the UK from NI and no customs or new regulatory checks. In essence there would be no change to existing trading arrangements.[25] Second, there would be no tariffs on UK internal trade. Third, there would be no new customs infrastructure in NI although there would be some new administrative processes including, for example, a new streamlined and simplified electronic import declaration requirement. Existing agri-food checks would continue, and facilities expanded, to reflect the single epidemiological status of the island of Ireland. Fourthly, and finally, NI would benefit from

[22] Available at Withdrawal Agreement (europa.eu).

[23] Available at Implementation of the Withdrawal Agreement (europa.eu). The sub-committee has responsibility to examine proposals raised by the North–South Ministerial Council and its six implementation bodies. See also the statement of the second meeting of this specialised committee available at Implementation of the Withdrawal Agreement (europa.eu).

[24] Available at The UK's Approach to the NI Protocol (publishing.service.gov.uk), paras 17–36.

[25] Ibid, para 22 at which it was noted that there would be an exception in those instances where there are binding international obligations on both the UK and the EU.

UK trade deals. The September meeting of the Joint Committee urged the UK to "accelerate its work on all aspects of the Protocol and in particular with regard to sanitary and phytosanitary controls; [and] customs-related IT systems…".[26]

As the transition period was coming to an end in December 2020 the Joint Committee received a number of unilateral declarations.[27] One of these from the UK was on goods and promised that the UK authorities would make available to the EU information on pre-departure and/or export declarations on certain goods moving from NI to the rest of the UK.[28] A further UK unilateral declaration outlined the approach to be taken for three months after the end of the transition period for various agri-food products (i.e. products of animal origin, composite products, food and feed of non-animal origin and plant and plant products) for which official certification was required for their import into the EU, namely that the UK would continue to apply current EU sanitary and phytosanitary legislation.[29] The scope of the declaration was limited to a restricted number of food suppliers who had to meet a range of trust criteria but did not apply to meat products which was the subject of a separate UK unilateral declaration. This outlined the conditions under which meat products (as defined by the declaration) would be brought into NI from Great Britain from 1 January to 1 July 2021.[30]

The March 3 statement by the Secretary of State for NI, Brandon Lewis, unilaterally extending the grace period expiring on 1 April for a period of six months prompted the Commission to initiate legal action against the UK.[31] The co-chair of the Joint Committee, Maros Šefčovič, considered the UK's action amounted to a violation of substantive provisions of the Protocol (Articles 5(3) and 5(4)) and the good faith obligation in Article 5 of the Withdrawal Agreement.[32] The response of

[26] Available at Press statement by Vice-President Maroš Šefčovič (europa.eu). See also statement from October 2020 meeting of the specialised sub-committee, available at Press statement following the third meeting of the Specialised Committee on Ireland and NI Protocol | European Commission (europa.eu).

[27] See Command Paper *The NI Protocol* (December 2020, CP 346) paras 9-48 reflect on the previous Command Paper and anticipate the unilateral declarations notified to the Joint Committee.

[28] Available at 3. Export declarations to publish.docx (europa.eu). See also Decision 6/2020 of the Joint Committee, [2020] OJ L 443/16.

[29] Available at 2. Export health certificates_UK+EU declarations_to publish.docx (europa.eu).

[30] Available at 1. Meat UK+EU declarations FINAL_to publish.docx (europa.eu). Meat products are defined in the declaration as being "minced meat of poultry, of ratites and of wild gamebirds, frozen or chilled; chilled minced meat from animals other than poultry; chilled meat preparations; and any unprocessed meat produced from meat initially imported in Great Britain from the EU's SPS area."

[31] For statement, see Written statements - Written questions, answers and statements - UK Parliament, See also statement from Lord Frost available at Lord Frost call with European Commission Vice President Maroš Šefčovič: 3 March 2021 - GOV.UK (www.gov.uk).

[32] Statement available at EU-UK Withdrawal Agreement (europa.eu). See also later statement on 15 March 2021 to Lord Frost, available at lettre_to_lord_frost_1532021_en.pdf (europa.eu).

the UK began to emerge in the July 2021 Command Paper entitled *NI Protocol: The Way Forward* with the Prime Minister commenting in the foreword:[33]

> . . . having reached a difficult compromise on the final text of the Protocol, we expected both sides to recognise the need to apply and administer it in a way that took account of the unique context of NI, as the Protocol itself requires. This was vital not just for trade and economic reasons, but also because of the sensitive issues around politics and national identity. We as a Government have been trying to do just that. But it has already become clear that it is not possible to operate these arrangements in a way that can be sustained, particularly not in the inflexible way the EU seems to want.

The solution advocated, after noting Article 16 of the Protocol, were proposals for a new and enduring consensus on the Protocol. That consensus would require three concerns to be addressed: the removal of burdens on trade in goods within the UK while managing the real risks to the EU Single Market; "how to ensure that businesses and consumers in NI can continue to have normal access to goods from the rest of the UK on which they have long relied"; and normalising the governance basis of the Protocol.[34]

The Command Paper offered a series of suggestions on how to treat trade in goods within the UK and the circulation of goods within NI. With respect to Customs, it suggested that the concept of "at risk" found in Article 5 should be built on to differentiate trade based on its destination; so, a trader based in Great Britain sending goods to NI would have the primary responsibility to declare the destination of those goods—NI or Ireland—with customs formalities only being necessary for goods destined for Ireland.[35] A similar regime would apply sanitary and phytosanitary (SPS) measures with a specific approach being adopted for live animals and certain plants and plant products which could be "an appropriately designed SPS agreement."[36] These arrangements would be backed up by "strong reciprocal data-sharing arrangements" with stronger oversight on SPS goods including labelling and penalties for non-compliance.[37] Export declarations for NI goods moving to Great Britain would only be required in very limited circumstances i.e. specifically controlled goods. The Command Paper also suggested a full regulatory regime in NI, i.e. "Goods, whether manufactured or SPS goods, should be able to circulate within NI if they meet either UK or EU rules, as determined by UK or EU regulators, and should be labelled accordingly."[38] Discussion of these proposals with the EU would require "a 'standstill' on existing arrangements, including the operation of grace periods in force, and a freeze on existing legal actions and processes, to ensure there is room to negotiate without further cliff edges, and to

[33] Command Paper (July 2021) CP 502, p. 3.

[34] Ibid, paras 39–41.

[35] Ibid, paras 47 and 48.

[36] Ibid, para 52.

[37] Ibid, para 55.

[38] Ibid, para 59. Paragraph 61 suggested that medicines should be removed entirely from the scope of the Protocol.

provide a genuine signal of good intent to find ways forward."[39] Whilst the Commission Vice-President Šefčovič recognised the need for creative solutions to the problems encountered with the Protocol, he indicated that this would not involve its renegotiation.[40]

Technical talks between the UK and the EU began in September with Lord Frost announcing that "the Government will continue to operate the Protocol on the current basis" so the grace periods then in force would continue.[41] In October the Commission published a series of non-papers suggesting additional flexibilities. The non-paper on customs suggested an expansion of the "goods not at risk of moving into the EU Single Market" in essence building on Decision 4/2020 of the Joint Committee in both its scope and the benefits it confers.[42] It is worth noting that the Commission noted that the UK had:[43]

> ... not provided any concrete economic evidence nor substantiated the precise difficulties faced resulting from the implementation of the agreed solution which would outweigh the benefits and opportunities that NI business has by remaining de facto part of the Union's Single Market for goods and are confirmed by a majority of NI businesses.

In contrast the non-paper on SPS listed the concerns of both the EU (e.g. lack of proper infrastructure and staff to perform border controls in NI) and the UK (disproportionately high administrative burdens on Great Britain-NI movements of SPS goods).[44] The solution advanced by the Commission would be NI-specific creating an Express Lane for the movement of goods from Great Britain to NI subject to a number of commitments to be assumed by the UK including, for example, the construction of permanent Border Control Posts. There would not be a complete abolition of checks or certification.

Although discussions continued into the autumn of 2021 no agreement had been reached to revise the Protocol. Lord Frost resigned in December 2021 and responsibility for the discussions with the EU passed to the Foreign Secretary, Liz Truss, who was assisted by Chris Heaton-Harris and later by James Cleverly. With the resignation of Boris Johnson as leader of the Conservative Party with effect from 6 September, Liz Truss became the Prime Minister, but her tenure was short being replaced by Rishi Sunak on 22 October with James Cleverly becoming the Foreign Secretary, and Chris Heaton-Harris the Secretary of State for NI. In NI, the Protocol was a major issue for Unionist parties in the Assembly elections in May 2022 but these did not lead to the formation of an Executive or the meeting of the Assembly as

[39] Ibid, para 77.

[40] Available at Statement by V-P Šefčovič on UK government announcement (europa.eu). See also Commission announcement of 6 September 2021 that legal proceedings against the UK would be proceeding, EU-UK relations (europa.eu).

[41] Available at Written statements - Written questions, answers and statements - UK Parliament.

[42] Available at attachment_iii_customs_non-paper.pdf (europa.eu). There was also a non-paper on Medicines, available at attachment_i_medicines_non_paper.pdf (europa.eu).

[43] Ibid, para 3.

[44] Available at attachment_ii_sps_non_paper.pdf (europa.eu), paras 1 and 2.

the Democratic Unionist Party (DUP), the largest Unionist party, did not nominate a deputy First Minister and declined to nominate a Speaker for the Assembly.[45] Before returning to the Executive and the Assembly, the DUP would like to see its issues with the Protocol addressed and resolved to its satisfaction.

4 Resolving Continuing Problems

Barely two weeks after the NI Assembly elections, the Foreign Secretary informed the House of Commons that although negotiations would continue with the EU, the Government would introduce a Bill allowing it to make changes to the Protocol.[46] The following month the Government released a Policy Paper outlining its legal position on the Bill.[47] Reflecting on the lack of progress in the negotiations with the EU, the Paper continued:

> In the meantime, the strain that the arrangements under the Protocol are placing on institutions in NI, and more generally on socio-political conditions, has reached the point where the Government has no other way of safeguarding the essential interests at stake than through the adoption of the legislative solution that is being proposed.

For the Government, this was evidence of a "state of necessity" that it had to respond to and the doctrine of necessity in international law provided a clear basis "to justify the non-performance of international obligations under certain exceptional and limited conditions."[48] Whilst it seems obvious that protecting the Good Friday Agreement could constitute an "essential interest", there is a question of whether that Agreement is in "a grave and imminent peril" and, indeed, whether the UK has "contributed to the situation of necessity."[49]

The Paper made it clear that the Government's position was without prejudice to Article 16 of the Protocol which allows for safeguard measures "if the application of

[45] Sinn Fein had emerged as the largest party so would nominate the First Minister. The previous First Minister (Paul Givan – DUP) had resigned in February 2022 triggering the resignation of the Deputy First Minister (Michelle O'Neill – Sinn Fein) and the Executive continued with limited functions until the election in May.

[46] Available at NI Protocol - Hansard - UK Parliament.

[47] Available at NI Protocol Bill: UK government legal position - GOV.UK (www.gov.uk).

[48] Ibid, the Paper cited the International Law Commissions 2001 Articles on State Responsibility, in particular Article 25 which states "1. Necessity may not be invoked by a State as a ground for precluding the wrongfulness of an act not in conformity with an international obligation of that State unless the act: (a) is the only way for the State to safeguard an essential interest against a grave and imminent peril; and (b) does not seriously impair an essential interest of the State or States towards which the obligation exists, or of the international community as a whole. 2. In any case, necessity may not be invoked by a State as a ground for precluding wrongfulness if: (a) the international obligation in question excludes the possibility of invoking necessity; or (b) the State has contributed to the situation of necessity." See Draft articles on Responsibility of States for Internationally Wrongful Acts, with commentaries - 2001 (un.org), pp 80–84.

[49] See, for example, Howse (2021), Available at SSRN: https://ssrn.com/abstract=3959075, p. 14.

the Protocol leads to serious economic, societal or environmental difficulties that are liable to persist, or to diversion of trade."[50] It must be noted that priority is to be given to safeguard measures that "least disturb the functioning of the Protocol. The July 2021 Command Paper had asserted the conditions to invoke Article 16 had already been met but negotiations with the EU had not led to suitable arrangements to resolve the difficulties. Moreover, the safeguard measures must be restricted in scope and duration so that the arrangements would be temporary rather than a permanent reworking of the obligations in the Protocol. Reflecting on Article 16, Howse concludes:[51]

> Absent regulatory harmonization, the only response to border control difficulties arising from the trilemma is to redouble working level cooperation and try to make the arrangements more efficient. Managing the temperature of political rhetoric and avoiding the legally untutored brandishing of Article 16 of a weapon would be positive steps. The EU at least seems still prepared to roll up its sleeves and work constructively for better outcomes on the ground, so the ball is in the UK court.

The NI Protocol Bill when published in June 2022 reflected the proposals made in the July 2021 Command Paper. It would establish a 'green channel' arrangement for goods staying in the UK for traders using the Trusted Trader Scheme and a 'red channel' for goods going to the EU with data-sharing and substantial penalties in the event of non-compliance.[52] The Bill would also establish a new 'dual regulatory' model to provide flexibility to choose between UK or EU rules. The Bill would also ensure the Government can set UK-wide policies on subsidy control and VAT and remove the role of the Court of Justice in dispute settlement. Two days after the publication of the Bill, the Commission announced that the infringement proceeding initiated after the publication of the July 2021 Command Paper would be taken forward and two new infringement proceedings would begin, reflecting the failure of the UK to carry out its obligations under the EU's SPS rules and for its failure to provide certain trade statistics data for NI as required by the Protocol.[53]

The EU also published two new proposals. The first of these was on Customs returned to the earlier proposal to amend Joint Committee Decision 4/2020 to provide simplified customs processes for trusted traders; the scope of the Trusted Traders Scheme would also be extended to businesses established in Great Britain and to more manufacturing sectors in NI.[54] The paper argued that these change

---

[50] Such measures according to Article 16 "must be limited to what is strictly necessary to remedy the situation, with priority given to those measures that least disturb the functioning of the Protocol." Article 16 was triggered by the EU with respect to the supply of medicines in January 2021, see NI Protocol: Article 16 and EU vaccine export controls (parliament.uk) but was withdrawn after widespread condemnation.

[51] Above n 47, p. 24 (footnote omitted which reference the October 2021 Commission proposals).

[52] Available at newbook.book (parliament.uk). See also the Government's explanation of the legislation, available at NI Protocol: The UK's solution (publishing.service.gov.uk).

[53] Available at Commission launches infringement proceedings against the UK (europa.eu).

[54] Available at Annex to the note SI(2022) 179 (europa.eu). See also uktf_factsheet_customs_final.pdf (europa.eu) a factsheet showing the effect of the suggested flexibilities.

would substantially reduce the customs requirements for Trusted Traders moving goods not at risk and would be assured by greater access to UK IT customs systems by EU representatives. The second paper dealt with SPS measures and suggested amendments to existing legal acts to effect reduced rates of official controls and simplified certification procedures covering authorised retailers in NI and their authorised suppliers in Great Britain.[55]

Negotiations between the UK and the EU continued over the final months of 2022 leading to an announcement by the Prime Minister and President of the Commission on 27 February 2023 that agreement had been reached on the way forward. The "Windsor Framework" they announced represented:[56]

> ... a series of practical and sustainable measures that the Government of the United Kingdom and the European Commission consider necessary to address, in a definitive way, unforeseen circumstances or deficiencies that have emerged since the start of the Protocol. They respond to the everyday issues faced by people and businesses in Northern Ireland, supporting and protecting the Good Friday or Belfast Agreement in all its parts.

The changes made by the Framework include a number proposed by the UK Government, in particular the green lane approach to internal trade i.e., goods imported into NI destined to remain there would be classified as not at risk of entering the EU through extensions to the trusted trader scheme—the NI Retail Movement Scheme will replace the Scheme for Temporary Agri-food Movements to Northern Ireland. As for goods moving from moving into the rest of the UK from NI, the framework reduced the export procedures and the use of labels to indicate that the goods are "Not for EU". For goods moving on into the EU—the red lane—there would be data-sharing arrangements to reduce paperwork alongside a new tariff reimbursement scheme for traders who could show that the goods were not destined for the EU. The Framework also recognises the importance of maintaining the island of Ireland as a single epidemiological unit with the grace period for veterinary medicines being extended to 2025 to allow for the negotiation of a long-term solution. Other changes include ensuring that NI has the same VAT and excise charges as the rest of the UK, a dual regulatory system for medicines, restoring the application of UK-wide rules for plants and plant products and changes to the rule on the use of subsidies.

Addressing the democratic deficit in the Protocol, the Framework introduces a means to offer democratic oversight on individual laws—the Stormont Brake—which allows the UK Government to veto the application of changes to EU customs, goods, and agriculture rules falling within the scope of the Protocol. If the matter cannot be resolved through the existing institutional structure, the Brake will operate on the basis of the Belfast Agreement's Petition of Concern which allows a matter to be raised based on 30 Assembly Members from two or more parties signing a

[55] Available at Annex to the note SI(2022) 179 (europa.eu). See also uktf_factsheet_animals_en.pdf (europa.eu) a factsheet showing the effect of the suggested flexibilities.

[56] Available at Political_Declaration_by_the_European_Commission_and_the_Government_of_the_United_Kingdom.pdf (publishing.service.gov.uk).

petition.[57] The Brake will used only in serious cases, i.e. changes that will have a significant impact specific to everyday life that is liable to persist. Any dispute about the application of the Brake will be resolved by arbitration. The introduction of a number of expert groups to promote greater stakeholder engagement with the existing institutional structure of the Protocol.[58] The Command Paper presenting the Windsor Framework as a New Way Forward concludes:[59]

> Taken as a whole, through this agreement we have put the arrangements for Northern Ireland on an entirely new footing: removing the barriers and burdens that gave rise to the perception of an Irish Sea border, and protecting those arrangements from being removed by the ECJ; protecting Northern Ireland's place in the UK internal market now and in the future; scrapping swathes of EU rules to support UK-wide policymaking in key areas of food safety, medicines, taxation and spending; and addressing the democratic deficit that was otherwise at the heart of issues with the original Protocol.

The UK Government concluded that the Framework was consistent with the Belfast Agreement (and the Act of Union) thus reflected the integral place of NI in the UK (and its internal market), whereas for the Commission the framework struck "the right balance between flexibilities and effective safeguards for the protection of the EU Single Market."[60]

There is a considerable amount of work to be done to implement the Framework, So, for example, arrangements relating to the implementation of the Framework were adopted by the Joint Committee in Decision 1/2023 on 24 March with further Decisions coming at its July meeting.[61] Work to be completed in the remainder of 2023 include, for example, putting in place a new trusted trader scheme by September and beginning in October the enhanced SPS inspection facilities in NI to be in place with the green and red lanes beginning to operate.[62] With the Green Lane not due to be fully operational until October 2024, there is time for problems with its operation to be addressed. The House of Lords sub-Committee on the Protocol on Ireland/Northern Ireland report on the Windsor Framework has

---

[57] See The Windsor Framework (Democratic Scrutiny) Regulations 2023 (legislation.gov.uk). See also The Protocol on Ireland/Northern Ireland (Democratic Consent Process) (EU Exit) Regulations 2020 (legislation.gov.uk) - a challenge to their lawfulness was rejected by the Supreme Court *In the matter of an application by James Hugh Allister and others for Judicial Review (Appellants) (Northern Ireland) and In the matter of an application by Clifford Peeples for Judicial Review (Appellant) (Northern Ireland)* [2023] UKSC 5.

[58] See for example Commission statement on Enhanced engagement with Northern Ireland stakeholders, https://commission.europa.eu/publications/commission-statement-enhanced-engagement-northern-ireland-stakeholders_en.

[59] Available at vFINAL- 2023 02 27 - Command Paper 1245 (publishing.service.gov.uk), para 71. It was also noted that the Government would not proceed with the NI Protocol Bill and the EU would not proceed in its legal actions against the UK.

[60] See https://ec.europa.eu/commission/presscorner/detail/en/qanda_23_1271.

[61] See [2023] OJ L 102/61. See also Decisions 2/2023 and 3/2023, [2023] OJ L 184/109 and 111.

[62] The Green Lane is to be fully operational by October 2024. Further details on aspects of the Framework were updated in 28 July 2023 see, The Windsor Framework - further detail and publications - GOV.UK (www.gov.uk).

identified a number of these problem areas as including, for example, meat for processing live poultry and dairy products and it also noted that there is time for the Government to address issues around the labelling of various products.[63] The Framework envisages more agreements, for example on veterinary medicines, so it is clearly a work in progress so further changes to the arrangements are anticipated. The sub-Committee Report concluded:[64]

> The Windsor Framework is the latest attempt to manage the implications of Brexit for Northern Ireland. The UK and the EU must ensure that they remain in close and productive dialogue, both with each other and with Northern Ireland stakeholders, maintaining a commitment to address all the issues that arise out of the Windsor Framework, and those issues which have yet to be resolved, not least for the benefit of all the people of Northern Ireland

Whilst dialogue will continue to resolve the problems with the Protocol, the Windsor Framework did not make sufficient changes to the Protocol to satisfy the concerns of DUP and thus allow for the restoration of the NI Executive and the Assembly.

5 Conclusions

In the aftermath of the approval of the Windsor Framework by the House of Commons, two days later the UK Foreign Secretary, James Cleverly, and European Commission Vice-President, Maroš Šefčovič, after a Joint Committee meeting on 24 March 2023 issued a joint statement welcoming the positive approach of both sides which led to the adoption of the Framework. They continued:[65]

> These arrangements address, in a definitive manner, the challenges in the operation of the Protocol on Ireland/Northern Ireland over the last 2 years and the everyday issues faced by people and businesses in Northern Ireland, while supporting and protecting the Good Friday or Belfast Agreement in all its parts, and protecting the integrity of the European Union's Single Market, and Northern Ireland's place in the United Kingdom's internal market.

The impression created is that the Windsor Framework has resolved the problems with the Protocol but, as noted above, the DUP, amongst others, continue to be dissatisfied with the outcome.[66] However, the joint statement also recognises that further work is needed to implement all aspects of the Framework and to address

---

[63] Available at House of Lords - Report from the Sub-Committee on the Protocol on Ireland/Northern Ireland: The Windsor Framework - European Affairs Committee (parliament.uk), paragraphs 69 and 85. See also paragraph 107 which notes the limited changes in the area of plants, seeds, machinery and trees.

[64] Ibid, paragraph 304.

[65] Available at Joint statement on the Withdrawal Agreement Joint Committee and Trade and Cooperation Agreement Partnership Council meetings, 24 March 2023 - GOV.UK (www.gov.uk).

[66] 29 MPs voted against the Framework in the House of Commons vote on 22 March 2023. See also an article written by MP Priti Patel criticising the Framework, available at The Windsor Framework will go down in history as a missed opportunity (telegraph.co.uk) and comments on the vote by the

further issues that may arise, for example, on veterinary arrangements. An opportunity may thus be found for the UK Government (and to a lesser extent the European Commission) to respond positively to concerns about the Windsor Framework whilst balancing the need to maintain the integrity of the EU Single Market and the Act of Union guaranteeing NI's place within the UK. Perhaps, in that spirit of optimism, the final words here should reflect the opening quote: "It is a far, far better thing that I do, than I have ever done; it is a far, far better rest that I go than I have ever known."

[**Post-script**—After a two year hiatus, the institutions of devolution in Northern Ireland were restored on 3 February 2024. The restoration was facilitated in part by the approval of the Windsor Framework (UK Internal Market and Unfettered Access) Regulation 2024 by the House of Commons on 1 February 2024.[67] The Regulations guarantee the unfettered access for Northern Ireland goods, either through Northern Ireland or Ireland, to the UK internal market, i.e. there will be no new checks, controls or administrative processes. In essence, the Green Lane in the Windsor Framework has been transformed into a UK Internal Market system which represents a movement towards the restoration of the arrangements existing before Brexit subject to the international obligations entered into by the UK.[68] Regulatory checks will be significantly reduced but not completely eliminated and there are still a number of other issues that remain to be addressed such as various horticultural and veterinary products. The Red Lane will continue to operate.

Politically, the Regulations seek to protect (and strengthen) Northern Ireland's place as part of the UK, for example through the establishment of an Independent Monitoring Panel and by strengthening the operation of the Stormont Brake.[69] Two new bodies will also be established an East-West Council and Intertrade UK with the latter having the mandate of supporting the development of trade within the UK.]

References

Duparc-Portier G, Figus G (2022) The impact of the new NI protocol: can NI enjoy the best of both worlds? Reg Stud 56(8):1404

Secretary of State for Northern Ireland, available at DUP has not come to terms with Brexit deal support, says Heaton-Harris - BBC News.

[67] Available at The Windsor Framework (UK Internal Market and Unfettered Access) Regulations 2024 (legislation.gov.uk).

[68] COM(2024) 57 Proposal for a Council Decision establishing the position to be taken on behalf of the EU in the Joint Committee established by the Agreement on the withdrawal of the UK from the EU as regards the amendment of the Decision No 1/2023 of the Joint Committee of 24 March 2023 laying down arrangements relating to the Windsor Framework. This allows goods within the UK's tariff rate quota to move into Northern Ireland.

[69] For details see Command Paper 1021 *Safeguarding the Union* Chapters 5 and 6. See also The Windsor Framework (Constitutional Status of Northern Ireland) Regulations 2024 (legislation.gov.uk).

Howse R (2021) "This is Not an Exit": the Article 16 safeguards in the Ireland/NI Protocol. Brexit Institute Working Paper Series, No 14/2021, NYU School of Law, Public Law Research Paper No. 22-03, NYU Law and Economics Research Paper No. 22-04

McCrudden C (ed) (2022) The law and practice of the Ireland/NI Protocol. Cambridge University Press, Cambridge

McMahon J (2018) Avoiding the backstop solution: NI and the EU Post-Brexit. UCD Working Papers in Law, Criminology and Socio-Legal Studies Research Paper No. 0518, available at SSRN: https://ssrn.com/abstract=3155145, pp 2–4

New Relationships for the Crown Dependencies and British Overseas Territories

Victoria Bell and Matthew Waddington

1 Introduction

Brexit did not just change the UK's relationship with the EU. It also changed the relationships with the EU[1] that had applied to the other territories related to the UK, namely the fourteen British Overseas Territories ("BOTs") and the three Crown Dependencies ("CDs") of Jersey, Guernsey and the Isle of Man.

This chapter considers how those relationships have changed, focusing particularly on the CDs, but also looking at the two BOTs that are geographically in Europe, namely Gibraltar and the Sovereign Base Areas in Cyprus (the "SBAs"). The chapter starts by considering the BOTs, briefly looking at the non-European BOTs before moving on to the SBAs and Gibraltar. Then it considers the CDs, particularly Jersey and the new trading arrangements, taking an in depth look at the change in relationship that Brexit has brought about between the CDs and the EU, but also between the CDs and the UK. It finishes by looking further into the future by considering how full independence from the UK, and the varied legal statuses of the different BOTs and CDs in relation to independence, colours the background to the directions that the BOTs and CDs might take in relation to the EU.

The authors do not speak for their employers.

[1] For convenience we refer to the EU throughout this chapter, including for events (such as UK accession) at times when the relevant body was the EEC or EC.

V. Bell (✉)
Law Officers' Department, States of Jersey, St Helier, Jersey
e-mail: V.Bell@lawofficers.je

M. Waddington
Legislative Drafting Office, States of Jersey, St Helier, Jersey
e-mail: matthew.waddington@gov.je

E. Guinchard, C. Panara (eds.), *The New Relationship between the United Kingdom and the European Union*, https://doi.org/10.1007/978-3-031-70652-3_11

The starting point is that the CDs and BOTs had a variety of different relationships with the EU, and they have been affected by Brexit in interestingly different ways. The BOTs and CDs do not form part of the UK,[2] but the UK is responsible for representing their interests internationally (with their consent, in the case of the populated territories) and is also responsible for their defence. With the exception of Gibraltar (see below), they did not vote for members of the European Parliament and did not have a vote in the UK's Brexit referendum, even though Brexit would affect them all. Each BOT and CD has its own legal system, and has had to adjust that to cater for the effects of Brexit.

A key issue in Brexit has been borders and relationships with immediate neighbours, and this issue has operated differently among the various BOTs and CDs. The UK itself has had to deal with the implications of its new land border with the EU, between Northern Ireland and the Republic of Ireland. The disputes over the Protocol for Northern Ireland have played a major role in the Brexit process and may or may not turn out to have been solved by the "Windsor Framework". Brexit has also played out politically (but not yet legally) as a factor in debates over Scottish independence. On a less grand scale there are also issues with borders for the territories considered in this chapter. The SBAs have a land border (virtually invisible on the ground) with the Republic of Cyprus, but that includes a harder border with the unrecognized "Turkish Republic of Northern Cyprus" (and two borders with the United Nations buffer zone—see below). Gibraltar has a land border with Spain (just north of where Gibraltar's airport runway similarly cuts across almost the full width of the peninsula). But at sea the UK has not claimed an Exclusive Economic Zone for either of those two BOTs. The CDs are islands, so there is no land border. Jersey and Guernsey each have a sea border with France (to which they are physically much closer than to the UK, whose territorial waters touch those of Guernsey but not Jersey). The Isle of Man sits in the middle of the Irish sea, but its territorial waters do not quite touch those of the Republic of Ireland (although the Isle of Man's territorial waters do touch each of the Marine Planning Areas that the UK allocates to Wales, Northern Ireland, Scotland and England respectively). Each of these borders and relationships has different sensitivities, and Brexit has affected almost all of them.

The governments and parliaments of each of the affected territories had to deal with the changes necessary to their law to make the best adjustments to suit them, often at very high speed given the way the Brexit process kept involving brinkmanship and last-minute decisions. Jersey's Legislative Drafting Office hosted a meeting of the Commonwealth Association of Legislative Counsel for jurisdictions to compare notes about their Brexit experiences, usefully summarised in Marsh-Smith (2019). Generally this subject has not received much academic attention, with exceptions like Alegre (2018). But these other perspectives on Brexit can shed new light on the broader question of the UK's relationship to the EU and the way the EU deals with third countries and exceptional territories.

[2] So they are not devolved administrations, but see below for comparisons with Northern Ireland and Scotland in relation to Brexit.

The CDs and BOTs share with the UK the "dualist" approach to international law, so their international treaty obligations, and EU obligations that do not have direct effect, need to be given effect in the domestic law of the CD or BOT. The relevant domestic legislation in the CDs and BOTs was often modelled to some degree on the equivalent UK legislation. But the closeness of the modelling depended on whether any EU law had direct effect in the CD or BOT, and whether there was a need to have the ability to use secondary legislation to implement EU law that the CD or BOT chose to apply (as opposed to being obliged to apply it). There is also a certain element of recycling in the EU provisions applied to each group of territories, again with significant points coming out of the variations in approach. At the crux on the EU law side was Article 355 of the Treaty on the Functioning of the EU ("TFEU") which governed the relationship of the CDs and BOTs with the EU (and still governs the EU's relationships with similar territories linked to the Netherlands, France, Spain and Portugal as the legacy of their imperial pasts). Article 355 does so effectively by setting up different categories of territory to which different relationships apply. Those categories include territories that are completely outside the EU, territories that are outside but with "associated" status, territories that are inside but as an "outermost region" (which has not applied to any of the BOTs or CDs), and territories for which there is a set of ad hoc arrangements (including being inside but with exclusionary exceptions, and being outside but with inclusionary exceptions). For the wider context of the various relationships, see Kochenov (2011) and Kochenov (2012).

In broad terms therefore, the different relationships between these varying territories and the EU can be traced by looking first at the historic relationship between the territory (or group of similar territories) and the UK (and any relevant neighbour of the territory), then at the arrangements made on applying EU law to the territory (in the relevant accession treaties and protocols, the amendments to TFEU, and the domestic legislation of the territory), and lastly at the equivalent arrangements on Brexit (in the Withdrawal Agreement and its Protocols, the amendments to TFEU, the coverage of the UK-EU Trade and Cooperation Agreement, and the domestic legislation of the territory). The trajectory traced by that development is likely to affect the course of future developments in the relationships of the territories with the EU, and with the UK.

2 The British Overseas Territories

2.1 The BOTs in General and the 12 Non-European BOTs

We will later look particularly at the two related, but different, case studies offered by the two British Overseas Territories ("BOTs") within the European continent. Those are the Sovereign Base Areas of Akrotiri and Dhekelia on the island of Cyprus (the "SBAs") and Gibraltar. They share with Northern Ireland the distinction of having the only land borders between the EU and the UK or its territories, but their relationships with the UK and EU are very different from each other. Before looking at them we turn now to the broad context of the relationship of the BOTs in general with the UK and EU.

Aside from the SBAs and Gibraltar, there are currently twelve other BOTs, making a total of fourteen. There were many more when the UK joined the EU,[3] at which point they were still referred to as colonies or dependent territories, before they were renamed by the UK's British Overseas Territories Act 2002.[4] The BOTs are the remains of the British Empire. That means they were conquered, or otherwise acquired by England or its successors (whereas in 1066 the Channel Islands were part of the Duchy of Normandy when it conquered England, establishing a different relationship—see below). For many decades the only convenient description of the law on the status of the BOTs was Roberts-Wray (1966), until 2011 when the first edition of Hendry and Dickson (2018) came out, after a revival of interest in the BOTs following a set of constitutionally interesting cases including Quark and Bancoult.[5] The current status of the BOTs is usefully summed up by Loft (2023).

The BOTs vary greatly, with some being uninhabited and some wholly or mainly used as military or communications bases. The others all make their own legislation, which is separate from that of the UK (but can be overridden by UK legislation). In particular, there is a core group of five Caribbean BOTs plus Bermuda which all have parliaments and most of which have financial services sectors.[6]

As with the CDs, Article 355 of TFEU governs the relations of the BOTs with the EU. Article 355(2) refers to Part 4 of TFEU, headed (before Brexit) "Association of the Overseas Countries and Territories", which governs the EU's relationship with "the non-European countries and territories which have special relations with Denmark, France, the Netherlands and the United Kingdom" (with the reference to the UK removed after Brexit). The countries and territories themselves are listed in Annex II to TFEU. As Annex II stood immediately before Brexit, it listed the twelve BOTs other than the SBAs and Gibraltar. The associated status did not apply any EU law as such to these BOTs. But it is worth noting that many territories outside the EU have chosen to implement some EU laws that do not apply to them (we will come back to this in looking at the CDs below). The most obvious case is data protection legislation, where a BOT or other non-EU country wants to obtain an "adequacy

[3]Twenty-four UK-related territories were named in Article 24 of the Act of Accession.

[4]That Act contains various provisions about the BOTs, but does not list them and instead refers to the list in Schedule 6 to the British Nationality Act 1981. The formal names of four of the BOTs reflect the fact that they are made up of more than one island—Pitcairn, Henderson, Ducie and Oeno Islands (only Pitcairn is inhabited); St Helena, Ascension and Tristan da Cunha (but these each have their own laws); South Georgia and the South Sandwich Islands; Turks and Caicos Islands. Also the SBAs are one BOT made up of the two Areas, Akrotiri and Dhekelia.

[5]R (Quark) v SoS for Foreign and Commonwealth Affairs [2005] UKHL 57 and R (Bancoult) v SoS for Foreign and Commonwealth Affairs (No 2) [2008] UKHL 61.

[6]The five Caribbean BOTs are Anguilla, the British Virgin Islands, the Cayman Islands, Montserrat, and the Turks and Caicos Islands.

decision" under Article 45 GDPR[7] to enable data to flow freely between it and the EU (and of course for data flows there is no difference how far the country is physically from EU territory). Those twelve BOTs all lost their "associated" status following Brexit, but this does not mark a major legal change in their relationship to the EU (but see below for possible future developments). The UK-EU Trade and Cooperation Agreement does not apply to the twelve non-European BOTs—see Article 774(3).

One significant difference brought about by Brexit, that affects all the BOTs and is shared with the UK, is that British citizens are no longer EU citizens. Each territory has a different history of its connection with the UK and the effects on nationality law, all of which is set out in detail in Fransman (2011). Briefly, in the nineteenth century the relevant status was "British subject", and it applied (at least in legal theory) across the British empire rather than just to those with a connection to the UK itself (immigration control was more guided by the class of travel by which a person arrived than by where a British subject came from). Then in the twentieth century legal distinctions started to appear, and the British Nationality Act 1981 gave a main status of "British citizen" for those with connections to the UK. It also gave various other types of status (not carrying significant rights to travel) for people without that direct connection, such as "British protected person", "British national (overseas)" and "British overseas citizen", but also "British subject" and "British overseas territories citizen". This meant the citizenship connected with the BOTs was not full British citizenship (but Gibraltarians could apply to register as full British citizens) and none of the other forms of status gave the holder EU citizenship.[8] Then the Falkland Islanders were given full citizenship after the Falklands war, and eventually the British Overseas Territories Act 2002 gave full British citizenship to all British overseas territories citizens (except those connected with the SBAs, who may have Cypriot citizenship instead). That meant people from BOTs obtained EU citizenship too, along with free movement rights.[9] Brexit now means that people who are British citizens through a connection with a BOT lost their EU citizenship in the same way as those who are British citizens from a connection with the UK.

[7] Regulation (EU) 2016/679 of the European Parliament and of the Council of 27 April 2016 on the protection of natural persons with regard to the processing of personal data and on the free movement of such data, and repealing Directive 95/46/EC (OJ L 119, 4.5.2016, p1).

[8] See the declaration by the UK government "on the definition of the term 'nationals'" annexed to the UK's Accession Treaty, and the updated 1983 version of that declaration after the British Nationality Act 1981 (OJ C 23, 28.1.1983, p1).

[9] See below on the odd twist that meant British citizens from BOTs could be better off than some of those from CDs, who did not benefit from EU free movement if they did not have sufficient connection to the UK.

2.2 Gibraltar

The position of Gibraltar in relation to the EU, and the effects of Brexit, are strikingly different from the rest of the BOTs and the CDs (and in some ways more like the position of Northern Ireland).[10]

Gibraltar traces its BOT status back to 1713 when Spain ceded Gibraltar to Great Britain in the Treaty of Utrecht (see the discussion of independence below for details on whether Spain has right of first refusal if the UK gives up sovereignty). Over 250 years later when the UK joined the EU, the model chosen for Gibraltar was the opposite of that for the CDs, in that Gibraltar would be in the EU with some exceptions (instead of out with exceptions). The exceptions were significant and included the customs union, the agriculture, fisheries and common commercial policies, and VAT. But this approach also meant that a great deal of EU legislation had to be enacted as Gibraltar legislation in fields that were not in practice applicable to such a small jurisdiction. To give domestic effect to EU law, Gibraltar enacted the European Communities Act 1972,[11] modelled closely on the UK's Act of the same name. Gibraltar was not mentioned by name in Article 355 TFEU, but was covered by the pre-existing paragraph (3), in line with the distinction drawn in that Article between "overseas" and "European" territories:

> The provisions of the Treaties shall apply to the European territories for whose external relations a Member State is responsible.

Unlike other BOTs, Gibraltarians[12] eventually became EU citizens with a vote in the EU Parliament (through a constituency of the UK). Despite the exceptions, Gibraltar was therefore, by a very great margin, the most integrated into the EU of all the BOTs and CDS, and the one where EU law operated most closely to the way a UK lawyer would expect.

Because Gibraltarians were unique among the BOTs and CDs in being eligible to vote as if part of the UK in elections for the European Parliament, they were also unique in having a vote in the 2016 Brexit referendum. They voted very heavily in favour of remaining in the EU but, unlike Scotland, they do not necessarily have the option of seeking independence as a way to re-join the EU (see below). To give domestic effect to Brexit Gibraltar therefore had to enact the European Union (Withdrawal) Act 2019,[13] which was similar to the UK's European Union

---

[10] See further Peralta (2019) and Mut-Bosque (2018).

[11] Gibraltar legislation is available at https://www.gibraltarlaws.gov.gi/. The 1972 legislation was originally styled an "Ordinance", but was re-styled as an "Act" after the 2006 change to the constitution. It was then repealed from 2021.

[12] Those who were "citizens of the UK & colonies" (or, later, BOT citizens)—see the declaration by the UK government "on the definition of the term 'nationals'" annexed to the UK's Accession Treaty.

[13] It also enacted the European Union Withdrawal (Application of International Agreements) Act 2019.

(Withdrawal) Act 2018 in repealing the 1970s legislation but then immediately reviving it with a savings provision for the Brexit transition period.

Gibraltar was a contentious issue throughout the Brexit negotiations over the proposed withdrawal agreement, with Spain threatening to veto the agreement entirely. Spain's bargaining position was helped by the approach of the EU Commission in saying that the planned UK-EU agreement could not apply to Gibraltar without Spain's agreement, notably allowing one member state to pursue its own agenda rather than taking a united EU approach. The most well-known Protocol to the Withdrawal Agreement is of course the one on Northern Ireland (which itself held up agreement and has subsequently been renegotiated), but two much smaller Protocols dealt with Gibraltar and the SBAs. To give the Withdrawal Agreement and Protocol domestic effect, Gibraltar then enacted the European Union (Withdrawal Agreement) 2020, reflecting the UK's European Union (Withdrawal Agreement) Act 2020. It amended Gibraltar's European Union (Withdrawal) Act 2019 and added a power to implement the Protocol.

However, the Protocol on Gibraltar left key issues still open for discussion between the UK and Spain. Diverging aims were apparent from the start, with Gibraltar seeking what it called a "differentiated solution" to cater for its unique situation, needing to keep both access to UK markets for its financial services and an open border for workers coming from Spain. The discussions were not productive, so Article 774(3) of the UK-EU Trade and Cooperation Agreement ended up saying "This Agreement shall neither apply to Gibraltar nor have any effects in that territory", so that the subject of Gibraltar was left to negotiations for a separate treaty. At the end of the Brexit transition period there was still no final agreement. The Spanish Government issued, and extended, "bridging measures"[14] to keep the status quo ticking over during the negotiations. Progress remained slow—for instance, it was only in July 2021, months after the end of the Brexit transition period, that the EU Commission adopted its "Recommendation for a Council decision authorising the opening of negotiations for an EU-UK agreement on Gibraltar", and the UK government gave evidence to a Parliamentary Committee in September of that year[15] that the UK view was that the EU proposal "directly conflicts with [the UK position,] undermines the UK's sovereignty over Gibraltar and cannot form the basis of negotiations". The UK issued press releases[16] on 21st March 2023 and 19th September 2024 about meetings between the UK, Gibraltar and Spain, both of which showed similarly little sign of further progress in the talks. The 2023 press release also contained a reference to preparing for the possibility of a "no-negotiated outcome", in an ominous parallel with the way the UK withdrawal negotiations were taken to the last minute with the threat of "no deal" as the default:

[14] See for example Government of Gibraltar press release 958/2021 at https://www.gibraltar.gov.gi/uploads/958-2021.pdf.

[15] See https://committees.parliament.uk/oralevidence/2782/html/.

[16] See https://www.gov.uk/government/news/foreign-secretary-meets-with-the-chief-minister-of-gibraltar-in-london.

> The ministers reiterated their shared commitment to work intensively to conclude UK-EU negotiations in respect of Gibraltar as soon as possible. A treaty would provide certainty for those living and working in Gibraltar and in neighbouring communities, and secure future prosperity for the whole region. ... the UK and EU continue to exchange proposals and work constructively towards an agreement ... The ministers, while committed to the successful conclusion of negotiations, agreed to continue preparations to ensure robust plans are in place for all eventualities, including a no-negotiated outcome.

Gibraltar's government has therefore had to maintain a constant state of preparation for a possible "no-negotiated outcome", with no certainty about key issues including Spain's continuance of its bridging measures at the border, the effects of political changes in Spain, and the possible impacts on the border of changes to come from the Schengen border code and the EU's (and UK's) moves towards electronic visas. These negotiations have been overshadowed by the negotiations on Northern Ireland, which do not offer a promising model for the prospects of reaching agreement.[17] This means that Gibraltar has gone from being the most integrated into the EU of all the BOTs and CDs, to a position where it is now the most difficult of them all to predict what might end up being the eventual relationship with the EU.

2.3 *Sovereign Base Areas of Akrotiri and Dhekelia in Cyprus*

The Sovereign Base Areas of Akrotiri and Dhekelia (the "SBAs") form one BOT. They are the remains of the former colony of Cyprus after the rest of the island became independent in 1960 as the Republic of Cyprus ("RoC"), and they have their own legal system[18] (like other BOTs). There is relatively little academic treatment of the SBAs, and they mostly attract attention from scholars interested in challenging their legitimacy (particularly following the International Court of Justice case on the British Indian Ocean Territory—see below on looking further into the future). A useful guide to how Brexit affects the SBAs is Hadjigeorgiou and Skoutaris (2019), and their pre-Brexit relationship with the EU is discussed in Laulhé Shaelou (2011).

It is important to note at the outset that, although the SBAs are often thought of as military bases, in fact the bases form only a small part of the territory (and the UK has other bases on the territory of the RoC), the rest of which is farmland with some housing and businesses. The boundaries were originally drawn to go around Cypriot villages, except for Akrotiri (at the entrance to the airbase) where the villagers were paid to leave. Over time the Akrotiri villagers returned, the other villages expanded across the borders, and the RoC asked the SBAs to use SBA territory to house Greek-Cypriot refugees after the 1974 partition of the island following the Greek

[17] In February 2023 the "Windsor framework" (Command Paper 806, February 2023) was agreed, and the progress of the UK's Northern Ireland Protocol Bill was paused. But the framework was opposed by the DUP a month later when put to the UK Parliament.

[18] SBA legislation is available at https://www.sbaadministration.org/home/legislation/01_02_09_08_INDICES/20100101_SBA_LEG_INDEX_U_JC.htm.

coup and Turkish invasion.[19] The result is that there is now a resident Cypriot population[20] (and extensive Cypriot-owned farmland and some business premises) that matches the size of the temporary population associated with the British forces (and is larger than that of Montserrat, and roughly twice the size of the civilian population of the Falkland Islands). This is further complicated by the fact that after 1974 one of the bordering villages, Pergamos/Beyarmudu, ended up in the "Turkish Republic of Northern Cyprus", and has similarly expanded.

It is worth also briefly putting the SBAs in the context of the other jurisdictions into which the island of Cyprus is currently split. Since the events of 1974 the government of the RoC only controls part of its territory. Much of the north of the island is now controlled by the "Turkish Republic of Northern Cyprus" (only recognised by Turkey, and not by the EU or UK). There is also a "buffer zone" controlled by the United Nations along the cease-fire line. At points the buffer zone is very wide and includes inhabited villages. There is no buffer zone where the "Turkish Republic of Northern Cyprus" meets the northerly border of the Eastern[21] SBA, and there are two crossing points between the Eastern SBA and the "Turkish Republic of Northern Cyprus", at Pergamos/Beyarmudu and Strovilia/Akyar. The Eastern SBA does also have two stretches of its border that adjoin the United Nations buffer zone, of which one is very short with no particular significance, south of Ayios Nikolaos. The other is alongside the inhabited "mixed" village of Pyla in the buffer zone, where there is free access to the buffer zone from the RoC-controlled area so that there are then no obvious indications of crossing back out of the buffer zone and into the SBAs (or vice versa) on the few through-roads.[22]

Because the SBAs are the continuation of the former colony of Cyprus, the laws that were in force in the colony carried over as the law of the SBAs, though they have mostly been repealed or amended since then. But the legal regime in the SBAs is also the subject of an international agreement between the UK and the RoC, contained in the Exchange of Notes known as "Appendix O" (from the way it was printed for the UK Parliament), associated with the 1960 Treaty of Establishment of the RoC. The exchange reproduces the "Declaration by her Majesty's Government Regarding

---

[19]The language used to describe these events and the current state of affairs has become highly politicised. Turkish Cypriots refer to the invasion as the "peace-keeping operation", while Greek Cypriots and many external observers put quotation marks around the names of the unrecognised entities set up by Turkey. We will refer to it as the events of 1974, and use the quotation marks, but the points made in this chapter do not depend on the view taken of the Cyprus problem.

[20]This led to village councils having to be established under SBA law—see the Akrotiri Community Ordinance 2001, the Akrotiri Village (Special Provisions) Ordinance 1966, the Paramali (Village Commission) (Election Constitution and Powers) Ordinance 1989, the Overlapping Communities Ordinance 2001, the Overlapping Municipalities Ordinance 2011, and their predecessors.

[21]Officially "the SBA of Dhekelia" (which, along with the SBA of Akrotiri further west, makes up the single BOT of the SBAs). But the two components are more usefully distinguished as the Western SBA and Eastern SBA, because Akrotiri and Dhekelia are villages and there are parts of other villages in each SBA.

[22]Including the main road taken by tourists from Larnaca Airport to the resort of Ayia Napa.

the Administration of the Sovereign Base Areas".[23] Under paragraph 2(III) the UK agrees "Not to create customs posts or other frontier barriers between the Sovereign Base Areas and the Republic". Under paragraph 3(2) the UK agrees that "The laws applicable to the Cypriot population of the Sovereign Base Areas will be as far as possible the same as the laws of the Republic". The result is that the border (or "boundary", as downgraded by those who challenge the legitimacy of the SBAs) is practically invisible on the ground, very much like a Schengen border (but see below as to the SBA boundary with the "Turkish Republic of Northern Cyprus"). As mentioned above, like other BOTs, the SBAs operate under the "dualism" approach to international law. So "Ordinances"[24] of the SBAs were needed to give effect to the UK-RoC treaty obligations, to the arrangements with the EU on the accession of the RoC, and to the subsequent Brexit arrangements.

When the UK joined the EU (before the events of 1974 and before the RoC had joined), the decision was taken to preserve the existing arrangements with the RoC (particularly the porous border) by excluding the SBAs from the EU. Article 26(3) of the Act of Accession amended the then Article 227 of the EEC Treaty to add paragraph (5)(b):

> This Treaty shall not apply to the Sovereign Base Areas of the United Kingdom of Great Britain and Northern Ireland in Cyprus.

That presented a striking contrast between the treatment of the SBAs, which are seen as European but were completely excluded, and the treatment of the non-European territories of the existing other member states and then of the UK, to which parts of the Treaties, or at least Associated status, were applied. A Joint Declaration on the SBAs was annexed to the UK's Accession Treaty to say that the relations between the SBAs and the EU would be "defined within the context of any agreement between" the EU and the RoC, but the RoC remained outside the EU for the next 30 years.

Then in 2004 the Greek Cypriots unexpectedly voted "no" in a reunification referendum sponsored by the United Nations (the "Annan Plan"), and the RoC joined the EU as a divided island. In order to meet the obligation to keep the laws the same as those of the RoC, the UK agreed that EU law on certain subjects should apply to the SBAs, mainly the customs territory, indirect taxation, agriculture, and special provisions on immigration for the borders. There were two potential models for the application of EU law, one from the CDs (not applying EU law, subject to exceptions that apply provisions) and one from Gibraltar (applying EU law, subject to exceptions that disapply provisions). The CD model was chosen, presumably based on experience over 30 years in the operation of the CD and Gibraltar systems.

---

[23] The Treaty of Establishment, together with the associated Exchanges of Notes, is available at https://www.sbaadministration.org/images/admin/docs/SBAA_Treaty_of_Establisment.pdf.

[24] Ordinances are the primary legislation of the SBAs. They are made by the "Administrator", who is the equivalent of the Governor in other BOTs, but the "Commander British Forces Cyprus" is always appointed as the Administrator.

So Article 355(5)(b) of TFEU provided for only partial application of the Treaties to the SBAs:

> (b) the Treaties shall not apply to the United Kingdom Sovereign Base Areas of Akrotiri and Dhekelia in Cyprus except to the extent necessary to ensure the implementation of the arrangements set out in the Protocol on the Sovereign Base Areas of the United Kingdom of Great Britain and Northern Ireland in Cyprus annexed to the Act concerning the conditions of accession of [. . .] the Republic of Cyprus [. . .] to the European Union and in accordance with the terms of that Protocol;

Notably this preserved "shall not apply" from the original provision, and therefore set out the form of the limitation for the SBAs in the opposite way to that for the CDs in Article 355(5)(c), although the difference appears to be political or cosmetic rather than legal or logical. For the CDs it is "the Treaties *shall* apply [. . .] *only* to the extent necessary to ensure the implementation of the arrangements", whereas for the SBAs that wording became "the Treaties *shall not* apply [. . .] *except* to the extent necessary to ensure the implementation of the arrangements". Perhaps with some political significance, in the rejected EU constitution the provision would have been changed in Article IV-440(6)(b) to match the CDs (*shall* apply only), but the subsequent Treaty of Lisbon left the wording as it was.

Provision for this was made in "Protocol No 3 on the Sovereign Base Areas of the United Kingdom of Great Britain and Northern Ireland in Cyprus"[25] attached to the 2003 Accession Treaty. Article 8 of that Protocol took pains to say its arrangements were particular to the SBAs and "shall not apply to any other territory of the Community, nor serve as a precedent, in whole or in part, for any other special arrangements which either already exist or which might be set up in another European territory".

To cater for the ongoing division of the island, another Protocol to the Accession Treaty, Number 10 "on Cyprus", disapplied the acquis from the Turkish-controlled North and referred to the North as "those areas of the Republic of Cyprus in which the Government of the Republic of Cyprus does not exercise effective control". It gave the Council power to "define the terms under which the provisions of EU law shall apply to the line between" the North and South,[26] and treated the SBA border with the North as an external border. This meant that the SBAs, without being a part of the EU as such, were controlling on the EU's behalf what was effectively an external border of the EU (the SBA crossing points into the North).

To give effect to the Protocol, and make the relevant elements of EU law part of SBA law, the SBAs enacted the European Community (Protocol Measures) Ordinance 2004. It was closely modelled on the UK's European Communities Act 1972, including giving domestic effect to anything that had direct effect in EU law and providing a power to implement other obligations (such as under Directives) using secondary legislation that could amend primary. A year later the SBAs enacted the

---

[25] OJ, L 236, 23.9.2003, p. 940.

[26] Council Regulation (EC) No 866/2004 of 29 April 2004 on a regime under Article 2 of Protocol No 10 of the Act of Accession (OJ L 161, 30.4.2004, p128).

European Community (Specified Measures) Ordinance 2005. This was to deal with the issue of EU legislation that was not covered by Protocol 3, but which should be given effect in the SBAs under Appendix O because it had effect in the RoC (including EU Regulations on non-Protocol matters, which the RoC did not need to enact domestically). It gave the SBAs power to implement that EU legislation by SBA secondary legislation, but with "exceptions, modifications or additions" to reflect the fact that Appendix O only required SBA laws to be the same as the RoC's "as far as possible", which was intended to ensure military needs could be catered for with provisions that were different from the RoC.

Article 7(3)-(4) of Protocol 3 specifically provided for the UK to delegate to the RoC the UK's functions under the Protocol (Appendix O had always encouraged delegation). The European Community (Specified Measures) Ordinance 2005 automatically delegated powers under the implemented EU legislation to officers of the RoC who exercised the equivalent powers in RoC territory. Then the Delegation of Functions to the Republic Ordinance 2007 added to the delegation provisions. That meant many Cypriots in the SBAs dealt with RoC officials under laws that were the same as the RoC laws, without it necessarily being obvious that in fact the laws were SBA Ordinances.

When the UK decided to leave the EU, this did not alter its obligations under Appendix O to keep SBA laws as far as possible the same as RoC laws, with RoC remaining a member state subject to EU laws. The Withdrawal Agreement ("WA"), under Article 3(1)(d), applies to the SBAs "to the extent necessary to ensure the implementation of the arrangements set out in" the original Protocol 3. The UK negotiated a new Protocol, to the WA, to cater for the SBAs by effectively providing for the continuation of the pre-existing arrangements, including for example continued jurisdiction for the ECJ in questions of applying EU law to the SBAs (see Article 1(2) of the Protocol). The WA only applied to the SBAs from the end of the Brexit transition period (see Article 185 of the WA).

The SBAs therefore enacted the European Union (Withdrawal and Implementation of Protocol) Ordinance 2020, which gives effect to the new Protocol and repeals the European Union (Protocol Measures) Ordinance 2004 (and the European Union (Withdrawal and Transition) Ordinance 2020), but leaves the European Union (Specified Measures) Ordinance 2005 in force. That was because the "specified measures" regime will still be needed to implement EU law not covered by the new Protocol, where that is needed under Appendix O to match the law of the RoC. The Protocol required further automatic delegation of functions to the RoC and this was provided for by enacting the Conferral of Protocol Functions on the Republic Ordinance 2020, which supplements and parallels the Delegation of Functions to the Republic Ordinance 2007.

The Protocol to the WA also preserves the position that the SBAs must treat the crossing points into the "Turkish Republic of Northern Cyprus" as an EU external border, as happened when both the UK and the RoC were EU member states. After Brexit the effect of the Protocol is that the UK is still filling this role even though it is no longer a member state itself.

Article 774 of the UK-EU Trade and Cooperation Agreement does not make any special provision about the SBAs, so it does not apply to them, because the WA and its Protocol already contain everything. This means the effect is very much of continuity of the previous regime on EU law and Appendix O, with some more delegation of functions to the RoC, in a relatively stable-looking settlement for the future (but see the discussion below on independence and possible cession of the SBAs to the RoC).

3 The Crown Dependencies

We turn now to the previous and future relationships between the EU and the Crown Dependencies ("CDs"), looking at how those relationships are affected by their relationships with the UK. The CDs are the Isle of Man and the Bailiwicks of Jersey and Guernsey.[27]

3.1 The relationship of the CDs with the UK and EU before the Trade and Cooperation Agreement

The CDs are parts of the British Islands,[28] but (like the BOTs) they are not and never have been parts of the UK. Each CD has its own legal system and legislation.[29]

As mentioned above, the UK is responsible for representing the interests of the CDs (and BOTs) internationally and is also responsible for their defence. But, as also mentioned above, the CDs were not acquired by conquest, cession or settlement like the BOTs, and in fact Jersey and Guernsey were part of the Duchy of Normandy which conquered England in 1066, so the relationship is different. The CDs insist

[27] The Bailiwick of Guernsey includes Alderney and Sark which each have their own legislative bodies. Together the Bailiwicks of Guernsey and Jersey are referred to as the "Channel Islands". In this chapter we use "Jersey" and "Guernsey" to refer to the whole of each Bailiwick.

[28] This is distinct from the geographic concept of the "British Isles" (which is sometimes loosely used to include the whole island of Ireland). The "British Islands" are just the UK and the CDs (not the Republic of Ireland, although it does form part of the Common Travel Area with the UK and CDs). See the matching definitions of "British Islands" in Schedule 1 to the Interpretation Act 1978 of the UK, the Schedule to the Interpretation (Jersey) Law 1954, the Schedule to the Interpretation and Standard Provisions (Bailiwick of Guernsey) Law 2016, and the Schedule to the Interpretation Act 2015 of the Isle of Man.

[29] Jersey legislation is available at https://www.jerseylaw.je/laws/current/Pages/search.aspx, Guernsey legislation at https://www.guernseylegalresources.gg/, and Isle of Man legislation at https://legislation.gov.im/cms/.

that the UK is not legally able to impose legislation on them without their consent or represent them internationally in ways they do not agree to.[30]

Whilst people from the CDs are British citizens,[31] they are not residents of the UK. Instead, CDs may be best described as self-governing dependencies of the Crown. This means that their relationships are with the person of the sovereign themselves. In the case of Jersey and Guernsey, this is in the context of the sovereign being heir to the Dukes of Normandy and in the Isle of Man, to the Lord of Mann. Thus, King Charles III is Head of State and the islands' respective Lieutenant Governors act as His Majesty's personal representatives.

The constitutional and legal relationship between the CDs and the UK had existed for centuries before the UK joined the EU, and had been built up by virtue of a series of Royal Charters, each granted by the reigning sovereign of the time. The relationship is broad but the items of particular interest in the EU context are the free movement of persons within the Common Travel Area (which also covers the Republic of Ireland) and the free movement of goods, which existed before the advent of the provisions which led to visa-free travel in the EU and membership of the EU customs territory.

The Charters had formed the backbone to UK-Jersey-Guernsey trading relations[32] and provided for a host of ancient rights and privileges, including that the Channel Islanders could export items grown, produced or manufactured in the islands to the UK duty free, with these freedoms finding reflection in the then contents of section 5 of the UK's Customs and Excise (General Reliefs) Act 1979 and now in Regulations made under section 126(5) and (6) of the UK's Finance Act 2016.[33]

The Isle of Man's history had always been distinct from its Channel Island cousins, because its status as a CD was settled only in 1765 by the Isle of Man Purchase Act which bought the feudal rights for the British Crown as Lords of Man. The Isle of Man and the UK had then later settled an Agreement on Customs and

---

[30] In 2010 the UK government stated that "The UK government is responsible for the Crown Dependences' international relations and ultimate good governance and has the commensurate power to ensure these obligations are met"—see "Government Response to the Justice Select Committee's report: Crown Dependencies" CM 7965. Birt (2017) lays out the various arguments for the contrary view taken by the CDs, dealing with the Justice Select Committee's report and the much older Kilbrandon Report, and covering all three CDs.

[31] Under section 50(1) of the UK's British Nationality Act 1981, the UK is defined for that Act's purposes to include the CDs, so birth in a CD confers British citizenship on the same basis as birth in the UK, and so on.

[32] As well as setting out certain facets of Crown Dependency autonomy, such as the status of Jersey and Guernsey as "Bailiwicks", exemption from English taxes and the right to import into England (now the UK) items grown, produced or manufactured in Jersey or Guernsey. These privileges were also summarised in the Report of the Civil Law Commissioners of 1861 and the charters are now translated in Thornton, Tim; The Royal Charters of Jersey 1341–1688; Woodbridge; Boydell Press; 2024.

[33] The Regulations are also made under sections 56 and 57 of the Taxation (Cross-border Trade) Act 2018 and section 11 of the Taxation (Post-transition Period) Act 2020.

Excise and Associated Matters in 1979,[34] which also brought the Isle of Man into the UK's VAT area (this was never the case for the Channel Islands).

As the UK prepared to join the EU, the CDs each debated the options for their future relationships. Ultimately, they chose not to join as full members but instead to have some elements of EU law apply to them on a bespoke basis. This special position is reflected in what was, immediately before Brexit, Article 355(5)(c) TFEU, which set out the parameters for this particular and partial application of the Treaties:[35]

> the Treaties shall apply to the Channel Islands and the Isle of Man only to the extent necessary to ensure the implementation of the arrangements for those islands set out in the Treaty concerning the accession of new Member States to the European Economic Community and to the European Atomic Energy Community signed on 22 January 1972

Protocol 3 to the UK's Act of Accession laid down in broad terms the exceptions where EU law would apply to the CDs, along with some supplementary provisions, becoming the embodiment of these new "arrangements". From 1973 to the end of 2020, the CDs' relationships with the EU functioned by virtue of this one Protocol.[36] In brief terms this meant that, while the UK was a member state, the CDs were *treated as* part of the EU for customs matters, quantitative restrictions and the trade in agricultural products. For all other purposes (such as financial services and data protection, for example) they were deemed to be "third countries"[37] as they had no treaty relationship with the EU for those purposes.

Each CD enacted domestic legislation to give general effect to the elements of EU law that were covered by Protocol 3. Jersey, for example, enacted the European Communities (Jersey) Law 1973.[38] As in the other territories discussed above, it was modelled on the UK's European Communities Act 1972, but much less closely because of the narrow scope of the Protocol 3 obligations. In fact, as originally enacted, it only gave effect to EU law that had direct effect, and did not include any power to make subsidiary legislation to implement relevant EU law such as Directives. That did not come till the European Communities Legislation (Implementation) (Jersey) Law 1996 was enacted, so in the meanwhile anything that needed legislation had to be dealt with under existing powers or by new primary legislation. The 1996 Law in particular allowed Jersey Ministers to make Orders to implement EU sanctions regimes (usually implementing United Nations sanctions), given the

---

[34] See https://www.gov.im/media/80147/cande-agreement-consolidated-version-2018-inc-annex.pdf.

[35] Taking the opposite approach to that for Gibraltar. See above for comparison with the framing of the similar provisions in Article 355 on the SBAs.

[36] For more on Protocol 3 in that period, see Sutton (2005).

[37] See also *Routier v Revenue and Customs Commissioners* [2019] UKSC 43 for further discussion on the term "third country". This case considered EU free movement of capital in relation to Jersey's status as a CD.

[38] Before that there was the European Free Trade Association (Jersey) Law 1960 and the European Communities (Jersey) Law 1972.

need for speed where financial assets are to be frozen. However, it also gave to Jersey's States Assembly (its parliament), and in some cases to its government, a power to implement EU legislation on a *voluntary* basis, where there was no obligation to do so under Protocol 3 (which applied to most of the acquis). As mentioned above, there are various advantages for even a third country to reproduce the effect of EU law in certain areas, such as where that may be necessary to enable trade with the EU. Data protection is a major example of that, but Jersey used primary legislation in that field, rather than relying on powers under the 1996 Law.[39] Perhaps the most obvious example of the trade-related use of these powers to implement EU legislation, outside of Protocol 3 fields, by secondary legislation under the 1996 Law is the Alternative Investment Funds (Jersey) Regulations 2012. Those Regulations gave effect to the necessary elements of Directive 2011/61/EU to enable cross-border trade with the EU in that field. However, the challenge of swift implementation of EU sanctions (mostly outside of Protocol 3), along with other factors, eventually led to the replacement of the 1996 Law by the European Union Legislation (Implementation) (Jersey) Law 2014. Later , Jersey moved to subject-specific primary legislation for sanctions in the form of the Sanctions and Asset-Freezing (Jersey) Law 2019.

When the UK voted for Brexit (as mentioned above, the CDs and the BOTs, other than Gibraltar, did not vote on the referendum), the CDs needed to work out their response. A crucial difference was that they already had their respective powers to implement EU law that they were not obliged to implement, and no particular political imperative to repeal the EU legislation. So instead of following the UK model of repealing the 1972 Act and then immediately reviving it by a saving provision for the Brexit transition period, Jersey was able to leave its 1973 Law in force until the end of that period. This meant instead that it enacted the European Union (Repeal and Amendment) (Jersey) Law 2018, which allowed secondary legislation by a Minister to set the time at which the repeal would come into force and to make necessary amendments (for both "deal" and "no deal scenarios"). The European Union Legislation (Implementation) (Jersey) Law 2014 was not repealed and remains in force, amended so that it enables Jersey to continue implementing EU legislation where that is useful, either as part of the ongoing post-Brexit changes to the relationship with the EU (see below on the consequences of the Trade and Cooperation Agreement) or for some other reason. Turning back to the examples mentioned above, the Data Protection (Jersey) Law 2018 and Alternative Investment Funds (Jersey) Regulations 2012 remain in force. So too does the Sanctions and Asset-Freezing (Jersey) Law 2019, but Jersey's Assembly has passed[40] the Sanctions and Asset-Freezing (Amendment No. 3) (Jersey) Law 2023 which will remove the ability to implement EU sanctions (leaving the powers instead to implement those of the UK and United Nations, and to make Jersey's own sanctions measures in areas such as terrorism). The result of this is that there has been no need for any

[39] See now the Data Protection (Jersey) Law 2018, which implements the EU's GDPR.
[40] Subject to Privy Council ratification, as at 1st May 2023.

equivalent of the complications involved in the UK's concept of "retained EU law" and its sunsetting of that law.

As with the BOTs and UK, Brexit meant British citizens in the CDs also lost their EU citizenship and associated free movement rights. But, oddly, some of them had not had full free movement rights anyway (making them worse off than BOT-based British citizens after 2002—see above). Protocol 3 on the CDs provided that those whose British citizenship came from birth in or other connection with the CDs would not have EU rights of free movement of persons or services, unless they had been ordinarily resident in the UK for five years or one of their parents or grandparents had British citizenship from a connection with the UK. In that sense Brexit meant that all British citizens in the CDs were in the same position again, as no longer being EU citizens. Meanwhile the "Common Travel Area", which pre-dated UK accession to the EU and allows visa-free travel between the UK, the CDs, and the Republic of Ireland, continues in force through the immigration legislation of each of those jurisdictions.

The Withdrawal Agreement applies, under Article 3(1)(c), to the CDs "to the extent that Union law was applicable to them before the date of entry into force of this Agreement". As the UK's status as a member state ended, Protocol 3 fell away as an automatic result of this change. But, under the Withdrawal Agreement, the Brexit transition period applied to the CDs' relationships under Protocol 3, meaning that the effect of Protocol 3 remained in place until the end of that transition period. Unlike in the case of the SBAs and Gibraltar, the Withdrawal Agreement did not include a new Protocol for the CDs. The CDs needed to be able to continue trading with the UK after Brexit, as well as considering their future relationship with the EU. The new trading arrangements with the EU are described in Bell et al. (2021) and are outlined in the following sections, along with the trading arrangements with the UK.

3.2 *Customs Matters: UK-CD Customs Union*

In the aftermath of the Brexit vote by the UK, the CDs needed to assess how their future interests may be best protected in an unknown and wholly new trading future. A key starting point was to understand fully the nature of the constitutional and legal position which had existed for centuries in relation to the free movement of goods - quite apart from those provisions which led to membership of the EU customs territory.

Regardless of some differences in histories between the CDs, their positions at the start of the Brexit process with regard to the free movement of goods were clear: that the respective goods relationships with the UK were centuries old and that the UK's withdrawal from EU membership must not adversely affect those relationships.

This resulted in the agreement of new arrangements for the CDs which were signed in 2018 in order to come into effect at the end of the Brexit transition period, whereby Jersey and Guernsey secured wholly new customs texts and the Isle of Man an Annex containing the same language as its sister jurisdictions which was added to their extant agreement (see above). Each new text is expressed as "*concerning the establishment and operation of the United Kingdom-Crown Dependencies Customs Union*" and, whilst not "*altering or affecting the constitutional relationship*" between the CDs and the UK, provided the backbone for a newly recognised union to cover "*all trade in goods involving the elimination between its members of customs duty on imports and exports and of any charges having equivalent effect, and the adoption of a common customs tariff in their relations with third countries.*" The primary drive behind this new UK-CDs Customs Union ("the Customs Union") was the enhancement of established freedoms and protection in a trading capacity post-Brexit where the outcome of any negotiations—with the EU or any other global partners—was mired in uncertainty for the foreseeable future. However, the formation of a "Union" also expressly recognised that the CDs are distinct jurisdictions with their own international identities separate from the UK.[41] Thus, they remain their own customs territories, with their own competent authorities and domestic processes through which the recognition and implementation of domestic or international obligations are given effect. With this in mind, the treatment of "Customs Law" in the Arrangements is approached from the angle of ensuring a form of "equivalence of outcome" between the jurisdictions within Union. Paragraph 10 to the Arrangements[42] sets this out clearly by establishing that:

1. Subject to any exceptions that may be agreed by the Competent Authorities of the United Kingdom and Jersey, the Government of Jersey will keep Jersey's Customs Law correspondent with that of the United Kingdom and will legislate to maintain that correspondence whenever necessary and, in particular, when changes are made in relevant United Kingdom Customs Law.
2. Compliance with the commitment in sub-paragraph 1 will require the introduction of legislation which requires Jersey Courts to have due regard to the relevant decisions of United Kingdom Courts when interpreting correspondent provisions of Jersey Customs Law.

With regard to the TCA and its effects in the CDs, the new Customs Union is a lens through which the new text must be understood and key for the CDs is the maintenance (in theory and in practice) of their respective autonomies in this wider trading context.

[41] See also the Framework Agreements for developing the international identities of each Crown Dependency: https://www.gov.je/SiteCollectionDocuments/Government%20and%20administration/R%20InternationalIdentityFramework%2020070502.pdf.

[42] Using the Jersey Arrangement as an example, but there are mirrored provisions in the Guernsey text.

3.3 *The World Trade Organization*

With the above in mind, the other essential component through which TCA obligations must be understood in their application to the CDs is that of the World Trade Organisation ("WTO"). Whilst each of the CDs had enjoyed membership of the General Agreement on Tariffs and Trade ("GATT") since 1948, only the Isle of Man had been part of the UK's membership of the WTO.[43] The WTO texts amount at around 60 agreements, annexes, decisions and understandings which make up six main parts: an Agreement Establishing the WTO ("the Marrakesh Agreement); agreements for three broad areas of trade (i.e. goods, services and intellectual property); dispute settlement provisions; and review mechanisms for member's trade, policies. Owing to their breadth, the WTO texts are often used as a baseline for free trade agreements around the world and accordingly, recognition of and compliance with that baseline is a prerequisite for many international trade negotiations. Jersey and Guernsey thus sought extension of the UK's WTO membership to themselves, this being communicated to the Director-General of the WTO on 15th October 2019,[44] and coming into effect at the same time as the new Customs Union. The notable timing had the further advantage of adding a protective mechanism to help deal with a "hard Brexit," had that been the final outcome of UK-EU negotiations.

Accordingly, since extension, the GATT, the General Agreement on Trade in Services ("GATS"), the Agreement on Trade-related Investment Measures ("TRIMS") and the Agreement on Trade-related Intellectual Property Measures ("TRIPS") all apply to the CDs as part of the global network of trade rules and, as with any rules system, participating jurisdictions have both the benefit and burden of obligations which are enforceable on the international stage.

Thus, whether it be in the context of the WTO Agreement commitments themselves or in the context of how they may be used to provide internationally understood platforms for new UK free trade agreement texts (such as the TCA), membership of the WTO marked a foundational legal milestone for the CDs.

3.4 *A New Trading Future: The TCA*

The next section of this chapter explores the emergence of the newly negotiated context for the CDs' international trading relations, as those jurisdictions which enjoy both autonomy and a set of international identities separate from the UK, but for which the UK will represent their interests globally, now itself as a state independent from the EU.

---

[43] The Isle of Man had the WTO agreements extended to them in 1997.

[44] See WTO Ref: WLI/100. Letter dated 4th January 2021.

The new UK-EU Trade Agreement ("the TCA")[45] came into effect on 1st January 2021 and marked the beginning of the new future of the CDs in their relationships with both EU partners and the UK. As the UK is a newly independent trading nation and the state responsible for representing the CDs' international interests, the text of the TCA provides for bespoke new provisions to facilitate the different context to the free movement of goods, this time being underpinned by international law rather than as a result of the UK's EU membership.

The UK published its "Approach to Negotiations" on 27 February 2020, with the negotiations getting under way on 2 March and only finally concluding on Christmas Eve. The reference to the CDs and the need to represent their interests was expressed as follows:

> 11. The Government will act in these negotiations on behalf of all the territories for whose international relations the UK is responsible. In negotiating the future relationship between these territories and the EU, the UK Government will seek outcomes which support the territories' security and economic interests and which reflect their unique characteristics.

4 CD Scoping

As the UK began to formulate its approach to the TCA negotiations, the CDs needed to crystallise their views swiftly as to their own negotiation asks and preferences. In broad terms, the CDs sought the maintenance of "continuity" as far as possible and the ability to pursue their interests in any new trading opportunities which the UK might secure. The States of Jersey's Brexit Report of June 2020 (Update) described the previous three months work in terms of ensuring that its offensive and defensive positions were actively considered by the UK whilst engaging with industry bodies to maximise preparations and ensure that "continuity".[46] One of the principal challenges was on agreeing the nature and scope of CD inclusion to be aimed for, given that the CDs each are predominantly "services" based, with a history of Protocol 3 being customs and agriculture focused (owing to the nature of their economies in the early 1970s). Accordingly, the approach ultimately adopted was to follow the goods-focused contents of Protocol 3 as a baseline and have the new trade text identify which of the specific chapters would apply directly.

The finalised version of the Territorial Scope text in the TCA is at Article 774[47] which sets out that:

> This Agreement also applies to the Bailiwick of Guernsey, the Bailiwick of Jersey and the Isle of Man to the extent set out in Heading Five of Part Two and Article 520.

---

[45] Trade and Cooperation Agreement between the European Union and the European Atomic Energy Community, of the one part, and the United Kingdom of Great Britain and Northern Ireland, of the other part (OJ L 149, 30.4.2021, p. 10–2539).

[46] Page 17.

[47] Part Seven, Final Provisions, Territorial Scope.

Heading Five to the text is specific to fisheries and this aspect to the TCA forms a substantive part to the new relationship which is very different in focus from Protocol 3. Article 520 is the provision which deals with geographical application and sets out the nature and mechanics of how the goods provisions of the agreement are to operate and be understood. In particular, the detail of Article 520(3) to (5) is helpful:

> 3. Subject to the exceptions contained in paragraph 4 of this Article, Chapters 1, 2 and 5 of Title I of Heading One and the Protocols and Annexes to those Chapters shall also apply, with respect to the United Kingdom, to the territories referred to in Article 774(2). For that purpose, the territories referred to in Article 774(2) shall be considered as being part of the customs territory of the United Kingdom. The customs authorities of the territories referred to in Article 774(2) shall be responsible for the application and implementation of these Chapters, and the Protocols and Annexes to these Chapters, in their respective territories. References to "customs authority" in those provisions shall be read accordingly. However, requests and communications made under these Chapters, and the Protocols and Annexes to these Chapters, shall be administered by the customs authority of the United Kingdom.
>
> 4. Article 110, Annex 18 and the Protocol on administrative cooperation and combating fraud in the field of Value Added Tax and on mutual assistance for the recovery of claims relating to taxes and duties shall not apply to the Bailiwick of Jersey or the Bailiwick of Guernsey.
>
> 5. Chapters 3 and 4 of Title I of Heading One and the Annexes to those Chapters shall also apply, with respect to the United Kingdom, to the territories referred to in Article 774(2). The authorities of the territories referred to in Article 774(2) shall be responsible for the application and implementation of these Chapters, and the Annexes to these Chapters, in their respective territories and relevant references shall be read accordingly. However, requests and communications made under these Chapters, and the Annexes to these Chapters, shall be administered by the authorities of the United Kingdom.

In other words, from a goods perspective, the treaty text provides that all of the following apply, including the attaching Protocols and Annexes of each[48]: Title I of Heading One, Chapter 1 (national treatment and market access); Chapter 2 (Rules of Origin); Chapter 3 (Sanitary and Phytosanitary Measures); Chapter 4 (Technical Barriers to Trade); and Chapter 5 (Customs and Trade Facilitation). However, with the exceptional profiles of the CDs in mind, the text also makes other appropriate references to ensure it is clear that whilst the UK is state party, those parts of the text which apply to the CDs do so with the consent of the CDs and are to be implemented and enforced by their own governments and institutions. Therefore, they have bespoke termination provisions at Articles 509(4) and 520(4), (7) and (8), and have certain specific competent authority references included. Thus, the treaty text provides in relation to references to "customs authority":

> the customs authorities of the territories referred to in Article 774(2) shall be responsible for the application and implementation of these Chapters, and the Protocols and Annexes to these Chapters, in their respective territories. References to "customs authority" in those provisions shall be read accordingly.

[48]Including Annexes 2 to 17 inclusive and the Protocol on Mutual Administrative Assistance in Customs Matters.

In other words, this example means that where a reference to "customs authority" would by its nature necessitate a reading of a singular authority, this provision displaces that presumption in order to protect the constitutional reality existing beneath the "UK" badging. Similarly, Article 520(3) provides that "the territories referred to in Article 774(2) *shall be considered as* being part of the customs territory of the United Kingdom," which in effect, carries the same meaning as being "treated as" (as opposed to actually "being"). This wording is an echo of Regulation 706/73 which, in its preamble and at Article 1(2), set out that "for the purpose of applying the rules referred to in paragraph 1, the United Kingdom and the Islands shall be treated as a single Member State."

From a constitutional standpoint, Article 520 (Geographical Application) also brings some other crucial provisions as Article 118 and its attaching Annex 18 (Authorised Economic Operators) are expressly excluded from applying to the Channel Islands, despite their goods and customs context. This is because Authorised Economic Operator[49] ("AEOs") status programmes are not presently in place in Jersey or Guernsey. This form of tailoring of the treaty text demonstrates both the obvious need to cater for the very particular territories which the UK also represents and further highlights the difficulties in how the contents of free trade agreements can be a challenging fit for small jurisdictions. However, the question then becomes (and remains for the future) one of considering how far in reality such tailoring should go and the questions of politics and political capital in balancing different and often conflicting jurisdictional profiles.

Another good example of this is in Article 520(4):

> the Protocol on administrative cooperation and combating fraud in the field of Value Added Tax and on mutual assistance for the recovery of claims relating to taxes and duties shall not apply to the Bailiwick of Jersey or the Bailiwick of Guernsey.

This inclusion was agreed again owing to the distinct systems of tax which exist between each of the CDs and the UK. In the case of Jersey and Guernsey, their fiscal autonomy goes back to the time of the Royal Charters and operationally and legally exclusion from this provision was clearly necessary. It also remains open to the Channel Islands then to consider whether, respectively, they would like to negotiate their own bilateral tax agreements in future (for example, under letters of entrustment[50]) and in what way. Their respective positions were further protected by a Declaration from the UK to this effect.

---

[49] AEO status is a certified authorization which is issued by customs administrations across the EU members and the UK.

[50] A "letter of entrustment" is an instrument by which the UK entrusts the government of a CD or BOT with the roles and responsibilities of conducting international negotiations on its own behalf, which is then accepted by the foreign country with which the CD or BOT negotiates directly.

5 Fisheries Provisions: Introduction

The new TCA articles dealing with fisheries for each of the CDs are found at Heading Five to the text and represent a real difference in relation to the previous Protocol 3 position. In brief, under Protocol 3, fisheries access and licencing provisions did not form any part of the extant EU treaty obligations affecting the CDs. However, the outcome of negotiations for the TCA resulted in goods and fish being treated as mutually dependant, meaning for the CDs that if they wanted to access the benefits of goods and customs inclusion, the trade package would include agreement on access and terms for fisheries. One particular challenge with this position, however, was the historically very different fisheries access profiles of each of the CDs. These differences (which are further explored below) meant that the degree of individual tailoring was significant in comparison with the approach to the goods and customs application discussed above.

With regard to Jersey, the existing treaty which governed Jersey-France fisheries arrangements was an agreement between "the Government of the United Kingdom and the Government of the French Republic concerning Fishing in the Bay of Granville"[51] ("the Granville Bay Agreement"). This Granville Bay Agreement, which was entered into by the UK on Jersey's behalf with its consent, was agreed before the Lisbon Treaty increased the competences of the EU. Therefore, the treaty itself was a member state bilateral text and provided for negotiated access to Jersey's territorial waters, which in 2002[52] had been extended out to twelve nautical miles[53] under the Territorial Sea Act 1987 (Jersey) Order 1997[54] (as further amended). The Granville Bay Agreement provided for access to Jersey waters between three to twelve nautical miles (and to French waters in the Bay of Granville, together known as "the Area") and allowed those with the valid licences and permits to fish in particular delineated zones.[55] Fisheries regulation of "the Area," except as otherwise provided, was premised on the idea that the Parties would look to agree measures by virtue of a "Joint Management Committee" to "govern fishing in the Area, on the

[51] Signed on 4th July 2000 and coming into force on 1st January 2004.

[52] In line with international norms under the United Nations Convention on the Law of the Sea.

[53] Subject also to the agreement of a median line with French territorial waters under the Agreement between the United Kingdom of Great Britain and Northern Ireland and the French Republic concerning the establishment of a Maritime Boundary between Jersey and France, 2000. This agreement was entered into by the UK on Jersey's behalf and with its consent in accordance with constitutional requirements. It should be noted that the TCA does not affect the delineation of territorial waters nor the median line and does not affect Jersey's territorial sovereignty over the rocks of its offshore reefs. Jersey's sovereignty in this regard was determined in 1953 by the International Court of Justice in *The Minquiers and Ecrehos case (France v United Kingdom)* ICJ Reports 1953, p47 at https://www.icj-cij.org/public/files/case-related/17/017-19531117-JUD-01-00-EN.pdf.

[54] This is an Order in Council extending a UK Act to Jersey, and as such it is available on the legislation websites of both Jersey and the UK.

[55] See https://treaties.fcdo.gov.uk/awweb/pdfopener?md=1&did=69746.

basis of the precautionary approach but having regard to socio-economic factors". It was then up to both sides to implement and promulgate the measures in their respective domestic laws.[56]

With regard to Guernsey, the previous position for fisheries was decidedly different from its Jersey cousins. Similar to Jersey, Guernsey had had its territorial waters extended out to twelve nautical miles under the Territorial Sea Act 1987 (Guernsey) Order 2019.[57] However, unlike in Jersey, the London Fisheries Convention 1964[58] had been applied to Guernsey and therefore governed the conditions of access for (non-Guernsey) fishers in Guernsey waters. The resulting nature of the access was based accordingly on historic fishing activity between 1953 and 1962 (as protected previously by the London Convention), and applies in the six to twelve nautical miles areas of Guernsey's territorial waters. The London Convention itself was renounced by the UK as part of the Brexit process in 2017 and therefore the new solution was required to maintain the activities engaged under the previous regime.

Finally, with respect to the Isle of Man, their territorial waters were also extended out to twelve nautical miles by virtue of the Territorial Sea Act 1987 (Isle of Man) Order 1991. Similar to Guernsey, the Isle of Man had seen the London Fisheries Convention extended to it which meant that EU fishermen could fish in the six to twelve nautical miles of Manx territorial waters. Therefore, this secured for EU fisherman the blueprint of their future access to the same extent as Guernsey. The end result was that, although the CDs had come to the fisheries negotiations from varied perspectives and historic backgrounds, the UK's renouncing of the London Convention, and the EU's increased competences for fisheries after the Lisbon Treaty, meant that all three CDs ended up in a similar position. This was especially so given that the prospects for a goods deal became intrinsically linked to what was on offer for fisheries.

6 New Arrangements on Fisheries

Article 502 of the TCA ("Specific access arrangements relating to the Bailiwick of Guernsey, the Bailiwick of Jersey and the Isle of Man") is the key provision for the new arrangements for access to CD waters for fisheries. It provides that:

> By way of derogation from Article 500(1) and (3) to (7), Article 501 and Annex 38, each Party shall grant vessels of the other Party access to fish in its waters reflecting the actual extent and nature of fishing activity that it can be demonstrated was carried out during the period beginning on 1 February 2017 and ending on 31 January 2020 by qualifying vessels

[56] See Granville Bay Article 4.

[57] As with its Jersey equivalent, this is an Order in Council extending a UK Act to Guernsey, and as such it is available on the legislation websites of both Guernsey and the UK.

[58] See https://assets.publishing.service.gov.uk/government/uploads/system/uploads/attachment_data/file/269708/Fisheries_Conv_March-April_1964.pdf.

of the other Party in the waters and under any treaty arrangements that existed on 31 January 2020.

Therefore, the new access in each case is based on the "actual nature and extent" of fishing activity "that it can be demonstrated was carried out" between 1st February 2017 and 31st January 2020 and under any treaty arrangements which existed on 31st January 2020 (i.e. under the Granville Bay Agreement and the London Convention). In a nutshell, the new TCA model aimed at a system of access which looks to be sustainable for the future whilst reflecting relevant and demonstrable prior activity. There was apparent nervousness on all sides, however, as to what this might mean in practice and how the rather bland language of the finalised treaty text might best be satisfied. In fact, such was the concern that on the 6th May 2021 Royal Naval vessels from both the UK and France arrived in Jersey territorial waters to monitor demonstrations by French fisherman where there had also been suggestions that St Helier's port could be blockaded in protest—this stand-off being dubbed "the Battle of St Helier".[59] Fortunately matters resolved but the processes involved to come to confirmed positions on new systems of access were only finalised in February of 2023, where all three CDs produced their "extent and nature" permits to sit alongside the suites of new licences.

Perhaps for Jersey most significantly, the fisheries changes brought about by the TCA bring back a unity of decision-making in terms of the management of the waters not seen during the Granville Bay Agreement period. This is because the "Joint Management Committee" system under the Granville Bay Agreement now no longer exists, so Jersey and the other CDs must manage their waters on a sole basis—although in accordance with Article 496 which calls on the Parties (the CDs for these purposes) to "decide on any measures applicable to its waters in pursuit of the objectives set out in Article 494(1) and (2), and having regard to the principles referred to in Article 494(3)" (which includes preservation of the "regulatory autonomy of the Parties").

7 Disputes: Particular Provisions for Fisheries

The TCA's provisions for dispute settlement are to some extent tailored for the CDs as although the main sections on dispute settlement under the agreement are found at Part 6 (Dispute Settlement and Horizontal Provisions), there are specific articles dealing solely with fisheries disputes. In particular, Articles 506 to 511 cover remedial measures and dispute resolution, data sharing, the Specialised Committee on Fisheries, termination, review clause and relationship to other agreements.

[59] For a further account see the editorial headed "Miscellany: The Battle of St Helier 2021" in the Jersey and Guernsey Law Review https://www.jerseylaw.je/publications/jglr/Pages/JGLR2102_Miscellany.aspx.

The term "Party" applies to the UK instead of the CDs on the face of the text. But the CDs' negotiation stances demonstrated their paramount concern to ensure that the provisions cater for their autonomy in their constitutional relationship with the UK, so that the UK is in a position to fulfil its duty to ensure that the CDs are involved in any of the dispute processes which may concern them. This is particularly important in the mechanics of the operation of the TCA, given the detail of these provisions, their tight turn-around times (such as the 14-day period with regard to complaint responses in Article 506), and the overall arbitration procedure requirements at Part 6.

Article 506 has a particular impact on the CDs, given their specific fisheries access arrangements (Article 502) and the effect on them of the notification periods relating to the importation and direct landing of fisheries products (Article 503). Article 506(2) provides that:

> 2. In relation to an alleged failure by a Party (the "respondent Party") to comply with Article 502, 503 or any other provision of this Heading in so far as it relates to the arrangements provided for in those Articles, the other Party (the "complaining Party"), after giving notice to the respondent Party:
>
> (a) may suspend, in whole or in part, access to its waters within the meaning of Article 502;
> (b) if it considers that the suspension referred to in point (a) of this paragraph is not commensurate to the economic and societal impact of the alleged failure, may suspend, in whole or in part, the preferential tariff treatment granted to fishery products under Article 21;
> (c) if it considers that the suspension referred to in points (a) and (b) of this paragraph is not commensurate to the economic and societal impact of the alleged failure, may suspend, in whole or in part, the preferential tariff treatment of other goods under Article 21.

Therefore, under the new arrangements, there are measures which can be taken by either side if there is a breach of the TCA access terms, with those measures being at all times "proportionate to the alleged failure by the respondent Party and the economic and societal impact" (Article 506(3)). A resulting measure may take effect "at the earliest seven days after the complaining Party has given the respondent Party notice of the proposed suspension," and the "Parties shall consult within the Specialised Committee on Fisheries with a view to reaching a mutually agreeable solution." There is then the 14-day period mentioned above (after the notification has been issued), with which the complaining Party must comply by way of challenging the alleged failure by "requesting the establishment of an arbitration tribunal under Article 739" (this is then treated by the arbitration tribunal as a "case for urgency"). It is notable that any suspension at the start of this process then only finally ceases to apply when the complaining Party is satisfied that the respondent is complying with its relevant obligations under the TCA or indeed that the arbitration tribunal ultimately finds in the respondent's favour. In any such dispute (offensive or defensive) arising in the future, the relevant CD's interests will need to be represented by the UK on the CD's behalf under their constitutional relationship.

8 Memoranda of Understanding Between UK and Each CD

Against the background of the constitutional relationship, the government of each CD also agreed a future-proofing Memorandum of Understanding with the UK government "in relation to trade with the EU and other relevant economic issues under the Trade and Cooperation Agreement."[60]

In each case, the resulting instrument is one of "political intent" and, whilst not legally binding, sets out the understanding between the participants on the principles regarding the TCA and future cooperation. It covers overall engagement expectations and the procedure and parameters for the new relationship in the event of a disagreement or dispute. Each MoU is careful to cite that it does not intend to "alter or effect the constitutional relationships", and it is guided by the principles already contained in the relevant "Framework Agreement" for developing international identity, agreed in 2007 between the UK and each CD.[61]

9 Future of CD-UK-EU Relationship and TCA

The UK-EU TCA applies in a much more limited way to the CDs than it does the UK and EU. In summary, the TCA only applies to the CDs in relation to trade in goods (to include customs procedures and the implementation and recognition of regulatory standards) and fisheries access to territorial waters. Given that the CDs are autonomous jurisdictions, implementation of any new treaty commitments which apply to them remains the responsibility of the relevant CD. The CDs and the UK will therefore need to continue to work together if they are to ensure the new TCA arrangements function as smoothly as possible for the benefit of all concerned. This point also applies to any future free trade agreements or other international commitments which the UK may embark on post-Brexit.

---

[60] See https://www.gov.je/SiteCollectionDocuments/Government%20and%20administration/MoU%20with%20the%20UK%20on%20the%20UK-EU%20Trade%20and%20Cooperation%20Agreement.pdf.

[61] See, for example, Annex 2 to the Memorandum submitted by Jersey's Chief Minister as written evidence to the Justice Committee of the UK Parliament's House of Commons for their "Eighth Report: Crown Dependencies HC 56-I" of 30 March 2010, at https://publications.parliament.uk/pa/cm200910/cmselect/cmjust/56/56we07.htm.

10 Looking Further Into the Future: Changing the Relationship with the UK as an Option for Changing the Relationship with the EU

One of the issues faced by the BOTs and CDs in the long Brexit process has been whether to push, or threaten to push, for complete independence from the UK in order to obtain a better result from the process. For instance, that could be an option aimed at joining the EU as full member States, but that would mean a radical departure from their pre-Brexit relationship with the EU. Alternatively, it could be aimed at trying to agree terms equivalent to their previous status, but that seems unlikely to be on offer from the EU. Lastly, it could be aimed at just achieving a better result overall than whatever is on offer from the UK or EU, but this too is influenced by the question of whether such small territories could prosper without any relationship with either the UK or the EU. Independence does not necessarily lead to severing all constitutional relations as there are alternatives like the "association" status between some Pacific island states and the United States of America or New Zealand, as considered in the Jersey context by Mariani (2013) and in relation to all the CDs by Mut-Bosque (2022). However, there is perhaps no obvious reason why the EU would consider negotiating any such status with any of the non-European BOTs (we will look at the CDs and European BOTs shortly).

Nevertheless, the issue of independence, and of BOTs or CDs creating their own relationship with the EU, remains important as a background factor influencing negotiations over the developing relationships. This bears comparison with the issue in Scotland over whether independence is desirable in part as a means of enabling Scotland to re-join the EU as an independent country.

10.1 Legal Obstacles to Independence as an Option for the SBAs and Gibraltar, and Possibility of Absorption into an EU Neighbour

The populated BOTs (but not the SBAs), and more so the CDs, now have a very high degree of autonomy, particularly as relates to their internal affairs (though the international nature of human rights makes it hard to draw a clear line as to what is purely internal and what involves international relations). Even in international relations, the UK now increasingly commonly agrees to give a BOT or CD a "letter of entrustment"[62] enabling the CD or BOT itself to negotiate agreements directly with other states, and those other states are increasingly willing to negotiate on that basis (though this did not happen over the Brexit negotiations with the EU). That helps reduce any pressure for full independence, in the sense of becoming a separate

[62] See above in relation to the CDs and the scoping of the TCA.

state recognised by the United Nations (in this there is a parallel inside the UK with the balance between devolution and independence).

Nevertheless, the option of full independence is still legally available for the twelve non-European BOTs and the CDs, forming an important background factor in negotiations. However, it does not apply straightforwardly to the two European BOTs because Gibraltar and the SBAs share one important legal feature, namely that in each case the UK sees itself as bound by international treaty to offer the territory to its neighbour first if the UK decides to relinquish sovereignty. For Gibraltar the neighbour is Spain and the obligation is contained[63] in the 1713 Treaty of Utrecht between Great Britain and Spain, by which Spain ceded Gibraltar to Great Britain. For the SBAs the neighbour is the Republic of Cyprus and the obligation is contained in an Exchange of Notes[64] "concerning the Future of" the SBAs, associated with the 1960 Treaty of Establishment of the Republic of Cyprus.

This feature of Gibraltar and the SBAs is in some senses parallel to the issue in Northern Ireland. There the neighbour is the Republic of Ireland and the treaty obligation is in Article 2 of the 1998 British-Irish Agreement.[65] Under that provision both countries agree to abide by the result of any future referendum in Northern Ireland on whether it should join the Republic of Ireland, which would mean re-joining the EU. Effectively this rules out any idea of independence for Northern Ireland on its own. The position is therefore similar to Gibraltar and the SBAs in that none of these three can become independent to form their own relationship with the EU, and instead if they leave UK control they will become part of their neighbouring member State and so part of the EU on the same terms as that neighbour (subject to any special agreement reached at the time, and subject to whether Gibraltarians

---

[63] The final sentence of Article X reads "And in case it shall hereafter seem meet to the Crown of Great Britain to grant, sell or by any means to alienate therefrom the propriety of the said town of Gibraltar, it is hereby agreed and concluded that the preference of having the sale shall always be given to the Crown of Spain before any others". See https://en.wikisource.org/wiki/Peace_and_Friendship_Treaty_of_Utrecht_between_Spain_and_Great_Britain#ARTICLE_X. Many Gibraltarians have taken the view that the modern international law principles of decolonisation and self-determination over-ride this pre-emption right given to Spain, so that Gibraltarians would be entitled to choose independence. See for example the 2023 address by a former Chief Minister to a United Nations seminar https://www.gibraltar.gov.gi/press-releases/right-to-self-determination-address-the-hon-sir-joe-bossano-kcmp-mp-to-the-united-nations-pacific-seminar-in-bali-3342023-8897.

[64] The Exchange of Notes is commonly known as "Appendix P" from the way it was printed for the UK Parliament. In it the UK first says it does "not intend to relinquish their sovereignty or effective control over" the SBAs (and the Republic says it "will not demand" that the UK "should relinquish their sovereignty"), but then the UK agrees with the Republic's statement that "In the event, however, that the [UK] ... should at any time decide to divest themselves of the aforesaid sovereignty or effective control over the [SBAs] or any part of them, it is understood that such sovereignty or control shall be transferred to the Republic of Cyprus".

[65] Formally the "Agreement between the Government of the United Kingdom of Great Britain and Northern Ireland and the Government of Ireland done at Belfast on 10th April 1998". See https://peacemaker.un.org/uk-ireland-agreement2003.

could make a successful case for self-determination over-riding the Treaty of Utrecht).

The position of each of the three is of course very different in political, as opposed to legal, terms. In Northern Ireland there are two communities, with those in favour of remaining with the UK currently in the majority, but with the likelihood of a future majority for joining the Republic of Ireland (and no significant drive for independence as such). In Gibraltar successive referenda have heavily rejected joining Spain, and there is no sign of that changing, given that even those who would favour independence would prefer the link with the UK if the only other offer is unification with Spain. In the SBAs the population is roughly evenly split between temporary UK personnel (and their dependants) and Greek-Cypriots who would favour joining the Republic of Cyprus (in principle, although there is the issue of whether that might lead to loss of income from spending by the British Bases), with no serious thought of independence. But this is complicated by the fact that the UK seems to have felt obliged to treat the Turkish-Cypriots as being included in its obligation to offer first refusal. In the United Nations' 2004 "Annan Plan" for reunification, the UK offered to cede parts of the SBAs to the proposed Greek Cypriot constituent state and other parts to the proposed Turkish Cypriot constituent state (with the rest retained).[66]

Hadjigeorgiou (2022) argues that the opinion of the International Court of Justice[67] in relation to Mauritius and the British Indian Ocean Territory (another BOT) significantly undermines the UK position on retention of the SBAs. The court rejected the practice of holding back part of a colony as a BOT for military use, so as to be able to grant independence to the rest, and Hadjigeorgiou points out that the RoC's submissions spelled out the parallels with the SBAs.[68] The UK has been negotiating conceding sovereignty over the British Indian Ocean Territory to Mauritius with a long lease back for the USA's military base (although elections in both Mauritius and the USA have thrown that process into doubt), which seems likely to

[66] See the Annan Plan's "Additional Protocol to the Treaty of Establishment" included as Annex II to the proposed "Treaty between Cyprus, Greece, Turkey and the United Kingdom related to the new state of affairs in Cyprus" at https://peacemaker.un.org/node/2961. For discussion see Hannay (2005) p. 207, who notes "Astonishingly there was no leak . . . And even more astonishingly neither side in Cyprus was able to identify any perfidious motives behind the British offer". For a suspicion of perfidy see Green (2003) p. 61, who anticipates the offer and suggests it could be made "in exchange for a reinforcement of the legal status of the land used for surveillance, which currently lies outside" the SBAs (no such condition was applied in the Annan Plan).

[67] See *Legal Consequences of the Separation of the Chagos Archipelago from Mauritius in 1965* (ICJ Advisory Opinion, 25 February 2019, General List No. 169) at https://www.icj-cij.org/case/169.

[68] Another striking parallel with the position of the SBAs (and with Gibraltar and Northern Ireland, as discussed above) is the fact that when the UK split this BOT from Mauritius, it gave undertakings to cede the territory to Mauritius if it was ever to relinquish sovereignty.

make it increasingly difficult for the UK to maintain its argument that it has a right to the SBAs in international law or that it needs BOT status to secure its bases[69].

It therefore seems unlikely that Gibraltar will be absorbed into the EU by becoming part of Spain. But there seems to be more of a substantive possibility that the SBAs could be absorbed into the EU by becoming part of the Republic of Cyprus.

10.2 The Non-European BOTs and Independence

Turning back to the other BOTs, there is less significance to Brexit for them because their relationship with the EU was relatively thin in the first place. Loft (2023) deals in part with the prospects of independence for the BOTs generally. But, even if the UK's handling of the ongoing fall-out of Brexit drives a non-European BOT to consider independence, there is little prospect of the EU seeing that former BOT as having any special case for a relationship with the EU that would match, or be stronger than, the relationship it had before Brexit. The Caribbean BOTs (particularly Anguilla and Montserrat) do have near(ish) neighbours that have varying relationships with France and the Netherlands, so in theory they could ask to unite with those territories to re-establish a relationship (albeit a different one) with the EU, but this appears unlikely.

There is also a very wide range of factors that make the question of independence operate differently for each of the non-European BOTs. In particular, South Georgia and the South Sandwich Islands is uninhabited and the subject of a sovereignty dispute with Argentina, while the Falkland Islands are the subject of the same dispute but are inhabited by a population that has voted heavily in favour of links with the UK. The British Antarctic Territory is uninhabited and subject to the 1959 Antarctic Treaty preventing any country making further claims. The British Indian Ocean Territory is currently entirely devoted to use as a military base (by the USA under a lease from the UK). It has been subject to a sovereignty dispute with Mauritius, and to negotiations for a treaty to pass sovereignty to Mauritius[70] (and

[69] For the progress of the negotiations see House of Commons Library Research Briefing Number 10115 at https://commonslibrary.parliament.uk/research-briefings/cbp-10115/ and HL Deb 19 December 2024, vol 842, col 398. On the point about not needing sovereignty to maintain bases, it is worth noting that under the Treaty of Establishment the UK has been entitled since RoC's independence to keep other bases in the territory of the RoC. These are referred to in the Treaty as "retained sites", and include the very visible radar and signals station at RAF Troödos at the top of the central mountain range of the island. It is also worth noting that, despite the focus of much of the political commentary on the British Indian Ocean Territory negotiations, none of these legal points apply to Gibraltar or the Falkland Islands, neither of which were carved out of a colony when it was given independence and neither of which were retained solely to host military bases.

[70] See above in relation to the SBAs.

there have been several cases[71] in UK courts brought by the Chagossian population who were moved to make way for the base). St Helena, Ascension and Tristan da Cunha form a single BOT, but Ascension has never had an indigenous population and serves as an airbase and communications centre.

Bermuda and the five Caribbean BOTs are probably the largest group of similar BOTs, as they are all inhabited, governed by elected governments, not subject to sovereignty disputes with neighbours, and reliant on financial services and tourism. The Brexit process caused strains in their relationship with the UK, but there are other sources of strain too, so that it is hard to predict what might push any of them to independence. As it stands, the UK is responsible for the "good governance" of the BOTs and can legislate for them. In extreme circumstances the UK can impose direct rule, as happened in the Turks and Caicos Islands in 1986 and again in 2009, but also more recently nearly happened in the British Virgin Islands—see Loft (2022).[72] Even if these moves, with or without issues over Brexit, do stir a pro-independence reaction in any of the non-European BOTs, it seems unlikely that any significantly new relationship with the EU will result.

10.3 The CDs: Plain(er) Sailing?

The Isle of Man has a pro-independence political party, Mec Vannin, but there is no real political equivalent in Jersey or Guernsey.[73] Nevertheless the subject is occasionally live among lawyers in the Channel Islands as shown by Bailhache (2012); Mariani (2013), and editorials in the Jersey and Guernsey Law Review.[74] There are also other alternatives to full independence, such as the "free association" relationships which Mut-Bosque (2022) considers adaptable to the CDs (but which do not appear to have sparked interest inside the CDs, beyond Mariani (2013)). If Brexit (in combination with other factors) does lead to Northern Ireland, or Scotland or both, leaving the UK then there could be an impulse to re-examine the UK-CD relationship too, though that would be a very indirect effect of Brexit. Unlike Gibraltar and the SBAs (or Northern Ireland) there is no international treaty entitling

---

[71] See for example R (Bancoult No 3) v Secretary of State for Foreign and Commonwealth Affairs [2018] UKSC 3.

[72] In fact the Virgin Islands Constitution (Interim Amendment) Order 2022 is still on the statute book, but has not been brought into force—see https://www.legislation.gov.uk/uksi/2022/627/made.

[73] Leaving aside the question of whether the Barclay brothers were aiming for independence for their island of Brecqhou in *R (Barclay) v Secretary of State for Justice* [2009] UKSC 9 and related litigation.

[74] In relation to Brexit see for example the editorials headed "The Battle of St Helier 2021", "Departure from the EU" and "Respecting Constitutions" in issues in 2019 and 2021.

any other country to claim sovereignty over the CDs if they did sever their constitutional links with the UK.[75]

A great deal of effort on all sides has gone in to setting up the CDs' positions in the Protocol and TCA, and the UK-CD trading agreements, so it seems likely that this will continue to develop on reasonably predictable lines. But there is always the possibility that one or more of the CDs could be provoked into seeking their full independence if the UK were to go too far in refusing to accommodate the CDs' interests in any further negotiations with the EU (or with any other treaty partners). It would be hard to imagine the CDs wanting to apply for full EU membership. But it also seems likely that, even if an independent CD sought a new lighter relationship, the EU would not be willing to agree to anything as favourable as the former Protocol 3 relationship. The difference in bargaining power between a lone CD (or even 2 or all CDs in combination) and the EU would be likely to mean that the EU would make demands, such as demanding an unpalatable price in relation to the financial services industries on which the CDs depend, in negotiating any new relationship. Equally if the fully independent CD still required a continuing relationship with the UK (such as through maintaining or replacing the current UK-CDs customs union), there would not be a free hand in negotiating that, because the EU will still be concerned that the UK should not allow goods to enter the EU by any uncontrolled back door through a CD (which is what led to the TCA and the UK-CD customs union—see above). All this seems to point to the CDs staying on a reasonably clear path, but Brexit has shown that there are no certainties.

11 Conclusion

Brexit has changed the relationships of the BOTs and CDs to the EU, and has affected their relationships with the UK, but in different ways. They vary both in the closeness of the future relationship and in the certainty and stability of the current situation. Broadly speaking the twelve non-European BOTs are now more like third countries, but their link to the EU was not strong in the first place. The CDs now seem to have a fairly settled relationship with the EU, particularly through their elements of the TCA, but things could change. The SBAs have a settled Protocol to the Withdrawal agreement and will continue to mirror the law of the Republic of Cyprus, which is a member State, so their relationship is very little changed (and although the precedent of the British Indian Ocean Territory may eventually see the SBAs ceded to the Republic of Cyprus, the factors influencing that are not directly related to Brexit). Meanwhile the odd one out is Gibraltar, where there is still (at the

[75] Jersey and Guernsey are surrounded on two sides by France, as they lie in the Granville Bay, where France has the nearby Isles Chausey. Jersey has uninhabited islands (the Minquiers and Ecrehos) whose status was considered by the International Court of Justice in 1953 (see above on CDs and fisheries). But despite occasional flag-planting escapades, there is no serious question of France claiming either Jersey or Guernsey if they were to seek independence from the UK.

time of writing) no settled post-Brexit legal relationship and where there are difficulties that in some ways echo those over Northern Ireland's relationship to the EU. We hope this tour of the BOTs and CDs helps illustrate the usefulness of studying them, in giving a different perspective on constitutional and EU law issues to add to the usual UK focus.

References

Alegre S (2018) Brexit, human rights and self-determination: a perfect storm in the British crown dependencies and overseas territories? Eur Human Rights Law Rev 4:311

Bailhache P (2012) Dependency or sovereignty? Time to take stock. Jersey and Guernsey Law Review, St Helier, Jersey

Bell V, Berry M, Burke J, Hodgett S (2021) Beyond Protocol 3: a rule-book for EU/Channel Islands Trade. Jersey Guernsey Law Rev 25:267

Birt M (2017) The power of the UK to legislate for the crown dependencies without consent - fact or fiction? Jersey Guernsey Law Rev 2017(2)

Fransman L (2011) Fransman's British nationality law. Bloomsbury, London

Green P (2003) Embracing cyprus: The Path to Unity in the New Europe. IB Tauris, London

Hadjigeorgiou N (2022) Decolonizing Cyprus 60 years after independence: an assessment of the legality of the sovereign base areas. Eur J Int Law 33(4):1125

Hadjigeorgiou N, Skoutaris N (2019) The status of the sovereign base areas in Cyprus following Brexit. Peace Research Institute Oslo (Cyprus Centre, Discussion Paper), Oslo

Hannay D (2005) Cyprus: the search for a solution. IB Tauris, London

Hendry I, Dickson S (2018) British overseas territories law, 2nd edn. Hart, Oxford

Kochenov D (ed) (2011) EU law of the overseas: outermost regions, overseas countries and territories associated with the Union, Territories Sui Generis. Kluwer Law International

Kochenov D (2012) The application of EU law in the EU's overseas regions, countries, and territories after the entry into force of the treaty of lisbon. Mich State Int Law Rev 20(3): 669–743

Laulhé Shaelou S (2011) The principle of territorial exclusion in the EU: SBAs in Cyprus: a special case of Sui Generis territories in the EU. Chapter 6 of Kochenov D (ed) (2011) EU Law of the Overseas: Outermost Regions, Overseas Countries and Territories Associated with the Union, Territories Sui Generis. Kluwer Law International

Loft P (2022) The potential for direct rule in the British Virgin Islands. House of Commons Library, Research Briefing Number 9538.

Loft P (2023) The overseas territories: an introduction and relations with the UK. House of Commons Library, Research Briefing Number 9706

Mariani S (2013) Jersey and the public international law dimensions of sovereignty. Jersey Guernsey Law Rev 17(1):20

Marsh-Smith L (2019) Conference report delivering Brexit: legislative Marathon or sprint? Jersey Guernsey Law Rev 1:76–86

Mut-Bosque M (2018) Ten different formulas for Gibraltar Post-Brexit. Dublin City University Brexit Institute Working Paper N6-2018 at https://ssrn.com/abstract=3212246

Mut-Bosque M (2022) Questioning the current status of the British crown dependencies. Small States Territ 5(1):55–70

Peralta P (2019) Life at the Fringe: Brexit and Gibraltar. Loophole 2:53–70

Roberts-Wray K (1966) Commonwealth and colonial law. Stevens, London

Sutton A (2005) Jersey's changing constitutional relationship with Europe. Jersey Law Rev 9(1)

Dispute Settlement Mechanisms and Brexit: Monumental Changes or Is It a Case of Much Ado About Nothing?

Tasnim Ahmed

One of the main obstacles faced by the EU, as it enters into international agreements with third countries is to determine if it can be bound by the jurisdiction of international judicial bodies, allowing these 'foreign' bodies in essence to replace the jurisdiction the Court of Justice of the European Union (CJEU). This may be whether, they be part of a treaty that deploys such mechanisms or they exist outside the context of the Treaties.[1] The Court has famously declared the autonomy of the EU legal order in many of its judgments. Primarily, the Court has retained its monopoly over the final interpretation of EU law and consequently, declared that many of the dispute settlement mechanisms established through international agreements concluded by the EU and third countries were not compatible with the treaties.[2] The 'autonomy principle' clearly presented a threat to any withdrawal agreement. Thus, this chapter will firstly assess the CJEU's stance on its exclusive competence concerning the interpretation of EU law. However to avoid isolation on the global level the Court has made some concessions to the EU-Canada Comprehensive Economic and Trade Agreement (CETA) Court albeit with restrictions. Secondly, the chapter will focus on the supervision conflict resolution provisions of the Withdrawal Agreement (WA), discussing the procedural aspects and the currency of the CJEU within the WA.[3] Furthermore, the dispute settlement

[1] Opinion 1/91, Opinion of 14 December 1991, Agreement, Agreement EEA, EU: C: 1991 490; and Opinion 1/92, Opinion of 10 April 1992, Agreement EEA II, EU: C: 1992:189, and Opinion 1/09 opinion of 8 March 2011, Draft Agreement on the creation of a unified patent litigation system, EU: C; 2011:123. See also Odermatt (2016).

[2] Polak (2021).

[3] Agreement on the Withdrawal of the United Kingdom of Great Britain and Northern Ireland from the European Union and the European Atomic Energy Community 2019/C 384 I/01.

T. Ahmed (✉)
Liverpool John Moores University, Liverpool, UK
e-mail: T.K.Ahmed@ljmu.ac.uk

E. Guinchard, C. Panara (eds.), *The New Relationship between the United Kingdom and the European Union*, https://doi.org/10.1007/978-3-031-70652-3_12

provisions of the Northern Ireland Protocol along side the updated Windsor Framework Agreement (WFA) will be analysed, as it is acknowledged that the Protocol is not a 'stand-alone agreement' but rather an integrated tool of the WA, which may qualify as a novice body of international agreements to be known as post-Brexit law.[4] Finally, the dispute settlement mechanisms within the Trade cooperation Agreement (TCA) will be discussed, highlighting a system that may have major effects such as the level playing field areas.[5]

The main findings are that as compared to the other dispute settlement mechanisms in EU international agreements, the WA will continue to have judicial intervention and resort to litigation before the CJEU. As the arbitral panel will continue to refer questions of EU law to the CJEU. The WA and the Protocol provide a peculiar 'compromise' relying on an intergovernmental approach based on mutual consent and arbitration alongside the continuous application of EU law and EU institutions, compared to the TCA's intergovernmental and supranational approach to governance.

1 Dispute Resolution Before the WA and TA

The EU allows for a dispute settlement provision within its bilateral agreements.[6] It has set in place various dispute settlement mechanisms, which generally reflect the WTO agreement or at least refer to the same. The agreements foresee that the parties will utilise consultations, which may lead to arbitration. The losing party will need to comply with the arbitral decision otherwise, the responding party may retaliate through removing benefits attached to the original agreement.

In the Achmea case, the CJEU decided that arbitration clauses within an Intra-EU Bilateral Investment Treaty (BIT) were incompatible with the autonomy of EU law.[7] The decision reiterated the CJEU's repeated stance on autonomy and protected its dominance. This was achieved through affirming its previous decisions, which had blocked the accession of the EU to the EEA Court, to the ECHR and the Unified

[4]This term is used in Larik and Wessel (2022). Protocol on Ireland and Northern Ireland. The Windsor Framework. https://commission.europa.eu/strategy-and-policy/relations-non-eu-countries/relations-united-kingdom/eu-uk-withdrawal-agreement/protocol-ireland-and-northern-ireland_en#protocol-on-ireland-and-northern-ireland. Also The Winsdor Framework: A new way forward. https://assets.publishing.service.gov.uk/government/uploads/system/uploads/attachment_data/file/1138989/The_Windsor_Framework_a_new_way_forward.pdf. Accessed on 29/10/2024.

[5]Trade and Cooperation Agreement between the European Union and the European Atomic Energy Community, of the one part and the United Kingdom of Great Britain and Northern Ireland, of the other part. OLJ 149 30.4.2021.

[6]For example, Comprehensive Economic and Trade Agreement (CETA) between Canada and the European Union OJ L 11, 14.1.2017.

[7]Judgment of 6th March 2018, Achmea, C-284/16, EU:C:2018:158.

Patent Court.[8] It is acknowledged, that the Achmea case focussed on an international agreement between two Member States and not the EU and a third country. Rather the issue in Achmea was that the BIT agreement required the tribunal to interpret EU law, whilst there was no mention of the CJEU. This was problematic because the Achmea tribunal could not utilise the Article 267 preliminary reference procedure, as this was only available to Member State courts and tribunals.[9]

In contrast to its previous rigid approach to protect the EU's autonomy, the CJEU within its Opinion 1/17 displayed more leniency towards dispute settlement mechanisms operating within the EU legal order.[10] It allowed the EU to utilise such dispute settlement mechanisms as long as they pose minimal threats to the judicial monopoly of the Court.[11] A permanent independent tribunal was established within the CETA agreement, which aimed to diverge from the traditional 'ad hoc' international dispute mechanisms towards 'independent, impartial and permanent courts'.[12] The CJEU held in its judgment that although the CETA tribunal was different to ad hoc tribunals in terms of its composition and dealing with cases, it had mandatory jurisdiction.[13] However, the CJEU found that the Member States could not set up tribunals, which may be outside the EU judicial system and had the jurisdiction to interpret or apply EU law (other than those of the agreement itself). Neither could the tribunals make awards that may prevent the EU institutions from operating within the EU constitutional framework.[14]

One of the features of the CETA tribunal it is that it is impartial; it is separate from the domestic courts of Canada, the Union and its Member States, which deems it to be outside the EU judicial system.[15] The tribunal does not have the jurisdiction to refer preliminary questions to the CJEU, the lack of power to issue preliminary references is testament to the fact that the tribunal is outside the judicial system.[16] The CJEU explicitly distinguished the CETA from the Patent Court by highlighting that the CETA Court would only interpret and apply the provisions of the agreement, unlike the patents Court, which may have to consider the general principles of law and fundamental rights.

Following Brexit, the initial British policy papers insinuated that Britain believed that the WA might be compared to other international agreements agreed between

---

[8] Riffel (2015), pp. 955–992.

[9] Andenas and Contartese (2019), pp. 157–191.

[10] CJEU, Opinion 1/17 Free Trade Agreement with Canada ECLI: EU:2019:341.

[11] Eva and Odermatt (2020), pp. 5–20.

[12] Lonardo (2022). See also Joint Interpretative Instrument on the Comprehensive Economic and Trade Agreement (CETA) between Canada and the European Union and its Member States OJ L11/3.

[13] CJEU, Opinion 1/17 Free Trade Agreement with Canada ECLI: EU: C2019: 341 para 194,195, 198.

[14] CJEU, Opinion 1/17;See also Opinion 1/91 EEA Agreement ECLI: EU 1990:490 paras 33-36; CJEU, Opinion 2/13 Accession to ECHR ECLI;EU: 2014:2454.

[15] CJEU, Opinion 1/17 Free Trade Agreement with Canada ECLI: EU:2019:341 para 14.

[16] CJEU, Opinion 1/17 Free Trade Agreement with Canada ECLI:EU:2019: 341 para 134.

the EU and third party states. This meant that the 'close relationship' did not require the jurisdiction of the CJEU emulating the CETA agreement.[17] However, the EU aimed to preserve the EU legal framework within the substantive content of the WA. Hence, the UK began to realise that any agreement resulting from the Brexit negotiations would require some dispute settlement mechanism in order to accommodate its enforcement and supervision. This would be followed by limitations on what the Union was able to agree to in this area.[18] Despite the UK ending the CJEU's jurisdiction on British territory, it did prove to be more accommodating; the dispute settlement mechanism agreed within the WA may be the most integrationist of the models set up to protect the EU legal order.

2 WA and Dispute Settlement: Halfway House?

Title III of Part Six of the WA contains the dispute settlement procedures. At the time of a dispute the Joint Committee, (containing members from the EU and the UK and its role includes the implementation of the WA) need to enter into consultations and reach a settlement, otherwise arbitration proceedings need to be initiated.[19] An arbitration panel needs to be set up within 3 months following the notice sent by the Joint Committee; failing any resolutions between the parties they can commence arbitration proceedings.[20] This request needs to be made in writing to the other party and the International Bureau of the Permanent Court of Arbitration (PCA) in the Hague.[21] Two of the arbitrators are nominated from the UK; two from the EU and one person selected by both parties. The panel needs to be established within 15 days of the request and should provide its ruling within 12 months from the date of its composition. This period may be lessened to 6 months for urgent cases. Any failures which lead to the parties not cooperating in good faith towards the composition of an arbitration panel, may lead to the PCA Secretary electing the arbitrators. This may be done within three months from the date of the request.[22]

Article 174 WA aims to protect the principle of autonomy by ensuring the monopoly of the CJEU through excluding any questions on the interpretation of EU law from the jurisdiction of the arbitral tribunals. Arguably, an EFTA type tribunal may have been more appropriate for the EU-UK WA, as the parties understood the CJEU to have the ultimate say on the interpretation of the EU legal order.[23] However, within the EEA context the parties decide if the case is referred to

---

[17] Page 4. Polak, Polly.

[18] Page 4. Polak, Polly.

[19] Art 170 WA.

[20] Art 170 WA.

[21] Art 170 WA.

[22] Art 171 WA.

[23] Brandtner (1992), pp. 300–328. Shermers (1992), pp. 991–1009.

the CJEU and not the arbitration tribunal.[24] This gives discretion to the WA arbitration panel to determine whether the matter is an EU law matter and once it does then it 'shall' refer. Reference by the WA arbitrational tribunal maybe sought for 'concepts' of EU law. Parties cannot compel the WA arbitration panel to make the reference to the CJEU; this retained control by the tribunal may pose threats to the autonomy of the EU legal order.[25] Rather the parties may request the tribunal to review its assessment, which may result in a hearing. Subsequently, the arbitration panel would need to provide a reasoned decision on whether or not it wold revert to the CJEU. However, it is important to note that the CJEU itself cannot compel the WA arbitration tribunal to refer the question of EU law to the Court, thereby this mechanism in essence fail to protect the EU's autonomy.

3 Dispute Settlement; Northern Ireland Protocol, the Windsor Framework and the Retained EU Law Act

As mentioned earlier one of the instrumental points featured within the post-Bexit debate evolved around the role of the CJEU. The UK focussed on abolishing the CJEU's jurisdiction over its territory. Whilst, the EU persisted on preserving the EU legal order. Therefore, admittedly the Protocol and the future of the CJEU's role remained the most contested within the UK.[26] The draft withdrawal Agreement 2018 published by the EU Commission intended to keep Northern Ireland in the common regulatory area combined with the EU customs territory.[27] For dispute settlement, it meant that EU law would still be applicable and the CJEU would still continue with its jurisdiction.[28] Unsurprisingly, it was rejected by the UK as it would pose a threat to 'the constitutional integrity of the UK'.[29]

The UK Government in response proposed the backstop agreement accompanied with a 'common rule book'. The proposal stated that the 'EU institutions, including the CJEU would no longer have the power to make laws for the UK'.[30] The rulebook would commit the UK to the relevant EU laws in support of harmonization but

---

[24] Art 113(3) Agreement on the European Economic Area. (1994).

[25] Art 174 WA.

[26] HM Government, Lord Frost Speech: Observations on the Present State of the Nation, Lisbon 12 October 2021. http://www.gov.uk/government/speeches/lord-frost-speech-observations-on-the-present-state-of-the-nation-12-october-2021. Last accessed 29/10/2024.

[27] European Commission Draft Withdrawal Agreement on the Withdrawal of the United Kingdom of Great Britain and Northern Ireland from the European Union and the European Atomic Energy Community TF50, 28 February 2018,33-Protocol on Ireland/Northern Ireland arts 3 and 4.

[28] Art 11 Protocol.

[29] Theresa May Rejects EU's Draft Option for Northern Ireland' BBC News (28 February 2018) http://www.bbc.com/news/uk-politics-43224785. Last accessed 29/10/2024.

[30] HM Government, 'The Future Relationship between the UK and the EU. Cm 9593 (July 2018) 84.

without a vote to change the rules.[31] This would result in the UK courts paying due regard to the CJEU's case law, thereby allowing the CJEU's jurisdiction from the backdoor. It specifically mentioned that 'only the CJEU can bind the EU on the interpretation of EU law. . . . ..there should be the option for a referral to the CJEU for an interpretation, either by mutual consent from the Joint Committee or from the arbitration panel'.[32] Following the EU's rejection of the UK back-stop proposal, the jointly published draft Withdrawal Agreement in 2018 reinforced the role of the EU institutions (including the CJEU) and the relevant EU legislation for Northern Ireland.[33] This endangered the UK's post-Brexit trade policies, as it would lead to the UK having to align its tariffs with the EU.[34] Following the rejection of the backstop; a resignation of a British prime minister; the single customs territory being scrapped; the Protocol states that 'Northern Ireland is part of the customs territory of the United Kingdom'.[35] However, this is far from the truth as the EU institutions and EU customs law are still prominent within the Protocol.[36]

The Northern Ireland Protocol although it is part of the WA, contains its own dispute settlement mechanism. The Protocol contains Article 12 titled 'Implementation, application, supervision and enforcement'; paragraph 1 in particular states that 'the authorities of the United Kingdom shall be responsible for implementing and applying the provisions of Union law made applicable by this Protocol to and in the United Kingdom in respect of Northern Ireland'. The EU has anticipated that under the protocol the EU institutions will have jurisdiction in customs and movement of goods; technical regulations; assessments; registrations; certificates; approvals and authorisations; VAT and excise; the single electricity market and state aid.[37] Here the 'institutions, bodies, offices, bodies and agencies of the Union shall have the powers conferred upon them by Union law'.[38]

Article 12(4) stipulates that '(in) particular, the CJEU shall have the jurisdiction provided for in the Treaties in this respect' and the 'second and third paragraphs of Article 267 TFEU shall apply to and in the United Kingdom in this respect'. This article amplifies the CJEU's position under the protocol, namely that in respect of Northern Ireland it has the jurisdiction to receive requests for preliminary hearings from the UK. Here, the provisions of the WA can be relied upon by the CJEU if they

[31] Ibid 89.

[32] Ibid 93.

[33] Art 14(4). Draft Agreement on the withdrawal of the United Kingdom of Great Britain and Northern Ireland from the European Union and the European Atomic Energy Community, as agreed at negotiators' level on 14 November 2018 TF50, 14 November 2018, 55-Protocol on Ireland/ Northern Ireland.

[34] Weatherill (2020), pp. 222,224.

[35] Art 4(1). Northern Ireland Protocol.

[36] Larik (2022).

[37] Protocol Art 7, Art 8, Art9 and Art 10.

[38] Ibid Art 12(4).

'meet the conditions for direct effect under Union law'.[39] In addition, under Article 12(5) 'acts of the institutions, bodies, offices and agencies of the Union adopted in accordance with paragraph 4 shall produce within the Union and its Member States'. Whilst interpreting the Protocol, the CJEU case law including cases decided during the transition period may also be applicable.[40] The Protocol allows the Commission to bring about infringement proceedings against the UK under Article 258 TFEU, with the UK potentially facing fines for non-compliance of the Court judgments.[41] Furthermore, the UK can bring about cases as a Member State as stated in Article 12(7):

> May represent or assist a party before the CJEU in such proceeding and shall in every respect be treated as lawyers authorised to practise before courts or tribunals of Member States representing or assisting a party before the CJEU.

On 27th February 2023 the UK and the EU made some revisions to the Northern Ireland Protocol called the Windsor Framework Agreement (WFA). In summary, the new rules allowed goods staying in Northern Ireland to be exempt from most checks and requirements (in the green lane). Whilst certain goods still may require physical inspections and medicines may be subject to dual regulation by both UK and the EU authorities.[42] The second change within the WFA allows for restrictions on EU subsidy rules for Northern Ireland and allows Northern Ireland's VAT rules to align with the rest of the UK. The final yet most important point of consideration for the purposes of this chapter is the WFA's consideration on the governance of the protocol. The WFA does not change the jurisdiction of the CJEU on the protocol. Although, in essence the aim of the agreement is to curtail the application of EU law in Northern Ireland. This may in the future lead to a decrease in the number of cases the CJEU may be requested to rule upon.[43] Rather, arbitration (not a CJEU hearing) would be the preferred method of dispute resolution between the parties if the UK triggers the 'brake' suspending the EU rule in question.

The UK's intention to move away from EU regulatory standards remain poignant through its plans on adopting the Retained EU law Bill which was enacted as the Retained EU Law Act (REUL) in July 2023 poses risks to the mutual trust between the parties.[44] There will be evitable barriers within Northern Ireland as time and time again questions will be raised on the CJEU's jurisdiction when examining the retained law. The EU will continue to question any regulatory divergence, which may threaten the integrity of the single market. The recent developments in the form

[39] WA, Art 4(1) (2).

[40] Protocol Art 13(2) and WA Art 4(5).

[41] Protocol Art 12(2).

[42] Spisak (2023). www.institute.global/insights/geopolitics-and-security/windsor-framework-what-has-been-agreed-and-what-it-means-northern-ireland-protocol. Last accessed 23/7/23.

[43] Peers (2023) www.EUlawanalysis.blogspot.com/2023/03/the-windsor-framework-limiting-scope-of.jtml. Last Accessed 29/10/2024.

[44] Retained EU Law (Revocation and reform) Act 2023. https://www.legislation.gov.uk/ukpga/2023/28. Last Accessed 29/10/2024.

of the WFA illustrate that the managing political and practical risks can only take place thorough a mutual understanding of the protocol.

As it stands, the REUL poses a threat to the CJEU's jurisdiction guaranteed within the Protocol and the WFA. The EU may have the option in the future to raise a dispute under the TCA if the bill is utilised to undermine the level playing protections placed by the parties via the TCA. Currently the UK courts are bound to apply CJEU case law for EU matters relating to the WA. They can utilise the preliminary proceedings procedure on matters relating to EU law application within Northern Ireland. However, the REUL intends to disrupt this process by providing UK courts with the discretion to disapply CJEU case law. This process would endanger the aim of the WFA, which is to eliminate trade barriers between British and Northern Irish products. The potential risk may be that Northern Irish businesses following EU regulations may be stung by GB producers adopting the set lower standards. The only way around this would be if the risk posing EU laws are maintained but then this would in return undermine the whole objectives of the REUL.

The Part Six WA dispute settlement provisions will also apply without prejudice to the provisions of the Protocol.[45] However, it may raise legal questions on whether the parties need to choose between utilising the Protocol or WA settlement provisions, or should they be applied in parallel or in sequence. In the case of the Protocol, the Article 13 'without prejudice' determines we are to assume that the ultimate choice exists with the parties on which dispute mechanism they prefer to deploy. With the WA parties can request arbitration when there is a breakdown in the Joint Committee negotiations. The CJEU continues to enjoy jurisdiction for citizens' rights; the arbitral tribunal should request a ruling from the CJEU on matters of EU law.[46] In contrast, the TCA under Article 737(1) expects the UK and EU to choose a settlement procedure, which both are parties to or utilise the TCA dispute settlement mechanisms. The Commission in March 2021 sent a letter to the UK claiming breach of Articles 5(3) and (4) of the Protocol on customs and the movement of goods and breach of the good faith clause under Article 5 of the WA. It initiated Article 258 TFEU proceedings under Article 12(4) of the Protocol and sent a letter under the WA procedure to the UK co-chair of the Joint Committee. Subsequently, the Commission paused the Article 258 proceedings in an effort to arrive to flexible solutions under the Protocol.[47] However, at the time of WFA, the joint political declaration of the EU Commission and the UK, the UK decided to drop the Northern Ireland Protocol and consequently the EU has done the same for its infringement proceeding.

[45] Protocol Art 13.

[46] Art 174(1) WA.

[47] European Commission press release, 'Withdrawal Agreement: Commission sends letter of formal notice to the UK for breach of its obligations under the Protocol on Ireland and Northern Ireland' Brussels, 15 March 2021. https://ec.europa.eu/commission/presscorner/detail/en/ip_21_1132. Last accessed 29/10/2024.

Larik argues that the WA should specifically deal with the breach of the WA procedures, and the CJEU needs to deal with any breaches of the Protocol via their set procedures. However, the CJEU's jurisdiction is limited under the Protocol under Articles 2(2)(5) and 7 to 10.[48] It seems unlikely that the WA's arbitral tribunal could not rule on any breaches of the Protocol as the WA dispute settlement provisions cover any agreements between the UK and the EU, this would cover the Protocol. The Commission itself would prefer the breaches within the Protocol to be addressed through the WA as the CJEU's jurisdiction may guarantee damages and compliance. This double protection of WA and Protocol being used together is sought by the EU as the UK has previously threatened to breach its obligations under the Protocol.[49]

4 TCA and Dispute Settlement

Title I of Part 6 (Articles 734 and 762) of the TCA provides the general provisions on dispute settlement. It stipulates that the CJEU does not have the jurisdiction to settle disputes amongst the parties. This also inhibits the arbitrators to make references to the Court on matters of EU law, unless it involves EU programmes.[50] It explicitly states that courts of each party 'shall have no jurisdiction' in resolving disputes under the TCA.[51] This may be seen as having the effect of restricting the CJEU carrying out a formal role within the context of the TCA.[52]

Chapter 2 of the dispute resolution provisions contain the procedural rules.[53] The process begins through the parties participating in good faith via consultations. The aim of these consultations is to agree to a mutually agreed solution regarding the highlighted breach of the TCA.[54] The respondent has to respond to the request for consultations within 10 days of the delivery date of the request. The parties unless if agreed otherwise need to complete the consultations within 30 days from that date.[55] Parties may place an urgent request for the time to be reduced to 20 days in circumstances such as dealing with seasonal services or perishable goods.[56] It is

[48] Page 224. Larik (2022).

[49] Ibid Page 225.

[50] P69. Peers (2022), p. 59.

[51] Art 754 (5).

[52] The UK Government on 16th August 2022 has initiated formal consultations with the EU, with regards UK's participation with the EU Science and Research Programme. The UK claimed this request was made following the EU's delays in implementing the agreement reached under the TCA. http://www.gov.uk/government/news/government-requests-consultations-with-eu-on-participation-in-eu-science-programmes. Last Accessed 29/10/2024.

[53] Art 738–745.

[54] Art 738.

[55] Art 738 (3) and (4).

[56] Art 735 (5).

noted that the time period is shorter than the WA which facilitates for 3 months of consultations between parties before arbitration can be formally adopted.[57]

The complaining party can begin the arbitration process if there has been no response to the request for consultations; if consultations reach a deadlock; if the consultations do not happen by the time of the deadline or if the parties omit them.[58] The TCA does not refer to any type of logistical support to be provided by the Permanent Court of Arbitration in the Hague. This is in contrast to the WA's reference to the Court in Article 170 for assisting with the selection of a chairperson from the agreed lists in the event of disagreements.[59] The arbitration panel will contain three arbitrators. There are default processes to ensure arbitrators are duly appointed to avoid any of the parties stalling the process.[60] The tribunal then needs to consult the parties regularly and make objective assessments on facts and the law to derive commonly agreed solutions.[61] The tribunal needs to provide a report within 160 days, which can be decreased by half in urgent circumstances.[62]

Modified dispute settlement rules also apply in the fisheries area. Article 506 refers to the general rules in fisheries. As the complainant files the notice he may suspend access to its waters in whole or in part; reduce tariffs on the fish; suspend in whole or in part the preferential tariff of other goods; suspend other trade obligations other than the level playing rules. This would have a knock on effect on the road transport rules. However, these sanctions would need to be proportionate to the respondent's alleged breach and considered in terms of their societal and economic impacts. Here there are possibilities to deploy fast track arbitration and utilise retaliation.[63]

The general provisions of the dispute settlement rules within the TCA are similar to the WA.[64] The objective of the rules is stipulated within Article 734 primarily being: 'to establish an effective and efficient mechanism for avoiding and settling disputes between parties concerning the interpretation and application of this Agreement and supplementing agreements with a view to reaching, where possible, a mutually agreed solution'.

The 'exclusivity' clause bears another striking resemblance with the WA. An involved party cannot take part in any type of dispute settlement mechanism other than that which is prescribed by the Agreement.[65] However the TCA provides exceptions to this rule namely via approving the WTO dispute resolution mechanisms. Hence, where there is a potential breach of a TCA obligation and 'a

[57] Art 170 WA.

[58] Art 739(1).

[59] Art 171 (5) WA.

[60] Art 740.

[61] Art 742/743.

[62] Art745(4)/744.

[63] Art 506(4) to (7).

[64] Chapter 1 of Title I Part Six (art 734–737).

[65] Art 736.

substantially equivalent obligation under another international agreement to which both parties are party including the WTO Agreement', the party lodging the complaint can choose the dispute forum.[66] Following this, the complainant party cannot issue proceedings against the measure that it wishes to challenge under any other international agreements. Unless it can successfully establish that, the originally selected forum cannot rule due to procedural or jurisdictional reasons.[67] Equally, parties retain the freedom to suspend their obligations after utilising the WTO dispute resolution mechanisms or alternative settlement forum.[68]

The general provisions are unduly limiting, as they do not apply in disputes on trade remedies, such as anti-dumping measures. If there are any references to the WTO then the relevant WTO dispute mechanisms would be applied.[69] The other exclusions listed under article 735 include cultural goods;[70] Part Three of the Agreement on Criminal Law;[71] the annex on medical products;[72] under the trade heading the rules on small and medium-sized business;[73] under the trade heading, Title X of Heading one of Part Two looking at regulatory cooperation;[74] the whole Part Four of the agreement on health security and 'cyber' matters[75]; the 'essential elements dealing with the EU/UK relationship.[76]

The general provisions also exclude some of the level playing field rules from the scope of dispute resolution rules.[77] There are various exclusions here including; taxation; subsidies rules; introductory rules; the 'future review' part of the rebalancing clause on future divergences on labour, environmental and subsidies law.[78] This in essence means that there are variations in the dispute resolution rules that do apply to the level playing field issues, and of those level playing issues that are excluded there are no alternative dispute settlement processes provided. It is argued by Peers that excluding issues from the general dispute settlement rules does

---

[66] Art 737 (1).

[67] Art 737 (2).

[68] Art 737 (4).

[69] Art 735 2(a).

[70] 735(2)(a).

[71] Art 735 (2) (f). This Part has its own dispute settlement rules, which are political.

[72] Art 735 (2)(b).

[73] Art 735 (2)(c).

[74] Art 735 (2) (d).

[75] Art 735 (2) (g).

[76] Art 735 (2) (h).

[77] Art 735 (2) (e).

[78] Art 735 (2)(e), excluding Art 355(1) and (2) and (4) (principles and objectives), Art 356(1) and (3) (right to regulate, precautionary approach and scientific and technical information) Chapter 2 of the Title XI of Heading One of Part TWO (Competition policy), Arts 371 and 372 (Independent authority or body and cooperation and Courts and tribunals) of Chapter 2 (Subsidy control), Chapter 5 of Title XI of Heading One of Part Two (Taxation- Level Playing Field) and Art 411 (4-9) (Rebalancing).

not allow for 'cross retaliation' for instance a party may not be retaliate trade provisions if they suspend criminal law obligations.[79]

Under Art 735 for the above mentioned excluded issues the parties may still resort to discuss the issues but not result to arbitration. However, the parties are bound by the TCA as not to use any other dispute settlement mechanisms falling outside the scope of the Agreement specifically for these excluded provisions. This means that the parties need to refer their disputes to the Partnership Council or applying the set rules contained in the Treaty. For example, for social security issues, dispute resolution cannot be utilised to settle 'individual cases'.[80]

In relation to the level playing field, some aspects are completely excluded from the dispute settlement rules, whilst some are subjected to all and finally some are subjected to a modified version of the rules.[81] For example, in the climate provisions; Chapter 6 and 7 of the level playing field rules on labour and environmental standards and Chapter 8 concerning the sustainable rules, all have special consultation procedures.[82] There are a specialist panel of experts replacing arbitrators.[83] Retaliation may be used in instances where there are breaches of non-regression clauses and labour and environment chapters.[84] In the case of subsidies, if it has caused a significant negative effect on trade and investment then the complaints can retaliate without prior approval by the arbitrators.[85] This is subject to challenge via the fast track basis, although the arbitrators can examine its compatibility with some rules set in the subsidies section.[86]

The TCA does confirm that arbitration rulings are binding but only apply between the parties.[87] It also sets out that the tribunal has no jurisdiction to rule on the legality of a measure under domestic law. Furthermore, no arbitration ruling may bind a domestic court as regards to interpreting domestic law.[88] The starting point on the procedural rules on enforcing arbitration rulings is that the party that has lost the action needs to take 'necessary measures to comply immediately with the ruling of the arbitration tribunal in order to bring itself in compliance' with the TCA.[89] It needs to inform the other party within 30 days of the measures it intends to comply

[79] P71 Peers (2022).

[80] Art 735(5).

[81] Art 735, Art 355(2), Art 760.

[82] Art 408.

[83] Art 409.

[84] Art 410.

[85] Art 374.

[86] Art 374 (9).

[87] Art 754 (2).

[88] Art 754 (4).

[89] Art 746 (1).

with or otherwise state a reasonable time for compliance.[90] If the parties cannot agree this time, then the arbitrators will rule within a period of 20 days.[91]

In the event of non-compliance the parties can ask the arbitrators to rule on whether true compliance did take place. Following this, the arbitrators need to respond within 45 days.[92] Non-compliance of an arbitration ruling can lead to compensation or the use of proportionate retaliation measures by the winning party.[93] More specifically retaliation can only take place for those areas in the TCA that are within the scope of the general dispute settlement provisions.[94] Retaliation may be used for breaches within the TCA in the areas of road or air transport/trade/fisheries/trade. If the breach is in road or trade transport then it acceptable for retaliation to occur in another title of the same heading of the economic part of the treaty if the party at loss feels that it would induce compliance. Hence, for example a breach in trade means that subject to parts of the trade rules not being part of the covered provisions, it can be sanctioned by a retaliation in services, digital trade, capital, intellectual property, public procurement or energy. If the losing party objects to the retaliation as an infringement of the principles of proportionality, or that the principles and procedures of cross retaliation have not been complied, then this may suspend the proceedings. However, the arbitrators need to provide a ruling on this point within 30 days.[95] Furthermore, breaches of the WA with regards to non-compliance of the arbitration rulings can be sanctioned under the TCA. As the TCA captures retaliation under a previous agreement, which indicates the reference made to the WA making it easier to enforce the WA.[96] Although retaliation is a temporary remedy until the parties settle or compliance is achieved.[97] In essence, if the winning party is sceptical of the compliance of the losing party this issue would again result in arbitration, providing the arbitrator 46 days to rule.[98]

Modified dispute settlement rules are also utilised in 'rebalancing'. In contrast to the unified dispute settlement provisions within the WA, the TCA contains various procedures in different sections, namely Article 411 which contains the rebalancing mechanism for 'material impacts on trade and investment'. Proportionate 'rebalancing' retaliation can be applied 'if material impacts on trade or investment between the parties are arising as a result of significant divergences' (divergences in future labour, environment or subsidies).[99] The TCA stipulates that the impacts have to be assessed relying on well-founded evidence. If parties fail to agree then the fast

---

[90] Art 205.

[91] Art 747 (2).

[92] Art 748 (2).

[93] Art 749(5).

[94] Art 749 (2).

[95] Art 749 (11).

[96] Art 749(4).

[97] Art 749 (13).

[98] Art 750(2).

[99] Art 411.

track consultations can be relied upon and the rebalancing retaliation can be imposed. There is no need for the arbitrators to declare any breaches of the TCA, with reasonable period for compliance before this retaliation to take place. The complaining party can within five days request for the arbitrators to determine whether or not the retaliation is compatible with TCA's rebalancing rules. The arbitrators need to rule within 30 days and the retaliation will need to discontinue if they rule against the same. If they agree with the retaliation then a 'return retaliation' may come in to existence.[100]

5 Concluding Thoughts

Within the context of the WA, the EU and UK finally agreed to combine the role of the 'politically inclined' joint Committee with arbitration and the CJEU. Despite, this the current model as it stands poses threats to the autonomy of the EU legal order. As, the complexity of the TCA negotiations also stemmed from yet 'another pinch point in the negotiations, that being the role of the CJEU'.[101] The British negotiators ruled out the Court's say in any form of dispute settlement or interpretation of the TCA, despite the EU's call that where there are matters of EU law then there is a clear obligation on the EU to refer to the CJEU for decisive rulings. Following the acceptance of the EU's stance for the WA, the UK was not willing to compromise, ultimately securing a dispute settlement mechanism, which omitted it. However, this had led to the UK accepting significant concessions at the price of the economy. Undoubtedly, the TCA has avoided the worst outcome of a non-agreement. The UK has still managed to move the EU from its starting points through securing the removal of the CJEU alongside, the extraction from the CFP and multiple exit clauses. However, it is noted that this by no means indicates that the UK has managed to secure its original position. At its best, the final treaty managed to take the rough edges of the EU's wish list, yet securing the UK to a governance and dispute settlement system with major effects.[102] Though the current situation may be challenging it will be utilised until either side provides an acceptable alternative; the actual test is to determine whether the UK will push the limit of the treaties against the amount of resilience, the EU will be prepared to accept. The WFA has provided EU concessions to the UK through some relaxation of rules on goods entering Northern Ireland from the UK and the VAT and subsidies rules. Yet, painfully for the UK the EU has yet again maintained the direct jurisdiction over EU law applied under the protocol. Resonating that, Northern Irish courts will remain to refer questions of EU law to the CJEU.

---

[100] Art 760.

[101] P119. Usherwood (2021).

[102] P120. Usherwood.

References

Agreement EEA, EU: C: 1991 490

Agreement on the Withdrawal of the United Kingdom of Great Britain and Northern Ireland from the European Union and the European Atomic Energy Community 2019/C 384 I/01

Andenas M, Contartese C (2019) EU autonomy and investor-state dispute settlement under inter se agreements between EU Member States: Achmea. Common Mark Law Rev 56:157–191

Brandtner B (1992) The Drama of the EEA – comments and opinions 1/91 and 1/92. Eur J Int Law 3(2):300–328

CJEU, Opinion 1/17 Free Trade Agreement with Canada ECLI: EU:2019:341

Comprehensive Economic and Trade Agreement (CETA) between Canada and the European Union OJ L 11, 14.1.2017

European Commission Draft Withdrawal Agreement on the Withdrawal of the United Kingdom of Great Britain and Northern Ireland from the European Union and the European Atomic Energy Community TF50, 28 February 2018

Eva K, Odermatt J (2020) The principles of autonomy and international investment arbitration: reflections on opinion 1/17. Quest Int Law 73:5–20

HM Government, 'The Future Relationship between the UK and the EU. Cm 9593 (July 2018) 84

Joint Interpretative Instrument on the Comprehensive Economic and Trade Agreement (CETA) between Canada and the European Union and its Member States OJ L11/3

Judgment of 6th March 2018, Achmea, C-284/16, EU:C:2018:158

Larik J (2022) Governance and dispute settlement. The protocol on Ireland/Northern Ireland. The law & politics of Brexit, vol IV. OUP, Oxford

Larik J, Wessel R (2022) The EU-UK Post-Brexit trade and cooperation agreement: forging partnership or managing rivalry? In: Lazowski A, Cygan A (eds) Research handbook on legal aspects of Brexit. Edward Elgar Publishing

Lonardo L (2022) The withdrawal agreement and the dispute settlement and the dispute settlement mechanisms of the European Union. Working Paper N.3-22

Odermatt J. (2016) When a fence becomes a cage: the principle of autonomy in EU external relation law. EUI Working Paper

Opinion 1/09 opinion of 8 March 2011, Draft Agreement on the creation of a unified patent litigation system, EU: C; 2011:123

Opinion 1/91, Opinion of 14 December 1991, Agreement

Opinion 1/92, Opinion of 10 April 1992, Agreement EEA II, EU: C: 1992:189

Peers S (2022) So close yet so far: the EU: UK Trade Cooperation Agreement. Common Mark Law Rev 59

Peers S (2023) EU law analysis. www.EUlawanalysis.blogspot.com/2023/03/the-windsor-framework-limiting-scope-of.jtml. Last Accessed 29/10/2024.

Polak P (2021): The dispute settlement mechanism in the EU-UK Article 50 withdrawal agreement and the principle of autonomy. Brexit Institute Working Paper No. 12-21

Protocol on Ireland and Northern Ireland. The Windsor Framework. https://commission.europa.eu/strategy-and-policy/relations-non-eu-countries/relations-united-kingdom/eu-uk-withdrawal-agreement/protocol-ireland-and-northern-ireland_en#protocol-on-ireland-and-northern-ireland

Protocol on Ireland/Northern Ireland.

Retained EU Law (Revocation and reform) Act 2023. https://bills.parliament.uk/bills/3340

Riffel C (2015) The CETA opinion and the European Court of Justice and its implications-not that selfish after all. J Int Econ Law 22(3):955–992

Shermers H (1992) Opinion 1/91of the Court of Justice, 14 December 1991; Opinion 1/92 of the CJEU 10 April 1992. Common Mark Law Rev 29(5):991–1009

Spisak A (2023) The Windsor framework-what has been agreed and what it means for the Northern Ireland Protocol. Tony Blair Institute for Global Change

The Winsdor Framework: A new way forward. https://assets.publishing.service.gov.uk/government/uploads/system/uploads/attachment_data/file/1138989/The_Windsor_Framework_a_new_way_forward.pdf. Accessed 29/10/2024

Trade and Cooperation Agreement between the European Union and the European Atomic Energy Community, of the one part and the United Kingdom of Great Britain and Northern Ireland, of the other part. OLJ 149 30.4.2021

Usherwood S (2021) 'Our European Friends and Partners'? Negotiating the trade and cooperation agreement. J Common Mark Stud 59

Weatherill S (2020) The Protocol on Ireland/Northern Ireland: protecting the EU's internal market at the expense of the UK's. Eur Law Rev 45:222, 224

Part III
A New Relationship to Forge

The UK and EU Security and Defence Relationship Post-Brexit

George William Lamb

1 Introduction

The UK and the EU face arguably the most challenging security and defence environment since the end of the Second World War (WW2). The UK's exit from the EU in January 2020 coupled with the ongoing war in Ukraine—Europe's first interstate war since WW2—has plunged the UK and the EU into a highly unpredictable and volatile state of affairs. Removed from the EU's legal framework, the UK now finds itself as a third party to the EU's Common Foreign and Security Policy (CFSP) and, in turn, its Common Security and Defence Policy (CSDP), in which it has been involved since 1992. Whilst the security and defence relationship between the UK and the EU has been difficult to define, aspects of it have almost certainly been mutually beneficial for both parties in various ways. Historically, although the UK has not always been the most active member when its come to EU security and defence, its role as one of the 'Big Two' military powers in the EU saw it become one of the biggest contributors of resources to CSDP missions, both in civilian and military missions. The UK's support for the CSDP and, in turn, the EU's access to Britain's vast military personnel, resources and expertise has bolstered the EU's military and diplomatic power, both on the continent of Europe and beyond. For the UK, on the other hand, its involvement in the CSDP has enabled it to save money, by pooling its resources to combat mutual problems it shares with the EU. Its involvement has also enabled it to capitalise on the EU's strong civilian, diplomatic and economic capabilities to help it in addressing conflicts in Europe and around the world. With the UK's withdrawal from the EU, and with no post-Brexit security and defence partnership having been agreed between the two parties, all of these mutual benefits are now in jeopardy.

G. W. Lamb (✉)
University of Salford, Salford, UK
e-mail: G.W.Lamb@salford.ac.uk

E. Guinchard, C. Panara (eds.), *The New Relationship between the United Kingdom and the European Union*, https://doi.org/10.1007/978-3-031-70652-3_13

This Chapter aims to answer the following four questions; firstly, it will seek to establish some context for a post-Brexit partnership. It will do this, firstly, by examining the UK's role in the development of the CSDP and then examining, historically, what have been the most difficult and beneficial aspects of the security and defence relationship between the UK and the EU for both parties. This Chapter will then seek to establish what the current position of the UK and the EU is post-Brexit, in terms of their positions on a post-Brexit security and defence partnership as well as identify the challenges and opportunities that now present themselves for the UK and the EU post-Brexit. Finally, this Chapter will turn its attention to the future of UK and EU security and defence and will seek to determine what kind of security and defence partnership between the UK and the EU is possible, if any. The Chapter will then conclude by assessing the merits of a post-Brexit security and defence partnership and whether such a partnership is one that is worth pursuing for both parties.

2 A Brief History of the UK's Security and Defence Partnership with the EU

As the EU has developed over time, slowly the member states have transferred increasingly more powers to the EU through the process integration. Whilst member states have been willing to transfer more sovereignty to the EU in certain areas they have been more reluctant to do so in other areas. One area in particular in which member states have been rather reluctant to give up more sovereignty is in the area of security and defence. The EU's powers in this area are limited and unlike the areas listed above, power rests firmly with the member states.

Security and defence has been a contentious issue in the development of the EU for one primary reason: a monopoly on violence is the hallmark of the nation state.[1] This idea was famously proposed by sociologist Max Weber, who, drawing on the previous works of philosophers such as Thomas Hobbes, Jean Jacque Rousseau and Jean Bodin, argued that the defining feature of the state was its '*monopoly on the legitimated use of physical force*'.[2] He argued that through its exclusive right to use, threaten, or authorize physical force against residents of its territory, and against its enemies abroad, a state is able to keep its citizens safe, and in doing so, this justifies its existence.[3] Whilst member states have been willing to transfer sovereignty to the EU in areas such as trade, energy and agriculture for example, almost all have viewed the transfer of sovereignty to the EU as a step too far. It has been regarded by many commentators in the field of EU studies that after transferring so much sovereignty to the EU already, the transfer of control over security and defence

[1] See Weber (1965)

[2] Weber (2015), p. 129.

[3] Weber, *Supra* 2.

policy by member states to the EU would mean surrendering the last element of what Weber defined as 'the state'. The relationship between a state's 'monopoly on violence', as Weber defined it, and its identity as a 'state' are therefore tightly intertwined and it is one of the primary reasons why member states have fought to retain control over EU security and defence policy.

Retaining this control has meant the relationship between the member states (including the UK) and the EU has been strained at times and has led to several stumbling blocks for the EU in the development of a security and defence policy. Since the end of the Second World War (WW2), the EU has been unable to develop any meaningful security and defence policy nor has it been able to acquire any effective means by which to enforce it. Whilst security and defence considerations played a major role in the early beginnings of the EU, with prominent federalists playing an integral part in its creation, the desires for deeper integration in these areas quickly diminished. This ultimately resulted is what exists today: a European security and defence policy under the full control of the EU's member states.

Defining the UK and EU's relationship in security and defence is a difficult task. It is a relationship which has at times been fruitful for both parties and which at others has been strained. As will be seen throughout the chapter, the UK has been one of the biggest opponents to integration in EU security and defence, yet, it has also contributed significant resources and personnel to many CSDP missions. Furthermore, whilst the UK has become the first member state to leave the EU, and has done so without agreeing a new security and defence partnership, it was one of the most influential member states in the establishment of the CSDP. As will be discussed in more detail below, during the history of the CSDP, the UK has at times been an active and an effective partner in EU security and defence, whilst at other times it has been arguably the biggest bulwark to further integration in this area.

2.1 *Early Beginnings:* European Coal and Steel Community 1950 to EDC

The ECSC was first conceived by French political economist (later President of the High Authority of the ECSC) Jean Monnet. Monnet, a federalist and advocate of European political unity, devised what became known as the 'Monnet Plan'. The plan outlined proposals for the reconstruction of France following the end of WW2. The plans primary proposal was French ownership of the coal and steel industries located in the previously German occupied area of the Ruhr and the Saar. The Monnet Plan would serve as the foundation for European integration and what would later become the EU. Bolstered by the Marshall Plan and US support for European multilateralism,[4] France was encouraged to make West Germany a partner in the rebuilding of France and the European continent. Building on Monnet's

[4]Milward et al. (1999), p. 335.

preparatory work, in 1950 French Minister of Foreign Affairs Robert Schuman presented a new plan for the reconstruction of Europe, later known as the 'Schuman Declaration'. Schuman called for the creation of an independent and common 'High Authority' to which France and West Germany could transfer control over their coal and steel industries. What was important about the Schuman Declaration was that it was not only concerned with rebuilding Europe economically but also uniting it politically. Schuman stated in his proposal that the 'federation of Europe' should be one of the most important aims of this project and that the pooling of coal and steel production would immediately provide for that foundation.'[5] The proposals made under the Schuman Declaration were later established in the Paris Treaty 1950, which created the ECSC and was ratified by six European states: France, West Germany, Italy, the Netherlands, Belgium and Luxembourg. Economically, the ECSC was a success and a major logistical achievement, however, its most lasting achievement was political in nature. The ECSC had permanently altered the psychology of Europe's nations: historical enemies were now irreplaceable partners and the integrated economies of these states now meant that war between them was not only undesirable but, as Schuman had hoped, 'materially impossible'.[6]

The UK did not form part of the original six signatories to the ECSC but it still played a role in the formation of the Community. In two speeches, then-PM, Winston Churchill, famously called upon Europe's nations to integrate under the ECSC. In 1946 Churchill delivered a speech, at the University of Zurich, in which he advocated for what he called a 'United States of Europe', urging European nations to forget what he called the "horrors of the past" and look towards the future by recreating what he described as the 'European family. In a later speech in 1948, to the European Congress in The Hague, Churchill advocated European integration to prevent the atrocities of the two world wars from ever happening again, calling for the creation of a Council of Europe as a first step towards that goal. Churchill's calls for European integration acted as a catalyst in the creation of the Council of Europe, which was established in May 1949.[7] Churchill would also use other speeches following the war, to discuss ideas such as a European army, which he believed could be utilised to protect the continent and provide European diplomacy.[8] Churchill is described by the European Commission as a major 'driving force' behind early European integration and as someone who was influential behind the founding of the ECSC.

Following the ECSC, the UK also extended its support to the formation of a European Defence Community (EDC). Talks of forming the EDC came about at the same time of the creation of the ECSC. For Western Europe, at this time, the threat of Nazi Germany had been replaced by the new threat of the Soviet Union.

[5] R Schuman, '*Schuman Declaration*' (1950) https://european-union.europa.eu/principles-countries-history/history-eu/1945-59/schuman-declaration-may-1950_en (accessed 06/07/19).

[6] *Ibid.*

[7] https://european-union.europa.eu/system/files/2021-06/eu-pioneers-winston-churchill_en.pdf.

[8] Find Churchill speech on European Army.

Furthermore, fear still surrounded Germany and its military ambitions, which many European states, including the UK, were keen to find ways to contain. These threats, coupled with the weak military and economic state European nations found themselves in, led to the members of the ECSC, and other Western European nations, including the UK, to call for continued US economic and military support.[9] In turn, in August 1949, the North Atlantic Treaty was signed between the US, Canada and ten West European countries: Belgium, Denmark, France, Iceland, Italy, Luxembourg, the Netherlands, Norway, Portugal and the UK. This was later upgraded to the North Atlantic Treaty Organisation (NATO) in 1950. Whilst the US sought to provide leadership in Europe, it had major military commitments beyond Europe, in particular the Korean War. The US was therefore keen for Europe to play its part and develop its own defence capabilities to relieve the burden on the US of providing Europe's security.[10]

In order to meet these expectations, the six member states of the ECSC agreed on the creation of the European Defence Community (EDC). The EDC was proposed by the then French Prime Minister Rene Pleven. Pleven proposed the creation of a defence community existing alongside the ECSC, incorporating the armies of six nations, including Germany and Italy, into an integrated supranational European army. Pleven's proposal became known as the 'Pleven Plan' and resulted in the EDC Treaty, which six member states of the ECSC signed in May 1952. The opening article of the Treaty stated that the EDC would be supranational in character, comprising of common institutions, a common armed force and a common budget. In reality, there were a number of obstacles in the way of the EDC and, although on the surface it appeared to be a fully integrated community, in reality the Member States were in control. The renewed sense of pride created as a result of the Allies' victory in WW2 and fear of German rearmament were also working against the EDC.[11] Falling upon France to be ratified, the EDC was rejected, fearing it was another unacceptable surrender of its national sovereignty.[12] Internal division combined with international developments—the death of Stalin in 1953 and the end of the Korean war had made the EDC project seem less urgent—eventually sealed the EDC's fate, and on 30th August 1954, the French National Assembly decided by 319 votes to 264 to postpone discussion of the EDC Treaty and, in effect, rejected it.[13] Instead, the EDC was replaced by the less supranational, and arguably weaker, Western European Union (WEU).

Although the EDC failed, the United Kingdom did give its support to the initiative. An official statement released in April 1954 by the then-UK government read "Her Majesty's Government in the United Kingdom of Great Britain and

[9] Keuklaire (2014), p. 12.

[10] *Ibid* at 39.

[11] Kanter (1970), p. 204.

[12] *Ibid.*

[13] This decision by the FNA became known by federalists as the 'crime of 30th August', as it destroyed what they perceived Europe's best hopes for a federal state.

Northern Ireland believe that the European Defence Community will be an essential factor in strengthening the defence of the free world through NATO, and desire to establish the closest partnership with it".[14] Furthermore, then Foreign Secretary, Anthony Eden, was quoted as saying that, although the UK government of the time felt the UK was precluded from the EDC, he was able to reaffirm his government's belief that the entry into force of the EDC Treaty was an essential factor in strengthening the European defence effort through NATO. Eden also stated that the UK reaffirmed its support for the EDC by signing a Treaty of Mutual Assistance and by subscribing to the Protocol to the North Atlantic Treaty and the Tripartite Declaration of May last year, stating that it was the UK's intention to arrange for the closest possible political liaison with the institutions of the EDC and military association with the European defence forces.[15]

2.2 *Forging the CSDP: Maastricht to St. Malo*

The UK was eventually brought into the fold of integration when it joined the European Economic Community in 1973, following referendum. Although always wary of European integration in security and defence, the UK played a crucial role in the development of the CSDP. One of the most significant developments in European security and defence came with the establishment of the CFSP under the Treaty of Maastricht. During discussions at the intergovernmental conference in Rome, although France and Germany pledged their support for a truly common CFSP, the UK made clear that it did not support a common defence policy. Maastricht and talks of a CFSP had stirred discontent in the ranks of then-Prime Minister, John Major's, Conservative Party. Labelled in the British media as the '*Maastricht Rebels*', 22 MPs rebelled against Major and the implementation of the Maastricht Treaty into British law in 1992.[16] Furthermore, a new Eurosceptic political party was on the rise in the form of the 'Referendum Party'. The party was set up by financier and tycoon Sir James Goldsmith, whose aim, as the Party's name suggests, was to force the government to hold a referendum on the UK's membership of the EU, following the ratification of Maastricht.[17] Although Maastricht had divided the Conservative Party and the nation, Major made his support for

[14] European Defence Agency (2012). https://eda.europa.eu/docs/default-source/eda-publications/eda_10years (accessed 13/08/19).

[15] https://api.parliament.uk/historic-hansard/commons/1953/jan/28/european-defence-community-british.

[16] Bowcott (2018) https://www.theguardian.com/politics/2018/jul/24/john-major-full-gloat-defeating-rebels-maastricht-european-union (accessed 05/04/20).

[17] Following the Referendum Party's disbandment in 1997 in wake of the sudden death of Sir James Goldsmith, UKIP—which existed alongside the Referendum Party, having been created in 1992—would scoop up most of the Eurosceptic electoral pot.

the Treaty clear. In a response to Irish Taoiseach, Albert Reynolds, Major thanked him, stating that it "felt good" to be a part of the new 'Union'.[18]

Whilst the Major government supported Maastricht, it was sceptical of the CFSP. As a result, a compromise was reached, in which the CFSP would become part of a so-called 'pillar structure': the first pillar consisted of the European Communities and provided a framework enabling powers for which Member States had transferred sovereignty in areas governed by the Treaty to be exercised by the Community institutions. The second pillar was the common foreign and security policy laid down in Title V of the Treaty. The third pillar was cooperation in the fields of justice and home affairs laid down in Title VI of the Treaty.[19] Titles V and VI provided for intergovernmental cooperation, with certain supranational features such as involving the Commission and consulting Parliament.

The objectives of the CFSP were to 'to safeguard the common values, fundamental interests and independence of the Union' and 'to strengthen the security of the Union and its Member States in all ways'. It also aimed 'to preserve peace and strengthen international security', 'to promote international cooperation' and 'to develop and consolidate democracy and the rule of law, and respect for human rights and fundamental freedoms'.[20] The Member States were to support this policy actively and unreservedly in a spirit of loyalty and mutual solidarity.

Whilst the Treaty provided for 'systematic cooperation between Member States on foreign and security policy issues', as the CFSP was made purely intergovernmental in nature, the European Council (Heads of State) and the Council of Ministers for Foreign Affairs, had overall control of the CFSP. Heads of State and Foreign Ministers must unanimously define a common position in areas of mutual interest between themselves. Each Member State holds a veto. Once a common policy is founded, HoS and/or Ministers may unanimously adopt joint actions and set out its aims and objectives and can decide these via qualified majority voting (QMV). In terms of the influence the EU has over the CFSP, whilst the Commission does not have, as it does in Community affairs, the right to put forward proposals upon which the Council must take a decision, it may refer matters to the Council. The economic means used in the conduct of foreign policy, however, do lie within its responsibility. The role of the European Parliament is also very limited. Whilst it can be informed about the CFSP, hold debates and can address questions and recommendations to the Council, the EU Parliament's role is solely consultative. The Court of Justice of the European Communities has no jurisdiction, since the Member States reject any legal involvement in the CFSP.

[18]Bowcott (2018) https://www.theguardian.com/politics/2018/jul/24/john-major-full-gloat-defeating-rebels-maastricht-european-union (accessed 05/04/20).

[19]Title VI, Treaty on European Union 1992 https://www.legislation.gov.uk/cy/eut/teu/title/VI/data.pdf (accessed 25/08/19).

[20]Title V, Treaty on European Union 1992 https://eur-lex.europa.eu/legal-content/EN/TXT/HTML/?uri=CELEX%3A11997M011 (accessed 25/08/19).

The UK was instrumental in the next phase of reinforcing the CFSP with the establishment of the EU's CSDP. Proposals for an independent European military capability came about at the St. Malo Summit of 1998 between the UK and France. Discussions had begun at the 1997 EU Council summit in Amsterdam. The UK and France took up opposing positions over proposals to integrate the quickly faltering WEU into the EU. France took the position that the WEU should be merged into the EU and fall under control of the Council, therby establishing an autonomous European defence capability. The UK, on the other hand, led by then-PM Tony Blair and his Labour government, opposed France's proposals and insisted on the institutional autonomy of the WEU. At a later conference in 1998, held in Portschach, Austria, the UK altered its position and called upon the EU to take on a stronger security and defence role by improving European defence capabilities. On 4 December 1998, following a two-day summit at Saint-Malo in France, the British and French governments issued a joint Declaration on European defence, stating that 'the Union must have the capacity for autonomous action, backed up by credible military forces, the means to decide to use them and a readiness to do so, in order to respond to international crises'.[21] The UK and France called for the EU to have access to 'suitable military means', whether European capabilities pre-designated within NATO or via multinational European means outside of the NATO umbrella.[22] The declaration at St. Malo led to the establishment of the 'Headline Goal' at Helsinki in 1999. Here, EU leaders sought to provide the EU with the autonomous ability to deploy 60,000 troops in 60 days for an operation lasting as long as one year to conduct the Petersberg Tasks. A deadline was set for December 2003, although this deadline was extended in 2001, before eventually being achieved in 2007. There has since been a new Helsinki headline goal in 2010. The UK—and France—through the St. Malo Declaration were therefore, in turn, instrumental in the creation of the EU's CSDP.

The agreement between France and the UK was surprising, both for the UK and France to agree on something related to Europe, but also because of the UK's explicit support for greater autonomy for the EU in security and defence. Euroscepticism, fear of German rearmament, and a strong Atlantacist outlook, in particular over European security and defence, made the UK's position at St. Malo all the more surprising the reference to multinational European military means outside the NATO framework marked a significant break with Britain's Atlanticist defence outlook.[23] For all the Euroscepticism that went before St. Malo, and all that would come after, the UK solidified its position in European history as a key nation behind the creation of the CSDP.

[21] Declaration on European Defence, British and French governments, Saint-Malo, 3–4 December 1998, paragraph 2.

[22] A Shearer.

[23] Shearer (2000), pp. 283–298.

2.3 The Legal Framework of the CSDP Post-Lisbon

Although the CSDP has evolved and there have been a number of landmark pacts and agreements (i.e. PESCO) since Lisbon, the 2009 Treaty still provides the overall framework for today's CSDP. Article 41 of the TEU outlines the funding of the CFSP and CSDP. The policy is further described in Articles 42 to 46, in Chapter 2, Section 2 of Title V ('Provisions on the Common Security and Defence Policy'), and in Protocols 1, 10 and 11 and Declarations 13 and 14. Under the former TEU, CSDP legal instruments could take the form of principles and general guidelines, common strategies, joint actions, common positions or decisions. Since Lisbon, these have been replaced with one instrument: decisions. Decisions incorporate all of the former and outline the actions that Member States should take. Although the clarity on this, there is still no mechanism for the Commission to monitor the implementation of CSDP decisions and the ECJ has no jurisdiction to condemn or imposes any penalties on the Member States for non-implementation.

As noted, the defining characteristic of the CSFP and CSDP, is its intergovernmental nature, making it distinct from the rest of the EU's supranational capabilities. To ensure Member States retain control over the CSDP, although there are some exceptions,[24] the Council of the EU is the key decision making body and almost all decisions are taken exclusively by unanimity. Article 24 of the TEU clearly states that:

> The common foreign and security policy is subject to specific rules and procedures. It shall be defined and implemented by the European Council and the Council acting unanimously, except where the Treaties provide otherwise. . .[25]

Further, although Lisbon did strengthen their influence somewhat, the Commission and the Parliament's roles are significantly reduced under the CSDP than in all other EU policy areas. The European Parliament does have the power to ask questions to the Council and the High Representative in relation to the CFSP and CSDP, and it can make recommendations on policy, however, the Parliament's questions and recommendations can be ignored.[26] The Parliament does have some power but only through its control over the EU budget. The Commission's role is also limited. Unlike other policy areas, it does not have the right of initiative under the CFSP or CSDP, although it does retain some influence through the HR's role as Vice President of the Commission.

The HR, supported by the EEAS, play a key role in the formation and implementation of the CSDP. As noted above, the High Representative is also one of the Vice-Presidents of the European Commission and chairs the Council of the EU when

[24]For example, the European Council can request for a decision to be taken under QMV, but the decision to request this must be taken by unanimity.

[25]Article 24, Lisbon Treaty 2009 https://eur-lex.europa.eu/resource.html?uri=cellar:2bf140bf-a3f8-4ab2-b506-fd71826e6da6.0023.02/DOC_1&format=PDF (accessed 03/09/19).

[26]Article 36, Lisbon Treaty 2009 https://eur-lex.europa.eu/resource.html?uri=cellar:2bf140bf-a3f8-4ab2-b506-fd71826e6da6.0023.02/DOC_1&format=PDF (accessed 03/09/19).

it sits in its Foreign Affairs configuration. The High Representative also attends European Council meetings, is Head of the EDA and represents the EU internationally, in organisations such as the United Nations. The EEAS, which supports the HR, works in co-operation with EU member states' diplomatic services. It is comprised of officials from the EU, as well as personnel from Member States' national diplomatic services.

As can be seen, EU external policy areas such as international trade, aid and sanctions are much more supranational. This is evident from the fact that decisions are made on the basis of QMV and the involvement of the Parliament and the Commission in the decision-making process is much greater. In these policy areas, Member States are not free to pursue their own individual policies as the legal competence rests partially or entirely with the EU. All bilateral or multilateral trading agreements with non-EU countries are negotiated solely by the European Commission and Member States cannot negotiate their own trade deals. Decisions on the issuing of sanctions against non-EU countries, meanwhile, follow a two-stage process: first, the Council of Ministers agrees—unanimously—to a framework for sanctions; then, the Commission and the HR/VP together draft more specific proposals, which are eventually agreed by the Council by Qualified Majority Voting.[27]

The decision-making in foreign policy and defence, on the other hand, is entirely intergovernmental. As noted above, decisions in this area are made on the basis of unanimity in the Council of Ministers and are implemented by the HR assisted by the EEAS, according to a framework set by Member States. Due to the requirement for unanimity, the EU as a whole cannot undertake any action in CFSP or CSDP if even one Member State dissents or vetoes. Unlike with international trade, aid and sanctions, Member States are able to pursue their own independent foreign policies outside of the EU.

3 UK Involvement in the CSDP: An Effective Partner?

3.1 The Iraq Invasion of 2003

Whilst the UK was instrumental to a great extent in the formation of the CSDP, its track record of cooperating under the CSDP umbrella has been mixed. The UK has, at times, been a reluctant partner with the EU in security and defence. Its Eurosceptic and Atlantacist outlook has made it favour its partnership with the US and its other bilateral partners when it has come to addressing global security and defence issues. This has also caused the UK to be, at times, an obstacle to integration. A notable example of this was the UK's response to the US-led invasion of Iraq in 2003.

[27] Foreign Affairs Committee, *Implications of the referendum on EU membership for the UK's role in the world* (2015) https://publications.parliament.uk/pa/cm201516/cmselect/cmfaff/545/54506.htm (accessed 10/09/19).

The US-led invasion provoked one of the biggest disputes amongst EU Member States in the history of the CSDP, and the UK was at the very centre of it. The US claimed the origins of its invasion of Iraq were triggered by the September 11th 2001 terrorist attacks on the World Trade Centre in New York. Following the attacks, there was an initial outpouring of solidarity by the EU Member States with the US. It was only until the US declared war on Afghanistan and Iraq, that dissent within the EU emerged. In October 2001, the US declared war on Afghanistan and a year later, in October 2002, declared war on Iraq also. A month later, the UN Security Council adopted Resolution 1441, calling upon Iraq to comply with its disarmament obligations, giving it a final opportunity to disarm not only the weapons of mass destruction (WMDs) it was suspected of having, but also the construction of prohibited types of missiles and the purchase and import of prohibited armaments, amongst other things.[28] The US and the EU were in agreement on the enforcement of Resolution 1441, however, both took opposing positions as to how to enforce it If Iraq did not disarm. The US on the one hand, took the position that it would enforce this change by leading a coalition of the willing to disarm Iraq and change the regime, led by Saddam Hussein, by force. The EU, on the other hand, particularly France and Germany, sought to enforce disarmament via UN weapons inspections, with the French Foreign Minister leading the calls for weapons inspections at the UN Security Council, which was met with applause by many of those attending.[29]

Whilst France and Germany represented the majority view of EU Member States, which was to oppose the war, the UK's position was much different. At the time, the UK faced mounting pressure from the EU, as well as its own citizens, to oppose US policy in Iraq. Then-PM, Tony Blair, faced one of the largest public anti-war demonstrations to date against the US declaration of war on Iraq, with 84% of the population opposing war in Iraq.[30] Despite the opposition to the invasion of Iraq,[31] the UK chose to side with the US and joined the coalition of the willing in the invasion of Iraq.[32] Fatally, the division resulted in one of the most embarrassing failures of the CFSP and CSDP in its history. The invasion of Iraq was an issue on which the majority of the EU agreed upon, yet the Member States were unable to form a consensus and united front when it came to the CFSP and the CSDP due to the UK's unwillingness to oppose the invasion. Iraq ultimately portrayed Europe as unstable, weak and divided when it came to handling global security and defence issues and the UK wad at the heart of that embarrassment.

Since 2003 and the first interventions in the Western Balkans, the EU has launched and run 36 operations and missions on three continents. As of May 2021, there were 17 ongoing CSDP missions and operations, 11 of which are civilian

[28] Resolution 1441.

[29] French Foreign Minister's speech at UNSC 2002.

[30] UK opposition to war in Iraq figure.

[31] Gallup International Iraq Poll 2003. Found at <http://www.gallup.com/poll/1633/iraq.aspx> accessed 03/08/14.

[32] McCormick (2007), p. 55.

and 6 military, involving around 5 000 EU military and civilian staff deployed abroad.[33] As discussed, the intergovernmental nature of the CSDP has made forming policy very difficult at times—Iraq is the prime example. As a result, although it has had many notable achievements, the CSDP's success to-date has been modest. When it comes to the CSDP, unanimous decision-making, and in turn Member States' right to veto policy, has placed the power in the hands of the EU's Member States. The opposing foreign policies of Member States has meant that, many times, vetoes have been invoked and a CSDP has ultimately failed to be formed, as in Iraq. Some Member States—such as France and Germany, for example—are more attuned to the CSDP and the concept of European defence. Furthermore, some Member States' foreign policies are very similar and, in turn, finding common ground in terms of the CSDP is much easier to find. Other Member States, however, are more opposed to the idea of European defence and have much different foreign policy interests in comparison to other Member States. It is this latter category that the UK has falls into.

In the years following Maastricht, development of EU security and defence was slow. Even after Lisbon, which did much to strengthen the power of the EU in security and defence, integration has moved at a slower pace relative to other policy areas. This has largely been due to the reluctance of Member States, such as the UK, to integrate further in this area. For the UK, the EU has been a key part of its foreign policy since its accession in 1973. The UK has had a long history of, at times, being a difficult member of the EU when it has come to security and defence. As was seen with Iraq, the UK's close ties to the US through the 'special relationship' has meant that it has always had a preference for developing a European identity within NATO, as opposed to duplicating NATO capabilities via a separate EU military capability. Despite its undisputed integral role in the establishment of the CSDP, successive UK governments have continued to advocate for the maintenance of the intergovernmental nature of the CSDP—and CFSP. For all the reforms under Lisbon and previous treaties, the UK has maintained its support for Member States' control over the CSDP via its veto powers and has resisted the 'communitisation' of the CSDP by preventing the Commission from taking a leading role in initiating policy proposals, and seeking to improve the effectiveness of the CFSP via greater use of the EU's own financial resources and power as a trading bloc.[34] Furthermore, its Atlantacist outlook has meant that the CSDP has not been at the core of its foreign policy and, as noted, the UK has placed its security and defence partnership with the US, NATO and other bilateral partnerships ahead of the one it shares with the EU.

The UK, overall, has made a modest contribution when it has come to the *military* side of the CSDP, however, in terms of its contributions to *civilian* missions (i.e. peacekeeping missions such as border control/observation and capacity building missions for third states), the story is a little different.

[33]EEAS, *Missions and operations* (EEAS, 2021) https://www.eeas.europa.eu/eeas/missions-and-operations_en (accessed 03/10/21).

[34]Whitman (2019), p. 3.

3.2 *EUBAM, Operation Sophia and the Libyan Civil War (2011-Present)*

One of the most notable examples of the UK having an effective involvement in the CSDP was in response to the Libyan Civil War, which began in 2011. Civil War broke out in Libya following the popular uprising by the Libyan people against the Libyan leader, Colonel Gadaffi. The conflict was part of the wider popular uprising which spread across the Middle-East in 2011, commonly referred to as the 'Arab Spring', in which other Middle-Eastern leaders, such as Tunisia's leader, Ben Ali and Egypt's Hosni Mubarak, were overthrown by their respective peoples.[35] The civil war in Libya resulted in months of fighting and bloodshed across the country, until eventually, in October 2011, Gadaffi, who had gone into hiding, was found and executed by rebel forces. Following the news of his death, the National Transitional Council leader, Prime Minister Mustafa Abdul Jalil, declared Libya's liberation. The fighting, however, did not come to an end following Gadaffi's death and rival rebel factions began to fight each other, both competing for overall control of the country. The Libyan Civil War continues to this day.

In its initial response to the conflict, the UK sought to address the conflict through NATO, via its bilateral partnership with France, a partnership which had recently been reinforced under the Lancaster House Treaties in 2010. The Treaties sought to bind the UK and France closer together in a shared security and defence partnership, which aimed at increased interoperability and cooperation between the two nations by setting up a joint military force and through the sharing of equipment and nuclear missile research centres.

The UK's response did not completely rule out the EU. Efforts were made by the UK and France to give mention to the CSDP in the Treaties. Under its stated five objectives, the two countries stated that they would make the CSDP one of the vehicles through which it would seek to achieve its joint objectives under Lancaster House.[36] The UK and France also made efforts to make the EU part of its initial response to the Libyan conflict. In the lead up to the invasion, the UK sought action against Gadaffi through the United Nations Security Council. On 26th February 2011, United Nations Security Council Resolution (UNSCR) 1970 was adopted unanimously by the UN Security Council (UNSC), condemning the use of force by the government of Gaddafi against protesters and imposed a number of international sanctions against his regime. The UNSCR also referred the state of Libya to the International Criminal Court.[37] The UK also sought the legal basis for intervention and the introduction of a no fly zone via the UNSC. On 17th March 2011, UNSCR 1973 was passed demanding an immediate ceasefire and authorizing the

[35] A term coined by American journalist Marc Lynch in 2011 to describe the spread of popular uprisings across the Middle East; See Lynch (2011) https://foreignpolicy.com/2011/01/06/obamas-arab-spring/ (accessed 05/01/21).

[36] Lancaster House Treaty, Article 1.

[37] S/RES/1970 (2011).

international community to establish a no-fly zone to protect civilians. The question was now how and by who the NFZ would be implemented.

Just days earlier, prior to the adoption of UNSCR 1973, the question of a NFZ and military intervention had been discussed at an extraordinary meeting of the European Council on 11th March. Prior to the meeting, William Hague addressed the House of Commons calling upon the EU to 'radically rethink its neighbourhood policy' and to take a 'bold and ambitious' approach to Libya.[38] In response to questions by the House, Hague affirmed his belief in the EU having a role in Libya, but argued that this should be in a civilian capacity.[39] Members of the House called on the EU to do more in response to the conflict.[40] The UK government's position was reaffirmed in a letter sent to the then EU Council President, Herman Van Rompuy, by Cameron and Sarkozy, calling on the EU to prepare to respond to the Libyan Conflict. The letter called upon the EU to undertake a number of tasks. These included supporting the NTC; to prepare to provide support for 'all possible contingencies'; to support a NFZ; to monitor the humanitarian situation in Libya and be ready to provide humanitarian assistance; to implement the arms embargo against Gadaffi; and to be prepared to provide support to displaced persons via financial and military assistance.[41] The meeting was attended by Foreign Secretary William Hague, who called upon the EU to put together a "bold, ambitious and historic plan for Libya" and to work on a coordinated basis with NATO.[42] He also called on the EU to assess what humanitarian assistance it could provide to Libya and to look at how the EU could transform its relationship with the region in order to incentivise change and ensure effective spending of EU funds.[43]

The UK's calls for the EU to prepare to play its part in the conflict were, however, met with a negative response. In an official declaration on 11th March 2011, the Council outlined the EU's position on the Libyan Conflict at that time.[44] The Council condemned the use of force by Gadaffi against the Libyan people and supported UNSCR 1970s referral of the Gadaffi regime to the ICC. It also called on Gadaffi to relinquish power and outlined its sanctions against the Gadaffi regime

---

[38] Hansard, House of Commons debate (7th March 2011).

[39] *Ibid.*

[40] Dr Andrew Murrison, Conservative MP for South West Wiltshire Conservative, criticized the HR and the EEAS during this session. He asked Hague: "If the EEAS has a point, it is surely to engage in a timely fashion in its very near abroad. Is my right hon. Friend aware of any action being taken by Baroness Ashton in advance of this Friday's meeting beyond cancelling a few visas and imposing a few trade sanctions?".

[41] '*Letter from David Cameron and Nicolas Sarkozy to Herman Van Rompuy*', Guardian UK, (London, 10 March 2011) https://www.theguardian.com/world/2011/mar/10/libya-middleeast (accessed 28/03/21).

[42] '*EU foreign ministers' meeting on Libya*', HM Gov (10 Macrh 2011) https://www.gov.uk/government/news/eu-foreign-ministers-meeting-on-libya (accessed 28/03/21).

[43] *Ibid.*

[44] Extraordinary European Council Declaration, (11 March 2011) https://ec.europa.eu/commission/presscorner/detail/en/DOC_11_2 (accessed 28/03/21).

and those supporting and connected with it. The Council also made assurances that it would help with Libya's transfer to democracy and with its rebuilding of its economy post-Gadaffi, as well as committing itself to providing humanitarian aid and to assist people fleeing the conflict and helping with border control. Finally, the Council committed the EU to enhancing its European Neighbourhood Policy, with a greater emphasis on the Southern Mediterranean region to ensure deeper economic integration, broader market access and political cooperation. Importantly, however, the Declaration left out any mention of a NFZ. Instead, it committed the EU to examine "all necessary options" if Gaddafi intensified his attacks on civilians.

To make matters more difficult, at the same Council meeting, High Rerpresentative Catherine Ashton was also reported as attacking Sarkozy's and Cameron's calls for military intervention and a NFZ, warning that a NFZ hat a no-fly zone could end up killing many civilians.[45] An official from her office also stated that Ashton believed the efficiency of a NFZ was very questionable.[46] Ashton's opposition to a NFZ was met with anger within the Conservative Parliamentary Party, and likely angered many other Eurosceptics within Cameron's government. In a statement to the House of Commons following the HR's comments, Conservative MP Bernard Jenkin addressed the PM and criticised Ashton, questioning 'what mandate' she had to give her opinions on the UK's proposals and arguing that she should seek to serve the Member States rather than pretending to lead them. Although Cameron laughed off the comments, Ashton's comments certainly would have made a CSDP operation even more difficult to achieve. Ultimately, the Council meeting ended without support for Cameron and Sarkozy's proposals, and the EU failed to bring about a CSDP operation to address the Libyan Conflict. The EU would eventually endorse UNSCR 1973 and, in turn, a NFZ, just days later, however, it ultimately came too late to bring together a CSDP operation.[47]

In early April 2011, the EU would eventually prepare for a military operation in Libya with the aim of supporting humanitarian assistance there. The operation was entitled EUFOR Libya and an Operational Headquarters was established in Rome. EUFOR Libya was to be deployed only on the condition if requested by the UN (specifically the Office for the Coordination of Humanitarian Affairs or OCHA). The UN, however, would never request the EU's assistance through EUFOR and, ultimately, the mission was never launched, leaving the EU without a response to the initial conflict. Although, as Liam Fox would make clear in a speech post-Gadaffi in October 2011, the UK wanted the NFZ and military intervention to be under the command of NATO,[48] it was clear the UK still wanted the EU to play a role via the

[45] Watt (2011) https://www.theguardian.com/politics/wintour-and-watt/2011/mar/15/eu-davidcameron (accessed 28/03/21).

[46] *Ibid.*

[47] Extraordinary European Council Declaration, *Supra* 44.

[48] Dr Liam Fox, Conservative Party Conference (2011) https://www.theguardian.com/politics/blog/2011/oct/05/conservative-conference-2011-live-coverage (accessed 02/04/21).

CSDP in addressing the conflict. Ultimately, the NFZ was led by France and the UK within the structures of NATO without the involvement of the EU.

Whilst the CSDP was not employed in the response to the initial conflict, the UK would utilise its partnership with the EU in addressing the post-conflict response. Prime Minister David Cameron, in an address to the House of Commons on 28th March 2011, spoke of the support the EU had eventually given to the intervention through its support of UNSCR 1973.[49] The PM claimed that the UK had been a primary reason why the EU came to support the conflict and claimed the UK had had a positive influence on the EU's renewed focus on the humanitarian crisis in Libya and in the Southern Mediterranean.[50] Cameron also took the opportunity during this session in the House to call on the EU to do more long-term in Libya and the rest of North Africa to put pressure on North African nations to do more to make their societies more open and more democratic.[51] Cameron argued the EU must offer these nations deeper economic integration, broader market access and greater political cooperation in return for evidence of this. Other government ministers joined Cameron in calling upon the EU to do more in addressing Libyan crisis. In a speech to the British Embassy in Berlin in May 2012, Hammond addressed the German Council on Foreign Relations regarding the UK government's perspective on the future of the CSDP.[52] Hammond called upon the EU to 'step up to the plate' to deliver security in the European neighbourhood and to stop being consumers of security but also producers of it. Hammond made the comments in light of the United States' new foreign policy direction, of turning its attention towards the emergence of China and Asia. Hammond argued that for the UK, the EU and the European nations, this meant taking more responsibility for security in the European neighbourhood. Hammond pointed to the Libyan conflict as an example, arguing that Libya exposed the imbalances and weaknesses of European NATO nations and that, without the US, Operation Unified Protector could not have been a success. Hammond called upon EU Member States to do more to act collectively and to work towards common positions, revealing a strong desire within the UK government to work with the EU the CSDP going forward. Furthermore, in June 2012, Minister for Europe David Liddington gave a speech specifically addressing the UK government's perspective on the CSDP.[53] The speech was one of the most comprehensive accounts of the UK government's approach to CSDP at the time. Liddington described the CSDP as a key component of European defence, that the UK was proud of what the CSDP has achieved to date and that it wanted to play a leading role in strengthening and sharpening CSDP. Liddington also outlined where the UK

---

[49] Hansard, House of Commons debate (28th March 2011).

[50] *Ibid.*

[51] *Ibid.*

[52] Phillip Hammond (2012) https://www.gov.uk/government/speeches/2012-05-02-shared-security-transforming-defence-to-face-the-future (accessed 08/04/21).

[53] Liddington (2012) https://www.gov.uk/government/speeches/eu-common-security-and-defence-policy-the-uk-perspective (accessed 08/04/21).

believed the CSDP could be a tool to address the Libya conflict, identifying this as helping Libya manage and control its borders, but also noting that this should not duplicate what 'other international actors' are doing. Finally, Liddington signed off by acknowledging the contribution that CSDP makes to UK security and defence, stating that the results of CSDP missions and operations 'matter' to the UK. The Cameron government's comments and responses during this session revealed that he valued and saw a place for the EU in helping to contribute to the effort in Libya in a civilian capacity as well as helping rebuild Libyan society post-conflict. This support for the EU's role in a post-conflict response culminated in two civilian CSDP missions in which the UK played a significant role.

Following the fall of Gadaffi and as a result of the ensuing conflict, Libya lost control of its land, air and sea borders and became a corridor through which migrants from across Africa could cross into Europe. The lack of border control also meant that Islamist terrorist groups were also able to enter the country. In response to this, on 22nd May 2013, the European Council passed a decision to launch EUBAM Libya, an integrated border management mission in Libya in partnership with Libyan authorities.[54] As a civilian crisis management mission with a capacity-building mandate, EUBAM assisted Libyan authorities at both strategic and operational levels to help the Libyan authorities to regain control of their borders. EUBAM was tasked with advising, training and mentoring Libyan counterparts in strengthening the border services in accordance with international standards and best practices, as well as advising Libyan authorities on the development of a national Integrated Border Management (IBM) strategy.[55] Although the missions HQ would be initially based in Tripoli, the mission was eventually downsized in 2014 due to the deteriorating security situation in Libya and the HQ relocated to Tunis, Tunisia. Its mandate would be amended a number of times, first in February 2016, when its mandate was amended to provide for a possible civilian capacity building and assistance crisis management mission in the field of security sector reform, focussing on police, criminal justice, border security and migration. The mandate was amended again in July 2017, when the Council extended the mandate of EUBAM Libya until 31 December 2018 to plan for a possible non-executive CSDP mission providing advice and capacity building in the fields of border management, law enforcement and criminal justice.

The mission to date has largely been unable to achieve its objectives due to the deteriorating crisis in Libya. After the relocation of its HQ to Tunis, the mission was placed into 'sleeper mode', meaning the mission was put on hold until seconded staff could safely return to Libya to carry out the mandate. EUBAM was able to return to Libya in September 2019 and re-establish its HQ there, however, its mandate remains unfulfilled and the Council recently extended the mission until 30th June

[54] Council Decision 2013/233/CFSP.

[55] '*About the EU's Border Assistance Mission in Libya*', EEAS, (15 September 2021) https://www.eeas.europa.eu/eubam-libya/about-eu-border-assistance-mission-libya-eubam_en?s=327 (accessed 04/12/21).

2023. That said, to reiterate, the focus of the Chapter is on the partnership between the UK and the EU, not the success of the individual missions. The partnership can be evaluated by analysing the contributions made by the UK. In the case of EUBAM, this was a civilian mission. It was therefore funded by the EU's CFSP budget, which is set by the European Parliament, through which all CSDP civilian missions are funded.[56] The UK's contribution to this budget is 15%—military missions are funded via the Athena Financing Mechanism, of which the UK's contribution is 16%. This will be looked at in more detail below. Although the UK's contribution of personnel to EUBAM was only small—4 border experts to a mission that was supposed to be 165 personnel at full operational capacity—its contribution in terms of finance was similar to the contributions made by France and Germany.

Although EUBAM is yet to fulfil its mandate almost 10 years on, it is clear that at the time of its launch in 2013, the mission was valued by the Cameron government in terms of the impact that it could have to help improve the security situation in Libya. Providing an update to the European Scrutiny Committee (ESC),[57] a year on from the mission's launch, Minister for Europe, David Liddington, gave his government's evaluation of both the importance of EUBAM and of the UK's contribution to it. Liddington described the UK's involvement as 'significant', listing examples of the UK's assistance such as providing a Deputy Head of Mission, Border Security Advisers, and training of Libyan border guards. Liddington also drew to the Committee's attention the fact that the UK contributes 15% to civilian missions. In an Explanatory Memorandum brought before the ESC, Liddington outlines a comprehensive list of the government's reasons why EUBAM is in the UK's interests.[58] The Memorandum states that Libyan border security is important for UK objectives of combating terrorism, arms dealing and people smuggling in the Southern Mediterranean and that EUBAM Libya makes an 'important contribution' to this. Liddington concedes that the first year of EUBAM was difficult, however, he goes on to defend the mission to the Committee by highlighting some of its achievements up to that date. Liddington described EUBAM as the most significant contribution to Libyan security to date and heralds the EU as Libya's lead partner on border security. Liddington also brought to the ESC's attention the achievements the mission has made in strengthening maritime capabilities of Libyan authorities and Navy and in building a stronger border network by strengthening telecommunications, information exchange and transport infrastructure, amongst other things. Speaking on how he saw the future of the mission and the UK's contribution, Liddington stated that the government wanted to see EUBAM further 'imbed itself' in Libya and the UK was prepared to continue to support the mission. The Committee ultimately agreed with Liddington's assessment of the mission and categorised EUBAM as 'politically

[56]Treaty of Lisbon (2009), Article 41(2).

[57]The ESC is a parliamentary select committee of the House of Commons which assesses the legal and/or political importance of EU documents deposited by the UK government in Parliament.

[58]ESC, Explanatory Memorandum (8th May 2014) https://publications.parliament.uk/pa/cm201314/cmselect/cmeuleg/83-xlv/8317.htm#note67 (accessed 10/04/21).

important'. The ESC would continue to support the UK's involvement until the UK's withdrawal of the EU in 2020.[59] EUBAM still exists and experts in the field still consider it an important mission, giving the EU a head start in supporting state structures for security when circumstances permit.

The second CSDP mission the UK played a significant role in in relation to Libya was EUNAVFOR Med Operation Sophia ('Operation Sophia'). This operation was launched in June 2015 in response to the continued Libyan conflict and the resulting migration, refugee and human trafficking crisis.[60] Sophia complemented EUBAM but was different to it in that it was a military CSDP operation. Through Sophia, the EU conducted a military crisis management operation contributing to the disruption of the business model of human smuggling and trafficking networks in Libya and the wider Southern Mediterranean. Its tasks included identifying, capturing and disposing of vessels and assets used or suspected of being used by smugglers or traffickers. Its mandate included patrolling the Southern Mediterranean seas to detect and monitor migration networks and to conduct boarding, search and seizure of vessels suspected of being used in human trafficking. In June 2016, Sophia's mandate was broadened to include the capacity building and training of the Libyan Navy and Coastguard, as well as contributing to information sharing and contribution to the implementation of the UN arms embargo in accordance with UNSCR 2292.[61] In July 2017 the Council extended the mandate of Sophia again to provide further and long-term training to the Libyan Coastguard as well as carry out new surveillance activities and information gathering on illegal trafficking of oil exports from Libya. In January 2019, Sophia's mandate was reduced and on 31st March 2020, it was replaced by a new mission EUNAVFOR MED Operation Irini.

The mission was responsible for 'neutralising' over 475 assets of human trafficking and rescued more than 40,000 migrants from the Mediterranean Sea. Against this, however, in 2017, the European Union Committee of the House of Lords in a report declared Sophia 'a failed mission'. The Committee stated that, although the mission had saved lives and apprehended assets, irregular migration into Europe increased by 18% in 2016 and 19% in 2017 compared to the previous year.[62] The report also claimed that Sophia had encouraged human trafficking, with human traffickers sending migrants into the Mediterranean in unseaworthy vessels with migrants believing they would be saved by the EU coastguard. This ultimately resulted in an increase in deaths of migrants. As a result, the Committee recommended the UK government to not renew the mandate of Operation Sophia. It did, however, encourage the UK and the EU to continue with its counter-migration efforts and even recommended the launching of a new CSDP mission to the southern border of Libya.

---

[59] *Ibid.*

[60] Council Decision (CFSP) 2015/778.

[61] Council Decision (CFSP) 2016/993.

[62] European Union Committee, '*Operation Sophia: a failed mission*' Report (2017) https://publications.parliament.uk/pa/ld201719/ldselect/ldeucom/5/503.htm (accessed 12/04/21).

Again, whilst the success of the EU's CSDP operations are important, regardless of the success of Operation Sophia itself, the focus here is on the security and defence partnership between the UK and the EU and whether it functioned well as a partnership or not. In terms of the UK's contribution of personnel, its contribution in this respect has been described as 'modest'.[63] That said, providing expert evidence to the House of Lords EU Committee, Angus Lapsley, Director, Defence and International Security, Foreign and Commonwealth Office (FCO), stated that the UK has contributed significantly in terms of financing and costs to Operation Sophia. As noted above, CSDP military operations are different to CSDP civilian operations in that they are not funded through the EU budget, rather, they are financed via the Athena mechanism.[64] Member States pay into Athena and their contribution is proportionate to the size of their economy (contributions are calculated according to a Gross National Income scale and varies from year to year). The Athena mechanism means that the EU Member States will, as a whole, cover what is commonly referred to as the 'common costs' of a mission, which includes things like the running costs of a HQ, travel expenses, IT systems etc. This has been estimated to generally only cover 10–15% of the costs of an operation.[65] The rest of the costs of the mission—85–90%—are paid for by the Member States participating in it. The UK's contribution of 16% to military CSDP operations is slightly higher than the contribution it makes to civilian CSDP operations (15%). Although the figure differs from year-to-year, in 2011, the common cost of operations funded by Athena was €34.7 million, of which the UK's share was €4.9 million. The equivalent figure for France was approximately €5.8m, and for Germany, approximately €7.2m.

It is unclear what the breakdown in costs of Operation Sophia were, however, by combining the UK's 14% contribution to 'common costs' via Athena and its 16% contribution to military CSDP operations, its contribution to Operation Sophia could be said to be in the region of 30% of the overall operation costs. Giving his expert opinion to the EU Committee in the House of Lords, Angus Lapsley argued that, on the basis of the EU's CSDP financing mechanisms, the UK made a "substantial monetary contribution" to Operation Sophia.[66] Lapsley also drew the Committee's attention to a £600,000 payment that the UK made towards Operation Sophia, to support the training of the Libyan coastguard. Although the UK's contribution of personnel to CSDP missions have, at times, been disproportionately low, in the case of Operation Sophia, Lapsely argues that the UK dedicated 'serious military assets' to this mission. In the case of Sophia, the UK provided survey vessels HMS Echo

---

[63] European Union Committee, '*Brexit: Common Security and Defence Policy missions and operations*', (2018) https://publications.parliament.uk/pa/ld201719/ldselect/ldeucom/132/13202.htm (accessed 12/04/21).

[64] Lisbon Treaty (2009), Article 41(2).

[65] '*Athena - financing security and defence military operations*', European Council https://www.consilium.europa.eu/en/policies/athena/ (accessed 15/04/21).

[66] European Union Committee, *Supra* 63.

and HMS Enterprise, the air-defence destroyer HMS Diamond, the frigate HMS Richmond, and with Merlin Mk2, AW159 Wildcat and AW Lynx Mk8 helicopters.[67] Furthermore, as highlighted in the UK's Brexit position paper on foreign policy and defence in 2017, the UK was also one of only a few Member States to have a ship continuously assigned an operation, provide personnel, and on top of its share of common costs, funded almost £600,000 for Libyan Coastguard training.[68] Although ultimately Operation Sophia was branded a 'failure' by the House of Lords in 2017, it was clear that, for the UK government at the time and the successive government of Primer Minister Theresa May, valued the impact that the EU and the CSDP could have in addressing the fallout of the Libyan Conflict. The level of the UK's contribution to the operation is testament to this.

3.3 EU Sanctions, EUAM and the Russian-Ukrainian War (2014-Present)

Another example of when the UK played an effective role within the CSDP was in response to the Ukraine conflict of 2014, following Russia's invasion and annexation of Crimea. Given the gravity of a potential nuclear conflict with Russia, from the very beginning of the 2014 conflict, the UK aligned itself closely with the EU to coordinate an effective response to the Ukrainian conflict, without resorting to hard military tactics. The UK's coordinated response with the EU to the Ukrainian crisis came in two-parts. The first came in the form of EU sanctions. In the initial phase of the conflict, then-Foreign Secretary William Hague, in a speech to the House of Commons, condemned the conflict and Russia's interference in it.[69] He spoke of the UK government's support for the announcement made by the EU's Foreign Affairs Committee, which condemned Russia's acts of aggression, called on Russia to immediately withdraw its forces to where they were stationed before the conflict, and to agree to the request by Ukraine for direct consultations under the Budapest memorandum.[70] Hague also outline his support for the €610 million in financial assistance the EU provided to Ukraine and stated that the UK would support future EU plans to provide further financial assistance to Ukraine. On 6th March 2014, the EU Council met to address the Ukraine crisis. The Council threatened Russia with economic sanctions, after announcing the freezing of the assets of the ousted

---

[67] '*EUNAVFOR MED Operation Sophia—Assets*', EEAS https://www.operationsophia.eu/media_category/assets/page/3/?deployment=any&tax=media_category&categories&nation&search_archive=filter#038;tax=media_category&categories=&nation=&search_archive=filter (accessed 16/04/21).

[68] '*Foreign policy, defence and development - a future partnership paper*', HM Gov, (2017) https://www.gov.uk/government/publications/foreign-policy-defence-and-development-a-future-partnership-paper (accessed 16/04/21).

[69] Hansard, House of Commons Debate (04 March 2014) c755.

[70] *Ibid.*

pro-Russian Ukrainian president Viktor Yanukovych and 17 other Russian officials.[71] Sanctions such as freezing talks regarding Russian visas and regulating relations between Russia and the EU.[72] European diplomats, however, conceded that the sanctions were more symbolic than substantive. At the summit, Cameron gave a speech to the Council, calling on the EU to act, drawing the Council's attention to the 70 years of peace the EU Member States had worked "so hard to keep".[73] Cameron called on the EU to start work on additional measures, such as travel bans and asset freezes.[74] Cameron acknowledged that getting agreement on CSDP is never easy, however, told the Council that the UK is proud to have "played an important part" in bringing the EU together over Ukraine.

Following the EU Council summit, Cameron updated the Commons on action being taken in Ukraine. The speech gave some insight to the value that he and his government placed in the EU's ability to address the Ukrainian conflict. In this speech, Cameron assured the Commons that, although the EU has not yet agreed to deploy these measures, they would be introduced if Russia did not open peace talks with Ukraine and if Russia tried to claim that referendum in Crimea about its future was legitimate. Cameron also gave his support to an increase in EU sanctions against Russia that would include a broad range of economic areas. Cameron also defended the EU's course of action, by trying dialogue with Russia first before implementing sanctions. He argued that the EU's approach was "not doomed to not work" and called up the EU Member States to provide a "strong, predictable and consistent" approach to the conflict.[75]

Following the sanctions made by the EU in March 2014, freezing the assets of 'certain individuals threatening the integrity, sovereignty and independence of Ukraine', no new sanctions were made against Russia until July 2014. In June 2014, following a meeting between EU foreign ministers, William Hague announced that, if the UK was not happy with Russia's response to a peace plan being offered by Ukraine, that the UK would be willing to support the imposition of more sanctions against Russia by the EU.[76] In turn, at a meeting of the European Council in July 2014, the EU concluded that Russia had not sufficiently implemented the steps set out in their previous conclusions, in which they had called on Russia to use its influence on the rebel groups and to stop the flow of militants and weaponry cross the border and to achieve rapid results in de-escalating the conflict.

As a result, the Council stopped the European Investment Bank and the European Bank for Reconstruction and Development from granting further loans in the

[71] This would be implemented via Council Decision 2014/145/CFSP 17th March 2014.

[72] Traynor (2014) https://www.theguardian.com/world/2014/mar/06/ukraine-crisis-european-leaders-emergency-summit (accessed 12/06/21).

[73] David Cameron, EU meeting on Ukraine Speech, (2014) https://www.gov.uk/government/speeches/eu-meeting-on-ukraine-david-camerons-speech (accessed 12/06/21).

[74] *Ibid.*

[75] Sparrow (2014) https://www.theguardian.com/politics/blog/2014/mar/10/gordon-browns-speech-on-further-devolution-to-scotland-politics-live-blog (accessed 14/06/21).

[76] Croft and Pawlak (2014) https://www.reuters.com/article/uk-ukraine-crisis-eu-idUKKBN0EY11L20140623 (accessed 14/06/21).

Russian Federation and instructed the European Commission to prepare a list of entities supporting the unrest by and to implement asset freezes and travel bans against them.[77] As Dr Tomila Lankina points out, the UK, without doubt, represented one of the stronger voices among EU member states advocating sanctions against Russia following its annexation of Crimea and proxy war in the Donbas.[78]

Following the shooting down of MH17, Cameron and the UK government stepped up their pressure on the EU to take a tougher stance against Russia. The then-UK Foreign Secretary, Philip Hammond (taking over from William Hague in July 2014) argued that asset freezes and travel bans could be imposed on close associates of Russian leader Vladimir Putin. Press reports at the time suggested that the UK government were pressing for 'tier three' sanctions. These are sanctions that target the whole sectors of a state's economy and impose arms trade bans.[79] Cameron stepped up his rhetoric on Russia and called on the EU to do more. He criticised European leaders who he alleged were hoping that the crisis "would go away".[80] He also criticised what he saw as a "reluctance on the part of too many European countries to face up to the implications of what is happening in eastern Ukraine" and that he saw this reluctance at the European Council meeting in July 2014. Over the next few days, the EU expanded its list of sanctions to include more Russian individuals and entities.[81] Eventually, on 28th July, the EU, the UK, along with France, Germany, Italy and the US, agreed to tier three sanctions against Russia, including restricting Russian banks' access to European and UK finance. This meant that EU nationals and companies could no longer buy or sell new bonds, equity or similar financial instruments with a maturity exceeding 90 days, issued by major state-owned Russian banks. These sanctions also included an embargo on the export and import of arms and related material, covering all items from the EU common military list and an export ban on goods and technology used for military ends. All of these measures were agreed to and supported by the UK.

The reaction to the use of sanctions against Russia was mixed—and still is to this day. There are some that argue that sanctions enable the EU's Member States to take effective action against Russia without resorting to military force. Others, on the other hand, argue that they only strengthen nationalistic feelings within Russia.[82]

---

[77] https://www.consilium.europa.eu/uedocs/cms_data/docs/pressdata/en/ec/143992.pdf.

[78] European Union Committee, '*The EU and Russia: before and beyond the crisis in Ukraine*.

[79] *Tier 3 sanctions: what are they*?', 6th report, (2015) https://publications.parliament.uk/pa/ld201415/ldselect/ldeucom/115/11509.htm (accessed 14/06/21).

[80] David Cameron, '*MH17 air disaster*' Speech, (2014) https://www.gov.uk/government/news/mh17-air-disaster-article-by-david-cameron (accessed 15/06/21).

[81] 15 additional persons and 18 new entities with a travel ban and assets freeze. In total, therefore, 87 persons and 20 entities were now under EU sanctions over the situation in Ukraine.

[82] Sir Tony Brenton, former UK ambassador in Moscow, argued that sanctions would be counter-productive, both because Vladimir Putin is riding high on nationalistic approval in Russia, and because they could force Russia to turn away from the West; See Brenton (2014) https://www.telegraph.co.uk/news/worldnews/europe/russia/10986630/Sanctions-wont-work-we-will-have-to-negotiate-with-Vladimir-Putin.html (accessed 20/06/21).

That said, following the 2014 EU and US sanctions against Russia, in 2015, Russia entered a recession, with Russia's Economy Ministry predicting a contraction of the Russian economy of 0.8%, as opposed to the previous expectation of a 1.2% growth in 2015.[83] Although sanctions had clearly had an impact, there appeared to be an appetite within Cameron's government and across the EU, to do more to help equip Ukraine in its fight against Russia.

The second part of the UK's coordinated response with the EU to the Ukrainian crisis came in the form of a CSDP mission: EUAM Ukraine. By July 2014, although sanctions were beginning to have an effect on Russia's occupation of Ukraine, there was growing pressure from within the Cameron government to see the EU do more to address the conflict in Ukraine. Writing in the Sunday Times, Cameron criticised the EU and its Member States for being 'slow to act' against Russia and called upon the EU to make its 'power, influence and resources count'.[84] Defence Secretary, Michael Fallon, speaking to the Daily Mail, warned Russia to get out of Ukraine and that, whilst he agreed sanctions were affecting the Russian economy, the UK would be willing to support more action through the EU to assist Ukraine.[85] Fallon also indicated the UK would be willing to give more military assistance to NATO member countries in Eastern Europe to help address the threat from Russia.[86] The UK would provide its own assistance to Ukraine via 'Operation Orbital' launched in October 2015, whereby the UK would provide bilateral assistance to the Ukrainian Government, which included the provision of non-lethal military equipment (defensive and designed to prevent further fatalities and casualties to Ukrainian forces).[87] The Operation would also include non-lethal training and capacity building, providing guidance and training to the Ukrainian armed forces through several advisory and short-term training teams. In all, the UK would send 100 personnel to Ukraine as part of the operation. In March 2015, the MOD set out the UK's overall policy with respect to military assistance to Ukraine, which stated that it would be the UK's policy to provide non-lethal assistance to Ukrainian armed forces, and that the MOD would continue to focus on support and assistance that will reduce fatalities and casualties amongst members of the Ukrainian armed forces, whilst building their capacity and resilience.[88]

---

[83] '*Russia warns of recession in 2015*', BBC News, (London, 02 December 2014) https://www.bbc.co.uk/news/business-30288739 (accessed 20/06/21).

[84] '*David Cameron criticises Europe for lack of action on pro-Russia separatists*', Guardian UK, (London, 20 July 2014) https://www.theguardian.com/politics/2014/jul/20/david-cameron-europe-russia-ukraine-mh17 (accessed 20/06/21).

[85] *Ibid.*

[86] '*Michael Fallon: UK to send troops to Baltic region*', BBC News, (London, 08 October 2015) https://www.bbc.co.uk/news/uk-politics-34472739 (accessed 20/06/21).

[87] House of Commons, '*Military Assistance to Ukraine 2014-2021*' Research Briefing, (2014) https://commonslibrary.parliament.uk/research-briefings/sn07135/ (accessed 20/06/21).

[88] *Ibid.*

While UK military assistance was bilateral in nature, the provision of equipment and training was undertaken in coordination with allies, primarily through NATO and the EU, through EUAM Ukraine.

The appetite within the Cameron government to provide non-lethal aid and assistance to Ukraine coupled with the pressure that Cameron and his ministers were putting on the EU to do more in Ukraine, played a significant role in the establishment of EUAM Ukraine. At an FAC meeting in July 2014, the Council, including the UK, discussed the situation in Ukraine following the downing of MH17 and adopted a decision launching the civilian CSDP mission European Union Advisory Mission for Civilian Security Sector Reform Ukraine (EUAM Ukraine). EUAM was mandated with mentoring and advising relevant Ukrainian bodies in the elaboration and implementation of renewed security strategies and cohesive reform efforts, in order to create sustainable security services delivering the rule of law. EUAM was also mandated with reorganising and restructuring Ukrainian security services in a way to help Ukraine recover control over them. The mission was also tasked with assisting in civilian security sector reform planning process. The HQ was initially in Kiev and it has had its mandate renewed and updated a number of times since 2014. Since the Russian invasion in February 2022, however, EUAM was no longer able to fully implement its mandate in Ukraine and remains on standby at the time of writing this Chapter.

In terms of financing, EUAM received a €2.68 million for the start-up of the mission and the Council allocated it a budget of € 13.1m for the first 12 months of the mission's two-year mandate starting on the 1st of December. In terms of personnel, EUAM consisted of 143 personnel. As EUAM Ukraine is a civilian mission, as noted above, the funding for the mission comes from the EU budget, of which the UK's contribution is 15%. In terms of personnel, the UK seconded 6 personnel to the mission for the duration of the mission. Again, in terms of the UK's personnel, the figure was well below what it should be sending (although it was one of the highest number of personnel it had sent to a CSDP civilian mission), however, its 15% share of the totally annual costs of the mission were, again, on par with France and Germany. In the case of EUAM, however, the value of the mission to the UK, is best looked at in what has been said about it since its launch.

Not long after the launch of EUAM, in May 2015, the UK General Election was held. In the lead up to the General Election, the Conservatives under Cameron published their 2015 Party Manifesto.[89] Europe was a key feature of the manifesto, mentioning the word 'Europe' a total of 85 times.[90] Overall, the key points made in relation to Europe in the manifesto were a scrapping of the Human Rights Act and an introduction of a British Bill of Rights and the promise of an in-out referendum on the UK's membership of the EU before the end of 2017. Like the 2010 manifesto, the

[89] Conservative Manifesto (2015) https://www.theresavilliers.co.uk/sites/www.theresavilliers.co.uk/files/conservativemanifesto2015.pdf (accessed 28/06/21).

[90] Sedghi et al. (2015) https://www.theguardian.com/news/datablog/2015/apr/14/what-conservative-manifestos-key-themes-reveal-about-partys-priorities (accessed 28/06/21).

2015 manifesto promised no further transfer of powers to the EU and ruled out any support for a European Army. That said, the manifesto did make promises that the UK would continue to use its membership of the EU to 'keep the UK safe'. Furthermore, although promises of a referendum were made, the manifesto clearly highlighted Cameron and the Party's position to remain in the EU and seek a 'new settlement' with the EU.[91]

In November 2015, following the Conservative victory in the 2015 General Election from which Cameron was able to establish a majority government, the UK government published its National Security Strategy and Strategic Defence and Security Review.[92] The Review spoke positively about the EU's complementary value to NATO and boasted about the UK's involvement in EU CSDP missions in Libya and Ukraine and the lead it took on sanctions against Russia in 2014, claiming the UK played a 'leading role in them'.[93] The Review also dedicated a section specifically to Ukraine, outlining what it has done with the EU to address the conflict. The Review expressed the desire and intention of the Cameron government to continue to work with the EU in Ukraine through EUAM and to continue to work with the EU to maintain the pressure of sanctions on Russia to comply with the commitments it entered into at the Minsk Summit.[94] The Review also highlighted the threats of both state-sponsored and non-state actors undermining the security and stability of the Western Balkans and Eastern neighbourhood, such as the spread of extremism and organized crime across Europe.[95] The Review outlined the Cameron government's intentions to continue to work with NATO and the EU, as well as bilaterally, to build greater resilience in the region, including through EUAM Ukraine. Concluding, the government assessed its own participation in the CFSP and CSDP stating that is was 'strongly in the UK's interests to work through the EU in foreign policy'.[96]

In the lead up to the Brexit referendum in 2016, Cameron made a number of speeches addressing what he saw as the threat Brexit posed to the UK's security. In May 2016, Cameron gave one of his few speeches relating to the UK's security and defence partnership with the EU. Cameron stated that EU membership meant strength, security and safety in the world for the UK.[97] Cameron also stated that "if you love this country and want to keep it safe" the UK's membership of the EU was one of the tools by which to do that. Cameron also argued that the EU

---

[91] Conservative Manifesto (2015), *Supra* 89, at 72.

[92] National Security Strategy and Strategic Defence and Security Review (2015) https://www.gov.uk/government/publications/national-security-strategy-and-strategic-defence-and-security-review-2015 (accessed 28/06/21).

[93] *Ibid.*

[94] *Ibid.*

[95] *Ibid.*

[96] *Ibid.*

[97] Cameron (2016) https://www.gov.uk/government/speeches/pm-speech-on-the-uks-strength-and-security-in-the-eu-9-may-2016 (accessed 01/07/21).

"amplifies" the UK's power in the world, and enables it to address security challenges. Cameron also devoted a significant portion of his speech to addressing the role the EU played in the UK's security and defence policy. He argued that the UK and the EU shared common threats that these affected both regardless of whether the UK was in the EU or not. He also argued that these threats required a shared approach by the UK and the EU. He reiterated his belief that NATO and the US were the alliances that the UK would always look to for its defence, however, he underscored his belief that the EU was a "vital tool" in the UK's "armory" to deal with its security and defence threats. Cameron also spoke of his fear of the unravelling of the EU following the UK's departure and a return to what he described as "turning the clock back to competing nationalisms". He also states that the Baltic States (i.e. Ukraine) would view the UK's departure from the EU with "utter dismay". He described closer security cooperation and utilizing the EU's soft-power tools as "essential" to addressing security and defence threats such as terrorism, organized crime and illegal migration. Cameron also drew attention to a message given by former heads of MI5 and MI6—Johnathan Evans and John Sawers—who said the UK was safer inside the EU. Cameron also made reference to EUAM Ukraine and argued that the idea that EU membership emasculated the UK's security and defence powers was complete nonsense. Cameron also used the UK's role in securing EU sanctions against Russia as an example of how the UK's membership of the EU provided it with greater impact in security and defence. He argued that without being in the EU, these sanctions could not have been secured and that he was fearful that the UK would lose the tool of EU security and defence. Cameron concluded by stating that the UK required the closest possible security and defence cooperation with the EU and that the UK was stronger and safer inside the EU.

Cameron's ministers also gave a number of speeches in the lead up to the Brexit referendum in 2016. Home Secretary (Cameron's successor as PM) Theresa May, said that it was her belief that remaining a member of the EU meant that the UK would be more secure from crime and terrorism.[98] At a meeting of the House of Commons Defence Committee, Michael Fallon told MPs that he believed leaving the EU would be an "extraordinarily irresponsible things to do at a very dangerous moment".[99] Speaking in relation to the Ukrainian conflict, Fallon said that the UK's departure from the EU would be "applauded in Moscow". Fallon argued that European security would be put at risk by the UK's departure, particularly in Ukraine. Fallon also praised EU sanctions and boasted of the "lead role" the UK played in securing them. Fallon argued that without the UK being a member of the EU, EU sanctions would not have been as tough as they were against Russia. In an

[98] Theresa May, '*UK, EU and our place in the world*' Speech, (2016) https://www.gov.uk/government/speeches/home-secretarys-speech-on-the-uk-eu-and-our-place-in-the-world (accessed 01/07/21).

[99] Norton-Taylor (2016) https://www.theguardian.com/politics/2016/may/24/brexit-absolutely-applauded-russia-putin-defence-secretary-michael-fallon (accessed 01/07/21).

interview on Brexit, Foreign Secretary Phillip Hammond outlined his position on the CSDP. He began by reiterating his position on ideas such as a European Defence Union and the European super state, describing these ambitions as "ridiculous" and that he was "deeply skeptical" prior to becoming Defence Secretary (his role before becoming Foreign Secretary in Cameron's cabinet).[100] Hammond, however, stated that, once he became Defence Secretary, and then Foreign Secretary, he began to see the value of the CSDP and realized what he described as the UK's significant influence and leading role within it. Hammond also recalls how he and High Representative Catherine Ashton became "really very conscious of how valuable this structure (CSDP) was to the UK". He also stated his belief that, once the idea of a European super state was stripped back, at the working level, what the UK had was an "extremely valuable forum which leveraged British power" that did not diminish British power but instead was a "multiplier". Hammond reaffirmed his view that he believed the UK was better off inside the EU. Cameron and his ministers were, therefore, clearly of the view that the UK's role in Ukraine through the CSDP, and in the CSDP in general, was a valuable one.

Although post-Cameron, in the UK's Brexit Position Paper of September 2017, the value placed on the UK's role in EUAM Ukraine during the Cameron premiership was clear.[101] The paper boasted of how the UK has worked closely with the EU to tackle its shared threats and to enhance European security. The Paper stated that the UK had accomplished a significant amount together with its European partners, including developing a stronger collective European defence effort and responding to Russian aggression in Ukraine.[102] The Review also stated that, by working with the EU institutions and other EU Member States, the UK was able to contribute significantly to European action on a range of recent international priorities, such as promoting reform in Ukraine through the EUAM Ukraine Operation. The Review also highlights the role played by the UK in EU sanctions against Russia. The Review describes EU sanctions as a 'vital and effective foreign policy tool' and that the UK took a particularly active role in driving policy on European stage, in support of its shared values with the EU and to tackle the UK and the EU's common threats. The Review also boasted the role played by the UK through the EU in holding Russia to account for its actions, with EU sanctions one of the UK's 'main foreign policy tools'. In terms of its role in EUAM Ukraine, the Review also states that UK played a lead role in the operation and was key in helping promote coordination between the EU and the US.

A report was also published in 2018, by the European Union Committee, looking at the UK's role in the CSDP post-Brexit. A number of EU security and defence experts were called to give evidence to the Committee. In one piece of evidence

[100] '*Philip Hammond Interview*', UK in a Changing Europe, (13 and 20 November 2020) https://ukandeu.ac.uk/interview-pdf/?personid=42190 (accessed 06/07/21).

[101] UK Brexit Position Paper (2017) https://www.gov.uk/government/collections/article-50-and-negotiations-with-the-eu (accessed 06/07/21).

[102] *Ibid.*

given at the meeting, European security expert, Dr Andi Hoxhaj, spoke on the value of EUAM Ukraine to the UK and the EU. Dr. Hoxhaj told the Committee that the UK's participation in the CSDP mission in Ukraine was in line with the UK's "geopolitical and national security" interests, because "organised crime and corruption" in these two countries posed "a direct threat to the UK".[103] Thus EULEX Kosovo and EUAM Ukraine contributed to the UK's priorities as set out in the UK National Strategic Assessment of Serious and Organised Crime 2016 and the SDSR 2015. Dr. Hoxhaj described the security threats emanating from Ukraine as a "real threat" to the UK and that EUAM Ukraine was vital in tackling these issues. Speaking on their view regarding the UK's involvement in EUAM Ukraine post-Brexit, Dr. Hoxhaj said that the UK should consider to continue to participate in EUAM and work closely with the EU in support of Ukraine to preserve its independence and territorial integrity. Dr. Hoxhaj concluded that it was their belief that it was crucial for the UK to support with assistance in Ukraine and continue to be part of the EUAM long-term. The report of the Committee concluded that, overall, CSDP missions and operations had made a significant contribution to a number of the UK's foreign policy priorities—including tackling piracy, promoting the rule of law, and peacebuilding in post-conflict states—and have been an important channel of UK influence.

4 Challenges and Opportunities

4.1 The UK and EU Position Post-Brexit

4.1.1 Under Theresa May

Since the occurrence of Brexit, the partnership now faces one of the most tumultuous periods in its history. It is unclear to what extent security and defence issues contributed to the UK's decision to leave the EU. What is clear, however, is that Leave was much more vocal on the topic and their narrative, in turn, reached a wider audience. Remain, on the other hand, as conceded by Cameron himself, did not do enough to advocate for the benefits of EU security and defence and the UK's role in it. In any event, on the 23rd June 2016, the British public voted to leave the EU by 51.9% to 48.1%.[104] Following through on his promise to resign as PM if Remain lost

---

[103] European Union Committee, '*Brexit: Common Security and Defence Policy missions and operations*', 16th Report of Session 2017-19, HL Paper 132, (2018) http://data.parliament.uk/writtenevidence/committeeevidence.svc/evidencedocument/eu-external-affairs-subcommittee/brexit-common-security-and-defence-policy-csdp-missions/written/77377.html (accessed 08/07/21).

[104] '*EU Referendum Results*', BBC News, (London, 23 June 2016) https://www.bbc.co.uk/news/politics/eu_referendum/results.

the referendum, Cameron announced his intention to resign on 24th June 2016, triggering a leadership race within the Conservative Party to select the new PM. On 13th July 2016, following the drop out of candidate Andrea Leadsom from the leadership race, Theresa May became the new leader of the Conservatives and new PM of the UK.

May had supported Cameron and had campaigned in favour of Remain. During the referendum, as Home Secretary to Cameron, May had argued that being a member of the EU "maximised" the EU's security and defence and warned against the UK's loss of access to the European Arrest Warrant and passenger name records (PNR) would make the UK less safe.[105] Even upon becoming PM, May vowed in her maiden speech that she would be a 'one nation prime minister', arguably positioning herself from the outset to the left of the hard-Brexiteers.[106] That said, May entered the leadership contest fully aware that the primary aim of the next PM would be to begin the process of leading the UK out of the EU. Launching what would be a short-lived campaign to become leader of the Conservative Party, on 11th July 2016, May vowed that there would be no attempts to remain inside the EU, no attempts to rejoin it "by the back door", and no second referendum.[107] May also promised that as PM she would make sure the UK would leave the EU and, coining the infamous phrase, that "Brexit means Brexit".[108] Furthermore, although little mention was made of the EU in her maiden speech as PM, May signed off vowing that the UK would "rise to the challenge" of Brexit and that the UK would "forge a bold new positive role" for itself outside the EU.[109]

May's intentions to take the UK out for the EU were unequivocal and, despite the political and legal attempts to stop Brexit, the UK was on straight path to leaving the EU. The first occasion at which May gave any mention of her government's perspectives on a post-Brexit security and defence partnership was at the Conservative Party Conference in October 2016. May gave speech outlining her vision for a 'Global Britain'.[110] In the speech, May stated that her government's vision for a partnership between the UK and the EU was one in which the UK and the EU were close friends and allies, but were the UK made its own laws and played its full part in promoting peace and prosperity around the world, beyond the EU. May gave a more detailed account of her government's plan for Britain in her Lancaster House speech

[105] May, *Supra* 98.

[106] Theresa May, Maiden Speech as PM, (2016) https://www.gov.uk/government/speeches/statement-from-the-new-prime-minister-theresa-may (accessed 15/03/22).

[107] Asthana (2016) https://www.theguardian.com/politics/2016/aug/31/no-staying-in-eu-by-back-door-theresa-may-brexit (accessed 15/03/22).

[108] *Ibid.*

[109] May, *Supra* 106.

[110] Theresa May, Conservative Party Conference Speech, (2016) https://www.conservativehome.com/parliament/2016/10/britain-after-brexit-a-vision-of-a-global-britain-theresa-mays-conservative-conference-speech-full-text.html (accessed 20/03/22).

in January 2017.[111] In this speech, May stated that her government wanted the UK to remain a friend and neighbour to the EU but also one that went out into the world to build relationships with new allies. May argued that the UK's vote to leave was not an attempt to "turn the clock back" and make Europe less peaceful. She also acknowledged the serious threats that Europe as a collective faced and vowed that the UK's intelligence capabilities would continue to help keep Europe safe from terrorism. May also stated that the British servicemen and women would continue to serve in bases across Europe. Further into the speech, May highlighted Britain and France's roles as the only 2 nuclear powers in Europe, as well their permanent seats on the United Nations Security Council, stating that the UK's armed forces were a crucial part of Europe's collective defence and that after Brexit, the UK wanted to be a good friend and neighbour to the EU. In terms of how this partnership would work, however, not much was said. May made clear that her government did not want partial or associate membership of the EU and that nothing but a complete withdrawal would suffice. That said, May stated that her government wanted the UK to cooperate more with the EU in security and defence post-Brexit.

A more detailed outline of May and her government's strategy came with the publication of the government's Brexit White Paper in February 2017, in which they formally set out their strategy for the UK to leave the EU.[112] On the topic of security and defence, the white paper had more of a focus on intelligence sharing and counter terrorism post-Brexit and the government's plans for a post-Brexit partnership in these areas were much more comprehensive. In terms of external defence, beyond the borders of Europe, their plans were less detailed. That said, their position on it could still be discerned. The white paper stated that the UK wanted to use its role as a nuclear power and as a permanent member of the UNSC to continue to work with the EU on foreign policy, security and defence. The paper stated that the UK would continue to play a leading role alongside EU partners in buttressing and promoting European security and influence around the world, however, it also stated that the UK would aim to enhance its bilateral relationships with European partners and beyond. The paper acknowledged the role the UK played in the CSDP and some of its achievements (referencing EUAM Ukraine, Libya and sanctions against Russia), however, it stated that it was the objective of the UK to ensure that the EU's role on defence and security was complementary to, and respected the central role of, NATO. The paper stated that post-Brexit, the UK would remain committed to European security and would aim to add value to EU foreign and security policy. No further details were given, however, on how that partnership might look. More detail was given to how the government saw the UK's continued role in NATO.

[111]Theresa May, '*The government's negotiating objectives for exiting the EU*' Speech, (2017) https://www.gov.uk/government/speeches/the-governments-negotiating-objectives-for-exiting-the-eu-pm-speech (accessed 20/03/22).

[112]'*The United Kingdom's exit from, and new partnership with, the European Union*' Policy Paper, HM Gov, (2017) https://www.gov.uk/government/publications/the-united-kingdoms-exit-from-and-new-partnership-with-the-european-union-white-paper/the-united-kingdoms-exit-from-and-new-partnership-with-the-european-union%2D%2D2 (accessed 01/04/22).

Just a month later, in March 2017, May sent a letter to President of the European Council, Donald Tusk, triggering Article 50 TEU, marking the beginning of the UK's withdrawal from the EU.[113] In the letter, May clarified her government's intentions for a post-Brexit security and defence partnership. May stated that the UK and the EU should work towards securing a comprehensive agreement and that the UK wanted to agree to a 'deep' and 'special' partnership, taking in both economic and security cooperation. The letter also stated that the UK recognised that Europe's security was more fragile at that moment than at any time since the end of the Cold War and that weakening the cooperation between the UK and the EU would be a costly mistake for the security of Europe's citizens—essentially May was warning against the risks of a no deal Brexit. May also confirmed that the UK's objectives for a post-Brexit partnership remain those set out in her Lancaster House speech of 17th January and the subsequent White Paper published on 2nd February (complete withdrawal from the EU), however, as noted above, no detail was included in either of these about a security and defence partnership. Although the letter revealed an appetite within the May government for a post-Brexit security and defence partnership, it lacked information on the finer details pertaining to the framework of any such partnership.

May's next speech on EU security and defence came later in the year, during a visit to Florence in September 2017.[114] In the speech, May stated that the UK would be the strongest friend and partner to the EU post-Brexit and insisted that the UK would continue to work with the EU on security. In the speech, May elaborated further on the new security partnership she wanted to see between the UK and the EU. May began by stating she believed cooperation on security and defence should be maintained and that the two parties should be as open-minded as possible about how they continued to work together. May acknowledged that there was no pre-existing model for co-operation between the EU and external partners which replicates the full scale and depth of the collaboration that existed between the EU and the UK on security, however, she stated that she believed it was vital that the two parties worked together to design a 'new' and 'dynamic' arrangement that went beyond the existing arrangements that the EU had in this area and drew on the legal models the EU previously used to structure co-operation with external partners in other fields such as trade. This framework, May suggested, should be in the form of a treaty. The Treaty, May suggested, should complement the bi-lateral relationships that the UK already has with European nations to promote common security. In terms of the content of the treaty, may was less clear. She stated that the treaty should be flexible and create a framework within which the two parties could cooperate. May also stated that the UK would seek to ensure that it was unprecedented in its

---

[113] '*Prime Minister's letter to Donald Tusk triggering Article 50*', HM Gov, (2017) https://assets.publishing.service.gov.uk/government/uploads/system/uploads/attachment_data/file/604079/Prime_Ministers_letter_to_European_Council_President_Donald_Tusk.pdf (accessed 01/04/22).

[114] Theresa May, '*A new era of cooperation and partnership between the UK and the EU*' Speech, (2017) https://www.gov.uk/government/speeches/pms-florence-speech-a-new-era-of-cooperation-and-partnership-between-the-uk-and-the-eu (accessed 04/04/22).

depth, in terms of the degree of engagement that the UK would aim to deliver. In terms of what the treaty would look to tackle, May stated that the UK would seek to include spreading the rule of law, dealing with emerging threats, handling the migration crisis, helping countries out of poverty and helping EU countries that are the victims of armed aggression, terrorism and natural or manmade disasters. May concluded by stating that the UK would be committed to the EU's security unconditionally. Again, whilst the speech indicated a clear commitment by the May government to establish a post-Brexit security and defence partnership, little was said about the substance of any arrangement.

With every speech, May revealed more about her government's intentions for a post-Brexit security and defence partnership with the EU. At the Munich Security Conference in 2018, May gave a clearer idea of what she wanted to have included in any partnership.[115] In the speech, May, once again, urged the EU to agree to a new security treaty with the UK. May stated again, that the UK had an "unconditional" commitment to European security that would not change after the country's departure from the EU. May honed in on the threats of cyberwarfare, terrorism and organized crime which she stated were European problems that demanded continued close cooperation on arrest warrants and intelligence sharing. May declared that the UK wanted the security pact to be signed fast, even before an agreement on the overall Brexit deal. Arguably giving an indication of her desire to broker a security and defence partnership with the EU, May also offered a big concession, stating that when cooperating with European agencies, the UK would be willing to respect the jurisdiction of the ECJ—something which hard-Eurosceptics in her Party had argued that the UK should take back control of its laws and judicial system and no longer be beholden to the rulings of the European court. "Another red line has gone pink," said Mark Leonard of the European Council on Foreign Relations.[116] As in earlier speeches, May again warned that if a security deal was not reached soon, or at all, both Europe and Britain would be less safe than they are today.

The speech, however, was a tale of two halves. It was clear that May's priority for any post-Brexit deal would be on internal security—combating counter-terrorism, human trafficking and the migration crisis, through cooperation with European agencies via things like the EAW and PNR. On external security post-Brexit, however, such as inter-state conflict, peacekeeping and humanitarian aid beyond the border of Europe, May appeared to have a different plan for the UK. In response to these external security challenges, May stated that she believed it was the defining responsibility of the UK to come together and reinvigorate the transatlantic partnership and the UK's other global alliances. May stated that as a permanent member of the UNSC and as a lead contributor of NATO, the UK had never defined its global outlook through the collective EU foreign policy, i.e. CSDP. May declared that the

[115]Theresa May, Munich Security Conference Speech (2018) https://www.gov.uk/government/speeches/pm-speech-at-munich-security-conference-17-february-2018 (accessed 04/04/22).

[116]Bennhold and Erlanger (2018) https://www.nytimes.com/2018/02/17/world/europe/uk-theresa-may-munich.html (accessed 05/04/22).

UK would be pursuing an independent foreign policy and would seek to engage with the EU in this respect via "ad hoc groupings". May did say that the UK would be willing to continue to engage with and contribute to CSDP missions where it was in the UK's interests. May stated that she believed there should, at a diplomatic level, be means for the UK and the EU to consult each other regularly. May stated that her government was keen to continue to work closely with the EU on sanctions, to enforce them and to develop them in the future. May also stated that the UK would be open to continuing to contribute to the EU development funds. All of this, however, May made clear would only be on an ad hoc basis and only when the UK felt it strengthened its interests and furthered its partnership with NATO. May concluded by stating her government was keen for the UK to continue working with the EU on R&D and developing Europe's defence capabilities—in defence, cyber and space—to meet future threats.

Following on from May's speech, the Government released a document entitled '*Foreign policy, defence and development—a future partnership paper*'.[117] This paper was a formal declaration by the Government of the speech made by the PM at the Munich Security Conference on the government's vision for a future security and defence partnership with the EU. The paper reiterated what May said, about the UK being committed to European security and defence and that the UK wanted to secure a future relationship that was deeper than any current third country partnership. It also reiterated May's vision for a partnership in which the UK could still contribute and engage in the CSDP but could do so on an ad hoc basis. Following on from this, a report was published by the European Union Committee, which considered the importance of the CSDP and CSDP missions to the UK's foreign policy priorities, and looked at how the UK could participate in and influence missions and operations post-Brexit. The Report made a number of conclusions and recommendations in respect of the UK's future participation in the CSDP. The Report found that, as the UK's foreign policy priorities were unlikely to change significantly upon leaving the EU, the UK would continue to derive value from participation in current CSDP missions and operations. The Report also concluded that the UK would require a higher level of political control to participate in military operations, more than any other third party has enjoyed before, in order to carry out the tasks required of it in these missions. The existing model for third country involvement in CSDP missions and operations would not give the UK the input and influence that it currently enjoys as a Member State. In turn, the Report concluded that it is unlikely that the remaining EU27 would be willing to allow the UK—as a non-Member State—a decision-making role on CSDP missions and operations, ruling out the May Government's aspirations for a deep partnership, including 'mandate development' and 'operational planning'. The Report also highlighted the fact that negotiations on the UK's

[117]'*Foreign policy, defence and development - a future partnership paper*', HM Gov, (12 September 2017) https://assets.publishing.service.gov.uk/government/uploads/system/uploads/attachment_data/file/643924/Foreign_policy__defence_and_development_paper.pdf (accessed 05/04/22).

withdrawal from the EU had not yet focused on foreign policy and defence, and had focused more on internal security. It also raised concerns over the fact that it was not yet clear how negotiations on foreign policy and defence co-operation were going to be structured, by whom they will be conducted, or how far they will be separated from the negotiations on future trade and other issues. The Report also raised concerns about the Government's lack of detailed proposals and called upon it to explain how its high-level aspirations for a post-Brexit security and defence partnership with the EU could be put into practice. The Report also warned the Government about relying too much on the UK's significant capabilities as leverage in the negotiations, given the fact that most CSDP missions and operations are at the lower end of the crisis management spectrum, with a focus on training and capacity building. The Report concluded, by recommending that, in the event of no post-Brexit security and defence partnership being agreed, as a last resort, the UK should seek to negotiate observer status in the EU's planning and decision-making bodies, such as the Political and Security Committee, for example—the merits this status will be evaluated in more detail below.

The response to the May government's aspirations for a security and defence partnership post Brexit were met with scepticism within the academic literature. Whitman argued that the UK government's aspiration of a deeper, unprecedented, treaty-based relationship on security, was fanciful and would be something very complicated to negotiate and would unlikely be something the EU would agree to.[118] Whitman argues that the complex distribution of EU security policy—operating on the basis of different degrees of integration between the member states, pursued across different institutions (with differing roles for the European Commission, other EU agencies and member states) and based upon different EU treaty articles—throws up complexities for negotiating a future trade relationship. Furthermore, Whitman argues that as the UK's external relations such as the environment, food security, energy and development policy—all of which contain security dimensions—had all been intertwined with EU policies, the scope of an EU-UK security treaty would be very broad. Whitman also argues that there would what he calls a 'docking problem' for the UK in terms of its involvement in the CSDP.[119] Whitman states that, whilst EU security and defence remains intergovernmental and Member States retain control over it, the evolution of Brussels-based decision-making and implementation structures of the CSDP and the fact that only member states can be members of the EU's key foreign, security and defence decision-making bodies (Foreign Affairs Council and the Political and Security Committee) makes the task of finding the UK a seat around the 'CSDP table' a very difficult one. May's proposals present a partnership within which the UK would engage with the CSDP as and when it felt it served its interests and have full decision making powers—essentially the UK would reap all of the benefits of CSDP yet pay nothing

[118]Whitman (2019).

[119]Whitman (2018), p. 6.

into it. As Whitman argues, it is unlikely the Member States would ever go for anything mirroring this.

Cardwell also makes a number of observations about the ambitions of the May government on EU security and defence.[120] Like Whitman, Cardwell does not think the EU will agree to a deal like the one presented by May. He argues that the UK should not assume that the EU will acquiesce to the UK's demands on security and defence simply because of the UK's military might. As noted above, the CSDP is more about soft-power capabilities and relies less on hard military tactics. That said, and as Cardwell concedes, the removal of the UK in the CSDP should not be underestimated. The UK has contributed significant resources and highly skilled personnel to these mission and, in turn, its absence will undoubtedly affect the success of future CSDP missions. This was also a view shared by other commentators such as Smith and Drent, who argue that the May government's proposals "created a bit more of a positive atmosphere" but that they "lacked specificity on what it means".[121] The FAC scrutinised the May government's position in a 2018 report on the future of UK diplomacy in Europe.[122] The response of government representatives seemed to underline the lack of detail in any of the government's proposals. When asked if the ambitions outlined in the UK position paper included observer status in the FAC or the PSC, the Foreign Secretary stated that "there is no Government position—we have not decided what we want to seek" and that the precise format for co-operation was subject to negotiation. FCO Permanent Under Secretary (PUS), Sir Simon McDonald, also gave a similarly unclear answer about the Government's position, stating that the government was "not making a pitch" for observer status in the FAC and the PSC and that the mechanisms would "emerge in the negotiations over the next 12 months". Furthermore, when asked to clarify the government's vision for a UK/EU security and defence partnership post-Brexit, the Minister for Europe stated that he could not "state categorically which rooms we are going to be in" and that there was a "spectrum of possibility". Ultimately, no deal was reached by the May government on security and defence, however, the overly ambitious proposals and the severe lack of detail in any proposals made by the May government as to a future security and defence partnership make it unsurprising that no deal was reached during this premiership.

[120]Cardwell (2017), p. 21.

[121]Smith (2017) http://ukandeu.ac.uk/brexit-and-british-foreign-policy-between-a-rock-and-a-hard-place/ (accessed 10/04/22) https://publications.parliament.uk/pa/cm201719/cmselect/cmfaff/514/51405.htm.

[122]'*The future of UK diplomacy in Europe*' Report, Foreign Affairs Committee (2018) https://publications.parliament.uk/pa/cm201719/cmselect/cmfaff/514/51405.htm (accessed 10/04/22).

4.2 Under Boris Johnson

During the final year of her premiership, May had struggled to convince her party and MPs across the Commons to support her EU Withdrawal Agreement Bill. Since December 2018, May's resignation following her failure to gain support for her Withdrawal Agreement had become a talking point within the Conservative Party and across the British media. After winning a vote of no confidence against her in December 2018, May had promised the Conservative Party that, if it supported her Brexit deal, she would resign. May's strategy, however, backfired, and in March 2019, her deal was rejected for, what was then, a third time, leading to a delay in the UK's withdrawal from the EU. In May 2019, May made one final attempt to obtain support from Parliament for her Brexit deal, this time promising a vote on whether to hold a second referendum on EU membership, if her EU Withdrawal Agreement Bill was passed. The offer was an attempt to gain support from Labour, however, it enraged hard-Eurosceptics within her party.[123] This led to one of her senior ministers, Andrea Leadsom, to quit her cabinet, adding to the pressure for her to go. In turn, on 24th May, May announced her resignation, triggering another Conservative leadership race within her party.

Favourite to replace her was her former Foreign Secretary, Boris Johnson, who had resigned from May's cabinet in July 2018 after opposing her Brexit plans drawn up at the PM's country retreat, Chequers.[124] As noted above, Johnson had been one of the leading advocates for Vote Leave. Whether a genuine Eurosceptic or not—Cameron had said of Johnson that he does not really believe in Brexit and had accused him of supporting Leave for personal gain[125]—Johnson represented the hard-Eurosceptic wing of the Conservative Party.[126] Upon May's resignation as PM, Johnson announced his leadership bid and joined the race to become the next PM. Whilst May had made clear her fear and opposition to a no-deal Brexit,[127] Johnson, in his launch speech for his leadership campaign, stated that he was open to the possibility of a no-deal.[128] During this speech, Johnson stated that he believed the UK must leave the EU on 31st October 2019—the deadline for reaching a

[123] '*Theresa May resigns over Brexit: What happened?*', BBC News, (London, 24 May 2019) https://www.bbc.co.uk/news/uk-politics-48379730 (accessed 11/04/22).

[124] Stewart (2018) https://www.theguardian.com/politics/2018/jul/09/boris-johnson-resigns-as-foreign-secretary-brexit (accessed 11/04/22).

[125] Cameron (2019), p. 652.

[126] Ironically, Johnson had supported the idea of an EU army when he was Foreign Secretary under Theresa May; See '*Boris Johnson says UK should support 'EU Army' in wake of Brexit*', Sky News, (London, 13 October 2016) https://news.sky.com/story/boris-johnson-says-uk-should-support-eu-army-in-wake-of-brexit-10615685 (accessed 11/04/22).

[127] Santolo (2019) https://www.express.co.uk/news/uk/1087286/Brexit-news-update-Theresa-May-motion-no-deal-brexit-ERG-andrew-bridgen (accessed 12/04/22).

[128] Johnson (2019) https://www.spectator.co.uk/article/full-text-boris-johnson-launches-his-tory-leadership-campaign (accessed 12/04/22).

withdrawal agreement—and that, whilst he was not aiming for a no-deal outcome, he would "prepare vigorously and seriously for no deal".

By July 2019, the leadership race had been narrowed down to Johnson and, former Health Secretary under May, Jeremy Hunt. Johnson won the election comfortably with 92,153 votes to his Hunt's 46,656.[129] In his first speech as PM, outside No.10 Downing Street on 24th July 2019, Johnson made only four references to Brexit and gave no detail about any future partnership with the EU in any area. Johnson vowed to take the UK out of the EU by 31st October 2019 and vowed that his government would do a new and better deal with the EU that would allow the UK to develop a "new and exciting partnership with the rest of Europe".[130] The following day, Johnson made his first speech to the Commons, committing to the 31st October 2019 date for Brexit and—whilst he stated he hoped for a renegotiation of the Withdrawal Agreement—he refused to rule out the possibility of a 'no-deal' Brexit.[131] Although Johnson had revealed his willingness to accept a no-deal, by 17th October 2019, Johnson's government had struck a deal with the EU. The new Withdrawal Agreement was brought before Parliament on 22nd October 2019 and, although the timetable for the beginning of the transition period is defeated, the Withdrawal Agreement Bill passes its second reading. Following the defeat of the timetable, the UK agrees a Brexit extension with the EU until 31st January 2020.

The Withdrawal Agreement set the terms of the UK's withdrawal from the EU and outlined the future of the UK and the EU's economic and trade relationship. The Agreement makes only two references to the CSDP (and CFSP), establishing that the UK will be bound by Chapter 2 Title V TEU (the Treaty establishing CSDP and Member States obligations) and will continue to contribute to the finance of the EDA and the costs of CSDP operations, amongst other things, until a new agreement is reached or 31st December 2020 (whichever came first).[132] The Withdrawal Agreement makes no mention of any terms for a future security and defence partnership or outline how either side want that partnership to look in the future. In turn, the failure to include any provisions pertaining to EU security and defence saw the UK leave the EU on 31st January 2020 without any deal secured with the EU on the future of UK and EU security and defence cooperation.

Following the passing of the Withdrawal Agreement in Parliament, a few days later on 30th October 2019, the Johnson government introduced the Early Parliamentary General Election Bill, which set the date for a General Election to take place on 12th December 2019. Although no mention was made of the CSDP in the

[129] '*Boris Johnson wins race to be Tory leader and PM*', BBC News, (London, 23 July 2019) https://www.bbc.co.uk/news/uk-politics-49084605 (accessed 12/04/22).

[130] Boris Johnson, '*First Speech as Prime Minister*' Speech, (2019) https://www.gov.uk/government/speeches/boris-johnsons-first-speech-as-prime-minister-24-july-2019.

[131] Boris Johnson, 'First Speech to Parliament as Prime Minister', (2019) https://www.reuters.com/article/us-britain-eu-leader-speech-text-idUSKCN1UK1JK (accessed 14/04/22).

[132] Agreement on the withdrawal of the United Kingdom of Great Britain and Northern Ireland from the European Union and the European Atomic Energy Community (Withdrawal Agreement) Article 127 and Article 156.

Withdrawal Agreement, the Conservative's manifesto for the 2019 General Election have some insight into where the Johnson government saw the UK's security and defence priorities. Under a section entitled 'We Will Strengthen Britain In The World', the manifesto stated that the Johnson government would bolster the alliances and institutions that it believed helped the UK project its influence and keep it safe. The alliances and institutions listed were the UN and the UN Security Council, NATO, the Commonwealth, Five Eyes, the G20, the G7, and the World Trade Organisation. The manifesto gave no mention of the EU or CSDP, arguably highlighting Johnson's intentions to steer the UK away from EU security and defence post-Brexit. Johnson and the Conservatives would go onto win the election with a Conservative majority, giving Johnson a mandate for 5 years until 2024.

To date, whilst the Johnson government has yet to agree a partnership with the EU in security and defence, their approach to any such agreement and how they may want that partnership to look, can be gleaned from a number of speeches and policy documents released by Johnson and his government. As a proponent of Vote Leave and an advocate for the hard-Eurosceptics of the Conservative Party during the Cameron and May premierships, it is unsurprising that Johnson does not hold the same esteem for EU security and defence as his predecessors, Cameron and May. Whilst Johnson had been uncomfortable (although willing) to leave the EU without a withdrawal agreement, it appears no agreement on security and defence was something he and his government had been prepared to accept for some time before the UK's departure. Back in early October 2019, the Spectator published a leaked 700-word memo from a Downing Street staffer on the state of the Brexit negotiations, which contained a warning that the UK might halt security cooperation with the EU if Brexit was not achieved by Johnson's deadline of 31st October2019.[133] The leaked memo and the Johnson government's position was met with criticism from former MI6 chief, Sir John Sawers, who has said Brexit negotiations had got to "an extraordinarily damaging state" and that any attempt to stop working with EU countries" in security and defence would be an act contrary to the UK's own self-interest. Regardless of the criticism it has received, it would seem, given the absence of any deal, the Johnson government is content to continue without a security and defence agreement with the EU.

This said, the Johnson government has given some indication of the type of partnership it would like with the EU in security and defence. In February 2020, the Johnson government released a policy paper setting out the UK's negotiating objectives, entitled 'Our approach to the Future Relationship with the EU'.[134] The Johnson government indicated that it is no longer seeking an institutionalised future UK-EU relationship in foreign affairs and defence and instead, it appears to be

[133] Sabbagh (2019) https://www.theguardian.com/politics/2019/oct/09/ex-mi6-chief-criticises-threat-to-withdraw-security-cooperation-with-eu (accessed 14/04/22).

[134] *'Our approach to the Future Relationship with the EU'* Policy Paper, HM Gov, (2020) https://www.gov.uk/government/publications/our-approach-to-the-future-relationship-with-the-eu (accessed 15/04/22).

favouring a flexible, ad-hoc approach. The negotiating objectives state that foreign policy will be determined "within a framework of broader friendly dialogue and cooperation between the UK and the EU". The document, however, made no direct reference to defence or participation in EU programmes such as the EDF and PESCO. Further detail about the Johnson government's approach to security and defence post-Brexit came with the publication of its 'Integrated Review of Defence and Security' in July 2021.[135] In the Review, the government outlined the UK's view for what it called a 'Gobal Britain' post-Brexit. The Review stated that the UK's European neighbours and allies remain vital partners and vowed that the UK would be the greatest single European contributor to the security of the Euro-Atlantic area to 2030. The government promised to 'work with its partners to defend common values, counter shared threats and build resilience in the European neighbourhood'. The government also states that it recognises the 'important role' played by the EU in the peace and prosperity of Europe and will seek to find 'new ways' of working with it on shared challenges—although, again, no detail is given as to what this new way of working might look like. The Review makes clear, however, that the UK will seek to pursue different political approaches to the EU in many areas where it suits its interests and reiterates the Johnson government's belief in NATO as the foundation of collective security in the Euro-Atlantic area. The Review does state, however, that when it came to the issue of Russia, the UK would continue to support closer practical cooperation between NATO and the EU. On the subject of EU security and defence, the Review concludes that the UK will cooperate with the EU on matters of security and defence as independent partners, where this is in our interest—mirroring the proposals made by May, in which the UK would seek to cooperate and engage with EU security and defence on an ad hoc basis.

The Johnson government's proposals appeared to support the proposals made by May—cooperating and engaging with the EU in security and defence on an ad hoc basis. Unlike May, however, Johnson appeared ready to accept no agreement with the EU on security and defence. In fact, much of what Johnson has done during his tenure as Prime Minister has suggested that he is looking to meet the UK's security and defence needs post-Brexit by building new alliances elsewhere—arguably putting his government's 2021 Integrated Security Review into practice. The outbreak of the Covid-19 pandemic halted any progress for the UK to make new security and defence pacts, however, as the world began to recover in mid-2021, and as restrictions began to be lifted, the Johnson government set about forming new security and defence partnerships around Europe and the rest of the world. Its first pact came with its new security and defence agreement with France. In the Integrated Security Review, the government stated that it would seek to pursue bilateral partnerships with European nations on security and defence, and one of these nations

[135] '*Global Britain in a Competitive Age: the Integrated Review of Security, Defence, Development and Foreign Policy*' Policy Paper, HM Gov, (2021) https://www.gov.uk/government/publications/global-britain-in-a-competitive-age-the-integrated-review-of-security-defence-development-and-foreign-policy/global-britain-in-a-competitive-age-the-integrated-review-of-security-defence-devel opment-and-foreign-policy (accessed 15/04/22).

mentioned specifically was France (others included Germany and Italy).[136] The Review mentions France 11 times, with the European Union gets only a few passing references, which arguably indicates the direction in which the Johnson government intends to steer the UK. In pursuit of these objectives, in July 2021, the UK and France signed a limited post-Brexit security treaty, entitled the 'UK-France Maritime Security Treaty', specifically aimed at protecting passengers on Channel ferries from terror attacks.[137] In a statement, the UK FCO said the agreement included sharing security information on potential threats, mounting swifter and stronger initial responses to serious security incidents, and cooperating more effectively in the aftermath of a terror attack or incident. The FCO also said that the treaty would enable the two countries' security services to work more closely together. The treaty also saw the UK pledge €62.7 million to reinforce police patrols on French beaches. At the same time as the agreement, a meeting with the French minister for Europe and Foreign Affairs, Jean-Yves Le Drian, UK Foreign Secretary, Dominic Raab, and Defence Secretary, Ben Wallace, the UK and France discussed potential future collaborations to address the migration crisis across the channel and the continued civil war in Libya. This piecemeal approach—forming individual agreements with other nations on an ad hoc basis in areas that suit the UK's interests—seems to be the direction in which Johnson is steering the UK. Although the treaty is a sign of progress for British and French relations, French officials are reported to have stated that the UK's approach of bypassing the EU and forming these bilateral partnerships is severely limiting, given the EU is the biggest standard-setter in the world on issues like trade and climate.[138] The relationship between the French President, Emmanuel Macron, and Johnson is also reported to be a sour one, with a former UK ambassador to France describing the relationship between the two nations as being as bad as they can remember.[139]

The Johnson government followed up its treaty with France with a new defence pact, this time with the creation of a trilateral defence partnership with the US and Australia, entitled AUKUS. The pact was announced on 15th September 2021 and focuses specifically on enhancing the military capabilities of all three parties in cyber, artificial intelligence and quantum technologies. Arguably the main feature of AUKUS is that it will enable Australia to build nuclear-powered submarines for the first time, a technology provided to it by the US. It has been viewed by commentators in the area as an effort to counterbalance the so-called threat of China.[140] In terms of UK and EU relations, it is not so much what the pact says that has soured the

[136] *Ibid.*

[137] Honeycombe-Foster (2021) https://www.politico.eu/article/uk-and-france-sign-post-brexit-channel-security-pact/ (accessed 16/04/22).

[138] Momtaz (2021) https://www.politico.eu/article/france-uk-relationship-entente-cordiale-emmanuel-macron-boris-johnson/ (accessed 16/04/22).

[139] *Ibid.*

[140] '*Aukus: UK, US and Australia launch pact to counter China*', BBC News, (London, 16 September 2021) https://www.bbc.co.uk/news/world-58564837 (accessed 16/04/22).

partnership between the two parties, but more whom it excludes. The exclusion of France from the pact, and the provision of nuclear submarine technology to Australia, caused the Australians to cancel their £48 billion submarine-building contract with France. The Pact was met with outrage from France, with the French recalling its ambassadors to the US and French Foreign Minister, Jean-Yves Le Drian calling it a "stab in the back".[141] The pact was also met with criticism from commentators in the field, with some arguing that AUKUS risked the UK becoming isolated from the EU and European states even more after Brexit.[142] Others have argued that the humiliation caused to France and the rest of the EU may also further intensify ambitions within the EU to develop a credible, independent European military force. Witney makes similar points about how the agreement will embitter relations between the UK and the EU and also points how, with the UK not directly benefiting from AUKUS, the UK will become ever more subordinate to the US in security and defence post-Brexit.[143]

Johnson's next port of call to build a new security and defence alliance was to India in April 2022. This was again in pursuit of pledges made in its Integrated Security Review to become 'the European country with the broadest, most integrated presence in the Indo-Pacific in support of trade, shared security and values'. During his first visit to India since becoming Prime Minister, Johnson and Indian Prime Minister, Narendra Modi, announced the new partnership agreeing to advance their new defence partnership to a 'new level', with a particular focus on maritime and industrial collaboration.[144] The partnership included new agreements on maritime information sharing, an invitation to the UK to join India's Information Fusion Centre (IMAC) in Gurgaon and an exercise programme which includes joint tri-lateral military exercises. The partnership also included new agreements on security and defence R&D, including commitments to build the Indian military's air, maritime propulsion and space and cyber capabilities. An agreement was also made to move the manufacturing of the MT30 Gas Turbine engine to India. Again, the new pact was an unequivocal statement by Johnson and his government as to where it intends to have the UK's security and defence needs met.

The Johnson government's latest security and defence alliance was created with Sweden and Finland in May 2022. The new defence pacts came in the wake of Russia's invasion of Ukraine in February 2022, which sparked a discussion within Finland and Sweden over NATO membership. The pact included an agreement between the UK, Finland and Sweden to come to each other's aid, should any of the three nations come under attack. Announcing the new defence pact, Johnson stated

[141] *Ibid.*

[142] '*View on Anglo-French relations*', The Observer, (London, 19 September 2021) https://www.theguardian.com/commentisfree/2021/sep/19/observer-view-on-anglo-french-relations-aukus-pact (accessed 19 September 2021).

[143] Witney (2021) https://ecfr.eu/article/aukus-after-the-sugar-rush/ (accessed 30/10/21).

[144] '*UK and India Prime Ministers announce Enhanced Defence Cooperation*', British High Commission New Delhi, HM Gov, (2021) https://www.gov.uk/government/news/uk-and-india-prime-ministers-announce-enhanced-defence-cooperation.

that the pact would become the "foundation of an intensification" of the three-party's security and defence relationship in other ways as well. In a statement released by the UK government, the UK intends to see a step-change in defence and security cooperation between the UK and Finland and Sweden, intensifying intelligence sharing, accelerating joint military training, exercising and deployments, and bolstering security across all three countries and northern Europe.[145] The UK government also announced that it hoped the new agreement will also see the UK bolster its collaboration on traditional threats facing all three nations, while working also with Sweden and Finland to tackle new geopolitical challenges, such as hybrid and cyber threats.[146] Although the agreement was almost entirely about countering the Russian threat northern and eastern European, as well as putting Finland and Sweden's NATO membership back on the table, the partnership's secondary ambitions for intensified cooperation and increased security and defence R&D, can also be viewed as another example of the UK bypassing the EU for bilateral partnerships with individual member states. The UK's pact with Finland and Sweden is yet another partnership in what is becoming a long list of new bilateral security and defence partnerships for the UK and is a strategy that Johnson shows no signs of detracting from any time soon.

The UK's new identity in international relations, with greater autonomy for international diplomacy, not just in security and defence but also in its foreign economic policy, it is difficult to determine how a future partnership with the EU might look like, if one will ever be agreed at all. As Whitman notes, the implication of the UK continuing with its current strategy is that there will be a divergence from the EU's norms, practices and ambitions in the security and defence field.[147] The longer this divergence occurs in, will increase—quite possibly to the point where a future security and defence pact with the EU may become impossible. As Whitman describes, the UK looks less likely to agree a security and defence pact with the EU and more likely to continue 'muddling through'. As Whitman notes, the current Integrated Security Review will define the UK's approach for the next decade. It would therefore be unsurprising to see any post-Brexit security and defence partnership with the EU in the next 10 years, or at least during Johnson's premiership. Whitman also highlights the politics of the Conservative Party, which he argues has become even more embittered with EU security and defence cooperation since Brexit and the election of Johnson as leader. A broadening and deepening of cooperation beyond trade policy will face significant opposition as the topic of EU security and defence cooperation is a taboo for many Conservative Party Members of Parliament and also for elements in the grass roots of the party, which has a

---

145 UK-Sweden Political Declaration of Solidarity (2022) https://www.gov.uk/government/publications/united-kingdom-sweden-statement-11-may-2022; UK-Finland Statement (2022) https://www.gov.uk/government/publications/united-kingdom-finland-statement-11-may-2022.

146 '*Prime Minister signs new assurances to bolster European security: 11 May 2022*', HM Gov, (11 May 2022) https://www.gov.uk/government/news/prime-minister-signs-new-assurances-to-bolster-european-security-11-may-2022 (accessed 17/04/22).

147 Whitman, *Supra* 118.

growing hard-Eurosceptic base.[148] At present, the prospects of a comprehensive UK/EU security and defence partnership remain slim.

5 Post-Brexit Developments

There have been a number of developments since Brexit, both on the UK's part and the EU's. These developments have the potential to create opportunities for a future security and defence partnership between the UK and the EU but they also have the potential to place in the way obstacles. Some developments are still evolving as of the date of publication of this book, whilst others have already occurred and come to nothing. All of the developments discussed, however, have had some impact on the UK and the EU's relationship and on the development of a post-Brexit security and defence partnership.

5.1 Developments Within the EU Post-Brexit

The EU has consistently made it clear that it wanted the UK to remain a part of the EU and that it will seek to have as close a partnership with it as possible post-Brexit. That said, however, the EU maintained throughout the negotiation process, and still to this day, that it any future partnership must also be in the best interests of the EU and the remaining 27.

5.2 EU's Global Strategy on Foreign and Security Policy (2016)

This approach by the EU is also taken to a future security and defence partnership with the UK. In 2016—coincidentally the same year as Brexit—the EU published its '*Global Strategy for the European Union's Foreign and Security Policy*' (EUGS), giving insight into the security and defence strategy it intends to pursue over the next couple of decades.[149] The EU produced its first security strategy back in 2003, with the adoption of the European Security Strategy (ESS) in 2003. The ESS worked as a narrative for the EU security and defence and provided it with a framework and a reference point when deciding on EU security and defence policy. As noted by

---

[148] Heppell (2012), p. 340.

[149] '*Global Strategy for the European Union's Foreign and Security Policy (EUGS)*' (2016) https://www.eeas.europa.eu/eeas/global-strategy-european-unions-foreign-and-security-policy_en (accessed 17/04/22).

Biscop, the ESS was important in that it ensured commonality amongst the 27 Member States, all of which had their own strategic security and defence cultures.[150] Since its adoption, there was a number of attempts to revise and update the ESS, however, it was not until 2014, with the appointment of Federica Mogherini as High Representative, that the HR finally received a mandate from the European Council to produce an entirely new strategy. As a result, the EUGS was presented to the European Council on 28th June 2016—just days after the Brexit referendum.

Like the ESS, the EUGS 2016 will guide the EU's foreign, security and defence policy for the foreseeable future and will also influence how it will negotiate and seek to frame any future security and defence partnership with the UK, and any other third-party for that matter. Under a section entitled 'Principles Guiding our External Action' in the EUGS, the EU sets out how its position on third-party partnerships, stating that the EU will seek to be a responsible global stakeholder, but will seek to share that responsibility by 'investing in its partnerships'.[151] The EU also states that 'co-responsibility' will be its guiding principle in advancing, what it describes as, the 'rules-based global order'. The EU states that it will reach out to states, regional bodies and international organisations and work with 'core partners', like-minded countries and regional groupings. The EUGS also states that the EU will partner selectively with players whose cooperation, it believes, is necessary to deliver global public goods and address common challenges.

The EUGS has appeared to give a new impetus to EU security and defence. The new High Representative, Josep Borell, echoed the EUGS statements on partnerships, when he identified building security and defence partnerships as one of his key priorities for his mandate upon being made HR.[152] Since the publishing of the EUGS, the EU has concluded Framework Partnership Agreements (FPAs)[153] with selected partner countries to facilitate their contributions to CSDP missions and operations. To date, the EU has signed 20 such agreements with third-party states, and 12 of these partners currently participate in 10 of the 17 established CSDP missions and operations. Beyond cooperation in the framework of CSDP missions and operations, the EU continues to organise bilateral dialogues on a regular basis with more than 20 countries, covering a broad range of security- and defence-related topics. In addition to all of this, the EU invested more than €900 million in assistance programmes with priority partner countries.[154] The aims of the EUGS to create more security and defence partnerships with third-party member states has also been supported by the FAC. In its conclusions of 18 May 2017, the Council stressed

[150] Biscop (2004), p. 16.

[151] EUGS, *Supra* 149, at 16.

[152] Borrell (2022) https://www.eeas.europa.eu/eeas/stronger-european-union-within-better-greener-and-safer-world-key-principles-will-be-guiding-0_en (accessed 20/05/22).

[153] The European Commission states that a Framework agreement is concluded as part of a long-term cooperation between the Commission and the partner with the aim to contribute to the objectives of the Union policy in the field of accreditation as referred to in the Preamble of the FPA.

[154] Weston and Maduraud (2021), p. 175 https://www.egmontinstitute.be/content/uploads/2021/06/CSDP-HANDBOO-4th-edition.pdf (accessed 20/04/22).

the importance of enhancing cooperation with partners, both with third countries and other international organisations.[155] Whilst the Council was keen to express its desire to build these partnerships, it underlined its belief that partnerships between the EU and third-party countries should be of mutual benefit and should contribute to strengthening the EU's security and defence efforts, while fully respecting the EU's institutional framework and its decision-making autonomy.

5.3 EU Strategic Compass (2022)

The EUGS also gave rise to the EU's Strategic Compass ('the Compass'), which was approved by the Council in March 2022.[156] As stated by the Council, the Compass gives the EU an ambitious plan of action for strengthening the EU's security and defence policy by 2030. Announcing the launch of the Compass, the Council stated that the Compass represented what it described as a 'quantum leap forward' in EU security and defence capabilities. The Council stated that an objective of the Strategic Compass was to make the EU a stronger and more capable security provider and to enhance the EU's strategic autonomy, as well as its ability to work with partners to safeguard EU values and security and defence interests. The Council states that one of the Compasses key objectives, and one of the four pillars it will be structured around is 'partnership' (the other four being action, investment, and security). In pursuit of that objective, the Compass states that the EU will seek to develop more tailored bilateral partnerships with like-minded countries and strategic partners, listing the UK amongst those potential partners.

5.4 EU's Negotiating Mandate (2020)

As well as revealing its desire to form a bilateral partnership with the UK post-Brexit, via the EUGS and the Compass, the EU gave some detail as to what type of partnership it envisaged with the UK. In February 2020, the Council adopted what it calls its Negotiating Mandate ('the Mandate'—also known as the 'Directives for the Negotiation of a New Partnership with the UK').[157] In the Mandate, the EU states that the envisaged partnership should enable structured consultations between the Union and the United Kingdom. The EU also stated that it believed its partnership

[155] Foreign Affairs Council, European Council, (18 May 2017) https://www.consilium.europa.eu/en/meetings/fac/2017/05/18/ (accessed 20/04/22).

[156] EU Strategic Compass (2022) https://data.consilium.europa.eu/doc/document/ST-7371-2022-INIT/en/pdf (accessed 20/04/22).

[157] EU Negotiating Mandate (2020) https://www.consilium.europa.eu/media/42736/st05870-ad01re03-en20.pdf (accessed 20/04/22).

should enable cooperation between the Union and the United Kingdom in third countries, including on consular protection, and in international organisations, notably in the framework of the United Nations, with a view to combining efforts in external action and management of global challenges. In relation to sanctions, the EU also states that any future partnership should facilitate dialogue and mutual exchange of information between the EU and the UK to ensure alignment of the UK and EU sanctions policy, when and where foreign policy objectives are shared, i.e. against Russia. In relation to the CSDP, the Mandate states that any future partnership should establish a framework in line with existing rules to enable the UK to participate on a case-by-case basis, however, that this should be upon *invitation* by the EU, and *only* in CSDP missions and operations open to third countries. The EU also states that, under any framework, and in the context of a CSDP mission or operation in which the UK participates in, the envisaged partnership should provide for interaction and exchange of information with the UK that are proportionate to the level of the UK's contribution. The UK recognises that it has been the EU's longstanding view that, as a third country, the UK cannot have the same rights and benefits as an EU Member State, and the EU's Negotiating Mandate makes that clear.[158] The EU seeks to ensure that any future partnership with the UK will preserve the autonomy of the EU's decision making, including in the shaping of its foreign and defence policies. There will be no standing invitation to participate in CSDP operations.

5.5 EU Security and Defence Ambitions Post-Brexit

The EU has made it clear, with the adoption of the EUGS, the Strategic Compass and the Negotiation Mandate, that it wants a post-Brexit security and defence partnership with the UK. Through its Negotiation Mandate, it has also given some detail as to how it would like that future partnership to look. These are all positive developments for the future of a UK/EU security and defence partnership. That said, since the UK's departure, although the UK's departure has undoubtedly been a blow to EU security and defence capabilities, its departure has also presented the EU with many opportunities. Although this thesis has highlighted where and when the UK and EU's security and defence relationship worked well, during its time as a member, as noted earlier in the thesis, the UK had been one of the biggest opponents to further integration in EU security and defence.[159] The UK was also a state around which other dissenting Member States could rally behind and oppose CSDP. This was most notable during the USA's invasion of Iraq, something which the UK supported in spite of formal EU opposition to the war. The EU and some of its Member States

[158] Mills (2020) https://commonslibrary.parliament.uk/brexit-next-steps-defence-and-foreign-policy-co-operation/ (accessed 21/04/22).

[159] Sweeney and Winn (2020), p. 232.

now see the UK's departure as an opportunity to deepen integration in security and defence and, in turn, there have been a number of developments since Brexit.

5.6 European Defence Fund (2017)

Following Brexit and the departure of the EU, another opportunity presented itself to the EU. In November 2016, the Commission released its 'Implementation Plan on Security and Defence'.[160] The Plan proposed the creation of a European Defence Fund (EDF) which it stated could 'support the financing of capabilities commonly agreed by Member States and with recognised EU added value'. It was calculated by the Commission that lack of cooperation between EU Member States in the field of security and defence costs up to 100 billion Euros every year and that an integrated military hardware procurement could save that money. To prevent this waste in spending and unnecessary duplication of capabilities, turn, in 2017, the Commission launched the EDF. The EDF supports support multinational cooperation in defence research and development. The EDF also provides matched funding to member state expenditure on cooperative multistate initiatives. The current EDF budget is 8 billion for 2021–2027, which will fund collaborative defence research and collaborative capability development projects.[161] The EDF has the potential to make a significant contribution to strengthening EU security and defence capabilities, especially if fully integrated with PESCO.[162] The EDF is also a clear sign of a push towards strengthening the European security defence capabilities and will be fundamental to any prospect of EU strategic autonomy.

5.7 Permanent Structured Cooperation (PESCO) 2018

Permanent structured cooperation (PESCO) in security and defence has been an ambition of the EU's since the failed ratification of the European Constitution. Although the EU Constitution failed, PESCO was revived under the Lisbon Treaty in 2009, which introduced the possibility for certain EU countries to strengthen their cooperation in military matters by creating permanent structured cooperation under Articles 42(6) and 46 of the Treaty on European Union (TEU). In order to do establish PESCO, the Treaty states that interested countries must intensively develop

[160] '*European Defence Action Plan: Towards a European Defence Fund*', European Commission, (30 November 2016) https://ec.europa.eu/commission/presscorner/detail/en/IP_16_4088 (accessed 22/04/22).

[161] '*About the European Defence Fund (EDF)*', European Commission https://defence-industry-space.ec.europa.eu/eu-defence-industry/european-defence-fund-edf_en (accessed 23/04/22).

[162] Sweeney, *Supra* 159 at 237.

defence capacities through the development of national contributions and their participation in multinational forces, in the main European equipment programmes and in the activities of the EDA in the field of defence capabilities development, research, acquisition and armaments. Interested countries must also have the capacity to supply combat units and support logistics for the tasks referred to in Article 43 TEU within a period of 5 to 30 days and, depending on needs, for a period of 30 to 120 days.[163] Following the UK's departure, PESCO was established by the Council on 11th December 2017, by 25 of the EU's 27 remaining Member States.[164] PESCO establishes a legal framework for these 25 Member States to jointly plan, develop and invest in shared capability projects, and enhance the operational readiness and contribution of armed forces. PESCO has not changed the intergovernmental nature of EU security and defence—Member States still retain full control over policy direction and decision-making when it comes to this area—however, PESCO now legally binds EU Member States to the commitments made under PESCO, to deepen defence integration, as opposed to political declarations to do so. To date, over 60 projects have been put forward by the participating Member States. In terms of third-party involvement, whilst membership of PESCO is only for those Member States who have undertaken the more binding commitments, third-party states may be invited to participate in PESCO projects upon meeting certain conditions. As noted by Witney, these new developments offers new capabilities and a "new promise of technological and industrial progress" for the EU in security and defence.[165]

PESCO, in fact represents one of the latest developments in UK/EU post-Brexit security and defence relations. In early November, the EU's High Representative Josep Borrell announced that the bloc had accepted the UK's request to join PESCO's military mobility project. Among PESCO's 60 collaborative projects, military mobility has the most countries involved, including 24 EU member states and three non-members, namely the US, Canada and Norway. The Dutch-led initiative aims at simplifying and standardising cross-border military transport logistics by enabling the unhindered movement of military personnel and assets within the borders of the EU, be it via rail, road, air or sea. Specifically, the PESCO project functions as a political platform which keeps member states aware of the work that needs to be done to achieve these objectives.

The UK joining PESCO's military mobility project represents the first post-Brexit formal engagement between the UK and the EU's CSDP. While this is undoubtedly a good sign for UK–EU rapprochement, it is still a long way from a return to institutionalised cooperation between the two parties. The issue of UK participation in PESCO initiatives has been sensitive since the country officially left the EU, with

[163] These tasks under Article 43 include joint disarmament operations, humanitarian and rescue tasks, military advice and assistance tasks, conflict prevention and peace-keeping tasks, tasks of combat forces in crisis management, including peace-making and post-conflict stabilisation.

[164] COUNCIL DECISION (CFSP) 2017/2315.

[165] Witney (2019) https://www.ecfr.eu/article/commentary_eur (accessed 22/04/22).

some Brexiteers fearing that accepting the conditions for third country involvement in PESCO would fail to deliver on the promise of Brexit and that the UK would be permanently tied to EU defence structures and principles, over which it would have no formal influence. Following a similar line of thinking, some commentators have recently gone so far as to suggest that the UK's participation in the military mobility project is part of a slippery slope towards joining an EU army. Besides overlooking the pragmatic reasons behind the UK's decision to join a European military mobility project at a time of war on the European continent and the transatlantic nature of this particular project, these claims fundamentally fail to grasp how PESCO is situated within the European defence architecture and its separation from EU supranational institutions.

It is likely that the UK's rationale for joining PESCO are related to the war in Ukraine and motivated by the need to send military kit to Ukraine faster and more easily, as well as equipment and troops to other vulnerable countries in Europe. Thus, there is high pragmatic value in the UK wanting to improve the speed at which its troops and kit can be deployed across Europe. The UK's joining of PESCO also falls in with the Johnson and May governments plans to engage in a flexible, ad hoc partnership with the EU on defence cooperation and where EU defence initiatives where they complement NATO activities. PESCO's military mobility project ticks these boxes.

Whilst the addition of the UK to PESCO is a sign that the UK is moving in the right direction, it is important not to overstate this development. The UK seeking to cooperate with European countries under the PESCO framework could potentially lead to further rapprochement with the EU and closer liaison with its CSDP structures, but it does not have to. For now, all that matters is that it is a sensible move which makes sense from the UK's perspective. This move will help the UK address the Ukrainian crisis much more easily. The move, overall is unsurprising This sort of cooperation is precisely the type of arrangement envisaged under Brexit: the UK liaising with European states where it is mutually advantageous to do so, and on issues mutually critical to European security.

5.8 European Intervention Initiative (2018)

Another significant development in security and defence since Brexit has been the creation of the European Intervention Initiative (E12). The E12 is a French-led initiative that was set out by President Macron in September 2017. In a speech given to Sorbonne University in Paris, Macron announced the launch of the E12 stating that it is as part of his vision for a "sovereign, united and democratic Europe".[166] The E12 has the aim of building a shared strategic culture that would

[166] Emmanuel Macron, Sorbonne University Speech, (2017) http://international.blogs.ouest-france.fr/archive/2017/09/29/macron-sorbonne-verbatim-europe-18583.html (accessed 23/04/22).

enhance the ability of its members to act together on missions as part of NATO, the EU, UN or other ad hoc coalitions. The project is resource neutral and makes use of existing assets and other joint forces available to its members. Participation in the E12 is by invitation only and a Letter of Intent launching the initiative was signed by nine European countries on 25 June 2018. Finland has since joined the EII, taking the current number of participating European countries to 10. Italy formally announced its willingness to join in mid-September 2019. The E12 was intended to be a flexible and non-binding forum of European states that are able, and willing, to engage their military forces when and where necessary in order to protect European security interests across the spectrum of crises, and without prejudice to the framework through which action is taken (i.e. the UN, NATO, the EU or as an ad hoc coalition). Macron has stated that it will not create a standing European force, nor does it envisage the creation of a new rapid reaction force. Participation in any of its specific initiatives, or any military operations that result, will be subject to sovereign national decision-making. The EII also intends to contribute towards ongoing efforts within the EU and NATO to deepen defence cooperation. In terms of the UK's involvement, it first signalled its intent to get involved in January 2018 following a Franco-British summit on defence cooperation and is one of the signatories to the Letter of Intent. Given that the EII is a defence initiative outside of the governance of the European Union, UK participation in it will not be affected in any way by Brexit, however, UK participation in an initiative that is so closely linked to EU defence projects, and PESCO in particular, has raised some concerns among pro-Brexit commentators who fear that the initiative could involve Britain in an embryonic European Army 'by the back door'.[167] The E12 has been considered as a huge boost to strengthening EU security and defence capabilities. Whilst it is outside the EU structures, it has been argued by some that it manages to get around the cumbersome EU processes institutional complexities, and inter-state wrangling, whilst still contributing to enhancing EU defence capabilities and autonomy.[168]

5.9 Aachen Treaty (2019)

A further significant development in EU security and defence was the signing of the Aahcen Treaty between France and Germany in 2019. Aachen was a reaffirmation of France and Germany's Élysée Treaty, or Treaty of Friendship. The Élysée Treaty was signed by French President, Charles de Gaulle, and German Chancellor, Konrad Adenauer, and was a declaration of friendship and cooperation between the two. The two parties agreed to institute regular meetings between French and German cabinet

[167] Mills (2019) https://commonslibrary.parliament.uk/research-briefings/cbp-8432/ (accessed 23/04/22).

[168] Mölling and Major (2018) https://www.egmontinstitute.be/why-joining-frances-european-intervention-initiative-is-the-right-decision-for-germany/ (accessed 24/04/22).

ministers and senior military officers, coordinate their foreign policies and agreed to establish programs in the realm of education teaching each other's language and culture.[169] In the new Treaty of Aachen, France and Germany have pledged to enhanced cooperation between each other on security and defence policies. The Treaty also reaffirms their foreign policy, security, and military cooperation, underscores their commitment to culture, education, and has established new initiatives on cross-border cooperation. Whilst the Treaty is largely symbolic, it is statement of intent from France and Germany on how they see EU security and defence in the future. The Treaty legally binds France and Germany to pursue further security and defence integration, policy coordination, and cooperation and sets out a road map for that. Furthermore, as arguably the two remaining leading Member States, it sends a signal to the rest of Europe, the world and, most notably, the UK, about their positive view of deeper integration in the EU and the direction they intend to steer Europe towards.[170]

5.10 Change in EU Rhetoric

The departure of the UK from the EU has clearly unlocked some—not all—of the EU's security and defence potential. Initiatives such as PESCO, EDF, E12, and Aachen, would almost certainly have been initiatives that the UK would have opposed had it still been a member, given its long standing policy of opposing further integration in EU defence. The rhetoric within the EU has changed also. Topics, once considered highly sensitive are being openly discussed by EU officials. Speaking to students at the Tsinghua University, China, HR Federica Mogherini said that, whilst the EU will lose an important member state, the UK will lose more than the EU.[171] Her successor, Josep Borrell, in a speech commenting on the first draft of the Strategic Compass in November 2021, stated that the EU has to become a 'security provider'.[172] Borrell also stated that European citizens want member states to improve their capacities in order to be more effective, and they want to project Europe in the world.

Following Brexit, the EU also started to attract pro-federalists to some of its top jobs. Upon the UK's decision to leave the EU, the European Parliament appointed Guy Verhofstadt as its representative on Brexit. Verhofstadt became the counterpart of the EU's chief negotiator, and chief negotiator of the Commission, Michel

[169] Dungan (2019) https://www.atlanticcouncil.org/blogs/new-atlanticist/france-germany-treaty-of-aachen/ (accessed 24/04/22).

[170] Perot (2019) http://www.egmontinstitute.be/the-aachen-mutual-defence-clause-a-closer-look-at-the-franco-german-treaty/ (accessed 24/04/22).

[171] Zavrsnik (2017) https://www.politico.eu/article/mogherini-britain-will-lose-more-from-brexit-than-eu/ (accessed 24/04/22).

[172] Brzozowski (2021) https://www.euractiv.com/section/defence-and-security/interview/europe-has-to-become-a-security-provider-says-eus-borrell/ (accessed 25/04/22).

Barnier. The two negotiators were tasked with presenting the EU's position in negotiations and approving any possible agreements on the conditions of the UK's departure. Prior to this role, Verhofstadt had been a prolific federalist, who once published a book entitled 'The United States of Europe' in 2006[173] which put forward the argument for a federal United States of Europe. Verhofstadt's position had not changed by the time he became a chief negotiator on Brexit for the EU. In an interview in May 2019, about his ambitions to take the EU's 'top job'—President of the Commission—Verhofstadt stated that he did not want a superstate, however, he stated that he saw nothing wrong with the idea of a United States of Europe and that he believed it would be a way to organize common action on a European level.[174]

As well as Verhofstadt, in December 2019, a fellow pro-federalist, Ursula von der Leyen, was elected as President of the European Commission. Although von der Leyen has backtracked on some of her past views, for a large part of her political career she had been a devote European federalist.[175] In an interview with Der Spiegel in 2011, von der Leyen stated that her aim as a politician "is the United States of Europe—modelled on federal states like Switzerland, Germany or the US".[176] She repeated this call for a United States of Europe again in 2016, stating that she imagined the Europe of her children and grandchildren "not as a loose union of states trapped by national interests".[177] Prior to becoming Presdient of the Commission, von der Leyen was defence minister in her native Germany, during which she pushed for greater security cooperation in the EU, advocating for European Defense Union and calling for the establishment of an "army of Europeans". During her time as Defence Minister, von der Leyen stated that "Europe must be able to act independently precisely in the areas where Europe must act independently".[178] On Brexit and the UK, von der Leyen has taken a much tougher stance than her predecessor, Tusk. She did not support a second referendum for the UK, stating that "as much as I would like to see the Brits stay in the EU, they voted to leave".[179] Giving some insight into how von der Leyen may approach any future security and defence negotiations with the UK, as defence minister, von der Leyen

[173] See Verhofstadt (2006).

[174] Jamieson and Harris (2019) https://www.euronews.com/2019/05/13/guy-verhofstadt-eu-presidential-hopeful-talks-to-euronews (accessed 25/04/22).

[175] Wiese (2019) https://www.politico.eu/article/ursula-von-der-leyen-rows-back-on-united-states-of-europe/ (accessed 25/04/22).

[176] '*Schuldenkrise: Von der Leyen fordert die Vereinigten Staaten von Europa*', Spiegel, (27 August 2011) https://www.spiegel.de/politik/deutschland/schuldenkrise-von-der-leyen-fordert-die-vereinigten-staaten-von-europa-a-782879.html (accessed 25/04/22).

[177] Bennhold (2019) https://www.nytimes.com/2019/07/05/world/europe/eus-top-pick-too-pious-for-feminists-too-feminist-for-conservatives.html (accessed 25/04/22).

[178] '*Ursula von der Leyen wirbt für "Armee der Europäer"*', Spiegel, (12 November 2018) https://www.spiegel.de/politik/ausland/ursula-von-der-leyen-wirbt-fuer-armee-der-europaeer-a-1238076.html (accessed 26/04/22).

[179] Gaugele (2018) https://www.morgenpost.de/politik/article215819939/Ursula-von-der-Leyen-Durch-den-Brexit-verlieren-alle.html (accessed 26/04/22).

stressed that, whilst she wanted the UK and the EU to still cooperate on security matters in the future, she would not allow special treatment for the UK post arguing that if the EU defines a special path for the UK, other partners like Norway would demand the same.[180]

5.11 Developments Within the UK Post-Brexit

5.11.1 Aukus Treaty (2021)

As well as developments occurring on the continent, there has been a lot of change from the UK perspective since Brexit. The Johnson government followed up its treaty with France with a new defence pact, this time with the creation of a trilateral defence partnership with the US and Australia, entitled AUKUS. The pact was announced on 15th September 2021 and focuses specifically on enhancing the military capabilities of all three parties in cyber, artificial intelligence and quantum technologies. Arguably the main feature of AUKUS is that it will enable Australia to build nuclear-powered submarines for the first time, a technology provided to it by the US. It has been viewed by commentators in the area as an effort to counterbalance the so-called threat of China.[181] In terms of UK and EU relations, it is not so much what the pact says that has soured the partnership between the two parties, but more whom it excludes. The exclusion of France from the pact, and the provision of nuclear submarine technology to Australia, caused the Australians to cancel their £48 billion submarine-building contract with France. The Pact was met with outrage from France, with the French recalling its ambassadors to the US and French Foreign Minister, Jean-Yves Le Drian calling it a “stab in the back”.[182] The pact was also met with criticism from commentators in the field, with some arguing that AUKUS risked the UK becoming isolated from the EU and European states even more after Brexit.[183] Others have argued that the humiliation caused to France and the rest of the EU may also further intensify ambitions within the EU to develop a credible, independent European military force. Witney makes similar points about how the agreement will embitter relations between the UK and the EU and also points how, with the UK not directly benefiting from AUKUS, the UK will become ever more subordinate to the US in security and defence post-Brexit.[184]

---

[180] Hellemann et al. (2016).

[181] ‘*Aukus: UK, US and Australia launch pact to counter China*’, BBC News, (London, 16 September 2021) https://www.bbc.co.uk/news/world-58564837 (accessed 16/04/22).

[182] *Ibid.*

[183] ‘*View on Anglo-French relations*’, The Observer, (London, 19 September 2021) https://www.theguardian.com/commentisfree/2021/sep/19/observer-view-on-anglo-french-relations-aukus-pact (accessed 19 September 2021).

[184] Witney (2021) https://ecfr.eu/article/aukus-after-the-sugar-rush/ (accessed 30/10/21).

5.12 *Finland, Sweden and India Partnerships (2022)*

Johnson's next port of call to build a new security and defence alliance was to India in April 2022. This was again in pursuit of pledges made in its Integrated Security Review to become 'the European country with the broadest, most integrated presence in the Indo-Pacific in support of trade, shared security and values'. During his first visit to India since becoming Prime Minister, Johnson and Indian Prime Minister, Narendra Modi, announced the new partnership agreeing to advance their new defence partnership to a 'new level', with a particular focus on maritime and industrial collaboration.[185] The partnership included new agreements on maritime information sharing, an invitation to the UK to join India's Information Fusion Centre (IMAC) in Gurgaon and an exercise programme which includes joint tri-lateral military exercises. The partnership also included new agreements on security and defence R&D, including commitments to build the Indian military's air, maritime propulsion and space and cyber capabilities. An agreement was also made to move the manufacturing of the MT30 Gas Turbine engine to India. Again, the new pact was an unequivocal statement by Johnson and his government as to where it intends to have the UK's security and defence needs met.

The Johnson government's latest security and defence alliance was created with Sweden and Finland in May 2022. The new defence pacts came in the wake of Russia's invasion of Ukraine in February 2022, which sparked a discussion within Finland and Sweden over NATO membership. The pact included an agreement between the UK, Finland and Sweden to come to each other's aid, should any of the three nations come under attack. Announcing the new defence pact, Johnson stated that the pact would become the "foundation of an intensification" of the three-party's security and defence relationship in other ways as well. In a statement released by the UK government, the UK intends to see a step-change in defence and security cooperation between the UK and Finland and Sweden, intensifying intelligence sharing, accelerating joint military training, exercising and deployments, and bolstering security across all three countries and northern Europe.[186] The UK government also announced that it hoped the new agreement will also see the UK bolster its collaboration on traditional threats facing all three nations, while working also with Sweden and Finland to tackle new geopolitical challenges, such as hybrid and cyber threats.[187] Although the agreement was almost entirely about countering the Russian threat northern and eastern European, as well as putting Finland and Sweden's

[185] '*UK and India Prime Ministers announce Enhanced Defence Cooperation*', British High Commission New Delhi, HM Gov, (2021) https://www.gov.uk/government/news/uk-and-india-prime-ministers-announce-enhanced-defence-cooperation.

[186] UK-Sweden Political Declaration of Solidarity (2022) https://www.gov.uk/government/publications/united-kingdom-sweden-statement-11-may-2022; UK-Finland Statement (2022) https://www.gov.uk/government/publications/united-kingdom-finland-statement-11-may-2022.

[187] '*Prime Minister signs new assurances to bolster European security: 11 May 2022*', HM Gov, (11 May 2022) https://www.gov.uk/government/news/prime-minister-signs-new-assurances-to-bolster-european-security-11-may-2022 (accessed 17/04/22).

NATO membership back on the table, the partnership's secondary ambitions for intensified cooperation and increased security and defence R&D, can also be viewed as another example of the UK bypassing the EU for bilateral partnerships with individual member states. The UK's pact with Finland and Sweden is yet another partnership in what is becoming a long list of new bilateral security and defence partnerships for the UK and is a strategy that Johnson shows no signs of detracting from any time soon.

The UK's new identity in international relations, with greater autonomy for international diplomacy, not just in security and defence but also in its foreign economic policy, it is difficult to determine how a future partnership with the EU might look like, if one will ever be agreed at all. As Whitman notes, the implication of the UK continuing with its current strategy is that there will be a divergence from the EU's norms, practices and ambitions in the security and defence field.[188] The longer this divergence occurs in, will increase—quite possibly to the point where a future security and defence pact with the EU may become impossible. As Whitman describes, the UK looks less likely to agree a security and defence pact with the EU and more likely to continue 'muddling through'. As Whitman notes, the current Integrated Security Review will define the UK's approach for the next decade. It would therefore be unsurprising to see any post-Brexit security and defence partnership with the EU in the next 10 years, or at least during Johnson's premiership. Whitman also highlights the politics of the Conservative Party, which he argues has become even more embittered with EU security and defence cooperation since Brexit and the election of Johnson as leader. A broadening and deepening of cooperation beyond trade policy will face significant opposition as the topic of EU security and defence cooperation is a taboo for many Conservative Party Members of Parliament and also for elements in the grass roots of the party, which has a growing hard-Eurosceptic base.[189] At present, the prospects of a UK/EU security and defence partnership are very slim.

5.13 UK Membership of PESCO

PESCO, in fact represents one of the latest developments in UK/EU post-Brexit security and defence relations. In early November, the EU's High Representative Josep Borrell announced that the bloc had accepted the UK's request to join PESCO's military mobility project. Among PESCO's 60 collaborative projects, military mobility has the most countries involved, including 24 EU member states and three non-members, namely the US, Canada and Norway. The Dutch-led initiative aims at simplifying and standardising cross-border military transport logistics by enabling the unhindered movement of military personnel and assets

[188] Whitman, *Supra* 118

[189] Heppell, *Supra* 148 at 340.

within the borders of the EU, be it via rail, road, air or sea. Specifically, the PESCO project functions as a political platform which keeps member states aware of the work that needs to be done to achieve these objectives.

The UK joining PESCO's military mobility project represents the first post-Brexit formal engagement between the UK and the EU's CSDP. While this is undoubtedly a good sign for UK–EU rapprochement, it is still a long way from a return to institutionalised cooperation between the two parties. The issue of UK participation in PESCO initiatives has been sensitive since the country officially left the EU, with some Brexiteers fearing that accepting the conditions for third country involvement in PESCO would fail to deliver on the promise of Brexit and that the UK would be permanently tied to EU defence structures and principles, over which it would have no formal influence. Following a similar line of thinking, some commentators have recently gone so far as to suggest that the UK's participation in the military mobility project is part of a slippery slope towards joining an EU army. Besides overlooking the pragmatic reasons behind the UK's decision to join a European military mobility project at a time of war on the European continent and the transatlantic nature of this particular project, these claims fundamentally fail to grasp how PESCO is situated within the European defence architecture and its separation from EU supranational institutions.

It is likely that the UK's rationale for joining PESCO are related to the war in Ukraine and motivated by the need to send military kit to Ukraine faster and more easily, as well as equipment and troops to other vulnerable countries in Europe. Thus, there is high pragmatic value in the UK wanting to improve the speed at which its troops and kit can be deployed across Europe. The UK's joining of PESCO also falls in with the Johnson and May governments plans to engage in a flexible, ad hoc partnership with the EU on defence cooperation and where EU defence initiatives where they complement NATO activities. PESCO's military mobility project ticks these boxes.

Whilst the addition of the UK to PESCO is a sign that the UK is moving in the right direction, it is important not to overstate this development. The UK seeking to cooperate with European countries under the PESCO framework could potentially lead to further rapprochement with the EU and closer liaison with its CSDP structures, but it does not have to. For now, all that matters is that it is a sensible move which makes sense from the UK's perspective. This move will help the UK address the Ukrainian crisis much more easily. The move, overall is unsurprising This sort of cooperation is precisely the type of arrangement envisaged under Brexit: the UK liaising with European states where it is mutually advantageous to do so, and on issues mutually critical to European security.

6 The Future of the Security and Defence Partnership

For the foreseeable future, a post-Brexit security and defence partnership between the UK and the EU looks unlikely. As discussed above, the two parties appear to be going in different directions on security and defence; the EU is focusing on deepening integration and developing its own capabilities within the Union, whereas the UK is developing its bilateral partnerships with European nations and nations beyond the borders of Europe, as well investing more in NATO (with the UK recently pledging to spend 2.5% GDP on defence by 2030 at the June 2022 NATO summit).[190] Furthermore, the terms of both party's proposals are a long way off from each other. The UK, on the one hand, seeks a partnership in which it can still make decisions on the CSDP but has the freedom to contribute to and finance those missions it feels suits its interests. On the other hand, the EU seeks a partnership in which it invites the UK to engage with and contribute to CSDP missions as and when it feels the UK's involvement can add value. As stated above, the EU has made clear that it will not make special arrangements for the UK and that any partnership must be in the EU's interests as well as the UK's. The EU will not allow the UK to 'have its cake and eat it'—reaping all the benefits of CSDP and contributing nothing to it (or contributing only to those missions it wishes to be involved in). As it stands, therefore, negotiations between the two on a post-Brexit security and defence partnership have reached stalemate.

Whilst it looks unlikely that a partnership will be formed in the near future, this has not stopped academics in the field from exploring what a future partnership could and should look like. Across the academic literature, a number of themes have emerged about the types of partnership the UK and the EU may engage in. Three types of potential partnership have emerged from the academic literature: tightly integrated, loosely integrated and detached. Whitman identifies and defines these three possible scenarios as for the UK in the CSDP post-Brexit as an '*integrated player*', an '*associated partner*', or a '*detached observer*'.[191] With the UK and EU's proposed terms in mind, starting with the 'integrated player' scenario, each scenario will now be looked at in more detail:

6.1 Integrated Player

As an integrated player, in order for the UK to take on this more integrated role, the EU would have to make a bespoke arrangement for it. As Cardwell states, in this scenario, the UK would take on what he describes as a 'reverse Denmark' (outside the EU but inside the CSDP), retaining involvement in EU battlegroups, CSDP

---

[190] Gallardo (2022) https://www.politico.eu/article/uk-pledge-2-5-percent-defense-end-decade/ (accessed 01/07/22).

[191] Whitman (2017), pp. 43, 48.

operations and in the FAC on relevant agenda items.[192] That said, under this scenario, the UK would lose its ability to make strategic decision-making relating to the CSDP. As a non-member states, the UK would be outside the mechanisms of the FAC, the Council, the Political and Security Committee and its working groups. Under this scenario, the UK would regain access to the EU's diplomatic and soft-power military capabilities, whilst the EU would also have access to the UK's hard-power military capabilities and expertise. With both party's foreign policies almost certainly remaining in correspondence with one another, it is likely that the UK's involvement in the EU's policy-making infrastructure would be a regular occurrence. At present, however, this type of arrangement sits outside the terms proposed by both parties and neither has made any indication yet that they would agree to such a partnership. This view was shared by a number of experts involved in the House of Lords' European Union Committee report on Brexit and CSDP missions and operations. Expert witnesses stated that could not foresee a role for the UK in CSDP decision-making after Brexit[193] and that a decision-making role for the UK would be an option that the EU would probably not be happy about.[194] Lord Ricketts, commenting in the Report, stated that the EU would always draw a line at EU autonomy.

A number of other similar scenarios have been suggested, which would enable the UK to have an integrated role within EU security and defence as a third-party state. This scenario was put forward by the European Union Committee in their report on CSDP post-Brexit. This partnership would require the UK to negotiate a privileged advisory or consultative role in the EU institutions, but without decision-making power and vetoes. This would mirror the type of partnership that Finland and Sweden currently have within NATO. Speaking to the EU Committee, expert witness, Andrew Lapsely, stated that these two nations, as non-NATO countries, have become very close partners within NATO and have been contributing to NATO operations. They have made broad intellectual and political contributions and, in some ways, have been more active than some allies within NATO. Finland and Sweden have become regular participants" in North Atlantic Council meetings, and while they do not have a formal decision-making role, these two states contribute to debate. Another integrated player scenario for the UK that was also suggested in the EU Committee's report was for the UK to have an early and permanent continuing consultation role, including an established mechanism for the UK to have influence and be part of the consultative process before any decisions are made by the EU Member States.[195] In this scenario, the UK could be involved thinking on policy

---

[192] Cardwell, (2017)*Supra* 120 at 23.

[193] 'Brexit: Common Security and Defence Policy missions and operations', 16th Report, European Union Committee, (2018) http://data.parliament.uk/writtenevidence/committeeevidence.svc/evidencedocument/eu-external-affairs-subcommittee/brexit-common-security-and-defence-policy-csdp-missions/written/77355.html.

[194] *Ibid.*

[195] *Ibid.*

early on when a crisis breaks out. It is not difficult to imagine that a similar sort of partnership could be agreed between the UK and the EU, with the UK participating in the debates at the meetings of the FAC and PSC, for example, but having no veto. Again, this type of scenario remains outside the terms proposed by the two parties.

6.2 Associated Partner

The second possible type of partnership the UK and the EU might have is where the UK is an associated partner to the EU. In this scenario the UK's position would similar to the position of Norway: having no membership of the FAC but participating in dialogue with the EU on policy and related issues.[196] Whilst it would still have the opportunity to participate in battlegroups and the European Defence Agency via special agreements, this would likely be a functional arrangement with little or no influence over policy-making. This would clearly be a much looser partnership with the EU in security and defence. Exchanges between the UK and the EU on security and defence policy would be on a dialogue basis, however, the UK would have no direct involvement in policymaking. The UK's involvement in the CSDP missions, both civilian and military, would require the two parties to sign an FPA, as discussed above, allowing the UK to join missions on a case-by-case basis, at the invitation of the EU. As Whitman states, under this scenario, the UK would relinquish its ability to have a direct influence on the development of EU security and defence policy.[197]

Academics in the field have described this as a partnership that would 'die out' quite quickly.[198] Others have argued that this model would be unlikely to satisfy the UK's interests and strategic ambitions in security and defence and would not be a good outcome for either party.[199] Representatives of the Johnson government have also made clear that this would not be something it would seek to engage in as the existing way in which the EU handles third countries would not allow the UK reasonable input.[200] The Global Europe Centre have made suggestions that there may be an opportunity for a rethink of the structure of FPAs so that it integrates partner countries at every stage of the planning and implementation of CSDP missions.[201] This would enable the UK to have a reasonable and proportionate degree of influence over what that operation was doing, however, the EU is yet to indicate whether this would be something it would be willing to do.

---

[196] Tardy (2014), pp. 6, 6.

[197] Whitman, *Supra* 191, at 7.

[198] European Union Committee, *Supra* 193.

[199] *Ibid.*

[200] *Ibid.*

[201] *Ibid.*

6.3 Detached Observer

The only other possible scenario for the UK, post-Brexit, is to become what Whitman defined as a 'detached observer'—in which the UK would not participate in any institutional formats and would be limited to participation in civilian missions on a case-by-case basis at the invitation of the EU.[202] This is essentially the position the UK finds itself in today. The UK's foreign, security and defence policy does not necessarily run counter to the EU's, however, it remains formally disconnected from strategic decision-making or policy making when it comes to EU foreign, security and defence policy. As Whitman argues, the UK may seek to influence the EU by building bilateral partnerships with EU Member States. This appears to be the approach that it is already taking, with its recent bilateral security and defence partnerships with Finland, France and Sweden. It is also possible that the UK could mirror the position taken by the US; participating in civilian CSDP missions on a case-by-case basis via a framework agreement on crisis management operations, allowing it to work in a separate mission alongside any CSDP missions, rather than being integrated into EU military deployments.[203]

Academics in the field have argued that the UK's diplomatic weight, military capabilities and prominent position in organisations such as NATO and the UN—as well as its special relationship with the US—would continue to count with the remaining 27 EU Member States on foreign security and defence policy, but that this would depend largely on what 'Global Britain' will mean in practice.[204] For these reasons, and its geographical location to continental Europe, the UK will undoubtedly have influence on the EU's security and defence policy from outside the EU. The level of influence that it will have, however, depends on how much it is willing to invest in ensuring it retains influence. The UK would have to invest in staff and financial resources in Brussels. The EU will still look to the UK for support. The EU engages regularly with the US beyond individual missions in forums such as the PSC in which representatives from the US are invited to participate in both formal and informal meetings. A similar sort of arrangement could be set up for the UK. Regardless of all of this, however, the fact still remains that the UK would have no direct influence on decision-making or policy formation.[205] As has been argued by some, agenda-shaping was difficult enough for the UK when it was a member—as argued earlier in the Chapter, it is very difficult to form policy due to the Member States' opposing foreign, security and defence policies. Being outside the EU now, shaping an agenda will be a very complex task for the UK.

It is likely that under this scenario, the UK will seek to make more of its bilateral partnerships with other European nations and nations beyond the borders of Europe, as has been evident with the partnerships the UK has recently forged with India,

---

[202] Whitman, *Supra* 191, at 7.

[203] *Ibid.*

[204] European Union Committee, *Supra* 193.

[205] Bakker et al. (2017) https://www.jstor.org/stable/resrep05446.5?seq=8 (accessed 27/04/22).

Finland and Sweden. Although the UK is planning to make more of its bilateral partnerships, it is useful to look at how one of their most famous bilateral partnerships, with France under the Lancaster house treaties, panned out, to gauge just how successful these might be. France is one of the European states the UK will most likely seek to build a stronger bilateral partnership with. It is now over ten years since the Lancaster House treaties, however, and the partnership that was developed between the UK and France under these treaties has had a mixed record. As the EU's two only nuclear powers, the two nations agreed to nuclear cooperation under one of the treaties. In pursuance of this aim, the two nations established the Teutates project, which had the aim of building a single shared facility in France for testing the safety and reliability of their nuclear warhead designs. Cameron forecasted several hundred million pounds of savings. By 2018, the UK and France were using the same vast radiographic machines for their national experiments. The full site is almost completed 2022, and the treaty is valid for 50 years. For this time, the UK and France will be mutually dependent for a critical aspect of their nuclear deterrents.

The main aim of the second treaty was to launch practical work in two areas: strengthening cooperation between the two armed forces, and joint procurement of equipment. One of the real success stories of the Lancaster House process has been much closer operational cooperation between the two militaries. The main vehicle for this was developing a Combined Joint Expeditionary Force (CJEF), capable of deploying a joint brigade-level force with air and naval assets and conducting high-intensity combat operations. Bringing this force up to full operating capability has involved regular joint exercises and exchanges of personnel. As a result, units across the two armed forces have trained together, communications problems have been ironed out, and personal links established up to senior levels. In turn, the two countries now have a fighting force which they could jointly deploy if the two governments decided to act together. In the meantime, the two armed forces are operating together increasingly often: from air strikes against the Islamic State in Syria, joint naval deployments, humanitarian relief and French participation in the UK-led NATO Enhanced Forward Presence in Estonia.

Progress on defence equipment cooperation has by contrast been disappointing. The initial high hopes that the UK and France could develop a joint Future Combat Air System have amounted to nothing thus far. Instead, France turned to a joint project with Germany on a next-generation fast jet, and the UK is pursuing the Tempest programme with Italy and Sweden. Cooperation on missiles has made more progress, particularly on a new anti-ship missile for the two navies, however, the ambitious plans for industrial cooperation between the UK and France have been a casualty of Brexit and the wider geopolitical environment. French energies under President Emmanuel Macron have turned towards European strategic autonomy, as has been discussed in this chapter.

In terms of the future of Lancaster House and the wider British/French security and defence relationship, the nuclear relationship is underpinned by the Teutates deal. There is scope for the two countries to consult more closely on nuclear deterrence. The CJEF has been successful in strengthening links between the armed forces. If European countries ever needed to deploy forces into combat, it would arguably be France and the UK in the lead.

Whilst Brexit does not weaken the case for Europe's two major military powers work together, in practice Brexit has pulled in them in opposite directions. Whilst the UK has joined a PESCO project, which signals progress, there is not a great deal of appetite in the UK government for structured dialogue with the EU on defence and security, while France is busy promoting EU-based autonomy. What is also striking is that the two governments did not plan a major event on the 10th anniversary of Lancaster House to celebrate the achievements and relaunch cooperation for another decade. That may partly be a casualty of the coronavirus pandemic but it is likely to be part of a larger breakdown in relations, almost inevitably a symptom of Brexit. For now, it would be wise to not expect too much to come from France and the UK in this field.

7 Conclusion

It is clear to see that the UK and the EU's security and defence partnership has been a turbulent one. It is a difficult partnership to define; at times it has worked extremely well for both parties and at others, it has not. Post-Brexit, it is difficult to determine the direction in which this relationship is heading and whether there will ever be a comprehensive post-Brexit security and defence agreement between the two parties. To reiterate, this Chapter aimed to answer the following four questions; firstly, what, historically, has been the most difficult and beneficial aspects of the security and defence relationship between the UK and the EU for both parties. It was established earlier in the Chapter, that the UK's role within the CSDP was a tale of two halves. For all the recent difficulties in the relationship between the UK and the EU, historically, the UK had been a staunch supporter of the development of an autonomous EU military capability. As far back as the 1950s, with the emergence of the ECSC, the UK had been vocal in its supported the establishment of such capabilities. It also played a significant role in the establishment of the CSDP itself in the 1990s, evident from the role it played at the St. Malo Summit. That said, in practice, when it came to working within the structures of the CSDP, the UK was at times a difficult partner. It was responsible for leading the EU to one of its most embarrassing moments in the history of the CSDP, when it sided with the US over its invasion of Iraq in 200, leaving the EU looking militarily redundant or, at best, weak on the world stage. The UK has historically been Atlantacist in its outlook, primarily due to the so-called 'Special Relationship' it shares with the US. In turn, it has consistently placed its relationship with the US and NATO as the primary vehicles within which to achieve its foreign policy and security and defence aims. This reluctance to work within the structure of the CSDP has been amplified under 13 years of Conservative governments, which have historically, always been predominantly Eurosceptic. Reluctance to cede too much power to the EU and fears of a European Army and

European super-state have been feelings which have only increased as time has gone on.

That said, there have been clear examples of where the UK and the EU have worked well together under the umbrella of the CSDP. The collective EU response to post-conflict Libya and the Russian invasion of Ukraine were prime examples of this. These two examples revealed a number of trends in the UK and EU's security and defence partnership. When it came to taking hard-military action, the UK favoured its own military capabilities and its bilateral ties with allies, as well as its role within organisations such as the UN and NATO, to meet these needs—although the UK did attempt to persuade the EU to respond to the initial conflict. In Libya, this was evident from the alliance it made with France under the Lancaster House Treaties of 2011 and the NATO intervention it and France led into Libya to quash the Gadaffi regime. That said, it was established that Cameron and the UK saw a role for the UK in the CSDP in the case of Libya, particularly in terms of helping rebuild Libyan society and sending humanitarian assistance. Cameron's soft-Eurosceptic position on the CSDP came to fruition in the UK's support for EUBAM and Operation Sophia in Libya, and the UK devoted significant resources and important personnel to these missions taking a leading role in the missions. Although the missions had difficulties in fulfilling their mandates, it is clear from both speeches made by Cameron and his ministers and Parliamentary committee reports that the UK valued these missions and, in turn, that they valued the CSDP's military and civilian capabilities. This was also true in the case of Ukraine in 2014. The UK found itself in a position with Russia, where hard-military power was not an option and the risk of nuclear war was too great. Ukraine was a clear example, like Libya, of how the UK benefited from the strong soft-power capabilities the EU possesses. Through sanctions and EUAM, the UK (via the EU) was able to provide an effective response to the Ukrainian conflict without coming into direct conflict with Russia. Furthermore, through its membership of the EU Council, it was also able to mount pressure on the EU and other Member States to implement tougher measures against Russia. It was also able to place its own military resources, personnel and experts on Ukrainian soil through the vehicle of the EU, presenting much less of a threat and provocation to Russia and, thereby, preventing itself from coming into direct conflict with Russia. Libya and Ukraine showed how the UK and EU's partnership through the CSDP worked well. The UK's involvement in these CSDP missions dispel, or go some way to dispelling, the argument that the UK and the EU's security and defence relationship was a negative one. It was certainly true that, at times, the relationship was strained, but there are clear cases where the partnership functioned well and where it was clear that both the UK and the EU valued the partnership between them. Chapter 2 therefore contends that this partnership did in fact work very well at times.

After providing some context by establishing the nature of the partnership in the past, the Chapter then sort to establish what the current positions of the UK and the EU is on a post-Brexit partnership, what challenges and opportunities present and what kind of security and defence partnership between the UK and the EU, if any, is possible. In terms of looking at how, if any, future security and defence partnership might look, it was clear that neither the May government or Johnson government have done enough to secure one. It was clear that security and defence was not at the top of either May of Johnson's priorities when it came to Brexit. It was clear from May's speeches and the policy documents of her government, however, that she valued the merits of a post-Brexit security and defence partnership. Her concessions and U-turns on the prospective arrangements indicated a strong desire within herself and within her government to get this deal done. Although May never formally said she would have like the UK to have continued contributing towards the CSDP, given her track record of concessions during her premiership, it would not have been outside the realms of possibility that May and her government would have conceded on this point. Her proposals for an ad hoc partnership, however, were too aspirational. The UK wanted to come and go as it pleased whilst having a full say in setting mandates, developing operations and deciding how they would be funded. Essentially May's proposals included a scenario in which the UK did not want to pay any of the cost towards the CSDP yet wanted to reap all of its benefits. This was fanciful at best and almost certainly something the EU is unlikely to have agreed. May's government had not conceded enough—the negotiations were always doomed to fail on these terms.

Johnson's proposals for a post-Brexit security and defence partnership echoed those made by May. What was clear from Johnson's speeches and his government's policy documents, was that, if it was to agree any post-Brexit security and defence partnership with the EU, that it would be one in which the UK could engage with the CFSP and CSDP on an ad hoc basis. Unlike May, however, Johnson appears comfortable with the current situation in which the UK has no security and defence agreement with the EU. Johnson's government has made it clear that it will look to the US, the UN, NATO, and the Five Eyes, amongst other alliances and organisations, for the UK's security and defence nees. Furthermore, in terms of building new alliances, the Johnson government has also made clear that it will look beyond the EU, evidenced by the UK's recent security and defence pacts with Finland, India, France and the establishment of Aukus. In stark contrast to Johnson, Cameron and May (May less so) did appear to recognise the merits of EU defence and, in May's case, tried to secure a deal. Given Johnson's hard-Eurosceptic rhetoric on the EU and Brexit, and given the strong mandate he received at the 2019 General Election, it would be unsurprising if no security and defence agreement was struck with the EU during his tenure as Prime Minister.

For the EU, from the outset of the UK's decision to leave the EU, with the publication of the EUGS and, more recently, the adoption of the Strategic Compass, it has made it clear that it wants to pursue security and defence partnerships with third-party states, including the UK. The publication of its Negotiating Mandate has given some detail as to what type of partnership it would seek to agree with the UK. Whilst these are all positive developments in terms of the UK and EU's future partnership, the EU's proposed partnership does not match up with that of the UK's, in terms of CSDP. Both parties agree that any future partnership should be on a case-by-case basis, or ad hoc, however, the two parties disagree on what basis that should be. Whereas the UK would like to have the option of being involved in all CSDP missions, and contributing only to those operations it decides serves its interests, the

EU would want that participation to be on the basis of an invitation from the EU. Furthermore, although the EU has not demanded that the UK contribute to the CSDP operations overall, it is likely that if it agreed to the UK having the option to be involved in all CSDP operations, it would likely not agree to the UK only contributing to those operations that it is involved in. Both parties are still a long way from agreement on what any future security and defence partnership may look, particularly when it comes to the UK's involvement in and contribution to CSDP operations. That said, whilst it wants to pursue a partnership with the UK, the EU appears to have discovered a new lease of life since Brexit. With the UK gone, the biggest bulwark to EU integration in security and defence has disappeared. The EU has been able to establish initiatives that, had the UK still been a member of the EU, would never have been achieved. Whilst the EU is a long way from becoming a defence union, it has certainly deepened and strengthened its security and defence autonomy. That said, the impact of the UK's departure should not be overstated and both parties look set to lose out in terms of their capabilities and influence around the world.

Whilst the UK and the EU do appear to be heading in different directions, the final section of this chapter has shown that there are viable options available to the two parties that, whilst they will not provide as good an arrangement as UK membership inside the EU, will mitigate many of the negative affects of Brexit. This Chapter argues that the UK and the EU should seek to negotiate a partnership in which the UK has a deeply integrated role (described by Whitman as an integrated player role) in EU security and defence. In this way, the EU will have access to the UK's hard-military power capabilities and expertise, whilst conceding some of its autonomy on policy making, and the UK will regain access to the EU's soft-power military and civilian capabilities, whilst respecting the EU's strategic autonomy and deepening integration in security and defence. It is unlikely that the UK will seek to engage in any other type of partnership other than one in which it can have some involvement in policy making and, as a result, this thesis argues that the integrated player model is the only viable option for both parties post-Brexit.

The UK and the EU's security and defence partnership has historically been a strained one at times. Following Brexit, the UK removed itself from the legal and political structures of the CSDP and the partnership is the loosest it has ever been in its history. That said, there are clear examples of how the partnership has worked well where it has served both the UK and the EU's security and defence objectives. Although there are many obstacles in the way of a future formal post-Brexit security and defence partnership, it does not change the fact that this is still a valuable partnership, from which both parties could continue to benefit. In turn, this Chapter concludes that this a partnership worth pursuing for both parties. A future partnership is not only viable but it is something that would be in the interests of both the UK and the EU. The security and defence partnership between the UK and the EU was an effective one and, so long as no post-Brexit partnership exists between the two parties, both the UK and the EU's security and defence capabilities and influence around the world are diminished. It would be prudent of the UK and the EU to come to an agreement on a formal security and defence partnership. Doing so would go a long way to making the UK, Europe and the world a much safer place.

References

Asthana A (2016) No staying in the EU by the back door, says Theresa May. Guardian UK, London (31 August 2016)

Bakker A, Drent M, Zandee D (2017) The UK as a non-member state in EU defence. Clingendael Institute (1 July 2017)

Bennhold K (2019) E.U.'s top pick: too pious for feminists, too feminist for conservatives. New York Times (5 July 2019)

Bennhold K, Erlanger S (2018) Theresa May, in Munich, calls for swift security pact and offers concession. New York Times, New York, (17 February 2018)

Biscop S (2004) The European security strategy. Implementing a distinctive approach to security. Sécurité & Stratégie, 82, 16

Borrell J (2022) A stronger European Union within a better, greener and safer world - key principles that will be guiding my mandate. Speech

Bowcott O (2018) John Major had a 'full gloat' after defeating rebels on Maastricht. Guardian UK, London (24 July 2018)

Brenton T (2014) Sanctions won't work – we will have to negotiate with Vladimir Putin. The Telegraph, London (24 July 2014)

Brzozowski A (2021) Europe has to become a security provider, says EU's Borrell. Euractiv (10 November 2021)

Cameron D (2016) UK's strength and security in the EU. Speech

Cameron D (2019) For the record. William Collins

Cardwell P (2017) The United Kingdom and the Common Foreign and Security Policy of the EU: from pre- Brexit 'Awkward Partner' to post-Brexit 'Future Partnership'? Croatian Yearb Eur Law Policy 13(13)

Croft A, Pawlak J (2014) Hague says EU ready for more Russia sanctions if necessary. Reuters (23 June 2014)

Dungan N (2019) The new treaty of Aachen: more than just a symbol? New Atlanticist (23 January 2019)

European Defence Agency (2012) 10 years of working together. EDA, p 8

Gallardo C (2022) UK defense spending to hit 2.5 percent of GDP by 2030, vows Boris Johnson. Politico, Madrid (30 June 2022)

Gaugele J (2018) Ursula von der Leyen: Durch den Brexit verlieren alle. Morgen Post (18 November 2018)

Hammond P (2012) Shared security: transforming defence to face the future. Speech, 2012

Hellemann A, Eichinger R, Starnick N (2016) Ist der Brexit wirklich so katastrophal? Bild, (25 June 2016)

Heppell T (2012) Cameron and Liberal Conservatism: attitudes within the Parliamentary Conservative Party and Conservative Ministers. Br J Polit Int Relat 15(3)

Honeycombe-Foster M (2021) UK and France sign post-Brexit Channel security pact. Politico, London (26 July 2021)

Jamieson A, Harris C (2019) Watch again: 'I don't want a superstate' says Verhofstadt. Euro News (13 May 2019)

Johnson B (2019) Leadership campaign launch. Speech

Kanter A (1970) The European defense community in the French National Assembly: a Roll Call analysis comparative. Politics 2(2):204

Keuklaire S (2014) The foreign policy of the European Union (2nd edn). Red Globe Press

Liddington D (2012) EU common security and defence policy: the UK perspective

Lynch M (2011) Obama's 'Arab Spring'?, Foreign Policy, London (6 January 2011)

McCormick J (2007) The European superpower. Palgrave Macmillan, p 55

Mills C (2019) The European intervention initiative (EII/EI2). UK Parliament, (23 September 2019)

Mills C (2020) Brexit next steps: defence and foreign policy co-operation. UK Parliament, (05 March 2020)

Milward A, Brennan G, Romero F (1999) The European Rescue of the Nation-state, 2nd edn. Routledge, p 335
Mölling C, Major C (2018) Why joining France's European intervention initiative is the right decision for Germany. Egmont, Brussels (15 June 2018)
Momtaz R (2021) Not much entente, barely cordiale: Franco-British ties in the doldrums. Politico, London (02 August 2021)
Norton-Taylor R (2016) Brexit would absolutely be applauded in Russia, says defence secretary. Guardian UK, London (24 May 2016)
Perot E (2019) The Aachen mutual defence clause: a closer look at the Franco-German Treaty. Egmont (26 February 2019)
Sabbagh D (2019) Ex-MI6 chief criticises threat to withdraw security cooperation with EU. Guardian UK, London (09 October 2019)
Santolo A (2019) BREXIT CHAOS as Theresa May issues no deal U-TURN – 'she wants to divide Brexiteers'. Express. London, (15 February 2019)
Sedghi A, Arnett G, Bengtesson H (2015) What Conservative manifesto's key themes reveal about party's priorities. Guardian UK, London (14 April 2015)
Shearer A (2000) Britain, France and the Saint-Malo declaration: tactical rapprochement or strategic entente? Camb Rev Int Aff 13(2):283–298
Smith K (2017) Brexit and British foreign policy: between a rock and a hard place. UK in a Changing World, (20 June 2017)
Sparrow A (2014) David Cameron's commons statement on Ukraine. Guardian UK, London (10 March 2014)
Stewart H (2018) May's plan 'sticks in the throat', says Boris Johnson as he resigns over Brexit. Guardian UK, London (09 July 2018)
Sweeney S, Winn N (2020) EU security and defence cooperation in times of dissent: analysing PESCO, the European defence fund and the European Intervention Initiative (EI2) in the shadow of Brexit. Defence Stud 20(3):232
Tardy T (2014) CSDP: getting third states on board. Eur Inst Secur Stud Brief 6:6
Traynor I (2014) Ukraine crisis: Crimea announces referendum on joining Russia. Guardian UK, London (06 March 2014)
Verhofstadt G (2006) The United States of Europe (The Federal Trust). Federal Trust for Education & Research
Watt N (2011) David Cameron mocks Cathy Ashton after 'rogue briefing'. Guardian UK, London (15 March 2011)
Weber M (1965) Politics as a vocation. Fortress Press
Weber M (2015) Weber's rationalism and modern society, translated and edited by Tony Waters and Dagmar Waters. Palgrave Books, p 129
Weston A, Maduraud F (2021) Partnerships in security and defence. In: Rehrl J (ed) Handbook on CSDP: the common security and defence policy of the European Union. Federal Ministry of Defence of the Republic of Austria, p 175
Whitman R (2018) UK foreign and security policy post-Brexit: the search for a European strategy. Swedish Institute of International Affairs, Stockholm, p 6
Whitman R (2019) The UK's European diplomatic strategy for Brexit and beyond. Int Aff 95(2)
Whitman RG (2017) The UK and EU foreign, security and defence policy after Brexit: integrated, associated or detached? Natl Inst Econ Rev 238:43, 48
Wiese Z (2019) Von der Leyen rows back on 'United States of Europe'. Politico (18 July 2019)
Witney N (2019) European Defence and the New Commission. European Council on Foreign Relations, London, (30 September 2019)
Witney N (2021) AUKUS: After the sugar rush. European Council on Foreign Relations (24 September 2021)
Zavrsnik G (2017) Mogherini: 'Britain will lose more from Brexit than EU'. Politico (20 April 2017)

Unlocking the UK's Digital and Services Economy Through Free Trade Agreements

David Collins

1 Introduction

The UK's departure from the European Union (EU) presented an opportunity for the country to establish an independent trade policy, a key component of which is the signing of preferential Free Trade Agreements (FTAs). As of early 2023, three years since 'Brexit' took full effect, more than 70 of these international agreements have been finalized covering just over 60% of the UK's global trade. While this falls short of the government's target of 80% coverage by the end of 2022,[1] it remains a remarkable achievement, especially given the complications associated with negotiations during the Covid-19 pandemic and the UK's relative lack of expertise in trade negotiation, having relied for this on the EU Commission for decades. In contrast to the EU, which requires the consent of multiple stakeholders for its FTAs through long periods of debates, the UK has a greater ability to customize its FTAs to its particular circumstances and, while it does engage in public consultations on trade agreements, these tend not to be exploited to frustrate treaty ratification by lobby groups or regional governments. The EU routinely takes many years to finalize its FTAs and has infamously abandoned some agreements, such as the Transatlantic Trade and Investment Partnership (TTIP) with the US because of resistance from minority agitators. As such, freeing itself from the EU was often cited as one of the UK's chief advantages of Brexit by the project's proponents.

The UK has therefore sought to achieve deeper trade liberalization with its trading partners through FTAs than it had done as a member of the EU. This is especially in relation to trade in services and digital for which the UK has comparative advantage

[1] Pickard (2022).

D. Collins (✉)
International Economic Law, City, University of London, London, UK
e-mail: David.Collins.1@city.ac.uk

E. Guinchard, C. Panara (eds.), *The New Relationship between the United Kingdom and the European Union*, https://doi.org/10.1007/978-3-031-70652-3_14

on the world stage. In 2021, services accounted for 80 per cent of the UK's economic output and 82 per cent of its employment.[2] Services trade has also grown remarkably in the past decade, a trend which has accelerated since the Covid-19 pandemic and the work from home revolution. The so-called Fourth Industrial Revolution of which the UK is an emblematic participant, predicated on automation, inter-connection and technology, requires an international legal framework that is predictable, flexible and accommodating of rapid change.

Trade in services depends heavily on how international data flows are regulated. Rules on cross-border data therefore impact heavily on services trade, for example, e-commerce and banking services, and finance, including blockchain/ cryptocurrencies. Cross-border data flows also affect innovation and by extension foreign investment. It is no surprise, then, that digital trade is an important element of the UK's trade policy. Information and Communication Technology (ICT) goods made up 4.1% of total UK exports of goods and 9.1% of total UK imports of goods in 2020. Moreover, potentially digitally delivered services comprised 74.9% of total UK exports of services and 58.8% of total UK imports of services over the same period.[3] Yet the management of data raises questions of safety and security which include issues privacy and consumer protection, such as data transfer, data storage, anonymization, data residency and cybersecurity. Trade agreements need to address trade liberalization and the wider public interest (e.g. safety and security). These concerns are often in conflict, requiring careful balancing in domestic trade policy, as disciplined by international law.

Services trade is poorly liberalized relative to trade in goods largely because of regulatory divergence.[4] Multilateral rules for trade in services under the World Trade Organization (WTO)'s General Agreement on Trade in Services (GATS) and various instruments touching on digital trade (such as the moratorium on customs duties on electronic transmissions) are generally less complete than they are for goods. Even in sectors where trade in services are notionally open, the failure to fully recognize the professional qualifications of services suppliers is a major obstacle. This results in much inefficiency in terms not only of trade barriers but also in compliance costs due to a lack of transparency and predictability.[5]

The UK has attempted to address these shortcomings through bilateral and regional arrangements concluded since its departure from the EU. Preferential FTAs concluded bilaterally or regionally are accepted as breaches of the WTO's Most Favoured Nation principle of equal treatment among all trading partners[6] provided that (in the case of services) these arrangements satisfy the requirements set out in GATS Article V, which essentially requires that the formation of the preferential trading arrangement must lower barriers to trade, have substantial

[2]Brien (2022).

[3]Digital Trade UK, 2020, Office of National Statistics (5 September 2022).

[4]World Trade Organization, World Trade Report 2019.

[5]See e.g. Willemyns (2022) Chapter One.

[6]GATS Art II.

sectoral coverage, and be notified to the WTO. Through its range of preferential trade treaties, the UK aims to establish an international legal framework to promote fair and open trade across a range of services sectors, from telecoms and digital technology to banking, financial and professional services.

This chapter will explore some of the UK's FTAs that have been negotiated, and in some cases signed, since formally departing the EU at the end of January 2020 at which point it was legally able to sign international trade treaties of its own accord. It will begin by examining UK FTAs that have already been concluded before turning to those which are currently under active negotiation. It must be conceded from the outset that achieving progress in the coverage of services and digital trade typically requires concessions in unrelated areas, such as tariffs and non-tariff barriers on goods or temporary movement of persons. While these matters are therefore unquestionably important in terms of the UK's trade policy, they will not be examined directly in this chapter.

2 UK's Concluded FTAs and Services/Digital Coverage

The UK has negotiated more than 70 FTAs since its departure from the EU, many of which (as with Canada) were trade continuity agreements (otherwise known as roll-overs) of pre-existing EU agreements. In the years following the Brexit vote, many believed that even the fairly straightforward, status quo preserving roll-overs would not be possible, given the EU's much greater bargaining strength and the size of its internal market compared to that of the UK.[7] Other FTAs, as with Australia and New Zealand (signed but not yet in force) were entirely new. While generally speaking the UK's FTAs have prioritized trade in goods, services and digital have been featured in all of them to varying degrees.

2.1 EU: The UK-EU Trade and Cooperation Agreement (TCA)

Among the most significant of FTAs for the UK is the Trade and Cooperation Agreement (TCA) with the EU, finalized at the end of 2020. The EU remains the UK's largest single trading partner and likely will do for some time, even though as a percentage of the UK's total trade this relationship has been in decline for years. While the TCA has a special status as an FTA because it represents the reframing of a disintegrated customs union and single market, it is still an FTA granting preferential treatment to the partner country than would be available under WTO MFN terms.

[7] See further Collins (2019).

The TCA has a digital trade chapter that is encouraging in that it contains a number of provisions designed to promote free flow of data, facilitating the supply of much cross-border services.[8] The chapter requires the UK and EU not to impose customs duties or tariffs on electronic transmissions (such as software) provided in its territory; not require businesses to obtain prior authorisation for any services purely because they are provided by electronic means; and not require the forced transfer of source code as a prerequisite to doing business in its territory. The TCA also contains material on data localization ensuring that signatories do not require that the use of computing facilities or processing of data takes place in its territory; not to make data transfers contingent on the use of computing facilities in its territory; and not to prohibit the storage or processing of data in the other party's territory.[9] Still, the TCA's rules on digital trade do not force the UK or EU to remove existing measures which might be regarded by some as barriers to trade. Many such measures are likely to continue to be permitted, primarily because of numerous public policy carve-outs. For example, although both parties make commitments on cross-border data flows, they remain able to impose conditions on transfers of personal data where these are considered justified to protect privacy. The EU's General Data Protection Regulation (GDPR) is very strict on this issue. For the time being, the UK has established the EU GDPR as part of its domestic law since leaving in the EU, enabling it to retain data equivalence with the EU.

The TCA's coverage for services is rather limited. Rather than open services sectors to supply by temporary movement of professionals (Mode 4 of services supply) through generous mobility provisions, the services chapter merely sets out frameworks through which qualifications of services providers may be recognized. Service suppliers, independent professionals and short-term business visitors must fall into one of the sectors listed in the annexes, while business visitors for establishment purposes and intra-corporate transferees are not subject to sectoral limitations. All categories of Mode 4 service suppliers are subject to country-specific reservations. These commitments are only somewhat more generous than those found in GATS. The EU also did not grant full equivalence to the UK's financial services, restricting the number and volume of transactions between the parties.

One area of modest success in the TCA is in relation to legal services, a £30 billion industry in the UK. The EU Lawyer's Establishment Directive (98/5/EC) ceased to apply to UK lawyers at the end of the transition period. UK lawyers seeking to provide legal advice in the EU must now deal with 27 separate regulatory regimes, as each Member State has its own rules relating to the legal profession. This means that a lawyer seeking to provide legal advice must satisfy the requirement of the relevant Member State they are seeking to enter. Encouragingly the principle of 'home title' practice was recognised in the TCA. Under the 'home title' principle, parties to the TCA agree to permit practice by lawyers of the other party under their home jurisdiction professional qualification with regards to advice on home country

[8] Title III Chapter 1.

[9] Article 201 et seq.

and public international law, as well as arbitration, conciliation and mediation both across borders and in person in the foreign country. On their own these are already sizable areas of the legal services market for most UK lawyers serving clients in the EU. Unfortunately, though, the TCA appears to contemplate a restrictive interpretation of the home title rules. The relevant part of the TCA (Annex 22) expressly refers to the categories of Contractual Services Suppliers (CSSs) and Independent Professionals (IPs) but it omits other key categories of business visitors such as Intra-Corporate Transferees (ICTs) and Business Visitors for Establishment/Investment Purposes (BVEP/BVIP). The legal services provisions in the TCA therefore appear only to apply to lawyers who qualify as either CSSs or IPs. This is a small group, excluding many of the services normally supplied on the crucial fly-in-fly-out basis, meaning that the foreign lawyer enters the country to represent a client in a brief transaction or arbitration hearing to leave again shortly thereafter. Article 194 of the TCA extends this to legal advice on home country (UK) and international law, but not host state law (the law of the relevant EU member state), unless that state wishes to grant this right, which typically requires registration and further qualifications.

When contemplating the TCA's coverage of services (as well as digital and other areas) it is important to recognize that the TCA is not a static instrument. It has future negotiations built into it, complete with specialized committees with the remit to further liberalization on a wide range of issues. For example, the TCA's Committee on Services, Investment and Digital Trade, which has met twice (in October 2021 and October 2022), has undertaken preparatory technical work for reviewing recommendations for mutual recognition submitted by professional bodies. It also received a joint recommendation for a Mutual Recognition Agreement (MRA) from the Architects Council of Europe and the UK Architects Registration Board, potentially precluding the need for requalification or other procedural impediments to cross-border delivery of services in that field.[10] It is a small step, but one which is indicative of a direction of travel towards less burdensome regulation of trade in other, more important sectors, such as legal services.

2.2 *The UK-Japan Comprehensive Economic Partnership Agreement (CEPA)*

The CEPA, which is primarily a roll-over of the EU-Japan agreement with some modifications, contains extensive provisions on services.[11] With regard to services commitments, CEPA adopts a negative list approach. This means that the list of services which cannot satisfy liberalisation obligations under CEPA (e.g. market

---

[10] The second Trade Specialised Committee on Services, Investment and Digital Trade under the EU-UK Trade and Cooperation Agreement Brussels, 20 October 2022 13:30 – 16:00 (BST)/ 14.30-17.00 (CEST) Borchette Center and via videoconference: Joint Minutes.

[11] Chapter 8.

access, national treatment, most-favoured-nation treatment, prohibition of nationality requirement for senior management and boards of directors, and prohibition of performance requirements) are listed as a reservation in an Annex to the agreement (Annex 8). Japan's reservations for existing measures for cross-border services and investment liberalisation in CEPA is identical to those found in the EU-Japan treaty. On the temporary stay and movement of natural persons for business purposes there have been some improvements in CEPA compared to the EU agreement.[12]

There are a number of provisions in CEPA's electronic commerce chapter reflecting new technologies, demonstrating that the UK takes liberalization of digital trade seriously and acting as a benchmark for future negotiations in this area with countries such as Canada and the US. Largely replicating the provisions of the EU-Japan FTA, these provisions include clarity on the disclosure of source code and cryptology; confirmation of the validity of e-contracts and e-signatures; overarching principles on access to and use of the internet; enhanced consumer protection/data protection provisions; clarity on use of government data and associated restrictions; a ban on unjustified data localisation.[13] The UK-Japan CEPA is arguably still weak with regards to rules on protecting personal information (at least from the perspective of regimes such as that of the EU) and clarity regarding consumer protections where safeguards may be enforced. There is also a lack of clarity regarding liability when digital transactions cross multiple platforms involving numerous actors or entities. This latter point can be restrictive for the regulated professions and financial services more generally. The digital trade provisions of the CEPA expressly do not apply to legal services delivered digitally (Art 8.70.5)—there is no other mention of legal services in the text of the CEPA.

2.3 *Australia and New Zealand FTAs*

The UK signed FTAs with both Australia and New Zealand—its first entirely new FTAs since Brexit. These are both comprehensive agreements with chapters covering services and digital trade as well as goods. The UK's FTA with Australia in particular attracted some criticism for being sub-optimal in relation to agriculture, where it was alleged that the UK surrendered more market access than it obtained. As with most modern FTAs, the coverage of services in the Australia and New Zealand agreements are modest, offering limited improvements upon GATS. The respective chapters on Cross-Border Trade in Services grant non-discrimination based on nationality and prohibit quantitative market access restrictions to most services, but there are numerous carve outs, for example, on services investment that involves the purchase of land and the delivery of social services such as public education, transport and health. The agreements prohibit Parties from requiring a

[12] See further, Morita Jaeger and Ayele (2020).

[13] Section F (Electronic Commerce).

service supplier of the other Party to establish or maintain a representative office or any form of enterprise, or to be resident, in its territory as a condition for the cross-border supply of a service, but again there are exceptions to this rule in certain sectors such as telecommunications.[14]

There are sensible rules for streamlining domestic regulation of services in the Australia and New Zealand FTAs, along the lines of that agreed in the WTO's new Domestic Services Regulation initiative, discussed further below. Parties to these agreements are encouraged, but not required, to recognize foreign qualifications of services providers, limited the capacity of professionals to supply services using expertise they have acquired at home (with legal services a good example, although 'home' state law practice is allowed). Both the Australia and New Zealand FTAs establish committees on trade in services with the UK with a view to negotiating further liberalization in the future. It is hoped that going forward, greater progress will be made in terms of temporary stay of business-people (beyond the current 90 days) as well as deeper recognition of foreign qualifications in professions such as legal services, precluding re-qualification or practice in certain fields.

The digital trade chapters of the Australia and New Zealand FTAs are world-leading, enabling free flow of data across borders and prohibiting data localization, with limited exceptions. Electronic contracts are also recognized as is cooperation on cybersecurity. The UK-Australia FTA also contains a novel "Innovation" chapter which outlines plans for cooperation in areas such as Artificial Intelligence and digital identities.[15] It will be interesting to see if this chapter, or something like it, appears in future UK FTAs and what initiatives they lead to. Cooperation in relation to digital technologies, such as AI, features in several of the UK's Strategic Approach statements for various upcoming FTAs. These elements can also be found in the UK-Singapore Digital Economy Agreement.

2.4 Singapore Digital Economy Agreement (DEA)

As two of the world's most digitally advanced economies, the UK and Singapore signed the Digital Economy Agreement (DEA) which came into force in June 2022. The DEA is modelled on the trilateral Singapore-Chile-New Zealand Digital Economy Partnership Agreement (DEPA) which is perhaps the most modern digital trade agreement in the world.[16] As digital-only agreement, the DEA was designed to open digital markets between the two countries, amending various provisions of the UK-Singapore FTA. The DEA includes guaranteed tariff-free flow of digital content,

[14] See generally UK-Australia Chapter 8 (Trade in Services) and UK-New Zealand Chapter 9 (Cross-Border Trade in Services).

[15] See generally UK-Australia Chapter 14 (Digital Trade) and UK-New Zealand Chapter 15 (Digital Trade).

[16] See further Soprana (2021), p. 143.

free flow of trusted data guaranteed protections for personal data and intellectual property and cheaper trade through the adoption of digital trading systems. Parties agree to support technologies such as electronic contracts and electronic signatures, eliminating costly paperwork and promoting transparency. Under Article 8.60 each Party shall maintain a legal framework governing electronic transactions consistent with the principles of the UNCITRAL Model Law on Electronic Commerce 1996 or the United Nations Convention on the Use of Electronic Communications in International Contracts. Electronic authentication is facilitated through the requirement that parties must not deny legal effect to e-contracts, e-invoices and bills of lading, secured with e-signatures.[17] The two countries will also cooperate on the use of single window systems to submit data to government and work towards the mutual recognition of digital signatures & authentication technologies, clearer rules to underpin the use of cross-border e-payments, adopting high international standards, encouraging the use of open APIs and promoting interoperability between different e-payment platforms.[18]

The DEA further ensures that there will be no customs duties on electronic transmissions.[19] It also prohibits unnecessary restrictions on the movement of data, including localisation requirements.[20] Both sides commit to maintaining existing high standards of data protection.[21] The DEA further prohibits the mandatory disclosure of software source code and algorithms[22] as a condition of market access. Both the UK and Singapore commit to making government-held data publicly available to support innovation, in particular by SMEs.[23] On online consumer protection, the DEA contains promises to maintain high regulatory standards to guard against fraudulent or misleading online practices.[24] The agreement also includes a range of provisions designed to support key growth sectors such as AI, fintech, regtech and lawtech, with dedicated dialogues established to support each rapidly growing sector.[25] There is an over-arching commitment to cooperate on matters relating to the digital economy.[26] Since the UK-Singapore DEA is a digital only instrument, it enables agreement on a narrower range of areas without requiring concessions in other, potentially contentious areas, such as tariffs on agricultural products. This approach may be worthwhile pursuing with other countries, as the US has done for example with Japan in the US-Japan Digital Trade Agreement. It is

[17] Art 8.61.

[18] Art 6.13.

[19] Art 8.59 (1). Note that this provision contains an exemption for digital services taxes under subsection (2).

[20] Art 8.61-G(2).

[21] Art 8.61-E.

[22] 8.61-K.

[23] Art 4.

[24] Art 8.61-M.

[25] Art 8.53 (fintech) and 8.61 (lawtech).

[26] Art 3.

probably more feasible in the case of digital trade than with services which engage many more regulatory issues across many sectors.

2.5 *Switzerland Temporary Services Mobility Agreement*

The UK-Switzerland FTA is a trade continuity agreement replicating the relationship that existed between the two countries prior to the UK's departure from the EU. Unfortunately, however, this FTA did not cover services. The UK was able to negotiate and sign the Switzerland Temporary Services Mobility Agreement (SMA) in 2020 which was extended until at least 2025. The SMA allows UK professionals, such as lawyers, to provide services in Switzerland for up to 90 days without a work permit or complete an economic interest test. The SMA also establishes a working group through which the UK and Switzerland aim to develop a comprehensive agreement on the recognition of professional qualifications for service suppliers operating in each other's markets.[27] While these entitlements merely replicate the arrangement that was in place between the two countries while the UK was a member of the EU, the SMA is mentioned here because it does not fully capture the nature of the relationship between the EU and Switzerland which is governed by a series of bilateral agreements.

3 Anticipated UK FTAs Covering Services/Digital

The UK plans to increase its economic engagement with the Indo-Pacific and this is evident in its ongoing trade agreements with partners in this region. Among the most important FTAs here are the bilateral one with India, and the mega-regional CPTPP (a 12-nation comprehensive free trade agreement signed by countries on the Pacific Rim comprising 15% of global GDP), both of which represent a key feature of the UK's economic diplomacy in the region. Under former Prime Minister Liz Truss, the UK had promised to complete negotiations to join the CPTPP by the end of 2022. Truss's predecessor, Boris Johnson, and Indian Prime Minister Narendra Modi in April set a goal to finish negotiating a bilateral free trade agreement by the end of October of the same year. The UK's current PM, Sir Keir Starmer appears keen to conclude the FTA with India but there is still no end date in sight.

[27] Art 16.

3.1 India

The UK and India concluded their sixth round of negotiations for an FTA in December 2022. The agreement is central to the UK's 'Pacific tilt'—a strategy designed to tap into the high growth currently enjoyed by that region.[28] Services and digital are key elements of the planned FTA. The UK's services exports to India amount to £3.2 billion per year and India has an expanding services sector which comprises more than half of its economy. The UK appears to be seeking to enhance these numbers by easing cross-border encouraging regulatory alignment, allowing the UK's financial and professional services businesses to offer expertise, increase trade into the Indian market.[29] On digital technology and innovation, the UK anticipates that the FTA will enable British and Indian businesses to pioneer innovative commercial ventures in fields such as emerging tech, artificial intelligence, and cybersecurity. The UK also seeks to stimulate collaboration between higher education institutions undertaking ground-breaking research through the FTA by including provisions which will enable higher quality interdisciplinary research in fields such as pharmaceuticals and life sciences.[30] Furthermore, the UK wishes to use the FTA to increase opportunities for UK business people to operate in India by enhancing opportunities for business travel while preserve the integrity of the UK's domestic immigration system.[31] India is urging the UK to ease work visa restrictions through the FTA which some believe could lead to a surge in immigration into the UK.[32]

The UK's strategic objectives for the Indian FTA state an objective of pursuing a comprehensive digital chapter that maximises opportunities for digital trade across all sectors of the economy, and businesses of all sizes including Small and Medium Sized Enterprises (SMEs). Much as seen in the UK-Singapore DEA, the UK further seeks predictable and open regulatory principles so that firms can access Indian digital markets freely and in fair competition. The UK also aims to secure commitments on free and trusted cross-border data flows, the prevention of unjustified data localisation, and maintain the UK's high standards for personal data protection along with the promotion of online consumer protection.[33] Accepting a prohibition on data localization may be particularly difficult for India, which has traditionally resisted these kinds of restrictions as an affront to its sovereignty and national security. There are, however, indications that India may be softening its stance on transfer and storage of sensitive data for certain safe countries,[34] which could include the

[28] 'UK-India Free Trade Agreement: The UK's Strategic Approach', UK Department of International Trade (undated) at 5.

[29] Ibid at 7.

[30] Ibid at 7.

[31] Ibid at 12.

[32] U.K. pushes Indo-Pacific trade deals to next year as dissent grows Nikkei Asia (23 Dec 2022).

[33] Strategic Approach at 13.

[34] Raghuraman (2022).

UK. Additionally, the UK-India FTA should facilitate more efficient and secure international trade through use of digital technologies, including through paperless trading and there will be an emphasis on cooperation on evolving areas of trade such as innovation and emerging technologies.[35] The successful conclusion of a UK-India FTA will likely depend on matters other than services and digital, notably the movement of professionals (as noted above), as well as agricultural subsidies. The protection of UK foreign investment in India is also likely to prove controversial given some of the difficulties that investors have experienced in India, particularly in relation to the Indian judicial system.[36]

3.2 Comprehensive Progressive Trans-Pacific Partnership (CPTPP)

Most significantly, formal talks on the UK's accession to the 11-nation CPTPP began in the summer of 2021 after several months of preliminary negotiations. The CPTPP consists of 30 chapters covering tariff reductions and rules on market access for goods as well as services and investment. It also includes disciplines on intellectual property, government procurement, digital trade, trade remedies, state-owned enterprises and SMEs. Accordingly, the CPTPP is an excellent example of a modern, comprehensive FTA in that it encompasses a breadth of topics, achieving economic integration across several countries of varying levels of development to a degree that would not be feasible multilaterally. It is widely recognized as the 'gold standard' FTA. Joining the CPTPP is vital from the perspective of the UK's global role as a champion of free trade because the CPTPP may eventually become a near-global regime for trade governance in conjunction, or perhaps in competition with the WTO.

Chapter 10 of CPTPP which covers services, like the TCA and the CEPA, adopts a negative list approach to the scheduling of market access and national treatment commitments, with all exceptions, restrictions or non-conforming measures listed in Annexes. This format is preferable to the positive list style of the GATS because under a negative list (where only explicitly identified sectors are protected) the default is that the sector is open to international supply, helping identify areas where restrictions remain to be addressed through future negotiations with a view to expanding overall market liberalisation. The negative list approach also opens up future sectors that have not yet been fully realised, such as those dealing with digital trade, and therefore cannot be outlined in a services schedule. Limits on services trade are contained in Annexes, specified for each member. CPTPP Parties commit to recognising the education or experience obtained as well as licences or certifications granted in a particular country for purposes of the fulfilment of criteria for the

[35] UK-India Strategic Approach, above n 28 at 13.

[36] Ranjan (2022).

authorization or certification of services suppliers. This obligation is also subject to exceptions set out in Annexes. For example, Australia has a number of exemptions enabling them to grant preferential treatment to indigenous services suppliers. The agreement further contains commitments on temporary entry to enable the travel of skilled people between Parties for the purpose of doing business, although all movement of temporary personnel remain subject to final approval from national immigration authorities and there are exemptions contained in country Annexes.

For legal services, the CPTPP is among the most progressive trading arrangements in the world. Many of the barriers to trade in legal services are behind the border, including domestic regulations around licensing, certification and requalification. The CPTPP specifically encourages member countries to allow foreign lawyers to operate on a temporary fly-in, fly-out basis and on a fully integrated basis with domestic lawyers. Moreover, the CPTPP's Professional Services Annex, especially paragraphs 9 and 10, sets out a principles-based framework on legal services to support medium and long-term reform of the regulation of foreign lawyers and the legal services sector. This is further enhanced by the creation of a professional services working group that supports the implementation of the framework across the jurisdictions.

On digital trade generally, the Electronic Commerce chapter of the CPTPP,[37] considered to be cutting-edge at the time it was concluded (but lacking some of the innovation material of more modern FTAs such as the DEA), commits Parties not to impose customs duties on digital products. The electronic commerce chapter of the CPTPP does not go as far as some of the digital trade chapters in the UK's new FTAs, such as that with Australia. The CPTPP does not protect algorithms, nor does it contain material on digital identities, for example. The CPTPP's electronic commerce chapter ensures electronic authentication and recognition of electronic signatures. There is also material on online consumer protection as well as access to the internet for the benefit of competition among network providers. This chapter also prohibits data localisation rules by which governments require businesses to store data on their territory, although there are exceptions from this prohibition where the restriction can be justified by public policy objectives, such as privacy protection. The CPTPP further recognizes the importance of protecting personal information, requiring each Party to have an effective enforcement of privacy rules. Ongoing controversies in this area regarding the competing approaches of China, the EU and the US suggest that this is an area where bespoke CPTPP plus (and potentially minus) commitments will be made in the future.[38]

The CPTPP's main privacy provision (Article 14.8.2) requires that parties adopt a legal framework for the protection of the personal information of the users of electronic commerce. A footnote to this provision states a party may comply with the obligation by adopting measures such as a comprehensive privacy, personal information or personal data protection laws, sector-specific laws covering privacy,

---

[37] Chapter 14.

[38] Ciuriak and Ptashkina (2020).

or laws that provide for the enforcement of voluntary undertakings by enterprises relating to privacy. There are also transparency requirements regarding the publishing of laws governing the use of personal information and protections available to the users of e-commerce.

The CPTPP also includes GATS Article XIV-style general exceptions which expressly cover privacy[39] requiring the satisfaction of a four-stage test which essentially mandates that the breach of the digital trade provision must be necessary to achieve 'a legitimate public policy objective' (term undefined and presumptively open-ended). This provision adds that the relevant measure must not be a 'disguised restriction on trade' evoking the chapeau of GATS Article XIV (the general exceptions provision of the GATS). GATS jurisprudence suggests that this will be a very difficult test to pass.[40] This suggests that the privacy justification in the CPTPP's digital trade chapter is not strong, although this may depend on how it is interpreted in practice through the CPTPP's dispute settlement. This same test applies, in slightly modified form, to the prohibition on data transfer restrictions and the prohibition on data localization rules.[41] Comparatively weak privacy rules in the CPTPP (in contrast to the EU's GDPR, for example) could be problematic for UK consumers who will need to trust that their data will not be misused in order to engage in e-commerce with CPTPP countries. Finally, Article 14.15 of the CPTPP requires parties to exchange information and share experiences on regulations, policies, enforcement and compliance regarding electronic commerce, including personal information protection. This could lead to progress in establishing enhanced norms on privacy, perhaps covering such issues as legal professional privilege. As CPTPP membership grows this cooperation could become vital to driving trade liberalization.

The UK has passed to the second stage of negotiations for accession during which its market access offers are being made. It is expected that the UK will accede to the CPTPP in 2023, although there has been some concern recently that the UK's agricultural market access offer has been insufficient.[42] It is difficult to assess whether there is a genuine risk that the UK's accession will not be successful because the process for CPTPP accession is lacking in detail. This is precisely why the establishment of practice, for example through the UK's accession, is so vital to the prospects of the agreement's enlargement in the future. Omission of the details from the treaty language may be pragmatic given the dynamic evolutionary nature of the accession practice. The CPTPP's accession process may need to be modified over time to adapt to changes in global trade and investment patterns as well as the nature of each applicant state. In this regard it is noteworthy that CPTPP negotiators expressly rejected a much more comprehensive text on accession, such

[39] Article 14.11.3.

[40] E.g. United States—Measures Affecting the Cross-Border Supply of Gambling and Betting Services, WT/DS285/AB/R (adopted on 20 April 2005).

[41] Arts 14.11 and 14.13.

[42] Horseman (2022).

as that contained associated with the Trans-Pacific Partnership,[43] the forerunner to the CPTPP. In applying to join the CPTPP, the UK must think strategically regarding which commitments it is prepared to make (for example zero tariffs on most goods) and which it is not (for example denial of recognition for certain professional qualifications) and to consider which compromises it may be expected to make with each Party as it seeks consensus support for its accession.[44]

3.3 Other FTAs Under Negotiation

The UK is currently engaging in negotiations for FTAs with Canada (building upon the rolled-over EU-Canada Comprehensive and Economic Trade Agreement, CETA) and Mexico. These two agreements should work in tandem with the UK's CPTPP accession given Canada and Mexico's membership in the Pacific mega-regional (along with New Zealand, Australia, Singapore and Japan, with which the UK has already signed bilateral FTAs). For services and digital, improving upon the existing Canada-UK Trade Continuity Agreement will focus on the adoption of digital trading systems, such as electronic invoicing. The current restrictiveness of the Canadian telecommunications market, which is highly concentrated, could pose a challenge for UK negotiators.[45] The UK is also pursing trade negotiations with Israel and with the Gulf Cooperation Council (a trade bloc consisting of Bahrain, Kuwait, Oman, Qatar, Saudi Arabia, and the United Arab Emirates). With Israel, the agreement will have a heavy focus on digital and technology because of the natural strengths of both countries in this area.[46] Each of the GCC countries has its own regulatory environment, requiring complex negotiations with each country as well as the GCC's Secretariat. At a general level, each of these planned FTAs aim to be comprehensive in nature covering services as well as goods and also making provision for digital trade, including cooperation in areas of innovation and technology.

The most important and highly anticipated of the UK's originally planned FTAs, and indeed a centrepiece of the UK's Brexit aspiration, was that with the United States. Unfortunately, the US under President Joe Biden appears to be less amenable to a UK FTA than his predecessor, partly as a consequence of the unsettled arrangement on the UK's land border with Ireland. An FTA with the US covering services would have been challenging in any circumstance given that the US appears to have de-prioritized FTAs as part of its international economic policy and also

[43] Art. 30.4.

[44] See further Collins (2023).

[45] 'UK-Canada Free Trade Agreement: The UK's Strategic Approach', Department of International Trade (undated) at 13.

[46] 'UK-Israel Free Trade Agreement: Strategic Approach', Department of International Trade (undated).

because some services, notably legal, are regulated at the state level, making country-wide market access implausible. In this regard it is noteworthy that the UK signed Memoranda of Understanding (MOU) in 2022 with three US states (Indiana, North Carolina and South Carolina) outlining intentions of cooperation in various fields, including technology and academic research 'to meet the needs of an innovative and digital economy.' Of course these are not true trade agreements—they do not create binding obligations under international law.

4 Conclusion

The UK has taken advantage of its independence from the EU to negotiate preferential free trade agreements with more than 70 partners in only a few years. While most of these FTAs have been roll-overs of EU agreements, needed merely for the UK to replicate what it lost from its EU membership, entirely new agreements are now being signed. Accession to the mega-regional CPTPP, expected in 2023, will be a landmark moment in the UK's post-Brexit trade policy, representing a deeper economic engagement with the fastest growing region of the world. Along with the anticipated Indian FTA, the UK's 'tilt' to the Indo-Pacific does not mean that it has chosen to neglect its closest neighbours. The UK-EU TCA remains the UK's most important bilateral trade treaty, designed to minimize trade barriers incrementally via ongoing negotiations across many sectors.

As a consequence of the UK's strongly service-focused economy and its evident commitment to capturing the growing global trend towards digital trade, services and digital will only become more important spheres of economic activity and therefore crucial points of focus in trade negotiations. Services tend to be more tightly regulated than goods and some areas, such as the recognition of professional qualifications for the temporary supply of services, require many years of negotiation and compromise. Likewise, while there is an encouraging momentum towards the establishment of key principles in the liberalization of digital trade, rapid changes in technology as well as contentious issues regarding the handling of sensitive data as it crosses borders, means that securing binding commitments in digital sphere will remain challenging. The UK must therefore continue to press for services disciplines in its bilateral agreements, including in areas such as financial and legal, and to drive forward an agenda of liberalization via free flow of electronic transmissions as well as bans on data localization. Obstacles to achieving these goals will be linked to concessions in other areas, especially agriculture, which has not been discussed in this chapter, and which is highly controversial because of domestic political pressures against zero tariffs and quotas. The UK's new FTAs contain frameworks which promote cooperation in areas like services and digital trade with a view to securing deeper commitments where they have not yet been forthcoming. While there may yet be life in the multilateral arena, as seen for example in the new WTO Services Domestic Regulation initiative, bilateralism and regionalism appear to be the best strategic way forward. Although much is yet to be achieved, the UK is well on its way to setting up a vibrant, dynamic network of FTAs which play to its strengths as a world leader in the modern knowledge economy.

References

Brien P (2022) Service industries: key economic indicators. House of Commons Library (24 March 2022)

Ciuriak D, Ptashkina M (2020) Toward a robust architecture for the regulation of data and data and digital trade. CIGI Paper, vol 240, issue 1

Collins D (2019) Brexit and international trade: the aspiration of global Britain. In: Ahmed T, Fahey E (eds) On Brexit: law justices and injustices. Elgar

Collins D (2023) The UK's Accession to the Comprehensive Progressive Trans-Pacific Partnership (CPTPP): legal obligations and political economy. Int Trade Law Regul 1

Horseman C (2022) London's 2022 CPTPP Accession Hopes Fade. Borderlex (28 September 2022)

Morita Jaeger M, Ayele Y (2020) The UK-Japan Comprehensive Economic Partnership Agreement: lessons for the UK's future trade agreements. UK Trade Policy Observatory (December 2020)

Pickard J (2022) UK government set to miss 2022 target on global trade deals. Financial Times (30 December 2022)

Raghuraman A (2022) India's data localization pivot can revamp global digital diplomacy. South Asia Source (5 December 2022)

Ranjan P (2022) Investment protection a must in India-UK FTA. The Hindustan Times (31 October 2022)

Soprana M (2021) The Digital Economy Partnership Agreement (DEPA): assessing the significance of the new trade agreement on the block. Trade Law Dev 13(1):143

Willemyns I (2022) Digital services in international trade law. Cambridge University Press

Environmental Cooperation in the Post-Brexit Era: Enhancing Collaborative Approaches for Environmental Protection and Conservation

Belen Olmos Giupponi

1 Introduction: Brexit and Its Implications for Environmental Law

The United Kingdom's withdrawal from the European Union (commonly referred to as Brexit) has resulted in substantial impacts on the country's environmental legislation.[1] At the time of the departure from the EU, UK environmental legislation was mostly EU legislation. While one of the main Brexit claims was that the UK could craft its own policies without being bound to observe the European Union's regulatory framework, British environmental law continues to be influenced by EU law in a number of areas.

Several important considerations arise then in the context of the UK-EU relations on environmental protection after Brexit. Drawing on scholarly research, one significant aspect to note is the introduction of the Retained EU Legislation (Revocation and Reform) Act[2] and of the sunset clause, which aims to modify and retain EU law within the UK legal framework.[3] The key provisions are primarily concentrated in

[1] Scotford and Bowman (2016), pp. 416–419. See, also, Jacquelyn MacLennan and Genevra Forwood, Environmental law after Brexit, 9 March 2021, available at https://www.whitecase.com/insight-alert/environmental-law-after-brexit (last accessed 31/01/2024) and Client Earth, Environmental Law & Governance Post-Brexit, available at https://www.clientearth.org/latest/documents/environmental-law-governance-post-brexit (last accessed 31/01/2024).

[2] Retained EU Law (Revocation and Reform) Bill, 8 June 2023, available at https://bills.parliament.uk/bills/3340 (last accessed 31/01/2024).

[3] 'Retained EU law' is a concept created by the European Union (Withdrawal) Act 2018. This act took a 'snapshot' of EU law as it applied to the UK at the end of the Brexit transition period on

B. O. Giupponi (✉)
International & European Environmental Law, Department Law & Social Sciences, Middlesex University, London, UK
e-mail: b.olmosgiupponi@mdx.ac.uk

E. Guinchard, C. Panara (eds.), *The New Relationship between the United Kingdom and the European Union*, https://doi.org/10.1007/978-3-031-70652-3_15

the initial three clauses, focusing on the retention of direct EU legislation.[4] Another significant element is the potential extension of the sunset clause, which pertains to Parliament's powers to modify legislation under a particular section.[5] This modification of the policy landscape introduces concerns of a potential "cliff edge" scenario where legislation could abruptly cease to apply. Certainly, the Retained EU Legislation Revocation and Reform Act plays a crucial role in shaping the overall dynamics of the UK's environmental policy landscape after Brexit.[6]

During the Brexit negotiations, environmental protection and climate change issues emerged as crucial points of contention in the post-Brexit scenario. The concept of "dynamic alignment" proposed by the European Union faced resistance from the United Kingdom, which sought to disengage from EU environmental standards following its withdrawal from the Union. Moreover, concerns were raised regarding the potential weakening of robust environmental standards in the absence of the oversight provided by the Court of Justice of the European Union (CJEU). During the time of the EU membership, the UK had frequently faced infringement proceedings in the area of environmental protection.[7] Now, due to these changes, there are asymmetries or divergent applications of environmental law.

The EU-UK Trade and Cooperation Agreement (TCA) marked a significant milestone in establishing a more constructive relationship and ushering in a new era of bilateral cooperation. As the specific provisions of the TCA were negotiated and finalized, particular attention was given to the intricate details of the new legal framework. Among the contentious issues were the inclusion of a "non-regression" clause, which aimed to prevent a decline in the level of environmental protection by the UK after the end of the transition period, with the commitment to maintain EU binding targets, and the adoption of re-balancing measures, among other significant aspects.

Furthermore, Title XXI of the UK-EU Agreement on the Level-Playing Field incorporates environmental law principles that the UK should respect and that are relevant to the application of environmental provisions, including the polluter pays principle and the precautionary principle. In other areas, such as the import and export of chemicals, there are specific TCA provisions on regulatory cooperation and transparency concerning, for instance, the classification of substances.

---

31 December 2020 and provided for it to continue to apply in domestic law, available at https://www.lawsociety.org.uk/topics/brexit/retained-eu-law (last accessed 31/01/2024).

[4]Additionally, the scheduled revocation set for the year 2023, the Retained EU Law (Revocation and Reform) Act received Royal Assent on 29 June 2023, marking the end of the legislation by the year's conclusion.

[5]Cater (2023) (last accessed 31/01/2024).

[6]Graeme Cowie, Research Briefing, Retained EU Law (Revocation and Reform) Act 2023, 28 July 2023.

[7]House of Lords - Brexit: environment and climate change - European Union Committee, House of Lords, Brexit: environment and climate change, https://publications.parliament.uk/pa/ld201617/ldselect/ldeucom/109/10903.htm (last accessed 31/01/2024).

Cooperation in the realm of environmental governance manifests itself in various ways, encompassing bilateral relations facilitated by committees and the inclusion of specific provisions in the legislation, such as sunset clauses. Notably, the Department for Environment, Food and Rural Affairs (DEFRA) and devolution issues have prompted discussions on enhancing environmental ambitions within the devolved administrations.[8] Particularly in Scotland, there is a pronounced drive for heightened environmental aspirations. Given the post-Brexit landscape, there arises a necessity to recalibrate inter-governmental relations within the United Kingdom to adapt to the new context.[9]

Amidst the implementation of post-Brexit legislations, apprehensions arose regarding the potential impact of the legislation and the imminent sunset date on environmental protection in the UK. The limited timeframe poses a significant challenge for parliament to adequately review, replace, or reiterate the extensive body of EU-derived environmental laws. This raises concerns about ensuring equivalent levels of environmental protection and conservation, which the UK is presently obligated to uphold.[10] The impending environmental legislation at the time of writing is supposed to help achieve the targets set out in the 25-Year Environmental Plan established in 2018 aimed at enhancing the natural environment.[11]

In turn, the Environment Act 2021 (EA) was finally enacted embodying the UK's new framework of environmental protection. This would help dissipate the potential risk of de-harmonization, i.e. of being subject to uneven standards. In terms of enforcement, the newly designed environmental policy after the adoption of the EA will fill a gap in this regard.

In terms of the implementation of international environmental agreements, it has been significantly affected by the repercussions of Brexit, leading to substantial transformations in the legal and institutional frameworks governing environmental governance in the United Kingdom in different sectoral areas.

In what regards access to environmental information, the Aarhus on Access to Information, Public Participation in Decision-Making and Access to Justice in Environmental Matters, was initially incorporated into the UK legal system through

---

[8] Department for Environment, Food and Rural Affairs: Policy paper 19 August 2020: Environment Bill - environmental targets, available at https://www.gov.uk/government/publications/environment-bill-2020/august-2020-environment-bill-environmental-targets#:~:text=Target%20framework&text=It%20requires%20government%20to%20set,forward%20by%2031%20October%202022 (last accessed 31/01/2024).

[9] Title XI. Level Playing Field for Open and Fair Competition and Sustainable Development. Article 305. Principles and objectives.

[10] J. Jones, The Retained EU Law (Revocation and Reform) Bill & The Environment, available at https://www.msbsolicitors.co.uk/the-retained-eu-law-revocation-and-reform-bill-the-environment/ (last accessed 31/01/2024).

[11] Office for Environmental Protection, Progress in improving the natural environment in England (2021/2022), updated on 19 January 2023, available at https://www.theoep.org.uk/report/progress-improving-natural-environment-england-20212022 (last accessed 31/01/2024).

the adoption of EU legislation.[12] However, following the UK's withdrawal from the European Union, it no longer falls directly under the jurisdiction of the European Court of Justice, which previously played a pivotal role in the interpretation and enforcement of the Aarhus Convention. As a consequence, the UK has undertaken the task of establishing new domestic mechanisms and processes to guarantee adherence to the Convention's provisions.

Likewise, the UK's departure from the EU has had ramifications for the transboundary dimensions of environmental decision-making and cooperation, necessitating the renegotiation of agreements and frameworks to sustain the effective implementation of the Aarhus Convention in the post-Brexit context. Scholars, such as Lee, have indicated that Brexit has eroded public participation under the Aarhus Convention.[13]

The implications of Brexit on UK environmental legislation have resulted in multifaceted consequences that warrant closer examination. Primarily, the withdrawal from the European Union has necessitated substantive alterations to EU-derived legislation within the UK's legal framework. To ensure regulatory continuity, the government has undertaken the task of amending or enacting new laws to address domains previously governed by EU regulations, such as air and water quality, waste management, and wildlife protection.

Moreover, the UK government has unequivocally expressed its steadfast commitment to upholding existing environmental standards following Brexit. It has articulated its intention to safeguard a high level of protection for both the environment and public health. In light of this commitment, the government has proposed the establishment of an independent watchdog (the Office for the Environment) endowed with the responsibility of overseeing and monitoring environmental regulatory practices, thus ensuring compliance with these robust standards.

Concurrently, the negotiation of new trade agreements by the UK subsequent to its departure from the EU introduces an additional dimension that could significantly impact environmental legislation. To maintain parity, the government has taken a firm stance, affirming its non-negotiable position of not compromising on environmental standards during trade negotiations.[14] The UK government seeks to establish and uphold a level playing field to prevent any potential dilution of environmental safeguards. In this regard, the Environment, Food and Rural Affairs Committee has emphasised that the government should formally commit to upholding animal welfare and environmental standards in all post-Brexit trade deals.

Furthermore, the UK's separation from the EU has resulted in the loss of access to certain EU funding streams that previously supported a range of environmental initiatives. In response, the UK government has proactively initiated the creation

[12] The Aarhus Convention, an international accord was signed by the UK on xx and entered into force on xx. The Aarhus Convention was signed by the United Kingdom (UK) on the 25th of June 1998 and ratified on 23 February 2005.

[13] See, Lee (2023), pp. 756–784.

[14] See, for instance, the reports on the Free Trade Agreement with Australia.

of new domestic funding mechanisms, which are designed to provide financial support for crucial environmental projects and initiatives, ensuring the continuity of environmental progress.

Lastly, the ramifications of Brexit extend to the recalibration of the UK's relationship with international environmental organizations. Notably, the UK's participation in the framework of other relevant international environmental treaties, such as the United Nations Framework Convention on Climate Change has necessitated a reassessment. The UK government, cognizant of the importance of global cooperation in addressing pressing environmental challenges, has underscored its unwavering commitment to continued collaboration on a global scale. Precisely, the collaboration between the UK and the EU will also extend to include participation in several Multilateral Environmental Agreements (MEAs). Globally, the importance of unified EU-UK leadership in addressing the climate crisis has been elevated within the context of international negotiations aimed at mitigating the most severe impacts of the climate emergency.

In an overall appraisal of the influence of Brexit on UK environmental legislation, one can say that the post-Brexit period in what concerns environmental protection is characterized by a comprehensive array of factors, encompassing legislative adjustments, the preservation of environmental standards, trade considerations, domestic funding mechanisms, and international cooperation. These facets collectively shape the landscape of UK environmental policy in the post-Brexit era, warranting rigorous analysis and evaluation.

Overall, the impact of Brexit on UK environmental legislation is still unfolding, and the full extent of the changes may not be apparent for some time. However, the UK government has signalled its commitment to maintaining environmental standards and protecting public health and has taken steps to ensure continuity in the regulation of key issues.

Against this backdrop, this chapter addresses the question of environmental protection in a post-Brexit context, from a multi-layered perspective, contemplating other areas of law with a bearing on environmental protection, such as trade and the environment. Within the analytical framework of this chapter, we embark on a comprehensive exploration of the prospective UK-EU dynamics in the post-Brexit landscape. This investigation is purposefully structured around the multifaceted environmental issues of convergence, divergence, and harmonization of norms. These elements serve as essential focal points, enabling us to discern and elucidate the intricate dimensions of environmental governance and cooperation between the United Kingdom and the European Union, as they navigate the challenges and opportunities arising in the aftermath of Brexit.

2 Unravelling Brexit: Assessing the Impact on the Legal Landscape of UK Environmental Law

Following the withdrawal of the United Kingdom from the European Union, there has been a concerted effort to preserve and uphold environmental laws and regulations that were previously governed by EU membership.[15] To this end, the UK government has implemented a series of legislative measures aimed at replacing and modernizing the environmental regulations previously established under EU law. One noteworthy example is the Environment Bill, which has undergone parliamentary scrutiny and introduced new initiatives to safeguard the environment.[16] These include setting targets for air quality improvement, addressing the issue of plastic pollution, mandating biodiversity net gain, redefining the contours of the energy policy, and defining strategic priorities to counteract the climate emergency. Ensuring compliance with retained EU legislation remains a significant priority during the post-Brexit era.[17]

The post-Brexit regulatory landscape in the UK encompasses several key areas. In the wake of Brexit, a discernible array of notable distinctions and modifications has emerged in the realm of environmental legislation when juxtaposed with the pre-existing European Union framework. These disparities can be observed in various areas.

Without delving into details, areas for enhanced regulation after Brexit include the regulation of chemicals and genetically modified organisms under the Chemicals (Health and Safety) and Genetically Modified Organisms (Contained Use) (EU Exit) Regulations 2019.[18] These regulations establish a comprehensive framework for ensuring the safe and responsible handling of such substances within the UK. Additionally, the UK Emissions Trading Scheme has been introduced as a replacement for the country's participation in the EU Emissions Trading System.[19] Designed to support the UK in achieving its carbon reduction targets, this scheme plays a crucial role in addressing climate change. Furthermore, the Conservation of Habitats and Species (Amendment) (EU Exit) Regulations 2019 have been implemented to update the UK's regulations for the protection of habitats and species, aligning them with the country's new post-Brexit realities.[20] Lastly, the Air Quality (Amendment) (EU Exit) Regulations 2019 have been enacted to ensure

---

[15] Lee (2017), pp. 155–164.

[16] Fisher (2020), pp. 163–189.

[17] https://www.legislation.gov.uk/ukpga/2021/30/contents/enacted (last accessed 31/01/2024).

[18] Burns et al. (2018).

[19] UK Government, *Participating in the UK-ETS*, 17 April 2023, available at https://www.gov.uk/government/publications/participating-in-the-uk-ets/participating-in-the-uk-ets (last accessed 31/01/2024).

[20] UK Government, The Conservation of Habitats and Species (Amendment) (EU Exit) Regulations 2019, available at https://www.legislation.gov.uk/ukdsi/2019/9780111176573 (accessed 9 June 2023).

that the UK's air quality regulations remain up to date, and effective following its departure from the EU.[21] These measures collectively reflect the UK's commitment to maintaining robust environmental standards and addressing key environmental challenges in a post-Brexit context.

In terms of legislative autonomy, which was at the heart of the Brexit claims. With the UK's withdrawal from the European Union, the UK has gained the ability to develop and amend its environmental laws independently. Although the UK government now has the authority to create domestic legislation tailored to its specific environmental priorities and challenges, a certain level of alignment is expected.[22]

With regard to the regulatory alignment; while the UK has retained many EU environmental laws through the European Union (Withdrawal) Act 2018, there have been certain modifications and adjustments to align them with the country's new regulatory framework. After that, the UK government has the freedom to adapt and refine environmental regulations to suit national circumstances and objectives. While certain regulatory mechanisms have been replicated by the UK, a comprehensive environmental policy strategy remained largely absent until the introduction of the Retained EU law (Revocation and Reform) Act, which aims to repeal all EU legislation by the conclusion of 2023.[23]

As a result of Brexit, the UK no longer falls under the jurisdiction of the European Court of Justice (ECJ), which previously played a role in interpreting and enforcing EU environmental laws. The CJEU has exerted a significant influence on the environmental policies the UK as a member state, historically dubbed as "Dirty man of Europe". The UK has replaced the monitoring of the CJEU by a new system. Instead, the UK has established its own legal mechanisms and institutions to oversee environmental governance and ensure compliance with domestic regulations.

The issue surrounding the preservation of environmental standards has been a subject of considerable contention and debate within scholarly discourse. The UK government has committed to maintaining high environmental standards post-Brexit. It has set out its own policies and frameworks to address issues such as air and water quality, waste management, biodiversity conservation, and climate change mitigation. While some standards may remain aligned with EU regulations, others may undergo modifications or diverge from the EU approach.

Some scholars argue that, in the post-Brexit area, we are witnessing a de-Europeisation of environmental law and policies. Drawing on empirical

---

[21] UK Government, The Air Quality (Amendment of Domestic Regulations) (EU Exit) Regulations 2019, available at https://www.legislation.gov.uk/uksi/2019/74/made#:~:text=Environmental%20Protection-,The%20Air%20Quality%20(Amendment%20of%20Domestic,)%20(EU%20Exit)%20Regulations%202019&text=The%20Secretary%20of%20State%20makes,)%20Act%202018(2) (last accessed 31/01/2024).

[22] See Gehring and Phillips (2018) (last accessed 31/01/2024).

[23] David Baldock, Environmental Regulation in the UK After Brexit Where Runs the River?, available at https://www.anothereurope.org/wp-content/uploads/2022/12/221214_Brexit_Spotlight_Analysis_final_online.pdf (last accessed 31/01/2024).

evidence, Burn et al. claim the concept of de-Europeanization as an analytical framework to identify the drivers and impediments of processes that entail moving away from European influence, suggesting that the insights garnered from this study may have broader applicability in diverse contexts. They posit that Brexit is more likely to result in disengagement and policy stasis in the environmental realm, with capacity emerging as a central explanatory factor.[24]

As for international environmental cooperation, Brexit has prompted a reassessment of the UK's international environmental commitments and collaborations. The UK now negotiates its own international agreements and partnerships in areas such as climate change, wildlife conservation, and sustainable development. This is perceived as an opportunity for the UK to shape its own environmental agenda and forge new alliances outside of the EU framework.

In a closely related area, trade and environment, as the UK establishes new trade relationships, considerations regarding environmental standards and regulations become crucial. The UK government aims to uphold environmental protections in trade agreements and maintain a level playing field to prevent potential environmental degradation resulting from increased trade activities.

On the flip side, the UK's departure from the EU has led to changes in access to funding programs and initiatives that previously supported environmental projects and research. The government has introduced new domestic funding mechanisms and frameworks to compensate for the loss of EU funding, ensuring continued support for environmental initiatives.

It is important to note that these differences between legal systems are subject to ongoing developments and may evolve further as the UK's environmental policies and regulations continue to shape the post-Brexit landscape.

One of the distinctive features of post-Brexit UK environmental law is the increasing importance of international environmental law for the United Kingdom. The UK is a party to many MEAs, and this remains unchanged in the face of Brexit.

3 Retaining EU Environmental Legislation in the UK: A Critical Analysis of Legal Mechanisms

Following Brexit, disparities in environmental laws and policies between the EU and the UK encompass not only divergent sectoral approaches but also variations in compliance mechanisms and enforcement strategies. These differences in compliance practices further contribute to the distinctiveness between the two regulatory frameworks in ensuring adherence to environmental standards and objectives. As the UK is no longer bound by the EU's environmental laws and policies, compliance monitoring takes place according to the UK rules.

---

[24] Burns et al. (2019), pp. 271–292.

In the post-Brexit period, one of the main objectives was to roll over as much EU environmental law legislation after Brexit. One of the areas of concern is the maintenance of environmental standards, as the EU is renowned for its stringent environmental regulations and Brexit removes the monitoring by the CJEU over compliance. While the UK has established its own set of environmental standards, there is uncertainty regarding its level of rigour compared to the EU's. The question of compliance arises, as it is essential to ensure that these standards are effectively implemented and adhered to. Divergencies are observed across the various sectoral areas.

In terms of climate change, the EU has made a commitment to achieving net-zero greenhouse gas emissions by 2050 and has implemented binding targets for emission reduction across its Member States. The UK has also made similar commitments, but there is a lack of clarity regarding binding targets beyond 2030, which raises concerns about the long-term trajectory of climate action.[25] Although there is the intention to maintain the level of ambition, the lack of a strict monitoring system could water down the commitments.[26]

Regarding nature and biodiversity conservation, the UK participated in the Natura 2000 network, encompassing a significant portion of its land area, to safeguard natural habitats and biodiversity. After Brexit, SACs and Special Protection Areas (SPAs) in the UK no longer form part of the EU's Natura 2000 ecological network.[27] Accordingly, The main points and processes of the 2019 Regulations, which amend the Habitats Regulations 2017 transpose the Habitats and Wild Birds Directives, to make them operable from 1 January 2021.[28] While the UK has developed its own system of protected areas, it remains uncertain whether it will match the scale and effectiveness of the EU's conservation efforts.[29]

In the domain of waste and recycling, the EU has set specific targets for waste reduction and increased recycling rates. Although the UK has comparable targets, there is a potential challenge in meeting them without the regulatory oversight previously provided by the EU. Plastic pollution remains at the centre of concerns.

Additionally, the regulation of chemicals poses another area of divergence. The EU's comprehensive chemical regulation system, known as REACH, covers the

---

[25] HM Government, Carbon Budget Delivery Plan, UK's sixth Carbon Budget, available at https://assets.publishing.service.gov.uk/government/uploads/system/uploads/attachment_data/file/1147369/carbon-budget-delivery-plan.pdf (last accessed 31/01/2024).

[26] UK enshrines new target in law to slash emissions by 78% by 2035, available at https://www.gov.uk/government/news/uk-enshrines-new-target-in-law-to-slash-emissions-by-78-by-2035 (last accessed 31/01/2024).

[27] CIEEM, Brexit changes to the Habitats Regulations for England and Wales, 4th January 2021, https://cieem.net/brexit-changes-to-the-habitats-regulations/ (last accessed 31/01/2024).

[28] Department for Environment, Food & Rural Affairs, Changes to the Habitats Regulations 2017, 1 January 2021 https://www.gov.uk/government/publications/changes-to-the-habitats-regulations-2017 (last accessed 31/01/2024).

[29] Wildlife and Countryside Link (2021): Achieving 30x30 Land and Sea, available at: https://www.wcl.org.uk/docs/WCL_Achieving_30x30_Land_and_Sea_Report.pdf (last accessed 31/01/2024).

entire life cycle of chemicals.[30] The UK has established its own regulatory framework, but its comprehensiveness in comparison to REACH is yet to be determined.

In summary, the future development of the UK's environmental laws and policies remains uncertain, and it is crucial to monitor their effectiveness in safeguarding the environment. The level of compliance and the ability to uphold high environmental standards will play a vital role in determining the success of the UK's environmental efforts post-Brexit as specifically discussed in the next sections.

4 Challenges and Obligations Faced by the UK in Complying with Environmental Regulations Post-Brexit

After Brexit, the UK government has established new systems to monitor compliance with environmental laws and regulations. A key legal instrument for the post-Brexit era, the UK Environmental Act sets out the "environmental principles" currently found in EU law; introducing Environmental Improvement Plans and creating the New Office for Environmental Protection (OEP), endowed with scrutiny and advice functions.[31] The Office for Environmental Protection was created by the need to respond to the need to update environmental legislation and, at the same time, to provide a stable framework. As part of its enforcement functions, the OEP deals with complaints and judicial review. In order to monitor compliance with environmental regulations after Brexit, the United Kingdom has implemented several mechanisms.

4.1 Landscape of Compliance with Environmental Law in the UK

Firstly, the UK government has enacted new domestic legislation to ensure adherence to environmental laws and regulations previously enforced by the European Union. Various government agencies have been subsequently tasked with enforcement, such as the UK Border Force, the Food Standards Agency, and the Health and Safety Executive.

[30] Department for Environment, Food and Rural Affairs (DEFRA) (2022c): UK REACH Extending data submission deadline, available at: https://consult.defra.gov.uk/reach-policy/consultation-on-extending-the-uk-reach-submission/supporting_documents/Impact%20Assessment%20IA.pdf (last accessed 31/01/2024).

[31] In 2021, the Environmental Act, as a newly enacted legal framework came into force, serving as the United Kingdom's updated architecture for environmental safeguarding, see https://www.legislation.gov.uk/ukpga/2021/30/contents/enacted (last accessed 31/01/2024).

Additionally, the UK government has introduced stricter border checks on goods entering the country. This includes verifying compliance with regulations related to food safety standards and product labelling requirements.[32]

To oversee compliance within specific sectors, the UK government has established new regulatory bodies.[33] Regular audits and inspections are conducted by the UK government to ensure compliance with laws and regulations. Businesses, such as food manufacturers and farms, are subject to inspections to verify their compliance with food safety standards.

Furthermore, on the international level, the UK government actively engages in information sharing with other countries and international organizations to enhance compliance. This includes sharing information on imports, exports, and potential non-compliant entities, thereby fostering collaboration in upholding regulations. Overall, the UK government has established new systems and processes to monitor compliance with laws and regulations after Brexit. These include domestic legislation, border checks, regulatory bodies, auditing and inspections, and information sharing.

Against this backdrop, in the UK the OEP plays an important role in protecting and promoting the country's natural environment. It is a governmental body responsible for ensuring that policies and practices related to the environment are effective, efficient, and consistent with the country's legal obligations and commitments.

The OEP's main responsibilities include providing advice and guidance to government ministers on environmental policy, monitoring the implementation of environmental policies, and carrying out research to support evidence-based decision-making. The OEP also works closely with other governmental bodies, such as the Environment Agency and Natural England, to coordinate environmental policy and enforcement.

In addition to these responsibilities, the OEP also works to engage with and educate the public on environmental issues. This includes providing information on how individuals and businesses can reduce their environmental impact, as well as promoting awareness of environmental challenges and opportunities.

Overall, the OEP plays a critical role in ensuring that the UK's natural environment is protected, preserved, and enhanced for the benefit of both current and future generations. Section 23(1) outlines its primary objective as follows: (1) The foremost aim of the OEP in the execution of its duties is to make contributions towards (a) safeguarding the environment and (b) the enhancement of the natural environment.

The report titled "Taking Stock: Protecting, Restoring, and Improving the Environment in England" presents a structured framework articulated by the OEP,

[32]To facilitate the monitoring of goods movement across borders, the government has implemented the Goods Vehicle Movement Service (GVMS), a system designed to track and monitor the movement of goods.

[33]One example is the Medicines and Healthcare products Regulatory Agency (MHRA), which is responsible for regulating medicines and medical devices.

consisting of six crucial building blocks. These building blocks encompass a spectrum of foundational elements essential for effective environmental management and conservation.[34] They include understanding the drivers and pressures impacting the environment, crafting a cohesive vision that guides future endeavors, establishing clear and measurable targets to gauge progress, formulating coherent strategies and policies that align with overarching goals, ensuring robust governance structures to oversee implementation and compliance, and instituting mechanisms for continuous monitoring, assessment, and transparent reporting of environmental outcomes. Together, these building blocks provide a strategic roadmap for advancing environmental sustainability and resilience across England.

It is noteworthy, however, that the OEP does not assume direct responsibilities for matters pertaining to environmental protection, such as environmental permitting, flood defense, or planning oversight. These functions continue to be vested within the purview of the relevant established public bodies or regulators. Instead, the OEP is entrusted with two overarching categories of functions: "Scrutiny and advisory functions" as delineated in sections 28–30 and "Enforcement functions" as delineated in sections 31–41.[35]

4.2 Proposals for Reinforcing Compliance with Environmental Law in the Post-Brexit Era

The creation of a dedicated forum for environmental EU-UK cooperation, or re-joining the EEA, could present steps towards robust maintenance of environmental standards on both sides of the channel.

As regards devolution, bearing in mind that environmental regulation is a devolved power in the UK, the prospective "shadowing" announced by some of the countries, may lead to different frameworks, adding another dimension and calling for reinforced cooperation and coordination in the post-Brexit context.

While Scotland has announced its intention to closely align with EU regulations, Northern Ireland, due to its formal alignment with the European Single Market in specific domains, has obligated itself to mirror certain facets of European environmental legislation.[36] The establishment of a specialized platform for fostering EU-UK environmental collaboration, or the prospect of re-engaging with the European Economic Area (EEA), could represent viable measures aimed at

[34] OEP, Taking stock: protecting, restoring and improving the environment in England, available at https://www.theoep.org.uk/report/taking-stock-protecting-restoring-and-improving-environment-england (last accessed 31/01/2024).

[35] Office for Environmental Protection- OEP (theoep.org.uk).

[36] Devolution after Brexit Managing the environment, agriculture and fisheries, https://www.instituteforgovernment.org.uk/sites/default/files/publications/IFGJ6070-Devoution-After-Brexit-180413-FINAL-WEB.pdf (last accessed 31/01/2024).

fortifying the preservation of environmental standards across both shores of the English Channel.

In the realm of prioritization of environmental issues, stipulated within the framework of the Environment Act, the mandate compelled the Government to formulate, no later than the 31st of October 2022, a minimum of one quantifiable objective within each of the four designated priority domains: specifically, air quality, biodiversity, water quality, and the optimization of resource employment coupled with waste reduction. Additionally, specific goals concerning crucial environmental areas are also encompassed within this ambit.

These objectives do not to remain in isolation but are to be bolstered by an arrangement of intermediate milestones, structured to span five-year intervals. The purpose of these interim targets is to chart a coherent trajectory towards the ultimate realization of the longer-term goals. Through this strategic arrangement, a continuous and systematic appraisal will be conducted, evaluating the extent to which the governmental endeavours align with its overarching aspirations for sustainable progress.

5 Autonomy or Deregulation: Has Brexit Led to a Paradigm Shift in the Approach to Environmental Law in the UK?

Delving into the main areas where the impact of Brexit on sectoral UK environmental legislation, there have been changes to the UK's environmental laws in light of Brexit. Although a significant portion of previous EU legislation has been preserved or substituted by new domestic legislation, new legislation enacted across UK nations has introduced nuanced changes. This is more appreciable in the fields of biodiversity, climate change targets, and energy transition.

Numerous challenges manifest in the absence of adherence to European Union (EU) principles, compounded by deregulation in some areas. Notwithstanding the implementation of the Environment Act 2021, an observable phenomenon of "regulatory environmental chill" has permeated various sectors.

Although the enactment of the Environment Act 2021 has provided a new legal framework post-Brexit in England and other UK nations, the implementation of environmental legislation in specific areas rests on the adoption of more detailed norms developing the framework legislation. As Macrory points out, "[i]n common with much of modern legislation, a number of the core provisions in the Act only provide a very broad framework, leaving the substantial detail to be found in subsequent regulations to be made by the Government. Examples include producer responsibility obligations (s 50), electronic waste tracking (s 58), hazardous waste (s 60), environmental recall of vehicles (s 74), amendment of water quality regulations (s 89), and amendment of Habitats Regulations (s 112)".[37]

Within the realm of secondary legislation, nuanced intricacies are embedded, particularly within air pollution regulations, which play a crucial role in delineating permissible thresholds. Such legislative frameworks encompass high-level commitments and serve as pivotal oversight mechanisms to ensure adherence and accountability. The autonomy is veiled within technical intricacies, often manifested through indirect measures. In the context of international obligations, the United Kingdom's adherence to EU law was more stringent, given its heightened binding nature. In contrast, international obligations tend to exhibit a degree of ambiguity, often leaning toward aspirational goals, coupled with comparatively weaker enforcement mechanisms.

An overall assessment of the environmental legislation adopted indicates that the UK is lagging behind the EU across a broad spectrum of environmental regulation, with the EU bolstering its legislation while the UK opts for weakening measures. In certain instances, environmental protections derived from EU law are removed.

The impending removal of EU-derived air pollution laws under the retained EU legislation, alongside the continued availability of numerous chemicals and pesticides banned within the EU but permitted in the UK, underscores a widening regulatory disparity between the two environmental law regimes. While the EU presses forward with initiatives such as carbon pricing and compensation schemes to ease the burden of transitioning to sustainable practices, the UK lags behind in implementing comparable measures. Moreover, the EU's stringent regulations on battery recycling contrast starkly with the UK's more lenient framework. Additionally, as the EU moves to address deforestation within supply chains, the UK's proposed scheme appears less rigorous and is scheduled for implementation a year later. This growing divergence between UK and EU environmental regulations raises concerns among businesses and environmental groups, exacerbated by the absence of a government body tasked with tracking and addressing these discrepancies.

Though the OEP is tasked with monitoring powers it does not possess the same level of independence as the European Commission. Hence the absence of a dedicated governmental body tasked with monitoring and assessing the divergence between the environmental regulations of the European Union (EU) and the United Kingdom (UK) leaves stakeholders, including citizens, industries, and environmental advocacy groups, uninformed about the magnitude of regulatory disparities.

Practically speaking, this regulatory disconnect translates into several concerning implications: firstly, the quality of water in the UK is anticipated to deteriorate compared to that of the EU; secondly, the levels of pesticides in British soil are expected to surpass those permissible under EU standards; thirdly, companies operating in the UK may produce and distribute products containing chemicals that have been deemed hazardous and restricted by EU regulations.

[37] Badger and Macrory (2022).

Moreover, the regulatory landscape has undergone significant alterations, exacerbating the gap between the environmental policies of the EU and the UK. Key policy changes include the elimination of EU-derived air pollution laws under the retained EU law bill, the continued availability of numerous chemicals banned within the EU for use in the UK, the legality of thirty-six pesticides in the UK that are prohibited in the EU, and the UK's lagging progress in reducing carbon emissions compared to the EU's implementation of carbon pricing measures. Additionally, the absence of financial assistance in the UK for individuals struggling to transition to environmentally friendly practices contrasts with the support provided by the EU. Furthermore, while the EU enforces stricter regulations on battery recycling, the UK's approach remains comparatively lenient. Lastly, while the EU moves to eliminate deforestation from its supply chain, the UK's proposed scheme is less stringent and delayed by a year, potentially leading to adverse environmental consequences.

5.1 Biodiversity, Conservation, and Protection of Nature After Brexit

Assessing the direct impact of Brexit on biodiversity in the UK is challenging due to its complexity, as this sector is influenced by a multitude of factors.[38] However, some potential impacts can be considered in a preliminary appraisal.

Precisely, one of the main concerns is the impact of Brexit on conservation efforts and environmental regulations. The UK was previously subject to EU environmental policies and regulations, such as the Birds and Habitats Directives, which aimed to protect biodiversity and habitat.[39] Following Brexit, the UK is no longer bound by these regulations, and it remains to be seen whether new policies will provide equivalent levels of protection. Areas that intersect with conservation, such as marine protection could be potentially at risk due to reduced levels of environmental protection.[40]

The UK has sustained a consistent commitment to protect biodiversity and has actively participated in various international forums, including the G7 and the Conference of Parties for the Biodiversity Convention.[41] The UK played a pivotal role in endorsing the "Leaders' Pledge for Nature", which was launched in September 2020, and all four UK nations have pledged their commitment to

[38] Gavin Lord, Biodiversity after Brexit: Agri-environmental policy in England after Brexit and private investment in ecosystem services, available at https://lup.lub.lu.se/luur/download?func=downloadFile&recordOId=8947290&fileOId=8947294 (last accessed 31/01/2024).

[39] Burns et al. (2019), pp. 271–292.

[40] Appleby and Harrison (2019), pp. 1–22.

[41] UN Biodiversity Conference (COP 15), Conference documents, available at https://www.cbd.int/conferences/2021-2022/cp-mop-10/documents (last accessed 31/01/2024).

safeguarding 30 percent of land and marine areas for biodiversity preservation by 2030.[42] Nevertheless, there remain doubts regarding the precise means by which this target will be achieved, particularly in England, and whether the requisite policies and financial allocations will be established to support this endeavour.

The UK Environmental Act 2021 introduces a ground-breaking framework for achieving net biodiversity gains, both domestically and internationally. Under this legislation, conservation efforts will extend beyond national borders, fostering biodiversity enhancements on shores and abroad.

A credit system, detailed in forthcoming regulations, will enable the offsetting of environmental impacts while facilitating on-site gains. This innovative approach envisions a market for these credits, whereby landowners can generate gains that are tradable commodities. Planning authorities will assume the role of brokers in this broad-based market, marking an exciting development in environmental management.

Statutory credits, earmarked for specified environmental purposes, promise to inject funds into conservation initiatives. Unlike traditional cap and trade systems, this framework allows for a more flexible approach, with a 10% provision for gains on the same site.

The envisaged statutory credits system, akin to carbon trading schemes, signals a significant shift towards incentivizing environmental stewardship while fostering biodiversity enhancements. This innovative market mechanism is poised to revolutionize biodiversity conservation efforts, aligning financial incentives with ecological imperatives.

Brexit also raises questions about the future of funding for conservation efforts. The EU has previously provided funding for a range of conservation projects in the UK, and the loss of this funding could have a significant impact on conservation efforts. Additionally, Brexit has the potential to affect migratory species that pass through the UK. Many migratory species rely on protected habitats in the UK, and any disruption to these habitats could harm their populations. Overall, the impact of Brexit on biodiversity in the UK is likely to be complex and varied, and it will take time to fully understand the effects. However, there is a need for continued investment in conservation efforts and a commitment to protecting biodiversity in the UK.

On the international level, the UK continues to be bound by the Convention on Biodiversity, which provides a specific framework setting out obligations for the contracting parties. The same considerations apply to the UK's participation in other biodiversity-related MEAs such as the Ramsar Convention.[43]

In other biodiversity-related areas, the UK has pioneered the adoption of new legislation. The Chemicals (Health and Safety) and Genetically Modified Organisms (Contained Use) (Amendment etc.) (EU Exit) Regulations 2019, which establish a framework for the regulation of chemicals and genetically modified organisms in the

[42] See https://www.leaderspledgefornature.org/ (last accessed 31/01/2024).

[43] Ramsar Sites in the UK and the UK's Overseas Territories & Crown Dependencies, available at https://jncc.gov.uk/our-work/ramsar-sites/ (last accessed 31/01/2024).

UK after Brexit.[44] The UK Emissions Trading Scheme replaces the UK's participation in the EU Emissions Trading System and aims to help the UK achieve its carbon reduction targets. In turn, the Conservation of Habitats and Species (Amendment) (EU Exit) Regulations 2019 update the UK's regulations for the protection of habitats and species in line with Brexit.

An interesting development is the adoption of a more comprehensive legal framework for the protection of nature in the EU.[45] In comparison to this, the UK is attempting to develop a strategy that revolves around the net gain strategy and through setting new targets for conservation.[46]

Accordingly, among the recent domestic legislative developments, one of the most notable pieces of environmental legislation is the incorporation of Biodiversity Net Gain within the purview of the Environment Act 2021, concomitant with the fortification of the legal obligation on public entities for the preservation and augmentation of biodiversity.[47] Upon its anticipated obligatory enforcement, potentially in November 2023, a substantial majority of planning permissions granted in England will necessitate the provision of a biodiversity net gain of not less than 10 percent, secured through enduring commitments spanning at least three decades. This alteration has engendered the introduction of a novel biodiversity metric designed to quantify net gain. Additionally, the Act puts forward a novel framework for conservation covenants and mandates the formulation of Local Nature Recovery Strategies, which are spatial strategies that pertain to nature—an innovation that elicited fervent advocacy from environmental non-governmental organizations.

Simultaneously, the progression toward the adoption of a fresh set of domestic targets remains underway. Among the most pivotal of these forthcoming benchmarks are the legally binding, long-term environmental biodiversity targets specifically designated for England. These targets are part of a broader set of environmental objectives as stipulated by the provisions of the Environment Act 2021. Nonetheless, it is anticipated that once these targets are endorsed, they are likely to bear resemblance to the terrestrial and marine biodiversity propositions advanced by Defra during a consultative exercise in March 2022, including one of the most pioneering propositions that entails a commitment to increase species by 10 percent by the year 2042.[48]

[44] Available at https://www.legislation.gov.uk/ukdsi/2019/9780111181539/contents (last accessed 31/01/2024).

[45] EU Commission (2022): Proposal for a Regulation on nature restoration available at https://environment.ec.europa.eu/publications/nature-restoration-law_en (last accessed 31/01/2024).

[46] Department for Environment, Food and Rural Affairs (DEFRA) (2022b): Nature Recovery Green Paper, available at https://consult.defra.gov.uk/nature-recovery-green-paper/nature-recovery-green-paper/ (last accessed 31/01/2024).

[47] Graham (2021).

[48] DEFRA 2022. Biodiversity Terrestrial and Freshwater Targets. Detailed Evidence report. 28th April 2022, available at https://consult.defra.gov.uk/natural-environment-policy/consultation-on-environmental-targets/supporting_documents/Biodiversity%20terrestrial%20and%20freshwater%20targets%20%20Detailed%20evidence%20report.pdf (last accessed 31/01/2024).

5.2 *Climate Change Law and Policy After Brexit*

Brexit has had a significant impact on UK climate change policy and legislation. Before Brexit, as a member of the European Union (EU), the UK had a range of climate change policies and targets that member states were required to adhere to. The existing legislation, the Climate Change Act 2008 dates back to that EU era.

One of the biggest impacts of Brexit on UK climate change policy has been the loss of access to EU funding for climate-related projects. The EU provided significant funding for research and development in areas such as renewable energy, energy efficiency, and carbon capture and storage, which has been crucial in advancing the UK's efforts to address climate change.

Brexit has also led to changes in the UK's domestic climate change policy. High expectations were set around climate change targets. In 2019, the UK announced the adoption of a binding objective to achieve net-zero greenhouse gas emissions by 2050. In 2019, the UK government set a legally binding target of net zero greenhouse gas emissions by 2050. This target is more ambitious than the target set by the EU, which is for a 40% reduction in greenhouse gas emissions by 2030. Public participation and consultation are at the heart of this new era of environmental law and policy in the UK.

This landmark development foreshadowed a series of progressive climate policies, particularly in the lead-up to COP26 in Glasgow in November 2021. Chief among these initiatives was the release of the "Net Zero Strategy: Build Back Greener", outlining a roadmap for decarbonising the UK economy by 2050, with a pronounced focus on actions to be taken by 2037.[49] While this strategy showcased leadership in certain aspects, such as the ambition to phase out fossil-fuelled heating systems by 2035 and halt the sale of new petrol and diesel vehicles by 2030, it was not without its critiques, particularly those coming from civil society and environmental NGOs due to the UK's reliance on unproven emission reduction technologies like carbon capture and storage plants.[50]

Whereas some of the previous climate change institutions survived Brexit, such as the independent Climate Change Committee, which represents the continuity in environmental policy established under the Climate Change Act 2008 and acknowledges the UK's alignment with the long-term temperature goal of the Paris Agreement, there is a significant stall in progress. The progress review submitted to Parliament in June 2022, it underscores the sluggish pace of advancement across several domains, noting that "tangible progress is lagging policy ambition", primarily due to various policy gaps. The report accentuates the imperative of closing these gaps, especially in areas like land use, potentially facilitated by new environmental

---

[49] Department for Energy Security and Net Zero and Department for Business, Energy & Industrial Strategy, Net Zero Strategy: Build Back Greener (19 October 2021), available at https://www.gov.uk/government/publications/net-zero-strategy (last accessed 31/01/2024).

[50] ClientEarth 2021, The "Greenwashing Files", available at https://www.clientearth.org/projects/the-greenwashing-files/drax/ (last accessed 31/01/2024).

legislation and the energy efficiency of buildings. Furthermore, it highlights the necessity for comprehensive strategies and detailed plans in waste management, land use, agriculture, and achieving complete electricity decarbonization by 2035.

There is the perception that Brexit has also allowed the UK government to have greater control over its own climate change policy, as it is no longer subject to EU regulations and directives. This has allowed the government to introduce policies that are more tailored to the UK's specific needs and priorities, such as the Green Industrial Revolution, which aims to create green jobs and accelerate the transition to a low-carbon economy.

However, Brexit has also created some uncertainties around the UK's future relationship with the EU on climate change. The EU is currently developing a new climate law, which includes a target of net zero greenhouse gas emissions by 2050, and it is unclear whether the UK will align with this target or develop its own separate target.

Equally important, the Strategy also faced scrutiny from a coalition of environmental NGOs, who questioned its legal compliance with the Climate Change Act. Specifically, the coalition pressed for detailed climate policies that would elucidate how the UK's legally binding carbon budgets would be fulfilled, including quantitative targets. Following a favourable ruling by the High Court in July 2022, the Government is obliged to amend the Strategy and provide clarity on how the proposed policies will effectuate the necessary changes to meet these targets.[51]

Overall, Brexit has had a significant impact on UK climate change policy and legislation, both in terms of the opportunities it has created and the challenges it has presented. The long-term effects of Brexit on the UK's ability to address climate change will depend on a range of factors, including the government's commitment to achieving its net zero target and its ability to develop effective policies to support this goal.

5.3 *Green Deal and the Just Transition Agenda*

After Brexit, the EU Green Deal and the UK Green Deal further differentiated as two separate initiatives aimed at addressing environmental challenges. The progressive departure of the UK coincided with the organisation of the COP26 in Glasgow which, up to a certain extent, shaped the future of the relations in what respect climate change.

The EU Green Deal is a comprehensive plan introduced by the European Commission in December 2019 to make the EU's economy sustainable and carbon-neutral by 2050. The plan includes a wide range of policy measures and investments

[51] ClientEarth, "We've won our case against the UK Government's inadequate net zero strategy", 19th July 2022, https://www.clientearth.org/latest/latest-updates/news/clientearth-are-suing-the-uk-government-over-its-net-zero-strategy/ (last accessed 31/01/2024).

to transform the EU's energy, transport, and agricultural systems, as well as initiatives to protect biodiversity and reduce pollution. The EU Green Deal is focused on the entire European Union and its member states, with the European Commission leading the effort to implement the plans.

On the other hand, the UK Green Deal was conceptualised as a policy framework introduced by the UK government in 2011 aimed at reducing carbon emissions and promoting sustainable growth. However, the UK Green Deal is no longer in operation, having been superseded by more recent policies and initiatives such as the Ten Point Plan for a Green Industrial Revolution, which was announced by the UK government in November 2020.[52] This plan includes measures such as investing in renewable energy, accelerating the transition to zero-emission vehicles, and upgrading buildings to improve energy efficiency. The Air Quality (Amendment) (EU Exit) Regulations 2019, updated the UK's air quality regulations to reflect its departure from the EU.

In the related area of energy efficiency, the UK's lag in energy efficiency compared to the European Union is exacerbating the ongoing cost-of-living predicament. Household electricity costs in the UK surpass those in several neighbouring EU nations by a considerable margin, exceeding at least 30 percent. This discrepancy can be attributed to the substantial reliance on gas as a primary energy source within the UK. Nonetheless, regulatory initiatives aimed at enhancing residential insulation and achieving heightened energy efficiency significantly trail behind the benchmarks set by the EU's Directive on the Energy Performance of Buildings. This EU directive has a specific goal of doubling the annual rate of building energy renovations by 2030, a milestone that the UK is notably behind in achieving.

In sum, whereas the EU Green Deal is a current, wide-reaching plan for transforming the EU economy to become carbon-neutral by 2050, at the moment, the UK Green Deal can be deemed as an almost defunct policy framework aimed at reducing carbon emissions and promoting sustainable growth, and the original proposal has been superseded by more recent policies such as the UK's Ten Point Plan.

5.4 Divergences in Other Environmental Areas

At the same time, the UK government has expressed a clear intent to diverge from EU-based environmental regulations, citing concerns over their perceived restrictiveness and administrative burdens (red tapes). This divergence manifests in several key areas, what could be narrowed down into three central domains.

[52] Department for Business, Energy and Industrial Strategy (BEIS) (2021): Net Zero Strategy: Build Back Greener, available at: https://assets.publishing.service.gov.uk/government/uploads/system/uploads/attachment_data/file/1033990/net-zero-strategy-beis.pdf (last accessed 31/01/2024).

With regard to environmental assessments, England is, in particular, moving away from EU-derived regulations governing Environmental Impact Assessments (EIAs) and Strategic Environmental Assessments (SEAs) for development projects. This proposed shift is outlined in the Levelling Up and Regeneration Bill, and aims to replace existing procedures with a more flexible "results-based" approach while ensuring continued assessments for select environmentally impactful projects.[53] This could result in an erosion of the level of protection pre-Brexit with the aim of attracting investments and facilitating projects.

In terms of Gene Editing and GMOs, the UK has already chosen to deviate from the EU in regulating gene editing and genetically modified organisms (GMOs). New legislation, such as the Genetic Technology (Precision Breeding) Bill, seeks to create a lighter regulatory framework for precision breeding techniques, including gene editing. This move is expected to attract investment, accelerate food development, and yield global benefits, but it faces opposition from various quarters.

Finally, in the area of chemical regulation, the UK's decision to depart from the EU's comprehensive chemical regulation regime, known as REACH, and establish an alternative domestic system under the Health and Safety Executive, represents a significant regulatory departure. This UK-based regime operates on a smaller scale and has limited resources and data access, potentially incurring governmental and industrial costs. The decision appears driven by ideological motives to disengage from EU institutions.

Through these divergences the UK seems to underscore the shift away from EU environmental norms, raising questions about their economic, administrative, and environmental implications, as well as potential consequences for future alignment with EU regulations.

6 Conclusions: It Takes Two to Tango, UK and Environmental Law After Brexit

After the United Kingdom's departure from the European Union, many of the environmental laws and regulations that were previously in place through EU membership have been retained in UK law.

The UK government has enacted a series of legislative measures aimed at supplanting or modernizing environmental regulations that were formerly governed by EU legislation. Among these measures, the Environment Act endeavours to usher in novel provisions designed to fortify environmental protection. These provisions encompass objectives encompassing air quality enhancement, strategies for mitigating plastic pollution, and mandates for achieving biodiversity net gain. Overall, while some changes have been made to UK environmental legislation as a result of

[53] Levelling-up and Regeneration Act, https://www.legislation.gov.uk/ukpga/2023/55/enacted (last accessed 31/01/2024).

Brexit, much of the previous EU legislation has been retained or replaced by new UK laws.

In the aftermath of Brexit, the landscape of environmental law has displayed a discernible lack of substantial deregulation, exhibiting varied trajectories contingent upon sectoral legislation. While certain measures have been undertaken, such as the UK's disengagement from the European Environment Agency and the regulatory framework of REACH pertaining to chemicals, the overarching trend signifies a limited scope of deregulatory initiatives. Notably, the United Kingdom's energy efficiency standards are comparably deficient vis-à-vis European counterparts, thereby exerting upward pressure on consumer pricing, and the palpable advancement towards the 2050 net-zero emissions target exhibits perceptible laggardness.

The trend toward deregulation gained momentum upon the unveiling of the Retained EU law (Revocation and Reform) Act, propounding an objective of expunging all EU legislation from the corpus of British statutes by the conclusion of 2023. This envisioned rollback of certain aspects within the domain of environmental law, particularly concerning developmental oversight, biodiversity preservation, and foundational environmental safeguards intertwined with agricultural and fisheries policies, stands as a pivotal departure from established policy paradigms. The forthcoming trajectory hinges upon the decisive interlude of 2025, coinciding with the prospective renegotiation of the Trade and Cooperation Agreement. This juncture portends the potential for introspection, encompassing a comprehensive re-evaluation of environmental repercussions stemming from the Agreement's provisions and, by extension, the broader ramifications of the Brexit phenomenon upon the legislative landscape governing environmental concerns.

References

Appleby T, Harrison J (2019) Taking the pulse of environmental and fisheries law: The Common Fisheries Policy, the Habitats Directive, and Brexit. J Environ Law:1–22

Badger C, Macrory R (2022) Environment Act 2021: text, guide and analysis. Bloomsbury

Burns C, Carter N, Cowell R, Eckersley P, Farstad F, Gravey V, Jordan A, Moore B, Reid C (2018) Environmental policy in a devolved United Kingdom: challenges and opportunities after Brexit. UK in a Changing Europe, London

Burns C, Gravey V, Jordan A, Zito A (2019) De-Europeanising or disengaging? EU environmental policy and Brexit. Environ Polit 28(2):271–292. https://doi.org/10.1080/09644016.2019.1549774

Cater L (2023) A post-Brexit regulatory 'bonfire' could scorch UK environmental protections. The UK's environmental regulations are in peril three years after it quit the EU. Politico, 1st February 2023. https://www.politico.eu/article/post-brexit-regulation-uk-environmental-protection-eu/

Fisher E (2020) Executive Environmental Law 83(1):163–189

Gehring M, Phillips F-K (2018) Brexit: the international legal implications | Paper No. 15 — February 2018, Brexit and Environmental Law: The Rocky Road Ahead, available at https://www.cigionline.org/sites/default/files/documents/Brexit%20Series%20Paper%20no.15_3.pdf

Graham T (2021) The Environment Act 2021: a guide for planners and developers. Bath Publishing

Lee RG (2017) Always keep a hold of nurse: British environmental law and exit from the European Union. J Environ Law 29(1):155–164. https://doi.org/10.1093/jel/eqx004
Lee M (2023) The Aarhus Convention 1998 and the Environment Act 2021: Eroding Public Participation. Mod Law Rev 86:756–784. https://doi.org/10.1111/1468-2230.12789
Scotford E, Bowman M (2016) Brexit and environmental law: challenges and opportunities. King's Law J 27(3):416–419. https://doi.org/10.1080/09615768.2016.1258779

The Anglicisation of Retained European Union Law

Mukarrum Ahmed

1 Introduction

The Retained EU Law (Revocation and Reform) Act 2023 ('the Act') was granted Royal Assent on 29 June 2023.[1] This chapter will discuss the Act's provisions on sunsetting, assimilation, departure from retained EU case law and delegated powers to restate, revoke or replace retained EU law with reference to the rules of retained EU Private International Law in the UK. Although the retained Rome I Regulation and the retained Rome II Regulation are 'assimilated direct legislation'[2] after the end of 2023 and not on the list of revoked legal instruments,[3] the Act nevertheless renders significant amendments to the status, content, and operation of retained EU law and mandates broad executive powers that could be used to achieve deregulation in the post-Brexit legal landscape. Retained EU law is a product of the EU (Withdrawal) Act 2018 ('EUWA 2018') and came into effect at the end of the UK's post Brexit transition period.[4] The cessation of a gradualist approach to the amendment and revocation of retained EU law has been given legislative effect by the Act.

[1] According to Section 23(3) the Act's short title is the 'Retained EU Law (Revocation and Reform) Act 2023'. The Act extends to England and Wales, Scotland, and Northern Ireland.

[2] Section 5 of the Retained EU Law (Revocation and Reform) Act 2023. At or before the end of 2023, assimilated direct legislation is referred to as retained direct EU legislation.

[3] EU-derived subordinate legislation and retained direct EU legislation listed in Part 1 and Part 2 of Schedule 1 of the Act is revoked at the end of 2023 under Section 1(1) of the Retained EU Law (Revocation and Reform) Act 2023.

[4] This chapter builds on the author's discussion of retained EU (Private International) law in Ahmed (2022).

M. Ahmed (✉)
Lancaster University Law School, Lancaster, UK
e-mail: m.ahmed25@lancaster.ac.uk

E. Guinchard, C. Panara (eds.), *The New Relationship between the United Kingdom and the European Union*, https://doi.org/10.1007/978-3-031-70652-3_16

Originally, the Bill that led to the Act proposed a controversial 'sunset clause'[5] that would have seen most (but not all) retained direct EU legislation (i.e. EU regulations, EU decisions and EU tertiary legislation) and EU-derived secondary legislation such as EU directives automatically repealed at the end of 2023, unless expressly saved. The original Bill included powers to delay expiry and to preserve legislation, but those decisions would have to be adopted by the end of 2023. The sunset clause was subject to criticism because it would have resulted in legislative uncertainty,[6] Parliament's weakened ability to scrutinise government proposals for replacing retained EU law,[7] and intolerable pressures on government departments/ devolved administrations.[8]

The proposed approach for revocation of legislative instruments changed during the Bill's Report Stage in the House of Lords. The unbridled ambition of the sunset clause was reined in by a narrower sunset schedule, which listed 587 pieces of retained EU law that were revoked at the end of 2023 pursuant to Section 1 of the Act. The remaining retained EU law was symbolically converted into assimilated law. Assimilated law is amenable to restatement, revocation, or replacement under new delegated powers until 23 June 2026.

Attempts were made, at Lords Report stage, to enhance Parliamentary scrutiny of the expiring 587 legislative instruments in Schedule 1. Lord Hope of Craighead proposed that a new Joint Committee should be able to review these instruments and if the Committee considered that revocation would represent a substantial change to the law, a debate on the floor of both Houses would be needed, and a vote to approve its revocation. Although the Government was defeated on this amendment at Lords Report stage, it was reversed in the House of Commons and was not revisited. Therefore, the enhanced scrutiny mechanism is not part of the Act.

[5] 'Sunset clauses—provisions that mean that a law or a particular part of the law lapse automatically on a fixed and precise date or after a specified and determined period of time': See Kouroutakis (2018).

[6] Sir Jonathan Jones KC in Hansard Society, 'Webinar: Unpicking the Retained EU Law Bill: What does it mean for Parliament?' (12 October 2022) <https://www.hansardsociety.org.uk/events/webinars/retained-eu-law-bill-parliament-what-does-it-mean> accessed 20 February 2024; 'The 'sunset clauses' in the REUL (R&R) Bill create a material risk to the stability of the UK legal system, its practitioners, and its end-users in areas of key policy…': See Bingham Centre for the Rule of Law, 'Joint written evidence submission to the House of Commons Public Bill Committee on the Retained EU Law (Revocation and Reform) Bill 2022' (16 November 2022) <https://bills.parliament.uk/publications/48723/documents/2531> accessed 20 February 2024; Bar Council, Retained EU Law Bill Briefing (n 7).

[7] George Peretz KC in Monckton Chambers, 'Webinar on the Retained EU Law Bill' (28 September 2022) <https://www.monckton.com/event/webinar-on-the-retained-eu-law-revocation-and-reform-bill/> accessed 20 February 2024. On a lack of democratic accountability in the Bill, see, The Bar Council, 'Retained EU Law (Revocation and Reform) Bill: Briefing for Peers' <https://www.barcouncil.org.uk/static/26e58174-6785-4bdf-94da497d9980f3be/Bar-Council-Briefing-for-Peers-Retained-EU-Law-Revocation-and-Reform-Bill-Feb-2023.pdf> accessed 20 February 2024.

[8] Cowie (2023).

In the post-transition phase of Brexit, the Rome I and II Regulations under the mantle of retained direct EU legislation constitute a new category of domestic law that is neither EU law nor English law *simpliciter*. It is a frozen-in-time remnant or 'snapshot' of EU law as of 31 December 2020.[9] The application and interpretation of retained direct EU legislation gives rise to its own set of challenges. Ultimately, fidelity to EU law must be balanced with the ability of Parliament and appellate courts to depart from retained EU law and develop their own law and jurisprudence. It will be argued that the legal transposition of the concept of 'retained EU law' into 'assimilated law' by jettisoning its special characteristics and encouraging the judiciary and executive to adopt a distinct path is an adaptation that will help domesticate this corpus of law even more easily. This should in turn simultaneously facilitate closer integration with English law and divergence from the peculiarities of European Union law. Although such a response to the ardent political rhetoric of Brexit is preferable to the regulatory void created by an all-encompassing sunset clause, it may nevertheless impact legal certainty and predictability generally and in international private law transactions and disputes involving contracts, torts, and other non-contractual obligations.

The chapter will commence with a discussion of retained EU law under the European Union (Withdrawal) Act 2018 and its conversion into assimilated law by virtue of the Retained EU Law (Revocation and Reform) Act 2023. An awareness of the specific characteristics of the latter is necessary for an understanding of the policy drive to anglicise (domesticate) retained EU law into assimilated law. This will be followed by a broad-brush depiction of Brexit's implications for private international law in the UK. In particular, the regime for the applicable law in civil and commercial matters at the transition, post transition and assimilated stages will be considered.

2 Retained EU Law

The UK government presented its plan to deliver Brexit in its White Paper, *Legislating for the United Kingdom's Withdrawal from the European Union*.[10] The White Paper noted that converting EU law into UK law would be insufficient to provide 'a smooth and orderly exit' because a large proportion of the converted law would not function properly when transplanted from the EU context to the new domestic context.[11] The EUWA 2018 therefore contains powers to enable corrections to be made to the new corpus of law to overcome this issue. The EUWA 2018 is a constitutionally significant statute because it repeals the European Communities

[9] See n 18 below.

[10] Department for Exiting the European Union, *Legislating for the United Kingdom's Withdrawal from the European Union* (White Paper, Cm 9446, 2017).

[11] Duhs and Rao (2021), p. 2.

Act 1972 and fills the void left by EU law across a large swathe of the UK statute book by creating a new legal category termed retained EU law in the domestic law of the UK. The concept of retained EU law ensures legal continuity and certainty in UK legal systems whilst also making provision for change where necessary.

The European Communities Act 1972 was repealed at 11 pm on 31 January 2020 when the UK ceased to be a Member State of the EU ('Exit Day').[12] The provision for a transition period extends from Exit Day till the 'IP completion day' at 11 pm on 31 December 2020.[13] During the transition period, EU law applies in the UK as if the UK had continued to be a Member State of the EU and:[14]

> shall produce in respect of and in the United Kingdom the same legal effects as those which it produces within the Union and its Member States, and shall be interpreted and applied in accordance with the same methods and general principles as those applicable within the Union.[15]

The policy of successive UK governments since the EU referendum was to ensure legal continuity between the law applicable before and after Brexit would take full effect.[16] To address the lacunas that would arise from an abrupt divorce of the coalesced European Union and UK legal systems, the EUWA 2018 made provision for the category of 'retained' EU law that will continue to be part of UK domestic law.[17] Retained EU law is neither English law nor EU law *simpliciter* but is a frozen-in-time remnant of EU law as of 31 December 2020.[18] The rules and principles applicable to retained EU law are laid down in the EUWA 2018 as amended by the EUWA 2020.

Retained EU law includes UK domestic primary and secondary legislation derived from EU law,[19] retained direct EU legislation such as EU Regulations, EU Decisions and EU tertiary legislation,[20] and directly effective 'rights, powers, liabilities, obligations, restrictions, remedies and procedures ... recognised and available ... by virtue of section 2(1) of the European Communities Act 1972'.[21] Decisions of the CJEU and UK courts prior to the end of 2020 interpreting the said

[12] Section 1 of the EUWA 2018.

[13] Article 126 of the EU Withdrawal Agreement 2020.

[14] Article 127(1) of the EU Withdrawal Agreement 2020.

[15] Article 127(3) of the EU Withdrawal Agreement 2020.

[16] See, principally, Department for Exiting the European Union, *The United Kingdom's exit from and new partnership with the European Union* (White Paper, Cm 9417, 2017), [1.1]; Department for Exiting the European Union, *Legislating for the United Kingdom's Withdrawal from the European Union* (White Paper, Cm 9446, 2017), [1.24].

[17] Section 3(1) of the EUWA 2018.

[18] The Secretary of State for Exiting the European Union described the approach as: '[taking] a snapshot of the body of EU law that currently forms part of the United Kingdom legal system and [ensuring] that it will continue to apply in the United Kingdom after we leave'. (HC Deb 7 September 2017, vol. 628, col. 342).

[19] Section 2 of the EUWA 2018.

[20] Section 3 of the EUWA 2018.

[21] Section 4 of the EUWA 2018.

EU laws also constitute retained EU law.[22] The post-Brexit CJEU jurisprudence will not be binding on the English courts,[23] but will continue to influence courts when interpreting the same piece of legislation.[24]

EU law that existed before IP Completion Day will continue in force and effect in the UK as retained EU law.[25] The category of retained EU law is susceptible to change and revocation pursuant to an express power to amend retained EU law.[26] Acts of Parliament enacted after the post Brexit transition period can expressly or impliedly repeal retained EU law.[27] Retained case law means decisions of UK courts and the CJEU as they had effect immediately before IP Completion Day.[28] Retained EU law is to be interpreted in accordance with retained case law and general principles of EU law.[29] General principles of EU law apply as retained EU law after IP Completion Day only if they had been recognised as such by a CJEU decision rendered before IP Completion Day.[30] An English court has no power after IP Completion Day to make references to the CJEU.[31]

The EUWA 2018 aims to balance the tension between continuity and change.[32] A significant example of the tension between continuity and change is found in the retention of a modified principle of supremacy of EU law.[33] The EUWA 2018 provides that the modified principle of supremacy does not apply to future domestic enactments passed on or after IP completion day,[34] but it does still apply after IP completion day to the interpretation, disapplication or quashing of any past domestic

---

[22] Section 6 of the EUWA 2018.

[23] Section 6(1)(a) of the EUWA 2018. This would apply to decisions of the CJEU given in relation to provisions forming retained EU law.

[24] Section 6(2) of the EUWA 2018. Arnold LJ considered that a judgment of the CJEU rendered after the post-Brexit transition period was 'highly persuasive' in *Tunein Inc v Warner Music UK Ltd* [2021] EWCA Civ 441, [91]; In similar vein, there was a reference to the 'non-binding persuasive effects' of EU law in *Lipton v BA City Flyers Limited* [2021] EWCA Civ 454, [65] (Green LJ).

[25] Section 3(1) of the EUWA 2018.

[26] Section 8 of the EUWA 2018.

[27] E.g. Fisheries Act 2020, sch 11. Section 5(1) of the EUWA 2018 clarifies that '[t]he principle of the supremacy of EU law does not apply to any enactment or rule of law passed or made on or after [IP completion day'.

[28] Section 6(7), of the EUWA 2018.

[29] Section 6(3) of the EUWA 2018.

[30] Section 5(6), Schedule 1, [2] of the EUWA 2018.

[31] Section 6(1)(b) of the EUWA 2018. It has the power until that date: Article 86 of the EU Withdrawal Agreement.

[32] Duhs and Rao (2021), pp. 4–5.

[33] The House of Lord Select Committee on the Constitution said in its report to the European Union (Withdrawal) Bill that it considered that it was 'impossible to see in what sense "the principle of the supremacy of EU law", set out in clause 5, could meaningfully apply in the UK once it has left the EU'. (Select Committee on the Constitution, *European Union (Withdrawal) Bill* (HL 2017- 09, 69), [88]). For the comparative characteristics of the modified principle of supremacy of EU law, see, Hancox (2021), p. 429.

[34] Section 5(1) of the EUWA 2018.

enactments passed before IP completion day.[35] The retention of the supremacy principle is ironic, considering the incessant political rhetoric that a newly liberated UK will regain its sovereignty. The reason for this preservation in relation to past legislation is that the supremacy principle is crucial for ordering the interaction between EU law and UK national law. Therefore, the principle of supremacy ensures clarity and coherence on the statute book by functioning as an overriding hierarchal rule, which takes precedence over contrary domestic law provisions.[36] However, it is difficult to see how the principle of the supremacy can operate in a domestic law context when its essential characteristics no longer apply. The principle of supremacy is a constitutional principle of EU law, which is a means for harmonising the law of Member States. It is an acknowledgement that the legal systems of the EU Member States have 'limited their sovereign rights'.

The CJEU has highlighted the legal implications of the supremacy of EU law in Popławski II:[37] 'the primacy principle requires, inter alia, national courts to interpret, to the greatest extent possible, their national law in conformity with EU law'. The possibility of disapplying incompatible national legislation only arises where the provision of EU law is directly effective.[38] A similar approach towards ensuring the compatibility of domestic law with EU law has been adopted by UK courts.[39]

As all legislation is an emanation of the politico-legal culture of a state, statutory interpretation of retained EU law will be informed by the fundamental change in the constitutional architecture of the UK.[40] At the risk of oversimplification, EU legislative instruments tend to be drafted in broad terms as compared to the common law's bootstraps or 'remedial' approach to statutory drafting where technical, detailed, and precise language is employed.[41] As a consequence, the EU approach to legislation necessitates a purposive approach to statutory interpretation. Purposive interpretation of EU law benefits from the CJEU's preliminary reference jurisdiction

---

[35] Section 5(2) of the EUWA 2018.

[36] Duhs and Rao (2021), p. 119.

[37] Case C-573/17 *Popławski II* EU:C:2019:53, [57]; In *Costa v ENEL* (6/64) [1964] ECR 585 the ECJ espoused the principle of supremacy of EU law and stated that EU law could not 'be overridden by domestic legal provisions, however framed, without being deprived of its character as [Union] law and without the legal basis of the [Union] itself being called into question'.

[38] Case C-573/17 *Popławski II* EU:C:2019:53, [60]-[62].

[39] Case C-213/89 *R. v Secretary of State for Transport Ex p. Factortame Ltd* EU:C:1990:257; [1991] 1 All E.R. 70; *R v Secretary of State for Transport Ex Parte Factortame (No 2)* (1991) 1 AC 603 (Lord Bridge); *Benkharbouche v Secretary of State for Foreign and Commonwealth Affairs* [2017] UKSC 62, [78] (Lord Sumption): 'a conflict between EU law and English domestic law must be resolved in favour of the former, and the latter must be disapplied'; *Benkharbouche v Embassy of the Republic of Sudan* [2015] EWCA Civ 33, [76]-[81]; *Fleming v Revenue and Customs Commissioners* [2008] UKHL 2, [2008] 1 WLR 195, [25] (Lord Hope): 'Disapplication is called for only if there is an inconsistency between national law and EU law. In an attempt to avoid an inconsistency the national court will, if at all possible, interpret the national legislation so as to make it conform to the superior order of EU law.'

[40] Sales (2023).

[41] Hartley (2005), p. 813; Forsyth (2005), p. 93.

under Article 267 TFEU but post IP completion day this is a 'red line' that cannot be crossed in relation to retained EU law. Without such assistance and when interpreting retained EU law should UK courts give precedence to the meta-telos of EU law or domestic rules of interpretation? The Explanatory Notes to the EUWA 2018 confirm that the intention of Section 6(3) is for the UK courts to adopt a purposive approach where the meaning of retained EU law is unclear or ambiguous.[42] However, there are aspects of CJEU reasoning which UK courts are not quite capable of mirroring. For instance, Spencer J has referred to the 'nightmare' of English courts applying 'the EU principle whereby the correct interpretation incorporates and encompasses all the various language versions' of the directive without the resources at the disposal of the CJEU.[43]

It is likely that a degree of divergence in the interpretation of the same legal provision will arise in cases where the UK courts cannot identify the purpose of retained EU law.[44] A homeward trend towards a more textual approach informed by the dictates of parliamentary sovereignty may prevent the courts from ignoring the precise words of a statute coupled with the need to curb judicial discretion.[45]

3 Departure from Retained EU Law

The UK Supreme Court is not bound by retained EU case law after IP Completion Day.[46] In deciding whether to depart or diverge from retained EU case law, the Supreme Court will employ the test it applies when invited to depart from one of its own decisions.[47] A court is not bound by any retained domestic case law that it would not otherwise be bound by.[48] It is clear that the usual doctrine of precedent which determines whether a domestic court is bound by the decision of another domestic court remains unchanged.

Other courts may be permitted, by Regulations made under Section 5A of the 2020 Act, to be not bound by retained EU law. This power has been extended to the English Court of Appeal and equivalent courts in the other UK legal systems.[49] The same test is applied by other courts to which the power to change retained EU law is extended to promote consistency of approach and legal certainty across the different jurisdictions in the UK.

---

[42] Explanatory Notes of the EUWA 2018, [111].

[43] *Greenway v Parrish & Ors* [2021] EWHC 1506 (QB), [44].

[44] Sales (2023).

[45] Ibid.

[46] Section 6(4)(a) of the EUWA 2018.

[47] Section 6(5) of the EUWA 2018.

[48] Section 6(4)(c) of the EUWA 2018.

[49] The European Union (Withdrawal) Act 2018 (Relevant Court) (Retained EU Case Law) Regulations 2020, SI 2020 No. 1525.

The UK Supreme Court test in deciding whether to depart from its own case law is set out in a House of Lords Practice Statement of 26 July 1966.[50] In summary, the test applied by the UK Supreme Court to depart from its previous case law is 'whether it appears right to do so'.[51] This test will also apply to depart from retained EU case law.[52] In deciding whether to depart from its own case law, the UK Supreme Court will have regard *inter alia* to 'the danger of disturbing retrospectively the basis on which contracts, settlement of property, and fiscal arrangements have been entered into'.[53] Lord Bingham has observed extrajudicially that 'the House could reject a bad rule in favour of a better, a power it has exercised, although very infrequently, where the interests of justice or the coherent development of principle appeared to demand revision of an earlier decision.'[54] By reserving the power for the highest appellate court, the role of precedent is preserved in the lower echelons of the judicial hierarchy.

Even outside the immediate context of retained EU case law, it has been argued that the Practice Statement should extend to the penultimate appellate court (Court of Appeal) as it cannot sensibly be confined to the judges in the final court of appeal (UK Supreme Court).[55] On the other hand, there is a strong consequentialist justification for the ruling that House of Lords precedents ought to bind all courts and to be reversible only by Parliament.[56] This latter approach retains the essential

---

[50] House of Lords Practice Statement (Judicial Precedent) of 1966 [1966] 1 W.L.R. 1234; [1966] 3 All E.R. 77.

[51] The Supreme Court has not re-issued the House of Lords' Practice Statement of 26 July 1966 (Practice Statement (Judicial Precedent) [1966] 1 WLR 1234) which stated that the House of Lords would treat former decisions of the House as normally binding but that it would depart from a previous decision when it appeared right to do so. The Practice Statement is 'part of the established jurisprudence relating to the conduct of appeals' and 'has as much effect in [the Supreme] Court as it did before the Appellate Committee in the House of Lords': *Austin v Mayor and Burgesses of the London Borough of Southwark* [2010] UKSC 28, [2011] 1 A.C. 355, [24], [25]. (Lord Hope of Craighead with whom Lord Brown and Lord Kerr agreed).

[52] Duhs and Rao, *Retained EU Law*, pp. 144–146.

[53] The Practice Statement (Judicial Statement) [1966] 3 All ER 77; [1966] 1 WLR 1234; [1966] 2 Lloyd's Rep. 151.

[54] Lord Bingham of Cornhill (2006), p. 62.

[55] Cross and Harris (1991), p. 114. Cf. *Young v Bristol Aeroplane Company Limited* [1944] 1 KB 718 (Lord Greene MR): The Court of Appeal is bound to follow its own decisions and those of courts of co-ordinate jurisdiction, and the 'full' court is in the same position in this respect as a division of the court consisting of three members. The only exceptions to this rule are: (1) The court is entitled and bound to decide which of two conflicting decisions of its own it will follow; (2) the court is bound to refuse to follow a decision of its own which, though not expressly overruled, cannot, in its opinion, stand with a decision of the House of Lords; (3) the court is not bound to follow a decision of its own if it is satisfied that the decision was given per incuriam, e.g., where a statute or a rule having statutory effect which would have affected the decision was not brought to the attention of the earlier court.

[56] *London Street Tramways Co Ltd v London County Council* [1898] AC 375 (Earl of Halsbury LC): 'a decision of this House once given upon a point of law is conclusive upon this House afterwards, and that it is impossible to raise that question again as if it was res integra and could be reargued, and

distinction between the judiciary and legislature.[57] A similar argument may be made in the different context of the retained jurisprudence of the CJEU that this corpus of law should only be amended by legislation.[58] However, the consequences of adhering to a strict doctrine of stare decisis have in turn been found sufficiently unsatisfactory for the House of Lords to have reversed itself on that point.[59] The extension of the legal provision to depart from retained EU law to the Court of Appeal renders the body of retained EU case law more susceptible to change than ordinary English law precedent. However, this extension mitigates the practical operational impact on the UK Supreme Court as it allows the Supreme Court to benefit from prior judicial deliberation by the Court of Appeal on complex legal issues.

Apart from legal provision for the UK Supreme Court and the Court of Appeal to not follow retained EU case law, judges sometimes rely on viable consequentialist arguments and arguments of principle, to apply a very narrow interpretation of a statutory provision.[60] On occasion and for similar justifications, judges also interpret the principle espoused by a precedent restrictively in order to 'distinguish' or 'explain' it from the point in issue in a given case.[61] In the words of Sir Geoffrey Vos MR, 'The common law is at its best when cases are decided by the finding of the facts in the particular case and by the application of the law applicable at the relevant time to those facts.'[62] Therefore, the possibility of distinguishing or explaining a particular statutory provision or precedent of retained EU law provides UK lawyers and courts the flexibility to work around retained EU law. Significantly, there is scope for not following retained EU case law where there are conflicting interpretations rendered in CJEU decisions and the law is not settled. In similar vein,

so the House be asked to reverse its own decision. That is a principle which has been, I believe, without any real decision to the contrary, established now for some centuries, and I am therefore of opinion that in this case it is not competent for us to rehear and for counsel to reargue a question which has been recently decided.' See, MacCormick (1978), p. 134.

[57] Dworkin (1962), p. 178.

[58] Whittaker (2021), pp. 484–485.

[59] Lord Rodger of Earlsferry (2004), p. 529, compares the intellectual context of the proclamation of the decree of papal infallibility of 18 July 1870 with the rule that the House of Lords was bound by its own decisions not being finally ordained until 1898. In that case only four Law Lords sat, the respondents' counsel was not called upon and Lord Halsbury delivered an extempore judgment that occupies less than three pages.

[60] For example, s. 4(4) of the Foreign Compensation Act 1950 in *Anisminic Ltd v Foreign Compensation Commission* [1969] 2 AC 147, [1969] 2 WLR 163 (HL). A unified 'contextual' approach to statutory interpretation was identified by Rupert Cross which was supported by dicta of the House of Lords. Cross suggested that the English approach involves not so much a choice between alternative rules as a progressive analysis in which the judges first consider the ordinary meaning of the words in the broad general context of the statute. The judges then moves on to consider other possibilities if the ordinary meaning leads to an absurd result. See Cross et al. (1995), p. 49.

[61] MacCormick (1978), pp. 219–224; Harris (1997), p. 183. See also, Dworkin (1962), p. 175.

[62] *Warner Music UK Ltd and another v TuneIn Inc* [2021] EWCA Civ 441.

retained EU case law that arrives at a conclusion without a well-reasoned analysis may be susceptible to being ignored.

In contrast to the common law's doctrine of precedent, the CJEU is not bound by its previous decisions:[63]

> The binding authority of precedent is not an inherent feature of the Union's judicial system. Although, in the interest of legal certainty and the uniform interpretation of Community law, the Community Courts endeavour in principle to give a coherent interpretation to the law, the general structure of both the Community legal order and the judicial system means that the Community Courts are not bound by their previous decisions.

Precedent provides some degree of certainty upon which individuals can rely in the conduct of their affairs.[64] If the power to depart is granted more extensively, it should be restricted to the Court of Appeal and its equivalents to help to mitigate the erosion of precedent.[65] A balance has to be struck between the policy aim of encouraging timely departure from retained EU case law, where appropriate, and the negative repercussions of driving re-litigation, and therefore caseloads, creating uncertainty and reducing confidence in the UK as a dispute resolution forum.[66] If the power to change retained EU law is extended to the High Court and equivalent courts and tribunals, it risks creating conflicting precedents within the judicial system and considerable legal uncertainty.

The test that the UK Supreme Court uses to depart from its own rulings has certain benefits in that the test is uncodified, the bar is necessarily high, and it will have the value of reinforcing legal clarity and certainty. This clarity, coupled with the quality of the judges who apply the case law, has traditionally been seen as a strength when making arguments about the UK as a favoured dispute resolution forum. However, the development of a test to depart from retained EU case law may assist courts. Ideally, the UK Supreme Court is best placed to provide a set of criteria for this purpose, taking account of both existing case law and the need to consider potential departures holistically. The Court of Appeal has had the opportunity to

---

[63] Opinion of AG Trstenjak in Case C-331/05 P *Internationaler Hilfsfonds e.V. v Commission of the European Communities* ECLI:EU:C:2007:191, [85]; See also, Opinion of AG Lagrange in C-28/62 *Da Costa en Schaake NV and Others v Administratie der Belastingen* ECLI:EU:C:1963:2, 44: '.... better for a court to interpret the law (the purpose for which it is setup) than to interpret its own decisions.'

[64] The Practice Statement (Judicial Statement) [1966] 3 All ER 77; [1966] 1 WLR 1234; [1966] 2 Lloyd's Rep. 151.

[65] See Ministry of Justice, 'Response to the consultation on the departure from retained EU case law by UK courts and tribunals' (CP 303, October 2020), <Response to consultation on the departure from retained EU case law by UK courts and tribunals (publishing.service.gov.uk)> accessed 20 February 2024. The paper concluded that it was appropriate to allow courts at the level of the Court of Appeal of England and Wales to depart from retained EU case law.

[66] Ibid, page 17.

offer guidance as to the proper approach for departing from retained EU case law in *TuneIn v Warner Music*.[67]

In TuneIn, Warner Music/Sony Music sued TuneIn for breach of copyright. The substantive legal issue addressed by the Court of Appeal was the concept of 'communication to the public' in copyright infringement, where Tunein offered online radio services. The concept of 'communication to the public' is employed both, in EU law and international conventions to which the UK is a party. As noted by Arnold LJ, the CJEU has addressed the meaning of the notion in question in 25 cases with more pending when the Court of Appeal rendered its own decision. The relevant legal issue for our purposes was whether the Court of Appeal should follow the jurisprudence of the CJEU or depart from it as it was permitted to do so by Section 6(3) of the EUWA 2018 and implementing Regulations.

Arnold LJ argued that the power should be exercised with caution, exactly as it is the case with departure from case law of the House of Lords and the Supreme Court. In the case at hand, despite being encouraged by the appellant, Arnold LJ opted to abide by the extant CJEU jurisprudence. Arnold LJ enumerated eight distinct reasons for a cautious approach to departing from CJEU case which warrant a closer examination:

There has been no change in the retained domestic legislation, so the relevant provision is garbed in the same language that was considered previously by the CJEU.[68]

The relevant international legislative framework has not changed.[69]

The CJEU had 'unrivalled experience' in confronting the relevant issue and has developed and refined its jurisprudence over time.[70]

Distinguished academic commentary was conflicting and did not provide a clear legal basis for departing.[71]

The case law from other courts in Commonwealth countries was materially irrelevant and could not offer settled or consistent guidance.[72]

A return to 'the drawing board' would create considerable legal uncertainty, where the appellant's own interpretation may not provide a clear defence to an infringement in any case.[73]

It is not sensible to depart from one CJEU case and not the remainder, later cases.[74]

[67] *TuneIn Inc v Warner Music UK Ltd* [2021] EWCA Civ 441. See also, *Lipton v BA City Flyer Ltd* [2021] EWCA Civ 454.

[68] *TuneIn Inc v Warner Music UK Ltd* [2021] EWCA Civ 441, [78].

[69] Ibid [79].

[70] Ibid [80].

[71] Ibid [81].

[72] Ibid [82].

[73] Ibid [83].

[74] Ibid [87].

The principal reason provided for departing from the CJEU jurisprudence was insubstantial and it was not clear that abandoning the CJEU's approach would assist the appellant because principles set out in other CJEU cases were enough to determine the issues against the appellant, and also because an alternative conclusion might be that linking to any content which had been posted without the requisite consent of the right holder would be an infringement.[75]

Sir Geoffrey Vos MR agreed with the outcome but confined himself to two reasons for not exercising the power to depart from retained EU law.[76] First, the courts should strive to interpret international conventions harmoniously.[77] Second, the CJEU's approach to the law of copyright infringement by 'communication to the public' is not restricting the proper development of the law nor is it leading to results which are unjust or contrary to public policy.[78]

4 Assimilated Law

Sections 1 and 2 of the Act provide for the sunsetting of retained EU law on 31 December 2023, after which 587 legislative instruments and an entire class of non-legislative retained EU law expired. Section 1 and Schedule 1 deal with the revocation of legislative instruments.[79] Section 2 deals with the revocation of law that has been retained pursuant to section 4 of EUWA 2018 (directly effective rights and obligations etc.).[80]

Sections 5(1)-(3) of EUWA 2018 is repealed by section 3 of the Retained EU Law (Revocation and Reform) Act 2023. The principle of supremacy of EU law and its modified version is abolished. Retained direct EU legislation (including retained EU regulations, EU decisions and EU tertiary legislation) will have to be read and given effect 'so far as possible' compatibly with domestic legislation, or failing that, 'subject to' all other domestic legislation. The duty of consistent interpretation in EUWA 2018, which gave precedence to retained EU law over domestic law has been reversed. Even if retained direct EU legislation became effective after domestic enactments, the latter will now take precedence. Retained direct EU legislation is downgraded and will have a lesser domestic legal status than domestic delegated legislation, whereas under the EUWA 2018 it takes (limited) priority over Acts of Parliament and delegated legislation passed before 2021.

This change will require key areas of domestic law to be reinterpreted after 2023. This will mainly affect the interpretation of retained EU regulations, so far as they

[75] Ibid [88].

[76] Ibid [196]-[197].

[77] Ibid [198].

[78] Ibid [201]-[202].

[79] Originally retained under sections 2 and 3 of EUWA 2018.

[80] Originally retained under section 4 of EUWA 2018.

have not expired. However, this new rule of legislative priority is subject to two significant exceptions. First, it does not apply to certain aspects of data protection law. In that context, retained direct EU legislation (most notably including the UK's version of the General Data Protection Regulation or UK GDPR) will continue to take priority in the event of conflicts. Secondly, regulations made under section 7 of the Retained EU Law (Revocation and Reform) Act 2023 by the executive,[81] could reinstate supremacy in relation to specific situations and instruments. This power to make regulations is a temporary one and expires on 23 June 2026.

Under section 4 the general principles of EU law will cease to be part of UK domestic law from 1 January 2024. The requirement to interpret retained direct EU legislation as per these general principles will therefore no longer apply. The general principles of EU law serve a gap filling role in the purposive statutory interpretation of EU law. They include, inter alia: fundamental rights, proportionality, legal certainty, equality before the law, legitimate expectations, and subsidiarity.

It is not clear from either the Act itself or its explanatory materials what principles the courts will be expected to use instead of the retained general principles of EU law, when construing the meaning and effect of assimilated law. Common law principles partly overlap with the EU general principles and would likely need to adapt to fill any lacunas.

The legal framework for departing from assimilated case law will enter into force via commencement regulations according to Section 22(3) of the Retained EU Law (Revocation and Reform) Act 2023. Section 6 of the Retained EU Law (Revocation and Reform) Act 2023 makes several amendments to section 6 of EUWA 2018. It confirms in primary legislation that appellate courts may depart from CJEU case law and provides (non-exhaustive) statutory tests for appellate courts when deciding whether to depart from CJEU case law and retained domestic case law. It also enables first instance courts, and tribunals, to refer points of law arising in retained case law to appellate courts for determination and enables law officers to make similar such references, or to intervene in cases concerned with departures from retained case law. The provisions relating to references and intervention by courts and law officers are not considered in this chapter.

Section 6(3) introduces a new statutory test for departing from pre 2021 CJEU case law for appellate courts. The test provides that, in deciding whether to depart from any retained EU case law, the court 'must (among other things) have regard to':

(a) the fact that decisions of a foreign court are not (unless otherwise provided) binding;
(b) any changes of circumstances which are relevant to the retained EU case law; and
(c) the extent to which the retained EU case law restricts the proper development of domestic law.

[81] All references to the executive in this chapter include UK Ministers or devolved authorities.

A corresponding provision in Section 6(4) introduces a statutory test to depart from retained domestic case law for appellate courts. A court may depart from its own retained domestic case law 'if it considers it right to do so having regard (among other things) to':

(a) the extent to which the retained domestic case law is determined or influenced by assimilated EU case law from which the court has departed or would depart;
(b) any changes of circumstances which are relevant to the retained domestic case law;
(c) the extent to which the retained domestic case law restricts the proper development of domestic law.

The Explanatory Notes of the Retained EU Law (Revocation and Reform) Act 2023 highlight that the (non-exhaustive) statutory criteria reflect some of the factors considered by the Court of Appeal in *TuneIn Inc v Warner Music UK Limited.*[82] However, it should be noted that in TuneIn, the Court of Appeal dismissed various arguments, that it should depart from CJEU case law in a copyright infringement dispute. Arnold LJ provided eight separate reasons why, in that case, such a departure was not necessary. The new statutory test is simultaneously a reductive statement of Arnold LJ's guidance in Tunein and open textured as it leaves considerable room for the exercise of discretion on the part of the judiciary. In relation to the former, it may be questioned whether there is a real and meaningful connection between the Court of Appeal decision and the new statutory test as the statutory language employed does not reflect the criteria laid down in the TuneIn judgment. Significantly, the other countervailing factors mentioned in the judgment that recommend a cautious approach against departure from CJEU case law find no place in the statutory test.[83] The test is effectively a 'nudge'[84] by Parliament to the judiciary encouraging it to depart from CJEU precedent 'that restricts the proper development of the law'.[85] It remains to be seen whether this rather permissive new test for divergence will alter judicial practice and the criteria applied in the Court of Appeal decision in *TuneIn*.

Indeed, the modification of the test by enumerating a set of factors for departing from retained CJEU case law encourages courts to forge their own distinct path. However, this expressly detracts from the sparingly used House of Lords practice direction, where a court would not simply ignore a previous decision in favour of a new outcome but would only develop the law where it was right to do so. It should be observed that judicial law making is retroactive whereas the legislation made by

---

[82] *TuneIn Inc v Warner Music UK Ltd & Anor* [2021] EWCA Civ 441; Explanatory Notes of the Retained EU Law (Revocation and Reform) Act 2023, [118].

[83] Philip Moser KC in Monckton Chambers, Webinar on the Retained EU Law (Revocation and Reform) Bill, 28 September 2022; Hancox (2021).

[84] Catherine Barnard in Monckton Chambers, Webinar on the Retained EU Law (Revocation and Reform) Bill, 28 September 2022.

[85] Sections 6(3) and 6(4) of the Retained EU Law (Revocation and Reform) Act 2023.

Parliament is prospective. Christopher Vajda KC has highlighted that in principle a departure is 'declaratory'[86] and therefore has retrospective effect till IP completion day.[87] However, legal uncertainty could be mitigated if the court decided that the judgment will have prospective effect only. That has been a characteristic of CJEU decisions with serious legal and financial repercussions.[88] This is a power that has never been exercised but is available at least in theory in exceptional circumstances where a retrospective overruling would have 'gravely unfair and disruptive consequences for past transactions'.[89]

The new test has wider implications for the separation of the judicial and legislative functions, the rule of law and parliamentary sovereignty.[90] From the perspective of those who longed for a newly 'liberated' UK, it would be ironic that 'taking back control' of laws after Brexit will involve the writ of an unelected judiciary as opposed to a sovereign Parliament.

It is argued that to preserve reasonable legal certainty and confidence in the legal system, UK courts will be expected to provide clear and well-reasoned explanations when they deem it appropriate to depart from purposive interpretations of retained EU law.[91] This should include reasoning to explain why a particular interpretation amongst other competing interpretations is preferable and how the interpretation aligns with the domestic legal system in the context of the case. Clear and transparent judicial decisions are essential in sustaining an optimal standard of legal certainty.

An extrapolation of the criteria enumerated in the Court of Appeal decision in *TuneIn* may offer guidance as to the non-exhaustive circumstances where courts may decide to depart from assimilated case law under the Retained EU Law (Revocation and Reform) Act 2023. In terms of a theory of adjudication, the tension between the category of 'fit' exemplified by assimilated case law and the category of

---

[86] According to Blackstone's declaratory theory of the common law 'if it be found that the former decision is manifestly absurd or unjust, it is declared not that such a sentence was *bad law*, but that it was *not law*': Sir William Blackstone, *Commentaries on the Laws of England* (1st ed, 1765) vol 1, 70. Cf. *Re Spectrum Plus Ltd (In Liquidation)* [2005] UKHL 41, [2005] 2 AC 680, [34] (Lord Nicholls of Birkenhead).

[87] Vajda (2021), p. 113.

[88] See, for instance, Case C-262/88 *Douglas Harvey Barber v Guardian Royal Exchange Assurance Group* EU:C:1990:209, [43]-[44].

[89] *National Westminster Bank plc v. Spectrum Plus Limited and others and others* [2005] UKHL 41, [2005] 2 AC 680, [40] (Lord Nicholls of Birkenhead). In *Re Spectrum Plus Ltd (In Liquidation)*, the House of Lords decided that *Siebe Gorman & Co Ltd v Barclays Bank Ltd* [1979] 2 Lloyd's Rep 142 (Slade J) was wrong and should be overruled. Cf. *Re Avanti Communications Limited (in administration)* [2023] EWHC 940 (Ch) (Johnson J).

[90] Cf. Lord Simonds' famous dismissal of Denning LJ's plea for a purposive approach to statutory interpretation as 'a naked usurpation of the legislative function under the thin disguise of interpretation' in *Magor and St Mellons Rural District Council v Newport Corporation* [1952] AC 189, 191.

[91] Sales (2023).

'justification' based on principle or policy in hard cases will result in the indigenous development of the corpus of assimilated law.[92]

In practice the category of 'fit' exerts a pull by the prioritisation of the overarching principle of legal certainty. Indeed, it is better to err on the side of caution and exercise judicial restraint in departing from assimilated case law.[93] The category of 'justification' could exert traction in several ways in either direction. For instance, a strong argument on the merits of the submissions for departure could be of significance. The benefits of regulatory alignment for a legal issue that could adversely impact trade between the UK and the EU could warrant harmonised interpretation. If the assimilated case is not well reasoned and lacks any sustained analysis of the issue that could be grounds for departure. The extent to which assimilated case law adopts an EU purposive interpretation of the legal provision and whether the purpose needs to be realigned for application in a UK domestic legal system that has diverged since Brexit could be relevant. A preponderance of assimilated case law considering the issue could be a relevant consideration and so could the constitution of the judicial panel in the assimilated decision. The nature and extent of the change in the law that the departure would cause, considering the separation of powers, and suitability of judge made law rather than Parliamentary intervention may be relevant. There could be rule of law and human rights implications as judicial law-making is retrospective.

The executive is accorded wide restatement, revocation, and replacement powers by the Retained EU Law (Revocation and Reform) Act 2023 in relation to secondary retained EU law and assimilated law.

The executive may restate secondary retained EU law until the end of 2023 and secondary assimilated law until 23 June 2026. The powers to restate legislation can be used to resolve ambiguities, remove doubts or anomalies or to facilitate improvement in the clarity or accessibility of the law.[94] Restatements can use 'words or concepts' that are different to those in the law being restated, giving the executive substantial discretion over the contents of restated legislation.[95] A restatement cannot include a blanket restatement of the principle of supremacy of EU law, or general principles of EU law.[96] However, an equivalent effect of these principles may be produced.[97] It appears, from section 12 of the Act, that assimilated law will, where necessary, be restated in a manner so as to recreate the effects of the general principles. These decisions would ultimately be those for the executive. Any restatement is not considered retained EU law and nor would it become assimilated law,

---

[92] See generally, Dworkin (1977) Chapter 4.

[93] It is 'of more consequence that a rule should be certain than whether the rule is established one way or the other': *Vallejo v Wheeler* (1774) 1 Cowper 143, 153; Lofft 631, 643; 98 ER 1012, 1017, 843 (Lord Mansfield).

[94] Section 13(3) of the Retained EU Law (Revocation and Reform) Act 2023.

[95] Section 13(2) of the Retained EU Law (Revocation and Reform) Act 2023.

[96] Section 13(5) of the Retained EU Law (Revocation and Reform) Act 2023.

[97] Section 13(6) of the Retained EU Law (Revocation and Reform) Act 2023.

and therefore restatements are not subject to the other executive powers of revocation or replacement.[98]

The restatement powers in sections 11 and 12 are Henry VIII powers,[99] as they can modify any enactment.[100] The practical significance of Henry VIII powers lies in the loss of public scrutiny and accountability for policy decisions that would usually occur when primary legislation is made by Parliament.[101] The Government has explained that this flexibility exists to enable restated law to be consolidated or codified in primary legislation, where appropriate.[102]

The executive has the power to revoke or replace secondary retained EU law until the end of 2023 and secondary assimilated law until 23 June 2026. Such legislation may be revoked without any replacement,[103] revoked and replaced with an appropriate provision achieving the same or similar objectives,[104] or even revoked and alternative provision made.[105] These are wide powers which will give the executive broad discretion to revoke or replace secondary retained EU law (or secondary assimilated law), including the ability to make policy changes through revocation and replacement. Any provision made through these powers must not increase the overall regulatory burden in a subject area.[106] Therefore, the provision may be deregulatory. The executive will also be able to make consequential amendments to any enactments including primary legislation and the provisions of the Act itself.[107]

---

[98] Sections 11(3) and 12(3) of the Retained EU Law (Revocation and Reform) Act 2023.

[99] Henry VIII powers provide the executive with a power to make changes to primary legislation by way of delegated legislation. In the EUWA 2018, there are several instances of the executive taking these powers, which have been used to update legislation to prepare for Brexit. These powers derive their name from The Statute of Proclamations 1539, in which Henry VIII acquired the right to pass laws directly, circumventing parliament.

[100] Section 13(7) of the Retained EU Law (Revocation and Reform) Act 2023.

[101] See Lord Judge, 'Ceding Power to the Executive; the Resurrection of Henry VIII' (12 April 2016) King's College London <https://www.kcl.ac.uk/archive/news/law/newsrecords/2015-16/ceding-power-to-the-executive%2D%2D-lord-judge%2D%2D-130416.pdf> accessed 20 February 2024.

[102] Explanatory Notes, [198].

[103] Section 14(1) of the Retained EU Law (Revocation and Reform) Act 2023; Explanatory Notes, [204].

[104] Section 14(2) of the Retained EU Law (Revocation and Reform) Act 2023; Explanatory Notes, [205].

[105] Section 14(3) of the Retained EU Law (Revocation and Reform) Act 2023; Explanatory Notes, [206].

[106] Section 14(5) of the Retained EU Law (Revocation and Reform) Act 2023; Explanatory Notes, [208], [213].

[107] Section 19 of the Retained EU Law (Revocation and Reform) Act 2023; Explanatory Notes, [235].

The Government insists that section 14 is not a Henry VIII power, because it can only amend secondary legislation.[108] Whilst this may be so, there could be an incidental impact on primary legislation. This is because regulations might revoke secondary legislation that, itself, made textual amendments to primary legislation.

These powers can be exercised with little or no Parliamentary scrutiny. The powers are controversial due to the substantial discretion they accord to the executive, and they attracted much debate during the Act's passage through Parliament - but the Act remained unamended. The powers are, however, constrained to revocation and replacement of laws that do not increase the overall regulatory burden in the estimation of the executive.

5 Brexit's Implications for Private International Law in the UK

Brexit was problematic for cross border civil and commercial judicial cooperation because the legal framework was based primarily on EU Regulations on jurisdiction, recognition and enforcement of judgments and the applicable law. The continued application of these EU Regulations in the post-Brexit civil judicial relationship between the UK and the EU was not possible because the Regulations derived their legal basis from an EU Treaty.[109] EU Regulations had been incorporated by reference via section 2 of the European Communities Act 1972. Once the UK left the EU and repealed the European Communities Act 1972, all EU law incorporated by reference, ceased to have effect.

Articles 66–69 of the Agreement on the withdrawal of the United Kingdom of Great Britain and Northern Ireland from the European Union and the European Atomic Energy Community, 19 October 2019,[110] contains provisions on jurisdiction, recognition and enforcement of judgments and the applicable law that apply during the transition period. The EU Withdrawal Agreement stipulates that, the Rome I Regulation shall apply in the UK in respect of contracts concluded before the end of the transition period.[111] The EU Withdrawal Agreement provides that, the Rome II Regulation shall apply in the UK in respect of events giving rise to damage, where such events occurred before the end of the transition period.[112] The remaining EU Member States will, of course, continue to apply the Rome I and II Regulations

[108] Delegated Powers Memorandum <https://publications.parliament.uk/pa/bills/cbill/58-03/0156/REUL_Bill_Delegated_Powers_Memorandum_20-09-22.pdf> page 28.

[109] Article 288 of the Treaty on the Functioning of the European Union (TFEU).

[110] EU Withdrawal Agreement.

[111] Article 66(a) of the EU Withdrawal Agreement.

[112] Article 66(b) of the EU Withdrawal Agreement.

in EU-UK relations during the transition period according to the principle of universal application.[113]

After the transition period elapsed, legislation provided that large swathes of EU law and EU derived law were carried forward into the UK statute book as retained EU law. The UK decided to incorporate the Rome I Regulation[114] and the Rome II Regulation[115] into domestic law at the end of the post-Brexit transition period with some minor and consequentialist amendments.[116] Contrary to the Brussels Ia Regulation, the Rome I and II Regulations do not require reciprocity and have an *erga omnes* effect. This means that EU Member State courts will apply the Rome I and II Regulations after Brexit to cases with a connection to the UK and vice versa.[117] The Rome I and II Regulations ensure legal certainty, deter forum shopping, and promote decisional harmony in cross border civil and commercial relations in the EU. The incorporation of the Rome I and II Regulations into English domestic law ensures continued regulatory alignment with the EU Member States in the significant area of the applicable law for cross border contractual and non-contractual obligations. The methodologically pluralist Rome I and Rome II Regulations offer a codified taxonomy that represents a significant improvement to the common law's piecemeal rules for determining the law applicable to contractual and non-contractual obligations.[118]

The provisions of the Rome I Regulation, the Rome II Regulation and the Rome Convention constitute retained EU law under the EU Withdrawal Act and are subject to the modifications laid down in the Law Applicable Exit Regulations.[119] These Regulations amend the existing EU legislation in order to convert them into the retained Rome instruments.[120] The EU Regulation on the negotiation of third country agreements with respect to contractual and non-contractual obligations is revoked.[121] On 29 January 2021, the UK government informed the European

[113] Article 2 of the Rome I Regulation and Article 3 of the Rome II Regulation.

[114] Regulation (EC) No 593/2008 on the law applicable to contractual obligations (Rome I), [2008] OJ L177/6 (hereafter Rome I Regulation).

[115] Regulation (EC) No 864/2007 on the law applicable to non-contractual obligations (Rome II), [2007] OJ L199/40 (hereafter Rome II Regulation).

[116] The Law Applicable to Contractual Obligations and Non-Contractual Obligations (Amendment etc.) (EU Exit) Regulations 2019, SI 2019 No 834. See Dickinson (2021), pp. 218–219.

[117] For the principle of universal application of Rome I and Rome II Regulations see, n 113 above.

[118] Briggs (2017).

[119] The Law Applicable to Contractual Obligations and Non-Contractual Obligations (Amendment etc.) (EU Exit) Regulations 2019, SI 2019 No 834.

[120] The Law Applicable to Contractual Obligations and Non-Contractual Obligations (Amendment etc.) (EU Exit) Regulations 2019, SI 2019 No 834, regs 2–9.

[121] The Law Applicable to Contractual Obligations and Non-Contractual Obligations (Amendment etc.) (EU Exit) Regulations 2019, SI 2019 No 834, reg 12. Regulation (EC) No 662/2009 is revoked.

Council of its view that the Rome Convention has ceased to apply to the UK and Gibraltar with the expiry of the transition period on 1 January 2021.[122]

The amendments that the Law Applicable Exit Regulations make to the text of the retained Rome I Regulation are mostly consequential and intelligible.[123] The reference in Article 2 (universal application) to the law of 'a Member State' is replaced by the law of 'the United Kingdom or a part of the United Kingdom'[124] and the application of Occam's razor omits Articles 22(2), 26–27 and 29.[125] However, the legislator has chosen to retain the elements of Article 3(4) and Article 7 that treat situations connected with EU Member States differently from other situations.

Under Article 3(4), retained EU law, as defined by the Withdrawal Act, cannot be derogated from by agreement by selecting a law that is not the law of a 'relevant state'[126] if all other elements relevant to the situation at the time of choice are located in a relevant state.[127] Therefore, mandatory rules of retained EU law will be applied by an English court where apart from the law chosen by the parties all other relevant elements are located in an EU Member State or the UK.[128]

Article 7 applies only to insurance contracts covering non-large risks situated inside the territory of a 'relevant state' and gives privileged status in certain respects to the law of the relevant states.[129] For instance, the parties to such a contract may choose, in accordance with Article 3, the law of any relevant state where the risk is situated, but not the law of any other country.[130] The retained Rome I Regulation will apply to contracts concluded as from 1 January 2021.[131]

---

[122] Letter of the UK Mission to the European Union dated 29 January 2021. <UK notifies that it considers the Brussels and Rome Convention to no longer apply to it – Conflict of Laws> accessed 20 February 2024.

[123] The Law Applicable to Contractual Obligations and Non-Contractual Obligations (Amendment etc.) (EU Exit) Regulations 2019, SI 2019 No 834, reg 10.

[124] The Law Applicable to Contractual Obligations and Non-Contractual Obligations (Amendment etc.) (EU Exit) Regulations 2019, SI 2019 No 834, reg 10(3).

[125] The Law Applicable to Contractual Obligations and Non-Contractual Obligations (Amendment etc.) (EU Exit) Regulations 2019, SI 2019 No 834, regs 10(8), (12), (13).

[126] Relevant state is defined for this purpose as the UK and all EU Member States: The Law Applicable to Contractual Obligations and Non-Contractual Obligations (Amendment etc.) (EU Exit) Regulations 2019, SI 2019 No 834, reg 10(2), restating Article 1(4) of the Rome I Regulation.

[127] The Law Applicable to Contractual Obligations and Non-Contractual Obligations (Amendment etc.) (EU Exit) Regulations 2019, SI 2019 No 834, reg 10(4).

[128] See Case C-381/98 *Ingmar GB Ltd v Eaton Leonard Technologies Inc.* [2000] ECR I-09305.

[129] The Law Applicable to Contractual Obligations and Non-Contractual Obligations (Amendment etc.) (EU Exit) Regulations 2019, SI 2019 No 834, reg 10(7).

[130] Article 7(3)(a) of the Rome I Regulation, as amended by the The Law Applicable to Contractual Obligations and Non-Contractual Obligations (Amendment etc.) (EU Exit) Regulations 2019, SI 2019 No 834. The passage of Article 7 into the retained Rome I Regulation may be questioned, given its unnecessary complexity and inextricable links with the internal market in insurance services.

[131] Article 66(a) of the EU Withdrawal Agreement.

The amendments made by the Law Applicable Exit Regulations to the text of the retained Rome II Regulation reflect a similar approach.[132] Articles 25(2), 29–30 and 32 are omitted[133] and most other provisions are amended by replacing references to 'Member State' with the 'United Kingdom'.

Article 6(3)(b) is amended to enable a party suing in a UK court to choose to apply the law of the forum to the claim if the UK market is amongst those directly and substantially affected by the restriction of competition, whether the defendant is domiciled in the UK or not. The law applicable under Article 6 may not be derogated from by an agreement pursuant to Article 14.

Article 8(2) is restricted to non-contractual obligations arising from infringements of pre-existing unitary Community intellectual property rights occurring before 1 January 2021 and to proceedings commenced before that date.[134] Read alongside the Withdrawal Agreement,[135] this change would seem to render Article 8-(2) obsolete going forwards. Where the event giving rise to damage constitutes the infringement of a unitary Community IP right, the 'country in which the act of infringement was committed' is located at the place of the initial act of infringement at the origin of the conduct complained of.[136] Before the exit date, the original Rome II Regulation will apply. For later events giving rise to damage, the law of the country for which the protection is claimed rule under Article 8(1) will apply to alleged infringements of unitary EU IP rights.[137] This will require the English court to identify the country, within a Member State, for which protection is claimed and to examine how the unitary right is given effect in that country through its implementation of EU law. The law applicable under Article 8 may not be derogated from by a choice of law agreement pursuant to Article 14.

Article 14(3), like the corresponding provision in Article 3(4) of the retained Rome I Regulation, is amended to prevent parties from derogating from retained EU law by selecting the law of a country beyond the 'relevant states' (defined as

[132] The Law Applicable to Contractual Obligations and Non-Contractual Obligations (Amendment etc.) (EU Exit) Regulations 2019, SI 2019 No 834, reg 11.

[133] The Law Applicable to Contractual Obligations and Non-Contractual Obligations (Amendment etc.) (EU Exit) Regulations 2019, SI 2019 No 834, regs 11(7), (10), (12). Oddly, reg 11(11) amends Art 31 to reflect the CJEU's decision in Case C-412/10 *Homawoo v GMF Assurances SA* [2011] I-11603, inserting 11 January 2009 as the reference date, even though the modified instrument will apply only to events giving rise to damage after 1 January 2021.

[134] The Law Applicable to Contractual Obligations and Non-Contractual Obligations (Amendment etc.) (EU Exit) Regulations 2019, SI 2019 No 834, reg 11(5).

[135] Article 66(b) of the EU Withdrawal Agreement which ensures the continued application of the Rome II Regulation for events giving rise to damage up to 31 December 2020. See also, Article 54, concerning the continuing effect of unitary EU intellectual property rights in the UK.

[136] Case C–24/16 *Nintendo Co Ltd v BigBen Interactive GmbH* EU:C:2017:724.

[137] See Case C-170/12 *Pinckney v KDG Mediatech AG* EU:C:2013:635, [2014] FSR 354.

including the UK and all EU Member States other than Denmark[138]) in situations that are otherwise entirely connected with the relevant states.[139]

It has been observed that over the course of time the interpretation of retained EU law and assimilated law is likely to diverge from the jurisprudence of the CJEU. This includes aspects of the UK's approach to the applicable law for cross border contractual and non-contractual obligations.[140] Therefore, it remains to be seen whether and to what extent common law choice of law concepts permeate or revisit potential areas such as characterisation, third country mandatory rules, scope of overriding mandatory provisions[141] and a liberal interpretation of the escape clauses in Articles 4(3) of Rome I and II. Broader questions relate to the scope of EU purposive interpretations of the Rome I and II Regulations premised on an internal market rationale when UK courts interpret the retained EU Regulations and assimilated law.[142]

The Brussels-Lugano regime has been revoked because a unilateral regime cannot replicate the multilateral jurisdiction and judgments framework premised on reciprocity or mutual trust between states. In its place, the common law jurisdiction of English courts is wider, the ancillary powers of English court are unfettered, and English judgments are less efficacious than would be the case if the UK was permitted to accede to the Lugano II Convention. Notwithstanding, the Brussels Ia Regulation's protective jurisdictional rules for consumer and employment contracts have been transplanted into domestic law by virtue of Sections 15A–D of the Civil Jurisdiction and Judgments Act 1982.[143] In applying and interpreting these provisions, an English court is to have regard to the principles laid down prior to Completion Day by the CJEU concerning Title II of the 1968 Brussels Convention or Chapter II of the Brussels Ia Regulation.[144] This means that decisions of the CJEU on the interpretation of the corresponding Articles of the Regulation will be treated

---

[138]The Law Applicable to Contractual Obligations and Non-Contractual Obligations (Amendment etc.) (EU Exit) Regulations 2019, SI 2019 No 834, reg 11(2), amending Art 1(4) of the Rome II Regulation.

[139]The Law Applicable to Contractual Obligations and Non-Contractual Obligations (Amendment etc.) (EU Exit) Regulations 2019, SI 2019 No 834, reg 11(6).

[140]For a discussion of potential areas where there could be a divergence in approach, see, Ahmed (2022), pp. 159–168.

[141]For a discussion on the application of mandatory rules post-Brexit, see Merrett (2021), pp. 352–354.

[142]Recital 1 of the Rome I and II Regulations. Cf. It is not always clear how some of the EU's initiatives can be said to be 'necessary for the proper functioning of the internal market'. Prominent English commentators expressed their doubts about the Rome II Regulation being necessary for the proper functioning of the internal market. Article 81 of the Treaty of Lisbon extended the competence of the EU over matters of private international law. Article 81(2) refers to the adoption of measures by the EU '*particularly* when necessary for the proper functioning of the internal market' (emphasis added). The wording suggests that an EU initiative need not be incontrovertibly necessary for the furtherance of the internal market. See Harris (2008), pp. 357–359.

[143]Civil Jurisdiction and Judgments (Amendment) (EU Exit) Regulations 2019.

[144]Section 15E(2)(a) of the Civil Jurisdiction and Judgments Act 1982.

as persuasive authority.[145] The courts may also consider and take account of the expert reports relating to the 1968 Brussels Convention.[146] The definition of retained EU law and the meaning and effect of a provision under Section 15(E)(2) of the Civil Jurisdiction and Judgments Act 1982 are inconsistent. As a result, common law jurisdictional concepts may assimilate into the interpretation of Sections 15A to 15D of the Civil Jurisdiction and Judgments Act 1982 more easily than the retained Rome I and II Regulations, where CJEU case law is still binding. However, the opposite may be observed about the concept of assimilated law under the Retained EU Law (Revocation and Reform) Act 2023, especially when the permissive provision on departing from CJEU case law becomes applicable via commencement regulations. A detailed discussion of the post-Brexit jurisdiction and judgments regime is outside the scope of this chapter.

6 Conclusions

The concept of assimilated law is a compromise between the sunset clause's all encompassing 'atomic' void and the more stable category of retained EU law. As such this fettered legal triumph of Heraclitus over Parmenides reflects the emerging socio-politico-economic autonomy of post-Brexit Britain. The Act's enactment may have settled the dust for the time being, but Brexit's long-term repercussions for the UK will persist. Those engaged in the study, practice and application of the law will have to grapple with the intricacies of the application of different regimes of EU law remnants in the devolved UK legal systems for several years to come.

Since a significantly large swathe of retained EU law has been converted into assimilated law, the simultaneous abolition of the supremacy principle, general principles and the enactment of the power to selectively mimic their effect is quite akin to approbation and reprobation. There are implications for separation of powers and parliamentary sovereignty where the executive and the judiciary are delegated powers to revoke, amend or replace retained EU law and assimilated law without adequate legislative restraints. In such circumstances, rule of law and human rights concerns could also arise.

The abolition of the supremacy principle, general principles, and retained EU rights and obligations by the Act may give rise to difficulties in interpretation. It is also unclear what role the courts might take with respect to legal interpretation and how far, if at all, they might wish to depart from assimilated case law. This means there is uncertainty as to whether what were thought to be settled legal issues may be re-litigated. It remains to be seen when the provisions facilitating the courts' departure from assimilated case law will come into force via commencement regulations. It is possible that the new permissive statutory test for departing from

[145] Ibid.

[146] Section 15E(2)(b) of the Civil Jurisdiction and Judgments Act 1982.

assimilated case law will come into effect after 23 June 2026 when the executive's powers to revoke amend or replace assimilated law expire.

In relation to the law applicable to cross border contractual and non-contractual obligations, the law is practically the same with some minor consequentialist amendments. Over the course of time, it seems likely that the UK approach will diverge from the EU Member States through judicial precedent and legislative reform. The liberal system of precedent created by Article 1(1) of Protocol No 2 on the Uniform Interpretation of the Lugano II Convention may offer a way forward in interpreting the assimilated Rome I and II Regulations by adopting a cautious approach that largely adheres to the notion of legal certainty. The courts of a Contracting State applying the Lugano II Convention 'pay due account' to the principles laid down by any relevant decisions on the Lugano Convention (1988), Brussels I Regulation (2001), Brussels Ia Regulation (2012), Brussels Convention (1968), and the Convention between the EU and Denmark applying the Brussels I Regulation to that Member State. However, the assimilated Rome I and II Regulations applied in the domestic legal context do not restrain recourse to a distinct approach to interpretation of assimilated case law.

References

Ahmed M (2022) Brexit and the future of private international law in English Courts. OUP

Briggs A (2017) Secession from the European Union and private international law: the cloud with a silver lining. Commercial Bar Association Brexit Lecture, 24 January 2017 <adrian_briggs_brexit_lecture.pdf (ox.ac.uk)>. Accessed 31 Aug 2021

Cowie G (2023) 'Retained EU Law (Revocation and Reform) Act 2023' (28 July 2023) House of Commons Library Research Briefing <https://researchbriefings.files.parliament.uk/documents/CBP-9841/CBP-9841.pdf>. Accessed 20 Feb 2024

Cross R, Harris JW (1991) Precedent in English law, 4th edn. Clarendon Press, OUP, p 114

Cross R, Bell J, Engle G (1995) Cross: statutory interpretation, 3rd edn. OUP, p 49

Dickinson A (2021) Realignment of the planets – Brexit and private international law. Praxis des Internationalen Privat- und Verfahrensrechts 213

Duhs E, Rao I (2021) Retained EU law: a practical guide. The Law Society

Dworkin G (1962) Stare Decisis in the House of Lords. Mod Law Rev 25:163

Dworkin R (1977) Taking rights seriously. Harvard University Press

Forsyth C (2005) The eclipse of private international law principle? The judicial process, interpretation and the dominance of legislation in the modern era. J Priv Int Law 1:93

Hancox E (2021) Interpreting the post-Brexit legal framework. Camb Law J 80:428

Harris JW (1997) Legal philosophies, 2nd edn. Butterworths, p 183

Harris J (2008) Understanding the English response to the Europeanisation of private international law. J Priv Int Law 4:347

Hartley TC (2005) The European Union and the systematic dismantling of the common law of conflict of laws. Int Comp Law Q 54:813

Kouroutakis A (2018) Sunset clause. In: Grote R, Lachenmann F, Wolfrum R (eds) Max Planck encyclopedia of comparative constitutional law. OUP

Lord Bingham of Cornhill (2006) 'The Judges: Active or Passive' (Maccabaean Lecture in Jurisprudence). Proc Br Acad 139:55

Lord Rodger of Earlsferry (2004) What are appeal courts for? Otago Law Rev 10:517

MacCormick N (1978) Legal reasoning and legal theory. Clarendon Press, OUP, p 134
Merrett L (2021) International employment cases post-Brexit: choice of law, territorial scope, jurisdiction and enforcement. Ind Law J 50:343
Sales P (2023) Retained EU law: purposive interpretation when the constitutional architecture changes. Annual Lecture of the UK Association for European Law (20 November 2023)
Vajda C (2021) The UK courts and EU law post-Brexit. Compet Law J 20:113
Whittaker S (2021) Retaining European Union law in the United Kingdom. Law Q Rev 137:477

Developments in Financial Services: UK and EU Approaches to Digital Finance

Jonathan McCarthy

1 Introduction

As with the areas of law discussed in the other chapters, the implications of Brexit for financial services in the United Kingdom and across the European Union remain to be fully revealed. However, if there is a salient aspect of modern financial services which especially highlights the potential future direction of the UK-EU relationship, it is digital finance, or FinTech (the use of technology in finance). Digital finance is a foremost policy concern for the UK and the EU in recent times. The changes which are occurring in contemporary finance—by virtue of increased digitalisation and adoption of technological innovations—signify that the course of UK-EU relations in respect of financial services will be particularly influenced by the approaches which are taken in regulating digital finance. As argued in this chapter, there are differences in the approaches of the UK and the EU regarding the regulation of digital finance. Yet, there are clear opportunities for enhanced collaboration and coordination of regulatory standards.

By focusing on digital finance and FinTech, Sect. 2 of the chapter provides an overview of modern UK and EU regulatory policies and initiatives. Section 3 describes how the UK and EU may adapt their regulatory positions towards technological innovations. Examples of technological developments will be identified and the role of the open banking regimes in the UK and the EU will be explicated. Section 4 evaluates the options for coordination and for standard-setting. By recognising the possibilities for improved collaboration in specific activities, not only can the future UK-EU relationship be strengthened, but much-needed regulatory clarity at an international level may also be facilitated. When appraising the

J. McCarthy (✉)
School of Law, University College Cork, Cork, Ireland
e-mail: Jonathan.McCarthy@ucc.ie

E. Guinchard, C. Panara (eds.), *The New Relationship between the United Kingdom and the European Union*, https://doi.org/10.1007/978-3-031-70652-3_17

necessity for greater collaboration, the respective merits of recent UK and EU approaches should be distinguished.

2 UK and EU Regulatory Policies and Initiatives

This section portrays the evolving measures for digital finance in the UK and EU in recent years. In view of the significance of technological innovations to financial services, it will be demonstrated that regulatory measures and policy initiatives have steadily gained impetus in the UK and the EU, regardless of the UK's exit from the EU.

2.1 UK Measures

The UK's focus on constructing a regulatory framework in support of innovation in finance gathered pace from 2015. Under the auspices of 'Project Innovate', the Financial Conduct Authority (FCA) took responsibility for implementing practical supports for FinTech firms. The measures were tailored towards firms that were interested in seeking formal authorisation as service providers. Such firms are keen to be afforded space within which to experiment and to trial new technologies and products, while assured that regulatory sanctions are not being imposed. As acknowledged by the FCA when summarising the 'lessons learned' following the initial introduction of the measures, unauthorised start-up firms were the most common applicants for entry to the FCA's regulatory sandbox.[1]

The FCA sandbox is the epitome of a regulatory technique that expressly aims to balance the promotion of innovation with the safeguarding of existing rules relating to consumer protection, market integrity and financial stability. By accepting cohorts of applicants since 2016, the sandbox enables entrants to test innovations in controlled settings with access to regulatory expertise and guidance. Applicants must fulfil eligibility criteria, based on whether an innovation is within the scope of the UK market, whether it represents 'genuine innovation', whether there is a benefit to consumers, whether the innovation is ready for sandbox testing (having refined a business plan and understood the existing regulatory requirements), and whether there is a definite need for the innovation to be subjected to testing in a sandbox environment.[2] As an indication of how the sandbox has grown into a fully-fledged

[1] FCA (2017).

[2] For a summary of the eligibility criteria, see https://www.fca.org.uk/firms/innovation/regulatory-sandbox/eligibility-criteria (date accessed: 30 October 2023).

and specialised component of UK financial regulation, it is estimated that there are almost 100 dedicated FCA staff for the sandbox alone.[3]

If a sandbox is the equivalent of a clinical trial for a technological innovation, an innovation hub is a relatively informal measure in providing firms and financial institutions with a designated point of contact for advice regarding compliance.[4] A more direct form of collaboration between supervisory authorities and private sector projects was exemplified by the Bank of England's 'FinTech Accelerator'. Launched in 2016, the initiative involved the Bank of England bringing proofs-of-concept to fruition with private firms.[5] Collaborative efforts between supervisors and market players are being maintained through FCA-organised 'tech sprints' and 'hackathons.'[6] In 2018 and in 2021, Green FinTech Challenges were used to test products and services by assisting in transitioning towards a sustainable or net-zero economy.[7]

A re-appraisal of the UK's policy direction in financial regulation was galvanised by the van Steenis 'Future of Finance' report for the Bank of England, published in 2019.[8] Although the report encompassed several aspects of contemporary finance, the repercussions of digitalisation and certain technologies were prominent in the findings. It was plainly expressed that "...Brexit or no Brexit, there are numerous areas where the Bank can make progress in the years ahead."[9] Ranging from facilitating the highly lucrative data economy (anticipated by the report to be valued at just under £100 billion by 2025) to protecting against cyber-risks and to embracing 'digital regulation', the report resulted in a Bank of England response which prioritised the delivery of a "world-class" RegTech and data strategy.[10]

The 2021 Kalifa Review of UK FinTech[11] represents the most thorough evaluation of current UK policies towards digital finance, notably because of its defined recommendations for overall post-Brexit policies. The review concentrated on reforms pertaining to policy and regulation, skills, investment, internationalisation, and national connectivity. The review contributes to the moulding of policy and regulation by demanding the creation of a comprehensive FinTech strategy, the establishment of a broadened 'scalebox' for FinTech firms, the introduction of a Digital Economy Taskforce, and the revision of the UK's trade policy (by integrating

---

[3] World Bank (2020a), p. 20.

[4] On the distinctive features of sandboxes and innovation hubs as suitable regulatory measures for FinTech, see particularly Zetzsche et al. (2017).

[5] See https://www.bankofengland.co.uk/speech/2017/the-boes-fintech-accelerator-what-have-we-done-and-what-have-we-learned (date accessed: 30 October 2023)

[6] See World Bank (2020b), pp. 25–26.

[7] See https://www.fca.org.uk/firms/innovation/green-fintech-challenge (date accessed: 30 October 2023).

[8] Bank of England (2019a).

[9] Bank of England (2019a), p. 8.

[10] Bank of England (2019b).

[11] Innovate Finance (2021).

issues of digital finance and assisting UK FinTech firms to become 'international champions').

As noted in Sect. 3 below, the Kalifa Review made proposals in respect of certain technologies and innovations. As will be elaborated on in Sect. 4, the scalebox recommendations are particularly instructive by bringing about an enhanced sandbox model. As a consequence of the recommendations, this sandbox is available on a rolling, or year-wide, basis, in conjunction with a permanent Digital Sandbox, which can be utilised to encourage partnerships between financial institutions and new market entrants.

The recommendations attest to the practically oriented mindset of UK regulatory measures on digital finance, but one which is increasingly combined with a more expansive, or visionary, attitude that may not have been as evident in the years prior to Brexit.[12] It could be argued that the espousal of an apparently broader perspective is more closely aligned to how EU measures have emerged during recent years.

2.2 EU Measures

Published in March 2018, the European Commission's FinTech Action Plan denoted the first concerted effort at EU level to devise a comprehensive policy approach towards emergent innovations in finance.[13] The Action Plan's avowed objectives were "to harness rapid advances in technology for the benefit of the EU economy, citizens and industry, to foster a more competitive and innovative European financial sector, and to ensure the integrity of the EU financial system."[14] However, the approach advocated through the Action Plan was decidedly cautious. For instance, against the backdrop of "a fast-moving environment" of technological innovations, it was articulated that "[o] verly prescriptive and precipitous regulation carries the risk of undesired outcomes", while acknowledging that refraining from regularly updating policy stances could impede the competitiveness of European finance in an increasingly globalised market. As a paradox to the idea of an Action Plan, the rather passive, 'wait-and-see' tone did seem to reveal reluctance, or, at least, ambivalence, about directly addressing unavoidable regulatory and legal concerns.[15]

If the Action Plan supported ongoing monitoring instead of making decisively proactive interventions to legislate for certain FinTech innovations, there were other initiatives which exhibit a gradual intensification of policy attention on issues of digital finance. Most of the EU measures which were complementary to the 2018

[12] The shift towards policy strategies is exemplified by the September 2021 publication of the UK Government's National AI Strategy, available at: https://www.gov.uk/government/publications/national-ai-strategy (date accessed: 30 October 2023).

[13] European Commission (2018).

[14] European Commission (2018), p. 18.

[15] See McCarthy (2019).

Action Plan were concentrated on particular technologies. The establishment of the EU's High Level Expert Group on Artificial Intelligence (AI) led to the formulation of guiding principles for ethical and trustworthy AI[16] and to the release of the Commission's 2020 White Paper on AI.[17] These steps culminated in the Commission's proposal of a Regulation to lay down harmonised rules on AI (a draft 'AI Act'), since enacted as Regulation (EU) 2024/1689.[18] The 2018 creation of the European Blockchain Observatory and Forum set foundations for further consideration of the purposes and benefits of blockchain technology and its variations, specifically distributed ledger technology (DLT).[19] Manifest outcomes of these initiatives are the enacted Regulation (EU) 2022/858, providing for a DLT pilot regime for financial market infrastructures (FMIs),[20] and the establishment of a European Blockchain Sandbox in 2023.[21]

Published in September 2020, the Commission's Digital Finance Strategy proved to be a markedly more ambitious endeavour than the previous Action Plan.[22] The scale of ambition was underscored by the introduction of a package of proposed measures of legislation which would be uniformly applicable to EU Member States.[23] The package consisted of three Regulation proposals and a separate Retail Payments Strategy. In addition to the entry into force of the DLT pilot regime for FMIs, Regulation (EU) 2022/2554 on digital operational resilience for the financial sector (Digital Operational Resilience Act (DORA))[24] and Regulation (EU) 2023/1114 on markets in crypto-assets (MiCA Regulation)[25] have both been enacted. An analysis of the legislative measures is outside of the scope of this particular chapter. Nonetheless, the expansive nature of the Digital Finance Strategy, in striving to

[16] See generally https://digital-strategy.ec.europa.eu/en/policies/expert-group-ai (date accessed: 30 October 2023).

[17] European Commission (2020a).

[18] Proposal for a Regulation of the European Parliament and of the Council Laying Down Harmonised Rules on Artificial Intelligence (Artificial Intelligence Act) and Amending Certain Union Legislative Acts, COM(2021) 206 final.

[19] See the EU Blockchain Observatory and Forum website at: https://www.eublockchainforum.eu/ (date accessed: 30 October 2023).

[20] Regulation (EU) 2022/858 of the European Parliament and of the Council of 30 May 2022 on a pilot regime for market infrastructures based on distributed ledger technology and amending Regulations (EU) No 600/2014 and (EU) No 909/2014 and Directive 2014/65/EU; OJ L 151.

[21] See https://ec.europa.eu/digital-building-blocks/wikis/display/EBSI/Sandbox+Project (date accessed: 30 October 2023).

[22] See https://finance.ec.europa.eu/publications/digital-finance-package_en (date accessed: 30 October 2023).

[23] McCarthy (2021).

[24] Regulation (EU) 2022/2554 of the European Parliament and of the Council of 14 December 2022 on digital operational resilience for the financial sector and amending Regulations (EC) No 1060/2009, (EU) No 648/2012, (EU) No 600/2014, (EU) No 909/2014 and (EU) 2016/1011; OJ L 333/1.

[25] Regulation (EU) 2023/1114 of the European Parliament and of the Council of 31 May 2023 on markets in crypto-assets, and amending Regulations (EU) No 1093/2010 and (EU) No 1095/2010 and Directives 2013/36/EU and (EU) 2019/1937; OJ L 150/40.

explicitly legislate for several facets of digital finance, will inevitably constitute a reference point for jurisdictions globally. Even the principle of 'same activity, same risks, same rules'[26] which underpins the Strategy should instigate discussion among international authorities as to whether suitably generalised regulatory responses can be taken towards constantly evolving innovations.

As direct legislative intervention, the package of measures from the Digital Finance Strategy corresponds to a broader set of EU policy goals, labelled as a 'Digital Compass', which is aimed at achieving a European 'Digital Decade' up until 2030. There are four core aspects to the objectives: developing skills; securing and sustaining digital infrastructures; improving digital transformation of businesses; and enhancing digitalisation of public services.[27] It could be argued that these kinds of overarching policy objectives for boosting digitalisation are purely aspirational, when contrasted with the specific requirements of legislative measures. However, an interwoven fabric of policy targets can ultimately strengthen the rationale for practical regulatory initiatives such as sandboxes.[28] Indeed, the EU's efforts to construct a cohesive policy and regulatory framework may offer an example for how the UK's post-Brexit initiatives could be honed to adapt to future innovations.

3 Adapting to Future Innovations in Financial Services

This section considers how present UK and EU approaches could adjust to ongoing and future technological innovations in financial services. The rather contrasting experiences of FinTech activity within the UK and the EU have influenced the approaches taken towards specific examples of technologies. It will be explained how open banking regimes in the UK and the EU will be pivotal in adapting to developments in payments services and transfers of customer data.

3.1 Examples of Technological Developments

The rate of FinTech activity has varied significantly between EU Member States.[29] While some EU Member States record higher concentrations of FinTech firms than others, the relative pre-eminence of UK FinTech has remained intact following Brexit. As stated in the Kalifa Review, the UK accounts for 10% of the global

[26] European Commission (2020b).

[27] See https://ec.europa.eu/info/strategy/priorities-2019-2024/europe-fit-digital-age/europes-digital-decade-digital-targets-2030_en (date accessed: 30 October 2023).

[28] McCarthy (2021).

[29] See especially World Bank (2022). For figures on the types of FinTech activity within the EU, see also Beck et al. (2022).

market share for FinTech and generates investment which is more than the next five European countries combined. The UK occupies third place internationally (behind the US and China) for investment in technology 'unicorn' start-up firms and the UK is also in third position for 'critically emerging' technologies (including AI and blockchain/DLT).[30]

In the years prior to Brexit, there is little doubt that the UK witnessed an astonishing expansion in FinTech activity and firms.[31] Before reports on an impending economic recession, empirical studies have seemed to indicate that UK investment in FinTech has maintained its pace ahead of EU Member States, with the UK's FinTech sector being characterised by specialised knowledge-based clusters, particularly in the City of London. Furthermore, findings have revealed that the numbers of firms intending to establish in the UK in the aftermath of Brexit have matched—and even exceeded—the numbers seeking to leave.[32] As a sign of the growth envisaged for forthcoming years, when recommending the establishment of a FinTech Growth Fund to assist firms to achieve public listing, the Kalifa Review referred to a survey finding that more than one-third of UK FinTech firms in 2019 wished to undertake an Initial Public Offering within five years.[33] However, the expectations that the UK will indefinitely retain its dominant status as a FinTech centre should be moderated. A substantial portion of the skills and expertise, which have been formative to FinTech growth in the UK, was linked to EU nationals as employees of UK firms and financial institutions.[34]

FinTech within the UK and the EU can be sub-divided to other functions. 'RegTech' is the use of technology by regulated institutions for regulatory purposes, such as fulfilling requirements on reporting, due diligence, and know-your-customer procedures. 'SupTech' is the use of technology by supervisory authorities for completing oversight obligations. Aside from the types of measures outlined in the previous section, the UK and EU have also pursued policies designed to facilitate adoption of RegTech and SupTech applications.[35]

AI, machine learning (ML) and advanced data analytics are forms of technologies—centred on algorithm-based and automated models—which should be most adept in enabling RegTech and SupTech to grow and to be utilised in an optimally efficient manner. To focus on AI as an example, the adoption of advanced technologies will be an incremental process within financial practices in the UK and the EU.[36] As evinced in the preceding section of this chapter, UK and EU policy

---

[30] Innovate Finance (2021).

[31] See Stolerman (2020).

[32] Kalaitzake (2022). On the numbers of financial services firms relocating, see also https://www.ey.com/en_uk/news/2022/03/ey-financial-services-brexit-tracker-movement-within-uk-financial-services-sector-stabilises-five-years-on-from-article-50-trigger (date accessed: 30 October 2023).

[33] Innovate Finance (2021), p. 53.

[34] Hall (2022).

[35] See McCarthy (2022).

[36] See Hoffmann and Nurski (2021), EBA (2021a), and McCarthy (2022).

measures have differed. Yet, for technologies such as AI, there is a sense that the same types of regulatory concerns and recommended actions are being identified on both sides.

To a large degree, the EU High Level Group's submission of ethics guidelines for trustworthy AI mirror the recommendations conveyed by the UK's van Steenis report in demanding "resilient and fair use" of AI, as accomplished through data governance, model validation frameworks, and accountability regimes.[37] The impact of the EU's AI Act will be to oblige human oversight for AI systems that can be categorised as 'high-risk' (as provided for within Article 14 of Regulation (EU) 2024/1689).[38] The need to ensure 'human-in-the-loop' oversight of AI-based procedures was reinforced by the final report of the Bank of England/FCA's AI Public-Private Forum in February 2022. To enhance the explainability of AI systems and to reduce the opacity which may envelop automated decision-making, the Forum recommended, *inter alia*, that centralised bodies within firms should be responsible for crafting AI governance standards.[39] By looking to place an onus on firms to voluntarily establish internal standards for the use of AI, this implemented recommendation should, in effect, serve the same purpose as the EU AI Act by incentivising firms to proactively take the initiative to clarify AI governance procedures.

A further example of technological developments, relevant to the UK and the EU, is the trialling and proposed launch of a central bank digital currency (CBDC). The European Central Bank has conducted advanced piloting of a digital euro[40] and the European Commission has proposed a Regulation for the legal establishment of a digital euro.[41] The UK's outlook towards a CBDC was comparably more hesitant, although the proposition has evidently gained greater support in recent times. For example, the van Steenis report could not "see a compelling case" for a CBDC, "given numerous uncertainties", ranging from legal ambiguities, apprehension over the use of a wide-scale CBDC, the effects on monetary transmission, and cybersecurity.[42] However, the Kalifa Review subsequently progressed to accepting that the introduction of a CBDC for wholesale use (for institutional use, rather than for retail use among the general public) could amount to a 'short-term win' in testing the viability of the CBDC proposal for broader use.[43]

The major move to initiate CBDC testing in the UK arrived in April 2021, as the Bank of England and HM Treasury announced the creation of a joint Taskforce to

---

[37] Bank of England (2019a), p. 61.

[38] Examples of high-risk AI systems are classified within Annex III of the EU's AI Act.

[39] Bank of England/FCA (2022).

[40] For example, see ECB (2022).

[41] Proposal for a Regulation of the European Parliament and of the Council on the establishment of a digital euro, COM(2023) 369 final.

[42] Bank of England (2019a), p. 33.

[43] Innovate Finance (2021), p. 29.

coordinate the exploration of a possible CBDC.[44] As numerous projects across jurisdictions internationally are directed towards designing retail CBDCs,[45] the UK's increased interest in a CBDC should aid cooperation and progress towards coordinated standards between the UK and the EU. These standards would be especially crucial to facilitating future cross-border payments, using different CBDCs, through shared and technically interoperable (possibly DLT-based) platforms.

3.2 *UK and EU Frameworks for Open Banking*

To maintain the future efficiency of payments, open banking frameworks will be decisive for customers and for providers alike. For the Basel Committee on Banking Supervision (BCBS), open banking is construed as "the sharing and leveraging of customer-permissioned data by banks with third party developers and firms to build applications and services." Although jurisdictions may opt to apply varying definitions of open banking, the primary technical grounds for open banking are Application Programming Interfaces (APIs). The BCBS ascribes quite a general interpretation to an API as "a set of rules and specifications for software programs to communicate with each other, that forms an interface between different programs to facilitate their interaction."[46]

The description of open banking implies the promise of such frameworks in accommodating innovations in financial services. By ensuring the seamless processing of customer data, an inherent quality of open banking should be its adaptability to technological innovations. However, in practice, there are significant numbers of jurisdictions which have not experienced any developments or initiatives in open banking.[47] The UK and the EU are two important examples as to how open banking can be refined in future and how open banking can be the basis for coordination between existing regimes, especially in the standardisation of APIs.

The second Payments Services Directive (PSD2)[48] is the legislative source for the EU's open banking regime. By Articles 66 and 67, third party providers are entitled to access data of bank customers' accounts for the purposes of Payment Initiation Services (PIS) and Account Information Services (AIS). Customer consent is necessary for data transfer. As specified in Article 94 of PSD2, data processing must be

[44] See https://www.bankofengland.co.uk/news/2021/april/bank-of-england-statement-on-central-bank-digital-currency (date accessed: 30 October 2023).

[45] See BIS (2022).

[46] BCBS (2019).

[47] BCBS (2019), Figure 1.

[48] Directive (EU) 2015/2366 of the European Parliament and of the Council of 25 November 2015 on payment services in the internal market, amending Directives 2002/65/EC, 2009/110/EC and 2013/36/EU and Regulation (EU) No 1093/2010, and repealing Directive 2007/64/EC; OJ L 337/35.

compliant with applicable data protection laws (particularly the General Data Protection Regulation (GDPR)[49]).

The UK's implementation of an open banking framework originated with the Competition and Markets Authority (CMA)'s Retail Banking Investigation of 2016 and the subsequent issuance of the CMA's Retail Banking Investigation Order 2017. Nine FCA-registered banks[50] were required to adopt secure and standardised APIs, but voluntary participation was permitted for smaller banks. The Open Banking Implementation Entity (OBIE) is the UK authority which is responsible for creating software standards and industry guidelines.[51] While PSD2 relates to data on the processing of payments, the UK framework applies to personal and small business current accounts. The UK rules encompass extensive informational requirements regarding branches and ATM locations, financial products, and relevant fees.[52]

As declared by the van Steenis report, "[t]he UK is the first country in the world to undertake this experiment, so the onus is on regulators to get it right, or adapt fast."[53] It is asserted by some commentators that "[t]hough PSD2 was a major development, the UK's open banking initiatives that followed were, in many respects, even more far-reaching."[54] On the other hand, the ideals of open banking have not always led to practical changes, specifically in making payments services more competitive and in improving the efficacy of APIs. Irrespective of the pioneering efforts of the UK and EU, there is still much to be done in maximising the benefits of open banking and in mitigating risks. For instance, studies of German banking data in the wake of PSD2's implementation found that the 'imposed innovation' of the open banking legislation did not deliver a conspicuous increase in innovative products from FinTech providers, that there was no indelible erosion in banks' traditional dominance in the payments services market, and that an accelerated use of secure APIs did not materialise.[55]

The European Commission's public consultations for the review of PSD2 and the EU's open banking framework were completed in 2022.[56] In the UK, the FCA

---

[49] Regulation (EU) 2016/679 of the European Parliament and of the Council of 27 April 2016 on the protection of natural persons with regard to the processing of personal data and on the free movement of such data, and repealing Directive 95/46/EC, OJ L 119.

[50] AIB, Barclays Bank, Bank of Ireland, Danske Bank, HSBC, Lloyds Banking Group, Nationwide Building Society, RBS Group, and Santander.

[51] See https://www.openbanking.org.uk/ (date accessed: 30 October 2023).

[52] For a background to the UK open banking measures in the context of broader initiatives, see Marimootoo (2020).

[53] Bank of England (2019a), p. 13.

[54] Nicholls (2019), p. 129.

[55] Radnejad et al. (2021).

[56] See the details regarding the Commission's targeted consultation on open finance and data sharing at: https://finance.ec.europa.eu/regulation-and-supervision/consultations/finance-2022-open-finance_en (date accessed: 30 October 2023) and the Commission public consultation on the review of existing EU rules on payments services at: https://ec.europa.eu/info/law/better-regulation/have-your-say/initiatives/13331-Payment-services-review-of-EU-rules/public-consultation_en (date accessed: 30 October 2023).

staged a 'Call for Input' on open finance, which closed in October 2020 and sought to determine reforms which may be needed for the benefit of consumers and for alleviating risks to market stability.[57] The reviews are obviously welcome in clarifying the kinds of amendments which could ameliorate open banking regimes. For instance, as a means of bolstering future use of sufficiently sophisticated APIs, industry-wide API standardisation was advocated by the European Banking Authority (EBA) in its response to the Commission's review of PSD2.[58]

The Commission subsequently released proposals for new legislative measures in 2023, consisting of a proposed PSD3[59] and a proposed Regulation on a framework for financial data access.[60] The Regulation proposal on financial data access is especially relevant to EU ambitions to promote data-driven finance. Rather than setting out common standards for APIs, the Commission favoured a uniformly applicable Regulation which would include requirements to oblige market participants to provide customers with data access 'permission dashboards', implement eligibility rules for access to customer data, and empower European Supervisory Authorities to issue guidelines. In turn, the responsibility should be on market participants to develop common standards for customer data and interfaces which are to be subject to mandatory access rules. As expressed in the original Commission proposal, "customers should be empowered to decide how and by whom their financial data is used and should have the option to grant firms access to their data for the purposes of obtaining financial and information services should they wish."[61]

As the EU reform proposals are entering the legislative procedures, a UK Joint Regulatory Oversight Committee (formed from the FCA, the Payment Systems Regulator (PSR), Treasury, and the CMA) has produced recommendations for the 'next phase' of UK open banking.[62] As reiterated through the recommendations, the rate of open banking payments has escalated (a doubling in amounts of payments was recorded in 2022, relative to 2021).[63] The thriving use of open banking and APIs is a primary factor behind the planned establishment of a future open banking entity in the UK, marking a transition from the previous OBIE. In enunciating a strategy for future open banking in the UK, the recommendations identify three central priorities to be delivered: the creation of a sustainable, competitive and strong ecosystem for open banking, the choice of effective methods of payments, and the

---

[57] https://www.fca.org.uk/publications/calls-input/call-input-open-finance (date accessed: 30 October 2023).

[58] EBA (2022).

[59] Proposal for a Directive of the European Parliament and of the Council on payment services and electronic money services in the Internal Market amending Directive 98/26/EC and repealing Directives 2015/2366/EU and 2009/110/EC, COM(2023) 366 final.

[60] Proposal for a Regulation of the European Parliament and of the Council on a framework for Financial Data Access and amending Regulations (EU) No 1093/2010, (EU) No 1094/2010, (EU) No 1095/2010 and (EU) 2022/2554, COM(2023) 360 final.

[61] Recital (2), Financial Data Access Regulation Proposal.

[62] Joint Regulatory Oversight Committee (2023).

[63] Joint Regulatory Oversight Committee (2023), para. 2.2.

scalable means of facilitating data sharing.[64] As stated by the Joint Regulatory Oversight Committee, roadmap themes and actions for achieving these aims include the levelling up of availability and performance (such as through data collection for APIs and, where necessary, the updating of requirements) and ensuring consumer protection (such as by guaranteeing appropriate dispute resolution processes).

There are larger regulatory concerns which are making evaluations and amendments of open banking frameworks even more necessary. The emergence of digital finance platforms—driven by Big Tech companies—proffers possibilities for a more expansive concept of 'open finance' than what currently exists through interactions between banks, payment service providers, and customers.[65] If Big Tech platforms are enabled to access customer accounts in the same manner as permitted through the UK and EU rules, the potential for profound systemic risk within financial services is also increased. For the sake of adapting appropriately to imminent transformations in the digital finance market and to the consequent regulatory challenges, the reviews of the open banking regimes should also have the effect of stimulating cooperation between the UK and EU, especially in standardising APIs and in cultivating standards on data access.

4 Coordination and the Setting of Standards

This section analyses the scope for coordination and standard-setting in the future relationship between the UK and EU in relation to digital finance. As the previous sections indicated why collaboration and convergence should be progressed, this section explains how specific collaborative mechanisms can be designed, particularly by referring to what has worked well for the UK and EU approaches over the past decade.

4.1 Collaborative Opportunities and the Role for Memoranda of Understanding

On 27 June 2023, the UK and the EU signed a Memorandum of Understanding to jointly establish a framework for regulatory cooperation in the area of financial services. According to the Memorandum of Understanding, the bilateral exchange of views and analysis is essential to preserving financial stability, market integrity, and protections for investors and for consumers.[66] A joint Regulatory Forum is to be

---

[64] Joint Regulatory Oversight Committee (2023), paras. 2.11 to 2.19.

[65] On the growth of digital finance platforms, see EBA (2021b).

[66] EU-UK Memorandum of Understanding on Financial Services Regulatory Cooperation (27 June 2023).

established in order "to serve as a platform to facilitate structured regulatory cooperation" and meetings are to be held on at least a semi-annual basis.[67] Contact points for each jurisdiction are to be designated to facilitate cooperation. Yet, it is clarified within the Memorandum of Understanding that "[d]iscussions in the Forum will not restrict the ability of either the EU or the UK to implement regulatory, supervisory or other legal measures that either considers appropriate."[68]

The 2023 arrangement is a starting point for further cooperation and collaboration in financial services, particularly in aspects of finance which are in the midst of ongoing technological changes and digitalisation. The terms and language of the Memorandum of Understanding appear to be intentionally general in scope, but minimal in detail. As observed by some commentators, the Memorandum of Understanding does not represent systematic equivalence. Instead, it is "a thin cooperation framework" and, for the foreseeable future, dialogue within the Joint Forum is likely to be a means by which potential equivalence decisions can reached in respect of financial services.[69]

Prior to the 2023 Memorandum of Understanding, a scarcity of equivalence decisions significantly restricted UK financial services firms' ability to access the Single Market, at the same time as European Economic Area firms are effectively passported for access to the UK market. UK firms have accordingly had to rely on temporary permission arrangements as they are being finalised.[70] The UK has agreed mutual recognition of regulatory standards with Switzerland and there are separate trade agreements and partnerships with jurisdictions such as Australia and Singapore. For digital finance specifically, FinTech 'bridges' are in existence with Australia, China, Hong Kong, Singapore and South Korea. However, the scope of these FinTech-related collaborative arrangements can be limited in practice.

As described by the Kalifa Review, FinTech bridges are 'unique' to particular jurisdictions, but the collaboration in question essentially entails "access to events, meetings and networking opportunities", referrals for regulatory approval, "introductions to buyers, investors, trade associations and institutions", advice, one-to-one mentoring from specialists and forms of grants or subsidies.[71] FinTech bridges do not possess explicit provisions for shared recognition of regulatory standards. As a glimpse of a more specialised avenue by which globalised collaboration could be nurtured, the Kalifa Review's FinTech International Action Plan recommended the creation of a collaborative hub for international firms "to identify partners and innovative new offerings and partnerships."[72] The hub's activities would

[67] EU-UK Memorandum of Understanding on Financial Services Regulatory Cooperation, paras. 1 and 2.

[68] EU-UK Memorandum of Understanding on Financial Services Regulatory Cooperation, para. 10.

[69] Beck and Petit (2023).

[70] For a summary of the effects of the lack of equivalence agreements for financial services firms, see further Hall (2022).

[71] Innovate Finance (2021), p. 38.

[72] Innovate Finance (2021), p. 75.

conceivably comprise of webinar sessions, contact information for professional services, and facilities for informal communication. The flexibility associated with the proposal may prompt engagement with individual firms, but it is not necessarily a spur towards coordinated regulatory standards.

It is preferably in the context of cooperation through international standard-setting bodies that regulatory clarity can be boosted at a global level. Engagement with international standard-setting can simultaneously help to build closer links between the UK and EU. The UK's participation in international standard-setting activities is considered to have been more active than that of the European Commission.[73] The FCA's chairing of the Global Financial Innovation Network (GFIN) is an emphatic example of the UK's willingness to steer collaborative projects at an international level.[74] In the activities of international institutions and agencies, the UK has been inclined to assume the role of an "independent player", entrenching strategies with certain bodies, but also showing a tendency to choose whom to side with.[75] This latitude in striking collaborative arrangements can flourish through the BCBS, the FSB, the International Organization of Securities Commissions (IOSCO), and the Financial Action Task Force (FATF), if there is adequate motivation to collaborate.

Memoranda of understanding, or cooperation agreements, between supervisory authorities in different jurisdictions have been utilised previously as a means of addressing regulatory fragmentation relating to cross-border FinTech activities. The parameters of a bespoke agreement rarely stray beyond the focus of whatever regulatory initiative is being stipulated. For example, a memorandum of understanding can be formulated exclusively to govern the terms of a regulatory sandbox which could be accessible to firms that are based in another jurisdiction. Otherwise, broader forms of cooperation agreements, which are principally concerned with information-sharing, would be analogous to the FinTech bridges which are currently operated by the UK.[76]

A model for a collaborative agreement on digital finance is provided by IOSCO's 'enhanced' Multilateral Memorandum of Understanding Concerning Consultation and Cooperation and the Exchange of Information.[77] As explicated by Lev Bromberg, Andrew Goodwin and Ian Ramsay, such formats for bilateral agreements are used by the US Securities and Exchange Commission (SEC), the Australian Securities and Investment Commission (ASIC), and New Zealand's Financial Markets Authority (FMA).[78] The content of an agreement should include relevant definitions,

[73] Stolerman (2020), p. 179.

[74] See generally https://www.thegfin.com/ (date accessed: 30 October 2023).

[75] Schilling de Carvalho (2022), p. 108.

[76] On the various features of memoranda of understanding and cooperation agreements, see European Supervisory Authorities (2018), section 2.2.3.

[77] See https://www.iosco.org/about/?subsection=mmou (date accessed: 30 October 2023)

[78] Bromberg et al. (2018).

purposes, principles, scope of coordination, confidentiality provisions, and term or duration.

Any prospective agreements involving the UK and EU should have an existing format to refer to. By couching collaboration within existing international standard-setting activities, the likelihood of achieving these agreements for regulatory cooperation can be improved. It should be conceded that 'soft law' manoeuvres are not a simple formula for resolving all possible regulatory dilemmas concerning digital finance in the UK, EU, and internationally. As regulatory issues regarding technology will transcend jurisdictional boundaries, memoranda of understanding and cooperation agreements are part of an overall approach—albeit a highly important part—in reaching coherent standards.[79]

As inevitable as the desire for competition will be in the economically turbulent years immediately after Brexit, competitive instincts will need to be relaxed for there to be some prospect of collaboration. To assist in promoting UK firms as international champions and to flexibly reflect "market dynamics", the Kalifa Review suggested that there should be a change in approach by the CMA's Digital Markets Unit when investigating (and, if necessary, sanctioning) mergers and acquisitions relating to FinTech firms under the UK's Competition Act 1998.[80] It is these intra-jurisdictional policy pressures which can affect convergence and coordination of international standards.[81]

Instead of being preoccupied with competition, there are patent examples of where the UK and EU can learn from one another. The proposed launch of a digital euro could lead to testing of multiple-CBDCs (mCBDCs) for use in cross-border payments. The UK may have perceptible interest in these testing activities if the idea of a CBDC is pursued.[82] Moreover, the EU's adoption of the DORA Regulation may foster international cooperation on cybersecurity standards, especially arising from the provisions requiring financial institutions to undertake threat-led penetration testing of systems.

4.2 *Credit Where Credit Is Due: Relative Successes of the UK and EU Approaches*

Because of the scale and ambition of the package of measures within the European Commission's Digital Finance Strategy, the seeming urgency of the EU's regulatory

[79] See further Bromberg et al. (2018), Yadav (2020), and Schilling de Carvalho (2022).

[80] Innovate Finance (2021), p. 9.

[81] On the issues arising from the CMA's scrutiny of FinTech M&As, see Schwarz and Bernstein (2022).

[82] For examples of collaboration between central banking authorities in mCBDC testing within the BIS Innovation Hub, see https://www.bis.org/about/bisih/projects.htm?m=3102 (date accessed: 30 October 2023).

approach to digital finance will be heeded by jurisdictions worldwide.[83] Each of the legislative pillars of the Strategy are targeted towards complex issues of contemporary FinTech: legally classifying crypto-assets and imposing suitable enforcement measures; shaping harmonised rules for digital operational resilience within the financial sector and compelling institutions to comply with requirements on testing and incident reporting; and putting in place a pilot regime that enables securities market operators to trial DLT as a novel technology which is expected to produce radical changes for the processing and recording of transactions. The parallel AI Act signals a determination to set clear rules for a technology which is imbued with as much opacity as potential benefits for financial services. Because of the sheer scope of the Strategy, there are undoubtedly features and regulatory concerns which resonate with the UK and with other jurisdictions, which, in turn, yields opportunities for international cooperation.

As set out in Sect. 2 above, there is plenty about the UK's focus on implementing feasible regulatory supports which can be informative for the establishment of the EU's DLT pilot regime, AI regulatory sandboxes, and other measures which are to function on a pan-EU basis. As argued in analyses of the UK's stance on FinTech regulation, the practical emphasis of UK initiatives is fundamentally tied to information, since "[e]ffectively, the UK adopted a regulatory approach which is oriented towards the capture of information."[84] Through the FCA sandbox and associated measures, the UK's regulatory outlook is influenced by a need to learn about emergent and advanced technological innovations and by guiding innovative businesses, products, and services towards market readiness and legal compliance. Policy agendas are vital for identifying longer-term objectives, but it is through practical measures, such as sandboxes, that regulators can appreciate the factors that contribute to innovation, in addition to understanding what may not work as effectively.

As a mechanism which the Kalifa Review recommended as a permanent feature of UK regulation, the FCA's Digital Sandbox initiative is illustrative of the types of schemes which could also be applied on an EU-wide footing. The Digital Sandbox was initially piloted for an 11-week period to February 2021. The second pilot was held from November 2021 to March 2022 and focused on applications for a sustainability-themed cohort of entrants, based on ESG (Environmental, Social and Governance) data and disclosure.[85] The pilots allowed participating firms to liaise with industry representatives within briefer (and, arguably, less constraining) timeframes than the standard FCA sandbox (which carries durations of six months at a time for testing). From the evaluations of the two pilots of the Digital Sandbox, it was envisaged that the next phase would direct attention towards the use of platforms

---

[83] As acknowledged by Zetzsche et al. (2021) and McCarthy (2021).

[84] Schilling de Carvalho (2022), p. 128.

[85] See the Digital Sandbox website at: https://www.fca.org.uk/firms/innovation/digital-sandbox (date accessed: 30 October 2023).

for SupTech.[86] With the intention of integrating the Digital Sandbox within an infrastructure of regulatory supports, the Kalifa Review recommendations also led to a scaling of the existing FCA sandbox, whereby applications are now being received throughout the year.

A Digital Sandbox-like programme is a practicable option for an EU-wide initiative. Although it is specific to a certain form of technology, a salutary pre-existing example is the European Blockchain Sandbox, which is committed to accepting 20 entrants annually. A programme which is open to all types of financial technologies would allow firms from across EU Member States to apply to participate in sandbox testing for a set period (limited to months) and to interact with sectoral representatives and experts. It would also offer lessons on how sandboxes can be implemented at a national level within Member States, for example, through an enacted AI Regulation. By scrutinising the results of the sandbox programme (as with the evaluations of the UK's Digital Sandbox), regulators would be equipped to gain a deeper understanding of the effects of sandbox participation for the future market growth of firms and for their ability to fully develop the technologies and applications which are being tested within the sandbox.

The future UK-EU relationship does not have to be distorted by competition between multiple sandboxes in different states. The search for empirical findings and appropriately granular data about sandbox outcomes—and about the results of regulatory measures generally—should be a common priority for the UK and the EU. By the same token, settling on tangible policy goals should also be a priority in the regulation of digital finance. The UK and EU have achieved much in both respects through their respective regulatory approaches. For the benefits of these approaches to be truly realised, the sharing of expertise and resources could be expedited through tailored agreements.

5 Conclusion

Rather than being devoted to attempting to summarise all potential issues regarding financial services, the chapter has deliberately focused on digital finance. Financial services are being steadily transformed by digitalisation and by various forms of advanced innovations. To a significant degree, the changing nature of the UK and EU regulatory approaches towards digital finance will determine the course of future UK-EU relations in financial services broadly.

As argued throughout this chapter, the features of the UK and EU approaches to digital finance show how there are considerable opportunities for collaboration and coordination of regulatory standards, beyond the somewhat scant detail of the 2023 Memorandum of Understanding. For digital finance, the future UK-EU relationship

[86] The Digital Sandbox evaluation reports are available at: https://www.fca.org.uk/firms/innovation/digital-sandbox (date accessed: 30 October 2023).

should not have to be predicated on competition. On the contrary, due to the borderless characteristics of modern technologies, the regulation of digital finance and FinTech can be best formulated through cohesive standards that are recognised and accepted by regulators internationally.

As the chapter commenced with an overview of the UK and EU regulatory policies and initiatives, some contrasting perspectives of the UK and EU can be discerned. The UK has gravitated towards practical measures and innovative experimentation with regulatory techniques. The EU has sought to shape overarching frameworks and objectives within which specific measures can then be implemented. The chapter pinpointed how the UK and EU approaches aim to adapt to ongoing innovations in finance. Open banking is ripe for growth, specifically in the types of technologies being utilised and in the forms of potent market players who could begin to further encroach into payments services.

The existing UK and EU regimes demonstrate that there is much that can be learned from the approaches that have been taken on both sides. As contended in the final section of the chapter, collaboration and coordination can occur within standard-setting activities through international bodies. Memoranda of understanding and cooperation agreements can be focal to post-Brexit regulatory arrangements on digital finance, especially when agreements are based upon specific initiatives. These initiatives could involve a cross-border sandbox, mCBDC trialling, the sharing of knowledge on the testing of the operational resilience of institutions' systems, and numerous other possibilities. Acknowledging the merits and relative successes of the UK and EU approaches is essential to progressing towards collaboration, even when—more than occasionally—this collaboration may not have been thought possible.

References

Bank of England (2019a) Future of Finance. Review on the Outlook for the UK Financial System: What It Means for the Bank of England (Chaired by Huw van Steenis)

Bank of England (2019b) New Economy, New Finance, New Bank. The Bank of England's Response to the van Steenis Review on the Future of Finance

Bank of England/FCA (2022) Final Report. Artificial Intelligence Public-Private Forum

BCBS (2019) Report on Open Banking and Application Programming Interfaces. Basel Committee on Banking Supervision, Bank for International Settlements

Beck T, Petit C (2023) Reboot of the UK-EU relationship in financial services regulation. VoxEU column (18 October 2023); available at: https://cepr.org/voxeu/columns/reboot-uk-eu-relationship-financial-services-regulation. Accessed 30 Oct 2023

Beck T, Cecchetti S, Grothe M, Kemp M, Pelizzon L, Sánchez Serrano A (2022) Will video kill the radio star? – Digitalisation and the future of banking. Report of the Advisory Scientific Committee No. 12, European Systemic Risk Board

BIS (2022) Using CBDCs across borders: lessons from practical experiments. Bank for International Settlements Innovation Hub

Bromberg L, Godwin A, Ramsay I (2018) Cross-border cooperation in financial regulation: crossing the Fintech bridge. Cap Mark Law J 13(1)spiepr A3B2 twbch ":":spiepr A3B2 twbch59–84

EBA (2021a) EBA Analysis of RegTech in the EU Financial Sector. European Banking Authority/Rep/2021/17
EBA (2021b) Report on the Use of Digital Platforms in the EU Banking and Payments Sector. European Banking Authority/Rep/2021/26
EBA (2022) Opinion of the European Banking Authority on its Technical Advice on the Review of Directive (EU) 2015/2366 on Payment Services in the Internal Market (PSD2), European Banking Authority Op/2022/06
ECB (2022) Progress on the Investigation Phase of a Digital Euro
European Commission (2018) FinTech Action Plan: For a More Competitive and Innovative European Financial Sector, COM(2018) 109 final
European Commission (2020a) White Paper on Artificial Intelligence – A European Approach to Excellence and Trust, COM(2020) 65 final
European Commission (2020b) A Digital Finance Strategy for the EU, COM(2020) 591 final
European Supervisory Authorities (2018) Report – FinTech: Regulatory Sandboxes and Innovation Hubs, ESMA/EBA/EIOPA JC 2018 74
FCA (2017) Regulatory Sandbox Lessons Learned Report. Financial Conduct Authority, London
Hall S (2022) The economics of UK financial services post Brexit. In: Portes J (ed) The economics of Brexit: what have we learned? Centre for Economic Policy Research Press, London
Hoffmann M, Nurski L (2021) What is holding back artificial intelligence adoption in Europe? Bruegel Policy Contribution, Issue 24/November 2021
Innovate Finance (2021) Kalifa Review of UK Fintech. London
Joint Regulatory Oversight Committee (2023) Recommendations for the Next Phase of Open Banking in the UK
Kalaitzake M (2022) Resilience in the City of London: the fate of UK financial services after Brexit. New Pol Econ 27(4)spiepr A3B2 twbch ":":spiepr A3B2 twbch610–628
Marimootoo R (2020) Is data to become a freely available resource? Comp Tel Law Rev 26(4) spiepr A3B2 twbch ":":spiepr A3B2 twbch91–95
McCarthy J (2019) What happens next? The EU's efforts in regulating the growth of FinTech. J Int Bank Law Reg 34(11)spiepr A3B2 twbch ":":spiepr A3B2 twbch404–410
McCarthy J (2021) Evaluating the EU's Digital Finance Strategy: ambitious glimpses of future regulation? J Int Bank Law Reg 36(9)spiepr A3B2 twbch ":":spiepr A3B2 twbch379–389
McCarthy J (2022) The regulation of RegTech and SupTech in finance: ensuring consistency in principle and in practice. J Fin Reg Compl 31(2)spiepr A3B2 twbch ":":spiepr A3B2 twbch186–199
Nicholls C (2019) Open banking and the rise of FinTech: innovative finance and functional regulation. Bank Fin Law Rev 35(1)spiepr A3B2 twbch ":":spiepr A3B2 twbch121–151
Radnejad AB, Osiyevskyy O, Scheibel O (2021) Learning from the failure of the EU Payment Services Directive (PSD2): when imposed innovation does not change the Status Quo. Rut Bus Rev 6(1)spiepr A3B2 twbch ":":spiepr A3B2 twbch79–94
Schilling de Carvalho P (2022) Retaining influence in post-Brexit international financial regulation: lessons from the UK's FinTech framework. J Fin Reg 8(1)spiepr A3B2 twbch ":":spiepr A3B2 twbch104–131
Schwarz D, Bernstein J (2022) Competition policy for FinTech M&A – what to expect when you're expecting – a FinTech M&A deal. J Int Bank Law Reg 37(10)spiepr A3B2 twbch ":":spiepr A3B2 twbch353–360
Stolerman K (2020) Rain or shine for London? Reexamining the Fintech Capital of Europe after Brexit. Boston Univ Int Law J 38(1)spiepr A3B2 twbch ":":spiepr A3B2 twbch157–182
World Bank (2020a) Global experiences from regulatory sandboxes. World Bank, Washington D.C.
World Bank (2020b) How regulators respond to Fintech. Evaluating the different approaches – sandboxes and beyond. World Bank, Washington D.C.
World Bank (2022) Fintech and the future of finance. World Bank, Washington D.C.

Yadav Y (2020) Fintech and international financial regulation. Vand J Transnatl Law 53(3)spiepr A3B2 twbch ":":spiepr A3B2 twbch1109–1146

Zetzsche D, Buckley R, Barberis J, Arner D (2017) Regulating a revolution: from regulatory sandboxes to smart regulation. Fordham J Corp Fin Law spiepr A3B2 twbch ":"23:31spiepr A3B2 twbch–103

Zetzsche D, Annunziata F, Arner D, Buckley R (2021) The Markets in Crypto-Assets Regulation (MiCA) and the EU Digital Finance Strategy. Cap Mark Law J 16(2)spiepr A3B2 twbch ":": spiepr A3B2 twbch203–225

Post-Brexit Cooperation in Higher Education and Research

The Changing EU-UK Relationship

L. Kortese and S. Garben

1 Introduction

Brexit gives rise to important questions concerning the UK's future position in, and influence on, higher education and research in Europe. It is safe to say that before its withdrawal from the EU, the UK was one of the established 'leaders' in both higher education and research in Europe. Through the intergovernmental Bologna Process, the UK successfully exported its higher education model consisting of the three-cycle structure bachelor-master-doctorate based on a market-driven approach to higher education to other EU Member States and beyond, to the benefit of its own competitive position on this newly created European Higher Education Area (EHEA).[1] Equally, the UK was one of the most successful contenders for EU Horizon 2020 research funding, ranking second out of all EU Member States.[2] As a 'net-importer' of EU students and academic staff, both its universities and the economy at large benefited from its continuous brain-gain.[3]

The UK's withdrawal from the EU has, of course, affected this position, although sometimes in perhaps quite subtle or indirect ways. In this context, Brexit can be said to have affected the relationship between the UK and EU at two different levels. On

[1] Garben (2018), p. 1294.

[2] European Commission (n.d.), United Kingdom Horizon 2020 Country Profile: United Kingdom. https://dashboard.tech.ec.europa.eu/qs_digit_dashboard_mt/public/extensions/RTD_BI_public_Country_Profile/RTD_BI_public_Country_Profile.html?Country=UK. Accessed 12 Nov 2024.

[3] See for example Zotti (2021), pp. 20–21.

L. Kortese (✉)
Utrecht University, Utrecht, Netherlands
e-mail: l.s.j.kortese@uu.nl

S. Garben
College of Europe, Bruges, Belgium
e-mail: sacha.garben@coleurope.eu

E. Guinchard, C. Panara (eds.), *The New Relationship between the United Kingdom and the European Union*, https://doi.org/10.1007/978-3-031-70652-3_18

the one hand, we can perceive a change in cooperation at the individual level where those persons involved in higher education and research cooperation such as students, researchers, and academics are concerned. On the other hand, Brexit has caused a change in the relationship between the UK and EU where it concerns policy cooperation in the context of systems such as the EHEA, European Education Area (EEA-2025), and European Research Area (ERA). Indeed, at system-level, the impact of Brexit may be considered rather limited, due to the peculiar 'mixed' governance structures of higher education and research in Europe, where the EU, the Council of Europe, the EU Member States in their own capacity, and other (both European and non-European) countries, cooperate alongside and with each other on closely interconnected initiatives and policies. As Sect. 2 will set out in more detail, this means, in particular, that the UK may have withdrawn from the EU and thus no longer takes (automatic) part in EU initiatives, many of these EU policies are in principle also open to non-Member States—and moreover the UK remains a member of the intergovernmental EHEA. It is in fact not so much directly caused by the withdrawal from the EU, but by the UK's specific policy decisions, that there has been much uncertainty about its (non-)participation in EU programmes such as Erasmus and Horizon Europe (respectively part of the EEA-2025 and ERA). That uncertainty has negatively impacted on students and academics in the UK. It is therefore the individual dimension where we see the most significant changes post-Brexit, where both the policy-decisions of the UK and the loss of EU free movement rights due to the withdrawal have curtailed the possibilities of students and academics. Section 3 considers the possibility to address the negative consequences of these changes for students, researchers, and academics and concludes this contribution.

2 The European Landscape of Higher Education and Research

2.1 The European Higher Education Area (EHEA)

Activities undertaken in the context of the EHEA find their origin in the well-known Bologna Process, which has effectuated some of the biggest changes to higher education seen in Europe in recent times, namely the structural harmonisation of higher education through the introduction of a three-cycle structure (bachelor, master, doctorate). The Bologna Process was initiated in 1998 by France, Germany, Italy and the UK,[4] who were quickly joined by another 25 countries in their initiative to create a "European area of higher education (EHEA) as a key way to promote

[4] Sorbonne Joint Declaration on harmonisation of the architecture of the European higher education system, Paris 25 May 1998.

citizens' mobility and employability and the Continent's overall development",[5] most notably through the adoption of a system of easily readable and comparable degrees, adoption of a two-cycle system,[6] and a credit transfer system such as the ECTS. The EHEA as such was launched in 2010 when the initial Bologna Process cooperation had grown from the original 29 participating countries to 47 countries.[7] The process can be considered an on-going platform for policy-making on higher education structured around regular ministerial conferences.[8] Over the course of the years, a total of twelve ministerial conferences have taken place, the results of which were laid down in communiqués acting as the basis for further action within the EHEA.[9] The Bologna Process and resulting EHEA continue to operate in this fashion.

The *modus operandi* of the Bologna Process and EHEA is peculiar since it was initiated—and continues to be—a form of voluntary, intergovernmental cooperation, yet is closely connected to both EU and Council of Europe law.[10] The 'soft law' character of the Bologna Process can in hindsight be considered remarkable, considering the extensive harmonisation it has achieved. It is furthermore remarkable that the initiative was undertaken outside the EU framework, even though it quickly included all EU Member states and related to the issues of student mobility and diploma recognition, on which the EU had legal competence, case law and policy. Space precludes a detailed account of the effects of the Bologna Process having taken place outside the EU legal framework. Suffice to say that the set-up of the Bologna Process and resulting EHEA led to a number of legitimacy problems fuelled by the initiative's close proximity to related EU policies and legal framework.[11] Indeed, various EU mobility tools, such as the European Credit Transfer System, have been 'imported' into the Bologna Process.

For the purposes of our analysis, however, the most relevant implication of the EHEA's non-EU status is that the UK's membership to the EHEA remains—in direct terms—unaffected by its withdrawal from the EU. The UK has been a founding

[5] Bologna Declaration of 19 June 1999 – Joint declaration of the European Ministers of Education.

[6] Originally a two-cycle system between undergraduate and graduate degrees, the system now has three cycles including that of doctorate as the third level. Coincidentally, the third level also constitutes the connection of the EHEA with the area of research since doctorates revolve around research practice.

[7] Budapest-Vienna Declaration on the European Higher Education Area, 12 March 2010.

[8] Garben (2018), p. 1296.

[9] For an overview of the different communiqués, see EHEA (n.d.). Ministerial declarations and communiqués. https://ehea.info/page-ministerial-declarations-and-communiques.

[10] The Council of Europe's Lisbon Recognition Convention was incorporated into the EHEA to give effect to the original Bologna objective aimed at overcoming obstacles to the mobility of students. The Convention provides principles and procedures for the academic recognition of higher education degrees and degrees giving access thereto. Convention on the Recognition of Qualifications concerning Higher Education in the European Region – European Treaty Series – No. 165.

[11] Garben (2011), Garben (2018), p. 1297, and Garben (2010).

member of the Bologna Process and resulting EHEA and continues to participate.[12] Equally, the UK continues to be a signatory to the Lisbon Recognition Convention—the only legally binding text connected to the EHEA—since that text originates from the Council of Europe and not the EU.[13] However, while the UK thus may continue to participate in the EHEA, its position within it will nevertheless be indirectly affected by its non-EU status. This is because the actual realisation of the EHEA and its *raison d'être*—i.e. the mobility of higher education actors—actually rests to a large extent on the achievement of EU free movement rights derived from the Treaties and secondary legislation, and these have been drastically curtailed due to the UK's withdrawal (see further Sect. 2.4 below). Furthermore, the fact that a range of EU policies, such as ECTS, form an integral or associated part of the Bologna Process, means that non-EU Member State participants in the Bologna Process do not have the same extent of influence compared to EU Member States, the latter having a direct say in the formulation of these EU instruments from the outset. In this area, it is not so much the question of legal coercion that is relevant, since neither EU soft law nor intergovernmental soft law like the Bologna Process gives rise to legally binding obligations—the issue is more political and subtle: who is in a position to coax and persuade other countries to take a certain direction. Structurally, it would seem that its loss of EU membership has negatively affected the UK's position as a policy-shaper.

2.2 EU Higher Education Policy (EEA-2025)

That same finding, that the UK's non-EU status will have caused a shift from a policy-making to a policy-taking position in the area of higher education, applies to the various EU policy instruments and frameworks in which the UK can still participate as a non-member, but not as a decision-maker.

Perhaps building on the imagery of an 'area' characterized by mobility as first evoked by the Bologna Process' EHEA, the EU has in the meantime developed the plan to establish a European Education Area by 2025 (EEA-2025)—which includes higher education and thus partially overlaps with the EHEA. The EEA-2025 initiatives serves as an overarching policy framework within which also pre-existing instruments (such as the Erasmus programme) are embedded. Its overall political approach focuses on strengthening the EU's core values such as the social market economy, democracy, freedom, diversity, human rights, and social justice.[14] In the

[12] EHEA (n.d.) United Kingdom. https://ehea.info/page-united-kingdom.

[13] Council of Europe (n.d.). Chart of signatures and ratifications of Treaty 165. https://www.coe.int/en/web/conventions/full-list?module=signatures-by-treaty&treatynum=165.

[14] Communication from the Commission to the European Parliament, the Council, the European Economic and Social Committee and the Committee of the Regions on achieving the European Education Area by 2025, COM(2020) 625 final, p. 1.

EEA-2025 strategy, much attention is given to stimulating investment in education in the EU post-COVID.[15] On a more substantive level, the EEA-2025 strategy is aimed especially at developing this area along six dimensions—one of which concerns higher education.[16] In this context, the EU's ambitions are related to, among others, deepening cooperation between higher education institutions and creating a suitable policy framework supporting such cooperation, strengthening the role of higher education institutions as core actors of the "knowledge square",[17] and automatic recognition of qualifications and study periods abroad.[18] This last point also concerns quality assurance of joint educational activities (e.g. double or joint degrees) and recognition concerning micro-credentials. Interestingly, according to the strategy to achieve the EEA-2025, this improved recognition and quality assurance: "would allow Member States to go deeper and faster in their cooperation, as compared to what they are able to do now in the context of the Bologna Process".[19]

The withdrawal of the UK means it is no longer part, as such, of the EEA-2025 initiative. There seems to be little reflection on the UK's position in EEA-2025 now or in the future, from either side.[20] Several of the EU instruments and policies that the EEA-2025 comprises—such as the Erasmus programme, Europass, the European Qualifications Framework (EQF) and the Council Recommendation on

[15] Through, among others, the Next Generation EU COVID-19 recovery fund, national level investments, and the Erasmus+ programme, European Structural and Investment Funds, and the Structural Reform Support Programme.

[16] COM(2020) 625 final, p. 5.

[17] In accordance with the strategy this concerns: "education, research, innovation and service to society, playing a key role in driving the COVID-19 recovery and sustainable development in Europe while helping education, research and the labour market to benefit from talent flows".

[18] COM(2020) 625 final, pp. 10–11.

[19] Ibid., p. 11.

[20] The core documents tracking achievements towards the EEA-2025 make no mention of the UK or a possible relationship. See for example the Communication from the Commission to the European Parliament, the Council, the European Economic and Social Committee and the Committee of the Regions on progress towards the achievement of the European Education Area, COM(2022) 700 final; Commission Staff Working Document Accompanying the document Communication from the Commission to the European Parliament, the Council, the European Economic and Social Committee and the Committee of the Regions on progress towards the achievement of the European Education Area, SWD(2022) 750 final; European Commission, Education and Training Monitor 2022: Comparative report (Luxembourg: Publications Office of the EU, 2022). In a similar vein, information from the UK side regarding its formal position towards the EEA-2025 appears limited with attention being dedicated primarily to the UK's decision not to take part in the Erasmus programme or issues related to its association to its participation in Horizon Europe (see Sect. 2.3 below).

Automatic Recognition[21] are, nevertheless, open for the UK to join, or follow. For each of these instruments, association of third countries is organised in a different way. The possibilities for association are the most extensive for the Erasmus programme. The corresponding regulation indicates in Article 19 that the programme as such is open to various categories of third countries, including European Economic Area members and an open category of third countries.[22] In relation to Europass, participation therein is open to European Economic Area members, acceding States, candidate States and potential EU candidate States in accordance with the European Economic Area Agreement or the accession agreements.[23] As far as the UK is concerned, this would mean that participation in Europass depends on it becoming a member of the European Economic Area. The same applies to the EQF and automatic recognition recommendations. In principle, these texts do not have EEA relevance. However, in the case of the EQF, the corresponding recommendation is taken up in Protocol 31 to the European Economic Area Agreement as a point on which the contracting parties shall seek to strengthen cooperation.[24] A last option, other than European Economic Area membership, appears possible as far as these recommendations are concerned. According to the European Parliament, the UK could take part in initiatives such as the EQF and automatic recognition recommendations on a voluntary basis.[25]

However, what is clear is that the UK's withdrawal from the EU also results in the solidification of its position as a policy-taker for these EEA-2025 initiatives. Despite this possibility to participate, the UK's third country status means that it will not be able to exert any influence on changes made to these EU instruments. Indeed, Brexit was considered to lead to a dramatic reduction in the UK's ability to shape EU legislation—especially in relation to formal decision-making avenues and represen-

---

[21] Council Recommendation of 26 November 2018 on promoting automatic mutual recognition of higher education and upper secondary education and training qualifications and the outcomes of learning periods abroad, [2018] OJ C 444/1. adopted on 26 November 2018 and seeks to promote automatic mutual recognition of higher education and upper secondary education diplomas (i.e. higher education diplomas and those giving access thereto) and the outcomes of learning periods abroad.

[22] Article 19(1)(a)(d) Regulation (EU) 2021/817 of the European Parliament and of the Council of 20 May 2021 establishing Erasmus+: the Union Programme for education and training, youth and sport and repealing Regulation (EU) No 1288/2013, [2021] OJ L 189/1.

[23] See Recital 31 and Article 10 Decision (EU) 2018/646 of the European Parliament and of the Council of 18 April 2018 on a common framework for the provision of better services for skills and qualifications (Europass) and repealing Decision No 2241/2004/EC, [2018] OJ L 112/42.

[24] See Article 4(8) Protocol 31 on cooperation in fields outside the four freedoms.

[25] The European Parliament thereby makes a reference to Turkey and its Qualifications Framework which makes a connection with Council Recommendation 2006/962/EC on Key competences for lifelong learning; see European Parliament Policy Department for Structural and Cohesion Polices (2018). *Research for CULT Committee – recognition of qualifications for educational and professional purposes: the impact of Brexit* (PE 629.180, November 2018). https://www.europarl.europa.eu/RegData/etudes/BRIE/2018/629180/IPOL_BRI(2018)629180_EN.pdf, p. 4.

tation in the EU institutions.[26] It is perhaps partially in light thereof, that the UK has not taken up this voluntary membership to EU policies enthusiastically post-Brexit. This applies most notably to the EU's research programme Horizon Europe (see further Sect. 2.3 below) and to the Erasmus programme.

Indeed, despite reassurance from Boris Johnson that participation in the Erasmus programme was to be maintained post-Brexit, the UK has withdrawn from it and has opted not to take part as an associated third country.[27] In its place, the UK has adopted the Turing Scheme which was met with resistance both from academia as well as politics.[28] Different from the Erasmus programme, the Turing Scheme has a global focus. Nevertheless, the scheme also has limitations—constituting an important reason for resistance prior to the scheme's adoption. For example, it only provides funding for UK students venturing outside the UK, meaning it does not cover incoming mobility.[29] This is particularly interesting viewed in light of the fact that the international character of the UK's higher education system has for an important part depended on incoming international students (under programmes such as Erasmus), rather than outgoing UK students.[30] As far as incoming mobility is concerned, the UK Government seemingly relied on universities and the sending states' governments to cover the fees of students coming to the UK.[31] In relation to outgoing mobility, the scheme does not guarantee all tuition fees are waived at hosting universities. More specifically, the UK Government expected these fees to be waived by hosting institutions, although ultimately left that decision to the individual institutions.[32] This means the Turing Scheme is mostly more extensive in geographical scope, but that its funding opportunities granted to individuals and institutions are more limited compared to the Erasmus programme. This has sparked concerns relating to the attractiveness of the UK as a destination for exchange students and ultimately the economic and cultural consequences connected to this.[33]

---

[26] For an overview of the consequences of Brexit for each of the institutions see Wright et al. (2020) Influencing the EU after Brexit - Institute for Government, https://www.instituteforgovernment.org.uk/sites/default/files/publications/influencing-EU-after-brexit_2.pdf. Accessed 23 January 2023, pp. 11 and 13–18.

[27] European Commission (n.d.) The UK and Erasmus+. https://erasmus-plus.ec.europa.eu/the-uk-and-erasmus.

[28] See, for example, Guibert and Rayón (2021) and Cardwell (2021). Concerns were also expressed by the Scottish Government where the Scottish Universities minister considered the Turing scheme a "watered down" version that did not support mobility to Scotland; see House of Commons Library (2021). *The Erasmus Programme* (Briefing Paper No. 8326, 6 January 2021). https://researchbriefings.files.parliament.uk/documents/CBP-8326/CBP-8326.pdf, p. 20.

[29] For a more detailed comparison see House of Commons Library (2022b). *The Turing Scheme* (No. 9141, 11 November 2022), https://researchbriefings.files.parliament.uk/documents/CBP-9141/CBP-9141.pdf, p. 28.

[30] Zotti (2021), pp. 20–21.

[31] House of Commons Library (2022b). *The Turing Scheme* (No. 9141, 11 November 2022), https://researchbriefings.files.parliament.uk/documents/CBP-9141/CBP-9141.pdf, p. 30.

[32] Ibid., p. 28.

[33] Ibid., p. 31.

Returning to the EEA-2025 and the EU's efforts in realising it, it is important to remark that policies for its achievement are not a stand-alone initiative. Instead, they work in synergy with other EU initiatives such as the European Skills Agenda, the renewed VET policy, and—especially relevant for higher education—the European Research Area (ERA, see below Sect. 2.3). Indeed, higher education institutions are considered especially well placed to connect the EEA-2025 with the ERA. To this end, the EEA-2025 strategy foresees the creation of a policy framework aimed at seamless and ambitious transnational cooperation between higher education institutions.[34] Specific measures proposed to achieve this objective concern strengthening of the European Universities Initiative, examining the feasibility of a European Degree, enhancing transparency in quality assurance tools at EU level to facilitate modular joint programmes in higher education institutions,[35] the development of a legal statute for university alliances,[36] achieving automatic mutual recognition by 2025,[37] and the stimulation of the research and innovation dimension of the European University alliances through Horizon Europe.[38] In 2022, a recommendation was adopted to further these objectives.[39]

This means that the EU is intensifying its education/higher education policy. Moreover, with these recent ambitious policy initiatives, the EU seems to be (re)-claiming a leadership role on those issues where the intergovernmental Bologna Process had caused it to lose the initiative for almost two decades. The EU is still supporting the EHEA and the Bologna Process, but instead of passively allowing its instruments and policies to be used in the context of the Bologna Process, it is subtly changing the narrative and approach, encouraging its Member States to "go deeper and faster"[40] compared to what they are able to do in the Bologna Process,[41] by

[34] Ibid., p. 19.

[35] This particular activity also involves a review of the existing Recommendation of the European Parliament and of the Council of 15 February 2006 on further European cooperation in quality assurance in higher education, [2006] OJ L 64/60.

[36] The European University Alliances (or other higher education cooperation) may experience particular challenges when cooperating transnationally. Issues identified can be linked to any aspect of cooperation ranging from student and employment relations to financing. Issues such as these originate from the differences in legislation, policy, and governance of national educational systems in the EU.

[37] In line with the Council Recommendation of 26 November 2018 on promoting automatic mutual recognition of higher education and upper secondary education and training qualifications and the outcomes of learning periods abroad, [2018] OJ C 444/1. Important to note that automatic recognition here mainly relates to the level of the degree a student is submitting to a higher education institution as evidence of prior learning. Since higher education institutions remain free to decide on substantive/programme specific admission criteria, automatic recognition does not cover such aspects.

[38] COM(2020) 625 final, pp. 21–23.

[39] Council Recommendation of 5 April 2022 on building bridges for effective European higher education cooperation, [2022] OJ C 160/1.

[40] COM(2020) 625 final, p. 11.

[41] Ibid.

means of developing the EEA-2025. From an EU perspective, it may well be that the EEA-2025 will eventually 'absorb' the EHEA in the future. These developments are detrimental for the UK's position in the European higher education landscape. Further and deeper integration of the higher education sector in the EU will inevitably have some impact on UK higher education actors. By not being part of it, the UK risks to miss out on lucrative opportunities for collaboration and exchange, and its higher education sector can be projected to lose some of the competitive advantages it previously held as a result, perhaps even globally. Furthermore, with the centre of policy gravity shifting away from the Bologna process and (back) to the EU, the UK will be further pushed into a policy-taker position.

2.3 The European Research Area

Due to the peculiarities of the development of EU competence, education and research have developed separately.[42] Whereas the EEA-2025 is still relatively new, the ERA originates from the 2000 Lisbon Strategy with which the EU was to become "the most competitive and dynamic knowledge-based economy in the world". Back then, research was considered in need of extra attention to better integrate and coordinate research activity at national and EU level to ultimately generate economic growth, employment, and social cohesion.[43] In line with Article 179 TFEU research is considered a shared competence allowing for harmonising legislation to be adopted. The ERA as such again has a strong correlation with the internal market aiming to create an area where there is free circulation of researchers, scientific knowledge and technology, while encouraging competitiveness. Article 179(2) TFEU furthermore shows that the ERA is broader than only universities,

[42] A prime example of how the two topics were considered separately can be found in the 1989 Commission v. Council case (Erasmus case). The Council had adopted the Decision establishing the Erasmus programme on the basis of Article 128 and 235 of the EEC Treaty. The Commission expressly opposed to the inclusion of Article 235 of the EEC Treaty, claiming the Erasmus programme could have been adopted exclusively on the basis of Article 128 on vocational training. By contrast, the Council (along with several Member States) held that Article 235 was necessary since some of the measures proposed under the Erasmus programme went beyond the topic of vocational training. Even though the Court initially followed its prior reasoning reiterating that university studies constitute a type of vocational training and are therefore covered by Article 128, it ultimately reached a different conclusion. This was mostly due to the overlap with research. The Court held that research needed to be included in the Erasmus decision to give sufficient reach to the programme's objectives. However, since this was not expressly covered by Article 128 EEC Treaty, the Court found the addition of Article 235 EEC Treaty as a legal basis appropriate. See Case 242/87 *Commission v. Council*, EU:C:1989:217, para. 35–36.

[43] For more detail see Communication from the Commission to the Council, the European Parliament, the Economic and Social Committee and the Committee of the Regions, COM(2000) 6 final and Council Resolution of 15 June 2000 on establishing a European area of research and innovation, [2000] OJ C 205/1.

covering also SMEs, research centres alongside universities and supporting efforts for cross-border cooperation.

Taking a closer look at the ERA strategy, four objectives are set to cope with some core challenges related to the twin transitions and recovery from the pandemic. In particular, these concern the prioritisation of investments, improving access to excellence, the connection between research and innovation and the economy (competitiveness), and deepening the ERA through enhanced circulation of knowledge.[44] To this end, the Commission has established a Roadmap consisting of 14 steps several of which are aimed at stimulating research investments, supporting and strengthening research practice, and strengthening research governance.[45] One of the roadmap steps furthermore involves the creation of a plan to create synergies between higher education and research by focusing on the role of universities.[46] Moreover, the ERA strategy and roadmap are supplemented by a *Pact for Research and Innovation in Europe* through which Member States have reinforced their commitment to the realisation of the ERA objectives.[47] In the Pact we may find the ERA's core values and principles such as freedom of scientific research, free circulation, and inclusiveness. One of the core areas for joint action is thereby defined as "Deepening a truly functioning internal market for knowledge". Whereas activities to attain this objective were previously geared primarily to supporting the mobility of individual researchers,[48] the internal market is currently understood to cover open science, research infrastructures, gender equality, knowledge valorisation, scientific leadership, and global engagement—in addition to efforts on improving research careers and mobility.

However, one crucial—and perhaps the most well-known—element of the ERA is its research funding provided through the Horizon Europe programme. More specifically, the Horizon Europe programme provides investments in research and innovation driving the broader policy objectives of the ERA forward. It does this by providing financial support to researchers and research collaborations expanding beyond higher education to also involve societal partners.[49] The programme itself is adopted by means of a regulation which confirms the EU's objective to strengthen its scientific and technological bases by strengthening the ERA in which, among others,

---

[44] Communication from the Commission to the European Parliament, the Council, the European Economic and Social Committee and the Committee of the Regions – A new ERA for Research and Innovation, COM(2020) 628 final, p. 5.

[45] See the Appendix of COM(2020) 628 final.

[46] COM(2020) 628 final, p. 16.

[47] Council Recommendation (EU) 2021/2122 of 26 November 2021 on a Pact for Research and Innovation in Europe, [2021] OJ L 431/1.

[48] See Garben (2018), p. 1303.

[49] COM(2020) 628 final, p. 6.

researchers, scientific knowledge and technology circulate freely and competitiveness is enhanced while research and innovation are promoted.[50] The Horizon Europe programme contributes to this main objective by providing research funding supporting the creation and diffusion of knowledge and technology, facilitating cooperation between research and societal partners, and by fostering innovation—to name a few.[51] The Horizon Europe programme provides funding along three pillars: Excellent Science (comprising ERC and MSCA), Global Challenges and European Industrial Competitiveness, and Innovative Europe—each of which having its designated budget.[52]

Even if the Horizon Europe programme is an EU initiative, participation in the programme is open to third countries. More specifically, members of the European Economic Area can accede subject to the conditions in the European Economic Area Agreement, as are acceding/candidate countries, European Neighbourhood Policy countries, and other third countries.[53] In case of this latter open category (which the UK falls under), the third country looking to accede must in any case have a good capacity in science, technology and innovation, be committed to a rules-based open market economy, and actively promote policies to improve the economic and social well-being of its citizens.[54] Association furthermore depends on the conditions laid down in the agreement dedicated to organising the participation of the third country concerned. One of the core conditions of such agreement dictates that the third country associated to the Horizon Europe Programme will not have any decision-making power over the EU programme.[55] In the case of the UK it therefore means that, although its research actors could be beneficiaries of Horizon Europe funding, the UK as such cannot exert any influence on the programme as such or the distribution of funding therein.

Despite this limitation regarding its decision-making power, it was clearly stated from early on in the Brexit negotiations that the UK was to remain part of the Horizon Europe programme, a message that initially brought optimism and an expectation that the UK would be able to participate on almost the same terms as before once financial matters were settled.[56] However, some of the initial optimism was soon replaced with concern since almost two years after the UK's formal exit from the EU the country's association to Horizon Europe had not been confirmed. In

[50] Recital 1 Regulation (EU) 2021/695 of the European Parliament and of the Council of 28 April 2021 establishing Horizon Europe – the Framework Programme for Research and Innovation, laying down its rules for participation and dissemination, and repealing Regulations (EU) No 1290/2013 and (EU) No 1291/2013, [2021] OJ L 170/1.

[51] Recital 2 Regulation (EU) 2021/695.

[52] Article 4 and 12 Regulation (EU) 2021/695.

[53] Article 16 Regulation (EU) 2021/695.

[54] Article 16(1)(d) Regulation (EU) 2021/695.

[55] See in particular Article 16(2)(c) Regulation (EU) 2021/695.

[56] See for example Corbett (2021), p. 21.

particular, association was connected to negotiations over arrangements concerning the Northern Ireland Protocol—itself unrelated to research.[57]

In order to cope with the uncertainty coming from the pending Horizon Europe association, the UK Government issued additional financial support in the context of the Horizon Europe guarantee scheme. In particular, this scheme was available to those who had successfully applied for a Horizon Europe grant before 31 December 2022 and were included as beneficiaries in the first proposal. An example of the uncertainty brought forward by the delayed association could be seen with ERC awardees. The lack of associated status meant that—once their ERCs were granted—they were faced with a decision: either to move to an EU country to conduct their ERC research or to decline their funding.[58] The Horizon Europe guarantee scheme therefore served as a safety net for those UK-based researchers who were successful in applying to Horizon Europe grant schemes, but could not receive the funding due to lack of an association agreement. Although this funding therefore mitigated the immediate gap created by lacking Horizon Europe funding, the national UK scheme did not have the same benefits a corresponding Horizon Europe grant has such as possibilities for mobility between countries, less prestige overall, less appreciation for co-creation in research, and less encouragement of international collaboration.[59] The latter aspect was thereby considered particularly liable to harm the international status of UK researchers—and ultimately UK research. Against this background, the UK Minister of State for Science, Research and Innovation announced the adoption of a package of £484 million in November 2022 "to invest in the UK R&D Sector to retain the best talent within the UK...".[60] When adopting the package a clear preference was expressed for association to the EU's R&D programmes, though recognising that the UK "cannot wait forever to invest the funding set aside for association in our world-leading R&D sector".

Ultimately, the wait persisted until 7 September 2023 when the European Commission and the UK finally reached an agreement on the UK's association to Horizon Europe.[61] The agreement is to take effect from 1 January 2024, meaning UK researchers can fully participate in calls under the Work Programme 2024 and

[57] Samarasekera (2022), p. 2257 and Guglielmi (2022), p. 253.

[58] See Amsen (2022), p. 1. A similar situation occurred in Switzerland after the country could not associate to Horizon Europe due to the end of talks over the Institutional Framework Agreement, see Guglielmi (2022), p. 252.

[59] Amsen (2022).

[60] Minister of State for Science (2022), Research and Innovation. Open letter – EU Programmes: Package of immediate investment for the UK's R&D sector. https://www.gov.uk/government/publications/eu-programmes-open-letter-on-a-package-of-immediate-investment-for-the-uks-rd-sector/eu-programmes-package-of-immediate-investment-for-the-uks-rd-sector.

[61] Joint Statement by the European Commission and the UK Government on the UK's association to Horizon Europe and Copernicus, 7 September 2023.

onwards.[62] This also means association does not immediately render the guarantee scheme obsolete since is continues to cover all Horizon Europe calls under the Work Programmes 2021–2023.[63] Therefore, despite the difficulties faced, there was a continued desire for association to Horizon Europe. Indeed, non-association would have led to the UK being considered a third country with researchers having less opportunities under Horizon Europe.[64] This would have also meant limited opportunities to host ERC and MSCA postdocs and—even if participation in Horizon Europe calls would be possible—researchers had to seek alternative sources of funding. Whereas some considered this alternative scheme an opportunity to develop a new research and innovation programme that could address some of the flaws seen in EU funding schemes,[65] the fact remains that the uncertainty concerning the UK's association to Horizon Europe risked damaging years of fruitful research cooperation conducted during the UK's EU Membership.

2.4 EU Free Movement Law

Whereas the EHEA, EEA-2025, and ERA as systems contain extensive policy initiatives to promote cooperation between Member States, much of their success is based on case law and legislation facilitating the freedom of movement of individuals as a means to give expression to cooperation at the system-level. It is ultimately this individual dimension where Brexit can be considered to have the most effects. Indeed, it must be emphasised that Brexit has given rise to challenges to the mobility of EU citizens into the UK and vice versa. Looking beyond the mere financial constraints coming from a lack of funding due to the UK's withdrawal from the Erasmus programme and its pending status as an associated country under Horizon Europe, it is clear that the UK has assumed a "true status" as a third country in the sense that EU free movement Treaty provisions and secondary legislation no longer apply. In the area of higher education and research this has a considerable impact on those students, researchers, and academics looking to move between the EU and UK to pursue their studies and research activities.

[62] See UK Research Office (2023). *UK Participation in EU Programmes for Research, Innovation, Earth Observation and Higher Education.* https://www.ukro.ac.uk/wp-content/uploads/2023/12/UK_association_factsheet.pdf.

[63] Department for Science, Innovation & Technology (2023) *Guidance – Horizon Europe and Copernicus programmes: 2023 UK-EU agreement explainer.* https://www.gov.uk/government/publications/horizon-europe-and-copernicus-programmes-2023-uk-eu-agreement-explainer/horizon-europe-and-copernicus-programmes-2023-uk-eu-agreement-explainer#the-future-of-the-uk-government-horizon-guarantee-scheme.

[64] Cavallaro (2022), pp. 1–2.

[65] Cavallaro (2022).

2.4.1 EU Free Movement Rights for Academic Actors

It is thanks to a combination of the case law of the Court of Justice of the EU (CJEU) and the Treaty provisions on free movement and non-discrimination that it has interpreted, that academic actors in the EU benefit from hard, enforceable rights that make a legal reality of the mobility so often loftily invoked in 'paper tiger' policy declarations that lack binding force.

Indeed, the CJEU can be said to have played a particularly important role in developing mobility rights for academic actors in the EU. The earliest example of this concerns the *Casagrande* judgment, which centered on the child of an Italian immigrant working in Germany who was refused an educational grant normally provided to German citizens.[66] The Court relied on Regulation 1612/68 (further elaborating the general right to free movement of workers designated in the EC Treaty) applicable to the father to deduce a right to the educational grant for the son by applying the principle of non-discrimination on the basis of nationality.[67] There were good arguments in that case to either consider that the regulation did not apply to education, or to consider the regulation to apply to education but then to annul it—considering it adopted *ultra vires*—as education was not a competence conferred on the EEC and instead remained with the Member States (or, in the case of Germany, the *Länder*).[68] Instead, the Court gave an interpretation focused on the effectiveness of the EU regulation and rights contained therein, with little regard to the 'absorbing' effects this would have on a policy area such as education.[69]

A decade later, in the seminal *Gravier* case, the Court was asked to rule on a French student having to pay an enrolment fee in Belgium that was not required from Belgian students.[70] The Court found that equal access to vocational training was guaranteed in the context of Regulation 1612/68. The CJEU thereby determined that vocational training constituted an indispensable element of the Community whereby access to such training was "in particular likely to promote free movement of persons throughout the Community, by enabling them to obtain a qualification in the Member State where they intend to work".[71] Accordingly, "any form of education which prepares for a qualification for a particular profession, trade or employment is vocational training, whatever the age and the level of training of the pupils or students, and even if the training programme includes an element of general education".[72] The Court later explicitly confirmed that this broad definition of vocational

[66] Case 9/74 *Casagrande*, EU:C:1974: 74.

[67] Case 9/74 *Casagrande*, EU:C:1974: 74, para. 14.

[68] Weiler (1991), p. 2240.

[69] Ibid, 2438–2241.

[70] Case 293/83 *Gravier*, EU:C:1985:69.

[71] Ibid., para. 23–24.

[72] Ibid., para. 30.

training was to also extend to higher education.[73] On this basis, the Court established a right to equal treatment for mobile students.

More specifically, the Court used the principle of non-discrimination on the basis of nationality in connection with the notion of EU citizenship to establish a right to access to education in other Member States. Here, a distinction should be made between access and pursuit of education. Whereas it is clear that the Court's case law led to a general right for mobile students to access education, subsequent case law showed that the Court took a different stance to matters essential to the pursuit of studies such as maintenance grants. This topic bears close connection to the right of residence of students regulated under the Citizens Rights Directive.[74] In principle, students enrolled to pursue studies at higher education institutions that are accredited or financed by the state have a right of residence in the host Member State.[75] Whereas persons residing in a host Member State on the basis of that Directive benefit from equal treatment on the basis of Article 24(1), that right is not unlimited for students. In accordance with Article 24(2) of the Directive, equal treatment is limited in the case of "maintenance aid for studies. . .consisting in student grants or student loans to persons other than workers, self-employed persons, persons who retain such status and members of their families". Based on the Directive, students would only get equal treatment regarding such grants once they obtain the status of permanent resident (an unlikely scenario in case of temporary mobility).[76]

Interestingly, the provisions of the Directive somewhat contrast the Court's case law. In *Bidar* the Court considered study maintenance grants to fall within the scope of the prohibition of discrimination on the basis of nationality—despite the limitation of Article 24(2) of the aforementioned Directive.[77] Subsequent cases nevertheless show that the move to a general right to study maintenance grants was not pursued further. Instead, much attention was given to students not becoming an unreasonable burden to the social assistance system[78] of the host Member States and to the need for a certain degree of integration—including multiple-year residence requirements—into the host Member State's society as pre-requisites for study maintenance grants.[79] It was previously pointed out that this distinction between access conditions and conditions such as maintenance grants gave rise to asymmetry

[73] Case 24/86 *Blaizot*, EU:C:1988:43 and Case 42/87 *Commission v. Belgium*, EU:C:1988:454.

[74] Directive 2004/38/EC of the European Parliament and of the Council of 29 April 2004 on the right of citizens of the Union to move and reside freely within the territory of the Member States amending regulation (EEC) No 1612/68 and repealing Directives 64/221/EEC, 68/360/EEC, 72/194/EEC, 73/148/EEC, 75/34/EEC, 75/35/EEC, 90/364/EEC, 90/365/EEC and 93/96/EEC, [2004] OJ L 158/77.

[75] Article 7(1)(c) Directive 2004/38/EC.

[76] See Article 24(2) Directive 2004/38/EC.

[77] Case C-209/03 *Bidar*, EU:C:2005:169, para. 42.

[78] A core requirement set by Directive 2004/38/EC in relation to non-economically active persons. See also Article 7(1)(b) of the Directive.

[79] These points were already introduced in *Bidar* (see para. 56–57) and further elaborated in subsequent case law. See also Case C-158/07 *Förster*, EU:C:2008:630.

between states, placing more obligations on states with highly subsidized education systems as opposed to states with more liberal education models with high tuition fees.[80] Taking the UK as an example of a country in which a liberal model of higher education is prevalent, this asymmetry between access and pursuit seen under EU law can be said to have previously worked to its benefit.

Over the course of the previous paragraphs it has become clear how the free movement of workers served as a basis to ultimately deduce an independent free movement right for students. However, the case law also shows that freedom of movement as such has an inextricable connection to education. This not only applies to workers, but also to the freedom of movement of other economically active persons such as self-employed persons (i.e. freedom of establishment). One area where the inextricability of this connection becomes particularly clear is that of the recognition of qualifications. Under the TFEU chapter on the right of establishment we find Article 53 TFEU on mutual recognition of diplomas which has been used extensively in the past to harmonize conditions for education and training for designated professions.[81] This extensive harmonization subsequently allowed for facilitated recognition of qualifications and ultimately mobility. Although the topic is generally considered to concern professionals, it undeniably has an effect on students as well—especially where it concerns the recognition of academic diplomas. Although academic recognition to access education is generally outside EU legislation,[82] the Court's case law again comes into play where such diplomas are recognized for professional purposes.

In *Kraus*, the Court ruled on the use of authorization procedures in Germany. These were required in order for a person with a foreign qualification to use an academic title that, though not necessary to access a profession, would prove advantageous for the exercise of a profession. The Court did provide that Community law set limits to Member States' powers meaning national law could not constitute an obstacle to the exercise of the fundamental freedoms.[83] Even if Member States were allowed to maintain authorization procedures to prevent the abuse of academic titles, these procedures had to fulfil a number of conditions to be

[80] Garben (2018), p. 1300.

[81] Present-day these harmonized conditions for education and training (also known as minimum training conditions) are found in Directive 2005/36/EC of the European Parliament and of the Council of 7 September 2005 on the recognition of professional qualifications, [2005] OJ L 255/22 as amended by Directive 2013/55/EU of the European Parliament and of the Council of 20 November 2013 amending Directive 2005/36/EC on the recognition of professional qualifications and Regulation (EU) No 1024/2012 on administrative cooperation through the Internal Market Information System ('the IMI Regulation'), [2013] OJ L 354/132 (the "Professional Qualifications Directive"). For more detailed discussion see Kortese (2020).

[82] Legislation in this area rather originates from the Council of Europe with the Convention on the Recognition of Qualifications concerning Higher Education in the European Region – European Treaty Series – No. 165 (Lisbon Recognition Convention).

[83] Case C-19/92 *Kraus*, EU:C:1993:125 , para. 28.

in conformity with the fundamental freedoms.[84] In a similar vein, the Court ruled in *Morgenbesser* that the academic qualifications of a former student seeking access to the profession of trainee lawyer had to be examined in accordance with the TFEU provisions on the free movement of workers and of establishment.[85] Even though Morgenbesser's academic qualifications were not covered by the relevant EU legislation, the Court determined that national authorities did have an obligation to examine them. Accordingly, the national authorities had to take into account all evidence of qualifications and conduct a comparative exercise with the qualifications required at national level.[86]

Maintaining the focus on the freedom of establishment, we find a further connection to the field of higher education. More specifically, in relation to the freedom of services and establishment as regards educational institutions.[87] It may be recalled that the exact organization of education is still very much a national affair. However, through its case law the Court also introduced a free movement element here. More specifically, the Court confirmed that the provision of private education qualifies as a service meaning that Member States cannot restrict free movement. Most recently, the application of the freedom of establishment and services was held to be applicable in the case of *Commission v. Hungary* concerning the Central European University (CEU).[88] The case concerned a new Hungarian law implementing additional requirements to the activities of foreign (non-EU) higher education institutions in the country. In this context, the core question concerned whether private educational activities could be considered as economic activity. Apart from reverting to its previous case law,[89] the Court also referred to the freedom of establishment of companies and branches to draw a parallel to institutions established in Member States providing education or training in return for remuneration in another Member State.[90]

[84] Ibid., para. 35.

[85] Case 3143/01 *Morgenbesser*, EU:C:2003:612, para. 56.

[86] This comparative exercise followed from previous case law of the Court in Case C-340/89 *Vlassopoulou*, EU:C:1991:193. In accordance with the doctrine developed in that case, national authorities must conduct a comparative exercise and—if sufficient correspondence is found—recognise the diploma. If insufficient correspondence is found, the host Member State must give the individual concerned the opportunity to show that he has the knowledge and qualifications which are lacking. Ibid., para. 67–71.

[87] Case C-76/05 *Schwarz and Gootjes – Schwarz*, EU:C:207:492 and Case C-153/02 *Neri*, EU:C:2003:614.

[88] Case C-66/18 *Commission v. Hungary*, EU:C:2020:792.

[89] Case C-153/02 *Neri*, EU:C:2003:614, para. 39.

[90] Case C-66/18 *Commission v. Hungary*, EU:C:2020:792, para. 162–163.

2.4.2 Situation Post-Brexit

The previous paragraph has shown the extent of the rights of academic actors under EU law—and correspondingly, their situation pre-Brexit. It was already remarked previously that it is this individual dimension where Brexit can be considered to have had the most drastic effects. Most importantly, the rights detailed in the previous section no longer apply to mobility between the UK and EU post-Brexit. This subsection discusses the consequences of this development.

To start, it is important to distinguish two situations, namely (1) the situation of EU and UK citizens residing outside their home Member State prior to Brexit or who moved during the transition period and (2) that of persons who moved after the end of the transition period. The former category of persons was initially still covered by EU free movement provisions through the Withdrawal Agreement until 31 December 2020.[91] During this transition period, EU citizens already resident in the UK were to apply for the EU Settlement Scheme which would result in settled status for those having already lived in the UK for a continuous 5-year period or pre-settled status.[92]

Post-transition period, the UK's withdrawal means that EU primary and secondary legislation ensuring, among others, residence rights and non-discrimination no longer applies. Therefore, the TFEU provisions on EU citizenship and free movement of workers, services, and establishment no longer apply. Neither do instruments such as Directive 2004/38/EC providing general provisions on residence for EU citizens. By contrast, instruments such as Directive 2016/801/EU will now apply to UK citizens moving to EU Member States since the UK is to be considered a third country. This means that students, academics, and researchers moving from the UK to the EU post-Brexit are likely subjected to national law procedures maintained for third country nationals (possibly originating from EU law as in the case of Directive 2016/801/EU). This application of national law is likely since Member States themselves remain free to adopt more advantageous rules for residence of third country nationals. Whereas EU secondary legislation on migration of third country nationals provides a minimum level of protection to non-EU citizens, Member States can still provide more rights or a higher level of protection. Nevertheless, third country status does entail that any more advantageous treatment depends on specific Member States—and is not guaranteed anymore as it previously was under EU free movement law. Furthermore, it is important to stress that this is bound to have an effect beyond the mere residence rights of UK citizens in the EU and may also affect the social security and access to study and maintenance grants to name a few.

While UK citizens will therefore be subject primarily to national law (possibly implementing EU secondary legislation on migration for third country nationals),

---

[91] See Article 126 of the Agreement on the withdrawal of the United Kingdom of Great Britain and Northern Ireland from the European Union and the European Atomic Energy Community, [2019] OJ C 384 1/1 (the Withdrawal Agreement).

[92] See UK Government (n.d.) Apply to the EU Settlement Scheme (settled and pre-settled status). https://www.gov.uk/settled-status-eu-citizens-families.

Points type	Relevant requirements to be met	Points
Study (must meet all)	• Confirmation of Acceptance for Studies requirement • Course requirement • Approved qualification requirement • Level of study requirement • Place of study requirement	50
Financial	Financial requirement	10
Language	Language requirement	10

Fig. 1 Points requirement for a student following from ST6.1 Immigration Rules Appendix Student

EU citizens in the UK are now also confronted with a complex scheme to regulate their residence and related rights. Concerns expressed prior to Brexit related to the anti-immigration atmosphere and approach adopted by prominent Brexiteers seem to have materialised, to the detriment of students, academics, and researchers.[93] Since the end of the transitional period EU citizens wishing to study or work in the UK must follow the point based immigration system. The system as such was not new, being introduced in 2008, but was updated following the Brexit referendum to form a unified set of work and study visa rules covering both EU and non-EU migrants.[94] The rules of the point-based system have furthermore been subject to updates since the end of the transition period and now include new routes for highly skilled workers and a graduate route for international students.[95]

The system as such is integrated into the Immigration Rules that have similar status to UK secondary legislation and lay down conditions for entry and residence for various categories of migrants.[96] Connected to the conditions for entry and residence are points awarded for certain attributes. To take students as an example, they must meet a number of validity requirements such as having paid relevant fees, having provided relevant biometrics, having proven their identity, and confirmation of acceptance for studies.[97] In order to then be eligible for a student visa, prospective students must first apply in time.[98] Additionally, they must be awarded 70 points following the scheme below (Fig. 1):

[93] Gromek Broc (2020).

[94] House of Commons Library (2022a). *The UK's new points-based immigration system* (Research Briefing No. CBP-8911, 27 September 2022), https://researchbriefings.files.parliament.uk/documents/CBP-8911/CBP-8911.pdf, p. 7.

[95] Ibid., pp. 14–15. See also the Immigration Rules Appendix Scale-up, Immigration Rules Appendix High Potential Individual, and Immigration Rules Appendix Graduate.

[96] Ibid., p. 13.

[97] ST1.2(a-d) Immigration Rules Appendix Student.

[98] ST4.1-ST4.3 Immigration Rules Appendix Student.

Since these requirements in sum amount to 70 points, it would appear students must essentially fulfil all the abovementioned criteria.[99] The Immigration Rules for students are thereby relatively straightforward. The situation can be said to be more complex for academics or researchers since they will be subject to different rules, such as the Immigration Rules on Skilled Workers, which cover a wider range of workers—and an evenly wide range of validity and eligibility requirements. It is thereby important to note that migrants may be subject to different Immigration Rules depending on the visa for which they are eligible and may thereby be eligible for multiple visas.[100]

All in all, the UK point-based system can be said to be covering a broad variety of migration routes. Nevertheless, it is also clear that it constitutes an administrative hurdle not seen under the EU free movement rules. Moreover, questions can be raised regarding the connection between various categories of migrants and the rights associated with their residence. It is therefore clear that Brexit has had far-reaching effects on the mobility of students, academics and researchers. This is a worrying development, especially considering the key function of the mobility of individuals in advancing higher education and research as such.

3 Concluding Reflections on the Future

Before Brexit, the UK's withdrawal from the EU was estimated to have limited effects on the UK's higher education and research at the system level since the direction of the discourse in both the EU context as well as in the EHEA was very much in line with the UK's market-based approach to higher education and research.[101] However, concerns were raised regarding the extent to which the UK could continue to benefit from the development of the continental European higher education systems into a market-model such as its own in the post-Brexit era.[102] This especially since the UK strongly benefited from student mobility from other EU Member States as well as financial support from EU funding programmes such as Horizon 2020. The chapter has discussed that since the unfolding of the UK's withdrawal, evidence may be found supporting the realisation of these concerns.

[99] See also ST6.1 Immigration Rules Appendix Student.

[100] The UK Government offers a practical tool on its website helping migrants find out whether they need a UK visa. A consultation of this tool using an EU Member State nationality and indicating the objective stay in the UK to be longer than six months to work as an academic or researcher yields a possible eligibility for *seven* different visas (skilled worker, global talent, government authorized exchange, senior or specialist worker, graduate trainee, scale-up worker, and high potential individual) each of which is subject to different Immigration Rules and corresponding validity and eligibility requirements. See UK Government (n.d.) Check if you need a UK visa. https://www.gov.uk/check-uk-visa.

[101] Garben (2018), pp. 1312–1316.

[102] Ibid., p. 1316.

In this context, it should be emphasised that the biggest issues related to Brexit and the areas of higher education and research manifest at the individual, rather than the system level. At system-level, the effects of the UK's withdrawal can instead be considered limited, as the UK continues to be part of the EHEA and can subscribe to some of the EU's instruments relevant to the EEA-2025 (formally or voluntarily depending on the instrument)—even if in the latter case it could be said to be in a 'rule-taking' rather than a 'rule-making' position. Compared to the EEA-2025 and EHEA, the effects of Brexit can be said to have a more direct and profound effect on cooperation in the ERA. An important reason for this lies in the fact that the ERA—although constituting system level cooperation—has a much closer connection to the individual level, affecting especially researchers and other academic staff thanks to the funding made available in the context of Horizon Europe as well as the ERA core objective to achieve an internal market for knowledge and researchers.[103] It is here where significant detrimental effects of Brexit on EU-UK cooperation appear the most prominent. This contribution has made clear that the UK's delayed association to Horizon Europe and non-participation in the Erasmus programme have (had) drastic effects on the mobility of individual students, academics and researchers seeking to move between the EU and UK—a situation compounded by the loss of mobility rights of academic actors in their capacity as student, researcher, teacher or academic institution under EU primary and secondary free movement law. This drastically curtails academic opportunity, with all the attendant consequences for the attractiveness and competitiveness of the UK higher education sector in particular, to the detriment its overall functioning.[104]

The core of the challenges in the area of education and research related to the UK's withdrawal are therefore for an important part centred on freedom of movement—a topic so central and controversial during the Brexit process. Whereas the UK and EU systems for higher education and research therefore seem to generally remain compatible, their relationship is strained by the limitations in exchanges brought on by the lack of freedom of movement and funding instruments in support thereof. In many ways it could be argued that "everybody loses" from this disintegration, as also EU citizens are negatively affected in their mobility options in and to the UK (although the impact is inevitably greater for the UK than it is for the EU). From a values perspective, this sector is one where openness, cooperation and mobility have been long-cherished hallmarks. The free circulation of knowledge and actors of knowledge is an ambition that long predates the EU and could be considered inherently beneficial for all concerned. As such, rather than treating this as a political bargaining chip (on either "side"), the UK and the EU should try to find a way to mitigate the negative consequences of their changed relationship for academia in general, and the individuals in particular.

---

[103] See Article 179 TFEU and Council Recommendation (EU) 2021/2122 of 26 November 2021 on a Pact for Research and Innovation in Europe, [2021] OJ L 431/1.

[104] Mayhew (2022), p. 179.

The most straightforward steps towards smoothening the relationship in this area in a way that directly benefits academic actors would be for the UK to become a member of the Erasmus programme—as was originally planned, even under Johnson's hard exit strategy. Although it would not resolve the UK's 'policy-taking' problem, it would allow it to benefit from the significant financial and institutional advantages these offer. More ambitiously, the EU and the UK could consider an agreement on cooperation in this area, providing reciprocal mobility rights to students, researchers and teachers as well as determining the UK's position in EEA-2025 and ERA instruments. As things stand at present, there does not seem to be much political priority accorded to this issue, however. Perhaps the most viable way forward is the UK becoming a member of the European Economic Area. As the negative consequences of exclusion from the internal market are more keenly felt by the UK every day,[105] European Economic Area membership may be the best way to become part of that once again (albeit as a policy-taker rather than a policy-maker),[106] would in fact go a long way towards resolving the rupture between the UK and the EU in the specific area of higher education and research as well.

References

Amsen E (2022) Broken Horizon: UK medical research struggling with funding and collaborations gap after Brexit. BMJ 378(2087):1–2

Cardwell J (2021) Erasmus and the Turing Scheme – a metaphor for Bexit? Parliament Mag:38–39

Cavallaro M (2022) Horizon Europe and Plan B research funding: turning adversity into opportunity. HEPI Policy Note 38

Corbett A (2021) Brexit is done: what next for UK higher education? Int High Educ 106:21–22

Department for Science, Innovation & Technology (2023) Guidance – Horizon Europe and Copernicus programmes: 2023 UK-EU agreement explainer. https://www.gov.uk/government/publications/horizon-europe-and-copernicus-programmes-2023-uk-eu-agreement-explainer/horizon-europe-and-copernicus-programmes-2023-uk-eu-agreement-explainer#the-future-of-the-uk-government-horizon-guarantee-scheme

Emerson M, Vahl M, Woolcock S (2002) Navigating by the starts: Norway, the European Economic Area and the European Union. CEPS Brussels, available at https://aei.pitt.edu/32566/1/5._Navigating_the_Stars.pdf

European Commission (n.d.) The UK and Erasmus+. https://erasmus-plus.ec.europa.eu/the-uk-and-erasmus

European Parliament Policy Department for Structural and Cohesion Polices (2018) Research for CULT Committee – recognition of qualifications for educational and professional purposes: the impact of Brexit (PE 629.180, November 2018). https://www.europarl.europa.eu/RegData/etudes/BRIE/2018/629180/IPOL_BRI(2018)629180_EN.pdf

[105] Polls have recorded a decline in support for Brexit in the UK. See e.g. https://yougov.co.uk/topics/politics/articles-reports/2022/11/17/one-five-who-voted-brexit-now-think-it-was-wrong-d.

[106] The policy-taking problem is one that all countries that are not member of the EU but that do participate in the internal market grapple with. On the EEA, see for instance Emerson et al. (2002). On EFTA, see Vahl and Grolimund (2006). For a discussion of the complex interactions, see Hillion (2018).

Garben S (2010) The Bologna Process: from a European law perspective. Eur Law J 16(2):186–210
Garben S (2011) EU higher education law: the Bologna process and harmonization by stealth. Wolters Kluwer, Alphen aan de Rijn
Garben S (2018) European higher education in the context of Brexit. Eur Pap 3(3):1293–1317
Gromek Broc K (2020) Brexit and its impact on the UK higher education sector and the rights of scholars and students. EU Law J 6(1):31–50
Guglielmi E (2022) EU grants restrict U.K. and Swiss research: rules on first grants from Horizon Europe highlight ongoing diplomatic disputes. Science 375(6578):252–253
Guibert JM, Rayón A (2021) UK's Turing Scheme: the challenges ahead. Int High Educ 106:23–24
Hillion C (2018) Brexit means Br(EEA)xit: the UK withdrawal from the EU and its implications for the EEA. Common Mark Law Rev 55:135–156
House of Commons Library (2021) The Erasmus Programme (Briefing Paper No. 8326, 6 January 2021). https://researchbriefings.files.parliament.uk/documents/CBP-8326/CBP-8326.pdf
House of Commons Library (2022a) The UK's new points-based immigration system (Research Briefing No. CBP-8911, 27 September 2022). https://researchbriefings.files.parliament.uk/documents/CBP-8911/CBP-8911.pdf
House of Commons Library (2022b) The Turing Scheme (No. 9141, 11 November 2022). https://researchbriefings.files.parliament.uk/documents/CBP-9141/CBP-9141.pdf
Joint Statement by the European Commission and the UK Government on the UK's association to Horizon Europe and Copernicus, 7 September 2023
Kortese L (2020) The recognition of qualifications in the EU: blurring the lines of competences between the internal market and education. Doctoral thesis, Maastricht
Mayhew K (2022) Brexit and UK higher education. Oxford Rev Econ Policy 38(1):179–187
Samarasekera U (2022) UK scientists warn over threat to Horizon funding. Lancet 399(10343):2257
UK Research Office (2023) UK Participation in EU Programmes for Research, Innovation Earth Observation and Higher Education. https://www.ukro.ac.uk/wp-content/uploads/2023/09/UK_association_factsheet.pdf
Vahl M, Grolimund N (2006) Integration without Membership. Switzerland's Bilateral Agreements with the European Union, Brussels, Centre for European Policy Studies. https://www.ceps.eu/?p=5273
Weiler J (1991) The transformation of Europe. Yale Law J 100:2405–2478
Wright G et al (2020) Influencing the EU after Brexit - Institute for Government, https://www.instituteforgovernment.org.uk/sites/default/files/publications/influencing-EU-after-brexit_2.pdf. Accessed 23 Jan 2023
Zotti S (2021) Academic mobility after Brexit: Erasmus and the UK post-2020. Eur J English Stud 25(1):19–33

The European Offices of the UK Local Authorities and Devolved Administrations After Brexit

Carlo Panara

1 Introduction

This chapter discusses the role of the Brussels-based offices of the UK local authorities and devolved administrations after Brexit. These offices are often referred to as the European offices of the UK 'regions' and so will they be hereafter. The aim of this chapter is to understand the current role of the offices and to identify what motivates some UK regions to maintain their offices in Brussels after Brexit. This study contributes, therefore, to the broader understanding of the impact of Brexit on the UK and the EU, but also of the continuing role of UK substate authorities in the EU after Brexit, and the continuing relevance of parts or aspects of EU law in the UK post-Brexit.

The European offices of the UK regions have been widely studied prior to Brexit. This is, however, the first and only study to date looking at these offices post-Brexit apart from my contribution to a book recently published, on which this chapter further builds and expands.[1] The Trade and Cooperation Agreement (TCA) is totally silent on local authorities and devolved administrations after Brexit. The only reference to a particular region and devolved administration can be found in the Northern Ireland Protocol attached to the Withdrawal Agreement. This lack of provisions about substate territorial authorities adds interest to research into an

I am grateful to my research assistants at Liverpool John Moores University, Dr Majida Ismael and Dr George William Lamb, for their invaluable help.

[1] Panara (2023), pp. 455–465. There is also an article that focuses on Scotland and Wales's direct engagement with the EU from 1992 to 2021, but not specifically on their Brussels offices. Minto et al. (2023).

C. Panara (✉)
University of Leicester, Leicester, UK
e-mail: cp481@leicester.ac.uk

E. Guinchard, C. Panara (eds.), *The New Relationship between the United Kingdom and the European Union*, https://doi.org/10.1007/978-3-031-70652-3_19

area of relations between UK subnational authorities, subnational authorities from the EU and EU institutions which has been considered inter alia in a report of the House of Lords.[2]

This study is also highly relevant to the theory of multilevel governance (MLG). The engagement of substate actors on the EU level has been widely researched, including that of local and regional authorities from the EU member states. There are, however, few and narrow-in-scope studies on the engagement with the EU of subnational authorities from non-EU countries[3] and, apart from the aforementioned exception, none on the engagement by UK substate authorities post-Brexit. This study will therefore contribute new knowledge on a hitherto largely unexplored aspect of the engagement with the EU by substate authorities from an important third country, the UK, during an unprecedented time of transition from EU membership to third country status, and will enrich MLG theory, so far mostly confined to the analysis of EU member states.[4]

The post-Brexit UK can repeal and replace EU laws.[5] Accordingly, at first glance there should be no need for UK substate authorities to seek to influence EU legislation and policy, for the simple reason that these are in principle no longer relevant to them. The supposed irrelevance in the UK of the laws of the EU tells us, however, only a part of the story and, whilst the law emanating from the EU lost its supremacy, direct and indirect effect, and other mechanisms to ensure compliance, it still remains an influential factor in the UK. The influence of EU law is not limited to what Birkinshaw calls the "legacy of European Public Law", by which he means the survival in UK law of principles and rules originating from the EU and from the case law of the European Court of Justice (ECJ).[6] Pursuant to the Northern Ireland Protocol annexed to the Brexit Withdrawal Agreement, as amended by the Windsor

---

[2]House of Lords European Union Committee, *Beyond Brexit: how to win friends and influence people*, 25 March 2019, pp. 30–31, available at https://publications.parliament.uk/pa/ld201719/ldselect/ldeucom/322/322.pdf (accessed January 2024). See also Institute for Government (2020), pp. 52–53, and Sandford (2016).

[3]These include studies on North Macedonia, Bosnia and Herzegovina, Turkey and EFTA countries: Hristova and Cekik (2015), pp. 23–38; Marciacq (2015), pp. 329–346; Özçelik (2017), pp. 171–199; Panara (2022), pp. 557–572.

[4]Hooghe and Marks (2001); Piattoni (2010); Greenwood (2011b), pp. 437–451; Rowe (2011); Greenwood (2014), pp. 1–16; Panara (2015); Tatham (2016).

[5]This results from the repeal of the European Communities Act 1972 by the EU (Withdrawal) Act 2018. See also the Retained EU Law (Revocation and Reform) Act 2023. Northern Ireland constitutes a partial exception in that certain EU laws regarding goods are still applicable there. See UK Supreme Court in *James Hughes Allister and others (First Appellants) and Clifford Peeples (Second Appellant) v the Secretary of State for Northern Ireland and others (Respondents)* [2023] UKSC 5.

[6]Birkinshaw (2020), pp. 829–830.

See the cases, all regarding the continuing relevance of the case law of the CJEU, *Chelluri v Air India Ltd* [2021] EWCA Civ 1953; *Lipton v BA City Flyer* [2021] EWCA Civ 454; *TuneIn v Warner Music* [2021] EWCA Civ 441; *Gladman Developments Ltd v SSHCLG & Corby BC; & Uttlesford DC* [2020] EWHC 518 (Admin); *Pearce v SoS for Business, Energy and Industrial Strategy* [2021] EWHC 326 (Admin).

Framework of February 2023, a range of EU rules concerning, inter alia, the standards of certain goods and state aid, continue to apply to Northern Ireland in relation to those goods that are destined for the EU market.[7] Moreover, the ECJ retains jurisdiction over the interpretation of these rules.[8] On the other hand, Scotland has chosen to maintain an alignment with EU laws by giving its ministers the power to issue regulations that mirror EU rules in a number of devolved sectors (environmental protection, animal health and welfare, plant health, equality, non-discrimination and human rights, social protection).[9]

These examples show how the impact of Brexit in the UK is asymmetrical, with some parts of the country maintaining an alignment with some of the rules originating from Brussels. Another aspect to consider is that the EU, with its 450 million people-strong Single Market, is the UK's largest trading partner by far.[10] Standards of quality and trade arrangements applicable to the bloc have an influence on trading partners outside the EU. Therefore, in addition to the impact of EU law on Northern Ireland and Scotland, it is likely that a significant, although less immediate or immediately visible, impact of EU standards in the rest of the UK will remain.[11]

The working hypotheses of this chapter are, first, that the UK offices post-Brexit are still interested in knowing, understanding and influencing EU policies in certain domains, although only Northern Ireland and Scotland are likely to engage in active lobbying. Second, that one of the most important reasons to remain in Brussels for some UK substate authorities is political, that is, that these authorities retain a presence in Brussels as testimony of the continuing importance of their relationship

[7] Annexes from 1 to 5 to the Northern Ireland Protocol attached to the Brexit Withdrawal Agreement of 24 January 2020 as amended by the Windsor Framework in February 2023.

[8] Article 12 of the Protocol.

[9] Section Part 1 of the UK Withdrawal from the EU (Continuity) (Scotland) Act 2021. See also the Policy Statement of the Scottish government of 22 July 2022. See: https://www.gov.scot/publications/uk-withdrawal-from-the-european-union-continuity-scotland-act-2021-july-2022-regulation-making-power-under-section-1-statement-of-policy/ (accessed March 2024). Examples of statutory instruments and secondary legislation enacted as a result of the Scottish Continuity Act include the following: the UK Withdrawal from the EU (Continuity) (Scotland) Act 2021 (Commencement No. 1) Regulations 2021; the UK Withdrawal from the EU (Continuity) (Scotland) Act 2021 (Commencement No. 2) Regulations 2021; the UK Withdrawal from the EU (Continuity) (Scotland) Act 2021 (Consequential Provisions and Modifications) Order 2021; the Public Interest Disclosure (Prescribed Persons) (Amendment) Order 2022; the Environment Act 2021 (Commencement No. 3) Regulations 2022; the Public Water Supplies (Scotland) Amendment Regulations 2022.

[10] In the 4 quarters to the end of September 2022, over 40 percent of UK exports of goods and services went to EU or EFTA countries (the second trading partner being the US with 20.8 percent). During the same period, nearly 50 percent of UK imports of goods and services came from EU or EFTA countries (the second importer being the US with 11.8 percent). See Office for National Statistics, *UK total trade: all countries, seasonally adjusted*, at https://www.ons.gov.uk/economy/nationalaccounts/balanceofpayments/datasets/uktotaltradeallcountriesseasonallyadjusted (accessed January 2024).

[11] An example is the recent decision by the UK to retain indefinitely the EU safety mark CE (Conformité Européenne) for a range of goods manufactured in Britain.

with the EU, as well as to partner up and network with substate authorities and organisations from the EU. Third, that the seeking of EU funding, which had been one of the key factors for the establishment of the offices in Brussels prior to Brexit, is far less relevant to the remaining offices, considering that currently, apart from the Peace Plus programme for Northern Ireland, the only funding scheme still available to UK regions is Horizon Europe.[12]

This chapter draws on evidence emerging from 35 semi-structured interviews, 5 Freedom of Information Act (FOIA) and 3 non-FOIA access requests. Fifteen interviews were completed between 2021 and 2023, alongside the 5 FOIA and 3 non-FOIA access requests. These concerned actors, both based in Brussels and in the UK, engaged in representing the interests of UK localities and devolved administrations in the EU. The chapter also draws on a focus group held in June 2016 with representatives of six UK offices and local authorities, as well as on 20 semi-structured interviews completed between July 2014 and April 2018. As a result, this study reflects the current post-Brexit situation, but also the developments that occurred in the sector of the UK offices between the period leading up to the actual exit from the EU and the present time. Additionally, representatives of the Committee of the Regions (CoR), of Core Cities UK (CCUK), the Secretary General at Eurocities, as well as representatives of the Council of European Municipalities and Regions (CEMR) and of the Conference of Peripheral and Maritime Regions (CPMR) were interviewed, and a wealth of strategy, policy and other official documents from the UK and the EU were consulted to cross-validate the findings emerging from the interviews. The result is a highly original study that fills an important gap in the knowledge regarding the new UK-EU relationship.

The next Sect. 2 will discuss the landscape before Brexit and will touch upon the history of the offices and their functions. The following section will look at the current situation, both in terms of number, size and structure of the existing offices (Sect. 3.1), as well as in terms of the most significant developments instigated by Brexit (Sect. 3.2). The final section will lay out the concluding remarks.

2 The European Offices of the UK Regions Prior to Brexit

The first UK region to open a liaison office in Brussels was Birmingham in 1984, followed in the same year by Strathclyde. In 1994 there were 20 substate offices from the UK, 18 of which had been established between 1988 and 1994.[13] These became 29 by 2009, a year that marks the beginning of the crisis of the Eurozone and of a

[12]The UK obtained recently (September 2023) associate member status of Horizon Europe. Associate membership of this scheme became achievable following the settlement through the Windsor Agreement of February 2023 of the dispute arising from the implementation of the Northern Ireland Protocol.

[13]Mawson et al. (1994), p. 740.

period of crisis, or at least a stalemate, in the EU integration process.[14] This growth mirrors the deepening of European integration and the expansion of Community (later Union) competences arising from the Single European Act of 1986, and subsequently the Treaty of Maastricht six years later, which established the EU. These developments, alongside the expansion of the European Regional Development Fund (ERDF), increased the opportunities for UK regions to engage with the EU institutions. The number of UK offices, and in particular of those from England, multiplied and reached its peak around 2009 also thanks to the funding made available for the offices by the Regional Development Agencies (RDAs). These were established by the Labour government through the RDAs Act 1998 and abolished in 2012 by the Tory-LibDem coalition government.

Following the Eurozone crisis that began in 2009, a significant portion of the UK public became increasingly disenchanted with the EU or turned altogether against EU membership. This led to the frequent questioning by local councillors and citizens of the cost to the taxpayer and the value for money of the Brussels-based offices.[15] As a result of the described developments (mounting Euroscepticism and especially abolition of the RDAs) by 23 June 2016, date of the Brexit referendum, the number of UK offices had already decreased to only 16,[16] and the size of some of these offices had become smaller in terms of number of staff and funding.[17]

Prior to Brexit, the Brussels-based offices of the UK regions had generally a fourfold function: promoting the image of the region in Brussels; seizing opportunities, particularly funding opportunities, arising from the EU for businesses and organisations from the region;[18] networking with other regions; monitoring and attempting to influence policy and legislative developments in Brussels.[19] The second and fourth functions (attracting EU funding to the region; monitoring and influencing policy) were probably the most important tasks in particular of the European offices of the English local authorities before Brexit.

Prior to Brexit lobbying and networking were the most common approaches by the European offices of the English regions to influencing EU decision-making. Lobbying targeted primarily the Commission and the MEPs, particularly those, irrespective of the member state of origin or political allegiance, who were chairs

---

[14] Committee of the Regions (2009); Greenwood (2011a), p. 186.

[15] See, for example, the FOIA request to Northamptonshire County Council by a citizen on 5 September 2011, https://www.whatdotheyknow.com/request/office_in_brussels (accessed January 2024).

[16] Panara and Varney (2017a), p. 155.

[17] Sykes and Lord (2011), pp. 486–489.

[18] The most important funding schemes for the UK local and regional authorities before Brexit were the ERDF, the European Social Fund (ESF), the Cohesion Funds, the European Structural and Investment Funds (ESIF), Interreg Europe, and Horizon 2020. Horizon was particularly important for UK universities and research institutions.

[19] On UK regions, see Macneill et al. (2007), pp. 406–407; Moore (2007), pp. 275–291.

On European regions in general, see Marks et al. (2002), pp. 1–23; Callanan and Tatham (2014), pp. 188–210; Trobbiani (2016); Tatham (2017), pp. 1088–1108; Tatham (2018), pp. 672–686.

or rapporteurs of relevant committees of the European Parliament.[20] The offices also used to work with the UK Permanent Representation to the EU (UKRep). This was effective given that the UK government held a seat in the Council of Ministers where it could vote on legislation. Networking with other EU regions, on the other hand, facilitated the creation of coalitions around common agendas relevant to the regions from various EU countries, as well as the sharing of best practice between these regions. The most important networks included Eurocities, CEMR, CPMR, and the European Regions Research & Innovation Network (ERRIN).[21] One important example of successful collective lobbying by some English regions in collaboration with other EU regions prior to Brexit, led to the inclusion of the so-called 'transition regions', i.e., those with a GDP between 75 and 90 percent of the average EU GDP, in the areas of intervention envisaged by Objective 1 of the ERDF.[22]

The offices are therefore a clear response to the impact on domestic law of the law and policies originating from the EU.[23] Their focus on influencing EU legislation and policy illustrates that there used to be a two-way process whereby not only EU law impacted on the UK, but also the UK government and substate units attempted to influence policy and legislative developments in the EU. The regional offices were indeed vehicles of this influence. The fact that the number and size of the offices varied significantly between the 1980s and 2016, is the result of the evolution of the EU integration process and of the relationship between UK and EU over the years, as well as of political dynamics entirely internal to the UK.

3 The UK Offices Post-Brexit

3.1 Number, Size and Structure of the Remaining Offices

At present (March 2024), four years since the UK left the EU, there are 9 UK regional offices in Brussels.[24]

There are five offices from England (there were 10 in June 2016[25]):

- Bristol & Bath Brussels Office
- London European Office

[20] Panara and Varney (2017b); Panara (2015), pp. 144–149.

[21] Sixteen UK cities, including London, Birmingham, Manchester and Bristol inter alia, still retain membership of Eurocities. Scotland and Wales still retain membership of the CPMR.

[22] Panara (2015), p. 151.

[23] Hooghe and Marks (2001), pp. 89–90.

[24] There is also a City of London Brussels Office which, however, represents the City of London Corporation. Since it does not represent a 'region', however, it is not relevant to this study.

[25] To these 10, one could add Access Europe Network, a London-based company with intermittent presence in Brussels, that facilitated access to EU funding by London boroughs and other stakeholders from London. The company closed in January 2017.

- Kent County Council in Brussels
- Greater Birmingham & West Midlands Brussels Office
- Local Government Association (LGA, this also represents 22 Welsh councils alongside 317 English councils).

Two further offices, the Cornwall Brussels Office and the Hampshire County Council's Brussels Office were closed relatively recently in 2021 and 2022 respectively.[26]

There are, additionally, three offices representing the devolved administrations and one representing the Scottish local authorities:

- Scottish Government representation in Brussels
- Wales in Europe representing the Welsh government
- Northern Ireland Brussels Office representing the Northern Ireland Executive
- Convention of Scottish Local Authorities (COSLA)

Three of the above indicated offices represent the devolved administrations; accordingly, only six UK offices represent local government authorities. This includes two associations of local authorities (LGA and COSLA), which shows how, due to the high operating costs of the Brussels offices, maintaining a presence in Brussels is more sustainable for groupings rather than for individual localities. Only four among the existing offices represent identified local government authorities, all from England (Bristol & Bath, London, Kent, Greater Birmingham & West Midlands). The Welsh Senedd (the Welsh Parliament) still has a desk in Brussels but in April 2022 we were informed that it had not used it for two years.[27]

Scotland engages with EU partners and the EU institutions through Scotland House, a Brussels-based location that hosts the Scottish Government representation in Brussels, as well as Scotland Europa, an organisation that represents 27 stakeholders including universities, various public bodies and private companies, and Scottish Enterprise, a non-departmental body that promotes economic development, investment and innovation in eastern and central Scotland.

The number of the Brussels-based offices, therefore, declined substantially compared to the years between the entry into force of the Treaty of Maastricht and the first decade of the 2000s (from 29 to the current 9). The number declined remarkably also compared to the period immediately preceding the Brexit referendum (23 June 2016), when there were as many as 16 offices. It is noticeable that a number of English regions traditionally very active in the Brussels arena, such as, Liverpool City Region, Greater Manchester CA, Cornwall, South of England, and East of England, closed their representations, whereas others, such as Northamptonshire County Council, have never followed up on their pre-Brexit plans to re-establish a liaison office in Brussels after its closure.[28] The reasons given in official documents

[26] See Report to the Leader of the Council, Cornwall Council, 30 June 2021; Hampshire County Council Decision Report, 27 January 2022.

[27] Head of Brussels Office, Welsh Government, 1 April 2022.

[28] Woods (2015).

for the closures include the changing focus of the UK international trade policy following Brexit, the fact that economic development funding and policy decisions have been moved from Brussels to London after Brexit, the desire to make savings, and that a more direct engagement with particular EU partners was more effective and appropriate for the region.[29] Other closures, though, were described as "ideological".[30] In relation to East of England European Partners Brussels Office, for example, it was highlighted that the cost to each partner council of running the office was small, and the closure was decided before the terms of Brexit had been agreed; therefore, before the possible benefits of retaining a Brussels-based office could be effectively factored in.[31]

The current number of UK offices is small compared to other third European countries. Two member states of the European Economic Area (EEA), as of 2021, had more regional representations, compared to the respective populations, than the UK (Norway, six; Iceland, one).[32] EEA membership implies that most EU Single Market rules, including those concerning free movements, apply to these countries, albeit not automatically. This means that these countries must incorporate all new relevant EU law into their domestic legal systems.[33] By contrast, the UK is no longer a member of the EU Single Market and the UK parliament is, in principle, at liberty to diverge from all European rules. Additionally, unlike EEA countries, UK organisations are eligible for a limited number of EU funding schemes (Peace Plus programme and Horizon Europe), which removed an important incentive for UK local authorities to engage directly in the Brussels arena.

A number of offices have been noticeably downsized compared to the pre-Brexit era, although the downsizing concerns only some English local authorities and not the devolved administrations. The Birmingham & West Midlands Office, for example, which is the oldest UK regional office in Brussels, counted 17 employees back in the 1990s, whereas currently has only one full-time staff and two interns. Similarly, London's European Office had three full-time staff and one half-time administrative support staff in 2017, but only one full-time employee at present. The downsizing of the London office, however, is not solely a by-product of Brexit, and therefore of the downscaling of the remit of the office, but also of the impact of Covid-19 that led to the reduction of the volume of affairs in Brussels for nearly two years.[34] The downsizing is also due to the cuts to central funding transferred to local

[29] See Report to the Leader of the Council, Cornwall Council, 30 June 2021; Hampshire County Council Decision Report, 27 January 2022; official response from Greater Manchester Combined Authority, 24 October 2022; response to FOIA request from Liverpool City Council, 28 November 2022.

[30] See Quinn (2019).

[31] Former Director of East of England European Partners, 6 September 2022.

[32] Panara (2022), pp. 557–572; Realfsen (2015).

[33] See Baudenbacher (2015, 2017).

[34] Head of London's European Office, 17 January 2021.

government,[35] as well as to the already mentioned abolition of the RDAs and, consequently, of the funding they supplied for the Brussels liaisons.

In terms of size, if one looks at the number of Brussels-based full-time employees, the number of permanent full-time staff for the existing English offices is usually of one full-time staff, occasionally with the support of some interns, with the exception of the LGA's Brussels Office that employs 2.7 permanent staff. The offices of the devolved administrations are bigger, given their wider political agendas, with the Northern Irish representation counting 9 staff (7 in Brussels and two in Belfast), Wales in Europe nine including two staff working in a partner office, and the Scottish Government 18.[36] The number of staff of the offices of the devolved administrations is similar to those of certain large regions with legislative powers from the EU, such as, the representation of the *Land* Baden-Württemberg, that comprises c.20 Brussels-based staff, or the delegation of Lombardy, that comprises six Brussels-based staff.[37] This shows the importance that the devolved administrations continue to attribute to the relationship with the EU, including Wales that in terms of continuing relevance of the EU laws is exactly in the same position as England, given that Wales, unlike Scotland, has not chosen to align with new laws originating from the EU.[38]

The current English offices are either entirely owned by one local authority (Kent County Council Office, London's European Office which is entirely owned by the Greater London Authority), or are the result of partnerships between local councils and various stakeholders, such as, the local universities and chambers of commerce (Bristol & Bath Office, Greater Birmingham & West Midlands Office). This second model was common among Brussels offices of the English regions prior to Brexit.[39] The offices of the LGA and of COSLA are entirely funded by councils from England and Wales or Scotland, respectively, which are members of these associations. The devolved administrations' representations are clearly organised as delegations to the EU, which is the model typically adopted by some EU regions with legislative powers (such as, the German *Länder*, the Italian regions and the Spanish Autonomous Communities inter alia).

The exit of the UK from the EU accelerated a trend, that was already taking place prior to the UK's departure from the EU, towards the erosion of the representation of the English territorial interests through the Brussels-based offices. In June 2016 there were 10 offices from England representing the interests of a multitude of partner stakeholder organisations. Table 1 below compares the landscapes in 2015–17 and at present. The picture that emerges, perhaps predictable but not entirely obvious in

[35] See Head of European and International Affairs, Birmingham City Council, 19 September 2023. See also the report by Atkins and Hoddinott (2022).

[36] The figure regarding Scotland reflects the situation in January 2022 and marks a marginal increase from April 2021 (17 staff by headcount, 16.8 FTE).

[37] Panara (2015), pp. 128–143.

[38] Minto and Morgan (2019), pp. 423–428.

[39] Panara and Varney (2017b).

Table 1 Partners, stakeholder representation and number of staff of the Brussels offices (Alongside the interviews with local officials and office representatives I completed during that period, the main source for 2015–17 is the document by Panara and Varney (2017b))

Office (June 2016)	Partners (period 2015–17)	Office and partners (2024)
Bristol Brussels Office	The office was founded by Bristol City Council in 2014 and later expanded to include the following six partners: – Bristol City Council – Bristol University – University of Bath – University of West of England – Business West (local chamber of commerce) – South Gloucestershire Council One full-time permanent staff (Head of Office) and occasionally interns on a temporary basis.	Still operational. Since 2019 became Bristol & Bath Brussels Office. There are only four partners left: – Bristol City Council – Bristol University – University of Bath – Business West One full-time permanent staff (Head of Office) and occasionally interns on a temporary basis.
Cornwall Brussels Office	Cornwall Council, Cornwall universities, Local Enterprise Partnership (LEP).	Closed in 2021
East of England European Partnership	East of England Local Government Association (52 local councils). Universities: University of East Anglia, University of Essex, Anglia Ruskin University. LEPs: Hertfordshire LEP, Greater Cambridge, Greater Peterborough LEP. In April 2017 Anglian Water became a partner of the Office.	Closed in 2019
Liverpool City Region Office	Liverpool City Region Combined Authority, Liverpool University, Merseyside Police, Merseytravel, Liverpool Vision.	Closed in 2020
Local Government Association Brussels Office	LGA members Two full-time members of staff engaging with lobbying in Brussels and one half-time office manager dealing with admin.	Still operational with the same membership. 2.7 FTE permanent staff.
London's European Office	The office is part of Greater London Authority (GLA). It used to represent a number of local stakeholders in addition to GLA: Transport for London (TfL), members of City Hall, Metropolitan Police, London Fire Brigade. In the past the office worked also with London NHS and London Higher, the umbrella body for London's universities. Three full-time staff and one half-	Still operational. It continues to represent GLA and TfL. TfL contributes half of the budget. One full-time staff (Head of Office).

(continued)

Table 1 (continued)

Office (June 2016)	Partners (period 2015–17)	Office and partners (2024)
	time administrative support staff in 2017	
Greater Manchester Brussels Office/New Economy Manchester	The Brussels Office was managed by New Economy Manchester, a company entirely owned by the local authorities of Greater Manchester.	The office was shared with Liverpool City Region for some time until closure in 2019.
Southern England Local Partners Brussels Office (SELP)	20 subscribers in total in 2015: 11 local authorities (the most important being Hampshire County Council), 4 local universities (including the University of Southampton), local LEPs, business intermediaries and other public and private stakeholders from Southern England.	Replaced by Hampshire Brussels Office until closure in 2022.
Kent County Council in Brussels	Kent County Council One full-time staff (Head of Office).	Still operational One full-time staff (Head of Office).
Greater Birmingham & West Midlands Brussels Office	Greater Birmingham Combined Authority, local authorities from the region, local universities. 17 employees in the 1990s and still c.10 in 2017.	Still operational, the universities are no longer partners of the office. One full-time staff (Head of Office) and temporary interns.

light of the claim to be building 'global Britain', is that Brexit has generated a more inward-looking local government sector that engages less with the EU and partners from the EU. Whilst this is only part of the story, given that not all the engagement by local authorities with partners from the EU takes place through the Brussels-based offices (for example, 16 UK cities still retain membership of Eurocities), there is no doubt that Brexit has caused a significant reduction in the representation of English territorial interests in Brussels.

At the same time, a parallel trend has taken place towards more cooperation between various UK representatives in Brussels through the creation in 2018 of a network of Brussels-based UK offices and organisations including the UK's Mission to the EU. The network, named UK Stakeholders Brussels, does not have formal terms of reference, a secretariat nor a membership fee. It is an informal forum for discussion of issues of common interest and for considering ways in which UK organisations may work together to maximise their collective influence. This development is judged positively by some office representatives.[40] The creation in 2020 of the Committee of the Regions-UK contact group responds in part to the same logic

[40] Director of Bristol & Bath Brussels Office, 30 November 2021.

of establishing more direct links between the territorial interests emerging from the UK and the EU (see further Sect. 3.2.2).[41]

3.2 *The Role and Activities of the Existing European Offices*

The typical activities of the Brussels-based offices of regions from EU countries include monitoring the EU policy horizon for information-gathering, influencing policy, chasing funding and networking with partners from the EU. Regions with legislative powers usually engage in lobbying of the EU institutions to influence policy, whereas substate authorities without such powers do so to a lesser extent.[42] In this paragraph, I will attempt to position the existing European offices of the UK regions in light of this knowledge emerging from past research and to identify developments and trends that have emerged since the UK left the EU.

3.2.1 Information-Gathering and Influencing Policy

All the UK offices still engage in monitoring the EU policy horizon in Brussels. Areas of interest include all the matters relevant to the devolved administrations, climate and environment legislation (including in particular air quality and vehicle emissions in the case of Greater London Authority), transport, trade arrangements, public procurement and state aid inter alia (see Table 2). Brexit itself became an additional subject of information-gathering for the offices. During the negotiations of the Withdrawal Agreement and of the terms of the new EU-UK relationship, this area of work included the monitoring of the relevant negotiations (East of England, Bristol, Cornwall, London, Birmingham) and, currently, the monitoring of any developments regarding the new relationship with the EU (Kent, Birmingham, Wales, Northern Ireland, COSLA).

The influencing of policy and lobbying activities the UK offices used to engage in prior to Brexit contracted significantly in the last three years, with some offices no longer engaging in direct lobbying of the EU institutions (LGA), others acknowledging that influencing EU policy became more difficult since the departure from the EU (London, Bristol), and others that either do not include lobbying/influencing policy among their current primary activities (Birmingham, Kent), or declare to be currently reconsidering this area of activity in light of the new UK-EU relationship (Wales). This change in the focus and practice of the regional offices is the product of a combination of factors. One is the more limited and more indirect relevance of EU law in the UK compared to the past. The other is linked to the difficulty of

[41] Schönlau (2021). See also Copeland and Minto (2023), pp. 501–518.

[42] Marks et al. (2002), pp. 1–23; Callanan and Tatham (2014), pp. 188–210; Tatham (2017), pp. 1088–1108; Tatham (2018), pp. 672–686.

Table 2 EU policy areas UK offices identify as relevant post-Brexit

Office	Policy areas (post-Brexit)
Bristol Brussels Office	Trade Higher Education Horizon Europe (if UK becomes associate member)
Local Government Association Brussels Office	Environment and waste Energy and climate change Social and labour laws Public procurement State aid
London's European Office	Transport Air quality
Kent County Council in Brussels	Monitoring Brexit Border arrangements and infrastructure required to manage border in Kent
Greater Birmingham & West Midlands Brussels Office	Trade Horizon Europe (if UK becomes associate member)
Northern Ireland Brussels Office	Health Education Areas covered by Northern Ireland Protocol Climate Horizon Europe (if UK becomes associate member) Peace funding (Peace Plus programme) Data protection Services (currently not covered in the Protocol) Justice matters (relevant because of the border with Ireland) Transport (relevant because of railways and buses crossing the border with Ireland)
Scottish Government	EU (Continuity) (Scotland) Act 2021: environmental protection, animal health and welfare, plant health, equality, non-discrimination and human rights, social protection. *Scotland's Global Affairs Framework*, 9 May 2022: climate action, renewable technologies, protecting biodiversity, development of green and digital jobs and skills, individual freedoms and democratic processes, keeping people safe, tackling poverty and inequality, Erasmus+ provided that Scotland can access the programme in future.
Wales	Brexit Trade Climate Environment Agriculture Fisheries Research and innovation Transport Health Anything relevant to Welsh language
COSLA	Local impact of TCA

influencing EU decision-making processes. This difficulty originates from being outside the EU, with the result that EU institutions are unlikely to consider demands arising from UK regions. These, however, remain members of various influential groupings, such as, Eurocities and the CPMR that attempt to shape EU policies in areas relevant to their membership.

English local authorities in particular see lobbying as too time-consuming and costly, as well as conducive to little results. This is clearly reflected in the current size of those English offices representing individual cities or regions (Kent, Bristol, London, Birmingham). With an average of only 1.0 FTE employee, these offices are not adequately staffed for this resource-intensive activity.[43] The exception in this context is the LGA with its 2.7 FTE employees, although even the LGA does not engage in direct lobbying of the EU institutions and continues to work with other local government associations from the EU, when they engage in lobbying in areas that could have an impact on UK policies, such as, environment and waste, energy and climate change, social and labour laws, public procurement, state aid.[44]

It is important to note, however, that the position of Northern Ireland, Scotland and Wales, the three devolved administrations, due to their constitutional status and legislative powers, differs from the position of local government authorities from England. Northern Ireland remains part of the Single Market for goods, therefore a range EU rules remain applicable to that region which in turn explains why Northern Ireland engages more than other UK regions in attempting to influence EU laws. Scotland, on the other hand, passed an Act enabling the Scottish Government to align Scotland with new EU laws in certain areas. This, alongside the stated intention to rejoin the EU as an independent country in the future,[45] explains the stronger engagement of Scotland with the EU institutions compared to other parts of the UK through Scotland House. Wales at present has a pro-European government,[46] but does not have a law promoting the alignment with laws emanating from Brussels, nor is it still part of the Single Market for goods like Northern Ireland. Accordingly, despite being a devolved administration with legislative powers, Wales does not

[43] The size of the Bristol & Bath Brussels Office has not changed significantly compared to that of Bristol Brussels Office prior to Brexit. The Office of Greater London Authority, however, moved from three full-time staff in 2017 to the current one only. Birmingham had 17 full-time staff back in the 1990s and c.10 in 2017–18, and only one currently. Kent had four full-time staff in 2002 and now only one.

[44] Local Government Association, response to FOIA request, 8 February 2021.

[45] See Scottish Government, *Scotland's Global Affairs Framework*, 9 May 2022, chapter 2 (Maintaining the closest possible relationship with the European Union). See also Scottish Government, *Steadfastly European: Scotland's Past, Present and Future*, 9 March 2021; and 'Nicola Sturgeon's speech launching the case for independence', 14 June 2022, at https://www.snp.org/nicola-sturgeons-speech-launching-the-case-for-independence/ (accessed March 2024).

[46] A small majority of Welsh voters (52.53%) voted in favour of leaving the EU in the referendum of 23 June 2016. The election of the Welsh Parliament (Senedd) held on 6 May 2021, however, returned a substantial pro-European majority.

include influencing EU law and policy among its current priorities, although maintaining good relations with the EU remains a political priority for Wales.[47]

It seems possible to conclude that the information-gathering by the offices continues to remain important. Despite the partial exception of two devolved administrations (Northern Ireland and Scotland), however, the direct lobbying and influencing policy strands disappeared or lost traction after Brexit.

3.2.2 Networking

Networking with other European local and regional authorities was prior to Brexit and remains post-Brexit an important area of activity for UK cities and regions, irrespective of their presence in Brussels. The most important networks and those our research concentrated on are Eurocities, CPMR and CEMR (see Table 3).

The Director of the Bristol & Bath Brussels Office suggests that networks became even more useful after Brexit:

> In the past, we did still have natural counterparts in the institutions whom we could talk to, so there were MEPs from the Southwest of the UK. The UK Government had a seat around the table with all the other Member States, so those direct channels of communication have of course disappeared compared to before Brexit, or at least dramatically reduced. And that's why networks are important and you also have to develop your connections. Other European cities and other European universities, if there's a specific issue, are able to talk to their MEPs or their government, but through these it may be possible to bring forward the agenda of UK local authorities.[48]

UK substate authorities, therefore, benefit from the EU status of their partners to obtain information which would not otherwise be otherwise, or easily, accessible. They also benefit from the political leverage that regions may have collectively on EU decision-making processes through these networks (COSLA in relation to CEMR; London, Birmingham, Bristol and others in relation to Eurocities). This is significant for MLG theory, traditionally exclusively focused on players from the EU, and confirms the finding that the engagement and influence of substate actors in the EU are not limited to those from the EU.[49]

The Head of the Welsh Brussels Office confirmed to us the importance of networks for influencing and shaping EU policy, but explained that Wales's membership of CPMR is not focused on generating influence on policy, but rather on raising the profile of Wales as a nation committed to certain EU agendas such as tackling climate change:

> So that's a network that we're increasingly finding is helpful to us, but again, a lot of their work is on influencing EU policies and programs, which to be honest, is not why we're still

[47] Head of Brussels Office, Welsh Government, 1 April 2022.

[48] Director of Bristol & Bath Brussels Office, 30 November 2021.

[49] Panara (2022), pp. 557–572. Minto et al. (2023), seems to me to converge in the same direction in relation specifically to Scotland and Wales post-Brexit.

Table 3 European networks (On European networks post-Brexit, see Bergstra et al. (2021))

Organisation	Summary description and areas of work most relevant to UK members	UK members (* indicates that they also operate an office in Brussels)
Eurocities	Eurocities is a network of c.200 cities from 38 countries with a focus on city government, environmental standards, air quality, culture, health. It is a forum for the sharing of best practice and a powerhouse for influencing EU policy. Birmingham was one of the founders of Eurocities in 1986.	Belfast Birmingham* Brighton & Hove Bristol* Cardiff Coventry Derry-Strabane Edinburgh Glasgow Leeds London* Manchester Newcastle Sheffield Sunderland Wolverhampton
Conference of Peripheral and Maritime Regions (CPMR)	This is a network organisation made up of more than 150 regions from across the UK and Europe, with a secretariat that supports its members to conduct joint lobbying on policy issues of common interests and which carries out a think-tank role on behalf of its members. Its remit comprises the economic development of regions with a specific focus on maritime, energy, connectivity and climate change.	Wales* Fife Council Aberdeenshire Council Cornwall terminated membership in 2021[a]
Council of European Municipalities and Regions (CEMR)	This is an organisation comprising 60 local government associations from 41 countries members of the Council of Europe. It operates in a number of fields, including regional policy, transport, environment, equal opportunities and governance. It also aims to influence draft EU legislation to ensure that the interests of local and regional authorities are taken into account in the legislative process.	LGA* Welsh Local Government Association* (WLGA retains a desk in Brussels) COSLA* Northern Ireland Local Government Association (NILGA)

[a] See Report to the Leader of the Council, Cornwall Council, 30 June 2021, para 2.10. This recommends that Cornwall Council should terminate the CPMR membership and engage in bilateral initiatives with neighbouring regions such as Brittany and Finistère councils in France and likeminded UK regions such as Wales, Cumbria, Dorset and others

in it. We're still in it because it's helpful to be connected to somebody in terms of telling our story in raising our profile, demonstrating our commitment to being European and I think our

> relationship with them is continuing to evolve in terms of each of us understanding what we want from each other.[50]

In addition to the above outlined rationales for networking (accessing information, influencing policy collectively, raising the profile of the region), there is a further dimension that deserves highlighting. Networks are also channels for the sharing of best practice in local governance and therefore for learning and cross-fertilisation between European regions (COSLA in relation to CEMR; London, Birmingham, Bristol and others in relation to Eurocities). The sharing of best practice is a two-way process. The Secretary General at Eurocities confirmed the value for cities from the EU in learning from UK partners due to the innovative solutions they often pioneer.[51]

What changed as a result of Brexit in relation to networking by UK local and regional authorities? A first change concerns the status of these authorities from EU to non-EU; for example, in the context of Eurocities, where UK cities became partner cities and do no longer enjoy the status of members,[52] or in the context of CPMR where UK regions are no longer eligible for EU funding, which limits significantly their involvement in cooperation projects.[53] Status aside, the most significant change after Brexit regards the focus of UK cities and regions participating in networks. This concerns predominantly the sharing of best practice rather than lobbying or influencing policy.[54] This is clearly a result of the more limited relevance of EU policies in the UK post-Brexit.

3.2.3 EU Funding

Prior to Brexit, UK regional offices used to provide support for funding opportunities emanating from the EU. The support included signposting and advising regional stakeholders, as well as, occasionally, assisting with the creation of the partnerships or consortia required, for example, for Horizon applications. This area of work (generating funding) is typically of key importance for the Brussels-based offices of regions from EU member states,[55] as well as for regions from some non-EU countries, such as, Norway and Iceland, which are EFTA and EEA members.[56]

---

[50] Head of Brussels Office, Welsh Government, 1 April 2022. The Head of European and International Affairs, Birmingham City Council, 19 September 2023, spoke along similar lines.

[51] Secretary General at Eurocities, 21 February 2023.

[52] UK cities cannot hold the presidency. They can chair working groups only if there is a co-chair from the EU. Additionally, there are limits to the number of UK cities in the Executive Group, given that only one out of the 12 cities in the Executive Group can be from outside the EU.

[53] Executive Secretary of Conference of Peripheral and Maritime Regions, 25 May 2023.

[54] Interim Policy Director at Council of European Municipalities and Regions, 10 May 2023; Executive Secretary of Conference of Peripheral and Maritime Regions, 25 May 2023.

[55] Rodríguez Pose and Courty (2018), pp. 199–219; Panara (2015), pp. 127–154; Rowe (2011), pp. 83–125; Burch and Gomez (2002), pp. 767–778.

[56] Panara (2022), pp. 557–572.

Until recently, however, with the exception of the Peace Plus Programme for Northern Ireland, the only EU funding available to UK regions post-Brexit was limited to legacy funding linked to EU projects approved before Brexit (Kent County Council, for example, managed some of this funding until 2023, whereas HEIs from Liverpool City Region are completing European Social and Investment Fund-funded projects). It emerges clearly from this research that the absence of substantial funding opportunities for UK stakeholders played a major role in the decision to close some Brussels-based offices,[57] as well as in the downsizing of others.

In September 2023, the association of the UK to Horizon Europe was finalised following the signing of the Windsor Framework in February 2023. This hopefully brought to a resolution the dispute arising from the implementation of the Northern Ireland Protocol and opened up again Horizon funding to UK HEIs and local authorities. The obtained associate membership of Horizon Europe is likely to relaunch the work of the offices in this field. This is, however, with the exception of the Peace Plus Programme, the only source of EU funding currently available to UK HEIs and local authorities, which means that the relevance of the Brussels offices as a vehicle to obtaining EU funding remains limited compared to the past. It appears therefore likely that the renewed availability of this funding may consolidate the role and position of the existing offices rather than leading to the opening or reopening of others.

3.2.4 Scratching Further Beneath the Surface: The Importance of Being in Brussels

The former representative of an office that was closed a few years ago told us that "there's no reason at the moment, there's no hook, there's no laws, there's no money, there's no institutions" for operating offices in Brussels. The same person wonders what the offices that survived until now are actually doing, since there are no policies to lobby the EU institutions on and no EU funding (the interview was conducted before the UK rejoined Horizon Europe):

> I think the only regions which have a real reason to still be in Brussels, are Northern Ireland and London, as in the Mayor's Office and the Greater London Authority and the City of London Corporation. The City of London Corporation is still in Brussels, and I get that completely because they are dealing with bilateral financial regulatory issues affecting the Square Mile. So that makes complete sense to me. The Greater London Authority, they only now have one guy – they used to have 5-6 – now they've got one. So, possibly that makes sense with London being the capital, but certainly the City of London should be there and

[57] Report to the Leader of the Council, Cornwall Council, 30 June 2021, p. 2; Hampshire County Council Decision Report, 27 January 2022, p. 2; former Director of East of England European Partners, 6 September 2022; Lead Officer International Relations, Liverpool City Region CA, 6 June 2023.

> Northern Ireland for obvious reasons. But everyone else, even I would struggle to really make that case. Fair enough, they've got the money, they can pay for it.[58]

Albeit phrased differently, the same suggestions surface in the closure documents of the Cornwall and Hampshire offices. Additionally, the fact that cities traditionally proactive in Brussels, such as, Greater Manchester CA and Liverpool City Region have decided to close their offices and do not currently have plans for reopening them, alongside the already mentioned decision by Northamptonshire County Council to abandon its plan to recreate a Brussels office, confirm that many see the potential return of an investment in an office in Brussels as limited or non-existent at present. Whilst things may change slightly as a result of the UK rejoining Horizon Europe, the broader picture remains the same since the structural funding is no longer available to UK regions.

A question mark, therefore, remains around what the added value of the Brussels-based offices could be in the current state of affairs of UK-EU relations. Some English offices include in their mission what one may summarily call 'promotion of the region'. The promotion of the 'country', or 'nation', is unsurprisingly deeply ingrained in the mission of the offices of the devolved governments in that they ultimately represent Wales, Scotland and Northern Ireland in Brussels. In relation to the existing English offices, this notion includes activities such as, "raising the profile of some of the local partners and of the cities and the region more broadly, and doing that with a view to identifying and leveraging EU opportunities locally by bringing back opportunities to the city and region" (Bristol), or seizing the opportunities arising from the wider 'Brussels ecosystem' ("Brussels is one of two cities in the world, that have this particular depth to their ecosystems, that is only really comparable to Washington. You have an incredible mix of regional representations, Member States, third-country missions, a variety of different business associations, sector organisations, corporate interests etc. and we are reimagining the way that we leverage those connections and it is already paying dividends", Birmingham).[59] It seems unrealistic, though, that investing in a Brussels-based trade representation would generate a profit before a significant number of years, an anecdotal example being Essex County Council that after 10 years of operating an office in China to this purpose, has only recently managed to break even on the initial investment.[60] The renounce by Greater Manchester CA to use the Brussels office as a platform for promoting trade and investment in the region corroborates the conclusion that this function alone could not justify maintaining an office in Brussels.[61]

---

[58] I anonymised this excerpt to protect the privacy of the office representative who made the statements. In 2016 the GLA's office had three FTE staff and one 0.5 FTE administrative support staff.

[59] Interviews of Director of Bristol & Bath Brussels Office, 30 November 2021, and of Director of Greater Birmingham & West Midlands Brussels Office, 14 January 2021.

[60] Interview of former Director of East of England European Partnership, 6 September 2022.

[61] Head of European Policy at New Economy Manchester, 2 March and 22 September 2017.

The international strategies of some local authorities, for example Greater Manchester Combined Authority, Bristol City Council and Liverpool City Region, emphasise the importance of international trade and relations.[62] Already during the Brexit negotiations, some English offices had begun refocusing from EU to international relations (East of England, Bristol). This transition from 'European' to 'international' is not fully reflected, however, in the current practice of the offices that still maintain a primary if not exclusive focus on the EU and on networking with other local and regional authorities from the EU.[63]

There seems to be, therefore, also a political motive underpinning the decision to stay in Brussels and to retain close links to the EU. Apart from Northern Ireland, that has obvious reasons for continuing to operate a Brussels-based representation due to the special regime created for that region by the Northern Ireland Protocol and the Windsor Framework, this is particularly apparent in the case of the devolved administrations, especially Scotland and Wales, whose international strategies highlight the critical importance of the EU to them and their identities.[64] It is worth noting, though, that Northern Ireland (64.4 percent of total goods exports), Scotland (59.1) and Wales (56.5) are respectively first, second and fourth among UK regions by share of goods exports to the EU.[65] Accordingly, the political eagerness on maintaining a close relationship to the EU is not a lone factor, but mirrors solid trade relations between these countries and the bloc.

The rationale for running Brussels-based representations is less straightforward in relation to the offices representing cities or regions from England (London, Bristol & Bath, Birmingham & West Midlands, Kent). London, Bristol and Bath were among the most pro-Remain areas in the UK in the 2016 referendum and have had 'pro-European' leaders since. The strong pro-European stance of these cities has certainly played a role in the decision to retain an office in Brussels. Since these cities voted overwhelmingly in favour of Remain in June 2016, challenges from local taxpayers and political turmoil regarding the operation of the Brussels offices are less likely than elsewhere in England. West Midlands and Kent, by contrast, were among the most pro-Leave, and in the case of Kent have mostly returned Conservative council majorities and MPs since 2016. The pro-European stance is therefore not an

---

[62] Greater Manchester, *Greater Manchester International Strategy 2022-2025*, no date but 2020; Bristol City Council, *Bristol: Global City – Working with the world for local and global benefit*, Strategy version 2 (refreshed 2022), May 2022; Liverpool City Region, *Internationalisation Strategy and Action Plan*, May 2019.

[63] In the case of Core Cities UK, the international dimension alongside the EU is clearly prominent. Core Cities UK that does not have a Brussels office, but works closely with Eurocities, as well as with city associations from various EU member states, and runs the U7, the city equivalent of the G7.

[64] See Scottish Government, *Scotland's Global Affairs Framework*, 9 May 2022, chapter 2 (Maintaining the closest possible relationship with the European Union); Welsh Government, *International Strategy*, 14 January 2020, pp. 4, 7–8, 14, 16, 23 inter alia. See also First Minister of Wales Drakeford (2022).

[65] Ward and Webb (2023), p. 27.

absolutely reliable predictor of the decision to operate a Brussels-based office (as demonstrated *a contrario* also by the fact that a city such as Liverpool, that voted by a large majority to remain in the EU, has nonetheless closed its Brussels office). It is then more appropriate to look at the unique circumstances of each region. In the case of Kent, for example, the geographical location on the Channel and the presence of the Tunnel mean that this region is the place where a high volume of transit of goods and people to and from the EU takes place. Birmingham and the West Midlands, on the other hand, have had close ties to the EU and partners there since the 1980s. Additionally, it is one of the UK regions trading more intensively with the EU, which explains why part of the focus of the office is about promoting trade and investment opportunities for stakeholders from this part of England.[66]

4 Concluding Remarks

The 'British Brussels offices sector' has noticeably scaled down since 2016. Brexit, however, has not marked the end of direct engagement with the EU by UK local authorities and devolved administrations through these offices. Although the UK has now left the EU, the ability by the EU to influence certain sectors of UK law and economy remains significant. The following are some examples of areas where the EU continues to influence UK laws:

- certain EU laws remain applicable, or relevant, to some parts of the UK (Northern Ireland, pursuant to the Northern Ireland Protocol and the Windsor Framework, and Scotland, pursuant to the UK Withdrawal from the EU (Continuity) (Scotland) Act 2021).
- A substantial number of 'retained' EU laws (renamed 'assimilated' EU laws) remained in force after 31 December 2023 according to the Retained EU Law (Revocation and Reform) Act 2023.[67] It will be important to understand the position of UK courts in relation to the interpretation of these laws. Section 6 (1) of the EU (Withdrawal) Act 2018, as amended by REUL (Revocation and Reform) Act 2023, establishes that UK courts or tribunals, obviously with the partial exception of those from Northern Ireland, are not bound by principles laid down or decisions made by the European Court after the end of the

[66] West Midlands is fourth in the UK by goods imports from the EU (57.2 percent of total) and sixth by overall worth of goods exports to the EU (fourth if one excludes Scotland and London, GBP 29.2 billion, 45.4 percent of total). Ward and Webb (2023), pp. 27–28.

[67] These are pre-Brexit laws (i.e., laws from prior to the expiry of the Brexit implementation period at the end of December 2020) and not the new EU laws that have come into effect since 1 January 2021 and that are not applicable to the UK, with the partial exception of Northern Ireland. The original plan of the UK government was to repeal c.4000 retained EU laws through the REUL (Revocation and Reform) Act 2023, but the Act repealed only c.800.

implementation period (31 December 2020). The following subsection, however, acknowledges some value to EU cases emerged after the expiry of the implementation period and, it would appear, potentially also to EU laws passed after that date if these are relevant to deciding the matter before the court or tribunal ("a court or tribunal *may have regard to anything done on or after implementation period completion day by the European Court, another EU entity or the EU* so far as it is relevant to any matter before the court or tribunal." Emphasis added.)

- One of the most important objectives pursued by the EU and the UK through the TCA is the achievement of 'frictionless trade' between the two. If in coming years frictionless trade with the bloc remains a priority for UK governments, this is likely to require that the UK retains most EU standards to prevent the creation of non-tariff barriers to trade. The more the regulatory standards on, for example, health, consumer, environmental protection diverge between the UK and the EU, the more frictions to trade could arise in case this undermines the 'level playing field' the UK and the EU aimed to establish through the TCA.[68]
- Finally, it is important to reflect on the consequences of the special regime for Northern Ireland. If standards diverge between the UK and the EU in the future, Northern Irish manufacturers and producers who intend to trade both with the EU and the rest of the UK could endure a competitive disadvantage because they would need to abide by different standards depending on the destination of their products. This too could motivate the UK government to mirror EU standards.[69]

The first working hypothesis set out at the beginning was that the UK offices post-Brexit are still interested in gathering information and, where possible, influencing EU policies in relevant domains, but that only Northern Ireland and Scotland, due to their current arrangements, still engage in direct lobbying of the EU institutions. Our findings confirmed in part this hypothesis. The evidence suggests that whilst all the existing offices still monitor EU policy developments, only Northern Ireland and Scotland Europa declare that it is their goal to engage in influencing EU policy. Apart from these notable exceptions, most offices have been morphing, therefore, into funding and networking offices delivering essentially consultancy work around these matters.[70]

The second working hypothesis was that one of the most important reasons to stay in Brussels for some UK local and regional authorities was political. Our analysis confirmed this hypothesis in part. Surely, the political motive ('remaining

---

[68] An example that was given during one of the interviews concerns the rules on vehicle emissions and safety. Whilst in theory the UK could pass its own rules and depart from EU standards, this is unlikely. Lower standards would lead to worse air quality in the UK than in the EU and this might not be politically sustainable in the UK, whereas higher standards would likely meet the opposition of domestic car manufacturers who could suffer from a competitive disadvantage. Interview of Director of London European Office, 17 January 2021.

[69] In 2022 64.4 percent of the goods exports from Northern Ireland went to the EU. See Ward and Webb (2023), p. 27.

[70] Head of Brussels Office, Convention of Scottish Local Authorities (COSLA), 30 March 2022.

in Brussels', 'remaining part of the EU family') is paramount to two devolved governments (Scotland and Wales), as well as to Birmingham and some pro-European cities such as Bristol and Bath. Our analysis, however, revealed a more complex mosaic of factors at play in the decision to remain in Brussels, concerning specifically each region or country; such as, the particular post-Brexit status of Northern Ireland, the fact that London is the capital of the UK and has a vital interest in certain EU policies, and the unique geographical location of Kent.

The third working hypothesis regarding the diminished importance of EU funding to the offices and to UK regions is fully confirmed by the circumstance that until the recent rejoining of Horizon Europe, with the exception of EU legacy funding and the Peace Plus programme (limited, however, to Northern Ireland) there were no other sources of funding available to UK local and regional authorities. The seizing of funding opportunities may play a bigger role in future decisions by UK regions to establish representation offices in Brussels, following the achievement of associate member status of Horizon Europe by the UK, although this funding is primarily relevant to universities and research institutions rather than to local authorities.

In relation to MLG theory, whilst it is apparent that the number of the offices, the range of the stakeholders they represent and the volume of activity is significantly smaller compared to the pre-Brexit period, it is also clear that UK local and regional authorities attempt to play a role in the EU, especially through the sharing of best practice and networking. Despite the limited direct impact of the UK local and regional authorities on shaping EU policies after Brexit, it is clear that they still attempt to play a role, be it in terms of cross-fertilisation through the sharing of best practice, be it through lobbying, albeit less effectively than in the past. This confirms that MLG in the EU must factor in the role of subnational agents from third countries instead of remaining solely focused on the input from actors from the EU.[71]

The other element that emerges from the collected evidence concerns UK MLG. As a result of being less active in the EU, but also as a result more in general of the smaller relevance of EU law and policy in the UK, it emerges that UK local and regional authorities became more London-focused. In a number of interviews, but also in several policy documents, it was highlighted that from now on it will be crucial for local authorities to focus on funding coming from London, as well as on influencing the Westminster government.[72] This does not mean that UK regions are more 'inward-looking' than in the past, given that they continue to have ambitious international strategies and, in some cases, remarkable international reach. It rather means that they largely lost their focus on the EU in favour of a more London-centric

[71] See, inter alia, as examples of this tendency, the excellent Simonato (2016), and Pazos-Vidal (2019).

[72] Report to the Leader of the Council, Cornwall Council, 30 June 2021, pp. 1, 2, 4; Interviews of former Director of East of England European Partnership, 6 September 2022, and of Head of London's European Office, 17 January 2021.

focus combined with a tendency to consider trade and wider exchange opportunities with countries outside the EU.

Original Empirical Data

(a) **Semi-structured interviews**

Before the Brexit referendum:

1. Director of Merseyside Brussels Office, 2 July 2014
2. Principal EU Funding at New Economy Manchester, 6 February 2015
3. Senior EU Policy Officer at London's European Office, 17 July 2015
4. Deputy Head of Local Government Association Brussels Office, 20 July 2015
5. Director of Access Europe Network, London, 29 July 2015
6. Head of City Office in Brussels, City of London Corporation, 20 August 2015
7. Director of Cornwall Brussels Office, 24 August 2015
8. Head of Southern England Local Partners, 16 November 2015

During the Brexit negotiations:

1. Head of European Policy at New Economy Manchester, 2 March 2017
2. Director of Bristol Brussels Office, 9 March 2017
3. Director of Cornwall Brussels Office, 21 March 2017
4. Director of East of England European Partnership, 24 April 2017
5. Senior EU Policy Office at London's European Office, 3 May 2017
6. Director of Liverpool City Region Brussels Office, 5 May 2017
7. Director of Cornwall Brussels Office, 5 July 2017
8. Director of East of England European Partnership, 18 September 2017
9. Head of European Policy at New Economy Manchester, 22 September 2017
10. Director of Bristol Brussels Office, 4 October 2017
11. Director of East of England European Partnership, 16 March 2018
12. Director of Bristol Brussels Office, 12 April 2018

After the conclusion of the Brexit negotiations:

1. Secretary General at Birmingham & West Midlands Brussels Office, 14 January 2021
2. Head of Office at London's European Office, 17 January 2021
3. Director of Bristol & Bath Brussels Office, 30 November 2021
4. Head of Brussels Office, Kent County Council, 4 February 2022
5. Senior EU Policy and Liaison Officer at Office of the Northern Ireland Executive in Brussels, 9 February 2022
6. Head of Brussels Office, Convention of Scottish Local Authorities (COSLA), 30 March 2022
7. Head of Brussels Office, Welsh Government, 1 April 2022
8. Former Director of East of England European Partnership, 6 September 2022

9. Policy Advisor at the Committee of the Regions, 25 November 2022
10. Leader at Dumfries & Galloway Council, European Policy Officer at COSLA, 21 February 2023
11. Secretary General at Eurocities, 21 February 2023
12. Interim Policy Director at Council of European Municipalities and Regions, 10 May 2023
13. Strategic Communications and Public Affairs Manager at Core Cities UK, 10 May 2023
14. Executive Secretary of Conference of Peripheral and Maritime Regions, 25 May 2023
15. Head of European and International Affairs, Birmingham City Council, 19 September 2023

(b) **Responses to Freedom of Information Act requests and other enquiries**

FOIA requests:

1. Local Government Association, 8 February 2021
2. Hampshire County Council, 29 April 2022
3. Scottish Government, 31 May 2022
4. Liverpool City Council, 28 November 2022
5. Scottish Government, 5 April 2023

Non-FOIA enquiries:

1. Greater Manchester CA, 24 October 2022
2. Scottish Parliament, 3 April 2023
3. Lead Officer International Relations, Liverpool City Region CA, 6 June 2023

(c) **Focus group**

Brussels, 29 June 2016: New Economy Manchester, Local Government Association, Access Europe Network, Bristol Brussels Office, East of England European Partnership, Northamptonshire County Council.

References

Atkins G, Hoddinott S (2022) Neighbourhoods services under strain. How a decade of cuts and rising demand for social care affected local services. Institute for Government, May 2022, https://www.instituteforgovernment.org.uk/sites/default/files/publications/neighbourhood-services-under-strain.pdf. Accessed Jan 2024

Baudenbacher C (ed) (2015) The handbook of EEA law. Springer

Baudenbacher C (ed) (2017) The fundamental principles of EEA law: EEA-ities. Springer

Bergstra M, Hagemeyer J, Karunska K (2021) Restoring "lost connections" between the EU and the UK as a consequence of Brexit through local and regional authorities. Committee of the Regions

Birkinshaw P (2020) European Public Law, 3rd edn. Wolters Kluwer

Bristol City Council (2022) Bristol: Global City – working with the world for local and global benefit. Strategy version 2 (refreshed 2022), May 2022

Burch M, Gomez R (2002) The English regions and the European Union. Reg Stud 36(7):767–778
Callanan M, Tatham M (2014) Territorial interest representation in the European Union: actors, objectives and strategies. J Eur Public Policy 21(2):188–210
Committee of the Regions (2009) Associations/Bureaux de Representation Regionale et Communale a Bruxelles: Repertoire. Committee of the Regions
Copeland P, Minto R (2023) European networks, domestic governance and the second-order effects of Brexit. Br Polit 18(4):501–518
Drakeford M (2022) After Brexit: the future of Wales in the UK and relations with Ireland and Europe, University College Cork Jean Monnet Lecture Series, 13 October 2022, https://www.youtube.com/watch?v=OHwNwE6i3TA. Accessed Jan 2024
Greater Manchester, Greater Manchester International Strategy 2022-2025, no date but 2020
Greenwood J (2011a) Interest representation in the European Union, 3rd edn. Palgrave Macmillan
Greenwood J (2011b) Actors of the common interest? The Brussels Offices of the Regions. J Eur Integr 33(4):437–451
Greenwood J (2014) The regional offices in Brussels. From "push and pull" to "place and partnership". Reg Cohes 4(3):1–16
Hooghe L, Marks G (2001) Multi-level governance and European Integration. Rowman & Littlefield
House of Lords, European Union Committee (2019) Beyond Brexit: how to win friends and influence people, 25 March 2019, https://publications.parliament.uk/pa/ld201719/ldselect/ldeucom/322/322.pdf. Accessed Jan 2024
Hristova L, Cekik A (2015) The Europeanisation of interest groups: EU conditionality and adaptation of interest groups to the EU accession process in the Republic of Macedonia. East Eur Polit 31(1):23–38
Institute for Government (2020) Influencing the EU after Brexit, January 2020
Liverpool City Region (2019) Internationalisation Strategy and Action Plan, May 2019
Macneill S, Jeffery C, Gibney J (2007) Changing dynamics of regional representation in Brussels: a case study of Birmingham and the West Midlands, 1984–2004. Reg Stud 41(3):403–414
Marciacq F (2015) Sub-state diplomacy in malfunctioning states: the case of the Republika Srpska, Bosnia and Herzegovina. Reg Fed Stud 25(4):329–346
Marks G, Haesly R, Mbaye H (2002) What do subnational offices think they are doing in Brussels? Reg Fed Stud 12(3):1–23
Mawson J (ed), John P, Birnie JE, Hitchens DMWN, Nel E (1994) Policy review section. Reg Stud 28(7):739–759
Minto R, Morgan K (2019) The future of Wales in Europe. Edinburgh Law Rev 23(3):423–428
Minto R, Rowe C, Royles E (2023) Sub-states in transition: changing patterns of EU paradiplomacy in Scotland and Wales, 1992-2021. Territory, Politics, Governance, published online on 15 May 2023
Moore C (2007) The impact of devolution on EU-level representation: British regional offices in Brussels. Reg Fed Stud 17(3):275–291
Office for National Statistics (2024) UK total trade: all countries, seasonally adjusted, at https://www.ons.gov.uk/economy/nationalaccounts/balanceofpayments/datasets/uktotaltradeallcountriesseasonallyadjusted. Accessed Jan 2024
Özçelik AO (2017) Analysing stages of subnational mobilisation across the European Union: the case of subnational administrations in Turkey. Reg Fed Stud 27(2):171–199
Panara C (2015) The sub-national dimension of the EU. A legal study of multilevel governance. Springer
Panara C (2022) The activities in Brussels of the local and regional authorities from European Free Trade Area countries. Reg Fed Stud 32(5):557–572
Panara C (2023) The European Offices of the UK local authorities and devolved administrations in Light of Patrick Birkinshaw's concept of European Public Law. In: Gromek-Broc K (ed) Public law in a troubled era: a tribute to Professor Patrick Birkinshaw. Kluwer Law International, pp 455–465

Panara C, Varney MR (2017a) Multi-level governance in the EU and EU democracy: democratic legitimacy, democratic accountability and transparency of the European offices of the English local authorities. Reg Fed Stud 27(2):153–170
Panara C, Varney M (2017b) A study on the transparency and accountability of the European Offices of the English Local Authorities in Brussels: Synthetising and Developing Good Practice Guidance (Liverpool and Hull, 9 June 2017, available from the author)
Pazos-Vidal S (2019) Subsidiarity and EU multilevel governance. Actors, networks and agendas. Routledge
Piattoni S (2010) The theory of multi-level governance. Conceptual, empirical, and normative challenges. Oxford University Press
Quinn B (2019) East of England local government agency to close Brussels office. The Guardian, 18 January 2019, https://www.theguardian.com/society/2019/jan/18/east-of-england-local-government-agency-to-close-brussels-office. Accessed Jan 2024
Realfsen F (2015) Swiss and Norwegian regions in Brussels: how and why do the regions from associated member-states of the EU mobilize in Brussels? Master Thesis, University of Bergen. https://bora.uib.no/bitstream/handle/1956/10403/135280027.pdf?sequence=1&isAllowed=y. Accessed Jan 2024
Rodríguez Pose A, Courty J (2018) Regional lobbying and structural funds: do regional representation offices in Brussels deliver? Reg Fed Stud 28(2):199–219
Rowe C (2011) Regional representations in the EU: between diplomacy and interest mediation. Palgrave-Macmillan
Sandford M (2016) Brexit and local government, House of Commons Library, 20 July 2016
Schönlau J (2021) Brexit: the sub-national dimension from the vantage point of the European Committee of the Regions. EU3D Research Papers, No. 19. https://www.eu3d.uio.no/publications/eu3d-research-papers/. Accessed Jan 2024
Scottish Government (2021) Steadfastly European: Scotland's Past, Present and Future, 9 March 2021
Scottish Government (2022) Scotland's Global Affairs Framework, 9 May 2022
Simonato A (2016) Multilevel Governance. Profili costituzionali. Il coordinamento tra Regioni, Stato e UE. CLEUP
Sturgeon N (2022) Nicola Sturgeon's speech launching the case for independence. 14 June 2022, at https://www.snp.org/nicola-sturgeons-speech-launching-the-case-for-independence/. Accessed Jan 2024
Sykes O, Lord A (2011) Whither a Europe of the (English) regions? Reflections on the prospects for the representation of English territorial interests in Europe. Local Econ 26(6–7):486–489
Tatham M (2016) With, without, or against the state? How European regions play the Brussels Game. Oxford University Press
Tatham M (2017) Networkers, fund-hunters, intermediaries, or policy players? The activities of regions in Brussels. West Eur Polit 40(5):1088–1108
Tatham M (2018) The rise of regional influence in the EU – from soft policy lobbying to hard vetoing. J Common Mark Stud 56(3):672–686
Trobbiani R (2016) European regions in Brussels: towards functional interest representation? Bruges Political Research Papers, College of Europe, No. 53
Ward M, Webb D (2023) Statistics on UK-EU Trade, House of Commons Library, 11 May 2023
Welsh Government (2020) International Strategy, 14 January 2020
Woods R (2015) Overview of the role and activity of the Northamptonshire European Office, 25 March 2015

Part IV
Conclusive Words

Towards a New Relationship Between the UK and the EU: A Truly Special One?

Emmanuel Guinchard

Whilst, following Brexit, the UK negotiated with the EU, and later ratified, a Trade and Cooperation Agreement (TCA), it seemed at times that the word 'Agreement' was being forgotten, with draft British Bills reneging on the binding commitments taken; that the word 'Cooperation' could be better replaced by 'Conflict' with some thundering declarations at the highest level of the UK Government; and that 'Trade' was finally not so important, not to say sacrificed (at least in the short term) on the altar of politics, with leading Brexiters claiming it never was about the economy. This time is past. A change of leaders within the UK has already moved the relationship from being acrimonious to being respectful, with the Windsor Framework being agreed in 2023 and subsequent progress made (such as the UK rejoining Horizon Europe). This is probably just the beginning.

Economically, it does not seem Brexit has been the success heralded by Brexiters and some may have felt short-changed (without even mentioning the Leave campaign's claim of 350 million pounds a week for the NHS). Brexit does not seem to have been catastrophic either. However, it appears that, overall, Brexit had a negative rather than a positive effect, the exact fall in GDP due specifically to Brexit varying according to economists.[1] Hence the insistence of some leading pro-Brexiters on the fact that either it was never about the economy (Lord Frost) or that Brexit has not been properly implemented (Nigel Farage). The current argument of Brexiters seems to be that Brexit will lead to a positive economic

[1] See notably Springford (2023), who discusses alternative views to his estimate that "the British economy is around 5 per cent smaller due to Brexit". These alternative views (Graham Gudgin, Julian Jessop and Jonathan Portes) range from a loss of 2.5 per cent GDP to negligeable costs and have also been criticised elsewhere (see for example Winters (2023) on Graham Gudgin, Julian Jessop and Harry Western). The common point is that one never talks of positive effects.

E. Guinchard (✉)
Liverpool John Moores University, Liverpool, UK
e-mail: E.R.Guinchard@ljmu.ac.uk

E. Guinchard, C. Panara (eds.), *The New Relationship between the United Kingdom and the European Union*, https://doi.org/10.1007/978-3-031-70652-3_20

outcome, but this effect is delayed and the path to this positive outcome is itself debated. Prime Minister Elizabeth Truss' attempt at deregulation failed loudly and appears unlikely to be repeated in the near future. The probable future Prime Minister of the UK, Keith Starmer, who leads the Labour party, has signalled that he would welcome a closer trading relationship with the EU should he be elected at the next general election (scheduled for 4 July 2024), whilst rejecting the country rejoining the EU Single Market. The British Chambers of Commerce have helpfully recently released a report on how to improve the trade relation with the EU. They suggest a three-fold approach: firstly, short-term solutions, to be implemented within 12 months (e.g. "an agreement on VAT cooperation with the EU");[2] secondly, medium term solutions, to be agreed in the early stages of the TCA review, whose date (2026) is fast approaching (e.g. delivering "further flexibility on travel for business purposes and the range of business activities which can be undertaken");[3] and finally more ambitious solutions, which are presented as long-term recommendations requiring a "more substantial review of the TCA",[4] in reality perhaps going beyond it at times (e.g. "Consider the convincing case for the UK rejoining the Lugano Convention, to allow businesses certainty on enforcement of civil and commercial judgements in the UK and the EU"[5]).

Although the position of the EU remains unknown at this time, it is likely that the introduction of stricter border controls from the UK in 2024, and their necessarily negative impact on EU traders, will encourage future trade discussions between the EU and the UK through amendments to the TCA (even if some requests from the British trade community appear unlikely to be met). Trade should therefore clearly constitute an important topic on the UK-EU agenda, and an improvement in the regulatory framework is expected. However, is it the most important topic if one looks at the UK – EU relationship not from the inside albeit from the outside, adopting a more global perspective?

Whilst the push for Brexit came from within the EU (by hypothesis the UK, at the time, was a Member State), and corresponded to a centrifugal movement, centripetal forces (starting with the invasion of Ukraine in 2022) are now at play and explain in no small part the positive evolution of the relationship between the UK and the EU. War (or a high-intensity conflict to use modern parlance) is no longer seen as a remote possibility, if not a likely scenario in a few years' time, as illustrated notably by declarations from the Chiefs of Staff of the Armed Forces of the three main European countries (France, Germany and the UK).

---

[2] British Chambers of Commerce (2024), p. 40. The aim is "to reduce the number of UK companies requiring a fiscal intermediary in the EU to conduct cross-border trade". The precedent of Norway is given.

[3] British Chambers of Commerce (2024), p. 41.

[4] British Chambers of Commerce (2024), p. 40.

[5] British Chambers of Commerce (2024), p. 42. Whilst European Civil Justice/European Private International Law had been included in the Withdrawal Agreement, the TCA does not cover this topic.

This is so despite the fact that all European armies seem to have severe difficulties: with recruitment; with equipment; with training and (perhaps to a lesser extent) with interoperability. A few examples, far from being comprehensive, may be given (whilst not forgetting the existence of some excellent units and the good will and strong patriotism of the vast majority of army personnel[6]). Thus, according to the 2023 Report from the German Parliamentary Commissioner for the Armed Forces (12 March 2024), the number of active personnel is slowly decreasing year on year. On 31 December 2023, there were 181,514 soldiers in the Armed Forces (including around 10,000 undertaking a voluntary military service), a decrease of 1522 in comparison to 31 December 2022.[7] The situation is particularly difficult for the German Navy, especially for its frigates where the gap in personnel reaches 50% at times.[8] Recruitment and retention are a major issue, with the living conditions a probable contributing factor, the Commissioner considering the infrastructures as disastrous.[9]

A similar situation affects the United Kingdom, starting the Royal Navy which had to decommission two (modernised or under modernisation) Type 23 frigates (HMS Westminster and HMS Argyll) in order to staff new ones (Type 26). The UK Armed Forces struggle to recruit adequately, and more people leave (16,000) than join (10,000).[10] The UK Ministry of Defence has itself admitted a shortage of trained personnel in several key areas such as "cyber, engineering, nuclear, digital, logistics,

---

[6]However, Islamism seems to gain ground from within some European armies: see for example the 'J'accuse!' of a former senior member of Belgian Security Services who, within an article very severely criticising Belgian politicians, points out that a Belgian Minister of Defence refused to launch an investigation into the penetration of the army by Islamists despite security services having brought forward the existence of several cases, all in the name of political correctness, i.e. the will not to 'stigmatise' the Muslim population within the army: "J'accuse un ancien ministre de la Défense de n'avoir pas autorisé une enquête approfondie sur l'islam radical au sein des forces armées afin de « ne pas stigmatiser la population musulmane au sein de l'armée » (dixit), alors même que nous avions connaissance de personnes radicalisées au sein de la « grande muette » (Snoeck 2016). The article follows the three coordinated Islamist attacks of 22 March 2016 in Belgium.

[7]German Parliament (Bundestag), Parliamentary Commissioner for the Armed Forces (2023), p. 38. The report focuses mostly on military personnel (equipment, living conditions, etc.), albeit also contains wider insights in the state of German Armed Forces. For a discussion in the German Parliament (Bundestag) on 25 April 2024, see the recording available at https://www.bundestag.de/dokumente/textarchiv/2024/kw17-de-wehrbericht-997908, Accessed 20 May 2024. The 2023 Report is currently only available in German. An English translation of the 2022 Report (64th Report) from 28 February 2023 is available at https://www.bundestag.de/resource/blob/949892/350e96fe32bce5146dbbf841d923c7eb/annual_report_2022_64th_report-data.pdf, Accessed 20 May 2024.

[8]German Parliament (Bundestag), Parliamentary Commissioner for the Armed Forces (2023), p. 39.

[9]German Parliament (Bundestag), Parliamentary Commissioner for the Armed Forces (2023), p. 6: "desaströs".

[10]UK House of Commons Defence Committee (2024), no 76 p. 32.

aviation and medical".[11] The recruitment crisis is such that, earlier in 2024, the British Chief of the General Staff publicly raised the idea of conscription in case of war before the idea being ruled out by Prime Minister Sunak.[12]

The British recruitment crisis feeds in into a wider readiness issue. In its February 2024 report on "Ready for War?", the British House of Commons Defence Committee, assessed the readiness of the UK Armed Forces, i.e. "the ability to deploy personnel and equipment within a set timeframe, for the personnel to be trained to use that equipment effectively and for the Armed Forces to be able to sustain the deployment until the mission is accomplished".[13] The Committee distinguishes 3 types of readiness: "the ability to deploy a force for a standing commitment or respond to a crisis" (operational readiness); "the ability to deploy and sustain a force that can fight at high intensity in multiple domains for a prolonged period of time" (warfighting readiness); and "the ability of the state to identify and utilise all the tools available to it to support a warfighting effort" (strategic).[14] The Committee assesses that only operational readiness is proven (albeit with overstretching issues); that warfighting readiness, probably the most crucial, is "in doubt"; and that strategic readiness is non-existent ("more of a concept under debate within Government").[15] Each Armed Force has its own set of deficiencies. However, there are common issues, besides the previously mentioned recruitment and retention concerns,[16] stockpiles,[17] utilisation of the reserve[18] and overtasking.[19] This is so despite the high reliance, and dependency, on foreign equipment (e.g. the most modern plane in service in the Royal Air Force and in the Royal Navy's Fleet Air Arm is the F-35 from primarily Lockheed Martin, USA[20]). If, for any reason, the supply of US equipment, including spare parts, were to be interrupted, the situation would be far worse. This is the situation of an army often, and rightly comparatively speaking, presented as one of the two (or three) best in Europe.

It will not therefore be a surprise that the European Union is not faring better. True, there has been a huge progress within the EU[21] on defence matters following the Ukraine invasion, with in particular the Act in Support of Ammunition

[11] UK Ministry of Defence (2023), A.v. p. 3 – see also p. 15.

[12] Lawless (2024).

[13] UK House of Commons Defence Committee (2024), Summary, p. 3.

[14] UK House of Commons Defence Committee (2024), Summary, p. 3; Report, no 9 p. 8 and ff.

[15] UK House of Commons Defence Committee (2024), Summary, p. 3.

[16] UK House of Commons Defence Committee (2024), no 73 p. 30 and ff.

[17] UK House of Commons Defence Committee (2024), no 67 p. 28 and ff.

[18] UK House of Commons Defence Committee (2024), no 79 p. 33.

[19] UK House of Commons Defence Committee (2024), no 82 p. 34.

[20] BAE Systems is also involved in the F-35 programme since its inception, supplying notably the rear fuselage or contributing to the electronic warfare suite (BAE Systems 2023). https://www.baesystems.com/en-uk/product/f-35.

[21] The same may be said of the United Kingdom.

Production (ASAP)[22] and the European Defence Industry Reinforcement through common Procurement Act (EDIRPA),[23] both adopted in 2023.[24] On 15 March 2024, the European Commission announced the selection of around 30 projects from the EU defence industry in five areas (explosives, powder, shells, missiles; and testing and reconditioning certification), for a total funding of €500 million under ASAP.[25] On the same day, the European Commission also released the EDIRPA Work Programme,[26] a major innovation.

However, this progress is only huge in comparison to the starting point. In absolute terms, the EU is very far from having a European Defence, whether in terms of capabilities, industry or cooperation. The fact that it could not (by far) honour its promise to deliver "one million rounds of artillery ammunition for Ukraine [...] within the next twelve months"[27] whilst North Korea has delivered one million shells to Russia is one of multiple examples of severe failings in defence matters, mostly due to decades of cuts in both financial and human resources as well as equipment and research (albeit not only as exemplified by the significant recruitment issue faced by all European armies). Another concrete and recent illustration of failings would be the unpreparedness of some European military units. For example, within a couple of weeks, several combat ships had to pause or cancel their operational deployment. Belgian frigate Louise Marie was supposed to deploy in the Red Sea on 12 April 2024 to protect shipping lanes from Iran-backed Houthis. This has now been postponed for an indefinite duration due to unsatisfactory training tests, relating to its protection against a drone attack, whilst in the Mediterranean.[28] Previously, in March 2024, Danish frigate Iver Huitfeldt faced several malfunctioning equipment, including radars and ammunition, and had to return

[22] Regulation (EU) 2023/1525 of the European Parliament and of the Council of 20 July 2023 on supporting ammunition production (ASAP), OJEU, L 185, 24.7.2023, p. 7, http://data.europa.eu/eli/reg/2023/1525/oj.

[23] Regulation (EU) 2023/2418 of the European Parliament and of the Council of 18 October 2023 on establishing an instrument for the reinforcement of the European defence industry through common procurement (EDIRPA), OJEU, L, 2023/2418, 26.10.2023, http://data.europa.eu/eli/reg/2023/2418/oj.

[24] On these instruments, see notably Bernard (2023).

[25] ASAP Results Factsheet, 15 March 2024, https://defence-industry-space.ec.europa.eu/regulation-support-ammunition-production-asap-aims-reinforcing-and-ramping-ammunition-production_en.

[26] Commission Implementing Decision of 15.3.2024 on the financing of the instrument for the reinforcement of the European defence industry through common procurement (EDIRPA) established by Regulation (EU) 2023/2418 of the European Parliament and of the Council and the adoption of the work programme for 2024-2025, C(2024) 1700 final, https://defence-industry-space.ec.europa.eu/document/download/8b38112b-a9e2-499e-bb1e-b8dbfc6dfb27_en?filename=EDIRPA%20Implementing%20Decision%20EN.pdf. The programme receives a 310 million euros funding.

[27] Council of the European Union, 20 March 2023, no 7632/23, "Delivery and joint procurement of ammunition for Ukraine", https://www.consilium.europa.eu/media/63170/st07632-en23.pdf. Missiles were also on the agenda, should Ukraine request them.

[28] Agence Belga (2024).

home. To be concrete, according to its Commanding Officer, regarding the ammunition, all shells onboard are 30 years old and therefore half of the ones fired by the two 76 mm turrets exploded prematurely[29]). In late February 2024, German frigate Hessen fired 2 missiles, which did not reach their target due to some malfunctioning. In this particular case, it was rather fortunate as the target was a drone, albeit belonging to the USA rather than Iran backed Houthis.[30] However, it does reveal some serious failings and in another context the consequences could have been very severe. The frigate is continuing its deployment. Other European navy units, whether from Member States of the EU (France) or outside (UK), have been more successful in repelling drone and missiles attacks from Houthis. However, it is also clear from the above that some European naval units are only combat-ready on the paper. This is concerning as sea denial is becoming much easier, for example with the use of multiple cheap drones capable of inflicting disproportionate damages to the perhaps high-value, but very limited in number, assets of the opponent. The current Houthi crisis in the Red Sea demonstrates the difficulty to even master what is, ultimately, a very limited threat in the meaning that it does not come from a power (e.g. Russia) or superpower (e.g. China) but from a small force backed up, it is true, by a regional power (Iran). The Ukrainiane use of drones or other low-value assets against the Russian navy is another example in point.

The above statements are merely an illustration of the severe difficulties faced by European armies and are in no way comprehensive. In brief, no European State (including in the EU or the UK) seems able to defend itself in a war (of 'high intensity' to use the new parlance). It is submitted that without cooperation, notably in terms of defence equipment, Europe will not be able to go back up the slope, unless it accentuates its dependency (already extreme for some countries) on the USA, thus renouncing to any idea of autonomy (independence is probably lost for the foreseeable future). This poor state of affairs concerning the defence of Europe should very strongly bring back the UK and the EU around a common sense of priorities.

The challenge, in our humble opinion, is on whether the UK accepts its full Europeanness in this respect and others, and whether the EU, without accepting back the UK in the Single Market (which it is in any case not officially currently interested in), accepts to grant it a unique status, reflecting its specificity.

What is needed, in other words, is a truly special relationship between the UK and the EU, with the understanding that it cannot exist (except in words) between the UK and the USA, or between the UK and Asia. At a time where the USA, since President Obama, is turning towards the Pacific rather than the Atlantic, does it make sense for the UK to seek to deepen its relationship with the USA after leaving its European neighbours? It does not seem to make sense to the USA, who have refused to engage

---

[29] Lagneau L (3 April 2024).

[30] Lagneau (29 February 2024). The article notes in fine that 24 h later the German frigate destroyed two drones at relatively short distance, which is interpreted as reflecting negatively on its ability to defend itself entirely satisfactorily.

in a Free Trade Agreement with the UK. As for defence matters, the USA are likely to need in the future strong allies rather than dependents. A strong Europe (EU and UK) defence-wise also benefits the USA. Turning towards Asia may bring some trade benefits to the UK, albeit it is unlikely that the UK will benefit in an Asian-led economic agreement from the senior position it had, and could have, in Europe. It is even less likely that the UK could benefit from a cooperation as deep as the one it could foster with the rest of Europe,[31] certainly not without accepting to relinquish the 'control' it claims to have regained from the EU.

The new leaders expected in both the EU and the UK in 2024, following the respective June and July elections, will have the difficult, albeit essential, task of seeing this special relationship through, without renouncing to the democratic values and human rights which are the soul of Europe.

References

Agence Belga (2024) La frégate Louise Marie doit peaufiner son entraînement avant de gagner la mer Rouge, 13 April 2024, https://www.rtl.be/actu/belgique/politique/la-fregate-louise-marie-doit-peaufiner-son-entrainement-avant-de-gagner-la-mer/2024-04-13/article/658341. Accessed 20 May 2024

BAE Systems (2023) F-35 – a trusted partner on the world's largest defence programme, https://www.baesystems.com/en-uk/product/f-35. Accessed 20 May 2024

Bernard E (2023) La communautarisation de la défense européenne dans le contexte de la guerre en Ukraine. Revue trimestrielle de droit européen 2023:325

British Chambers of Commerce (2024) BCC-Trade-and-Cooperation-Agreement-Three-Years-On, https://www.britishchambers.org.uk/policy-campaigns/global-britain/our-impact/trade-and-cooperation-agreement-three-years-on/. Accessed 20 May 2024

German Parliament (Bundestag), Parliamentary Commissioner for the Armed Forces (2023) Report (65th Report), 12 March 2024, https://dserver.bundestag.de/btd/20/105/2010500.pdf. Accessed 20 May 2024

Lagneau (29 February 2024) Mer Rouge : La frégate allemande Hessen a failli abattre un drone américain, https://www.opex360.com/2024/02/29/mer-rouge-la-fregate-allemande-hessen-a-failli-abattre-un-drone-americain/. Accessed 20 May 2024

Lagneau L (3 April 2024) La frégate danoise Iver Huitfeldt a eu des problèmes de radar et de munitions lors d'une attaque houthie, https://www.opex360.com/2024/04/03/la-fregate-danoise-iver-huitfeldt-a-eu-des-problemes-de-radar-et-de-munitions-dune-attaque-houthie/. Accessed 20 May 2024

Lawless J (2024) The U.K. government says it has no plans to introduce conscription, after the head of the British Army said a "citizen army" would be needed to fight a future war with a country like Russia, 24 January 2024, https://www.independent.co.uk/news/british-army-ap-britain-rishi-sunak-london-b2484111.html. Accessed 20 May 2024

Snoeck B (2016) J'accuse ! l'attentat que les services craignaient. Tribune Libre no 62 (March 2016), https://cf2r.org/tribune/jaccuse-lattentat-que-les-services-craignaient/. Accessed 20 May 2024

[31] Cooperation with selected partners such as Japan for a 6th generation plane is currently taking place. It does not undermine the general idea here expressed.

Springford J (2023) Are the costs of Brexit big or small?, Center for European Reform. Insight, 09 May 2023, https://www.cer.eu/insights/are-costs-brexit-big-or-small. Accessed 20 May 2024

UK House of Commons Defence Committee (2024) Ready for War? HC26, 4 February 2024, https://committees.parliament.uk/publications/43178/documents/214880/default/. Accessed 20 May 2024

UK Ministry of Defence (2023) Agency and Agility: incentivising people in a new era. A review of UK Armed Forces incentivisation by Rick Haythornthwaite, June 2023, https://assets.publishing.service.gov.uk/media/648ad6b8b32b9e000ca967c9/Incentivising_people_in_a_new_era_-_a_review_of_UK_Armed_Forces.pdf. Accessed May 2024

Winters LA (2023) Is it really true that Brexit has had no harmful effects? UK Trade Policy Observatory, 17 February 2023, https://blogs.sussex.ac.uk/uktpo/2023/02/17/is-it-really-true-that-brexit-has-had-no-harmful-effects/. Accessed 20 May 2024

The manufacturer's authorised representative in the EU is Springer Nature Customer Service Centre GmbH, Europaplatz 3, 69115 Heidelberg, Germany. If you have any concerns regarding our products, please contact ProductSafety@springernature.com

Printed and bound by CPI Group (UK) Ltd, Croydon, CR0 4YY
01/10/2026
02225950-0019